The Darker Angels of Our Nature

The Darker Angels of Our Nature

*Refuting the Pinker Theory
of History & Violence*

*Edited by
Philip Dwyer and Mark Micale*

BLOOMSBURY ACADEMIC
LONDON • NEW YORK • OXFORD • NEW DELHI • SYDNEY

BLOOMSBURY ACADEMIC
Bloomsbury Publishing Plc
50 Bedford Square, London, WC1B 3DP, UK
1385 Broadway, New York, NY 10018, USA
29 Earlsfort Terrace, Dublin 2, Ireland

BLOOMSBURY, BLOOMSBURY ACADEMIC and the Diana logo are
trademarks of Bloomsbury Publishing Plc

First published in Great Britain 2022

Cover design: Graham Ward
Angel of Death statue, Wroclaw, Poland. A monument to the victims of the
Katyn massacre, 1940. Alejandro Montecatine/Shutterstock.com

A catalogue record for this book is available from the British Library.

Library of Congress Cataloging-in-Publication Data
Names: Dwyer, Philip G., editor. | Micale, Mark S., 1957- editor.
Title: The darker angels of our nature: refuting the Pinker theory of history & violence /
edited by Philip Dwyer and Mark Micale.
Description: London; New York: Bloomsbury Academic, 2021. | Includes
bibliographical references and index. |
Identifiers: LCCN 2021000369 (print) | LCCN 2021000370 (ebook) |
ISBN 9781350140608 (hardback) | ISBN 9781350140592 (paperback) |
ISBN 9781350140615 (epub) | ISBN 9781350140622 (ebook)
Subjects: LCSH: Pinker, Steven, 1954- Better angels of our nature. | Violence–History. |
Violence–Historiography. | Violence–Psychology.
Classification: LCC HM1116 .D385 2021 (print) | LCC HM1116 (ebook) |
DDC 303.609–dc23
LC record available at https://lccn.loc.gov/2021000369
LC ebook record available at https://lccn.loc.gov/2021000370

ISBN: HB: 978-1-3501-4060-8
PB: 978-1-3501-4059-2
ePDF: 978-1-3501-4062-2
eBook: 978-1-3501-4061-5

Typeset by Deanta Global Publishing Services, Chennai, India

To find out more about our authors and books visit www.bloomsbury.com and
sign up for our newsletters.

CONTENTS

PART FIVE Coda

ILLUSTRATION

CONTRIBUTORS

David A. Bell is a historian of early modern France, with a particular interest in the political culture of the Old Regime and the French Revolution. From 1990 to 1996, he taught at Yale, and from 1996 to 2010 at Johns Hopkins, where he held the Andrew W. Mellon chair in the Humanities, and served as Dean of Faculty in the School of Arts and Sciences. He joined the Princeton faculty in 2010. He has been the recipient of fellowships from the Guggenheim Foundation, the American Council of Learned Societies and the Woodrow Wilson International Center for Scholars. He is the author of six books, including *Lawyers and Citizens* (Oxford, 1994), *The Cult of the Nation in France* (Harvard, 2001), *The First Total War* (Houghton Mifflin, 2007) and *Rethinking the Age of Revolutions: France and the Birth of the Modern World*, with Yair Mintzker (Oxford, 2018). His latest book is *Men on Horseback: Charisma and Power in the Age of Revolutions* (Farrar, Straus, Giroux, 2020).

Joanna Bourke is Professor of History at Birkbeck, University of London, and a Fellow of the British Academy. She is also the Global Innovation Chair at the University of Newcastle (Australia, 2017–21). She is the principal investigator on a five-year Wellcome Trust-funded project entitled 'SHaME' (Sexual Harms and Medical Encounters). She is the prize-winning author of thirteen books, as well as over 100 articles in academic journals. She is a frequent contributor to TV and radio shows, and a regular correspondent for newspapers. She has published *The Story of Pain: From Prayer to Painkillers* (Oxford, 2014), and *Wounding the World: How Military Violence and War-Play Are Invading Our Lives* (Virago, 2014).

Sara M. Butler is King George III Professor in British History at the Ohio State University. She is the author of three books: *The Language of Abuse: Marital Violence in Later Medieval England* (Brill, 2007), *Divorce in Medieval England: From One to Two Persons in Law* (Routledge, 2013) and *Forensic Medicine and Death Investigation in Medieval England* (Routledge, 2015). She has also written on a variety of other subjects such as abortion, infanticide, juries of matrons, regulation of the medical profession and suicide.

Robert T. Chase is Associate Professor of History at Stony Brook University, State University of New York (SUNY). He is the author of *We Are Not*

Slaves: State Violence, Coerced Labor, and Prisoners' Rights in Postwar America (University of North Carolina Press, 2020) and the editor of *Caging Borders and Carceral States: Incarcerations, Immigration Detentions, and Resistance* (University of North Carolina Press, 2019). His work on the history of prison and policing reform and state violence has been featured on national media programmes through radio, newspapers and television, including MSNBC, CNN and NPR, *Newsweek*, *Washington Post*. He is currently working on a history of sheriffs in the US South and Southwest.

Philip Dwyer is Professor of History and the founding director of the Centre for the Study of Violence at the University of Newcastle. He has published widely on the Revolutionary and Napoleonic eras, including a three-volume biography of Napoleon. He is the general editor (with Joy Damousi) of the four-volume *Cambridge World History of Violence* and co-editor of the *Cambridge History of the Napoleonic Wars*. He is currently engaged in writing a global history of violence.

Caroline Elkins is Professor of History and African and African American Studies at Harvard University, a visiting professor of business administration at Harvard Business School and the founding director of Harvard's Center for African Studies. Her first book, *Imperial Reckoning: The Untold Story of Britain's Gulag in Kenya* (Henry Holt, 2005), was awarded the 2006 Pulitzer Prize for General Non-Fiction. She is a contributor to *The New York Times Book Review*, *The Atlantic* and *The New Republic*. She has also appeared on numerous radio and television programmes including NPR's *All Things Considered*, BBC's *The World* and PBS's *Charlie Rose*. She is currently working on two projects: one examining the effects of violence and amnesia on local communities and nation-building in post-independent Kenya; the other analysing British counter-insurgency operations after the Second World War, with case studies including Palestine, Malaya, Kenya, Cyprus and Nyasaland. Professor Elkins teaches courses on modern Africa, protest in East Africa, human rights in Africa and British colonial violence in the twentieth century.

Linda Fibiger is Senior Lecturer in Human Osteoarchaeology at the University of Edinburgh and Programme Director of the MSc in Human Osteoarchaeology. She has published widely on bioarchaeological perspectives on violence and conflict, experimental bioarchaeology, reconstructions of past lifeways and the promotion of professional standards, ethics and legislation in bioarchaeology. She is currently involved in the European-funded The Fall of 1200 BC project for which she is leading the analysis of human skeletal remains from the Balkans, with a particular focus on population relationships, lifestyle and indicators of crisis and conflict.

Nancy Shields Kollmann is William H. Bonsall Professor in History at Stanford University; she specializes in early modern Russian history with an emphasis on the history of law, represented in *By Honor Bound. State and Society in Early Modern Russia* (Cornell, 1999) and *Crime and Punishment in Early Modern Russia* (Cambridge, 2012). Her *The Russian Empire 1450-1801* (Oxford, 2017) surveys the growth and governance of the Russian empire as a Eurasian 'empire of difference'. She is currently working on visual sources of early modern Russia, both produced in Russia and in European travel accounts, maps, and pamphlet literature.

Dag Lindström is Professor of History at Uppsala University in Sweden. He has conducted research on the history of crime since the 1980s and is co-author (with Eva Österberg) of *Crime and Social Control in Medieval and Early Modern Swedish Towns* (Uppsala, 1988). Lindström has published widely in the field of urban social and cultural history from Medieval times to the early nineteenth century. He is co-editor (with Alida Clemente and Jon Stobart) of *Micro-Geographies of the Western City, c.1750-1900* (forthcoming, 2021) and co-author (with Göran Tagesson) of *Houses, Families, and Cohabitation in Eighteenth-Century Swedish Towns* (forthcoming, 2021). His more recent research includes a Nordic comparison of homicide between the seventeenth century and the present. The results will appear in Janne Kvivouri et. al, *Homicide in Deep Time: Nordic Homicide from Early Modern to Present Era* (forthcoming 2021).

Mark S. Micale is Emeritus Professor of History at the University of Illinois in Urbana-Champaign. His fields of specialization include modern comparative European intellectual and cultural history; post-Revolutionary France; the history of science and medicine, especially the mental sciences; psychoanalytic studies; masculinity studies; and historical trauma studies. He is the author or editor of seven books, including *Beyond the Unconscious* (Princeton, 1993); *Discovering the History of Psychiatry* (Oxford, 1994); *Traumatic Pasts: History, Psychiatry, and Trauma in the Modern Age, 1870-1930* (Cambridge, 2001); *The Mind of Modernism: Medicine, Psychology, and the Cultural Arts in Europe and America, 1880-1940* (Stanford, 2003); *Enlightenment, Passion, Modernity: Historical Essays in European Thought and Culture* (Stanford, 2000); and *Hysterical Men: The Hidden History of Male Nervous Illness* (Harvard, 2000). After thirty years of teaching – at Yale, the University of Manchester and the University of Illinois – he retired in 2017 and now lives in Los Angeles.

Susan K. Morrissey is Professor of History at the University of California, Irvine. She is a specialist in Russian history, and has published books and articles on student radicalism, suicide, and terrorism, including *Heralds of Revolution: Russian Students and the Mythologies of Radicalism* (Oxford, 1998) and *Suicide and the Body Politic in Imperial Russia* (Cambridge, 2006). She is currently writing a monograph about political violence in late imperial Russia.

Matthew Restall is Edwin Erle Sparks Professor of History and Director of Latin American Studies at Penn State University. He was recently the Greenleaf Distinguished Professor at Tulane University and president of the American Society for Ethnohistory. He is a former National Endowment for the Humanities, John Carter Brown Library, Institute for Advanced Study at Princeton, Library of Congress and US Capitol, and Guggenheim fellow. He edits *Hispanic American Historical Review* and book series with Cambridge and Penn State university presses. His two dozen books in six languages include *The Maya World* (Stanford, 1999); *Maya Conquistador* (Beacon Press, 1999); *Seven Myths of the Spanish Conquest* (Oxford, 2003); *The Black Middle* (Stanford, 2009); *2012 and the End of the World* (Rowman & Littlefield, 2012); *The Conquistadors* (Oxford, 2012); and *When Montezuma Met Cortés* (Ecco/HarperCollins, 2018), which won the 2020 Howard Cline Prize. His newest books are *Return to Ixil: Maya Society in an Eighteenth-Century Yucatec Town* (University Press Colorado, 2019); *Blue Moves* (Bloomsbury, 2020); and *The Maya: A Very Short Introduction* (Oxford, 2020).

Elizabeth Roberts-Pedersen is Senior Lecturer in History at the University of Newcastle. She has published on several elements of the history of modern warfare, including international volunteering, discipline and military medicine. Her book examining the effects of the Second World War on the theory and practice of psychiatry, funded by an Australia Research Council Discovery Early Career Researcher Award (DECRA), is forthcoming with Cambridge University Press.

Corey Ross is Professor of Modern History at the University of Birmingham. He is the author of numerous works on modern Europe, global environmental history and modern empire. His most recent book, *Ecology and Power in the Age of Empire* (Oxford, 2017), won the American Historical Association's George Louis Beer Prize. He is currently writing a book on the history of European imperialism through the lens of water, with the support of the Leverhulme Trust and National Endowment for the Humanities.

Daniel Lord Smail is Professor of History at Harvard University, where he works on deep human history and the history and anthropology of Mediterranean societies between 1100 and 1600. His current research approaches transformations in the material culture of later medieval Mediterranean Europe using household inventories and inventories of debt collection from Lucca and Marseille, and he is also embarking on a study of slavery in later medieval Provence. His books include *Legal Plunder: Households and Debt Collection in Late Medieval Europe* (Harvard, 2016), *On Deep History and the Brain* (University of California Press, 2008) and *The Consumption of Justice: Emotions, Publicity, and Legal Culture in Marseille, 1264-1423* (Cornell, 2003).

Eric D. Weitz is Distinguished Professor of History at City College and the Graduate Center, City University of New York. His most recent book is *A World Divided: The Global Struggle for Human Rights in the Age of Nation-States* (2019). His other major publications include *Weimar Germany: Promise and Tragedy* (2007; Weimar Centennial (third) edition 2018); *A Century of Genocide: Utopias of Race and Nation* (2003; reprint with new foreword 2014); and *Creating German Communism, 1890-1990: From Popular Protests to Socialist State* (1997), all with Princeton University Press. *Weimar Germany* was named an 'Editor's Choice' by *The New York Times Book Review*. Weitz edits a book series for Princeton, *Human Rights and Crimes against Humanity*.

Michael Wert is Associate Professor of East Asian History at Marquette University. A specialist in early modern and modern Japan, he is the author of *Meiji Restoration Losers: Memory and Tokugawa Supporters in Modern Japan and Samurai* (Harvard, 2013). He is currently working on a manuscript that uses critical theory to analyse martial 'fantasy', violence and ideology.

PREFACE

This book has a somewhat convoluted history. Mark Micale and I first met in Newcastle in 2017 when he was invited to come and work at the Centre for the History of Violence (as it was then known). I recall being in his office when he showed me an article in the *Sydney Morning Herald* about a tweet posted by Bill Gates, the founder of Microsoft and one of the richest people on the planet. In it, Gates told college students, who were then completing their studies in great numbers across North America, that they should read Pinker's *Better Angels of Our Nature*. '[Steven Pinker] shows how the world is getting better', Gates proclaimed. 'Sounds crazy but it's true. This is the most peaceful time in human history.' 'That matters', Gates added, 'because if you think the world is getting better, you want to spread the progress to more people and places'.[1]

We were taken aback; as historians we knew that Pinker's thesis was problematic. We also knew that his book, *Better Angels of Our Nature*, had been critiqued quite extensively by a wide variety of scholars from across the social sciences but, interestingly, by very few historians. This was a little puzzling given that the core of Pinker's thesis is in fact historical. Mark and I decided it was time to weigh into the debates and present an alternative view, one that countered some of the more egregious claims made by Pinker. We quickly assembled a team of historians from different fields and published the articles in a special issue of the journal *Historical Reflections/Réflexions Historiques* at the end of 2017.[2] Antoinette Burton kindly facilitated our initial contact with the journal's editorial board. Comprised of eleven articles of around 5,000 words each, the special issue appears to have resonated with the readers of the journal, so much so that the publisher, Marion Berghahn, decided to reprint the articles as a collection of essays, titled *On Violence in History*.[3]

Even before the reprint had come out, Mark and I were already thinking of transforming the articles into a collection of chapters, by choosing some of the best and extending the length to around 8,000 words, and by then

---

[1] *Sydney Morning Herald*, 16 May 2017.
[2] Philip Dwyer and Mark S. Micale (eds), special issue, 'History, Violence, and Steven Pinker', *Historical Reflections/Réflexions historiques*, 44, no. 1 (Spring 2018).
[3] Philip Dwyer and Mark S. Micale (eds), *On Violence in History* (New York: Berghahn, 2019).

inviting other scholars to fill in some of the historical gaps. This collection of chapters is the end result of that endeavour. The chapter by Nancy Kollmann remains the same as originally published in *Historical Reflections*, but the chapters by Linda Fibiger, Sara Butler, Caroline Elkins, Joanna Bourke and Daniel Smail are included here in a modified and expanded form. Philip Dwyer and Mark Micale have provided a new introduction and have both entirely rewritten their own chapters. Nine new chapters have been added, those by Dag Lindström, Eric Weitz, David Bell, Robert Chase, Philip Dwyer and Elizabeth Roberts-Pedersen, Susan Morrissey, Matthew Restall, Corey Ross and Michael Wert. We think they significantly add to the critique of Pinker's narrative, make a case for how history should be written and researched, as well as challenging and questioning the declinist thesis of violence in history.

Despite *Darker Angels of Our Nature*'s generous selection of eighteen chapters, we obviously cannot claim comprehensive coverage. Readers will no doubt think of other countries (China and Brazil, especially) and other topics (such as religion and violence or cyber-violence) that could rewardingly have been included. An entire second volume of chapters could in fact be devoted to other sorts and sites of violence, including several we originally had in mind but were compelled to leave out because of space limitations. We need also to acknowledge a serious gap in the book's coverage, a gap that we tried, patiently but alas unsuccessfully, to fill. Nazism and Stalinism may well be the paradigmatic cases of state-sponsored mass civilian violence in modern times. The historical scholarship on these overlapping subjects is voluminous and very rich. Nevertheless, the chapter we commissioned on German fascism as a system of violence never materialized and, as editors of the project, we finally had to move forward without it, an omission that, as professional historians of modern Europe, we feel most keenly.

We would like to thank Maddie Holder for giving us the opportunity to publish this collection of chapters and thereby to introduce the debates around Steven Pinker and his thesis to, hopefully, a much wider audience. Mark would like additionally to thank his former colleagues in the University of Illinois history department for their many suggestions about the project – in particular, Clare Crowston for raising the issue of prison violence, Rod Wilson for insisting on the significance of Japanese history to the global history of violence, Mark Steinberg for bringing Susan Morrissey's work on emotions history to our attention and Carol Symes for hosting a lively evening discussion. We heartily thank all the contributors to the collection, those who have agreed to rework existing pieces, and those who have come on board, entering the fray, so to speak, by challenging popularly held views. We hope that these chapters will inspire students and readers, and more broadly, lovers of history, wanting to see how historians go about their craft, to think more critically about the present.

Philip Dwyer, Newcastle
Mark Micale, Baltimore

1

Steven Pinker and the nature of violence in history

Philip Dwyer and Mark S. Micale

The huge commercial success of Steven Pinker's *The Better Angels of Our Nature: The Decline of Violence in History and Its Causes*, which first appeared in 2011, took many in the academic world by surprise. There was nothing that predisposed it to being on the bestseller lists. It is over 800 pages long, the text is quite dense, and there are over 100 charts and graphs that are supposedly based on a rigorous choice of data and a 'commitment to objectivity'. The overarching argument of the book is that violence in the world has declined significantly over the years, a counter-intuitive argument to those familiar with the history of the twentieth century. Pinker is not the first to argue for the long-term decline of violence, but he is certainly the most successful writer to do so.[1] Moreover, he goes further than anyone else by arguing in the Preface to *The Better Angels* that the decline in human violence over the past 10,000 years, as he chronicles it, 'may be the most important thing that has ever happened in human history', and that 'we may be living in the most peaceable era in our species' existence'.[2]

---

[1]Others include Azar Gat, *War in Human Civilization* (Oxford: Oxford University Press, 2006); Joshua S. Goldstein, *Winning the War on War: The Decline of Armed Conflict Worldwide* (London: Dutton, 2011); and Ian Morris, *War!: What Is It Good For?: Conflict and the Progress of Civilization from Primates to Robots* (New York: Farrar, Straus and Giroux, 2014). Manuel Eisner, 'Long-Term Historical Trends in Violent Crime', *Crime and Justice*, 30 (2003): 83–142, also argues that violence in Western Europe from the sixteenth century through to the early twentieth century has declined. For a critique of these views, see Michael Mann, 'Have Wars and Violence Declined?', *Theory and Society*, 47, no. 2 (January 2018): 37–60.
[2]Steven Pinker, *The Better Angels of Our Nature: The Decline of Violence in History and Its Causes* (London: Allen Lane, 2011), xxi.

In some respects, his book falls within the genre of non-fiction that attempts to explain the complexities of the world to the lay reader, such as Jared Diamond's *Guns, Germs and Steel*, Yuval Harrari's *Sapiens*, Peter Frankopan's *The Silk Roads* or even Thomas Piketty's *Capital in the Twenty-First Century*. These books share a cluster of traits: in an age of specialized technical knowledge, they offer sweeping accounts of human nature and human history that synthesize masses of information organized around a few provocative themes, presented with popular appeal and marketability in mind. But that really is where the comparison must end.

Let's take as an example Pinker and Piketty. The two authors have entirely different purposes and messages. Piketty sets out to demonstrate how capitalism is one of the main drivers of inequality in the world and how extreme inequalities give rise to the kind of discontent that can undermine democratic values. Pinker's take on the world, in both *The Better Angels* and in a subsequent 700-page tome published in 2018, *Enlightenment Now: The Case for Reason, Science, Humanism, and Progress*, was the exact opposite. Both of Pinker's books are panegyrics to capitalism, or more precisely to what Pinker dubs 'gentle commerce'. Pinker goes so far as to deny, against the consensus of other social scientists, that economic inequality – that is poverty – is a form of violence, even though overwhelming evidence shows that such inequality leads to poor health outcomes and early deaths, a fact illustrated most recently and starkly in the epidemiological fate of Covid-19 victims in Britain and the United States. Moreover, inequalities can generate violence, as has become apparent over the past few decades when looking at just one aspect of the systemic racism that exists in many Western countries, the relationship between law enforcement agencies and ethnic communities. In a number of Western countries – Australia, Britain, France and the United States – minorities are often over-represented in both the numbers of incarcerated and the numbers killed by the police. It would surprise many people to know that the country with the highest rates of indigenous incarceration in the world is Australia.[3]

In Pinker's mind, socio-economic inequality, like violence, is a problem that can be and is being solved. If in *The Better Angels* we are now living in the most peaceful era in human history, in *Enlightenment Now* life is simply getting better all the time, due mostly to the global spread of what the author takes to be enlightened values. 'We' are much better off because of 'Newborns who will live more than eight decades, markets overflowing with food, clean water that appears with a flick of a finger and waste that disappears with another, pills that erase a painful infection, sons who are not sent off to war, daughters who can walk the streets in safety, critics of the powerful who are not jailed or shot, the world's knowledge and culture

---

[3]https://theconversation.com/factcheck-qanda-are-indigenous-australians-the-most-incarcerated-people-on-earth-78528.

available in a shirt pocket'.[4] We leave to one side the question of who the 'we' is that he claims to speak for, but suffice it to say that from Pinker's rosy vantage point, the signs of advancement towards a future conflict-free utopia are plain to see, including in the latest update of his iPhone.

Pinker's critics and his response

Upon its publication a decade ago, *Better Angels* received divided reviews, some of them strongly favourable but many of them sharply critical. In contrast, Pinker's follow-up book, *Enlightenment Now*, has been almost entirely panned, including in a number of long, scathing and exceptionally well-informed critiques by international authorities on the historical Enlightenment.[5] *Enlightenment Now* lays bare the motivating ideology underpinning both Pinker works. Apparently not satisfied with the commercial success of *Better Angels*, Pinker seems to have been genuinely surprised and angered by his critics. *Enlightenment Now* is partly a response to these critics that attempts to tether Anglo-American free-market economics to his idea of Enlightenment values (i.e. science, progress and humanism). It must be frustrating that academics don't see 'reason' as he does and simply accept the proposition that the world is getting steadily and demonstrably better, including less violent. Pinker's explanation for the negative reaction to his latest treatise is to characterize his critics variously as nihilists, Marxists, post-modernists and anti-utopians. Indeed, Pinker rails against 'intellectuals' who '*really* hate progress. It's not that they hate the *fruits* of progress. . . . It's the *idea* of progress that rankles the chattering class'. The term, 'chattering classes' was coined in the 1970s by the conservative British journalist Auberon Waugh and popularized by President Richard Nixon; it is intended to denigrate commentators who disagree with you and who claim to speak with authority.

Precisely because progress is one of Western civilization's core ideas, its long and rich intellectual history has been written many times. As readers of these histories know, the *idea* of progress is extraordinarily fraught, both intellectually and ideologically. Historians have been at pains to point out that any 'Whiggish' interpretation of history and human progress – that is, the presentation of history as an inevitable and universal march towards

---

[4]Steven Pinker, *Enlightenment Now: The Case for Reason, Science, Humanism, and Progress* (New York: Penguin Books, 2019), 4.

[5]See, for example, Peter Harrison, 'The Enlightenment of Steven Pinker', 20 February 2018, https://www.abc.net.au/religion/the-enlightenment-of-steven-pinker/10094966; David A. Bell, 'The Power Point Philosophe: Waiting for Steven Pinker's Enlightenment', *The Nation*, 7 March 2018; Samuel Moyn, 'Hype for the Best: Why Does Steven Pinker Insist that Human Life Is On the Up and Up?' *The New Republic*, 19 March 2018.

greater freedom, democracy and Enlightenment – is bound to distort the historical reality and to misrepresent the enormous variations in both the pace and the nature of cultural change. It will come as no surprise that whether one thinks things are getting better or worse in the world very much depends on one's personal perspective, and that in turn may very well depend on who you are and where you live. The Enlightenment, as Pinker understands it, has not spread to all parts of the world. We are not even going to raise at this point the profound question of whether civilization, including modern Western civilizations, necessarily rests on deep systemic violence for both its creation and maintenance. Others would argue contra-Pinker that if there has been demonstrable progress in the quality of human life, this has been as much in spite of as due to capitalism.[6] Others again, as is evident in the chapters by Caroline Elkins and Matthew Restall in this collection, highlight the proliferation of 'crimes against humanity' carried out by the Western powers against the indigenous peoples of the world, which were made possible principally by modern industry, technology and weaponry during the same time when, Pinker claims, violence has been ebbing in the Western world.

Leaving all that to one side, Pinker's tirade is surprisingly dismissive of academics who have spent their whole lives researching, teaching and publishing in their specialized fields, and who are lumped together as the 'chattering classes', 'those who intellectualize for a living'. This is a bit much coming from a man who works at one of the world's most prestigious universities and who has literally toured the world spruiking his thesis. The chattering classes are in fact Pinker's fellow university professors, including two in this volume from his home institution, Harvard University.

In some respects, Pinker's emotive responses are a form of intellectual gaslighting, directed at those who question and criticize his methods, sources and conclusions.[7] Rather than engage in an exchange of ideas – the very essence of the Enlightenment form of truth seeking – he caricatures and then ridicules those who engage with his ideas. As criticism of his two books has mounted, Pinker has gotten shriller and sillier. His critics, he charges, are part of a 'quasi-religious ideology . . . laced with misanthropy, including an indifference to starvation, an indulgence in ghoulish fantasies of a depopulated planet, and Nazi-like comparisons of human beings to

---

[6]See Jeremy Lent's blog: https://patternsofmeaning.com/2018/05/17/steven-pinkers-ideas -about-progress-are-fatally-flawed-these-eight-graphs-show-why/; Sidney Pollard, *The Idea of Progress: History and Society* (New York: Basic Books, 1969); Morris Ginsberg, *The Idea of Progress: A Reevaluation* (Westport: Greenwood Press, 1972); Robert A. Nisbet, *History of the Idea of Progress* (New York: Basic Books, 1980); Arthur M. Melzer, Jerry Weinberger and M. Richard Zinman (eds), *History and the Idea of Progress* (Ithaca: Cornell University Press, 1995); Matthew W. Slaboch, *A Road to Nowhere: The Idea of Progress and Its Critics* (Philadelphia: University of Pennsylvania Press, 2018).
[7]Our thanks to Elizabeth Roberts-Pedersen for this idea.

vermin, pathogens, and cancer'.[8] Say what? And in an interview published in 2018 in *The Guardian*, he further bloviates:

> One of the surprises in presenting data on violence was the lengths to which people would go to deny it. When I presented graphs showing that rates of homicide had fallen by a factor of 50, that rates of death in war had fallen by a factor of more than 20, and rape and domestic violence and child abuse had all fallen, rather than rejoice, many audiences seemed to get increasingly upset. They racked their brains for ways in which things could not possibly be as good as the data suggested, including the entire category of questions that I regularly get: Isn't X a form of violence? Isn't advertising a form of violence? Isn't plastic surgery a form of violence? Isn't obesity a form of violence?[9]

This is the kind of hyperbole one finds in a culture war. It is also dishonest. No respected scholar has claimed that advertising, cosmetic surgery and obesity are forms of violence. The contributors in this volume, however, believe that any conscientious and ethically up-to-date account of violence in the past and present, especially one that claims comprehensive coverage, should include such human behavioural phenomena as interpersonal violence, environmental violence, violence against indigenous people, violence in prisons, human trafficking and cyber-violence, to cite only several omissions in Pinker's world view.

Truth be told, Pinker's critics are not attacking him because they are perverse, or contrarian, or because they belong to an imaginary cabal of overeducated progress haters. In any field of secular knowledge, bold new theories or interpretations are invariably subjected to evaluation by a community of peers who rigorously examine its method, observations and findings. Some of these new interpretations (whether in physics, biology, psychology, history or the law) stand the test of time and become the shared consensus of knowledge. Others endure in part after being revised by critical input from fellow professionals, a process of intelligent re-evaluation that is ongoing. Yet others fade away under critical scrutiny. It is called 'the scientific method'. Apparently, Pinker feels that his ideas are beyond the basic process of hypothesis testing. Instead of evaluating the idea content of his books, he has expected audiences just to 'rejoice' that, like some prophet or Prometheus-figure, he has delivered the truth to us about the past, present and future of humanity.

---

[8]Pinker, *Enlightenment Now*, 122.
[9]Andrew Anthony, 'Steven Pinker: "The way to deal with pollution is not to rail against consumption"', *The Guardian*, 11 February 2018, https://www.theguardian.com/science/2018/feb/11/steven-pinker-enlightenment-now-interview-inequality-consumption-environment.

Pinker characterizes his critics by charging that 'To look at the data showing that violence has gone down and say "Violence has gone up" is to be delusional'.[10] Using the language of psychopathology to dismiss a critic is something a professor of psychology should know better to do. The quite sane collection of historians in this book do, however, question in an altogether rational manner some of the assumptions Pinker makes, the accuracy of his data and, hence, the conclusions upon which his grand transhistorical thesis is based. They question whether violence, and especially violence across huge swathes of time, can in fact be measured accurately, not least because through history a great deal of interpersonal violence is hidden from public view and is grossly under-reported, and whether that violence can be compared meaningfully across myriad cultures. They question Pinker's understanding of what violence is; they question whether we are biologically predisposed towards violence; and they object to the oversimplification of the subject. We do this precisely because we know that violence, in all of its multifarious manifestations, continues to be such a fundamental problem in the contemporary world and that to work towards its diminution requires an accurate and honest understanding of human aggression in our collective past.

'Reason', like 'progress', is a major theme running through both *The Better Angels* and *Enlightenment Now*. To paraphrase the late seventeenth-century English political philosopher, John Locke, part of the problem is that Pinker confounds 'judgment and opinion', which is how Locke defined 'reason', with 'knowledge and certainty'.[11] Knowledge is an ever-evolving body of work; there can be no certainty in anything, and the publication of research outcomes can change overnight the way scholars think about a period, an object or an event. It is not only a question of keeping up to date with the most reliable information and the best analyses; it is also a matter of deep, carefully acquired knowledge of a subject and the debates in any particular field. Pinker patently does neither of these things.

Statistics and the past

In the current age of overspecialization, books with a panoramic scope and big new ideas that attract a general readership are admirable cultural accomplishments. As our opening citations of Diamond, Piketty and Harrari suggest, we ourselves are enthusiastic readers of the best works in this genre. That is why we believe that while Pinker's popularity is perhaps understandable, it deserves rebuttal from the very community of experts

---

[10]Pinker, *Enlightenment Now*, 45.
[11]For a discussion of 'reason' see Peter Harrison, 'The Enlightenment of Steven Pinker', citing Locke's classic *Essay Concerning Human Understanding* (1689).

who are trained and tasked to study the past professionally. At its core, Pinker's arguments (as the subtitle of *Better Angels* indicates) are historical; this is why the contributors to this collection are historians or historically oriented anthropologists or sociologists. All of them take offence at seeing their field mishandled. In places, our language might appear strong, but the stakes are high. We do not lightly seek a polemic. Some of our colleagues would rather not engage with Pinker in the belief that his work does not warrant a response; but to not do so would be to leave the field open to someone who uses the rhetoric of science irresponsibly in the pursuit of a particular agenda that is neither acknowledged nor proven.

As is amply demonstrated by the essays in this collection, there are a multitude of objections to Pinker's thesis. The first has to do with his use of statistics. This is a recurring criticism that appears in a number of chapters throughout this collection.[12] As Dag Lindström points out in his chapter, Pinker's use of statistics is sometimes on solid ground, but it is often based on limited and problematic evidence. Despite the discourse of science and objectivity that Pinker deploys, his use of quantitative data throughout *Better Angels* is shockingly shoddy. Pinker considers his figures in absolute terms, that is, as though 'facts' are hard and fast and cannot be questioned. He presents himself as someone who 'soundly appraise[s] the state of the world', by counting.[13] His unexamined assumption is that the data by definition is accurate and numbers 'speak for themselves', when, as many of the authors in this collection decisively demonstrate, it is often neither accurate and representative nor self-evident. Even Pinker admits that 'it is legitimate to question how accurate and representative the numbers truly are'.[14]

Like many of the eighteenth-century European Enlightenment thinkers whom Pinker lauds, we are sceptical; we take with more than a pinch of salt anyone who presents their findings with the kind of conviction – if not blind faith – in the idea of neutral, value-free statistics. To paraphrase the most famous of those Enlightenment philosophes, Voltaire, 'at least confess you are as ignorant as I am'.[15] The main challenge is not that statistical information about historical violence is inherently faulty; it is rather that what he measures is frequently shifting, partial and often

---

[12]Other critiques of Pinker's use and misuse of statistics can be found in Edward S. Herman and David Peterson, 'Reality Denial: Apologetics for Western-Imperial Violence', https://www .globalresearch.ca/reality-denial-apologetics-for-western-imperial-violence/32066; and Pasquale Cirillo and Nassim Nicholas Taleb, 'The Decline of Violent Conflicts: What Do the Data Really Say?' *Nobel Foundation Symposium 161: The Causes of Peace*, https://www.fooledby-randomness.com/pinker.pdf.

[13]Pinker, *Enlightenment Now*, 42–3.

[14]Pinker, *Enlightenment Now*, 43–4.

[15]Cited in Nicholas Hudson, 'Are We "Voltaire's Bastards?" John Ralston Saul and Post-Modern Representations of the Enlightenment', *Lumen*, 20 (2001): 111–21, here 116.

hugely under-reported. Linda Fibiger points to Pinker's misuse of a single archaeological site – Vedbaek in Denmark – where twenty-one human skeletons have been uncovered dating from the Mesolithic era (from about 13,000 to 4,000 BC), and in which there is some evidence of violent deaths. Pinker concludes that the site is representative of *all* prehistory. That is problematic to say the least, especially if you start to compare it with other regions in the world. In Britain, for example, human remains for the Mesolithic are rare and often incomplete. You cannot, therefore, make a generalization about all of human prehistory based on the findings of one or even a few sites, especially when information surrounding these societies and these deaths is lacking.

Even in our own era, in advanced technocratic countries where bureaucracies keep good records, statistics can be incomplete or flawed. These are what are referred to as 'dark figures', unrecorded or undiscovered crime. Take, as any number of countless possible examples, sexual assault and drink-fuelled violence. Despite what Pinker says about rates of sexual assault declining over the years, the number of rape cases has actually increased, and as Joanna Bourke in this collection maintains, they are greater now than during the Middle Ages.[16] Moreover, drink-fuelled violence that occurs on weekends in big cities involving people who end up in accident and emergency departments is also prevalent but largely under-reported. Even when it is reported, it almost never ends up in court. In one particular survey of an emergency department in a British hospital, the incidence of domestic violence – women assaulted in their own home, usually after an argument – was higher than that reported in the British Crime Surveys, while most other assaults involving alcohol-fuelled violence took place in the street or in pubs and nightclubs.[17] There is no doubt that a survey of any similar emergency ward in any large modern city would provide comparable figures of higher rates of violence than that reported by police departments. A fundamental skill of the professional historian is to assess and acknowledge the nature of their source material, and therefore what sorts of knowledge about the human past can and cannot be gleaned responsibly from it.

Pinker virtually never questions his own data or indeed the sources he uses. This habit is so egregious that at times it is difficult to know whether he accepts every account he reads that serves his purpose, or whether some of it is tongue-in-cheek. Again, one famous example must suffice. Early in *The Better Angels*, Pinker refers to the Old Testament story of Cain killing his brother, Abel. 'With a world population of exactly four', Pinker quips,

[16]Joanna Bourke, 'The Rise and Rise of Sexual Violence', 236–5; Hans Peter Duerr, *Obszönität und Gewalt. Band 3: Der Mythos vom Zivilisationsprozeß* (Frankfurt am Main: Suhkampf, 1993), 411.

[17]Jonathan Shepherd, 'Violent Crime in Bristol: An Accident and Emergency Department Perspective', *The British Journal of Criminology*, 30, no. 3 (1990): 289–305.

'that works out to a homicide rate of 25 per cent, which is about a thousand times higher than the equivalent rates in Western countries today'. Although Pinker knows the Biblical story not to be true, he insists on citing it as factual, rather than symbolic, just to illustrate his main thesis that 'sensibilities towards violence' have changed over time. How exactly is anyone's guess and is in any event a complete misreading of the Bible from both a literary and a historical perspective.

A further lesson about this topic can be drawn from Sara Butler's chapter. When it suits his argument, all material is uncritically accepted by Pinker; in a parallel move, any contradictory or disconfirming evidence he consistently ignores, dismisses or rejects. Let us take as an example the Spanish Inquisition, which Pinker claims killed 350,000 people. This is totally erroneous. As any scholar of early modern Europe now knows, what is called the Spanish Inquisition was much less punitive than was once thought, although just how punitive it was is a matter of contention. One historian estimates that during the 350-year period that was the Inquisition (from around 1478 to 1834), about 1.8 per cent of those who were brought to trial were actually executed across the whole of the Spanish Empire from Sicily to Peru. That admittedly comes to a total figure of around 810 executions, even if many thousands more death sentences were passed. It is a death rate that was actually lower than the courts in the rest of Europe. That figure has been suggested by the historian Joseph Pérez, a leading authority on the subject.[18] What is odd about this is that Pinker actually cites Pérez in a footnote, which leads one to wonder if he either missed the figure in question or if he is cherry-picking higher estimates because they buttress his argument. This is an old, transparent tactic: dramatize your point, and contrast it as sharply as possible with its negative opposite, even if that requires parody, simplification or distortion.

Other forms of violence

Another example of Pinker's fast-and-loose use of 'data' is modern slavery and human trafficking. In *The Better Angels*, Pinker blithely dismisses any concerns one might have about human trafficking in our own time with the assertion that there can be no comparison between it and the Atlantic slave trade, meaning that the latter event is exponentially more violent than the former. The Atlantic slave trade involved millions of people, predominantly

---

[18]Joseph Pérez, *The Spanish Inquisition* (New Haven: Yale University Press, 2006), 173. And for a discussion on the difficulty of assessing the number of executions, see Henry Kamen, *The Spanish Inquisition: An Historical Revision* (London: Phoenix Giant, 1998), 67–8. Kamen argues that it is unlikely that more than 2,000 people were executed for heresy in Spain over that whole period.

sub-Saharan Africans, being kidnapped from their homelands and transported under horrific conditions to the faraway Americas and into a form of lifelong physical bondage from which there was no escape. In contrast, he states, modern-day human trafficking is usually not for life and is often imbricated in contemporary migration movements.[19]

Regions with poverty, armed conflict and high numbers of displaced people are the best recruiting grounds for coerced labour today as are women, adolescents and children without parents. Because of the shadowy nature of the activity, it is difficult to obtain exact figures. According to the latest statistics by the International Labour Organization (ILO) and the Walk Free Foundation, there are more than 40 million people in the world today who are 'forced to work, through fraud or threat of violence, for no pay beyond subsistence'.[20] This is what the ILO calls the 'underside of globalization'. Around 30 per cent are trafficked for sex, while 70 per cent are in situations of forced labour. There is no doubt that what Harold Hongju Koh calls 'the new global slave trade' flourishes today and that it continues to evolve in order to cater to rising consumer demand in the world for cheap goods and cheap sex. Each year it generates many billions of dollars in profits and is judged one of the fastest growing transnational criminal businesses. Migrant smuggling is a related illegal practice and source of injury and death.

'Today, of course, slavery is illegal for everyone', Pinker states, as if this mere pronouncement will make the problem vanish.[21] But laws express legislative and humanitarian ideals, not realities. The European Union, the United Nations, the US Senate and State Department, and religious leaders of the Anglican, Buddhist, Hindu, Jewish and Muslim faiths have all recognized and issued proclamations against the trafficking of human beings in our own time. To contain the counterevidence to his thesis that our time is the most peaceful ever in the history of humanity, he is compelled to dismiss or downplay new forms of violence that were not recorded in the past. The evidence of these practices that is provided by researchers working on the problem, Pinker asserts, is 'pulled out of thin air and inflated for their advocacy value', mainly the expression of an overheated moral crusade. Because today we do not find Africans who are physically in chains being sold openly in the marketplaces of Charleston, Havana or Rio di Janeiro,

---

[19]Pinker, *Better Angels*, 157–8.
[20]Monique Villa, *Slaves Among Us: The Hidden World of Human Trafficking* (London: Rowman and Littlefield, 2019), 2; Kevin Bales, *Disposable People: New Slavery in the Global Economy* (Berkeley: University of California Press, 1999); and Louise Shelley, *Human Trafficking: A Global Perspective* (Cambridge: Cambridge University Press, 2010). See also, Harold Hongju Koh, 'The New Global Slave Trade', in Kate E. Tunstall (ed.), *Displacement, Asylum, Migration* (Oxford: Oxford University Press, 2006), 232–55. A related problem is the global traffic in human organs. See Nancy Scheper-Hughes and Loïc Wacquant (eds), *Commodifying Bodies* (London: Sage, 2002).
[21]Pinker, *Better Angels*, 649.

he ignores other forms of human enslavement. This manoeuvre is perhaps made easier for him because the most active regions of trafficking today include West Africa, the Arabian Peninsula and Southeast Asia, that is, sites outside of the West.

In a related irony, Pinker appears oblivious to the short-term and long-term psychological damage inflicted on victims by the various trafficking industries, an omission that is a wee bit problematic coming from one of the world's most prominent professors of psychology. The whole concept of psychological violence – that is, trauma induced in a wartime or civilian setting – is absent from Pinker's purportedly comprehensive account of violence in our time. Pinker's idea of violence is, in fact, quite narrow, and is limited to actual physical, intentional violence. That is why Mark Micale has elsewhere highlighted much of what is left out – colonial violence and violence against indigenous peoples, as well as violence of an environmental, biological or technological nature.[22] And, of course, there are the billions of animals that are slaughtered every year, often in inhumane conditions (no irony intended), in order to satisfy consumer demands for cheap meat and the fast-food industry. These sorts of numbers sit uncomfortably with the idea that we are living in the most peaceful era in human history. It's this kind of nexus between violence towards nature and violence towards humans, forcefully underlined by Corey Ross in this collection, as the planet faces a surge of 'environmental violence', that helps us see violence in another light.

The examples we have adduced earlier highlight what specialists working in the field of violence studies would consider a fundamental problem with Pinker's overall approach. He sees violence as a static thing that can always be measured. Scholars, on the other hand, see violence as a process that morphs in time as societal attitudes change, as what was once acceptable becomes no longer acceptable, as violence, used as a tool, is adapted and shaped to meet different ends in different circumstances. Forms and practices of violence change, and new technology often enhances its intensity, as the history of modern warfare illustrates all too well.

In a parallel fashion, the internet has become a site of child sexual exploitation in ways that few of us care to realize and certainly in ways that never existed even a decade ago. Online trading and sharing of images and videos of children being sexually abused and tortured has increased dramatically over the last twenty years. Indeed, the problem has skyrocketed since 2014 when it was thought the number of images reached the million mark. As of 2018, tech companies identified over 45 million images and videos of children being sexually abused on the internet, some as young as three or four years of age, some even younger. Since around 2000, sex

---

[22]Mark S. Micale, 'What Pinker Leaves Out', *Historical Reflections/Réflexions historiques*, 4, no. 1 (Spring 2018): 128–39; reproduced in Philip Dwyer and Mark S. Micale (eds), *On Violence in History* (New York and Oxford: Berghahn, 2020), chap. 11.

abuse scandals have roiled religious, educational, and athletic organizations, and in recent years high-profile national scandals have come to the fore in Ireland, Australia, and the United States, among many other locations. These criminal abusive practices were previously unseen, unreported, and undocumented; they therefore are treated dismissively in Pinker's feel-good story about the decline of violence in the world today.

Does the avalanche of new coverage of this subject in our own time indicate that there are more paedophiles in the world or that such people can now gain access to material more easily or that more such criminal acts are reported to authorities? Does that mean more children are being abused and assaulted than ever before? It is difficult to determine. Pinker, however, again thinks he knows for sure; he argues that human rights' watchdogs just look harder and in more places for abuse.[23] 'We can be misled into thinking that there is more abuse to detect', and he assures us that historical levels of sexual and physical abuse of children are on the way down.[24] This is another example of a manifestation of violence whose terrible extent has only recently been discovered and documented. What we can say with some degree of certainty is that criminal elements – including those spreading hate speech and terrorist propaganda – have been able to exploit the internet exponentially in ways that largely avoid most forms of prosecution. It cannot, however, be excluded from a comprehensive accounting of violence in our own time.

Interpreting history and violence

Yet another objection to Pinker's history is that he treats all past atrocities equally, as if the only thing that mattered was the death count. These atrocities, in all their enormous variety, are wrenched out of their defining historical context, and neither the period during which they occurred nor the surrounding cultural circumstances are given any consideration. In his chapter on indigenous violence in the Americas in this collection, Matthew Restall points out that the all-too-familiar claim that the Aztecs sacrificed forty people a day in gory public rituals is nonsense, while the long-standing religious meaning of human sacrifice within Mesoamerican societies is completely ignored. Pinker even analyses in similarly simplistic terms historical events that readers tend to be much more familiar with. Proportionally speaking, according to Pinker, the Second World War was the ninth-deadliest conflict of all time, whereas the Arab slave trade and the Atlantic slave trade rank as No. 3 on his hit list of world historical atrocities.

---

[23]Pinker, *Enlightenment Now*, 207.
[24]Pinker, *Enlightenment Now*, 229.

Now, not only is comparing distant and very different time periods problematic in general – recall Pinker's own refusal to contemplate modern slavery on those very grounds – but it is a failure to consider the crucial historical conditions and circumstances surrounding those two vastly different events. The Second World War occurred over a concentrated six-year period in the second quarter of the twentieth century in Europe and the Far East during which the cataclysmic events that were Auschwitz, Dresden and Hiroshima unfolded. The Atlantic slave trade triangulated Western Europe, sub-Saharan Africa, North and South America and the circum-Caribbean. It extended over hundreds of years, and its main motivation was economic gain. No two historical events are ever equivalent, but the Second World War and the Atlantic slave trade are surely apples and oranges. If we want to measure the depth and significance of a past event of mass violence, it defies logic to simply compare the number of deaths involved. It is also disconcerting to find that some events, like deaths of the twentieth-century world wars, are judged relative to world population, whereas rates of death in warfare in non-state and state societies are not.[25]

Surely, killing rates in the past, insofar as they are knowable, are one, but only one, indication of both the intensity and horror of a particular event. The Holocaust serves as a glaring example. Astoundingly, Pinker discounts the Nazi genocide as a central or even significant event in the development of long-term human violence by hiding the atrocity in world population figures. Ten or eleven million people killed in Nazi concentration camps in the span of only a few years may not seem like much as a proportion of the world's population. The Holocaust takes on an entirely different perspective if comprehended as a proportion of the population of Central and Eastern Europe. Worse still, Pinker argues that the 'hemoclysm' – an odd term that Pinker draws from the self-proclaimed 'atrocitologist', Matthew White, to denote the mid-twentieth-century world wars – was a 'fluke'.[26] Yes, a fluke, part of the random distribution of wars that were somehow an exception to the rule. Apart from the fact that such a view is highly offensive, scholars across the disciplinary spectrum would beg to differ. Here is the sociologist Siniša Malešević:

> The twentieth-century casualties of inter-polity violence total more than 120 million and, as such, they constitute around two-thirds of all war deaths for the last five thousand years on this planet. Simply put, in the last hundred years we moderns have killed twenty-two times more

---

[25]See the graph in Pinker, *Better Angels*, 53.
[26]Pinker, *Better Angels*, 207–8. Pinker himself realizes just how outlandish this might appear when he qualifies the statement with the caveat, this way of thinking might seem like 'monstrous disrespect to the victims'.

individuals than our precursors did in 4,900 years. Hence, the modern age is the true age of mass slaughter.[27]

Some of the finest thinkers of the past seventy-five years have tried to ponder the moral meaning of this event of state-sponsored mass violence against civilians. For Pinker, the Holocaust is only a statistical-historical aberration.

There is more to it than that, however. Pinker's overarching narrative is based on the thesis of a German sociologist, Norbert Elias, called the 'civilizing process'. To sum up a complex thesis in one sentence is unfair to Elias, who is crucial to Pinker's thesis, both to explain declining rates of violence and to convey a general sense of 'moral progress'. But as Dwyer and Roberts-Pedersen demonstrate in their chapter, Elias is anything but the unheard-of scholar Pinker takes credit for pulling out of obscurity. Not only has Elias inspired a generation of scholars who have produced a whole body of work, most of which seems to have passed over Pinker's head, but the 'civilizing process' as a theoretical explanation is used quite uncritically by Pinker to support his interpretation of violence in human history.

Let's point to two problems. First, one of the biggest criticisms of Elias' 'civilizing process', one which was also directed at Pinker, is that it is Western centric. When Pinker talks of the world, he is generally referring to Western industrialized nations. The histories of the rest of the world, as the contributions by Michael Wert, Nancy Kollman, and Eric Weitz clearly demonstrate, do not follow Pinker's unilinear trajectory. They are emblematic of a bigger problem in that Pinker's schema does not work for non-Western parts of the globe. Second, scholars who have used the 'civilizing process' have always assumed that violence and civility are mutually exclusive, and that indeed they are diametrically opposed forces.[28] History tells us that this is simply not so, and a case in point is the SS. The leaders of the *Einsatzgruppen*, the special mobile killing units on the Eastern front during the Second World War, responsible for the deaths of anywhere between 1.5 and 2 million people, were a highly cultivated, highly educated elite within the cadres of the Nazi party.[29] When looking at the biographies of these men, it is difficult to see how people like Pinker can maintain that 'civility' leads to a decrease in violence.

Can these disparities in interpreting history be explained as mainly differences in perspective? Perhaps to some degree. Asking if we think

---

[27]Siniša Malešević, 'Forms of Brutality: Towards a Historical Sociology of Violence', *European Journal of Social Theory*, 16, no. 3 (July 2013): 11.
[28]Siniša Malešević, *The Rise of Organised Brutality: A Historical Sociology of Violence* (Cambridge: Cambridge University Press, 2017), 134.
[29]Christian Ingrao, *Believe and Destroy: Intellectuals in the SS War Machine* (Cambridge: Polity, 2013).

society is better or worse than before, more or less violent than in the past, is after all a classic 'glass half full or half empty' question. A recent article in the *Proceedings of the National Academy of Sciences*, however, suggests that as population scales up, per capita casualties of violence scale down, regardless of governance, shared commerce or technology.[30] Pinker discounts this argument because it only looks at one kind of violence and doesn't explain what he believes to be an overall decline. A different perspective can help explain why modern conflicts don't involve as many people in modern societies as in the past, even without considering the great increase in the lethality of modern warfare over the past century.

During the Cold War, there was a shift away from wars between nation states to civil wars. Most of the wars that have been fought since 1944 – and there have been over 140 of them – have been 'small' but protracted and very bloody civil wars that involve the so-called great powers only indirectly. Syria is a case in point, with the United States, Russia, Iran and Saudi Arabia all fighting directly or indirectly. Far more people die in the aftermaths of civil war than during the conflict itself as a result of disease, lack of food and shelter, and suicide.[31] The fact that modern wars result in fewer casualties does not mean that violence is in decline, only that the nature of warfare has dramatically evolved. Some see these smaller conflicts as 'New Wars' characterized by the privatization of the military, the ability of rebel armies to finance their activities through the selling of drugs or natural resources, and the apparent loss of the monopoly of violence by states.[32] Pinker, on the other hand, seems to think that war, like violence, is a constant phenomenon throughout history. The fact that wars now have lower casualty rates is not a symptom of a more peaceful era, but rather it is indicative of a highly professionalized (small armies have replaced millions of conscripts) and a highly technologized military (think of drone strikes).[33]

It is all too easy to judge the past from our own perspectives. When we see through the eyes of the modern West, all violence becomes cruel, barbarous and sadistic. As a result, there is a certain victimization of people at the receiving end of violence, whether 'legal' and justified, as in the case of the execution of someone condemned to death for murder, or in the case of a

---

[30]Rahul C. Oka, et al., 'Population is the Main Driver of War Group Size and Conflict Casualties', *Proceedings of the National Academy of Sciences*, 11 December 2017, E11101–E11110. See also Dean Falk and Charles Hildebolt, 'Annual War Deaths in Small-Scale versus State Societies Scale with Population Size Rather than Violence', *Current Anthropology*, 58, no. 6 (2017): 805–13; and Tanisha M. Fazal, 'Dead Wrong?: Battle Deaths, Military Medicine, and Exaggerated Reports of War's Demise', *International Security*, 39, no. 1 (Summer 2014): 95–125.
[31]Bill Kissane, *Nations Torn Asunder: The Challenge of Civil War* (Oxford: Oxford University Press, 2016).
[32]Mann, 'Have Wars and Violence Declined?', 51; Herfried Munkler, *The New Wars*, trans. Patrick Camiller (Oxford: Polity, 2005); and Mary Kaldor, *New and Old Wars: Organized Violence in a Global* Era (Cambridge: Polity, 1999).
[33]Malešević, *The Rise of Organised Brutality*, 152–3.

Mesoamerican sacrificed to the gods in Tenochtitlan, even if they have gone to their deaths willingly. This implicit victimization, which runs throughout Pinker's books, prevents us from understanding the past through the eyes of others.

Consider a more particular historical example, the suicide-murder of Margrethe Christensdatter, a Danish woman who in 1741 decided to murder a nine-year-old girl, rather than commit suicide, knowing that she would be found guilty and executed for her crime.[34] In mid-eighteenth-century Denmark, suicide-murders were religiously motivated; the perpetrators feared hell if they committed suicide but understood that if found guilty of murder and condemned to death, their souls would be saved as long as they were true Christian believers. That is why Margrethe had no fears or doubts when she mounted the scaffold. Just as interesting are the remarks of a young pastor, Henrik Gerner, who witnessed her execution and later wrote in his memoirs:

> This was of course a revolting event, and God save any honourable person from such destiny; but nevertheless there is something good, evangelical and pleasant in it, and it is a great example of the faithful shepherd's unending forbearance and patience in saving the lost souls.

In this instance, the person being executed is not the victim of a brutal state apparatus bent on showing its raw power but an individual who uses the state for their own spiritual salvation. Similarly, sixteenth-century magistrates during the Reformation who ordered the torture and execution of fellow Christians deemed heretical, believed themselves to be acting from the highest motives of Christian charity.[35] The historical figure of Margrethe is not just a statistic: her story becomes comprehensible only with contextual knowledge.

These kinds of insights transform our understanding of the past and demonstrate that when historians study violence through the eyes of contemporary witnesses, they end up posing a very different set of questions. What actually is violence (nowhere posed or answered in *The Better Angels*)? How do people perceive it in different time-place settings? What is its purpose and function? What were contemporary attitudes towards violence and how did sensibilities shift over time? Is violence always 'bad' or can there be 'good' violence, violence that is regenerative and creative? If Pinker had seriously engaged with any of those questions, we would have had a much more credible, sophisticated and interesting book.

---

[34]Tyge Krogh, *A Lutheran Plague: Murdering to Die in the Eighteenth Century* (Leiden: Brill, 2012), 1–5.
[35]Brad S. Gregory, *Salvation at Stake: Christian Martyrdom in Early Modern Europe* (Cambridge, MA: Harvard University Press, 1999), esp. chap. 3.

To be clear, no one, least of all the professional student of history, disagrees that the past was violent. Medieval law recommended public executions, burning, branding, blinding, drowning and castration for felonies, and all devout Christians were encouraged to attend executions as a deterrent from choosing a criminal lifestyle. If violence is a learned trait, medieval men certainly learned it at home. Christians were encouraged to commit acts of self-violence in the form of flagellation and starvation, while husbands were expected to discipline their wives, children and servants. But as with human prehistory, Pinker ludicrously exaggerates the violence that took place during the European Middle Ages. There were tremendous variations across the whole of the continent during this thousand-year epoch. Public executions, for instance, did not attract mass crowds and did not become public spectacles until the late Early Modern period. Executions were rare and small affairs, and the witnesses took part in a sort of Christian drama of salvation, as we have seen in the tragedy of Margrethe, in which both the condemned and the witnesses had defined roles as the condemned person's soul was reconciled with the Christian community before death. As a matter of historical fact, we cannot even say with any certitude that people in the Middle Ages were 'more violent' or 'less violent' than we are today.

Conclusion

Raw data, as we have been at pains to point out, is only made meaningful through interpretation, a basic truism that seems to elude Pinker. Numbers rarely 'speak for themselves'. In 2018, the Violence Research Centre at Cambridge University released an intriguing digital map. The map carefully plots murders that took place in London between 1300 and 1340.[36] The data was gathered by historians from the Coroners' Rolls – the legal records of investigations into 'unnatural deaths', including homicides, suicides and accidents.[37] The map plots 142 deaths over that forty-year period in a city that the map's researchers estimate to be around 80,000 people. The number of yearly deaths then fluctuated between 13 and 22 per year, with an average of 16 annual deaths over the four decades. If we accept the population figure of 80,000, then we come to a homicide rate of around 20 in 100,000. Interestingly, Manuel Eisner, one of the project's team members, is a good deal more circumspect about his conclusions on the map's web page than he

---

[36]Manuel Eisner, 'Interactive London Medieval Murder Map', Institute of Criminology, University of Cambridge, https://www.vrc.crim.cam.ac.uk/vrcresearch/london-medieval-murder-map.
[37]Barbara Hanawalt, 'Violent Death in Fourteenth-and Early Fifteenth-Century England', *Comparative Studies in Society and History*, 18, no. 3 (1976): 297–320; R. F. Hunnisett, *The Medieval Coroner* (Cambridge: Cambridge University Press, 1961); and R. R. Sharpe (ed.), *Calendar of Coroners Rolls of the City of London, AD 1300-1378* (London: R. Clay and Sons, 1913).

has been in media interviews. On the internet site, we read that the rate is 'about 15-20 times more than what we would expect in a UK city of equal size in our times, but a lot lower than the rates that are currently found in some of the most violent cities in the world'. Another historian, Warren Brown, has looked at historical data on violence across England and has come to a different conclusion. As 'counterintuitive' as it might seem, he argues that

> thirteenth-century England as a whole was not significantly more violent than the US or EU around the turn of the twenty-first century. Warwick may have been thirteenth-century England's Washington DC, while Bristol suffered homicide rates only slightly higher than many places in the modern EU. All of this is to say that while much of the US or EU experiences far less violence than much of thirteenth-century England, some city dwellers in the United States and some inhabitants of Russia endure about the same level. And some parts of thirteenth-century England experienced levels of violence little different from those found in much of the west today.[38]

Brown further concludes, as do many of the contributors to this volume, that medieval societies, indeed one could argue all past societies, were *differently* violent. That is, violence was used differently in different situations, according to what was considered acceptable and what was not. The question then is not 'how violent was such and such a period', but rather, 'how was such and such a period violent?'

Readers might consider the debates between Pinker and the growing chorus of his critics to be primarily a disparity in how different knowledge fields do their work, or a difference in ideas, or of conceptions of humanity. There may be some truth to this observation. We have been at pains, however, to point out that Pinker – despite his hard data, just-the-facts rhetoric – has a hidden ideological agenda, one with powerful present-day implications. His work is a defence of neoliberalism and the capitalist world system, of the overwhelming benefits of the free-market and Western civilization. Now, one can argue that capitalism, democracy and free trade have brought tremendous gains to the West, but it is equally undeniable that those gains have been achieved at the expense of the rest of the world, an exploitation that continues today. Many of today's conflicts in Africa are intimately connected with global capitalism.

In Pinker's mind, Western civilization and capitalism are inherently good, rather than violent, unequal and unjust. Violence is an aberration, but never a symptom of capitalism's relentless, global ascent. This book critiques Pinker

---

[38] Warren Brown, *Violence in Medieval Europe* (Harlow: Longman Pearson, 2011), 5.

not because his overarching thesis that life today is less violent than before is necessarily wrong. It may well be the case for some people living in some places of the Western World, including the sphere that Pinker personally inhabits, but we do not have a fundamentally pessimistic view of human nature. We do not believe, in contrast to Pinker, that violence is innate, nor do we believe in a view of the world that sees humans as intrinsically violent. As such, we offer these chapters in the best spirit of critical questioning and inquiry that was the core of the Enlightenment project. If *The Better Angels* and *Enlightenment Now* are history, they are very bad history. The best response to the attention these books have unfortunately attracted seems clear: to assemble a generous sampling of scholarship by an international cast of distinguished historians who demonstrate the work of true historical scholarship at its finest.

PART ONE

Interpretations

2

The inner demons of *The Better Angels of Our Nature*

Daniel Lord Smail

In the final stages of preparing this chapter for publication, I had an illuminating exchange with a colleague in the field of evolutionary psychology whose work I admire and respect. I had asked him whether he would be kind enough to read and fact-check several paragraphs that provide a short overview of recent trends in the field of evolutionary psychology. Those paragraphs seemed fine to him, which was good. But his email closed on an odd note, for he mentioned that he was a 'bit sad' to read my critique of *The Better Angels of Our Nature*. The use of the word brought me up short. I felt that I had made an interesting case, grounded in argument and evidence, to the effect that the tools used by Pinker to measure the decline of violence are inadequate to the task. What was there to be sad about?

However trivial this exchange, it demonstrates how the polarization of the political sphere today has settled into the sphere of knowledge, dividing the humanities from the sciences. Studies by psychologists have demonstrated the degree to which people evaluate truth claims not so much by evidence as by the degree to which those claims are consonant with social goals and political affiliations.[1] In this case, my colleague probably felt sad because

[1] See, inter alia, Hugo Mercier and Dan Sperber, *The Enigma of Reason* (Cambridge, MA: Harvard University Press, 2017). I am grateful to Daniel Mroczek and Matthew Liebmann for their thoughts and suggestions and to the students of Anthropology/History 2059 for their insightful contributions to the broader themes of this chapter. Many thanks to friends and colleagues, including Philip Dwyer, Mark Micale and Julia Adeney Thomas, for their valuable feedback on an earlier draft.

he learned that I belonged to the other tribe. On my side, I felt that my reasoned arguments were like popguns aimed against the wall of faith that surrounds the enduring belief in the decline of violence.

Faith in the decline-of-violence thesis is widespread in the general public. The popularity of the best-selling *Better Angels* arose because it told people something they already wanted to believe in. In Western societies, belief in the decline of violence is rooted in Hobbesian understandings about the brutishness of primitive societies. It is a prominent theme in some of the earliest history textbooks and readers, first published more than a century ago. Belief in the decline of violence was further amplified in the twentieth century by theories such as the 'killer ape' hypothesis proposed by Raymond Dart, the paleoanthropologist who helped found the new field of African paleoanthropology starting in the 1920s.[2] The belief is particularly strong among certain members of the scientific community for whom the decline of violence is a component of a broader belief in the existence and goodness of progress.

Once upon a time, historians also believed in progress, and felt it was their duty to heap praise upon it, especially in textbooks and curricula that extolled the values of Western civilization. But we have for the most part lost this sunny sense of optimism. As a graduate student in the late 1980s, I was taught that the first serious doubts about progress arose in the wake of the Holocaust, as historians began to confront the horrors of the Nazi era and found that they could not be squared with a belief in Western civilization. More recent trends in historiography, I am told, point to the shocking calamities of the Great War as the moment when scholars began to raise the first doubts about the idea of progress.[3] To indigenous peoples today, of course, progress, as defined by Westerners, was never more than convenient excuse for taking their land. In the same way that one person's justice is another person's vengeance, progress exists only in the eye of the beholder. One of the things that history never used to do very well was to see things from others' points of view. In recent decades, we have done a lot better, and the lessons we have gained have been sobering.

To cast doubt upon the possibility of progress is not to question the fact of change. In living systems, change is common and easy to explain; what's hard to explain is stasis. Many trends in the human past, moreover, have the appearance of directionality, in part because many kinds of change are associated with a path that is taken from which there is no turning back. There is a significant difference, for example, between the human world of the Pleistocene and the human world of today. But change is not progress. Progress is a moral claim, to the effect that today's world is better than the

---

[2]Dart's arguments were popularized in an influential work by Robert Ardrey, *African Genesis: A Personal Investigation into the Animal Origins and Nature of Man* (London: Collins, 1961).
[3]Paul Valéry, 'La crise de l'esprit', *Nouvelle Revue Française*, 13 (1919): 321–37.

world of the past. In the same way that no palaeontologist would ever claim that today's creatures are better than dinosaurs, fewer and fewer historians are inclined to say that today's world is morally better than the past.

A belief in moral progress, in point of fact, is an outlier in Western historiography, since Western historians writing before the nineteenth century rarely assumed that there had been any moral progress over time. Only in the second half of the nineteenth century was the concept of progress brought into the narratives of history in a serious way. This being the case, the field of history has been retreating from the idea of progress for about as long as it upheld that idea. But when history began to shed the vision of progress and abandon the Western civilization course through which it had once been mediated, it created a serious interpretive vacuum for people whose moral cosmology relies on a belief in progress. If you happen to believe in the values of Western civilization, it must have been disturbing to discover that historians were no longer willing to peddle it. Who, then, will be your champion? Who will hold firm in the belief in progress when the historians have abandoned it?

In 2011, Steven Pinker took up the mantle with the publication of *The Better Angels of Our Nature*, and has since developed those arguments further in *Enlightenment Now: The Case for Reason, Science, Humanism, and Progress*.[4] Both books offer a spirited defence of Western civilization and do so through the writing of history. I open my door to anyone who believes that the study of the past can bring clarity. Like most of my colleagues in the profession, I don't believe that history should belong only to the historians. As the chapters in this volume demonstrate, some historians have bristled at Pinker's efforts to make a contribution to history, but this is not because historians are inhospitable. The problem is that Pinker is indifferent to the basic tenets of academic hospitality, like a guest who tracks mud into the house, puts his feet on the table and spills ash on the carpet. These violations of hospitality seem peculiar, given Pinker's belief in the civilizing function of manners. Much of his recent work has an equally paradoxical quality. He deploys a set of heuristic devices – that is to say, images and motifs which are designed to evoke visceral responses – instead of careful and reasoned analyses. He argues so passionately on behalf of reason that he cannot see how he treats his opponents with the violence and contempt that by his own argument are qualities appropriate to the barbaric human past.

Inspired by the dichotomy that informs *Better Angels*, I shall divide these remarks into two sections, the first of which addresses some of the book's excellent qualities. Like Pinker, I believe that the brain–body system is an actor in the making of history, and have long been an admirer and user of

---

[4]Steven Pinker, *The Better Angels of Our Nature: Why Violence Has Declined* (New York: Viking, 2011); Steven Pinker, *Enlightenment Now: The Case for Reason, Science, Humanism, and Progress* (New York: Viking, 2018).

some of Pinker's prior scholarship. Where Pinker draws on his own expertise in the cognitive sciences, there is much to commend in the book. But *Better Angels* is also characterized by some inner demons. These arise when the author's passion for his subject overwhelms his capacity to do due diligence when it comes to researching and understanding the human past.

The better angels of *Better Angels*

In the second half of the nineteenth century, in the wake of the time revolution that accompanied the 1859 publication of Charles Darwin's *On the Origin of Species*, the bottom dropped out from the world's chronology, leaving European historians teetering on the edge of the vast abyss of time.[5] Nineteenth-century European cosmology was a brittle thing, so tightly strung onto the 6,000-year time frame allotted by interpretations of the Book of Genesis that the discovery of deep time should have shattered that cosmology into a thousand shards. That it did not is one of the most remarkable happenings in the history of Western historiography. Between 1850 and 1950, the short chronology of shallow history was not abandoned. Instead, it was translated into a secular key, as the origins of human history were moved from the biblical Garden of Eden to ancient Mesopotamia. This sleight of hand allowed Euro-American historians to avoid the difficult task of learning how to narrate human history in deep time.

This shift was never more than a stop-gap solution. By arbitrarily dividing the full span of human history into two non-communicating phases, the time of biology and the time of history, Western historians succeeded for a while in preserving the 6,000-year chronology. They did so, however, at the cost of losing sight of the rest of human time. In recent years, the inadequacy of a chronological framework that excludes the human Pleistocene has become increasingly clear. The stories we tell about a number of topics – including gender, social hierarchy, poverty, material culture and the environment, indigeneity, trust, religion and many others – cannot be adequately told without reference to the deep human past.

In recent years, some historians have begun to propose new ways to link humanity's deep past with the present, and their work has joined a veritable flood of books written by non-historians.[6] At its best, *Better Angels* makes

---

[5]I have written about this fascinating story in the opening chapters of *On Deep History and the Brain* (Berkeley: University of California Press, 2008). See also Andrew Shryock, Daniel Lord Smail, Timothy K. Earle, et al., *Deep History: The Architecture of Past and Present* (Berkeley: University of California Press, 2011).

[6]Works by historians include David Christian, *Maps of Time: An Introduction to Big History* (Berkeley: University of California Press, 2004); Felipe Fernández-Armesto, *Humankind: A Brief History* (Oxford and New York: Oxford University Press, 2004); Yuval N. Harari, *Sapiens: A Brief History of Humankind* (London: Harvill Secker, 2014).

an original contribution to this literature, using the history of violence as an organizing thread. The narrative arc of *Better Angels* is dominated by the trope of decline, in this case the decline of violence, and, like all narrative arcs, this one is based on quantitative claims. This brings us to one of the most interesting methodological challenges associated with the writing of humanity's deep history, namely the fact that the evidence we use necessarily changes across the long span of human time, in the hand-off from palaeontology and human evolutionary biology to archaeology and history. How do we commensurate findings based on evidence drawn from independent lines of inquiry?

Pinker rises to the challenge by offering a single proxy for violence, namely the rate of homicide or violent death, and then attempting to marshal all available data, regardless of domain or methodology, in order to measure change over time. Scientists use a 'proxy' whenever the thing they want to measure is not itself directly measurable. By way of example, we cannot measure actual temperatures in previous eras of earth's history, but we can extrapolate changes in temperature from the changing ratio of oxygen isotopes found in oceanic cores. Violence, in much the same way, is not directly measurable, hence the need for a proxy. Some archaeologists and anthropologists have expressed reservations about the reliability of the data he uses to describe rates of violent death in the earliest historical periods, as discussed by Linda Fibiger in her chapter in this volume.[7] As a medieval historian, I have no particular objection to the claim that the homicide rate in later medieval Europe was high relative to today. My own concern, described further on in this chapter, addresses the appropriateness of a proxy that excludes the many forms of structural violence, often non-lethal, that afflict women, the poor and the disempowered. But either way, this is a good and healthy debate. To reiterate, *Better Angels* offers a bold new model for linking the many eras of the human past into a single history.

As suggested earlier, the narrative arc of *Better Angels* is defined by decline. This isn't entirely accurate as a characterization, however, because Pinker also deploys a very different type of narrative explanation based on a form I shall call the 'slider'. Let me explain. The 'better angels' and 'inner demons' of the book are heuristic devices for conveying more complex ideas. The first term refers to the human capacity for cooperation, altruism and empathy; its counterpart describes the human propensity for tribal hostility, suspicion and violence. Both predispositions, according to Pinker,

---

[7]See Nam C. Kim, 'Angels, Illusions, Hydras, and Chimeras: Violence and Humanity', *Reviews in Anthropology*, 41, no. 4 (2012): 239–72; R. Brian Ferguson, 'Pinker's List: Exaggerating Prehistoric War Mortality', in Douglas Fry (ed.), *War, Peace, and Human Nature: The Convergence of Evolutionary and Cultural Views* (Oxford: Oxford University Press, 2013), 112–31.

emerged in the evolutionary past.[8] But although all humans have the weird capacity to be both angels and demons at the same time, the intensity of the predisposition is variable. To a significant degree, environmental or cultural circumstances are able to play up the angels and play down the demons, or vice versa.

Now array these predispositions at the ends of a single behavioural spectrum and add a slider that can be moved left or right, depending on biographical or historical circumstances. Any individual will be located somewhere on the spectrum. More interestingly, you can characterize whole populations by averaging the propensities of all the individuals in the group. This is a dramatically simplified reduction of a complicated situation, of course, but it makes the point. The central historical explanation of *Better Angels* describes a movement of the slider from violence to peace.

From time to time, I find myself discussing this interesting argument with students and colleagues. Almost invariably, it turns out that no one gets the basic idea. The reason, I think, is that Pinker's critics often view him as a genetic determinist, as someone who believes that genes make us do things in the absence of free will. But this critique is not accurate, at least where *Better Angels* is concerned. The arguments of the book, instead, are built on the claim that culture matters. In particular, Pinker claims that the forces responsible for moving the slider from the demonic towards the angelic can be located in the cultural changes associated with the rise of civility, manners and education in the West. There was nothing preordained about this, and no guarantee that the slider, henceforward, will remain on the angelic side. 'Declines in violence', Pinker argues in a sentence that is often not noticed by his critics, 'are caused by political, economic, and ideological conditions that take hold in particular cultures at particular times. If the conditions reverse, violence could go right back up'.[9] Far from being a teleology, the dominant narrative of *Better Angels* is founded on the idea that the path forward in time is not fixed but can take odd or accidental turns.

Why do some readers miss this point? To appreciate what Pinker is arguing, it helps to be familiar with the latest trends in the field of evolutionary psychology. At the risk of oversimplifying a complex and interesting subject, let me define a distinction between the evolutionary psychology of the 1990s and that of today. The earlier form, which I call Evolutionary Psychology 1.0, was based on the thesis of massive modularity. Scholars in the field assumed that many forms of human behaviour are governed by hard-wired modules that arose in the brain over the course of human evolution.[10] Thus,

---

[8] See also Robert M. Sapolsky, *Behave: The Biology of Humans at Our Best and Worst* (New York: Penguin, 2017).

[9] Pinker, *Better Angels*, 361.

[10] See the critical overview in David J. Buller, *Adapting Minds: Evolutionary Psychology and the Persistent Quest for Human Nature* (Cambridge, MA: MIT Press, 2005).

we are afraid of the dark not because the unlit basement is dangerous but instead because the ancestral night was full of leopards who ate us. The gene-centred approach to human cognition and human behaviour characteristic of EP 1.0 was founded on the idea that although culture changes rapidly, genes change slowly or not at all. Blindly and dumbly, they continue to prime us to behave in an environment that no longer exists.

Given that Pinker's best-selling 1997 work, *How the Mind Works*, was one of the leading texts in EP 1.0, readers are not at fault for associating him with the idea that genes are destiny.[11] But unbeknownst to some of its critics, the field of evolutionary psychology has undergone a shift in recent years towards EP 2.0, which offers a more nuanced and less deterministic explanation for human behaviour. Consider, by way of example, Jonathan Haidt's work of moral psychology, *The Righteous Mind*.[12] Haidt argues that all people are capable of having five moral senses. That much is a given. But the intensity of the moral sense is not fixed *a priori*. Instead, given cultures or environments are capable of overactivating some of the moral senses and deactivating others. By way of analogy, think of a painter who has five pigments at her disposal and uses them to greater or lesser degrees, or sometimes not at all. Since the moral senses can be activated to greater or lesser degrees, this means that every human subpopulation, and indeed every individual, has a unique moral canvas. In point of fact, evolutionary psychology has always acknowledged a significant degree of cognitive plasticity. The chief difference between EP 1.0 and EP 2.0 is that the recent scholarship, in line with the latest research coming out of cognitive neuroscience and related fields, has been emphasizing plasticity to a greater and greater degree.

Historical explanation, lately, has been troubled by the difficulty of explaining how the universal fits with the particular; this is one of the legacies of a short chronology that excluded the deep human past from the time of human history. Scholars in the history of emotions, for example, have claimed that anything that is universal must be invisible to history, a discipline concerned with explaining change in the past. As Barbara Rosenwein has put it, 'if emotions are, as many scientists think, biological entities, universal within all human populations, do they – indeed can they – have much of a history at all?'[13] Jan Plamper has acknowledged that it might well be true that emotions 'possess a constant, transhistorical, and culturally generalized foundation'. But since history is interested in what

---

[11]Steven Pinker, *How the Mind Works* (New York: Norton, 1997).

[12]Jonathan Haidt, *The Righteous Mind: Why Good People Are Divided by Politics and Religion* (New York: Pantheon Books, 2012).

[13]Barbara H. Rosenwein, 'Problems and Methods in the History of Emotions', *Passions in Context: International Journal for the History and Theory of Emotions*, 1 (2010), published online at http://www.passionsincontext.de, accessed 16 March 2018.

varies in human cultures, he argues, these universals are 'uninteresting' and at best 'trivially true'.[14] I admire their work, but I think the historical philosophy that undergirds it doesn't fully capture all that is interesting in the relationship between the universal and the particular. The slider model developed by Pinker and many other scholars these days offers a device for making universals visible to historical practice. In this regard, *Better Angels* is very good to think with.

The inner demons of *Better Angels*

In turning to the inner demons of *Better Angels*, I shall put on the hat I wear as a historian of later medieval Europe, a period portrayed with withering scorn in *Better Angels*. Europe between the years 1250 and 1500 was a foreign country, and they did things differently there. Some of those things were admirable. Their diet consisted of completely organic and locally sourced foods, and no one suffered from opioid addiction. In the absence of dietary sugar, diabetes was rare. People took care of their friends and family and recycled nearly everything that came into the household. Some of the other aspects of life were maybe not so admirable, at least to us. But the past is past. We study it today in order to understand another world on its own terms and to learn more about the endless ways in which humans have been human. With this in mind, consider the Middle Ages as depicted in *Better Angels*:

> Medieval Christendom was a culture of cruelty. Torture was meted out by national and local governments throughout the Continent, and it was codified in laws that prescribed blinding, branding, amputation of hands, ears, noses and tongues, and other forms of mutilation as punishments for minor crimes. Executions were orgies of sadism, climaxing with ordeals of prolonged killing such as burning at the stake, breaking on the wheel, pulling apart by horses, impalement through the rectum, disembowelment by winding a man's intestines around a spool and even hanging, which was a slow racking and strangulation rather than a quick breaking of the neck. Sadistic tortures were also inflicted by the Christian church during its inquisitions, witch hunts, and religious wars. Torture had been authorized by the ironically named Pope Innocent IV in 1251, and the order of Dominican monks carried it out with relish. As the *Inquisition* coffee table book notes, under Pope Paul IV (1555–9), the Inquisition was 'downright insatiable – Paul, a Dominican and one-time Grand Inquisitor, was himself a fervent and skilled practitioner of torture and atrocious mass murders'.[15]

---

[14]Jan Plamper, *The History of Emotions: An Introduction*, trans. Keith Tribe (Oxford: Oxford University Press, 2015), 32–3.
[15]Pinker, *Better Angels*, 132.

Yow. It is difficult to know where to begin. On a factual level, executions in later medieval Europe were rare on a per capita basis; the same is true for judicial torture. It's not that the kind of stuff described by Pinker never happened; by the sixteenth and seventeenth centuries, it's fair to say that rates of torture and execution had risen from 'rare' to 'very uncommon'. But a 'culture of cruelty'?

So, where did Pinker go wrong? He has fallen victim to something psychologists have described as the availability heuristic, where impressions that are striking and ready-to-hand in pop culture overwhelmed his duty to deal responsibly with the literature in the field. Although Sara Butler has already dealt fully with Pinker's shortcomings in this volume, let me add some additional thoughts by drawing attention to the scholarly literature that Pinker has cited as evidence for this portrayal. One of the references is mentioned in the passage: a 'coffee table book'. Huh? The endnote refers to a source identified in the bibliography in this way: 'Held, R. 1986. *Inquisition: A selected survey of the collection of torture instruments from the Middle Ages to our times*. Aslockton, Notts, U.K.: Avon & Arno'.[16] You can do the next bit on your own: go to the Library of Congress or another authoritative repository and try to authenticate the book's existence. In fairness to Pinker, you will find a related title by Mr Held, and in this book you can find a passage that is similar to the one cited.[17] But I have only this to say about the real book: it is not very good.[18] Another citation in *Better Angels* takes you to the work of an author who, alarmingly, was once a professional sword-swallower.[19] Several other citations inspire more confidence at first blush, but problems happen when you read further. A book chapter by the legal scholar Sanford Levinson, for instance, offers no support for the claims that Pinker attributes to it.[20] Most problematically, you will search *Better Angels* in vain for the formative book on European law and torture by the legal historian John Langbein, or the nuanced and thoughtful rebuttal to Langbein offered by the medieval historian Edward Peters.[21] Neither book is

---

[16]Pinker, *Better Angels*, 751.

[17]Robert Held, Marcello Bertoni and Amor Gil, *Inquisition: A Bilingual Guide to the Exhibition of Torture Instruments from the Middle Ages to the Industrial Era, Presented in Various European Cities in 1983-87* (Florence: Qua d'Arno, 1985), 14.

[18]Among medieval historians, it is widely known that the supposed instruments of torture (a) post-date the Middle Ages and (b) are often fake. For a debunking of the 'pear of anguish' (*Better Angels*, 131; *Inquisition*, 132–3), see Chris Bishop, 'The "Pear of Anguish": Truth, Torture and Dark Medievalism', *International Journal of Cultural Studies*, 17, no. 6 (2014): 591–602.

[19]Daniel Mannix, *The History of Torture* (Sutton: Phoenix Mill, Stroud, Gloucestershire, 2003). For an obituary identifying his days as a carnival performer, see http://www.nytimes.com/1997/02/08/arts/daniel-mannix-85-adventure-writer.html, accessed 22 February 2021.

[20]Sanford Levinson, 'Contemplating Torture: An Introduction', in Sanford Levinson (ed.), *Torture: A Collection*, (Oxford: Oxford University Press, 2004), 23–43.

[21]John H. Langbein, *Torture and the Law of Proof: Europe and England in the Ancien Régime* (Chicago: University of Chicago Press, 1977); Edward Peters, *Torture*, expanded edn (Philadelphia: University of Pennsylvania Press, 1996).

hard to find. Here is one of the rules of academic hospitality: when you enter
another discipline, take time to cite the appropriate literature.

At a basic level, Pinker is wrong about the facts he has presented, at
least where medieval Europe is concerned. This inattentiveness to the rules
for assembling and citing evidence is troubling in a work that otherwise
extols the virtues of Western reasoning. One of the tenets of Enlightenment
philosophy is that the subjects of knowledge are obscured from us by a haze
of suppositions, myths and misdirections. Some of the haze results from the
mischievous activity of sword-swallowers and other charlatans. Some of it is
produced by common-sense reasoning that just happens to be wrong. Either
way, truth lies beneath the veneer of appearance, and scholars do research
in order to peel back the veil.

Why did Pinker's predisposition to demonize the medieval European
past overwhelm his duty to practise responsible scholarship? I have puzzled
a great deal over this. Like Butler, I think that the answer lies partly in
the fact that Pinker needs a barbaric Middle Ages. In *Better Angels*, the
period occupies what the anthropologist Michel-Rolph Trouillot famously
called the 'savage slot'.[22] What Trouillot meant is that for some kinds of
anthropological or historical arguments, there just have to be savages, so
the savages are conjured into existence regardless of whether they are real
or not. What is especially curious is that Pinker's need to demonize the
Middle Ages leads him into a profound logical inconsistency. In Chapter 2,
he praises 'Leviathan', the coercive apparatus of the state, as the first of
several historical forces responsible for bringing down the supposedly high
levels of prehistoric violence.[23] The threat of punishment, supposedly, helped
tamp down the rage circuitry. In Chapter 4, though, Pinker takes torture and
spectacles of execution, the very tools used by Leviathan to control excessive
violence, and recategorizes them as evidence for primitive or unbridled
violence. The savage slot, like some dark shadow, always follows a step
behind as Pinker moves forward in time.

Why must there be savages? I have come to believe that Pinker's *a priori*
commitment to a belief in past violence is driven to a large extent by his
visceral reaction to pain and suffering. He is genuinely horrified by the
suffering that is inextricably associated with life in nature (e.g. p. 32). Like
a shaman, he slides readily into the bodies of other animals – the starling
torn apart by the hawk; the horse tormented by insects – and feels their pain.
He demonizes the human past because he assimilates it to the horrors of a
natural world that is filled with misery and suffering. In this view, history
describes the story of how humanity clawed itself out of the nightmarish

---

[22]Michel-Rolph Trouillot, 'Anthropology and the Savage Slot: The Poetics and Politics of Otherness', in Richard G. Fox (ed.), *Recapturing Anthropology: Working in the Present* (Santa Fe:
School of American Research Press, 1991), 17–44.
[23]An instance can be seen in Pinker, *Better Angels*, 35.

world of natural selection. Thanks to the blessed constraints of civilization, we have been rescued from the ravages of the diseases and animals that once preyed upon our bodies and from the violence of our fellow humans. The savage slot, in this world historical vision, is occupied by nature itself.

As all this suggests, *Better Angels* is not a work of history. It is better understood as a work of moral and historical theology, where nature, in the immortal words of the character played by Katharine Hepburn in *The African Queen*, 'is what we are put in this world to rise above'. Nature, not sin, is the source of all that is evil and violent, and the coming of civilization plays the role of the saviour. I am in no position to comment on these moral claims. On the question of whether the study of the past is compatible with moral theology, however, I stand with Stephen Jay Gould, who addressed the temptation to moralize the past in his 1982 essay, 'Nonmoral Nature'. Gould's essay explores a question that agonized the theologians and naturalists of nineteenth-century Europe: 'How could a benevolent God create such a world of carnage and bloodshed?' The question arose because naturalists had brought to light many features of the natural world that seemed utterly revolting to Victorian moralists and incompatible with the idea of a beneficent deity. A noteworthy example, discussed in Gould's essay, was the behaviour of parasitical ichneumon wasps whose larvae consume their paralysed hosts from the inside out, preserving essential organs until the very end.

Here is Gould's answer to the conundrum: 'Nature contains no moral messages framed in human terms. Morality is a subject for philosophers, theologians, students of the humanities, indeed for all thinking people. The answers will not be read passively from nature; they do not, and cannot, arise from the data of science.'[24] Like the naturalist who studies not only koala bears and gentle earthworms but also parasitical ichneumon wasps, slave-making ants and infanticidal Hanuman langurs, the historian comes across things that are admirable and things that are ugly. But it is crucial to understand that ugly things are there not because the society that evinces them is *past*. They are there because humans, like every other living organism, are capable of doing things that are ugly. Remember the lesson of the slider – which in this area of the book Pinker himself seems to have forgotten – according to which any movement along the spectrum that stretches from peacefulness to violence has no built-in trajectory that follows the ticking of time. Instead, the condition of any society, or any individual, stutters left or right along the spectrum according to a complex array of social, economic and environmental factors. Just as important, an approach that selectively highlights certain things in order to satisfy an *a priori* commitment to a violent and ugly past will generate blindness or indifference to all that was

---

[24]Stephen Jay Gould, 'Nonmoral Nature', *Natural History*, 91, no. 2 (February 1982): 19–26, here 26.

simultaneously good and praiseworthy. Pinker has no idea that there were good people in the Middle Ages.

Let us pause and take stock of where we are. The European Middle Ages were not nearly as violent as Pinker has made them out to be. Contributions to this volume suggest that similar interpretive problems extend to other historical eras. Dag Lindström's contribution to this volume, for example, takes a close look at the graphs and tables presented in *Better Angels* and shows how Pinker failed to consider other explanations for changes in the data, including changing methods for recording homicide and changes in medical practice. To argue with Pinker over the numbers, however, is to accept that violent death, the proxy chosen by Pinker and others to measure violence over time, is appropriate to the task. But is it? Are there other ways of defining violence that might lead to a different set of conclusions?

To appreciate some of the problems associated with Pinker's chosen proxy, begin by imagining a world in which all people have been imprisoned in physiological or mental shackles and thereby rendered incapable of doing violent acts. This is the world imagined by the great authors of twentieth-century dystopian fiction, such as Evgeniĭ Zamiatin, Aldous Huxley and George Orwell.[25] To an outside observer, this would appear to be a spectacularly violent world in which the rate of violent death is extremely low. More realistically, consider a society in which human slaves are procured and treated with brutality – shackled, whipped, raped, humiliated, subjected to social death – but pains are taken to ensure that they don't die. Such conditions apply to the 24.9 million people today who, according to estimates of the International Labour Organization, have been trapped in forced labour.[26] The kind of violence that can lead to death is only one of many different kinds of behaviour that we intuitively recognize as being violent, and is not necessarily the worst.

In *Better Angels*, the semantic narrowing of 'violence' arises because Pinker, in search of a proxy, chose to associate violent acts with (male) genetic predispositions, in this case predispositions that operate through the rage circuitry and other organs of violence.[27] The problems here are obvious. To take an example, any objective measurement of pain and suffering would conclude that the American meat-packing industry is violent.[28] Apart from a brief section concerned with animals (465–73), however, Pinker's definition of violence is primarily restricted to humans. Beyond that – and with the

---

[25]Evgeniĭ Ivanovich Zamiatin, *We* (New York: Modern Library, 2006); Aldous Huxley, *Brave New World* (New York: Alfred Knopf, 2013); George Orwell, *1984* (New York: Signet Classic, 1977).

[26]See https://www.ilo.org/global/topics/forced-labour/lang--en/index.htm, accessed 22 February 2021.

[27]See, for example, Pinker, *Better Angels*, 497–509.

[28]Peter Singer, *Animal Liberation: A New Ethics for Our Treatment of Animals* (New York: HarperCollins, 1975).

major exception of war deaths and torture – his definition revolves around forms of violence that could be processed by the criminal justice system. Given this bias, Pinker defines violence according to a vector that proceeds from the aggressor to the victim. The victim, in this scenario, is passive and invisible.

Now think about this very carefully: Why should we accept an understanding of violence centred on the rage circuitry of the aggressor rather than the pain centres of the victim? The violence that is done to animals in the American meat-packing industry is a case in point, because although it is exceedingly violent, it involves, to the best of my knowledge, no rage whatsoever. Taking a victim-centred perspective would allow us to consider the micro- and macro-aggressions that make the present day feel violent to African Americans and other minority groups.[29] It would also bring into view the forms of slow or structural violence that operate against the poor and the disempowered.[30] As described by Rob Nixon, slow violence arises when the poor suffer disproportionately from things that affect the environment, such as toxic chemicals, acidified oceans and rising waters. It is 'slow' because the effects of violence precipitate out over years or decades rather than minutes and therefore don't hit the front pages or end up in the crime statistics. Slow violence, in turn, is a component of a larger field of structural violence, which includes forcible displacements, not-so-subtle forms of sexual coercion and persistent social degradations. 'The poor', as Paul Farmer has pointed out, 'are not only more likely to suffer; they are also more likely to have their suffering silenced'.[31] When the poor die, those deaths add nothing to the body counts in Pinker's tables because the violence involved, such as malnutrition and displacement, is invisible to a definition of violence that has been arbitrarily restricted to war and criminality. A victim-centred perspective would allow us to include the fact that many women experience forms of non-lethal violence in the workplace and elsewhere in the public sphere. I am not claiming that these kinds of violence have necessarily increased in the last century or two. My claim is that the decline in violent death since the Middle Ages or for that matter since the Pleistocene may seem less important when measured against a baseline comparison of the enduring forms of structural violence. However

---

[29]Bernard E. Harcourt, *Illusion of Order: The False Promise of Broken Windows Policing* (Cambridge, MA: Harvard University Press, 2001); Elizabeth Kai Hinton, *From the War on Poverty to the War on Crime: The Making of Mass Incarceration in America* (Cambridge, MA: Harvard University Press, 2016).

[30]Johan Galtung, 'Violence, Peace, and Peace Research', *Journal of Peace Research*, 6, no. 3 (1969): 167–91; Rob Nixon, *Slow Violence and the Environmentalism of the Poor* (Cambridge, MA: Harvard University Press, 2011).

[31]Paul Farmer, 'On Suffering and Structural Violence: A View from Below', *Race/Ethnicity: Multidisciplinary Global Contexts*, 3, no. 1 (2009): 11–28, here 25.

awful violent death might be, after all, it is experienced at a rate far lower than the routine injuries and humiliations of structural violence.

If we define violence from the victims' point of view, the appropriate measure of violence will be the victims' quantum of pain and humiliation. I can readily imagine the objection to this: pain and suffering, in past societies, are not directly measurable. *But neither is violence.* We always have to resort to proxies. This being the case, why not favour a victim-centred proxy, such as chronic stress, that can bring structural violence into the equation? In the archaeological record, chronic stress can be measured indirectly using evidence of stature and damage to hard tissue in joints and teeth. In the twentieth century, chronic stress can also be measured using simple proxies such as life span, obesity, heart disease and rates of opioid addiction.[32] What we learn is that chronic stress is associated with poverty and the condition of being disempowered. Crucially, what may matter is not absolute poverty but relative poverty. As Amartya Sen pointed out in 1999, African Americans as a whole are wealthier than the inhabitants of the state of Kerala in India. But Sen reports that the health outcomes of African Americans were worse than those of the Keralans, a situation arising from their condition of relative poverty.[33] If what matters is relative rather than absolute poverty, there are grounds for believing that structural violence has increased over the last half millennium.

And now to perhaps the most important question of all: Why should it matter that violence has declined? That such a decline, on the face of it, may seem to be inherently a good thing is the best reason for taking a close look at the matter, since common-sense intuition, as Einstein once demonstrated so clearly, does not always provide an accurate depiction of how the world really is. As discussed earlier in this chapter, authors of dystopian fiction, with the noteworthy exception of Aldous Huxley, have found it easy to imagine a world where violence has declined but the people are nonetheless miserable. In Pinker's grand historical vision, the decline of violence is itself a proxy for something else, namely happiness. Because there is less violence, people are happier now. Or at least, people *ought* to be happier, and would be so if those dang historians would do their job and stop trying to persuade people that modernity is so bad.

Many arguments about progress turn out to be ideas about the advance of happiness. But all such arguments, Pinker's included, fail to account for one of the most important findings of recent decades of research in the psychology of well-being. We are accustomed to the world we inhabit, and our measures of happiness and contentment are defined by the parameters of the possible in the present day. Our subjective well-being is anchored at

---

[32]See, inter alia, Jörg Niewöhner, 'Epigenetics: Embedded Bodies and the Molecularisation of Biography and Milieu', *BioSocieties*, 6, no. 3 (13 June 2011): 279–98.
[33]Amartya Sen, *Development as Freedom* (New York: Knopf, 1999), 21–4.

a set point determined by our personality traits.[34] Life events – winning the lottery, suffering injury in an accident – will cause feelings of happiness to wax or wane.[35] But a kind of psychological elastic constantly pulls us back to our set point.

Contrary to what Pinker indirectly suggests, subjective well-being is not determined by intermittent experiences such as violence. Though it can be permanently affected by a number of structural factors, notably including the structural violence described earlier, subjective well-being is determined primarily by the attachments we form with family, friends and things. The subjective well-being of a man or a woman living in the Pleistocene, for example, would have been determined by the experience of living in a warm, supportive and rewarding social environment, and not by the group's objective state of poverty, or by the dangers of the night, episodic violence or sleeping on the damp ground. The personality traits associated with subjective well-being could not have evolved if humans in the past were never happy, as the dark vision of *Better Angels* would have us believe.

Pinker has confused history with biography. In a rhetorical gesture of great power, he has invited the reader to imagine living a life that has spanned the centuries from the Middle Ages to the present, like an immigrant who has left the horrors of the Third World for the comforts of America. But this is a phantom argument. Whole populations, across their generations, can never have this experience, because it happens too slowly. In every era, people calibrate their sense of well-being to the conditions of the day. Think of it this way: a hundred years hence, medicine may have cured our sneezes and our itches. But unless your great-grandchildren are lucky enough to experience this change during their lifetimes, the absence of sneezes and itches will not make them any happier than you are. Although history can and does tell a story of constant change in human society, technology, and material culture, subjective well-being is historically invariant. This important point has been made by Darrin McMahon, the historian of happiness.[36] The point is worth arguing, but if McMahon is right and Pinker is wrong, then long-term shifts

---

[34]David G. Myers and Ed Diener, 'Who Is Happy?', *Psychological Science*, 6, no. 1 (1995): 10–19; David Lykken and Auke Tellegen, 'Happiness Is a Stochastic Phenomenon', *Psychological Science*, 7, no. 3 (1996): 186–9; Robert A. Cummins, 'Can Happiness Change? Theories and Evidence', in Kennon M. Sheldon and Richard E. Lucas (eds), *Stability of Happiness: Theories and Evidence on Whether Happiness Can Change* (London: Academic Press, 2014), 75–97. For criticisms of set-point theory, see Bruce Headey, 'The Set-Point Theory of Well-Being Needs Replacing: On the Brink of a Scientific Revolution?', *SSRN Electronic Journal* (2007). doi:10.2139/ssrn.1096451; Richard E. Lucas, 'Adaptation and the Set-Point Model of Subjective Well-Being', *Current Directions in Psychological Science*, 16, no. 2 (2007): 75–9.
[35]Philip Brickman, Dan Coates and Ronnie Janoff-Bulman, 'Lottery Winners and Accident Victims: Is Happiness Relative?', *Journal of Personality and Social Psychology*, 36, no. 8 (1978): 917–27.
[36]Darrin M. McMahon, *Happiness: A History* (New York: Atlantic Monthly Press, 2006), 466–80.

in levels of violence can have no impact on aggregate levels of subjective well-being. The past was never a vale of tears, and no decline in violence will bring greater happiness.

I am all in favour of doing a deep history of violence. This history, though, needs to place the victim, not the aggressor, at the front and centre of history. From the victims' point of view, violence is an inescapable feature of human life, even if, like sex or eating, the forms that it takes are variable. Deeply entangled in relations of power and dominance, violence is durable and protean. It operates in plain sight and also in the nooks and crannies of human relations. In light of the deep history of violence, it is incumbent upon us to be aware of the presence of violence, to recognize its forms and to find ways to work against it.

3

Pinker and the use and abuse of statistics in writing the history of violence

Dag Lindström

In *The Better Angels of Our Nature*, Steven Pinker claims that 'violence has declined over long stretches of time' and that we may actually be living in 'the most peaceable era in our species' existence'.[1] Without any further hesitation, Pinker also declares non-state societies to have been far more violent than modern state societies, 'even in their most war-torn centuries'.[2] 'If the past is a foreign country, it is a shockingly violent one. It is easy to forget how dangerous life used to be, how deeply brutality was once woven into the fabric of daily existence'.[3] Pinker presents various diagrams and graphs in support of these claims. Serious analyses of long-term changes in the prevalence of violence certainly have to include quantitative evidence, but the ways in which Pinker uses statistics are highly problematic.

The subtitle of Pinker's book declares that this is about 'the decline of violence in history and its causes'. It is true that we have strong evidence for a massive long-term decline in deadly interpersonal violence at least in Western Europe from the sixteenth century to the mid-twentieth century. This transition was tentatively identified already in 1981 by Ted Robert Gurr in a famous article in which he compiled quantitative evidence from

---

[1]Steven Pinker, *The Better Angels of Our Nature: The Decline of Violence in History and Its Causes* (London: Allen Lane, 2011), xvi.
[2]Pinker, *Better Angels*, 52.
[3]Pinker, *Better Angels*, 1.

England covering the thirteenth to the twentieth centuries.[4] Subsequently, similar transitions have been observed in other European regions, although with varying chronologies.[5] In a series of studies, Manuel Eisner has compiled a growing number of quantitative observations of historical homicide rates. Eisner's analyses confirm a long-term decline in homicide in Europe between the mid-sixteenth and the early twentieth century. They furthermore confirm different long-term trajectories in different regions, and that there has been numerous and recurrent surges and counter-trends interrupting the main trend towards lower homicide levels.[6]

Establishing the long-term decline in European homicide has been a major scientific achievement.[7] The long-term decline in deadly interpersonal violence continued (in the Western world at least) until around the 1960s. After that, homicide rates slightly increased until the 1990s and then started to decline again. Nothing of this is very controversial among researchers today. This knowledge is extremely important as certain media, certain politicians, and various agents of moral panic, tend to describe the present situation in extremely gloomy terms, often pointing at supposedly increasing crime rates in general and violence in particular. The picture sometimes painted of our society as rapidly heading towards social breakdown is simply not compatible with what we actually know about the historical trajectories of deadly interpersonal violence.

My aim here is not to question the long-term decline in European homicide. So, what is the problem with Pinker's thesis? Shouldn't we all be happy about

---

[4]T. R. Gurr, 'Historical Trends in Violent Crime: A Critical Review of the Evidence', *Crime and Justice: An Annual Review of Research*, 3 (1981): 295–350. See also Lawrence Stone, 'Interpersonal Violence in English Society 1300-1980', *Past and Present*, 101 (1983): 22–33.

[5]For Example, J. S. Cockburn, 'Patterns of Violence in English Society: Homicide in Kent, 1560-1985', *Past and Present*, 130 (1991): 70–106; Pieter Spierenburg, 'Faces of Violence: Homicide Trends and Cultural Meanings, Amsterdam, 1431-1816', *Journal of Social History*, 27, no. 4 (1994): 701–16; Eva Österberg, 'Criminality, Social Control, and the Early Modern State: Evidence and Interpretations in Scandinavian Historiography', in Eric A. Johnsson and Eric H. Monkkonen (eds), *The Civilization of Crime: Violence in Town and Country since the Middle Ages* (Urbana and Chicago: University of Illinois Press, 1996), 35–62; Heikki Ylikangas, Jens Christian V. Johansen, Kenneth Johansson and Hans Eyvind Næss, 'Family, State, and Patterns of Criminality: Major Tendencies in the Work of the Courts, 1550-1850', in Eva Österberg and Sølvie Sogner (eds), *People Meet the Law: Control and Conflict-Handling in the Courts. The Nordic Countries in the Post-Reformation and Pre-Industrial Period* (Oslo: Universitetsforlaget, 2000), 57–139.

[6]Manuel Eisner, 'Modernization, Self-control and Lethal Violence: The Long-Term Dynamics of European Homicide Rates in Theoretical Perspective', *The British Journal of Criminology*, 41, no. 4 (2001): 618–38; Manuel Eisner, 'Long-Term Historical Trends in Violent Crime', *Crime and Justice*, 30 (2003): 83–142; Manuel Eisner, 'From Swords to Words: Does Macro-Level Change in Self-Control Predict Long-Term Variations in Levels of Homicide?', *Crime and Justice*, 43, no. 1 (2014): 65–134.

[7]See also Pieter Spierenburg, *A History of Murder: Personal Violence in Europe from the Middle Ages to the Present* (Cambridge: Polity Press, 2008); Robert Muchembled, *A History of Violence: From the End of the Middle Ages to the Present* (Cambridge: Polity Press, 2012).

the good news? Well, as is often the case, things are more complicated than the good news might at first indicate. My primary concern here relates to Pinker's use, and sometimes abuse, of quantitative and statistical evidence. Quantitative evidence is mobilized in a careless and sometimes misleading way. To be more precise, Pinker markets a global grand narrative with high claims based on often limited and problematic quantitative evidence. Some of his conclusions are solid, while others are dubious. He often neglects the many problems associated with historical and prehistorical quantifications, he tends to ignore evidence pointing in other directions, and he sometimes conducts rather pointless long-term comparisons.

From homicide to violence in general

Pinker systematically uses homicide as a proxy for violence in general. He is certainly not the only person to do this. Contrary to many other crimes, homicide is considered fairly easy to count. Dark figures, that is the amount of unrecorded or undiscovered crime, are expected to be low. Killing another person has been considered unlawful in almost all societies, and homicide is usually regarded as a crime less dependent on specific cultural contexts than many other crimes. For these reasons, homicide is widely considered suitable for cross-cultural and long-term studies.[8] Nevertheless, the crucial issue as to whether there is a fixed relation between homicide rates and the general prevalence of violence in a society has seldom been explicitly discussed.[9] Pieter Spierenburg is one of very few historians who have explicitly argued for an immediate correspondence between homicide rates and more moderate forms of violent crime, especially concerning the long-term trends; homicide rates are the only reliable indicator of the total amount of violence in a society. It should be emphasized that Spierenburg's argument is purely theoretical and not based on empirical analyses.[10] The Finish historian, Petri Karonen, has analysed registered homicides in relation to other violent crimes in a sample of Early Modern towns in the Swedish realm. His observations do confirm certain correlations, but they also indicate significant differences between regions and variations over time.

---

[8]C.f. Eisner, 'Long-Term Historical Trends in Violent Crime', 93f.

[9]One of few examples is Österberg, 'Criminality, Social Control, and the Early Modern State', 43–8, where some similarities are observed in the long-term trends of registered homicides and non-lethal violence in Sweden.

[10]Pieter Spierenburg, 'Long-Term Trends in Homicide: Theoretical Reflections and Dutch Evidence, Fifteenth to Twentieth Centuries', in Johnsson and Monkkonen (eds), *The Civilization of Crime*, 74; Pieter Spierenburg, 'Violence and the Civilizing Process: Does It Work', *Crime, History and Societies*, 5, no. 2 (2001): 87–105, here 92. See Richard McMahon, Joachim Eibach and Randolph Roth, 'Making Sense of Violence? Reflections on the History of Interpersonal Violence in Europe', *Crime, History and Societies*, 17, no. 2 (2013): 5–26, here 10.

When, for example, homicide rates declined in the seventeenth century, the registered numbers of other violent crimes tended to increase in the Finnish part of the realm.[11]

Pinker's main argument is a general long-term decline in violence throughout human history, and the quantitative evidence he presents essentially concerns homicides and warfare. Referring to Eisner, Pinker also identifies homicide as a reliable index of violence. Eisner, however, declares that his 'analyses is based on the assumption that homicide may be cautiously construed as an indicator only of serious interpersonal violence'.[12] It certainly seems reasonable to assume a correlation between homicide and violent crimes in general. It also seems reasonable to expect this correlation to be fairly stable within a specific society. In cross-cultural comparisons and in long-term analyses, however, such an assumption is less convincing.[13] One must also take into consideration here the fact that Pinker goes far beyond crime. He has global claims about violence in general, covering human history from ancient times to the present. The point is not that Pinker is necessarily wrong. It is possible that homicide is a good proxy for violent crime or even for violence in general. But we do not know, and we certainly do not know if it holds for cross-cultural comparisons and long-term analyses.

Europe and the world

Most of the available quantitative evidence for a long-term decline in homicide rates is extracted from (Western and Northern) European sources. Pinker, however, places the rest of the world into the general Western European pacification narrative. Evidence derived from a specific context is used as a general model for a global trajectory.[14] In doing this, Pinker seems to apply a rather outdated diffusion model; a civilizing process started in a Western European epicentre, than spread to other parts of the continent and later also to the rest of the world. What Pinker describes might of course be a general pattern in human history, but we do not know for sure, and the quantitative evidence he presents cannot prove it.

In order to underpin his general thesis, Pinker presents two maps, one showing European average homicide rates for the nineteenth century and

---

[11]Petri Karonen, 'Trygg eller livsfarlig? Våldsbrottsligheten i Finlands städer 1540-1660', *Historisk Tidskrift för Finland*, 80, no. 1 (1995): 1.11; Petri Karonen, 'A Life versus Christian Reconciliation: Violence and the Process of Civilization in the Kingdom of Sweden, 1540-1700', in Heikki Ylikangas, Petri Karonen and Martti Lehti (eds), *Five Centuries of Violence in Finland and the Baltic Area* (Columbus: Ohio State University Press, 2001), 85–132, here 104–10.
[12]Pinker, *Better Angels*, 62; Eisner, 'Long-Term Historical Trends in Violent Crime', 94.
[13]Cockburn, 'Patterns of Violence in English Society', 104–5.
[14]Pinker, *Better Angels*, 85–91.

the other for the early twenty-first century.[15] It is true that for parts of Western and Southern Europe these maps indicate a substantial drop in homicide. On the other hand, they also indicate increased homicide rates for parts of Eastern Europe and Russia. Another problem is that the homicide rates refer to mean national figures, while many of the state borders have been radically recast between to the two maps. For example, the Habsburg Empire has been divided into a number of independent nation states with various contemporary homicide rates, and neither Poland nor the Baltic countries existed as independent states in the nineteenth century. From much of East and Southeast Europe, where there are indications of actually increasing homicide rates, we have very limited information that far back in time. Accordingly, we do not know what kind of homicide trajectories these regions have experienced.

Pinker also presents a global map showing national homicide rates in 2004.[16] It confirms huge variations in global homicide rates. These variations in fact cover the same range as the Western European long-term homicide decrease. Pinker is not very explicit about how the pacification model is applied to the non-European world, and he does not present any figures proving similar global trajectories as in Western Europe. He even admits that we largely lack reliable long-term global figures. Nevertheless, he claims the present world to be less violent than ever before.

From ancient times

Not only has Pinker far-reaching global claims, he also aims at grasping the overall trajectory of violence from the very early stages of human civilization until the present, and he does this in primarily quantitative terms. In this operation, Pinker is indeed much bolder than the average historian or anthropologist. His basic narrative is about a global reduction of violence, a reduction that can be traced back to prehistorical time.

Pinker criticizes previous perceptions of pre-state societies as fundamentally peaceful and harmonious. This is not a unique position. Both archaeologists and anthropologists have long been interested in analysing prehistoric violence, as a result of which the role of violence in deep time has been fundamentally reassessed.[17] We certainly need figures and numbers

---

[15]Pinker, *Better Angels*, 86.

[16]Pinker, *Better Angels*, 88.

[17]See for example Lawrence Keeley, *War Before Civilization* (New York: Oxford University Press, 1996); Debra L. Martin and David W. Frayer (eds), *Troubled Times: Violence and Warfare in the Past* (Amsterdam: Gordon and Breach 1997); I. J. N. Thorpe, 'Anthropology, Archaeology, and the Origins of Warfare', *World Archaeology*, 35, no. 1 (2003): 145–65; Mike Parker Pearson and I. J. N. Thorpe (eds), *Warfare, Violence and Slavery in Prehistory* (Oxford: Archaeopress, 2005); Ian Armit, 'Violence and Society in Deep Human Past', *The British Journal*

when analysing violence in pre-state and prehistoric societies. It is important to know how many cases a conclusion is based on, it is important to relate homicide cases to population sizes and time spans, and it is necessary to evaluate whether individual examples are extraordinary exceptions or if they fit into more general patterns.

Pinker's figures include both warfare deaths and homicide rates, and they demonstrate fundamental differences in rates of violence between non-state and state societies. This statistical evidence may at first seem compelling. Presented figures confirm a dramatic drop in the prevalence of violence. However, things are not as clear-cut and simple as Pinker wants us to believe. A number of serious objections can be raised against the way he collects his information, how he produces statistical evidence and how he uses these figures to argue for his thesis. He has also been heavily criticized for relying on exaggerated secondary interpretations, cherry-picking exceptional cases and ignoring many studies pointing at different conclusions. In addition, it has been systematically argued, contrary to Pinker, that widescale archaeological evidence does not show that war was generally ubiquitous, and that war only gradually became common over a long period of time.[18]

Pinker commences his argument by citing a number of nineteenth- and twentieth-century ethnographic reports, illustrating excessive violence performed within non-state societies. These reports, however, are of limited value for general conclusions about violence in non-state societies throughout history. A fundamental problem is the so-called 'tribal-zone dilemma', that is, ethnographic documentation that primarily refers to societies already deeply affected by contacts with aggressive colonial state powers. It has been established that these types of reports cannot be utilized to reach conclusions about pre-state societies in general.[19] Although this objection specifically concerns qualitative evidence, it is relevant also for Pinker's uses of quantitative evidence.

In Figure 2-3 (53), he compares the number of deaths in warfare per 100,000 people in a set of non-state societies and state societies. All the non-state figures are from the nineteenth and twenties centuries, and we can assume that that they all represent societies profoundly affected by contacts with state societies. These figures are real, but they cannot be generalized in the way Pinker does into conclusions about non-state societies regardless of temporal and geographic contexts. With the exception of Central Mexico

---

of Criminology, 51, no. 3 (2011): 499–517; Sarah Ralph (ed.), *The Archaeology of Violence: Interdisciplinary Approaches* (Albany: State University of New York Press, 2012).

[18]R. Brian Ferguson, 'Pinker's List: Exaggerating Prehistoric War Mortality', in Douglas Fry (ed.), *War, Peace, and Human Nature: The Convergence of Evolutionary and Cultural Views* (Oxford: Oxford University Press, 2013), 112–31; R. Brian Ferguson, 'The Prehistory of War and Peace in Europe and the Near East', in Fry (ed.), *War, Peace, and Human Nature*, 191–240.

[19]Armit, 'Violence and Society in Deep Human Past', 503f. See also in this collection the chapter by Linda Fibiger, 'Steven Pinker's "Prehistoric Anarchy": A Bioarchaeological Critique', 107–24.

1419 to 1519 Pinker includes no state figures before the nineteenth century. Some available figures indicate that warfare losses in Early Modern state societies could be much higher compared to the figures Pinker presents. These losses were often not so much caused by battlefield deaths as by diseases. In the case of Sweden, it has been calculated that around 50,000 men were lost in total during ten years of warfare from 1621 to 1632. This should be related to a population of approximately 1 million people. The death rate here would be around 500 per 100,000 people.[20] This is much higher than any of Pinker's state society figures, and it is much higher than many of his non-state figures as well. It has been estimated that these losses brought Sweden close to a demographic collapse in the 1630s, and it can be questioned whether a society could possibly on a long-term basis bear war losses of the dimension Pinker presents for some non-state societies.

In Figure 2-2 (49), Pinker compares deaths in warfare between non-state and state societies, calculated as the percentage of all deaths caused by warfare. It is important to examine what these figures actually represent. Pinker is rather brief concerning how the various rates have been generated, but we have every reason to be sceptical about statistical evidence that goes as far back as 10,000 BC. A first obvious obstacle is the concept of warfare. If we do not know how warfare is defined and identified some 12,000 years ago, how can we measure the numbers of victims of warfare? Pinker is not very informative here. Pinker's figures themselves illustrate a related problem. Some of the state society figures are identified as 'battle deaths', others are 'war deaths' and 'wars and genocides', and some are not specified at all. Which deaths should actually be counted as deaths in warfare, and how can contemporary war deaths be compared with prehistorical war deaths? The choice of examples is of course crucial as well. It is no big surprise that the rate of war deaths in the United States in 2005 (one of Pinker's examples) was extremely low. If regions with battlefield areas had been chosen, the results (including civilian casualties) would obviously have been quite different, and Bosnia in 1992–5, Rwanda in 1994 and Syria in the 2010s most certainly would have provided us with other rates than the ones chosen by Pinker. On the other hand, we would of course not dream of using them as representative contemporary examples.

For the twentieth century, it is possible to calculate fairly reliable global long-term averages. The presented figures for non-state societies, on the other hand, rely heavily on a set of very limited samples. Pinker presents three different sets of non-state examples in his statistical presentation. The

---

[20]Sven A. Nilsson, *De stora krigens tid. Om Sverige som militärstat och bondesamhälle* (Uppsala: Uppsala universitet, 1990), 21f. See also Jan Lindegren, 'Frauenland und Soldatenland. Perspektiven auf Schweden und den Dreissigjährigen Krieg', in Benigna von Krusenstjern and Hans Medick (eds), *Zwischen Alltag und Katastrophe. Der Dreissigjährigen Krieg aus der Nähe* (Göttingen: Vandenhoeck and Ruprecht, 1999).

first one is composed of evidence from prehistoric archaeology, represented by twenty-one different sites covering a time span from about 12,000 BC to the eighteenth-century AD, that is, around 14,000 years. They represent both 'hunter-gatherers' and 'hunter-horticulturists' groups. The next set is composed of information from eight recent or contemporary hunter-gatherer societies, and the third set is composed of ten examples of societies with a mix of hunting, gathering and horticulture. It is not clearly indicated what chronologies the third set represents. From what has already been indicated earlier, Pinker's second set of quantitative evidence is not very useful for general conclusions about hunter-gatherer societies.

Concerning the archaeological evidence, Pinker informs the reader that the figures are based on analyses of skeletons.[21] This is an extremely brief description given the many problems and possible pitfalls connected with the construction of prehistoric death rates based in archaeological evidence.[22] To begin with, the coverage of archaeological analyses is extremely uneven and such evidence tends to be very fragmentary. In this case, analysing skeletons more precisely means observing injuries on human bones. Prehistoric societies, however, often did not bury their dead in easily identified cemeteries. We often do not know at all if the analysed individuals are representative for a larger population. In many societies it was custom to burn the dead. And even when that was not the practice, the degree to which bones have survived varies a lot.[23] As Wayne E. Lee points out, information from single sites confirms the presence of violence early in history, but they cannot tell us much about the general frequency of violence.[24] We simply do not know if they represent exceptional events, when, for example, one group took over territory and resources from another group, or if these actions were frequently recurring. There is an obvious risk here of transforming the exceptional into the normal, but in all cases we must admit that we do not know.

To generate valid rates, it would be necessary to estimate the gross number of deaths and to assess whether the analysed sample of bones is somehow biased. For example, are individuals killed in battle or victims of massacres more likely to be found and analysed compared to people who died of natural causes? In addition, it is crucial to know the absolute number of individuals on which the rates are calculated. Very small numbers of deaths and limited populations undermines the validity of the calculated rates, because in very

---

[21]Pinker, *Better Angels*, 48.

[22]Researchers have emphasized the importance of being cautious in the interpretations of archaeological evidence of violence. See, Debra L. Martin and David W. Frayer, 'Introduction', in Martin and Frayer (eds), *Troubled Times*, xiii–xxi, here xiv; Armit, 'Violence and Society in Deep Human Past'.

[23]Armit, 'Violence and Society in Deep Human Past', 505–7.

[24]Wayne E. Lee, *Waging War: Conflict, Culture, and Innovation in World History* (Oxford and New York: Oxford University Press, 2016), 18f.

small populations even single cases may heavily influence rates calculated as percentages per 100,000 people.[25] Information about numbers is necessary in order to evaluate whether it is meaningful at all to compare these figures with contemporary figures based on populations of hundreds of millions or even billions of people. Pinker does not provide any such information. It is, however, clear that at least some of the cited archaeological sites represent only very few individuals. A famous example from Sudan, 12,000–10,000 BC, includes no more than fifty-nine individuals of which at least twenty-four display injuries indicating intentional killing, possibly warfare.[26] This can of course be calculated as 41 per cent war deaths in Sudan, but the absolute numbers are so small that the result is useless as an average for 2,000 years within such a large territory. It would be even more ridiculous to use this as an indicator for the prevalence of violence in non-state societies in general, and it is rather meaningless to compare this figure with contemporary global rates.

Categorization is a fundamental dimension of quantitative evidence. Pinker builds his argument on a simple dichotomy between non-state and state societies. This approach produces several deficiencies in the statistical evidence. Pinker's grand narrative presumes a fundamental transition in the prevalence of violence in human societies and that this shift came about long before the Medieval/Early Modern period. The long-term decline has not been a trajectory of a slow and steady reduction through the millennia but a fundamentally discontinuous process where the major transition is directly connected to the appearance of the centralized state. Hence, the distinction between non-state and state societies is crucial in Pinker's narrative.[27]

One effect of this is that Pinker undermines some of his own critique against previous perceptions of a peaceful past. No one claims that all non-state societies have been peaceful and that warfare started only with the emergence of states. The suggested peacefulness has rather been associated with a specific type of non-state societies: hunter-gatherer societies. The development of warfare has frequently been identified as a long-term effect of the Neolithic Revolution (i.e. the gradual development of agriculture) and with the emergence of sedentism. A common scientific position is that warfare, even if it occurred before the Neolithic, became more frequent, more sophisticated and more institutionalized during that era.[28] Information

[25]Cf. Eric Monkkonen, 'New Standards for Historical Homicide Research', *Crime, History and Societies*, 5, no. 2 (2001): 5–26, here 7f.

[26]Thorpe, 'Anthropology, Archaeology, and the Origins of Warfare', 152f; Lee, *Waging War*, 19f. In addition, it is not possible to establish home many single incidents those 24 individuals represent.

[27]Pinker, *Better Angels*, 42.

[28]See for example Doyne Dawson, 'The Origins of War: Biological and Anthropological Theories', *History and Theory*, 35, no. 1 (1996): 1–28, here 26–8; Keith F. Otterbein, *How War Began* (College Station: Texas A & M University Press, 2004); Jonas Christensen, 'Warfare in

derived from an arbitrary sample of pre-state societies, regardless of time and place, is a weak argument against an assumed general peacefulness of hunter-gatherer societies specifically.

Pinker himself completely dismisses the Neolithic Revolution as a main divide in the history of violence. According to Pinker, 'it makes no sense to test for historical changes in violence by plotting deaths against a timeline from the calendar.' Agriculture, Pinker argues, developed at different times in different regions and spread only gradually, and 'societies cannot be dichotomized into hunter-gatherer bands and agricultural civilizations'.[29] Why this is necessarily wrong remains somewhat obscure. Anyway, Pinker predicts a transition from non-state to state societies to have been the crucial step towards reduction of violence, and he sets off to compare 'hunter-gatherers, hunter-horticulturalists, and other tribal peoples (from any era) on one side, and settled states (also from any era) on the other'.[30] This manoeuvre actually comes close to circular reasoning; the non-state/state transition appears both as a starting point for the analyses and as a result. The non-state/state dichotomy might be intended as a hypothesis, but it is not made clear how such a hypothesis would then be tested.

Violence rates from various non-state societies are lumped together by Pinker in order to verify the basic thesis of a fundamental shift between non-state and state societies. Several of the archaeological sites in Pinker's figure (3.4 here) cover hundreds or even thousands of years. Possible variations over time are thereby erased, although there is substantial evidence of huge differences between various non-state societies, long-term fluctuations and even considerable increases. Herbert Maschner has conducted a long-term evaluation of archaeological evidenced of lethal violence in the North West coast of North America. The results show increasing levels of violence over time, for example, related to the introduction of the bow and arrow (100–500 AD), which resulted in a substantial rise in intergroup violence.[31] Other analyses indicate that both the development of sedentism and changes in group sizes and complexity have substantially increased the prevalence of violence.[32]

Pinker overlooks important distinctions and oversimplifies his typologies, he divests himself of the possibility to identify trajectories other than the

---

the European Neolithic', *Acta Archaeologica*, 75 (2004): 129–56; Lee Clare and Hans Georg K. Gebel, 'Introduction: Conflict and Warfare in the Near Eastern Neolithic', *Noe-Lithics*, 10, no. 1 (2010): 3–5.

[29]Pinker, *Better Angels*, 40–7, quotation from 42.

[30]Pinker, *Better Angels*, 40–2, 47f.

[31]Herbert Maschner, 'The Evolution of Northwest Coast Warfare', in Martin and Frayer (eds), *Troubled Times*, 267–302.

[32]Paul F. Reed and Phil R. Geib, 'Sedentism, Social Change, Warfare, and the Bow in the Ancient Pueblo Southwest', *Evolutionary Anthropology*, 22, no. 3 (2013): 103–10; Lee, *Waging War*, 30–5.

non-state/state shift, and he systematically interprets the figures to fit his grand narrative. The presented percentages of warfare deaths in prehistoric societies vary between 0 and 60 per cent. If we can trust those figures, one obvious conclusion would be that prehistoric non-state societies represent huge variations in terms of violence. These variations appear to have been much stronger than between different state societies.[33] (This can of course be a completely false conclusion, as the presented state society figures are averages based on huge populations, sometimes even on a global level, while the non-state figures represent individual sites or communities.) In addition, Pinker does not analyse possible differences between hunter-gatherers and agriculturists. He simply avoids this issue, although his own figures seem to indicate that hunter-horticulturists have been more violent than hunter-gatherers, that is, increasing the prevalence of violence.[34] Several researchers how also emphasized how variable the prevalence of violence has been in different non-state societies, and that it is impossible to generalize about violence in non-state societies. Because of this, it is also extremely problematic to assume one single linear trajectory from non-state to state societies.[35] If we really want to analyse how violence has developed through history and identify what factors that have produced significant change, we need to consider both local variations and various long-term trajectories.

Early historical homicide rates

It is not only prehistoric and non-state homicide rates that are problematic. Medieval and Early Modern rates must also be treated with caution. Manuel Eisner emphasizes that historical homicide data 'should not be regarded as precise measurements'.[36] The German historian Gerd Schwerhoff takes this scepticism one step further when characterizing estimated medieval homicide rates, presented as incidents per 100,000 people, as an example of 'pseudo-objectivity'. There are simply too many uncertain parameters; homicide categories change over time, figures are based on a variety of sources and jurisdictions, and population figures are notoriously uncertain.[37]

---

[33]Cf. Armit, 'Violence and Society in Deep Human Past', 505, emphasizing the wide range of social forms in prehistoric societies.

[34]Pinker, *Better Angels*, 49.

[35]For example, Thorpe, 'Anthropology, Archaeology, and the Origins of Warfare', quotation from 159; Armit, 'Violence and Society in Deep Human Past'; Amy E. Nivette, 'Violence in Non-state Societies: A Review', *The British Journal of Criminology*, 51, no. 3 (2011): 578–98, here 580–2.

[36]Eisner, 'Modernization, Self-control and Lethal Violence', 628.

[37]Gerd Schwerhoff, 'Criminalised Violence and the Process of Civilization: A Reappraisal', *Crime, History and Societies*, 6, no. 2 (2002): 103–26, here 106–13. See also Cockburn, 'Patterns of Violence in English Society', 101–6.

Medieval and Early Modern homicide rates are not equivalent with contemporary statistics. It is extremely important to recognize this. Usually, figures get more and more inexact the further back in time we go. We move from statistical evidence to quantitative estimations. The latter are often based on incomplete records, limited surveys, obscure judicial capacities and insufficient information about population figures. The possible effects of these deficiencies are not always obvious; do they lead to over or underestimated homicide rates? In any case, we need to be cautious when comparing present homicide statistics with calculated homicide rates from the distant past.

Generally, we have fairly reliable homicide rates from many areas in Western Europe stretching as far back as the later sixteenth century. When we move beyond that point, things get more problematic. It should be admitted that we do have a fairly large amount of estimated homicide rates even for the Middle Ages, and with few exceptions they point to very high homicide rates (ranging from about 5 to over 100 homicides per 100,000 people).[38] However, we still have to rely on what Eric Monkkonen calls 'spotty knowledge': a number of singular studies, often limited in time, in population and in geographical scope. In addition, estimations are often based on sources of very different type and quality.[39] Data series covering longer sequences of time are rare, and it is difficult to assess how much the picture depends on small population studies. It is, therefore, difficult to assess the extent to which available rates are representative for larger regions, large populations and long periods of time. There is a strong urban bias in available medieval homicide rates, often with an emphasis on larger towns (with more than 5,000 inhabitants).[40] Concerning Sweden, for example, data from the fifteenth, sixteenth and early seventeenth centuries are heavily dominated by urban contexts.[41] This is a time when townspeople made up not more than a few percentage at most of the total Swedish population. The earliest estimated rural homicide rates in Sweden (fifteenth century) range from 4 to 14 homicides per 100,000 people, while estimated urban homicide rates from the fifteenth and sixteenth centuries range from around 10 to 80 homicides per 100,000 people.[42]

---

[38]Eisner, 'Long-Term Historical Trends in Violent Crime', 100f. Eisner mentions about 100 different medieval estimates in 2003.

[39]Monkkonen, 'New Standards for Historical Homicide Research', 7–9; Schwerhoff, 'Criminalised Violence and the Process of Civilization', 106–9.

[40]Eisner, 'Long-Term Historical Trends in Violent Crime', 100.

[41]Österberg, 'Criminality, Social Control, and the Early Modern State', 44.

[42]Österberg, 'Criminality, Social Control, and the Early Modern State', 44f; Jonas Liliequist, 'Violence, Honour and Manliness in Early Modern Northern Sweden', in M. Lappalainen and Hirvonen (eds), Crime and Control in Europe from the Past to the Present (Helsinki: Academy of Finland: 1999), 174–202, here 74–81.

We have reason to believe that urban bias would tend to overestimate average homicide levels.[43] During certain times of the year, urban populations tended to increase substantially as people other than the permanent residents migrated to towns for shorter or longer periods. Many urban court records also include homicides not committed in the town, and they frequently include homicide cases involving individuals who were not urban residents but visitors in the town. Fairs and markets attracted numerous visitors, and these occasions also attracted crime and violence.

Until around the mid-seventeenth century there are huge variations in estimated European homicide rates (roughly between 5 and 100 homicides per 100,000 people). After that time, the variations are reduced to 1 to 10 homicides per 100,000 people.[44] It is difficult to judge whether this represents larger local, regional and temporal variations in homicide levels farther back in time or if these variations are more haphazard and dependent on, for example, the quality of surviving sources or the intensity of law enforcement. These estimated homicide rates nevertheless tell us two things. First, medieval homicide rates generally were substantially higher than in the nineteenth and twentieth centuries. Second, it would be difficult to establish any long-term trajectories for the Middle Ages.

In chapter 3, titled 'The Civilizing Process', Pinker moves on to identify and explain a continuing homicide decline from the High Middle Ages to the twentieth century. Figure 3-4 (64) demonstrates a steady long-term decline of homicide rates in Western Europe from around 1300. The graph is based on figures presented by Manuel Eisner and extracted from his *History of Homicide Database*.[45] But, again, things are more complicated than Pinker wants us to believe, and his use of statistical evidence is rather misleading. The figures presented by Eisner actually indicate a peak in the fifteenth century. The available average rates are substantially lower for both the thirteenth and fourteenth centuries, and for the sixteenth century, compared to the fifteenth century. Eisner's figures furthermore indicate a possible English increase from the thirteenth to the fourteenth century, a similar increase in Germany/Switzerland, and a sixteenth-century increase in Sweden.[46] There might have been substantial long-term variations during the Middle Ages, with possible periods of increases and peaks. It is also possible that homicide levels did not change much during this period. We still cannot reach safe any definitive conclusions about this. Pinker nevertheless concludes a European decline from 1300 on. This decline is furthermore specified for various regions (Figure 3-3, 63).

---

[43]See for example McMahon, Eibach and Roth, 'Making Sense of Violence', 8.

[44]Eisner, 'Long-Term Historical Trends in Violent Crime', 95–101.

[45]Pinker, *Better Angels*, 64; Eisner, 'Long-Term Historical Trends in Violent Crime', 99.

[46]Eisner, 'Long-Term Historical Trends in Violent Crime', 99. See also McMahon, Eibach and Roth, 'Making Sense of Violence', 8.

Here, Pinker indicates a steady decline from around 1300 in England, the Netherlands, and Germany and Switzerland. Pinker builds on Eisner's figures.[47] But Eisner lacks figures for England between the late fourteenth and early sixteenth centuries and therefore concludes that 'the precise period when the secular downturn started cannot be identified'. Eisner's Dutch figures start around 1400, and the scattered German and Swiss figures rather points towards a peak around 1400. Eisner's own conclusion is that 'the existing data make solid conclusions impossible' concerning Germany and Switzerland. The data indeed seems to confirm a dramatic homicide decline starting in the fifteenth century. But this probably only reflects variations in the types of sources used for the documentation of homicides. It is even possible that the trend towards lower homicide rates, as in Italy, did not really take off until the early nineteenth century.[48] Schwerhoff emphasizes that research has established a decrease from the sixteenth to the eighteenth century in some parts of Europe, but we do not have solid evidence for a long-term decline already from the High Middle Ages.[49]

It is important to be aware of how uncertain many pre-modern homicide rate calculations actually are. One of the more well-known early and frequently cited medieval examples is Carl I. Hammer's study of fourteenth-century Oxford, which yielded homicide rates of over 100 per 100,000 people.[50] Monkkonen has pointed to the fact that the estimated population was only 6,000 people. This means that one or two extra homicide cases would have greatly impacted on the homicide rate and a few unusual years could easily distort the whole result. Furthermore, Hammer's calculations are based on only four years. He did analyse records from six years but decided to leave two of them out because homicides were substantially fewer, and he concluded that these records were probably incomplete. No one has made a follow-up study over a longer period of time. Monkkonen clearly demonstrates the problems associated with calculations based on chronologically limited studies of small urban populations, and how easily they can lead to highly overestimated homicide rates.[51]

One reason for overestimated urban homicide rates is the fact that homicides committed at other places sometimes were registered in urban court records. Occasionally, researchers have recalculated homicide rates on the basis of homicides committed only in the specific town. For one Swedish town (Vadstena), the result has been homicide rates ranging between 20 and

---

[47]Pinker, *Better Angels*, 63f.
[48]Eisner, 'Long-Term Historical Trends in Violent Crime', 95–103.
[49]Schwerhoff, 'Criminalised Violence and the Process of Civilization', 112.
[50]C. I. Hammer Jr, 'Patterns of Homicide in a Medieval University Town: Fourteenth-Century Oxford', *Past and Present*, 78 (1978): 3–23.
[51]Monkkonen, 'New Standards for Historical Homicide Research', 7f.

60 per 100,000 people in the late sixteenth and early seventeenth centuries, instead of 60 to 80 killings.[52]

It has already been mentioned that many early homicide rates are based on few cases and very small populations. Several early Swedish homicide rates from the fifteenth, sixteenth and early seventeenth centuries are based on not more than one or two killings during periods of ten to fifteen years and estimated populations of just a few thousand people at the most. This means that one or two extra homicides in a ten-year period would dramatically increase homicide rates calculated as incidents per 100,000 people. In addition, population figures are usually estimated on the basis of tax rolls. They usually do not register the population but households. The usual procedure to estimate population is to count the number of households and then multiply this figure with an assumed average household size. These average sizes should be regarded as qualified guesses, at best. The fact is that we don't know. More recent analyses of urban populations in early seventeenth-century Sweden, based on a wide combination of various sources instead of only tax records, point at populations more than twice the size usually assumed.[53] The early seventeenth-century Vadstena rate of 77 homicides per 100,000 people would then be reduced to probably less than 20, when homicides not committed in the town have been omitted and the population size has been calibrated. This is still a high figure confirming the long-term decline. But it puts things in a slightly different perspective.

Pinker focuses on his grand narrative of a general secular decline in violence. Variations and differences are important to the extent that the long-term decline started at different times in different regions, but Pinker generally avoids discontinuities and divergent trajectories that do not fit into his narrative.[54] There is a well-documented and well-known divergence between Finland and Sweden that can be identified at least form the mid-eighteenth century on. At that time Sweden and Finland were parts of the same kingdom with the same legislation and identical court systems. In Sweden, the homicide rates continued to decrease over time. In Finland, on the other hand, homicide rates increased and reached a level of more than 8 per 100,000 people in the 1920s, which is substantially higher than most calculated sixteenth-century Finnish homicide rates.[55] The relatively low Finnish sixteenth-century figures resemble some calculated sixteen-century

---

[52]Österberg, 'Criminality, Social Control, and the Early Modern State', 44; Karonen, 'A Life versus Christian Reconciliation', 99, 107, 123.

[53]Dag Lindström, 'Homicide in Scandinavia: Long-Term Trends and Their Interpretations', in Sophie Body-Gendrot and Pieter Spierenburg (eds), *Violence in Europe: Historical and Contemporary Perspectives* (New York: Springer, 2008), 41–64, here 48f.

[54]Pinker, *Better Angels*, 62.

[55]Heikki Ylikangas, 'What Happened to Violence? An Analysis of the Development of Violence from Medieval Times to the Early Modern Era Based on Finnish Source Material', in Ylikangas, Karonen and Lehti (eds), *Five Centuries of Violence in Finland and the Baltic*, 1–84, here 3, 8.

Swedish rates from more remote northern areas pointing at levels under 4 homicides per 100,000 people.[56] These observations do not fit well into a single coherent narrative of a decline in secular violence primarily caused by state building and the civilizing process.

From figures to Elias

Pinker claims that Norbert Elias is the only major social thinker who has been able to explain the long-term decline in violence. He furthermore claims that available homicide rates confirm the civilizing theory; 'it made a surprising prediction that turned out to be true' and 'the Civilizing Process passed a stringent test for a scientific hypothesis'.[57] In other words, figures confirm Elias. These are, however, problematic statements.

First, Pinker does not provide a correct description of scientific debates when claiming Elias' ideas to be 'the only theory left standing'.[58] Helmut Thome, for example, extensively discusses Émile Durkheim's theories about collectivism versus individualism and anomie as possible explanations of the long-term trends; declining collectivism made individuals less inclined to use violence, while on the other hand absence of norms, disputed norms or contradicting norms (anomie) cause increasing violence.[59] Many historians have emphasized the Early Modern state building process as a crucial factor behind declining homicide rates, without necessarily referring to Elias. Increasing state monopoly of violence, judicial professionalization, expanding social trust and growing faith in institutions has been analysed also without Elias' theoretical framing.[60] It is true that Elias' civilizing theory has been widely referred to by historians of violence. According to Eisner, it is even 'the most prominent framework discussed by those historians of

---

[56]Liliequist, 'Violence, Honor and Manliness in Early Modern Northern Sweden', 74–81.

[57]Pinker, *Better Angels*, 61, 78, 81.

[58]Pinker, *Better Angels*, 6. See also in this collection the chapter by Philip Dwyer and Elizabeth Roberts-Pedersen, 'Steven Pinker, Norbert Elias and *The Civilizing Process*', 87–104.

[59]Helmut Thome, 'Explaining Long-Term Trends in Violent Crime', *Crime, History and Societies*, 5, no. 2 (2001): 69–86. See also Heikki Ylikangas, 'Major Fluctuations in Crimes of Violence in Finland: A Historical Analysis', *Scandinavian Journal of History*, 1, no. 1 (1976): 81–103; Ylikangas, Johansen, Johansson and Næss, 'Family, State, and Patterns of Criminality', 77; Eisner, 'Modernization, Self-Control and Lethal Violence', 632–3.

[60]See for example Heikki Ylikangas, 'Reasons for the Reduction of Violence in Finland in the Seventeenth Century', in Lappalainen and Hirvonen (eds), *Crime and Control in Europe*, 165–73; Ylikangas, Johansen, Johansson and Næaa, 'Family, State, and Patterns of Criminality', 115–23; Ylikangas, 'What Happened to Violence?'; Lindström, 'Homicide in Scandinavia', 56–7; Randoph Roth, *American Homicide* (Cambridge, MA: Harvard University Press, 2009), 61–107; Matthew Lockwood, *The Conquest of Death: Violence and the Birth of the Modern English State* (New Haven and London: Yale University Press, 2017); Jeppe Büchert Netterstrøm, 'Criminalization of Homicide in Early Modern Denmark (16th to 17th Centuries)', *Scandinavian Journal of History*, 42, no. 4 (2017): 459–75, here 467–8.

crime who are interested in explaining this long-term trend'.[61] However, paying attention to Elias does not mean unconditional acceptance of his theories. Far from all historians would agree with Pieter Spierenburg that Elias 'offers the only theoretical framework which easily accommodates the empirical evidence on the long-term decline of homicide'.[62] Critical examination and cautious discussions have been more common. Many historians obviously regard this issue as far too diverse and complicated to be reduced to one singular explanation the way Pinker claims.[63] Some historians have explicitly rejected the civilizing theory.[64] And some have actually paid limited attention to Elias.[65]

Second, Pinker does not provide statistical evidence that proves the civilizing theory. He claims that the theory 'made a surprising prediction that turned out to be true' and that it explains the European homicide decline from the Middle Ages to the present.[66] It is important in this context to remember that Elias himself did not make any such predictions. He did not intend to explain long-term trends in violent crime. It was not until much later, when historians of crime started to identify a long-term homicide decline, that some of them took an interest in Elias' theories as a possible explanation.[67] Pinker's use of statistics is again deceiving. At first, the various graphs and statistical calculations demonstrating the long-term decline in homicide rates may seem convincing. However, the mere observation of a certain change does not in itself tell us anything about the causes behind the

---

[61]Eisner, 'Modernization, Self-Control and Lethal Violence', 619.

[62]Spierenburg, 'Violence and the Civilizing Process', quotation from 87. See also Spierenburg, 'Long-Term Trends in Homicide', 63–105; and Spierenburg, A History of Murder, 5–7. See also Dwyer and Roberts-Pedersen in this collection, 87–8, 95 and 97–100 for additional examples of this position.

[63]Ylikangas, Johansen, Johansson and Næss, 'Family, State, and Patterns of Criminality', 79; Thome, 'Explaining Long-Term Trends in Violent Crime', 70–4; Eisner, 'Modernization, Self-Control and Lethal Violence'; Maria Kaspersson, '"The Great Murder Mystery" or Explaining Declining Homicide Rates', in Barry Godfrey, Clive Emsley and Graeme Dunstall (eds), Comparative Histories of Crime (Cullompton: Willan Publishing, 2003), 72–88, here 82–3; Lindström, 'Homicide in Scandinavia', 55–6; Muchembled, A History of Violence, 28–9; McMahon, Eibach and Roth, 'Making Sense of Violence'; Netterstrøm, 'Criminalization of Homicide in Early Modern Denmark', 467–8; Eisner, 'From Swords to Words'.

[64]Martin Dinges, 'Gewalt und Zivilisationsprozess', Traverse, 2, no. 1 (1995): 70–81; Schwerhoff, 'Criminalised Violence and the Process of Civilization'; Gerd Schwerhoff, 'Violence and the Honour Code: From Social Integration to Social Distinction?', Crime, History and Societies, 17, no. 2 (2013): 27–46, here 28–30. See also Jonathan Davies, 'Introduction', in Jonathan Davies (ed.), Aspects of Violence in Renaissance Europe (London and New York: Routledge, 2013), 1–16, here 4 with referred literature.

[65]See for example Cockburn, 'Patterns of Violence in English Society'; James Sharpe, 'Crime in England: Long-Term Trends and the Problem of Modernization', in Johnsson and Monkkonen (eds), The Civilization of Crime, 17–34; Randolph Roth, 'Homicide in Early Modern England 1549-1800: The Need for Quantitative Synthesis', Crime, History and Societies, 5, no. 2 (2001): 33–67: Lockwood, The Conquest of Death.

[66]Pinker, Better Angels, 61, 78.

[67]Thome, 'Explaining Long-Term Trends in Violent Crime', 70–1.

change. Declining homicide rates does not prove that the civilizing theory is the correct (and only important) explanation. There are many possible explanations for high homicide rates in the Middle Ages and the sixteenth century, and there are many possible explanations for declining homicide rates during the following centuries. None of them can be ruled out just by counting the number of homicides.

Other kinds of analyses are needed in order to prove that high homicide rates were related to a civilization deficit and that decreasing homicide rates were caused by increasing self-control and a growing sense of empathy.[68] Such analyses could be performed, but they are not included in Pinker's argument. Generally, more elaborated quantitative studies would be welcome. In order to explain variations and long-term changes, we need more information than just the number of incidents. We need systematic information about motives, modes of killing, course of events, contexts, offender–victim relations and so on.

Conclusion

Steven Pinker has an extremely positive and hopeful message. His grand narrative is certainly interesting. However, he underpins it with quantitative evidence that is sometimes not very convincing. Pinker might be right in many of his conclusions. The problem is that presented quantitative evidence often does not prove his claims. Sometimes his use of statistical evidence is even misleading. He underestimates and neglects fundamental problems and he disregards many pitfalls related to long-term and cross-cultural comparisons. He builds far-reaching conclusions on sometimes very fragile quantitative evidence. He over-interprets, simplifies, cherry-picks and even adjusts available quantitative documentation to fit and support his grand narrative. He avoids evidence pointing in other directions. This is a pity because we do need more qualified, nuanced and diverse quantitative analyses of violence and homicide in history. We need that to understand the long-term historical changes, and we also need it to understand and explain violence in our contemporary society.

---

[68]Pinker, *Better Angels*, 169.

4

Progress and its contradictions

Human rights, inequality and violence

Eric D. Weitz

'I claim to be a human rights man', wrote the American abolitionist William Lloyd Garrison in 1853.[1] Frederick Douglass also knew that the struggle against slavery was a part of the 'great doctrine of Human Rights', as Angelina Grimké declaimed, both of them linking together women's rights and slavery abolition. 'The rights of the slave and of women', she continued, 'blend like the colors of the rainbow'.[2] On a more mundane level, in the 1960s the great British historian E. H. Carr could only imagine the practice of history so long as it was firmly tied to a belief in progress, and that meant a liberal order and the panoply of advances in science, society and the economy that characterized Great Britain and the West since the eighteenth century.[3] Steven Pinker would find all these expressions grist for his mill of

---

[1]Quoted in Kathryn Kish Sklar, 'Human Rights Discourse in Women's Rights Conventions in the United States, 1848-70', in Pamela Slotte and Miia Halme-Tuomisaari (eds), *Revisiting the Origins of Human Rights* (Cambridge: Cambridge University Press, 2015), 163–88, quote 182.
[2]Frederick Douglass used the phrase 'human rights' in an article, 'Reconstruction', in the *Atlantic Monthly* (December 1866), reprinted in *The Life and Writings of Frederick Douglass*, vol. 4, ed. Philip S. Foner (New York: International, 1975), 198–9, 202. For Grimké see Ana Stevenson, 'The "Great Doctrine of Human Rights": Articulation and Authentication in the Nineteenth-Century U.S. Antislavery and Women's Rights Movements', *Humanity*, 8, no. 3 (2017): 413–39, quote 413.
[3]E. H. Carr, *What Is History?* ed. R. W. Davies (1961; Houndsmills: Macmillan, 1986).

continual human progress. Slavery has been abolished, women have the right to vote in almost every country on the planet, and society has progressed medically, technologically and economically in ways Carr, writing in 1961, could never even have imagined.

So far so good. Yet a historian has to feel uneasy with the triumphant bell-ringing that runs through Pinker's two recent books.[4] It would require an army of research assistants to engage Pinker on his preferred battleground of statistics. I shall not take that route and would not even if I had an army at my disposal. Nor does it help to challenge Pinker by marching down the dour, depressive, opposite-running one-way road and arrive at an end-station where all we see is the human condition marked by failure, stagnation and violence. So argue a number of academics and journalists who contend that human rights are on the wane; have altogether failed; are utopian in character and therefore undermine the real world of politics; divert attention from more critical social issues like inequality; or are Western-based and therefore necessarily imperialist in character.[5]

In the realm of human rights, there has been great progress since the eighteenth century. On that most general statement we can stand with Pinker. For all their limitations and half-hearted (at best) implementation, human rights remain our best hope for constructing the kind of peaceful, just and egalitarian society that Pinker wants, a society where people are respected and afforded recognition no matter what their specific gender, nationality or race and everyone has access to the basic necessities of life and enjoys the freedom to express themselves, to work and build and create as they wish, to join with others as they desire, and to be free of the scourge of violence and forced displacement.[6]

Yet human rights advances have neither been simply positive nor easily obtained. Rather than engage Pinker on the battleground of statistics, I want to develop a critique based on two conceptual shortcomings in his work. The first entails his honey-coated understanding of the Enlightenment as a philosophical movement. Human rights today certainly rest upon the

---

[4]Steven Pinker, *The Better Angels of our Nature: Why Violence Has Declined* (New York: Viking, 2011), and *Enlightenment Now: The Case for Reason, Science, Humanism, and Progress* (New York: Viking, 2018).

[5]See, for example, Samuel Moyn, *Not Enough: Human Rights in an Unequal World* (Cambridge, MA: Belknap Press, 2018); idem, *The Last Utopia: Human Rights in History* (Cambridge, MA: Belknap Press, 2010). Eric A. Posner, *The Twilight of Human Rights Law* (Oxford: Oxford University Press, 2014); Stephen Hopgood, *The Endtimes of Human Rights* (Ithaca: Cornell University Press, 2013). For a very effective challenge to such critiques, see Kathryn Sikkink, *Evidence for Hope: Making Human Rights Work in the 21st Century* (Princeton: Princeton University Press, 2017), and Beth A. Simmons, *Mobilizing for Human Rights: International Law in Domestic Politics* (Cambridge: Cambridge University Press, 2009). On the French debates, see Justine Lacroix and Jean-Yves Pranchère, *Le Procès des droits de l'homme: Généalogie du scepticisme démocratique* (Paris: Seuil, 2016), which is highly critical of the francophone opponents of human rights. Lacroix and Pranchère's position is very similar to my own.

[6]This is the argument of my book, *A World Divided: The Global Struggle for Human Rights in the Age of Nation-States* (Princeton: Princeton University Press, 2019).

Enlightenment's promotion of liberty and the rights of the individual. Yet the same Enlightenment figures who advocated liberty also limited its scope through their drive to categorize the human population based on racial and gender hierarchies. Their arguments along these lines were not mistakes or oversights, and hardly innocent of political effects. They were intrinsic to the Enlightenment investigation of the nature of the human species. The division of human beings into civilized and barbarian lay at the centre of Enlightenment thought and *enabled* human rights violations and outright violence against those deemed incapable of rational and progressive thought. The point here is not to debunk the Enlightenment in toto, rather, it is to recognize the complexities and contradictions that lie at the heart of Enlightenment philosophy, all of which Pinker so blithely ignores. If we are to get closer to a world more and not less infused with human rights, the underside of the Enlightenment still has to be recognized and challenged. And that is no simple task given the global rise of right-wing populism and the huge number of migrants and refugees worldwide.

The second critique is related. In his two books, Pinker offers an assemblage of trends that make for the decline in violence, such as the transition from hunter-gatherer to agricultural societies, the increasing dimensions of rational thought, the 'civilizing process', the long peace of the European nineteenth century, among others. Together, they trigger the 'better angels of our nature'. But trends do not make an explanation; the causative factors for each is not clear, and we have little sense of who exactly is pushing forward these developments. It all seems like a natural unfolding from barbarism to civilization. If only it were all so easy. Pinker soars over the hard, political struggles that Black slaves, women, Korean citizens and so many others engaged to *create* the realm of liberty – with all its limitations – in the real world. In those struggles, the incidence and intensity of violence was often huge, and those events do not appear in statistical tables on murder rates or the number of wars that have been fought in the modern period. Forced-feedings of suffragettes, death squad activities in Guatemala, tortures in American prisons, crimes against humanity and war crimes in the Great Lakes region of Africa, not even counting the Rwandan Genocide of 1994 – a cascade of examples can easily be summoned. Nowhere do they come into Pinker's world view. And they cry out for recognition because we can never simply assume – as Pinker does – that the human condition will naturally and inevitably improve.

Enlightenment

For Pinker, Enlightenment means a commitment to the 'ideals of reason, science, humanism, and progress'.[7] And so it does. But one of the central

---

[7]Pinker, *Enlightenment Now*, 4, and generally 3–14.

questions for Enlightenment figures was who, precisely, has the capacity for reason and therefore can explore and understand science, humanism, and progress? Who, then, has the 'right to have rights?' as Hannah Arendt asked in 1951. She was preceded by the German Enlightenment philosopher Johann Gottlieb Fichte, who wrote in 1796: 'The one true right that belongs to the human being . . . [is]: the right . . . to acquire rights'.[8] Which civilians and combatants come under the Hague and Geneva conventions and are therefore protected from the worst ravages of warfare? More than a generation of scholarship on the Enlightenment, much of it by feminist historians and political theorists, has shown just how limiting was the Enlightenment view when it came to matters of race and gender.

Since the Columbian encounters beginning in the 1490s, Europeans strove to make sense of a world far more diverse than they had ever known.[9] The globe became more tightly linked by the movement of peoples and commodities, even more so when steamships and railroads came along in the nineteenth century. Epic population migrations and the forced enslavement of Africans meant that well over 100 million people left their homelands, not just in Europe but in Asia and Africa as well. Individual travellers also found their way around the globe. They were scientists, businessmen, missionaries, government emissaries and adventurers. They wrote journals, newspaper articles, memoirs and books, some widely read. They created the pathways of communication that made the larger world known to literate publics in their home countries. Sometimes they experienced these encounters personally, taking passage on merchant ships or government-sponsored explorations, as did, for example, the great naturalists Alexander von Humboldt and Charles Darwin. Others, like the French philosopher Montesquieu, rarely set foot outside their estates or villas. They sat in their libraries and read travel literature and scientific accounts, genres that became wildly popular in the eighteenth and nineteenth centuries and reflected about what this wider world signified for Europeans and for the human condition generally.[10]

Africans, Asians and Middle Easterners did much the same. Confronted with Western power, products and ideas, they reconsidered some of their own scientific, religious and political beliefs. They did not just receive Western ideas; they developed their own syncretic reform movements that blended

---

[8]Hannah Arendt, *The Origins of Totalitarianism* (1951; Cleveland: Meridian, 1958), 300, 296, and J. G. Fichte, *Foundations of Natural Right: According to the Principles of the Wissenschaftslehre* (1796), ed. Frederick Neuhouser, trans. Michael Baur (Cambridge University Press, 2000), 333. Arendt makes no reference to Fichte's formulation, nor do any of the major Arendt scholars.

[9]Some of what I write below is drawn from Eric D. Weitz, *A Century of Genocide: Utopias of Race and Nation* (2003; Princeton: Princeton University Press, 2015); and idem., *A World Divided*.

[10]For the East Asian example, see Jürgen Osterhammel, *Unfabling the East: The Enlightenment's Encounter with Asia*, trans. Robert Savage (1998; Princeton: Princeton University Press, 2018).

and adapted new models emanating from the West with their indigenous traditions. Fath 'Ali Shah, who ruled Persia from 1797 to 1834; Mehmet Ali, the effective leader and ultimately khedive of Egypt from 1805 to 1849; a series of Ottoman sultans beginning with Selim III in 1789 – all recognized the need for reform.[11] Every traveller, Western or Eastern, Northern or Southern, was deeply attuned to human difference – between people in one's home country and those in the destination regions, and within those same lands.[12] This was hardly a new phenomenon. The works of Thucydides and Herodotus ripple with descriptions, some quite fanciful, of different people in the known world, and the same is true of educated Chinese and Arab travellers in the medieval period.

Two factors, however, were different in the eighteenth- and nineteenth-century encounters. Europeans and North Americans who journeyed outward often – not always, but often – sought evidence for dividing the human species along racial lines. Classification of the natural world had been a defining characteristic of the Scientific Revolution and the Enlightenment, and it carried over into the nineteenth century. Naturalists like Humboldt and Darwin closely observed rock formations, vegetation and fish and animal species. Most could not refrain from commenting as well on society and politics.[13] Like Carolus Linnaeus, the great eighteenth-century Swedish scientist and master of classification, they drew links from their analysis of the natural to the human world.[14]

From the determination to categorize all flora and fauna in the world, it was but a short step to categorizing human beings in a similarly rigorous, supposedly scientific manner. Linnaeus was among those who posited a racial division of the human species. That division was never innocent;

[11]On these nineteenth-century developments, see the magisterial works of Jürgen Osterhammel, *The Transformation of the World: A Global History of the Nineteenth Century*, trans. Patrick Camiller (Princeton: Princeton University Press, 2014), and C. A. Bayly, *The Birth of the Modern World, 1780-1914: Global Connections and Comparisons* (Malden: Blackwell, 2004), along with the powerful article by Sebastian Conrad, 'Enlightenment in Global History: A Historiographical Critique', *American Historical Review*, 117, no. 4 (2012): 999–1027. Bayly emphasizes the growing uniformity of social practices and political and economic developments around the world as well as the greater complexity of societies. Osterhammel is more attuned to difference. In regard to state power, Bayly's formulation is insightful: '[States] had to trench into areas of society that had formerly been autonomous' (7).

[12]For Persian and Middle Eastern travellers to Europe in the early nineteenth century, see Alexander Bevilacqua, *The Republic of Arab Letters: Islam and the European Enlightenment* (Cambridge, MA: Belknap Press, 2018); Nile Green, *The Love of Strangers: What Six Muslim Students Learned in Jane Austen's London* (Princeton: Princeton University Press, 2016). Also interesting is Rifā'ah Rāfi' al-Ṭahṭāwī, *An Imam in Paris: Account of a Stay in France by an Egyptian Cleric (1826-1831)*, trans. Daniel L. Newman (London: Saqi, 2004).

[13]On Humboldt, see the magnificent biography by Andrea Wulf, *The Invention of Nature: Alexander von Humboldt's World* (New York: Knopf, 2016).

[14]See Lisbeth Koerner, *Linnaeus: Nature and Nation* (Cambridge, MA: Harvard University Press, 1999).

it was always hierarchical, always categorized some people – inevitably Europeans – as capable of higher learning and rational thought, and others as barbarians. Linnaeus identified the European as 'ingenious', the Asian 'melancholy' and the African 'crafty, lazy, careless'.[15] Such an interpretation commingled easily with John Locke's emphasis on observation and Montesquieu's division of the human species into immutable groupings based on geography and climate. Unsurprisingly, Montesquieu praised the inhabitants of the north, the well-governed English and Scandinavians who had created liberty from its origins in the Germanic tribes. But Africans, he wrote, were beyond the pale: 'It is hardly to be believed that God, who is a wise Being, should place a soul, especially a good soul, in such a black ugly body. It is so natural to look upon colour as the criterion of human nature.' In these two brief sentences, Montesquieu made four significant moves in the direction of race thinking. He gave eternal characteristics to human groups based on skin colour; argued that physiognomy, outward appearance, expresses inner being; made one group, Africans, incapable of ever joining the circle of the elect; and 'naturalized' skin colour as a marker – 'it is so *natural*', he wrote. Hence, the correct political order had to reflect particular racial properties.[16]

A fully developed theory of race required a new science of humankind. This is what anthropology, an Enlightenment invention, provided. Enlightenment thinkers fervently sought to redefine the place of humankind in nature. Their critique of Christianity had undermined the primacy of religious dogma, setting human beings adrift in a sea of uncertainty. They had to be re-anchored, and a de-sanctified, presumably scientific 'nature' provided the weight.[17]

The key figure in the emergence of the new discipline of anthropology was Johann Friedrich Blumenbach (1752–1840), whose work, *On the Natural Variety of Mankind*, insisted on both the unity of the human species and the diversity within it, a diversity that only could be accounted for through rigorous scientific observation. His 'epoch-making catalogue of human races', in Peter Gay's words, included just five, each assigned to its own region of the globe – Caucasian, Mongolian, Ethiopian, American and Malay.[18] For

---

[15]Quoted in Ivan Hannaford, *Race: The History of an Idea in the West* (Washington, DC: Woodrow Wilson Center Press, 1996), 204.

[16]Quoted in Hannaford, *Race*, 26.

[17]As David Brion Davis, *The Problem of Slavery in Western Culture* (Ithaca: Cornell University Press, 1966), 446, writes: 'Insofar as the Enlightenment divorced anthropology and comparative anatomy from theological assumptions, it opened the way for theories of racial inferiority'. See also, Emmanuel Chukwudi Eze (ed.), *Race and the Enlightenment: A Reader* (Cambridge, MA: Blackwell, 1997); and Nell Irvin Painter, *The History of White People* (New York: Norton, 2010), chaps. 5 and 6.

[18]Peter Gay, *The Cultivation of Hatred: The Bourgeois Experience Victoria to Freud*, vol. 3 (New York: Norton, 1993), 72.

the next 200 years, just about down to the present day, scientists would dispute the number and types, but not the effort to define and categorize races. Blumenbach's own collection of skeletons, the raw material of his scientific researches, would only be rivalled by the anthropologists of the nineteenth century who began to collect skulls and measure the cranium as a way of determining race-linked intelligence.[19]

The German Enlightenment figure Johann Gottlieb Fichte perfectly embodies the contradictions at the heart of the Enlightenment.[20] In *Foundations of Natural Right*, published in 1796, Fichte argued that the notion of a single individual, existing solely onto himself, is nonsensical. The I is irreducible, but the I always exists in conjunction with others. 'The human being . . . becomes a human being only among human beings', he wrote.[21] The social and the individual are inextricably bound; intersubjectivity is a necessary condition of the world.

Precisely from this egocentric vantage point, Fichte makes a profound contribution to the development of human rights thinking: the I has to recognize that others deserve the same set of rights.[22] Fichte situated the origins of rights not in some universal landscape, whether it be moral, theological or political, not in some original state of nature, but in the self-acting, self-conscious I that has to grant others the same rights. Fundamental here is a notion of mutual recognition [*Anerkennung*] that would play such an important role in Hegel and then in late twentieth-century philosophy, notably in the philosophy of Emmanuel Lévinas.[23] A reasoned world can only be constructed by free men together. Individual and collective freedom, individual and collective self-determination are inextricably bound together.

But Fichte's thought, for all its intersubjectivity, for all its refreshing, universalist tone, poses immediately the problem that always stalks the Enlightenment and human rights thinking: Who is eligible to enter into the charmed circle of those endowed with the capacity to posit themselves and to exercise freedom? Fichte wrote: 'The concept of individuality determines a *community*, and whatever follows further from this depends not on me alone, but also on the one who has by virtue of this concept – entered into

---

[19]See Stephen Jay Gould, *The Mismeasure of Man,* revised edn (New York: Norton, 1996).
[20]See, Eric D. Weitz, 'Self-Determination: How a German Enlightenment Idea Became the Slogan of National Liberation and a Human Right', *American Historical Review*, 120, no. 2 (2015): 462–96.
[21]Fichte, *Foundations*, 37.
[22]See Manfed Kühn's discussion in, *Johann Gottlieb Fichte: Ein deutscher Philisoph, 1762-1814* (Munich: Beck, 2012), 300–1, as well as Anthony J. La Vopa, *Fichte: The Calling of the Self and Philosophy* (Cambridge: Cambridge University Press, 2001), 305–17. As Fichte wrote, 'The source of this [mutual] obligation is certainly not the moral law; rather, it is the law of thought'. Fichte, *Foundations*, 47.
[23]See Samuel Moyn, *Origins of the Other: Emmanuel Lévinas between Revelation and Ethics* (Ithaca: Cornell University Press, 2005).

community with me. . . . We are both *bound* and *obligated* to each other by our very existence.'[24] But who, precisely, constitutes the community?

In two critical arenas, Fichte's universal subject is immediately undone: when he writes about women and the family, an entire section of *Foundations*, and when he turns his attention to the German nation, as he did amid the Napoleonic occupation of Germany in the first years of the nineteenth century. Always attuned to the philosophical and political events around him, Fichte responded to the calls for equal rights for women that had been articulated in England and France in the wake of the French Revolution, if not yet in Germany. Moreover, he was self-critical enough to recognize the obvious question that arose from his egocentric philosophy: Do women have the capacity to develop the free, rational I, to become self-determining individuals?

Not quite. Fichte's writings on women and the family are his least convincing, a mix of philosophical pretension with the rank prejudices of the day.[25] 'The one sex', he wrote, 'is entirely active, the other entirely passive. . . . [I]t is absolutely contrary to reason for the second sex to have the satisfaction of its sexual drive as an end.'[26] Instead – no surprise here – the sexual drive in women exists only for them to bear children. The woman achieves dignity by surrendering herself to her husband, by becoming the means of his sexual satisfaction, out of which she derives meaning in life.[27] In the process, she cedes to him all her property and rights.[28] 'The husband represents her entirely, from the state's point of view, she is completely annihilated by her marriage. . . . In the eyes of the state, her husband becomes her guarantee and her legal guardian; in all things, he lives out her public life, and she retains only a domestic life.'[29] A woman, he went on, 'cannot even think about exercising her rights directly on her own'.[30] She was self-determining only by freely entering into a marriage of her choice. Afterward, her husband self-determines for her, rendering the concept truly meaningless. Fichte's universalism would be undone even more dramatically in his writings on Germany. After the turn into the nineteenth century, amid the Napoleonic occupation of the German lands, Fichte took the social dimension of his thought to a new level. The universal I became, in essence, the German nation. In that way, Fichte moved the concept of self-determination, the focus of all his intellectual striving, from a purely

---

[24]Fichte, *Foundations*, 45.
[25]La Vopa, *Fichte*, 345–67, is perhaps too generous to his subject on this matter. More critical is Isabel V. Hull, *Sexuality, State, and Civil Society in Germany, 1700-1815* (Ithaca: Cornell University Press, 1996), 314–23.
[26]Fichte, *Foundations*, 266.
[27]Fichte, *Foundations*, 269.
[28]Fichte, *Foundations*, 271.
[29]Fichte, *Foundations*, 282.
[30]Fichte, *Foundations*, 299.

individualist concept to a collectivist one. By the time of the famed *Addresses to the German Nation* in 1807 – unfortunately the work for which he is most known – his thought moved from egocentricity, to the universal man, to the national man. Ultimately, in Fichte, the 'right to have rights' became restricted to those men belonging to the German nation – at least for those living in the German lands.[31]

No Enlightenment figure ever denied the essential unity of the human species, and Johann Gottfried Herder specifically rejected the terminology of race. But Herder was virtually alone. The problem that preoccupied them, the more telling reality, was the diversity of human beings and the division into 'civilized' and 'barbarian'.[32] That diversity was rooted in nature, in God's creation, expressed first in language, then in culture, and then in political guise through the state. Herder and Fichte wrote about people and nations. By defining a people as a closed community whose ties to one another were primordial – based in language and culture – the concepts they developed and the language they deployed slid easily into racial categories. A racial understanding of human diversity became even more prominent after the mid-nineteenth century. All sorts of commentators drew on Darwinian ideas to promote 'scientific' racism – even though much of the science was rank prejudice. In this sense, there existed in the West a 'racial international', a way of thinking about human diversity based first in the Enlightenment that transcended national borders.

The point here, again, is not to debunk the Enlightenment, to replace Pinker's starry-eyed optimism with a dismal reading of the past. Instead, it is to show the Enlightenment *in its complexity*. Yes, as a set of ideas the Enlightenment is absolutely critical to advances in human rights. At the same time, the Enlightenment discounting (at best) of the rational capacities of women and everyone but Europeans contributed to some of the worst violations of human rights over the next two centuries. Because of the belief in inherent Black and female inferiority, the Enlightenment enabled slaveholders to defend the institution and the advocates of male superiority to deny women entrance into the public sphere. It enabled the worst of all possible consequences of race thinking, namely genocide, as in the

---

[31]For a recent reading of Fichte that is more sophisticated but, ultimately, emphasizes his nationalism to the exclusion of much else, see Helmut Walser Smith, *The Continuities of German History: Nation, Religion, and Race across the Long Nineteenth Century* (Cambridge, MA: Cambridge University Press, 2008), 58–73. But see Isaac Nakhimovsky, *The Closed Commercial State: Perpetual Peace and Commercial Society from Rousseau to Fichte* (Princeton: Princeton University Press, 2011), which provides an insightful reading of Fichte's republicanism and views of the state that in some ways runs parallel to my argument here. Nakhimovsky shows how Fichte argued that a true republicanism, which would also be the foundation of international peace, could only be founded when the state limited the functioning of the market, established autarky (a closed, self-sufficient economy) and guaranteed work for everyone.
[32]For Britain, see the pioneering work of George Stocking, *Victorian Anthropology* (New York: Free Press, 1987).

vicious annihilation campaign pursued by the German military against the Herero and Nama people of German Southwest Africa (today Namibia). As 'barbarians', these Africans did not come under the purview of Geneva Convention, as the chief agent of genocide, Lt General Lothar von Trotha, wrote.[33]

One can imagine Pinker's response. Ultimately, he would say, slavery was abolished, women won the right to vote, international law now encompasses all civilians and Namibia is independent. To which one can only answer: Yes, but at what great cost? How many lives snuffed out, and how many bodies tortured and maimed because of the underside of Enlightenment thought? And how great are the lingering effects today, as in the realm of rampant inequality? Pinker travels only on the sunny side of the street. Lucky for him. But the street-world of politics is much broader and often deluged with hailstorms.

Politics and struggle

History moves in many directions at the same time. And it is surely not by ideas alone that it moves. Pinker argues that his assemblage of trends invoke our more humane characteristics. In reality, those trends *represent* an overall development he has already defined. His reasoning is circular. We need a much better handle on the causes and agents of historical change.

Ideas are critical, and the rivers of communication advanced globally in the eighteenth and especially the nineteenth century, pushed along by newspapers, railroads, steamships and telegraph lines. The places of communication expanded around the globe, in coffee houses, madrassas and teahouses.[34] Yet the greater depths of communication cannot alone explain how human rights and other forms of progress came about.

Let me use one example, drawn from my book, *A World Divided* – the abolition of slavery in Brazil.[35] Slavery as an institution thrived through all of recorded history and in virtually every known society. Virtually all of the Western European countries made huge profits off of the slave trade and slave labour. Britain in particular drew immense wealth from its sugar plantations in the Caribbean, worked by African slaves, which provided capital to underwrite the Industrial Revolution. Around 12.5 million Africans were forcibly moved in the trans-Atlantic slave trade from 1501 to

---

[33]Quoted in Gesine Krüger, *Kriegsbewältigung und Geschichtsbewußtsein: Realität, Deutung und Verarbeitung des deutschen Kolonialkriegs in Namibia 1904 bis 1907* (Göttingen: Vanden-hoeck and Ruprecht, 1999), 65.
[34]Osterhammel, *The Transformation of the World*; Bayly, *The Birth of the Modern World*; Conrad, 'Enlightenment in Global History'.
[35]Weitz, *World Divided*, chap. 4.

1867, nearly 1.9 million of them between 1801 and 1825, entwining the histories of Africa and the Americas.[36] Only slowly and very reluctantly did the British elite respond to the emergence of abolitionist sentiment at the end of the eighteenth century. Finally, in 1833, parliament voted to end slavery in the British Empire. Only in 1888, with abolition in Brazil, was bonded labour eliminated in the Americas. (At least as a public matter. Many forms of human trafficking, especially of women, remain today, meaning that something like slavery persists in many parts of the world.)

How did abolition come about? A huge, sophisticated historiography exists, but Pinker is hardly alone in presuming that abolition was a natural, inevitable unfolding of history since the eighteenth century.[37]

I think not. In reality, it took determined action, first by slaves themselves, who resisted slavery through rebellion and flight, and then by a segment of the elite that organized an abolitionist movement tied into the international anti-slavery organization headquartered in London. The third factor was comparatively mundane – the more or less blind workings of the market that eviscerated the support for bonded labour among those in the sugar-producing regions who could no longer afford to buy and keep slaves. In these struggles, the level of violence exercised by slaves, masters and the state was intense, but nowhere does that kind of violence get recorded in the statistics Pinker uses. Nor does he take into account the complex legacies of abolition and other human rights advances. In Brazil, the legacy of slavery and the manner of abolition spawned the huge inequality that still define Brazilian society today.

The great majority of Africans taken to the New World, some 95 per cent, were enslaved in Brazil and the Caribbean.[38] Rio de Janeiro was the largest

---

[36]David Eltis and David Richardson, *Atlas of the Transatlantic Slave Trade* (New Haven: Yale University Press, 2010), 4–5.

[37]The literature on abolitionism is vast. See multiple works by David Brion Davis, including *The Problem of Slavery in the Age of Emancipation* (New York: Knopf, 2014), and *The Problem of Slavery in the Age of Revolution* (Ithaca: Cornell University Press, 1975); Seymour Drescher, *Abolition: A History of Slavery and Antislavery* (Cambridge: Cambridge University Press, 2009); Adam Hochschild, *Bury the Chains: Prophets and Rebels in the Fight to Free an Empire's Slaves* (Boston: Houghton Mifflin, 2005); and Rebecca Scott, *Slave Emancipation in Cuba: The Transition to Free Labor, 1860-1899* (Pittsburgh: University of Pittsburgh Press, 2000). Clarence-Smith, *Islam and the Abolition of Slavery*, demonstrates the diverse influences that led to abolition in the Islamic world, including Western pressure as well as Muslim traditions. Modern scholarship on slavery and its abolition begins with Eric Williams, *Capitalism and Slavery* (Chapel Hill: University of North Carolina Press, 1944).

[38]On Brazilian slavery and its society and polity in general, I draw especially on Emilia Viotti da Costa, *The Brazilian Empire: Myths and Histories* (Chapel Hill: University of North Carolina Press, 2000); Herbert S. Klein and Francisco Vidal Luna, *Slavery in Brazil* (Cambridge: Cambridge University Press, 2010); Stuart B. Schwartz, *Sugar Plantations in the Formation of Brazilian Society: Bahia, 1550-1835* (Cambridge: Cambridge University Press, 1985); Robert Edgar Conrad, *The Destruction of Brazilian Slavery, 1850-1888*, 2nd edn (1972; Malabar: Krieger, 1993); and some of the essays in Kenneth Maxwell, *Naked Tropics: Essays on Empire*

port of the slave trade, taking even more slaves than New Orleans. By best estimates, Brazil took 41 per cent of all African slaves.[39] In 1864, there were 1,715,000 slaves in Brazil, 16.7 per cent of the population.[40]

As early as 1719, Count Pedro de Almeida, the captain general of the province Minas Gerais, wrote to King João V, lauding the successful suppression of a slave revolt. However, worrying signs remained.

> Since we cannot prevent the remaining blacks from thinking, and cannot deprive them of their natural desire for freedom; and since we cannot, merely because of this desire, eliminate all of them, they being necessary for our existence here, it must be concluded that this country will always be subjected to [the] problem [of slave rebellions].[41]

The Count went on to note that the sheer numerical domination of slaves gave them the courage to rebel, while the geography offered them countless places to hide.[42]

One hundred years later, little had changed. Masters and their slaves in Brazil exist in a 'a state of domestic war', wrote one government official in 1818.[43] Another five decades on and the situation was no better. Slave rebellions were an ever-present danger, a 'volcano that constantly threatens society, a bomb ready to explode with the first spark', wrote a Brazilian legal scholar in 1866.[44]

'Death to Whites! Long live Blacks!', slave rebels cried out in Bahia, Brazil, in 1835, sometimes extending their killing slogans to mulattos as well.[45] Hardly a call for *human* rights. The Bahian rebels were Muslim. They wanted to end *their* enslavement, not slavery in its entirety. After their expected victory, they envisaged enslaving other Blacks and mulattos.[46] These slave resisters did not seek a fulfilment of liberalism's universalist promise of citizenship rights for all. Nonetheless, slave rebels, in Bahia in 1835 and

---

and Other Rogues (New York: Routledge, 2003. For the state of the historiography as of the 1990s, see Stuart B. Schwartz, *Slaves, Peasants, and Rebels: Reconsidering Brazilian Historiography* (Urbana: University of Illinois Press, 1992), 1–38. Klein and Luna, *Slavery in Brazil*, offer a more recent synthesis of the historiography.

[39]David Brion Davis, *Inhuman Bondage: The Rise and Fall of Slavery in the New World* (New York: Oxford University Press, 2006), 104.

[40]Davis, *Inhuman Bondage*, 324.

[41]'Excerpt from Count Pedro de Almeida to King João V (of Portugal), 1719', in Robert Edgar Conrad (ed.), *Children of God's Fire: A Documentary History of Black Slavery in Brazil* (Princeton: Princeton University Press, 1983), 394–7, quote 396–7.

[42]Conrad, *Children of God's Fire*, 396–7.

[43]An adviser to King João VI, quoted in Conrad, *Children of God's Fire*, 359.

[44]Quoted in Conrad, *Children of God's Fire*, 241.

[45]For some examples, João José Reis, *Slave Rebellion in Brazil: The Muslim Uprising of 1835 in Bahia*, trans. Arthur Brakel (1986; Baltimore: Johns Hopkins University Press, 1993), 40, 47, 56, 121, 122.

[46]Reis, *Slave Rebellion in Brazil*, 120–3.

in many other, smaller rebellions that permeated the Brazilian landscape, by their actions, demanded, at the very least, to be treated as human beings. They claimed for themselves the dignity that comes with the recognition of the other, the basis of all human rights claims. They directly challenged the institution that served as the most consistent and brutal violator of rights, that so thoroughly assaulted the dignity of the individual that nothing was left except a commodity, bought, sold, exchanged and brutalized at will. Until the totalitarian and genocidal states of the twentieth century, nothing stood in such absolute contradiction to the principles of citizenship and rights as slavery. The *abolition* of slavery was the greatest human rights advance of the nineteenth century.

Slave resistance made Brazil inherently unstable, but slaves were unable to win their emancipation by their actions alone. In Brazil, another mobilization was necessary – of members of the elite who had come to believe that the modern, liberal Brazil they desired and the slave society in which they lived stood in stark contradiction to one another. Only by emancipating slaves could Brazil progress and take its rightful place among the civilized nations of the world, they believed.

In his great work, *O Abolicionismo*, and in hundreds of other writings and speeches, Joaquim Nabuco, Brazil's preeminent abolitionist, gave powerful voice to the long-standing criticism that the slave system had created in Brazil 'demoralization and inertia . . . servility and irresponsibility . . . despotism, superstition, and ignorance' among masters as well as slaves.[47] Like other major abolitionists, Nabuco commanded great rhetorical powers to depict the lash on the back, the mere drops of milk left to a slave child after the mother has nursed the master's children, the endless agony and sorrow of slavery.[48]

Yet a wistful tone runs through Nabuco's writing, as if he wished that Brazil could have been created without Blacks.[49] That sentiment signalled the limits of Nabuco's liberalism. His was not a celebration of Brazil's multiculturalism (as we would now call it), but a grim coming to terms with reality. As slaves produced mixed-race children for the master, they multiplied, and the 'vices of African blood came into widespread circulation throughout the nation'. The major result was the 'mixing of the servile

---

[47]Joaquim Nabuco, *Abolitionism: The Brazilian Antislavery Struggle* (1883), trans. and ed. Robert Conrad (Urbana: University of Illinois Press, 1977), 9–10.

[48]Nabuco, *Abolitionism*, 10, 19. See also the first great Brazilian abolitionist statement, by Brazil's first prime minister, José Bonifacio de Andrada e Silva, in 1823, excerpts in Conrad, *Children of God's Fire*, 418–27.

[49]Nabuco, *Abolitionism*, 98–103. Another abolitionist L. Anselmo da Fonseca, in his *A Escravidão, o Clero e o Abolicionismo*, was even more hostile towards Blacks. But that did not stop him from opposing slavery.

degradation of the one [Blacks] with the brutal arrogance of the other [whites]'.[50]

As the abolitionist movement developed in the 1860s, 1870s and 1880s, the sugar economy in the northeast declined, making the possession of slaves uneconomical for many plantation owners. Then slaves took matters into their own hands. Not by rebellion, but in massive flight, a runaway slave movement with few parallels in the sordid history of slavery. It was an extraordinary development, akin to a general strike.[51] Slaves simply fled the coffee plantations, first in small numbers, and then in droves. Brazil's vast and often difficult geography offered them numerous places to hide. Meanwhile, a Brazilian version of the underground railway offered runaways shelter and protection.

Finally, on 13 May 1888, parliament passed an emancipatory act, simple and clear: 'From the date of this law slavery is declared extinct in Brazil. . . . All provisions to the contrary are revoked'.[52] Slaveholders received no compensation. Princess Imperial Regent Isabel signed the law because her father, Dom Pedro II, was in Portugal. 'The victory was so sweeping and unexpected that the enthusiasm of the people overflowed all bounds', wrote the abolitionist A. J. Lamoureux. 'The streets [of Rio] have been continually crowded, business almost wholly suspended . . . over a hundred thousand people in the streets on Sunday . . . nothing but enthusiastic joy, good temper, and good order.'[53] In the northern city of São Luis, newly liberated slaves swarmed the streets for a week, covered in flowers and palms, singing and dancing.[54] Music echoed through the cities, crowds surged in parades.

But what about after slavery? Despite the hopes of many, Brazilian ex-slaves were not even offered the prospects of the 40 acres and a mule promised to freed American slaves. Brazilian slaves were on their own, and that meant, most often, going back to work on plantations as technically free but poverty-stricken individuals. And that legacy remains today. Brazil has one of the highest indices of social inequality in the world. Between 1960 and 1990, the top 10 per cent of the population enjoyed an 8.1 per cent increase in income, and the bottom 50 per cent a decrease of 3.2 per cent. In 1990, the top 10 per cent of the population possessed nearly half the income of the country, an increase of 10 per cent since 1960. Black mean income in 1960 was less than half that of whites, with mixed-race people's mean income closer to the Black than the white level. In 1950, over half the Black population but only one-quarter of the white population

[50]Nabuco, Abolitionism, 98.
[51]Sidney Chalhoub, 'The Politics of Ambiguity: Conditional Manumission, Labor Contracts, and Slave Emancipation in Brazil (1850s-1888)', International Review of Social History, 60, no. 1 (2015): 161–91, here 164.
[52]Text of the law in Conrad, Children of God's Fire, 480–1.
[53]Quoted in Conrad, Destruction of Brazilian Slavery, 205.
[54]Conrad, Destruction of Brazilian Slavery, 205.

was illiterate. (In 2015, the overall adult literacy rate was 92.05 per cent.[55]) Careful analyses have demonstrated that the low mean income of Blacks is not only related to poor education or dead-end jobs; sheer discrimination against Blacks provides much of the reason.[56] Despite some narrowing of the spread between wealthy and poor over the last twenty-five years, Brazil sits at place 19 of 150 countries on the scale of unequal income distributions.[57]

Social inequality in Brazil largely aligns with race. Those at the top are disproportionately white – radically so – those at the bottom largely Black. Around the year 2000, Afro-Brazilians constituted 44 per cent of the population. At the University of São Paulo, the most prestigious institution of higher education, the student body numbering in the thousands included less than twelve Afro-Brazilians, and even fewer faculty members.[58] Brazil's *favelas*, the sprawling shantytowns on the edges of all Brazilian cities, have grown dramatically since 1960 as poorer, Black Brazilians pour into the city from the countryside. Today, 23–24 per cent of Rio's population lives in these impoverished neighbourhoods.[59]

All of this in a country that had no formal, legal racial discrimination and segregation, as did the United States and South Africa.[60] Yet an intense race consciousness prevails in Brazil. When a government agency in 1976 asked Brazilians to identify their skin colour, 134 different classifications came up, including pure white, bronzed tan, cashew-like, orange, Black, greenish, high pink and many others.[61] One scholarly study identified 500 categories.[62] For many years, the slogan and ideology of Brazil as a 'racial democracy' masked, at least in public discourse, the severe inequalities that defined

[55]https://countryeconomy.com/demography/literacy-rate/brazil, accessed 18 March 2020.
[56]Figures from Anthony W. Marx, *Making Race and Nation: A Comparison of the United States, South Africa, and Brazil* (Cambridge: Cambridge University Press, 1998), 171–2, 254, and Thomas E. Skidmore, *Brazil: Five Centuries of Change*, 2nd edn (New York: Oxford University Press, 2010), 189.
[57]See the World Bank figures at https://data.worldbank.org/indicator/SI.POV.GINI/. and the CIA's inequality list (based on the same GINI index used by the World Bank) at https://www.cia.gov/library/publications/the-world-factbook/rankorder/2172rank.html, both accessed 15 May 2018.
[58]Skidmore, *Brazil*, 199.
[59]https://catcomm.org/favela-facts/, accessed 18 March 2020. For important and gripping cinematic renderings of life in the favelas and the legacies of slavery, see *City of God* (2002, directed by Fernando Meirelles and Kátia Lund), and *Black Orpheus* (1959, directed by Marcel Camus).
[60]Along with Marx, *Making Race and Nation*, for other important comparative studies of race, see Patrick Wolfe, *Traces of History: Elementary Structures of Race* (London: Verso, 2016), and George M. Fredrickson, *Racism: A Short History* (Princeton: Princeton University Press, 2003), though the latter addresses the United States, South Africa and Nazi Germany, the three states with legally enshrined racism not Brazil.
[61]Brazilian Institute of Geography and Statistics, 'What Color Are You?', in Robert M. Levine and John J. Crocitti (eds), *The Brazil Reader: History, Culture, Politics* (Durham: Duke University Press, 1999), 386–90.
[62]Wolfe, *Traces of History*, 113–14, citing the study by Marvin Harris and Conrad Kotak, 'The Structural Significance of Brazilian Categories', *Sociologica*, 25 (1963): 203n.

the lives of Black and mixed-race people, and limited the appeal of Black identity mobilizations. Left-wing parties, like Lulu's (Luiz Inácio Lula da Silva) Workers' Party (PT), have emphasized class issues and have been loath to discuss race or to develop policies of redress that are oriented specifically towards the Black and mixed-race population.

The emancipation of Brazilian slaves marked a huge advance. It came about largely through popular activism, slave resistance and flight. Slaves posed a constant threat to liberal Brazil, but slaves could not liberate themselves. They needed support. That came from well-placed abolitionists, who built a parallel movement, one that tapped into international anti-slavery activism. The final blow came when slavery proved no longer economical in major areas of the country. However partial were the rights that Blacks received in 1888, they at least received the most basic right – to be recognized as free persons.

More than anything else, the ideology and practice of race, in Brazil and many other places around the globe, shattered the universalist claims of liberalism, sharply delimiting those who had the right to have rights. The belief in inherited Black inferiority, founded in Enlightenment thought then strengthened by so-called racial science, long outlasted the abolition of slavery. The close identity of race and class left many Blacks and mulattos subject to deep-seated prejudices and a market economy that sometimes proved nearly as harsh as slavery itself, especially when, in the nineteenth and early twentieth centuries and, more recently, with the rise of neoliberalism, a classical liberal perspective refused to adopt any kind of social policies that would have mitigated the workings of the market.

Abolition was a great achievement, but the line between slavery and freedom was not always as clear and firm as abolitionists, and slaves themselves, had hoped. And the legacy of slavery remains. Formal, legally enshrined rights are of fundamental importance. But they also require social capacities – the arguments of Martha Nussbaum and Amartya Sen – and a socially egalitarian order for people fully to exercise the rights laid out for them in constitutions and laws.[63]

History is far more contradictory and complex than Steven Pinker allows. There have been gains in the realm of Enlightenment and human rights. They are critically important and need to be defended. But the achievements have by no means been uniform and steady, and hardly linear. In order to establish a more peaceable, egalitarian and humane world, we need to understand the complexities and not presume that life is always on an upward trajectory.

---

[63]See Martha C. Nussbaum, *Creating Capabilities: The Human Development Approach* (Cambridge, MA: Belknap Press of Harvard University Press, 2011); and Amartya Sen, *Development as Freedom* (New York: Knopf, 1999).

5

Pinker's technocratic neoliberalism, and why it matters

David A. Bell

Nature seemed to have wisely arranged for men's follies to be fleeting, but books immortalize them.

MONTESQUIEU[1]

Catastrophe can sometimes function as a particularly pointed form of book review. In 1710, for instance, the philosopher Gottfried Wilhelm Leibniz published *Theodicy*, in which he argued that humanity lived in 'the best of all possible worlds'.[2] When an earthquake destroyed the city of Lisbon in 1755 taking at least 10,000 lives, commentators (first and foremost Voltaire, in *Candide*) presented the event as a decisive refutation of Leibniz's thesis.[3] Exactly 200 years after Leibniz, the Anglo-American journalist Norman Angell published his best-selling *The Great Illusion*, which asserted that military power had become 'socially and economically futile' and predicted the imminent arrival of perpetual peace.[4] Four years later, the most

---

[1]'La nature semblait avoir sagement pourvu à ce que les sottises des hommes fussent passagères, et les livres les immortalisent.' Charles Louis de Secondat, baron de La Brède et de Montesquieu, *Lettres persanes*, 2 vols (Paris: Bureaux de la Publication, 1880), i. 160.
[2]Gottfried Wilhelm Leibniz, *Theodicy: Essays on the Goodness of God, the Freedom of Man, and the Origin of Evil*, ed. Austin M. Farrer, trans. E. M. Huggard (New York: Cosmo Classics, 2009 [1710]), 228.
[3]Voltaire, *Candide, or Optimism*, trans. John Butt (London: Penguin, 1947 [1759]), 32–3.
[4]Norman Angell, *The Great Illusion: A Study of the Relation of Military Power to National Advantage* (New York: G. Putnam's Sons, 1913 [1910]), ix.

destructive war yet seen in human history broke out. And in 2018, Harvard psychologist Steven Pinker published *Enlightenment Now*, in which he claimed that 'societies have become healthier, wealthier, freer, happier, and better educated' than ever before, and that the trends would continue.[5] Two years later a global pandemic struck that took over 2,500,000 lives in just one year and forced governments to impose draconian shutdowns that devastated economies worldwide. In a chapter on 'existential threats' to humanity, Pinker had devoted less than a paragraph to the threat of pandemic, although he did provide a list of 'falsely predicted pandemics' that had been 'nipped by medical and public health interventions'.[6]

Books, though, have a remarkable way of surviving this sort of review. Leibniz – whose argument was far more subtle and thoughtful than Voltaire's broad satire of it – remains a pillar of the Western philosophical canon. Norman Angell received a knighthood in 1931 and the Nobel Peace Prize two years later. As for Steven Pinker, the pandemic did not cause him to retract any of the assertions in *Enlightenment Now*. Readers now had more reasons than ever to doubt his sunny predictions for the human future, but his faith in the power of science and his condemnation of what he awkwardly called 'the stupidification of science in political discourse' may well have seemed more attractive than ever.[7]

Indeed, there is reason to think that in the post-2020 world, the political vision underpinning Pinker's work – what I would call 'technocratic neoliberalism' – may also become more attractive than ever. This is, as I will show, a vision of a world where social movements and the messy, unruly aspects of democratic politics are kept within the tightest possible bounds (Pinker has what he himself calls a 'minimalist conception' of democracy).[8] Decisions about social organization and the distribution of goods are instead determined as much as possible by the autonomous, impersonal action of free markets and the rational decisions of well-informed experts. The pandemic of 2020 did not only remind the entire world of the importance of scientific experts. It also highlighted the shortcomings of democracy, as populist demagogues denounced established science, and in the process facilitated the spread of the deadly Covid-19 virus. But modern democracies face a wide variety of challenges, and it would be a grievous error to uncritically apply lessons learned from the pandemic to other, very different ones.

For these reasons, it is still very much worth subjecting Pinker's political vision to strong scrutiny. It is not a vision that he himself has ever expounded upon in a systematic manner. He is not a political philosopher and does not

---

[5]Steven Pinker, *Enlightenment Now: The Case for Reason, Science, Humanism, and Progress* (New York: Viking, 2018), 324.
[6]Pinker, *Enlightenment Now*, 307.
[7]Pinker, *Enlightenment Now*, 387.
[8]Pinker, *Enlightenment Now*, 204.

pretend to be. He is a psychologist who wants to correct what he sees as mistakes in the way most people perceive and interpret the world around them. As he writes: 'Humans today rely on cognitive faculties that worked well enough in traditional societies, but which we now see are infested with bugs.'[9] His is the work of debugging. But his books nonetheless contain strong assumptions about what the world really does look like, how it works, and which policies will do the most to ensure that the positive trends Pinker discerns will continue. In other words, the work is, in fact, inescapably political. At the same time, it is also contradictory, for technocracy and neoliberalism do not actually fit together very well. They share an important common element, but they also reflect very different visions of social and economic organization, which emerged at very different moments in recent history. Pinker, by casting himself as a psychologist correcting humanity's cognitive biases, and not laying out the political implications of his work in a systematic manner, has managed to avoid confronting this contradiction.

The closest that Pinker himself has come to claiming a political vision is when he states, in the first chapter of *Enlightenment Now*, that he is 'channelling a body of beliefs and values that had taken shape more than two centuries before me . . . the ideals of the Enlightenment'. As many critics have noted, Pinker never systematically discusses actual Enlightenment authors, and refers to them only in passing. Indeed, some have charged him with having very little understanding of the actual historical moment that goes by the name of the Enlightenment.[10] Ironically, Pinker's technocratic neoliberalism does have two clear eighteenth-century precedents. But they are not ones that he cites, and he may not even be aware of the second. The contradictions and ultimate failure of this second precedent, however, help to show why we can expect so little from its twenty-first-century Pinkerian counterpart.

What is neoliberalism?

Pinker's neoliberalism is the more obvious part of his political stance. True, 'neoliberalism' itself is an admittedly slippery term that in present political discourse has often degenerated into little more than a term of abuse. Here, I use it to mean, first, a faith derived from older ('classical') liberal thought that free markets are the most efficient and economically productive way

---

[9]Pinker, *Enlightenment Now*, 25.
[10]See for instance Jessica Riskin, 'Pinker's Pollyannish Philosophy and Its Perfidious Politics', *Los Angeles Review of Books* online, 15 December 2019, https://lareviewofbooks.org/article/pinkers-pollyannish-philosophy-and-its-perfidious-politics/, accessed 29 May 2020; David A. Bell, 'The PowerPoint Philosophe: Waiting for Steven Pinker's Enlightenment', *The Nation*, 7 March 2018.

to distribute goods and services in a society. This faith is coupled with a readiness to accept high levels of inequality in exchange for maximum possible economic growth, with a strong distrust of taxation, regulation, economic planning and nationalization, and with a distinct hostility to labour organization. 'Neo-'liberalism distinguishes itself from its classical ancestor by its particular emphasis on freeing the financial sector of the economy from restraint, by its tolerance for so-called 'creative destruction', and by its insistence that free trade operate on a global level, with goods and services freely circulating at maximum possible speed and volume across the world. It also expresses in even more intense form what Pierre Rosanvallon has called classical liberalism's vision of a world largely free from politics – a world where self-regulating, self-organizing market mechanisms determine the most important social configurations and patterns of distribution, leaving ordinary citizens with little or no recourse to political action.[11] While still an imperfect label, 'neoliberalism' does roughly describe the ideological programmes put in place by the Thatcher and Reagan governments of the 1980s in the United Kingdom and the United States, respectively, central elements of which remained largely unchallenged by successive governments of opposing parties (i.e. the Democrats of Bill Clinton and the 'New Labour' of Tony Blair).[12]

Pinker's attraction to neoliberal ideas comes through clearly in two chapters of *Enlightenment Now* entitled 'Wealth' and 'Inequality'.[13] In the first, he seeks to demonstrate the massive explosion in human wealth over the past two centuries and to explain it by reference to three factors: technological innovation, institutions that promoted and protected free markets, and the triumph of 'bourgeois virtue' over value systems that had disdained wealth creation.[14] Throughout, he praises the prodigious wealth-creating capacity of free-market economies, contrasting them to what he calls 'collectivization, centralized control, government monopolies and suffocating permit bureaucracies'.[15] He praises globalization for lifting billions of humans out of poverty, although the statistics he relies on use the United Nations' definition of 'extreme poverty' of $1.90 per day, which is obviously far too low for many countries, and does not take into account the

---

[11]See especially Pierre Rosanvallon, *The Demands of Liberty: Civil Society in France since the Revolution*, trans. Arthur Goldhammer (Cambridge, MA: Harvard University Press, 2007).

[12]On neoliberalism, see Angus Burgin, *The Great Persuasion: Reinventing Free Markets since the Depression* (Cambridge, MA: Harvard University Press, 2012); and Daniel Stedman Jones, *Masters of the Universe: Hayek, Friedman, and the Birth of Neoliberal Politics* (Princeton: Princeton University Press, 2012). See also David Harvey, 'Neoliberalism as Creative Destruction', *Annals of the American Academy of Political and Social Science*, DCX (March 2007): 22–44.

[13]Pinker, *Enlightenment Now*, 79–96, 97–120.

[14]Pinker, *Enlightenment Now*, 82–4.

[15]Pinker, *Enlightenment Now*, 84.

condition of hundreds of millions who live perilously close to this line.[16] He also insists that economic inequality does not matter, as long as all people benefit from economic growth. 'Income inequality', he states baldly, 'is not a fundamental component of well-being'.[17] He does insist on the need for a robust social safety net, including some sort of national health insurance (Pinker, it will be remembered, is Canadian). At the same time, he repeatedly expresses scorn for 'the left' because of 'its contempt for the market and its romance with Marxism', and he bashes the alleged 'progressophobia' of 'intellectuals' in general.[18]

Strikingly, Pinker gives little consideration to the political and social consequences of extreme economic inequality. In the spring of 2020, the 400 wealthiest Americans possessed as much wealth as the bottom 64 per cent of the US population, while the 2,153 wealthiest people on the globe possessed as much wealth as the poorest 4.6 billion.[19] Such massive discrepancies exacerbate the power of the wealthiest to influence or even to buy elections, to determine government policies, to structure systems of education, taxation, transportation for the benefit of their own social, ethnic and religious groups, and much else. The extraordinary power that accrues to the super-wealthy thanks to their wealth also frequently undermines the rules of free and equal competition that supposedly govern the free marketplace. Neoliberal capitalist democracies, it could be said, have a distinct tendency to degenerate into capitalist oligarchies. In the second decade of the twenty-first century, two of the world's three superpowers – Russia and China – arguably fit this latter category, and the third, the United States, showed signs it was moving in the same direction.

The technocratic vision

Technocracy, like (neo-)liberalism, also has a long history. The idea of applying the principles of science and engineering to resolve political problems dates back at least to the Enlightenment, although very few actual Enlightenment thinkers ever advocated anything remotely similar. Rather, the idea was attributed to Enlightenment thinkers by their enemies, who accused them of forcing an imperfect humanity onto the Procrustean bed of abstract philosophical principles, treating humans as broken machinery in

---

[16]Pinker, *Enlightenment Now*, 87.

[17]Pinker, *Enlightenment Now*, 98.

[18]Pinker, *Enlightenment Now*, 364, 39–52.

[19]CNBC report, 1 May 2020, at https://www.cnbc.com/2020/05/01/us-billionaires-boost-wealth-by-406-billion-as-markets-rebound.html; Max Lawson et al., 'Time to Care: Unpaid and Underpaid Care Work and the Global Inequality Crisis', Oxfam International, 20 January 2020 at https://www.oxfam.org/en/research/time-care?cid=aff_affwd_donate_id78888&awc=5991_1590673503_3ddaf06111012760d0b87d5c5fb0dbb9, both accessed 28 May 2020.

need of expert repair.[20] But as Sophia Rosenfeld has recently stressed in her book *Democracy and Truth: A Short History*, many Enlightenment thinkers certainly recoiled from the idea of entrusting ordinary people with political power. From Voltaire, who called 'more than half the habitable world . . . two-footed animals who live in a horrible condition approximating the state of nature', to Madison, who wanted to entrust power to the men with the 'most wisdom' and 'most virtue', to the French *idéologues*, who believed in a science of ideas that had more than a little in common with Pinker's 'cognitive debugging', many eighteenth-century figures made the case for what Rosenfeld calls 'the social and political utility of a distinct cohort of the learned'.[21] This is the first Enlightenment precedent for Pinker's work. As Rosenfeld further points out, over the course of the nineteenth and twentieth centuries advocates for this sort of 'cohort' increasingly cast it less as a moral and wise elite and more as a class of technical experts whose superior scientific knowledge and reasoning skills would allow them to solve the increasingly technical problems of increasingly complex societies.[22]

In the decades after the Second World War, these technical experts seemed to be in the ascendant. In *The Coming of Post-Industrial Society*, published in 1973, the sociologist Daniel Bell argued that as services, theoretical knowledge and information technology became the principal motors of the economy in developed countries, displacing heavy industry, this 'new class' would achieve unprecedented social and political influence.[23] Operating from think tanks, universities and large corporations, the experts would guide social and economic planning, providing direction to elected officials. Europe seemed to offer an example of this path, in such institutions as France's ultra-powerful École Nationale d'Administration (ÉNA) and its Commissariat Général du Plan. The Communist bloc, meanwhile, with its massive bureaucracies and supposedly 'scientific' central planning, seemed to represent a hypertrophied version of government by experts. The phrase 'the new class' in fact first gained popularity after the Yugoslav politician–turned dissident Milovan Djilas used it as the title of a book analysing Communist systems in Eastern Europe.[24]

The technocratic vision, like the neoliberal one, is a vision of government without politics. In the extreme case, that of the Communist dictatorships

---

[20]See on this subject Darrin M. McMahon, *Enemies of the Enlightenment: The French Counter-Enlightenment and the Making of Modernity* (New York: Oxford University Press, 2001), 18–53.

[21]Sophia Rosenfeld, *Democracy and Truth: A Short History* (Philadelphia: University of Pennsylvania Press, 2019), 44, 51, 59, 49.

[22]Rosenfeld, *Democracy and Truth*, 42–91.

[23]Daniel Bell, *The Coming of Post-Industrial Society: A Venture in Social Forecasting* (New York: Basic Books, 1973). The author of the present chapter is Bell's son.

[24]Milovan Djilas, *The New Class: An Analysis of the Communist System* (New York: Praeger, 1957).

claiming to govern in accord with scientific principles, political life was forcibly suppressed. In France, Charles de Gaulle imagined his Fifth Republic as a state in which a powerful president, advised by the technocrats of the ÉNA, would set the broad lines of social and economic development from a position far above the political fray. Even in the United States, in the heyday of theorizing about the 'new class', thinkers like Bell (who himself wrote as an analyst, not an advocate of technocracy) imagined ranks of highly trained technical experts from places like MIT, IBM and the Brookings Institution guiding the federal government towards their rationally chosen goals.

Steven Pinker does not express his advocacy of technocracy as explicitly as he does his advocacy of neoliberalism. Throughout his work he praises science as a key to human progress, but this alone hardly qualifies him as a technocrat. What does qualify him is that he does not, in the end, recognize a fundamental difference between scientific and technological questions, on the one hand, and political ones, on the other. He has a consistent tendency to assert that serious political disputes do not hinge on differences of moral values, or of social priorities, or of historical interpretation, but rather on correct versus erroneous evaluation of data. In one of his concluding chapters, on 'reason', he repeatedly scolds voters for their 'irrationality' and 'ignorance' of the issues before them.[25] No one would deny that voters often fail to instruct themselves adequately, or to use their reason sufficiently, but Pinker fails to acknowledge that most of the great issues facing modern democracies do not in fact have 'correct', far less quantitative answers that a better-informed use of reason can discern. Voters make their choices, however apparently irrational and uninformed, on the basis of a large number of factors, including, crucially, their fundamental political and moral values, and their sense of which candidates share these values and have earned their trust. As an American voter, I believe passionately in the extension of the Medicare programme to the entire population of the United States. I will argue for it as both a moral and a practical necessity, but I recognize that opponents of the idea are not necessarily ignorant and incorrect – they hold different principles from me and interpret the same facts in a different manner.

Is Steven Pinker ready to make a similar concession? It is hard to believe this, when he writes in *Enlightenment Now*: 'To make public discourse more rational, issues should be depoliticized as much as is feasible'.[26] Unfortunately, most of the 'issues' facing the public in democratic societies cannot and should not be 'depoliticized' because their 'solution' depends fundamentally on the vision voters have for how society should be constituted – which is to say, it depends fundamentally on politics. Ever the psychologist concerned with cognitive malfunction, Pinker insists on the need for 'effective training

---

[25]Pinker, *Enlightenment Now*, 351–84.
[26]Pinker, *Enlightenment Now*, 382.

in critical thinking and cognitive debiasing' to facilitate the desired process of depoliticization.[27] Liberate people from their cognitive 'biases', and they will see the correct, rational, scientific solution to the issues before them. Yet even assuming that such 'debiasing' is possible, we cannot free people of their moral values and visions of how society should be organized. We cannot free them of politics.

To be sure, Pinker himself devotes considerable space to political matters in *Enlightenment Now*, but the way he does so is revealing. His chapter entitled 'Democracy' presents the spread of democratic governments throughout the world as an additional indicator of overall human progress.[28] But he praises democracy above all for finding a way between the Scylla and Charybdis of anarchy and tyranny and for giving citizens 'the freedom to complain'.[29] He briefly evokes 'a civics-class idealization of democracy in which an informed populace deliberates about the common good and carefully selects leaders who carry out their preference'. But he then immediately comments: 'By that standard, the number of democracies in the world is zero in the past, zero in the present, and almost certainly zero in the future.' He defends this remarkably cynical statement by invoking 'the shallowness and incoherence of [most] people's political beliefs', their ignorance and irrationality. He prefers, as already noted, a 'minimalist conception' of democracy that does not equate it with self-governance, with citizens using a political process to pursue their common good.[30] Progress cannot follow from such a collective pursuit of the good, he insists (how naïve!). It follows from citizens staying out of the way as experts show how to resolve issues that have been successfully 'depoliticized'.

Pinker's discussion of capital punishment in Europe and America, at the end of the chapter on democracy, illustrates these points perfectly. In his view, the campaign to end capital punishment, which he sees as a rational and desirable goal, was an elite, expert project from start to finish: 'The ideas trickled down from a thin stratum of philosophers and intellectuals to the educated upper classes.' In Europe, these ideas won approval despite, not because of, democracy, 'because European democracies did not convert the opinions of the common man into policy. The penal codes of their countries were drafted by committees of renowned scholars'. A similar process did not take place in the United States, because 'the United States, *for better or worse*, is closer to having government by the people for the people' (emphasis added).[31] Yet even in America, Pinker believes, the experts will ultimately have their way. In his conclusion to the discussion, and to the

---

[27]Pinker, *Enlightenment Now*, 379.
[28]Pinker, *Enlightenment Now*, 199–213.
[29]Pinker, *Enlightenment Now*, 205.
[30]Pinker, *Enlightenment Now*, 204.
[31]Pinker, *Enlightenment Now*, 210.

chapter, he paraphrases Martin Luther King, Jr.: 'there really is a mysterious arc bending towards justice.'[32]

One is left wondering about the myriad social movements, almost entirely absent from the 576 pages of *Enlightenment Now*, that fought for equal rights, an end to slavery, improved working conditions, a minimum wage, the right to organize, basic social protections, a cleaner environment and a host of other progressive causes, generally without waiting for ideas to 'trickle down' from the experts. The arc bending towards justice is no mystery. It bends because ordinary people force it to bend, through political action. In short, in both his neoliberal and technocratic guises, Pinker has little confidence that ordinary people can successfully choose forms of social and economic organization that will further their well-being. Better to leave 'the common good' to the impersonal action of growth-generating free markets, or, alternately, to trained experts.

Remarkably, Pinker does not recognize the contradiction between these two approaches. Technocracy and neoliberalism may not only express an aversion to ordinary citizens using the political process to pursue the common good but also represent fundamentally opposed visions of social and economic organization. In no sense do technocrats want to allow independent markets to self-organize, to self-regulate and to determine the distribution of goods and services through their own autonomous operation. Technocrats want to determine the optimum form of distribution by conducting rational and well-informed analyses. They may tolerate market systems, but they do not entirely trust them. It is no coincidence that the neoliberal triumphs of Margaret Thatcher and Ronald Reagan did not take place during the heyday of the technocratic vision in the 1960s and 1970s. To the contrary, they took place at a time when this vision had come to be widely seen as a failure. In the late 1970s, under the pressure of the oil shock and the end of the long post-war economic expansion, technocracy and economic planning were increasingly perceived as rigid, petrified, overly bureaucratic and deeply inefficient. In their campaigns, Thatcher and Reagan cast government itself as the enemy. In a very real sense, their neoliberal movements arose over the ruins of post-war forms of technocracy.[33]

More recently, American centrists seeking to limit the effects of 'creative destruction' on actual American citizens have often turned back to technocracy as a remedy for neoliberalism's excesses. For instance, after the 2008 financial meltdown and subsequent recession, the Obama administration mostly did not pursue punitive measures against the financial firms whose recklessness had sparked the crisis, and it did not try to restructure the financial sector as a whole. It concentrated its efforts on

---

[32]Pinker, *Enlightenment Now*, 213.
[33]See Tony Judt, *Postwar; A History of Europe since 1945* (New York: Penguin, 2007), 535–41.

technical, regulatory fixes such as the Dodd-Frank Act.[34] One of Obama's most important advisers was Steven Pinker's Harvard colleague Cass Sunstein, who advocated the pursuit of reform through the careful, expertly designed 'nudging' of public behaviour in a wide variety of arenas. In Samuel Moyn's description, Sunstein looks very much like Pinker in his attempt to reconcile a fondness for free markets with strong technocratic instincts, and especially in his disdain for politics: 'When it comes to government helping people achieve fulfillment, Sunstein insists that technocrats must rule. With a palpable sense of relief, he has confessed that he finds politics mostly a distraction and not so much about contending collective visions of the good life or about calling out the oppression that claims to expertise can mask.'[35]

The opposition between technocracy and neoliberalism became clearest in the sector of the economy which Bell and other analysts in the 1970s had seen as the principal arena for the triumph of the 'new class': information technology. Starting in the 1980s, this sector exploded in wealth and social importance, but it did not do so under the leadership of white-coated experts from MIT and IBM. It did so under the leadership of swaggering upstart capitalists, many of whom (most obviously, Steve Jobs of Apple) infused their firms with a distinctly counter-cultural vibe even as they took full advantage of neoliberal globalization and accumulated massive reserves of wealth.[36] The famous Apple television advertisement from 1984, caricaturing IBM's customers as an army of drones marching in lockstep to a totalitarian leader, in scenes drawn straight from Orwell's *1984*, and Apple as a brightly clad young woman freeing them from ideological slavery, perfectly expressed this shift.[37] The woman may not have looked like a symbol of neoliberal capitalism, but in fact she was precisely that. Neoliberalism vanquished technocracy.

An eighteenth-century precedent

Pinker's contradictory attempt to marry technocracy to neoliberalism may seem a classic twenty-first-century phenomenon, but it does have a fascinating eighteenth-century precedent. As already noted, many eighteenth-century thinkers had a pronounced suspicion of popular, democratic political action,

---

[34]See Ganesh Sitaraman, 'The Collapse of Neoliberalism', *The New Republic*, 23 December 2019.

[35]Samuel Moyn, 'The Nudgeocrat: Navigating Freedom with Cass Sunstein', *The Nation*, 3 June 2019.

[36]See on this subject Fred Turner, *From Counterculture to Cyberculture: Stewart Brand, the Whole Earth Network, and the Rise of Digital Utopianism* (Chicago: University of Chicago Press, 2006); Margaret O'Mara, *The Code: Silicon Valley and the Making of America* (New York: Penguin Press, 2019).

[37]Video available on https://www.youtube.com/watch?v=VtvjbmoDx-I, accessed 28 May 2020.

but this suspicion hardly distinguished them from a long line of predecessors stretching back to the Greeks. One particular school of eighteenth-century thinkers, however, did try to combine a faith in rule by learned elites with a faith in free markets. This was the school known as the Physiocrats, which first took shape around the French court physician, François Quesnay, and came to include such notable figures as the reforming statesman Anne-Robert Turgot, and the mathematician and revolutionary politician, the Marquis de Condorcet. Also known as the 'Economists', the Physiocrats helped to develop economic thought as a distinct body of knowledge, advocated free trade and first popularized the phrase 'laissez faire, laissez passer'. Synthesizing a wide range of earlier philosophical and religious writings whose authors had developed the notion of 'self-organizing systems', they postulated that markets, when left to their own devices, naturally produced a stable but dynamic economic equilibrium. As one of the most popular Physiocratic writers, Pierre-Paul Le Mercier de la Rivière concluded: 'the world thus runs by itself.'[38]

Yet even as the Physiocrats preached the virtues of free markets (often with cult-like fervour), they also remained loyal servants of Old Regime France's absolute monarchy and refrained from any serious advocacy of political liberalization. Turgot, in his brief tenure as the effective French prime minister between 1774 and 1776, attempted to implement an ambitious reform programme that included freeing the price of grain and abolishing the main privileges and monopolies of French trade guilds. He also proposed the creation of a series of new representative institutions, but solely as consultative bodies that would bring information and the opinions of the educated public to the attention of the central administration. Turgot's vision of government was very much that of the rational, top-down management of society by expert administrators such as himself.[39]

Turgot's tenure, instructively, ended in disaster. His attempts at economic liberalization led to widespread popular unrest, while the lack of any concomitant political liberalization meant that he failed to develop a constituency among the burgeoning numbers of French people who had come to see the creaky structures of French absolutism as both inefficient and oppressive.[40] At the same time, the reforms undercut his support among that other portion of the French public which still imagined French government

---

[38]See Jonathan Sheehan and Dror Wahrman, *Invisible Hands: Self-Organization and the Eighteenth Century* (Chicago: Chicago University Press, 2015), 249–57, quote from 251.

[39]On Turgot, see Douglas Dakin, *Turgot and the Ancien Régime in France* (London: Methuen, 1939). For his political vision, see especially Keith Michael Baker, *Inventing the French Revolution: Essays on French Political Culture in the Eighteenth Century* (Cambridge: Cambridge University Press, 1990), 109–27, 153–66.

[40]See Steven L. Kaplan, *Bread, Politics and Political Economy in the Reign of Louis XV*, 2 vols (The Hague: Martinus Nijhoff, 1976).

as the paternalist, patriarchal rule of an all-powerful king beneficently overseeing the well-being of even the least of his subjects. In less than two years, court enemies profited from this lack of support to engineer Turgot's downfall. His reforms were mostly reversed, contributing to the background of political confusion and paralysis against which, thirteen years later, the French Revolution would begin.

An example from twenty-first-century American politics shows how contemporary technocratic reform can run into very much the same sort of political disaster. Barack Obama, on taking office in 2009, concluded that political opposition would make it impossible for him to reform American healthcare through the implementation of a full, taxpayer-supported national insurance scheme of the sort that existed in Canada or many Western European countries. Instead, he and his advisers crafted the programme known as Obamacare, which rested on free-market principles and obliged citizens to purchase private health insurance (it built on ideas first developed by the right-wing Heritage Foundation, and first implemented by a Republican governor, Mitt Romney, in Massachusetts).[41] As a technocratic tweak to the grievous deficiencies of the existing American healthcare system, Obamacare actually worked quite well. It reduced the proportion of adult Americans under sixty-five without healthcare coverage from 22.3 per cent in 2009 to just 12.4 per cent by 2016.[42] But it quickly ran into massive political opposition. Right-wing populists eager to discredit and defeat Obama seized on it as a classic example of 'elite', arrogant experts imposing abstract, unworkable and harmful ideas on an unsuspecting public. The error-prone debut of the system, and the widespread perception that the American government was denying citizens free choice in healthcare matters only strengthened this reaction, which fuelled a large-scale repudiation of Obama's Democrats in the mid-term elections of 2010. Ultimately, it also contributed to the populist wave that brought Donald Trump to power in 2016. But Obamacare's reliance on free-market mechanisms, the need to pay high deductibles and wildly shifting, unpredictable prices, and the reform's very presentation as a tweak, meant that Democrats had great difficulty generating active political support for it.[43] The fervent young volunteers who campaigned for the socialist Bernie Sanders in 2016 and 2020, inspired in large part by his call for 'Medicare for All', never marched for Obamacare.

---

[41] See Catherine Rampell, 'If the GOP Built Their Ideal Health-Care System ... It'd Be Obamacare', *Washington Post*, 28 March 2019.

[42] Abby Goodnough et al., 'Obamacare Turns 10. Here's a Look at What Works and Doesn't', *New York Times*, 23 March 2020.

[43] See Goodnough et al., 'Obamacare Turns 10'.

Conclusion

Steven Pinker has understandably attracted a large and enthusiastic audience for his books. His writing is engaging, amusing and provocatively counterintuitive. No less a figure than Bill Gates has described *Enlightenment Now* as 'my new favorite book of all time'.[44] But the existence of a large and appreciative readership does not mean that an equally large constituency endorses Pinker's vision of technocratic neoliberalism. The readers appreciate the book's prose qualities, take comfort from its reassuring message of human advancement (or, at least, they did until the spring of 2020) and also in some cases probably enjoy its snarky, knowing dismissals of intellectuals, particularly left-wing humanists. The contradictions, limitations and potentially maligned side effects of its technocratic neoliberalism are far more difficult to discern.

But the contradictions, limitations and side effects are there. Both technocracy and neoliberalism, while not incompatible with democratic systems of government, nonetheless have in common their suspicion of actual democratic politics, defined as the process by which a body of equal citizens can deliberate upon and collectively devise measures to pursue the common good. Neoliberalism, as noted, is built upon the faith that a wide range of social and economic questions are better regulated by the impersonal, autonomous, self-organizing mechanisms of the free market than by such democratic procedures. Technocracy is built upon the faith that most citizens simply do not have sufficient learning or analytical ability to make reasonable, informed choices about many of the crucial questions facing hyper-complex modern societies.

In practice, however, neither neoliberalism nor technocracy have proven as stable and functional as their advocates have hoped. The enormous inequalities generated in contemporary neoliberal economies have ramifications that go far beyond simple monetary imbalance. Millions have found themselves in precarious jobs, at the mercy of their employers' algorithms, unable to improve their lot. And the enormous political influence that so easily follows upon enormous wealth pushes societies in the direction of oligarchy. Technocracy, meanwhile, tends to petrify, to cordon off learned experts from the rest of the population to such an extent that they become trapped in their own echo chambers, deaf to the concerns of a general public they consider ignorant and irrational.[45] In both cases, the bulk of the population comes to feel powerless, frustrated, resentful, angry. It is a recipe for a dangerous populist reaction, and this reaction has followed,

---

[44]Bill Gates, 'My New Favorite Book of All Time', *GatesNotes: The Blog of Bill Gates*, 25 January 2018, https://www.gatesnotes.com/Books/Enlightenment-Now, accessed 29 May 2020.
[45]See on this especially, Rosenfeld, *Democracy and Truth*, 77–91.

in country after country, since the middle of the century's second decade.[46] The 'depoliticization' that accompanies technocratic neoliberalism has led, in practice, to an angry and dangerous repoliticization. In the United States, this repoliticization made itself felt so deeply during the first months of the 2020 pandemic that even basic, unquestioned matters of science and public health, such as the ability of face masks to slow the progress of a dangerous viral infection, became politicized.

Modern, complex societies need free markets, and they need very high levels of technical expertise. But we need to recognize that ordinary citizens, however imperfect their knowledge and reasoning abilities, need to have a say – an equal say – in determining the nature of the common good and in deciding the best overall way to pursue it. We need further to recognize that the common good itself cannot be determined by an algorithm or a spreadsheet. Human well-being has many different possible elements. The common good is determined by reflecting on moral values, on history, on experience. Poetry may offer better assistance than a calculator. Above all, it is crucial to remember that without the freedom truly to govern themselves – without politics – ordinary people will not always peacefully and quietly obey the dictates of the market or the precepts of the experts (or even the experts' 'nudges'). They will turn, in frustration, to the demagogues. Far from moving ever closer towards Enlightenment, as Steven Pinker believes, societies will turn back towards an all-too-familiar darkness.

---

[46]See notably Jan-Werner Müller, *What Is Populism?* (Philadelphia: University of Pennsylvania Press, 2016).

6

Steven Pinker, Norbert Elias and *The Civilizing Process*

Philip Dwyer and Elizabeth Roberts-Pedersen

The Better Angels of Our Nature is steeped in what many consider to be an unwarranted optimism in the future. One of many 'reasons to be cheerful', Pinker tells us, is that contrary to the horrors of our nightly news bulletins, we walk the streets safer than ever before. While this is not the first time that Pinker has posited a sustained and significant decline in violence in modern societies, *The Better Angels of Our Nature* lays out his case in extensive if contested statistical detail, arguing that there has been a 'tenfold-to-fiftyfold' decrease in rates of homicide in Western Europe since the sixteenth century.[1] He appears to have been inspired to think in terms of downward trends by a graph of declining homicide rates in England, calculated by Robert Ted Gurr in 1981 and part of a broader effort by historical criminologists to quantify long-term patterns in interpersonal violence. It was their data, Pinker writes, that convinced him that there was 'an underappreciated story

[1]See Steven Pinker, *The Blank Slate: The Modern Denial of Human Nature* (New York: Viking, 2002), 166–9, 320, 330–6 and Steven Pinker, *The Better Angels of Our Nature: The Decline of Violence in History and Its Causes* (London: Allen Lane, 2011), xxiv. For a critique of Pinker's use of statistics, see the chapter in this collection by Dag Lindstrom, 'The Use and Abuse of Statistics in Writing the History of Violence', 39–56. Our thanks to Markos Carelos for preliminary research carried out with funds from the Centre for the Study of Violence at the University of Newcastle.

waiting to be told'.[2] In doing so *The Better Angels of Our Nature* draws heavily on the work of the German sociologist Norbert Elias and his theory of 'the civilizing process', first set out in a book of the same name published in 1939.

According to this theory, increasing mastery of psychological 'drives' towards impulsivity – best demonstrated by the aristocratic adoption of elaborate rules of courtly etiquette – and the spread of princely authority, centralized administration and economic ties over larger and larger territories resulted in an increasing 'pacification' of key societies in Western Europe by the early modern period. For many historical criminologists and crime historians, murder is understood as an impulsive, if irrational, act. In mapping homicide rates in the same era, Elias' ideas about the development of self-restraint have provided important theoretical ballast for data sets that are often uneven or incomplete. It is unsurprising, therefore, that an interpretation of Elias is also crucial to Pinker's thesis, both to explain declining homicide rates and to convey a general sense of 'moral progress'.

Elias' *The Civilizing Process* was no doubt appealing to Pinker in other ways as well. To a large degree, Elias' methodology mirrors the synthesis of historical reflection and contemporary psychology the *Better Angels* promotes. Both authors trade in meta-narratives, and seek to explain changes in human behaviour over large time scales through the coalescence of interior and exterior factors – what Elias calls 'internal' and 'external' 'restraints', and what Pinker describes as 'endogenous' and 'exogenous' 'forces'.[3] (Both Elias and Pinker appear to be working on the assumption that emotions come in just two varieties: expressed and repressed.[4]) For Pinker, the 'Civilizing Process' (he always uses the term in capital letters) 'provides a large part of the explanation for the modern decline in violence not only because it predicted the remarkable plunge in European homicide' but also because it made correct 'predictions' about two other 'zones' where the civilizing process never fully penetrated: the working classes, and the developing world, which Pinker otherwise refers to as 'inhospitable territories of the globe'.[5] Chapter Three of *Better Angels* is premised almost entirely on applying Elias' civilizing process and the later concept

---

[2]Pinker, *Better Angels*, xxvi–xxvii. See Robert Ted Gurr, 'Historical Trends in Violent Crimes: A Critical Review of the Evidence', *Crime and Justice: An Annual Review of Research*, 3 (1981): 295–353.

[3]Elias refers to *Selbstzwänge* (self-restraints) and *Fremdzwänge* (foreign or external constraints). Without the constraints, humans would remain' brutish animals'. Norbert Elias, *The Civilizing Process: Sociogenetic and Psychogenetic Investigations*, trans. Edmund Jephcott (Oxford: Blackwell, 1994), 117–19, 156–7, 159–60, 168–9, 365–87, 415–21, 447; Pinker, *Better Angels*, xviii, xxv, 73–4, 174, 278, 292, 440, 476, 477, 578, 585, 609, 686.

[4]Carolyn Strange and Robert Cribb, 'Historical Perspectives on Honour, Violence and Emotion', in Carolyn Strange, Robert Cribb and Christopher E. Forth (eds), *Violence and Emotions in History* (London: Bloomsbury, 2014), 11–13.

[5]Pinker, *Better Angels*, 81.

of 'informalization' to an analysis of homicide rates from the early modern period to the present day, including the vexed case of the United States, where the homicide rate does not outwardly conform to the downward trajectory of European societies. Indeed, that Elias is so central to Pinker's overall thesis perhaps explains why he has appeared reluctant to engage seriously with the considerable scholarship critiquing Elias' work and its interpretation.[6]

In this chapter, we want to consider the reception of Elias and his civilizing process in Western scholarship, the significant criticisms of the theory, and the way Pinker's interpretation of Elias shapes the optimistic position advanced in *Better Angels*. Far from being what Pinker describes as 'the most important thinker you have never heard of', Elias has been widely acknowledged as a major theorist since his principal works were rediscovered in the 1970s.[7] From this period onwards, he enjoyed considerable prominence in German, French and Anglophone scholarship, not just among the criminologists and crime historians mentioned earlier but also among sociologists and political theorists seeking encompassing explanations for large-scale social transformations. As Anthony Giddens pointed out some years ago, there is a veritable 'Norbert Elias industry' that has kept many academics very busy.[8] Historians, particularly those working on the history of emotions and the history of manners and civility, have also engaged with Elias' ideas, though their opinions are more divided.[9] While many recognize the power and originality of his work, many others dispute the empirical basis on which it rests, and others reject altogether the idea that a single overarching mechanism can ever explain the complexities of the past. It is therefore a little disingenuous for Pinker to tout Elias as an unassailed, if underappreciated, authority on the decline of violence in the

---

[6]See Pinker's response to Benjamin Ziemann, 'Histories of Violence', *Reviews in History* (review no. 1232), where Ziemann noted that historians have largely rejected Elias' characterization of medieval European societies as 'simplifying' and 'naïve' and cited an influential article by Gerd Schwerhoff as illustrative. In his reply, Pinker characterized Schweroff as 'a single historian who has made this accusation', ignoring the body of forgoing critical literature cited by Schweroff. See Steven Pinker, 'Author's Response', point 6 and Gerd Schweroff, 'Zivilisationsprozess und Geschichtswissenschaft. Norbert Elias Forschungsparadigma in historischer Sicht', *Historische Zeitschrift*, 266 (1998): 561–605.
[7]Pinker, *Better Angels*, 59.
[8]Anthony Giddens, '*The Society of Individuals*: Norbert Elias, Michael Schröter and Edmund Jephcott', *American Journal of Sociology*, 98, no. 2 (1992): 338.
[9]See for example Keith Thomas, *In Pursuit of Civility: Manners and Civilization in Early Modern Europe* (New Haven and London: Yale University Press, 2018), xiii–xiv, 19–21, 53–6. Thomas notes Elias as a 'looming intellectual presence' in the field, while also acknowledging that his work has 'some well-known limitations' (p. xiii). Penny Russell, *Savage or Civilised? Manners in Colonial Australia* (Sydney: NewSouth Books, 2010), 9–10, suggests that while Elias is fundamental to any discussion of the history of manners, his focus on printed rules of etiquette are of limited value in contexts where rules of conduct were forged far from the metropole.

West. This characterization not only minimizes the acclaim Elias eventually received in the latter part of his career but also risks obscuring the robust and ongoing critiques of his work, including Elias' own profound discomfort with a key corollary of his theory – the state's monopolization of the use of force.

Elias had tragic, intimate knowledge of the implications of the state's consolidation of the means of violence, circumstances that are inseparable from the interpretation of *The Civilizing Process* and his later works. One of the many German-Jewish intellectuals forced out of the universities after the Nazi takeover, he wrote *The Civilizing Process* in exile in London. The only child of a respectable Jewish family in Breslau, he lost both parents during the war, his father dying of natural causes in 1940 and his mother murdered in Auschwitz in 1941. While Pinker does acknowledge this important personal context in *Better Angels*, he largely underplays the degree to which these searing experiences informed Elias' views on the relationship between violence and the state, including the degree to which the Second World War and the Holocaust could be explained within the context of an ongoing 'civilizing process'. As we shall see, it is difficult to believe that Elias would have shared Pinker's blithe optimism about human betterment, as well as *Better Angels*' broader complacency about the extent of state-sanctioned killing in the twentieth century. For Elias, humans were always 'becoming' civilized – a process without end, 'never completed and always endangered'.[10] For this reason it is important to distinguish Elias' theory of the civilizing process from the account Pinker gives of it.

Elias and *The Civilizing Process*

By Elias' own account, the origins of *The Civilizing Process* lie in the library catalogue of the British Museum, which Elias visited nearly every day after arriving as an exile in London in 1935. With a small grant from a Jewish refugees' committee and some 'rather vague' ideas about a book he might write, he began browsing the catalogue and calling up any title that looked interesting.[11] By this method he found the 'books of etiquette' and *manuels de savoir-faire* that became so central to Part Two of the first volume of *The Civilizing Process*, which focused on 'changes in conduct, manners and feelings of embarrassment' between the medieval and early modern

---

[10]Elias, *The Civilizing Process*, 447; and idem., *The Germans: Power Struggles and the Development of Habitus in the Nineteenth and Twentieth Centuries*, trans. Eric Dunning and Stephen Mennell (Oxford: Polity Press, 1996), 173.

[11]Norbert Elias, *Reflections on a Life*, trans. Edmund Jephcott (Cambridge: Polity Press, 1994), 53–5.

period.[12] For Elias, the history of these developments was significant in two respects. First, changes in attitudes towards things such as table manners and bodily functions signalled related changes in people's affective lives, in particular their capacity for self-control and restraint. Second, the spread of elaborate rules of etiquette had a distinctly political dimension: evidence of the 'courticization' (*Verhölichung*) of the aristocracy, the process by which the absolutist state stripped the nobility of its martial prerogatives and subordinated it to royal directives and laws. With their autonomy reduced and their use of violence curtailed, nobles displaced their aggressiveness into competition for elite status, all the while regulating and ritualizing interpersonal violence through things like codes of honour and duelling. Here Elias presents the workings of the French court as paradigmatic, arguing that during the sixteenth and seventeenth centuries adherence to codes of refined behaviour and self-restraint replaced fighting prowess as the marker of high status. These behaviours were copied in the lesser courts of Europe and by the emergent French bourgeoisie, who consulted *manuels de savoir-faire* for guidance on correct behaviour. Over the course of centuries, and in parallel with the development of more complex judicial systems and policing, elite notions of masculine behaviour evolved into a general disdain of interpersonal violence as no longer compatible with 'civilized' behaviour.

Elias argued that this represented a major shift in the 'emotional economy' of Western Europe, one he characterized in Freudian terms as a collective strengthening of the superego.[13] Indeed, Elias' ideas about 'civilization' are closely tied to those elaborated by Freud in his *Civilization and Its Discontents*, which appeared in 1930. Freud argued that civilization came about because humans were able to suppress their biological drives or instincts. The greatest impediment to culture, the one thing that could lead to the disintegration of civilization, was man's tendency to aggression, which was innate.[14] It was only by 'internalizing' those instincts, and in particular aggression, that civilization could come about. Elias took this psychic structure one step further, and linked the rise of the state and state control to the development of self-control – the mastery of impulsivity via what Elias described as 'foresight or reflection'.[15] In contrast to Freud, who believed that civilization was based upon biological processes, Elias believed that

---

[12]Elias, *The Civilizing Process*, 63.
[13]Elias, *The Civilizing Process*, 106.
[14]Sigmund Freud, *Civilization and Its Discontents*, trans. Joan Riviere (London: Hogarth Press, 1930), 85–6, 102, 105. Of equal importance seems to have been Freud's *The Future of an Illusion*, first published in 1927. See Robert van Krieken, *Norbert Elias* (London: Routledge, 1998), 18.
[15]Elias, *The Civilizing Process*, 239.

affect regulation was learned in specific relationships with others.[16] For Elias, these 'affective changes' at the level of the individual reflected and reinforced political and economic developments that tended towards consolidation of both territory and authority. The 'monopoly of physical force or violence' (*Gewaltmonopol*) was one; the monopolization of taxation, emblematic of greater commercial interdependence, was another; the culmination of these tendencies in the creation of ever larger and internally coherent political and economic formations was a third. Put another way, one of the central tenets of the civilizing process is the idea of the internalization of emotions, of an imposition of self-constraint, coupled with an evolution in the complexity of the state and its control over its citizens. The civilizing process thus goes hand in hand with modernization, or as Elias called it, 'the progress of the west'.[17]

In making this argument Elias was not just interpreting the past but making a claim for an empirically informed and historically conscious sociology, one that took seriously the psychological lives of individuals and the effects of emotions and behaviours on society at large. During his long academic apprenticeship in Germany, he had come to understand the leading lights of the discipline as still preoccupied with the ramifications of Marx's materialist conception of history for the interpretation of society and social processes. At Heidelberg, Alfred Weber espoused a liberal humanist position that elevated culture above economics but barely concealed a distorting 'personal metaphysics'; his mentor Karl Mannheim pursued a theory of knowledge that, to Elias, threatened to 'relativize everything'.[18] Focusing instead on the evolving relations between psychic processes and social structures held out the possibility of explaining not only change over time but also the internal dynamics of contemporary societies.

Elucidating and defending this interdependency was key. For Elias, society could only exist as a collection of individuals in relationship with each other, tied together, in both economic and social terms, in 'chains of mutual reliance', a sort of network of interdependent human beings.[19] Yet Elias' claims about the methodological virtues of *The Civilizing Process* also suggest two broader, related but largely unresolved questions: first, the extent to which Elias understood his theory to apply beyond the specific context of Western Europe (and, perhaps more accurately, the French court and its imitators) in the medieval and early modern periods; and second,

---

[16]See Jonathan Fletcher, *Violence and Civilization: An Introduction to the Work of Norbert Elias* (Cambridge: Polity Press, 1997), 42–4.

[17]Elias, *The Civilizing Process*, 7.

[18]Elias, *Reflections on a Life*, 104–20; Van Krieken, *Norbert Elias*, 14–18.

[19]Robert van Krieken, 'Norbert Elias and Emotions in History', in David Lemmings and Ann Brooks (eds), *Emotions and Social Change: Historical and Sociological Perspectives* (London: Routledge, 2014), 22; J. Carter Wood, *Violence and Crime in Nineteenth-Century England: The Shadow of Our Refinement* (London: Routledge, 2004), 15–16.

the degree to which Elias regarded the civilizing process as a desirable and necessary step of human development. Here the evidence is mixed, perhaps because Elias was constantly revisiting his own positions. Certainly at times Elias underlined that he did not believe in some sort of linear progression in history, even if the civilizing process has often been interpreted that way.[20] By this view the civilizing mechanism is blind, composed of fits and starts, with no guarantee of its ultimate success nor prospect of an endpoint, and with no moral commentary attached.[21] In this interpretation, too, Elias is ambivalent about the process he describes, particularly its culmination in the triumph of the state and its capacity to wield deadly force.

By another view, however, *The Civilizing Process* vacillates between treating 'civilization' as an ideological, Western invention, the means by which 'the barbarian' is created, and as a normal and even desirable state of being.[22] The chronology underpinning *The Civilizing Process* necessarily implies a 'directional' narrative in which the Renaissance marks a turning point in the affective lives of Europeans, cleaving them off from both past European societies and non-Western societies yet to follow in Europe's footsteps.[23] This has caused numerous critics to accuse Elias, like Max Weber before him, of promoting a kind of Eurocentric determinism, as well as reproducing racialized hierarchies of 'civilized' men and 'savages'.[24] While his supporters have defended him against such charges, and some scholars have attempted to apply the theory to other parts of the world, the accusation has nevertheless remained central to critiques of Elias.[25] The theory has found little resonance in historiographies outside of the Western world.

---

[20]Pieter Spierenburg, 'Elias and the History of Crime and Criminal Justice: A Brief Evaluation', *IAHCCJ Bulletin*, 20 (Spring 1995): 20–3; Eric Dunning, Patrick Murphy and Ivan Wadding-ton, 'Violence in the British Civilizing Process', in Eric Dunning and Stephen Mennell (eds), *Norbert Elias*, 4 vols (Sage: London, 2003), ii. 5–34, here 5–9.

[21]Elias, *The Civilizing Process*, 383–4. See van Krieken, *Norbert Elias*, 65–6; Fletcher, *Violence and Civilization*, 44.

[22]Elias, *The Civilizing Process*, 39, 41; Fletcher, *Violence and Civilization*, 45–7.

[23]Nicole Pepperell, 'The Unease with Civilization: Norbert Elias and the Violence of the Civilizing Process', *Thesis Eleven: Critical Theory and Historical Sociology*, 137, no. 1 (2016): 6 and throughout; Jack Goody, *The Theft of History* (Cambridge: Cambridge University Press, 2006), 161–2.

[24]Goody, *The Theft of History*, 154–79.

[25]See, for example, Eiko Ikegami, *The Taming of the Samurai: Honorific Individualism and the Making of Modern Japan* (Cambridge, MA: Harvard University Press, 1995); Johan Gouds-blom, Eric Jones and Stephen Mennell, *The Course of Human History: Economic Growth, Social Process and Civilization* (London: Routledge, 1996), esp. chap. 6; Stephen Mennell, *The American Civilizing Process* (Cambridge: Polity, 2007); and Roderic Broadhurst, Thierry Bouhours and Brigitte Bouhours, *Violence and the Civilising Process in Cambodia* (Cambridge: Cambridge University Press, 2015).

Reception and critiques

Speculation about the Eurocentrism of *The Civilizing Process* underscores the degree to which scholars have engaged with Elias' work since new editions and translations became available in the 1970s. It is true that the first edition of *The Civilizing Process*, published as two volumes in 1939 by a straightened Swiss publishing house, received limited attention in the context of the outbreak of the Second World War. Unable to find secure academic work (and at one point interned as an enemy alien), Elias really was an important thinker no one had ever heard of. But, once Elias established himself at the University of Leicester in the mid-1950s, his reputation as a teacher and a scholar grew rapidly, as did interest in the themes of his pre-war writings, which found contemporary expression in his analysis of sport, 'informalization' and the theory of 'figurations' more generally. Elias' British collaborators – particularly Eric Dunning and Stephen Mennell – were key interlocutors; the Dutch scholar Johan Goudsblom also did much to promote and defend Elias' work.[26] A new German edition of *The Civilizing Process* published in 1969 and French and English translations in the 1970s and early 1980s reflected a growing appreciation of Elias as a sociological theorist. Elements of *The Civilizing Process* also fit with developments in historical theory and practice. In France, for example, Elias' erudite treatment of the evolution of manners, published as *La Civilisation des moeurs* in 1973, mirrored the *Annales* school's preoccupation with *mentalités*, an affinity that has continued in Elias' appeal for a number of historians of emotion.[27] In its reflections on the production of knowledge and the relations between the idea of 'civilization' and the self-image of the West, *The Civilizing Process* also arguably echoed elements of French post-structuralist and postmodernist thought gaining prominence during this period. Tellingly, François Furet, Roger Chartier and Pierre Bourdieu all sang its praises – an ecumenical endorsement that perhaps reflected historian Arlette Farge's wry observation that the theory of the civilizing process was *un prêt à penser* (ready to think), a play on the phrase *prêt à porter* (ready-to-wear clothes) that implied the theory's widespread but shallow appeal. It also helped that the largely favourable portrayal of the early modern French court in *The Civilizing Process* (a view now disputed by historians) was relentlessly juxtaposed to the coarser norms of the German principalities.[28]

---

[26]See, for example, Stephen Mennell and Johan Goudsblom, 'Civilizing Processes—Myth or Reality? A Comment on Duerr's Critique of Elias', *Comparative Studies in Society and History*, 39, no. 4 (1997): 729–33.

[27]See the collection of essays in Lemmings and Brooks, *Emotions and Social Change*.

[28]Daniel Gordon, 'The Canonization of Norbert Elias in France: A Critical Perspective', *French Politics, Culture & Society*, 20, no. 1 (2002): 68–94, here 69. For a critique of Elias' depiction of early modern France, see Stuart Carroll, *Blood and Violence in Early Modern France* (Oxford: Oxford University Press, 2006), 5–6, 307–11.

In Germany itself the reception of Elias' work was more mixed, with robust critiques issued by Gerd Schwerhoff and Martin Dinges on the grounds that both Elias' history and psychology were outdated.[29]

As we have already indicated, from the 1980s onwards historians of crime also found *The Civilizing Process* to be a compelling and convenient explanation for phenomena they saw written in the data. This is despite the fact that Elias' treatment of interpersonal violence (such as murder and assault) is less thoroughgoing and more generalized than his treatment of the evolution of the state's monopoly of violence and its corollaries, such as changes in the conduct of warfare. Elias used the term *Angriffslust* (literally, 'the lust for attacking someone' or aggressiveness) very broadly, to encompass the cruelty of knights in wartime, the feuding of the medieval burghers and the impulsivity of ordinary people who were 'quick to draw their knives'.[30] Nevertheless, a number of scholars have adapted Elias' theory in an attempt to explain long-term patterns of interpersonal violence specifically, including Robert van Krieken, Jonathan Fletcher, Eric Johnson, Eric Monkkonen, Jeffrey Adler and in particular Pieter Spierenburg, who was one of the first to introduce Elias to historians of crime and who became one of his most ardent champions.[31]

Not all crime historians have wholeheartedly endorsed Elias' theory, however. The French historian Robert Muchembled suggests that not everything can be explained by the civilizing process and that in France the reduction in homicide was not entirely related to courtly etiquette and that the decline began much earlier, from the 1580s onwards, though he does agree with Elias about the importance of the nobility in initiating it.[32] In his

---

[29]See Hans Peter Duerr, *Nacktheit und Scham* (Frankfurt am Main: Suhrkamp Verlag, 1988); Schwerhoff, 'Zivilisationsprozess und Geschichtswissenschaft'; and Martin Dinges, 'Formenwandel der Gewalt in der Neuzeit. Zur Kritik der Zivilisationstheorie von Norbert Elias', in Rolf Peter Sieferle and Helga Breuninger (eds), *Kulturen der Gewalt. Ritualisierung und Symbolisierung von Gewalt in der Geschichte* (Frankfurt am Main: Campus, 1998), 171–94.

[30]See for example Elias, 'On Changes in Aggressiveness,' in Elias, *The Civilizing Process*, 161–72.

[31]Robert van Krieken, 'Violence, Self-discipline and Modernity: Beyond the Civilizing Process', *Sociological Review*, 37 (1989): 193–218; Fletcher, *Violence and Civilization*; 'Introduction', in Eric A. Johnson and Eric H. Monkkonen (eds), *The Civilization of Crime* (Urbana: University of Illinois Press, 1996), 1–13; as well as Helmut Thome, 'Modernization and Crime: What Is the Explanation?', *IAHCCJ Bulletin*, 20 (Spring 1995): 31–48. Spierenburg was associated with the Norbert Elias Foundation in Amsterdam (Norbert Elias Foundation: http://norbert-elias .com/en/). Jeffrey Adler questions the utility of the civilizing process when examining homicide in American cities – in Chicago, for example, the effort to reduce violent behaviour actually led to a significant increase in the homicide rate – only to eventually conclude that it reflected the success of the process: Jeffrey S. Adler, '"Halting the Slaughter of the Innocents": The Civilizing Process and the Surge in Violence in Turn-of-the-Century Chicago', *Social Science History*, 25, no. 1 (Spring 2001): 29–52; and idem., *First in Violence, Deepest in Dirt: Homicide in Chicago, 1875-1920* (Cambridge, MA: Harvard University Press, 2006).

[32]Robert Muchembled, *A History of Violence: From the End of the Middle Ages to the Present* (Cambridge: Polity, 2012), 28–9. Elias is very vague about the developmental stages of the

work on the history of violence in England, James Sharpe is more critical of the civilizing process than some of his peers, while Randolph Roth argues that declines and spikes in violence are explained not by 'civilization', but by the ability of the state to bring people to justice and to defend life and property.[33]

These reservations point to a wider conceptual question about the degree to which *The Civilizing Process* can accommodate revisions in historical understanding of the suppositions on which it rests. In the preface to the first edition, Elias wrote that he did not want to make 'a theory of civilization in the air', that his arguments would proceed from 'documents of historical experience'.[34] How does the theory measure up now, if elements of the history are in dispute? For example, Elias' portrayal of medieval people as 'childlike', 'emotive' and lacking in self-control, which Pinker unquestioningly accepts, draws heavily on Johan Huizinga's *The Waning of the Middle Ages*, published in 1919.[35] Both accounts are now understood to be one-dimensional caricatures of people whose emotional lives were as complex and varied as those in the period that followed. We know, too, that much of the supposed spontaneous violence of the medieval period, far from being irrational or inchoate, was often defined by cultural norms and unfolded according to predictable cultural scripts.[36] Do these inaccuracies about the medieval period nullify the theory as a whole? What about Elias' relative neglect of religion as a factor in subjective experience, or the relegation of the bourgeoisie to the role of mere imitators, or the marginal role accorded to the working class?[37] Do problems with chronology and periodization matter? What if the character and extent of violence in the

---

state; scholars have argued that courtly behaviour had much earlier origins, in Germany not France, than Elias was aware. See C. Stephen Jaeger, *The Origins of Courtliness: Civilizing Trends and the Formation of Courtly Ideals, 939–1210* (Philadelphia: University of Pennsylvania Press, 1985).

[33]See James Sharpe, *A Fiery & Furious People: A History of Violence in England* (London: Random House, 2016), 29; Randolph Roth, 'Does Better Angels of Our Nature Hold Up as History?', *Historical Reflections/Réflexions Historiques*, 44, no. 1 (2018): 94–5.

[34]Elias, *The Civilizing Process*, x and xiv.

[35]Van Krieken, *Norbert Elias*, 28. Krieken goes so far as to argue that Elias' *The Civilizing Process* is best understood while reading it alongside Huizinga's *The Waning of the Middle Ages*. On Pinker's misrepresentation of the medieval period, see Sara Butler, 'Getting Medieval on Steven Pinker: Violence and Medieval England', 125–41, in this collection.

[36]Jonas Liliequist, 'Violence, Honour and Manliness in Early Modern Northern Sweden', in Mirkka Lappalainen and Pekka Hirvonen (eds), *Crime and Control in Europe from the Past to the Present* (Helsinki: Hakapaino, 1999), 174–207.

[37]On religion, see George Mosse, 'Review: Norbert Elias. *The Civilizing Process: The History of Manners*', *New German Critique*, 15 (1978): 180–1; and Andrew M. McKinnon, 'The Sacramental Mechanism: Religion and the Civilizing Process in Christian Western Europe with Particular Reference to the Peace of God Movement and Its Aftermath', in Andrew McKinnon and Marta Trzebiatowska (eds), *Sociological Theory and the Question of Religion* (Farnham: Taylor & Francis, 2014), 105–26. McKinnon argues that the Catholic Church contributed to constraining, shaping and channelling warrior elites' drive to violence. For a critique of the

early modern period suggests not a lessening of the violent impulses of the medieval period but their increase? The religious wars of the sixteenth century, the exterminatory aspects of many imperial endeavours and an increase in European homicide rates, which peaked in the first half of the seventeenth century, all occurred during a period Elias designates as one of increasing self-restraint. These problems do not render the theory worthless, but they do make it highly contestable, calling into question its internal coherence and the conclusions that spring from it. Moreover, the fields of history, political science and psychology have evolved substantially over the eighty years since Elias' work was first published so that most of the premises, not to mention the empirical bases underlying the 'civilizing process', can, if not be dismissed outright, then at least be called into question. Since the 1930s, scholars have rethought concepts such as the connection between the citizen and the state; the Weberian notion of the 'monopoly of violence' and the manner in which punishment was meted out; the development of the self and its association to violence and the emotions in the early modern and modern eras; and the relevance of Freudian ideas to history. Today, the precepts on which the theory of the civilizing process was built are beginning to look unsound.

Pinker's use of *The Civilizing Process*

While scholars' engagement with and critique of Elias' work has been extensive, Pinker has used *The Civilizing Process* expansively and uncritically to support his interpretation of violence in human history. Pinker makes much of Elias' powers of prediction, for example, arguing that *The Civilizing Process* was the only theory that 'anticipated' the work of historical criminologists like Ted Gurr, Manuel Eisner and J. S. Cockburn, whose empirical findings on falling homicide rates began to appear and gained currency in the 1970s and 1980s. In this way Elias has passed a 'stringent test for a scientific hypothesis'.[38] But Pinker has this backwards. *The Civilizing Process* does not 'predict' a fall in homicide rates; as we have noted, Elias mentions this kind of interpersonal violence only a handful of times. At most *The Civilizing Process* implies the *possibility* of a decline in interpersonal violence, but only as a corollary of a broader mechanism by which Western Europeans learned to control the outward expression of their inner drives, a process which in turn reinforced the authority of the state and its instruments. That this *caused* a decline in the murder rate is an extrapolation made by others, not the substance of the theory itself.

---

book's account of class relations, see R. J. Robinson, '"The Civilizing Process": Some Remarks on Elias's Social History', *Sociology*, 21, no. 1 (1987): 1–17.
[38]Pinker, *Better Angels*, 78.

Pinker also glosses over Elias' use of Freud to reflect his own preferred 'theory of mind', described in *Better Angels* as 'a synthesis of cognitive science, affective and cognitive neuroscience, social and evolutionary psychology, and other sciences of human nature'.[39] Elias' Freudianism was thoroughgoing – he was in analysis for many years in London, was formally trained in group therapy and for a time even practised as a group therapist – but Pinker downplays its influence on *The Civilizing Process*, assuring the reader that Elias 'stayed away from Freud's more exotic claims', and only used his theories to understand the psychology of self-control and empathy. Similarly, and in a rather transparent attempt to separate Elias from his postmodernist admirers (always, for Pinker, the undifferentiated *bêtes noires* of rational inquiry), Pinker also minimizes the degree to which Elias relies on culture, and not just biology, as an explanation for changes in human behaviour. 'To his credit', writes Pinker, 'Elias leapfrogged academic fashion in not claiming that early modern Europeans "invented" or "constructed" self-control.' Rather, '[h]e claimed only that they toned up a mental faculty that had always been a part of human nature but which the medievals had underused.'[40] It is true that Elias, the former medical student, took biology seriously. But in *The Civilizing Process* the separation between a biological capacity for self-control and the cultural meanings attached to it is not so cut and dried. Indeed, for Elias, *ideas* about self-control and its exercise were at least as important as the mechanism itself in explaining the pacification of West European societies. In particular, they were central to Western Europeans' view of themselves as 'civilized', that is, to a shared self-image based on a mutual and culturally mediated understanding of self-control and its meanings (and, in that sense, one partially 'constructed' by beliefs as much as objective reality). This insistence on the mutually reinforcing relationship of biology and culture underlines both the fragility of this self-control and its inhibitions on violence should circumstances change and the capacity for pronouncements about widespread self-control to disguise more subterranean forms of violence.

Pinker also goes to some lengths to apply aspects of the civilizing process to the recent past, and in particular trends in homicide data from the 1960s, when there was a distinct rise in the murder rate in the United States, a peak in the early 1970s, before coming down and then rising again until it reached another peak in 1991.[41] Could there be, Pinker wonders, a connection between the counterculture's 'glorification of dissoluteness', a concomitant

---

[39]Pinker, *Better Angels*, xxi.
[40]Pinker, *Better Angels*, 73.
[41]Nathan James, 'Recent Violent Crime Trends in the United States', Congressional Research Service, 20 June 2018, https://fas.org/sgp/crs/misc/R45236.pdf; and Alexia Cooper and Erica L. Smith, 'Homicide Trends in the United States, 1980-2008', U.S. Department of Justice, November 2011, https://www.bjs.gov/content/pub/pdf/htus8008.pdf.

decline in manners, and an increase in violence in daily life during the 1960s and early 1970s? Here his reasoning becomes slightly confused. He is eager to co-opt the notion of 'informalization', a concept developed by Elias and collaborators such as Cas Wouters (whom Pinker cites), to describe the reduced emphasis on formal rules of etiquette in modern daily life during this period. The point of informalization, however, was not that it signalled a reversal of the civilizing process, but rather the opposite: that self-control had become so ingrained in people's psyches that behaviour signalling the existence of that self-control – complex rules at table, formalities in dress and speech, for example – was no longer necessary.[42]

In his analysis of the American homicide rate, Pinker conflates informalization with 'decivilization', characterizing the 1960s as a period of lowered inhibitions, diminished self-restraint and consequent moral decline. While declining values – defined by Pinker in an extraordinarily politically conservative manner, such as rising divorce rates and births out of wedlock – and vulgar pop culture may not have been the direct cause of an increase in violence, 'there are plausible causal arrows from the decivilizing mindset to the facilitation of actual violence'.[43] These decivilizing effects (in concert with the not-insignificant effects of poverty and discrimination, which Pinker tangentially acknowledges) hit African American communities particularly hard.[44] Thankfully, there was a 'recivilizing' movement in the 1990s.[45] When the counterculture petered out, the civilizing process was 'restored to its forward direction'.

This turnaround came about in part because of mass incarceration ('almost certain to lower crime rates', although Pinker admits that the argument is not 'watertight'), increased policing and a change in sensibilities.[46] Here Pinker appears sanguine about both the longer-term effects of mass incarceration on Black communities and the ongoing continuity of the American murder statistics, now returned to their civilized trajectory. Homicides rates in the United States do seem to have plateaued between 1999 and 2008. But, as history repeatedly attests, it is always possible to speak too soon. Another uptick appears to be taking place since 2015, although it is too early to tell yet just how far it will go.

In addition, rates of suicide – an act of violence against the self, though one understudied in the history of homicide literature – seem to be rising steadily and is a trend that Pinker completely ignores. (The only mention of suicide in *The Better Angels of Our Nature* is limited to suicide terrorism.[47])

---

[42]Cas Wouters, *Informalization: Manners and Emotions since 1890* (Los Angeles: SAGE Publications, 2007).
[43]Pinker, *Better Angels*, 114, 115, 127.
[44]Pinker, *Better Angels*, 115.
[45]Pinker, *Better Angels*, 116–28.
[46]Pinker, *Better Angels*, 125.
[47]Pinker, *Better Angels*, 353–61.

Recent research points to an inverse relation between homicide and suicide, that is, as homicide numbers decline, numbers of suicides increase. This began to happen in Europe during the middle of the seventeenth century and into the eighteenth, so that today some 800,000 people in the world commit suicide each year, compared to some 385,000 homicides. The relation between homicide and suicide is not universal, but it is clear in many modern societies, including in developing nations such as Sri Lanka, and may have something to do with the internalization of concepts of male honour.[48] The implications for the 'civilizing process' have yet to be explained.

If Pinker is quick to declare 1960s America as decivilized, he is strangely resistant to doing the same to the example that inspired the concept: Nazi Germany. Indeed, Pinker tends to downplay what is painfully evident to historians of the twentieth century and a cause of lifelong anguish for Elias himself – the implications of the civilizing process for our understanding of state-directed violence, including the kind perpetrated by the Nazis between 1933 and 1945. Elias grappled with this 'German question' his entire career; later in life he indicated that he was partly motivated to write *The Civilizing Process* in order to better understand the rise of the Nazis, whose initial excesses he had witnessed at close quarters while a young academic at Frankfurt University.[49] Elias' most definitive statements on this topic are in *The Germans*, a collection of essays published in 1989, shortly before his death. In these pieces, Elias positioned Nazism and the Holocaust as a 'regression' or 'rebarbarization' of German society – what later commentators have understood to be a kind of 'decivilizing spurt' (*Schub* in German) or reversal.[50] Elias argued that Nazism tapped into a deep and distinctively German nostalgia for *satisfaktionsfähigkeit* – an aristocratic code of honour dating from the eighteenth century, in which an offence demanded satisfaction through duelling.[51] This widespread consensus that a perceived insult required a violent (if ritualized) response made defeat in the First World War and the subjugation implicit in demilitarization acutely painful. The *Freikorps*, private extreme-right paramilitary units that appeared after the defeat in 1918, were the epitome of this tendency, which the Nazis then extended and racialized. Under these conditions, the

---

[48]Pieter Spierenburg, *A History of Murder: Personal Violence in Europe from the Middle Ages to the Present* (Cambridge: Polity, 2008), 158–61; Peter Mayer, 'Comparative Reflections on *The Civilizing Process*', in Lemmings and Brooks (eds), *Emotions and Social Change*, 233–51, here 241–4; Hugh P. Whitt, 'The Civilizing Process and Its Discontents: Suicide and Crimes against Persons in France, 1825-1830', *American Journal of Sociology*, 116 (2010): 130–86.
[49]Elias, *The Germans*, xi, 445–6.
[50]Elias, *The Germans*, 1; Jonathan Fletcher, 'Towards a Theory of Decivilizing Processes', *Amsterdams sociologisch Tijdschrift*, 22, no. 2 (October 1995): 283–97; and Stephen Mennell, 'Decivilizing Processes: Theoretical Significance and Some Lines for Research', *International Sociology*, 5, no. 2 (1990): 205–23.
[51]Eric Dunning and Jason Hughes, *Norbert Elias and Modern Sociology: Knowledge, Interdependence, Power, Process* (London: Bloomsbury, 2013), 107–8.

self-restraint instilled over centuries disintegrated rapidly, in a process that demonstrated the disturbing 'vulnerability of civilization'.[52]

While there are problems with the explanations Elias sets out in *The Germans* – if centuries of psychological *habitus* could be overthrown so quickly, how real was it to begin with? – his theorizing at least acknowledged the need to try and account for the catastrophe of Nazism via the mechanisms described by *The Civilizing Process* itself. That work, after all, purported to demonstrate a pacification process that was thoroughgoing, anchored in a general mastery of psychological drives, and applicable both to individuals and to societies as a whole. A cataclysmic war and genocide in the heart of civilized Europe called all this into question. Pinker, on the other hand, treats the civilizing process as if it was only ever intended to apply to rates of homicide – in other words, to the one kind of violence that seems to retrospectively validate the theory. Like other accounts of the history of homicide that use Elias' civilizing process as explanatory, in *Better Angels* Pinker must quarantine these 'one-on-one homicides', perpetrated within the bounds of the nation-state, from genocides (often perpetrated by the nation-state on 'others' and therefore invisible in crime statistics), in order to prove a putative reduction in violence. On this basis Pinker suggests that perhaps Elias need not have bothered with the arguments he proposed in *The Germans*, since 'in Germany during the Nazi years the declining trend for one-on-one homicides continued'.[53] By this logic the civilizing process went on, like time's arrow, through the political violence of the 1930s, through the Second World War, through the Holocaust. It was thrown off course not by the piles of corpses in Europe, but by the hippies and their bad manners. The numbers say so.

That the official homicide rate within Germany declined at the same time as some German citizens and their collaborators murdered millions of people at the lips of mass graves or gassed them to death, first in mobile wagons and then later in purpose built death camps, is hardly a consoling thought. It also underlines just how problematic it is to use homicide figures as some sort of singular measure of violence in a society.[54] But the insistence on such a distinction is wholly characteristic of Pinker's tendency to reduce the catastrophic, state-directed violence of the first half of the twentieth century to a statistical blip in an otherwise heartening trajectory. Rather than be driven to despair by the fact of its occurrence, Pinker seems to suggest, we

---

[52]Elias, *The Germans*, x.
[53]Pinker, *Better Angels*, 79. See also Eric A. Johnson, *Nazi Terror: The Gestapo, Jews and Ordinary Germans* (New York: Basic Books, 1999), on the question of crime in Nazi Germany.
[54]See Barbara A. Hanawalt, 'Obverse of the Civilizing Process in Medieval England', *IAHCCJ Bulletin*, 20 (Spring 1995): 49–60, here 52.

should instead be happy that in the several decades since 1945, there has not been another genocide of comparable scale.[55]

Similarly, and in the context of this statistical view, Pinker's alternative to Elias' writing on Nazism – that it and the Holocaust are not examples of 'decivilization' but rather a demonstration of how the 'compartmentalization of the moral sense', in concert with high levels of ideology and coercion, can lead to wars and genocides 'even in otherwise civilized societies' – suggests a broader willingness to retrofit explanatory frameworks to the contours of his data. (This includes the 'no Hitler, no Holocaust' thesis, invoked at several points as though it is uncontested.[56]) Indeed, having contextualized the Holocaust numerically, Pinker seems largely unconcerned by the reams of scholarship seeking, as Elias did, to understand and interpret the genocide within the history of violence and progress in the West. Indeed, as critics of both *Better Angels* and his more recent *Enlightenment Now* have pointed out, he is vehemently resistant to accounts suggesting that there may be a connection between the industrialized killing of the Holocaust and the 'rational' precepts of modernity, leading him to mischaracterize all utopian ideologies (except democracy) as products of the counter-Enlightenment.[57] For historians trained to value nuance over bald assertion, the case is far from closed on either score.

Conclusion

Even if we accept the existence of a civilizing mechanism working away over centuries, the concept is an ambivalent one that contains within it the 'the potential to unleash the forces it would label "barbaric" on an unprecedented scale'.[58] Indeed, the brutality of two world wars and twentieth-century dictatorships is one of the paradoxes of the rise of the modern state: the expansion of the state and its monopoly over violence (à la Weber and Elias) may be responsible for increased public order and security for its citizenry, but

---

[55]Pinker, *Better Angels*, 377. He makes a similar argument in relation to the mass warfare of the twentieth century, suggesting that *apart from* the millions and millions of deaths in wars and their associated genocides, the 'enduring moral trend' of the period was 'a violence-averse humanism' (p. 192).

[56]Pinker, *Better Angels*, 209 and 343.

[57]See Pinker, *Better Angels*, 777–8; 231–2 and 643; Benjamin Ziemann, 'Histories of Violence', https://reviews.history.ac.uk/review/1232; Peter Harrison, 'The Enlightenment of Steven Pinker', *ABC Religion & Ethics*, 20 February 2018, https://www.abc.net.au/religion/the-enlightenment-of-steven-pinker/10094966 and Paul Corey, 'Steven Pinker and the Ambivalence of Modernity', http://anamnesisjournal.com/2014/01/steven-pinker-ambivalence-modernity-critique-better-angels-nature-violence-declined/.

[58]Ian Burkitt, 'Civilization and Ambivalence', *British Journal of Sociology*, 47, no. 1 (1996): 135–50, here 142.

at the same time the capacity of the state to inflict destruction has increased dramatically, so that it is responsible for some of the worst crimes of the twentieth century – genocide, ethnic cleansing on a massive scale, starvation, massacres and mass murder.[59] Elias found this destructive potential of the modern state – both the means of pacification *and* 'a dangerous instrument' – troubling.[60] Pinker appears far less concerned.

It is obvious, however, that Elias has had a significant impact, not just on Pinker, but on the way scholars understand the association between psychic processes and social transformations, including the history of violence in the West. In this sense the civilizing process has proved resilient, and scholars across disciplines still engage with elements of the theory and suggest ways in which his model might be reworked, revised and improved. As we have seen, however, there are questions around the applicability of the model to an understanding of violence, questions that Pinker should have engaged with. A number of historians have argued that there is no empirical evidence that the modern economy, the modern state, modern manners or modern science have had any long-term impact on humanity's predisposition to violence. On the contrary, scholars have argued that the scale of collective brutality dramatically increases with the rise of modern social organizations, while the scale and the character of interpersonal violence remains essentially the same.[61] Similarly, there is an argument that as the state increased its hold and as some forms of violence declined, other forms became far less public and much more private.[62] Put another way, violence evolves and changes, not just quantitatively but also qualitatively. It is, however, impossible to measure with any degree of accuracy those forms of violence that are private – especially domestic violence, child abuse, sexual assault and rape – largely because they are either not reported or significantly under-reported. It does seem to be the case, however, that when the state is very centralized (as we see in totalitarian states), or on the contrary when the state is absent, violence tends to be high.[63]

How do we view the present moment? Europeans today are as capable as ever of interpersonal violence and in certain circumstances, as we have seen with any number of wars and civil wars over the last century, can be just as

---

[59]Pieter Spierenburg, 'Toward a Global History of Homicide and Organized Murder', *Crime, Histoire & Sociétés / Crime, History & Societies*, 18, no. 2 (2014): 102–3; Alvin W. Gouldner, 'Doubts About the Uselessness of Men and the Meaning of the Civilizing Process', *Theory and Society*, 10, no. 3 (May 1981): 413–18.

[60]Cited in Burkitt, 'Civilization and Ambivalence', 140.

[61]Siniša Malešević, 'Forms of Brutality: Towards A Historical Sociology of Violence', *European Journal of Social Theory*, 16, no. 3 (July 2013): 1–19.

[62]Mark Cooney, 'The Privatization of Violence', *Criminology*, 41, no. 4 (2003): 1377–406.

[63]On the difficulties in measuring sexual violence, see the chapter in this collection by Joanna Bourke, 'The Rise and Rise of Sexual Violence', 236–51; and Mark Cooney, 'From Warre to Tyranny: Lethal Conflict and the State', *American Sociological Review*, 62 (1997): 316–38.

murderous as their forebears. The spread of literacy, refined manners and involvement in national and international economic markets has not made all that much of a difference to rates of violence over the last 200 years, despite Pinker's assertion to the contrary. For Pinker, there are two choices: either the world is 'a nightmare of crime, terrorism, genocide, and war' or it is 'by the standards of history . . . blessed by unprecedented levels of peaceful coexistence'.[64] It is true that judged by the 'standards of history' many of us in the privileged West live lives wholly unlike those of our sixteenth- and seventeenth-century counterparts. But it is surely worth reflecting on what *meaning* we place on that change. As we have argued, Pinker and Elias diverge significantly on this point. For Elias, the civilizing process is contingent and reversible. Pinker, on the other hand, uses Elias' concept of the civilizing process in a manner for which it was never really intended – to explain the putative, long-term decline in violence and to project it into the future. If this not an outright distortion of Elias, it is also not a particularly thoughtful or sophisticated use of his theory. Whether one thinks that the civilizing process is, in the words of Gerd Schwerhoff, the 'last theoretical dinosaur' of its kind, or whether it is the 'only theoretical framework' that can explain violence, the time has probably come to treat Elias as 'an important social and cultural figure of the 1930s and 1940s, but not as a guide for present-day historical research'.[65]

---

[64]Pinker, *Better Angels*, xix.
[65]Schwerhoff, 'Criminalized Violence and the Process of Civilisation', 11; Spierenburg, 'Violence and the Civilizing Process: Does It Work?', 90; Barbara H. Rosenwein, 'The Uses of Biology', *Cultural and Social History*, 4, no. 4 (2007): 553–8.

PART TWO

Periods

7

Steven Pinker's 'prehistoric anarchy'

A bioarchaeological critique

Linda Fibiger

Steven Pinker's *The Better Angels of Our Nature* is not the first work to put bioarchaeological evidence (i.e. data resulting from the scientific analysis of human skeletal remains) at the heart of its argument for high levels of violence in the past.[1] Lawrence Keeley's *War Before Civilization* did exactly that, using skeletal and ethnographic studies when revisiting the prehistoric narrative on violence to reject the image of a pacified past.[2] Pinker simply reused most of the skeletal studies featured in Keeley's work. Since its publication in 2011, Pinker's thesis has been heavily criticized on the basis of its statistical inferences, which use percentage deaths in war of up to 60 per cent in select archaeological and ethnographic studies.[3] Most recently, scholars have demonstrated that Keeley's and Pinker's percentage-based approach of simply considering the number of those engaged in violent conflict and the proportion of those killed by violent acts is not a sufficiently robust indicator for comparisons across time. They suggest that

---

[1]Steven Pinker, *The Better Angels of Our Nature* (New York: Viking, 2011).

[2]Lawrence H. Keeley, *War before Civilization: The Myth of the Peaceful Savage* (New York and Oxford: Oxford University Press, 1996).

[3]Pasquale Cirillo and Nassim N. Taleb, 'On the Statistical Properties and Tail Risk of Violent Conflicts', *Physica A: Statistical Mechanics and Its Applications*, 452 (2016): 29–45; and Dean Falk and Charles Hildebolt, 'Annual War Deaths in Small-Scale versus State Societies Scale with Population Size Rather than Violence', *Current Anthropology*, 58, no. 6 (2017): 805–13.

units with larger population sizes (mostly states) produce more casualties 'per combatant than in ethnographically observed small-scale societies or in historical states', meaning that modern states are not any less violent than their archaeological predecessors.[4]

Numbers and percentages are at the heart of Pinker's argument, while their method of calculation and lack of contextualization form the basis of the criticism levelled against him. The issue of numbers and frequency calculations will resurface in the context of bioarchaeological analysis in the following text, but it is terminology which will be considered first, followed by a critical exploration of bioarchaeological data generation, analysis and interpretation. These underpin much of Pinker's argument for prehistoric violence. His superficial treatment and understanding of key ideas and concepts weakens the impact of his thesis that we have simply been evolving from a brutal (pre)historic past towards a significantly more peaceful present. In his failure to consider the potential of bioarchaeology (and indeed history) to explore the experiential and contextual qualities of violent events, he reduces the (pre)historic past, and those who inhabited it, to mere statistical props for his larger narrative, rather than considering the skeletal remains of the individuals he refers to as the most direct and poignant evidence for past lifeways.

Reading the prehistoric record

What is prehistory?

Prehistory denotes the period prior to written records. A lack of contemporary text, however, does not mean that prehistory is silent. Centred on the study of past human societies through their material remains, the prehistoric archaeological record is rich and diverse, as are the materials that constitute it.[5] These range from the mineral to the organic, the portable (tools, ornaments) to the monumental (temples), the secular (field systems) to the sacred (burial mounds) and the permanent (megaliths) to the more transient (seasonal camps) – with the borders between these categories and spheres rather fluid and hybridization common. It is precisely this diversity that makes archaeology and prehistory, especially at a multiregional or a global level, an important discipline. It takes a long-term perspective when addressing important and often timeless questions, such as human expansion and settlement, changing

---

[4]Rahul C. Oka, Marc Kissel, Mark Golitko, Susan Guise Sheridan, Nam C. Kim and Agustín Fuentes, 'Population Is the Main Driver of War Group Size and Conflict Casualties', *Proceedings of the National Academy of Sciences*, 114, no. 52 (2017): E11101–E11110.
[5]Chris Scarre (ed.), *The Human Past: World Prehistory & the Development of Human Societies*, 2nd edn (London and New York: Thames & Hudson, 2009), 27.

environments and adaptation, conflict and cooperation.[6] When including deep prehistory, that is, the period of development of hominids into modern humans, this means a record going back roughly 2 million years, though archaeological (human-made) remains become more widely evident after the end of the last Ice Age around 12,000 years ago.[7]

Archaeology as a discipline developed from an antiquarian, artefact-based approach that left little room for theory or interpretation. This was followed by processual or new archaeology, which redefined archaeology as a science that aimed to understand the complex cultural and environmental dynamics driving change and adaptation, as well as post-processual approaches. New archaeology criticized the dominance of natural science data and widened the interpretative scope to include questions of, among others, gender, materiality and identity.[8] Today's archaeology is a multidisciplinary subject with increasing specialization; ancient DNA analysis in particular has brought the natural sciences back to the very forefront of archaeology and prehistory.[9]

The prehistoric record is by no means unbiased. Evidence is not equally distributed in space and time, and just like social anthropologists, archaeologists of prehistory and beyond have wrestled with the notion that 'there is no such thing as objective knowledge' and that 'archaeological interpretations are influenced by society, culture, and self-interest'.[10] This may become even harder to avoid when studying prehistory, simply because it involves peoples, places and events further removed from our own experiences – a point which will be revisited in view of Pinker's treatment of this period. At the same time, prehistoric archaeology is constantly evolving, both in methods and in the nature and extent of the evidence available, to overcome some of these challenges. Its long-term and inclusive approach, particularly with regard to bioarchaeological/skeletal evidence, does not claim to be complete, but is much more likely to inform us about a wide section of society, including both sexes, all ages and diverse socio-economic groups, than many historical, written sources.

Talking about prehistory and bioarchaeology

Prehistoric archaeology and bioarchaeology combine a variety of social and natural science approaches, which rely on clear, unequivocal language when

[6]Scarre, *The Human Past*, 28.
[7]Chris Stringer and Peter Andrews, *The Complete World of Human Evolution* (London: Thames & Hudson, 2005), 10.
[8]Bruce Trigger, *A History of Archaeological Thought* (Cambridge: Cambridge University Press, 2006).
[9]Kristian Kristiansen, 'Towards a New Paradigm? The Third Science Revolution and Its Possible Consequences in Archaeology', *Current Swedish Archaeology*, 22 (2014): 11–34.
[10]Trigger, *History of Archaeological Thought*, 2.

trying to identify, classify, analyse and interpret what is in many cases a fragmented, incomplete and complex record to re-create past human activity. This does not mean archaeology or its terminology is universal. Examples for variation are regional chronologies and systems of periodization, which are underpinned by more widely accepted conventions, ethical and professional frameworks and operational procedures (such as *The Vermillion Accord on Human Remains*). In archaeological terms, prehistory encompasses a vast period of tens of thousands of years. Its traditional periodization highlights apparent changes in aspects of material culture (Stone Age, Bronze Age, Iron Age), and is also punctuated by shifts in subsistence (such as the introduction of agriculture), settlement patterns (permanent rather than seasonal settlements) and societal organization and administration (such as urbanization).[11]

Pinker, on the other hand, presents 'prehistory' as a universal term, a unifying or global expression used to refer to non-state societies and the 'anarchy of the hunting, gathering and horticultural societies in which our species spent most of its evolutionary history to the first agricultural civilizations with cities and governments, beginning around five thousand years ago'.[12] His main focus is on hunter-gatherer/horticultural societies and beyond, but this means different things to different regions at different times. In Europe, for example, written history begins with ancient Greece in the southeast, but in the more northern regions the Vikings were still part of the prehistoric Iron Age during the Middle Ages.[13] The transition to agriculture, as another example, certainly did not equal the universal emergence of cities and governments that Pinker claims, highlighting that patterns as well as exceptions are a guiding feature of (pre)historic discourse. This shines a rather poor light on Pinker's literacy and understanding of the period of human history that forms the cornerstone of his argument for a decline in violence.

Take, for example, the table illustrating the percentage of deaths in warfare in non-state and state societies that Pinker provides (on p. 49) in order to demonstrate just how violent prehistoric and hunter-gatherer societies were compared to state societies. Twenty-two sites in the table list warfare deaths at prehistoric sites. Overall, they make up a rather incoherent sample.[14] One of those sites is Vedbæk, a small Danish cemetery in which only two of a total of twenty-one individuals presented skeletal changes indicative of violence. This translates into a percentage figure of violent deaths of 9.5 per cent (although for some reason it shows as around 12 or 13 per cent on Pinker's table). People were buried at this site in the fifth millennium

---

[11]Scarre, *The Human Past*.
[12]Pinker, *Better Angels*, xxiv.
[13]Scarre, *Human Past*, 27.
[14]Pinker, *Better Angels*, 49.

BC, which for the region means they belong to the Mesolithic (i.e. hunter-gatherer dominated) Ertebølle horizon (named after its type site in Jutland), representing complex hunter-gatherer-fisher groups with settlement sites (some of which were probably occupied year-round).

A single site from Denmark is not representative of the non-state prehistoric horizon in a Northern European context, and it is certainly highly problematic comparing or even grouping it with geographically and temporally removed sites from India, Africa and North America that join Vedbæk in Pinker's table. All of these sites have been selected purely, one imagines, because the findings have been published in English. Indeed, all non-state references can be gleaned from two works, one by Keeley, which has been already mentioned, and the other by Azar Gat, both of which are English-language summary works; primary data is wholly absent.[15]

As for the variability of the prehistoric record, a completely different picture for the Mesolithic emerges when we cross the North Sea into Britain. In Britain, no Mesolithic cemeteries have to date been excavated; human remains are usually found disarticulated and in a variety of mostly non-funerary contexts so that the complete skeletal record for the whole period (c. 4000–2300 BC) consists of fewer skeletal remains than the single site of Vedbæk. Skeletal remains provide the most direct evidence for violence in prehistory, especially in times and places where specialized weapons may not exist or fortified architecture is absent.[16] Of course, we can only analyse them where we find them, but it would be difficult to make a broad statement about cross-regional or continental trends of violent interaction in prehistory from the remains of twenty-one individuals found in a small cemetery. To put this in perspective, this author's own bioarchaeological investigation of violence in Neolithic Europe involved the analysis of over 1,000 individuals from over 150 sites spanning a period of over 3,000 years. Even at that much larger scale, this only meaningfully reflects on the prevalence and importance of violence in the specific region covered by the research, which saw endemic levels of violent interaction which included both fatal and non-fatal incidences.[17] This is at odds with Pinker's bold statements about whole continents based on a very limited evidence that

[15]Keeley, War before Civilization; Azar Gat, War in Human Civilization (New York: Oxford University Press, 2006).

[16] John Robb, 'Violence and Gender in Early Italy', in Debra L. Martin and David W. Frayer (eds), Troubled Times: Violence and Warfare in the Past (Amsterdam: Gordon & Breach, 1997), 111–44; Philip L. Walker, 'A Bioarchaeological Perspective on the History of Violence', Annual Review of Anthropology, 30 (2001): 573–96.

[17]Linda Fibiger, Torbjörn Ahlström, Pia Bennike and Rick J. Schulting, 'Patterns of Violence-Related Skull Trauma in Neolithic Southern Scandinavia', American Journal of Physical Anthropology, 150 (2013): 190–202; Linda Fibiger, 'Conflict and Violence in the Neolithic of North-Western Europe', in Manuel Fernández-Götz and Nico Roymans (eds), Conflict Archaeology: Materialities of Collective Violence in Late Prehistoric and Early Historic Europe (New York: Taylor & Francis, 2018), 13–22.

focuses purely on fatalities as an indicator of violence. How this approach of Pinker's misconstrues the impact and meaning of violence will be further discussed later in the chapter.

Defining violence and war

These kinds of figures raise other interesting questions like, what is violence, and how do we define, recognize and measure it? The term 'violence' in its primary, dictionary-defined meaning is the 'exercise of physical force so as to inflict injury on, or cause damage to, persons or property'.[18] This is in line with many of the current anthropological definitions of violence.[19] There are, of course, other forms of violence which entail 'emotional, psychological, sexual or material damage' rather than bodily harm. Physical injury oftentimes can result in emotional and psychological damage, and different cultural norms exist for what actually constitutes violence, which include emotional and psychological maltreatment or structural violence.[20] Pinker's measure of violence in terms of fatalities only, death as the result of visibly violent injury, is rather limited in this context.

While the skeletal marker of an injury committed with a particular weapon and particular force may be the same whether committed in prehistory or committed today, its meaning as 'violent' cannot be assumed to be universal, and is likely to have been interpreted and defined differently in the prehistoric past from how we view it today. This is not disputing the impact of pain, suffering and potential longer-term consequences of and injury inflicted by (an)other human being(s), but it questions how this particular type of interaction would have been defined, given a particular context. How do we define violence, especially when viewing prehistory through our modern observer bias?

The subtitle of Pinker's book refers to the history of violence, but it is warfare that features large in his narrative and is applied universally to a

---

[18]Oxford English Dictionary. Available at: https://www.oed.com/oed2/00277885, accessed 15 January 2020.

[19]Jon Abbink, 'Preface: Violation and Violence as Cultural Phenomena', in Jon Abbink and Göran Aijmer (eds), *Meanings of Violence: A Cross Cultural Perspective* (Oxford: Berg, 2000), xi–xvii; John Archer, 'Introduction: Male Violence in Perspective', in John Archer (ed.), *Male Violence* (London: Routledge, 1994), 1–20; David Riches (ed.), *The Anthropology of Violence* (Oxford: Basil Blackwell, 1986).

[20]Claus Bossen, 'War as Practice, Power, and Processor: A Framework for the Analysis of War and Social Structural Change', in Ton Otto, Henrik Thrane and Helle Vandkilde (eds), *Warfare and Society: Archaeological and Social Anthropological Perspectives* (Aarhus: Aarhus University Press, 2006), 89–102; Dave Grossman, *On Combat: The Psychology and Physiology of Deadly Conflict in War and Peace* (PPCT Research Publications, 2004); Christian Krohn-Hansen, 'The Anthropology of Violent Interaction', *Journal of Anthropological Research*, 50 (1994): 36781.

variety of contexts and data sets, ranging from violence-related skeletal trauma data in prehistoric grave sites to death statistics from the world wars. It raises questions about the concept of warfare, what actually constitutes true evidence for its presence, and how it may vary depending on the context and period. This is an underdeveloped but important aspect in Pinker's argument.

Available definitions of warfare arise from anthropological, archaeological, historical and military studies and place different emphases on social, tactical and physical aspects, varying degrees of specificity and complexity and different scales of conflict. Physical force and domination are recurring features in existing characterizations of warfare, as are its link to groups or defined units.[21] Additional identifying features frequently examined are lethality, territoriality and duration.[22] At other times, warfare is defined exclusively as a state activity.[23] All of these attributes are valid and important considerations, but they are varied and not universally present in Pinker's data sample.

The scale of feuding and raiding, common expressions of conflict in pre-industrialized, preliterate small-scale societies like those of the earlier prehistoric periods may well be characterized by 'organised fighting' involving planning, direction and an expected set of lasting results.[24] It may also see the application of the 'use of organised force between independent groups' and therefore be defined as warfare according to some of the current anthropological definitions.[25] This does not mean that it is always possible to distinguish its presence and consequences, at least archaeologically, from one-off violent events and other forms of interpersonal violence such as one-to-one fights, punishment, torture and domestic violence. The scale and intensity of a conflict may not necessarily be accurately reflected in the archaeological record, and warfare as scaled, organized, long-term group

---

[21]Göran Aijmer, 'Introduction: The Idiom of Violence in Imagery and Discourse', in Abbink and Aijmer (eds), *Meanings of Violence*, 1–21; Quincy Wright, 'Definitions of War', in Lawrence Freedman (ed.), *War* (Oxford: Oxford University Press, 1994), 69–70; R. Brian Ferguson, 'Introduction: Studying War', in R. Brian Ferguson (ed.), *Warfare, Culture and Environment* (Orlando: Academic Press, 1984), 1–81.

[22]Joshua S. Goldstein, *War and Gender: How Gender Shapes the War System and Vice Versa* (Cambridge: Cambridge University Press, 2001); Carol R. Ember and Melvin Ember, 'War, Socialization, and Interpersonal Violence – A Cross-Cultural Study', *Journal of Conflict Resolution* 38 (1994): 620–46; James R. Kerin, 'Combat', in Lester R. Kurtz (ed.), *Encyclopedia of Violence, Peace and Conflict*, 2nd edn (San Diego: Academic Press, 1998), 349.

[23]David Warbourton, 'Aspects of War and Warfare in Western Philosophy and History', in Otto, Thrane and Vandkilde (eds), *Warfare and Society*, 37–55.

[24]Robert O'Connell, *Ride of the Second Horseman: The Birth and Death of War* (Oxford, Gordon & Breach, 1995).

[25]Herbert D. G. Maschner and Katherine L. Reedy-Maschner, 'Raid, Retreat, Defend (repeat): The Archaeology and Ethnohistory of Warfare on the North Pacific Rim', *Journal of Anthropological Archaeology*, 17 (1998): 19–51.

conflict will need critical levels of human casualties or material destruction to be visible archaeologically and/or bioarchaeologically.[26]

In the face of such different ideas about underlying concepts as well as the actual practice of warfare, the main function of Pinker applying the term universally across time and space appears to be its superficial simplicity, its familiarity and its popular accessibility in a work that is situated across the popular/academic divide. Warfare also suggests a sense of scale that – when considering the discussions on Vedbæk and on the statistical validity of some of the data in Pinker's work – may be misleading. It does also, even unintentionally, dramatize, perhaps even sensationalize, the topic in a way that the term 'violence' may not to the same degree.[27]

Why do we fight?

There is no question that skeletal evidence for interpersonal violence goes back as far as the origins of humans themselves, indicated by traces of potential non-accidental and predominantly cranial trauma from a number of hominid and early modern human skeletal specimens.[28] Throughout the history of *Homo sapiens* 'no form of social organisation, mode of production, or environmental setting appears to have remained free from interpersonal violence for long' – a statement which is in broad agreement with Pinker's work.[29]

Potential reasons for and explanations of aggressive behaviour, physical violence and warfare have been central to anthropological discourses on conflict and can be broadly divided into three main explanatory models: biological, cultural and materialist.[30] Unfortunately, discussions on these models have not always succeeded in addressing problems such as

---

[26]Donald F. Tuzin, 'The Spectre of Peace in Unlikely Places: Concept and Paradox in the Anthropology of Peace', in Thomas Gregor (ed.), *A Natural History of Peace* (Nashville: Vanderbilt University Press, 1996), 3–33; Patrick S. Willey, *Prehistoric Warfare on the Great Plains: Skeletal Analysis of the Crow Creek Massacre Victims* (New York: Garland, 1990).

[27]Robert K. Dentan, 'Recent Studies on Violence: What's in and What's Out', *Reviews in Anthropology*, 37 (2008): 41–67.

[28]Charles F. Merbs, 'Trauma', in Mehmet Y. İşcan and Kenneth A. R. Kennedy (eds), *Reconstruction of Life from the Skeleton* (New York: Alan R. Liss, 1989), 161–89; Christoph E. Zollikofer, Marcia S. Ponce De Leon, Bernard Vandermeersch and François Lévêque, 'Evidence for Interpersonal Violence in the St. Cesaire Neanderthal', *Proceedings of the National Academy of Sciences of the United States of America*, 99 (2002): 6444–8.

[29]Walker, 'A Bioarchaeological Perspective on the History of Violence', 573.

[30]Maschner and Reedy-Maschner, 'Raid, Retreat, Defend (repeat)'; Pia Nystrom, 'Aggression and Nonhuman Primates', in Mike Parker Pearson and Nick J. N. Thorpe (eds), *Warfare, Violence and Slavery in Prehistory* (Oxford: Archaeopress, 2005), 35–40; Andrew J. Strathern and Pamela J. Stewart, 'Anthropology of Violence and Conflict, Overview', in Lester Kurtz (ed.), *Encyclopedia of Violence, Peace and Conflict*, 2nd edn (San Diego: Academic Press, 2008), 75–86.

distinguishing cause from effect, or short-term individual and collective motivation for violence from long-term 'differential survivability' of a particular course of violent or non-violent action.[31] This puts some of Pinker's more generalizing, almost monocausal statements on the origins, functions and prevalence of interpersonal violence and warfare on shaky ground. Multiple levels of causality and various context and culture-specific factors may prove to make causal linkages inconclusive and detract from the complex interaction between biological, cultural and ecological factors.[32] This problem is not something that receives the critical reflection it deserves by Pinker.

Biological perspectives on violence

While Raymond Dart's and Robert Ardrey's 'killer ape hypothesis', which dates from the 1940s and 1950s and which presents aggression and violence as the driving force behind human evolution, has long been discredited, the notion of some biological roots for aggression and violence persists, receiving more recent support through DNA analysis.[33] Aggression is a natural part of animal behaviour and biological explanations of aggression highlight its potential evolutionary advantages by maximizing reproductive success through elimination of competitors – giving it a functional role arising from some prehuman tendencies.[34] Many species are largely unable to kill members of their own species because of what has been termed a 'violence immune system' in the midbrain.[35] Fighting and killing between

---

[31]Simon Harrison, 'War', in Alan Barnard and Jonathan Spencer (eds), *Encyclopedia of Social and Cultural Anthropology* (London: Routledge, 2002), 561–2; Ferguson, 'Introduction: Studying War', 1–18.

[32]Bruce Knauft, 'Violence and Sociality in Human Evolution', *Current Anthropology*, 32 (1991): 391–428; Ton Otto, 'Conceptions of Warfare in Western Thought and Research: An Introduction', in Otto, Thrane and Vandkilde (eds), *Warfare and Society*, 23–8; Strathern and Stewart, 'Anthropology of Violence and Conflict, Overview', 80.

[33]Robert Ardrey, *African Genesis: A Personal Investigation into the Animal Origins and Nature of Man* (London: Collins, 1961); Frans B. M. De Waal, 'Primates – A Natural Heritage of Conflict Resolution', *Science*, 289 (2000): 586–90; Keith F. Otterbein, *How War Began* (College Station: Texas A&M University Press, 2004), 22f.; Richard W. Wrangham, 'The Evolution of Coalitionary Killing', *Yearbook of Physical Anthropology*, 42 (1999): 1–30; Christopher J. Ferguson and Kevin M. Beaver, 'Natural Born Killers: The Genetic Origins of Extreme Violence', *Aggression and Violent Behaviour*, 14 (2009): 286–94; José María Gómez, Miguel Verdú, Adela González-Megías and Marcos Méndez, 'The Phylogenetic Roots of Human Lethal Violence', *Nature*, S38 (2016): 233–7.

[34]Nystrom, 'Aggression and Nonhuman Primates'; Goldstein, *War and Gender*, 135; Deepa Natarajan, Han De Vries, Dirk-Jan Saaltink, Sietse F. De Boer and Jaap M. Koolhaas, 'Delineation of Violence from Functional Aggression in Mice: An Ethological Approach', *Behavior Genetics*, 39 (2009): 73–90; Wrangham, 'The Evolution of Coalitionary Killing'.

[35]Kenneth R. Murray, Dave Grossman and Robert W. Kentridge, 'Behavioral Psychology of Killing', in Kurtz (ed.), *Encyclopedia of Violence*, 166–73.

humans, therefore, require a strong motivation as well as conditioning and training.[36] The biological model suggests that natural selection favours the tendency to attack and potentially kill if resulting benefits are sufficiently high, primarily in a system of intergroup relationships. This relies on observations of social animals, primarily primate species, with some primate species showing skeletal evidence for interpersonal violence very similar to that recorded in prehistoric human populations.[37]

The variability of violence, aggression and peaceful interaction throughout human history, however, strongly supports the notion that factors other than evolutionary or genetic heritage play an important part in the 'human potential for peace and violence'. It prompted the United Nations to issue the 'Seville statement' in 1986, which condemns the belief that man is violent by nature.[38] People do what they do at a certain time and in a certain context, which requires very individual, contextual considerations for conflict and violence. These considerations of individuality are missing throughout Pinker's narrative, which is largely presented through a psychological evolutionary lens.

Cultural perspectives on violence

At the heart of cultural explanations for violence is its definition not only as a physical act but as social action, means of communication, interaction and learned cultural behaviour pattern.[39] This approach makes cultural context the prime determinant for the nature of violence and conflict. It accepts the human potential for violence, but views it as ultimately developed and constrained by rules and societal conduct.[40]

There is little doubt that individual development is hugely influenced by social learning and skills acquired early in life, and these provide some of the foundations for behavioural patterns and responses, violent and non-violent,

---

[36]Grossman, *On Combat*; Barry Molloy and Dave Grossman, 'Why Can't Johnny Kill?: The Psychology and Physiology of Interpersonal Combat', in Barry Molloy (ed.), *The Cutting Edge: Archaeological Studies in Combat and Weaponry* (Cheltenham: History Press, 2007), 188–202.
[37]De Waal, 'Primates – A Natural Heritage of Conflict Resolution'; Robert Jurmain and Lyn Kilgore, 'Sex-Related Patterns of Trauma in Humans and African Apes', in Anne L. Grauer and Patricia Stuart-Macadam (eds), *Sex and Gender in Paleopathological Perspective* (Cambridge: Cambridge University Press, 1998), 11–26.
[38]Bruce Bonta, *Peaceful Peoples: An Annotated Bibliography* (Metuchen: Scarecrow, 1993); Walter Goldschmidt, 'Peacemaking and Institutions of Peace in Tribal Societies', in Leslie E. Sponsel and Thomas Gregor (eds), *The Anthropology of Peace and Nonviolence* (Boulder: Lynner Rienner Publishers, 1994), 109–31; David Adams (ed.), *The Seville Statement on Violence: Preparing the Ground for the Construction of Peace* (UNESCO, 1991).
[39]Aijmer, 'Introduction'; Bossen, 'War as Practice, Power, and Processor'; Otto, 'Conceptions of Warfare in Western Thought and Research'.
[40]John Keegan, *A History of Warfare* (New York: Knopf, 1993), 387; Maschner and Reedy-Maschner, 'Raid, Retreat, Defend (repeat)'.

in adulthood.[41] Fry's statement that 'peace begins in the nursery' certainly has some validity but individual parenting style is only one influential factor concerning the potential for violence.[42] Community environment and encouragement, as well as the toleration or discouragement of violence, is an influential societal and therefore cultural factor.[43] Human community and group identification, in combination with the ethnographically documented influence of learned mistrust or fear of strangers and outsiders to the group may also foster the concept of a dualist world view, an 'us' and 'them' attitude, with its ultimate culmination in intergroup violence.[44] Specific situational dynamics aside, culturally determined structural conditions, such as political or social systems without centralized power, may also facilitate the escalation of conflict into violent interaction in the absence of individuals or groups responsible for negotiating non-violent resolution. On the other hand, centralized powers may, of course, mobilize large numbers of combatants for much larger-scale conflicts.[45] This highlights social-political complexity as a contributing factor in the development and scale of violent interaction, an observation clearly supported by Pinker, who unfortunately fails to consider that this can work both ways when it comes to the development and scale of conflict (i.e. more complex does not equal less violent).

Material perspectives on violence

Material interests and resource competition, in combination with ecological and environmental factors, are some of the most frequently cited and ethnographically documented explanations for violent conflict in small-scale societies. Crops, livestock, land, water, access to exchange networks and trade all present coveted or necessary, potentially limited, oftentimes locally centred natural and social resources worth fighting for. Added to this list can be the competition for human resources, such as women or slaves.[46] Many

---

[41]Ember and Ember, 'War, Socialization, and Interpersonal Violence', 620–46; Goldstein, *War and Gender*, 135.

[42]Douglas Fry, 'Maintaining Social Tranquility: Internal and External Loci of Aggression Control', in Sponsel and Gregor (eds), *The Anthropology of Peace and Nonviolence*, 133.

[43]Alfred Blumstein, 'Violence: A New Frontier for Scientific Research', *Science*, 289 (2000): 545.

[44]R. Brian Ferguson, 'Explaining War', in Jonathan Haas (ed.), *The Anthropology of War* (Cambridge: Cambridge University Press, 1990), 26–55.

[45]Blumstein, 'Violence'; Jürg Helbling, 'War and Peace in Societies without Central Power', in Otto, Thrane and Vandkilde (eds), *Warfare and Society*, 113–39.

[46]Harrison, 'War'; Helbling, 'War and Peace in Societies without Central Power'; Keegan, *A History of Warfare*; 9; Knauft, 'Violence and Sociality in Human Evolution', 391–428; Keith F. Otterbein, 'Killing of Captured Enemies: A Cross-Cultural Study', *Current Anthropology*, 41 (2000): 439–43.

social goals such as status, prestige or revenge are frequently underlined by material objectives that compensate for the potential costs of violent interaction.[47] All of the above would have been important components in the prehistoric groups Pinker is referring to, and it is in these broadly material interests and in the question of gain, both material and personal, that we may find explanations for much of the skeletal evidence for interpersonal violence recorded during the period.

Two of the main factors that may upset the balance of natural economic resources are environmental and ecological fluctuations and/or population pressure, both of which can change resource balances and initiate increased competition and conflict. These are all issues that have been highlighted repeatedly for prehistory but which receive scant mention in Pinker's narrative, mostly, one would guess, due to his previously identified illiteracy when it comes to reading and understanding the prehistoric record.[48] Some researchers have presented warfare as a mechanism to correct the potential environmental imbalances and pressures on local and regional natural resources by controlling population numbers for a particular area. Population growth is limited and rebalanced through casualties, and/or populations are scattered over a wider area in the course of conflict. Even though resource pressures have a documented role to play, the use of violence cannot necessarily be defined as a consciously applied method of population control but may be an unpremeditated by-product of violent interaction and conflict in particular cases.

The complexity of violence

The aforementioned outline of biological, cultural and materialist explanations for violent interaction have demonstrated that it is difficult to isolate any one particular factor as the definitive origin of a violent event in a given context or find a universally applicable explanation for why and how often people fight. Explanations of violence should not be a question of deciding for either nature or nurture, as 'man is neither, by nature, peaceful nor warlike, and some conditions lead to war, others do not'.[49] Rather, violence as a variable form of human behaviour is shaped by a complex

---

[47]Ferguson, 'Explaining War', 29.

[48]Jean Pierre Bocquet-Appel, 'Paleoanthropological Traces of a Neolithic Demographic Transition', *Current Anthropology*, 43 (2002): 637–50; Rebecca C. Redfern, *Injury and Trauma in Bioarchaeology: Interpreting Violence in Past Lives* (Cambridge: Cambridge University Press, 2017), 62ff; Martin Smith, Rick Schulting and Linda Fibiger, 'Settled Lives, Unsettled Times – Neolithic Violence', in Garrett G. Fagan, Linda Fibiger, Mark Hudson and Matthew Trundle (eds), *The Cambridge World History of Violence, Vol. I: The Prehistoric and Ancient Worlds* (Cambridge: Cambridge University Press, 2020), 79–98.

[49]Keith F. Otterbein, 'The Origins of War', *Critical Review*, 2 (1997): 251–77.

interaction of biological factors, environmental conditions and social experiences that may obscure the line between cause and effect.[50] Social, economic, demographic and psychological needs may influence ultimate societal goals and more proximal individual motivation for the application of physical force, whether fatal or not. The further we go back in time, the more difficult it may be to disentangle this complex web.[51] The main message here is to keep in mind that models that explain violent interaction in one society or population group cannot be readily applied to another and that many of the needs or goals proposed as explanations for violence may be of a rather short-term nature. This is an important point with regard to Pinker's claim of universality when discussing violence, no matter what period and context. It may be hard for the individual or group to grasp long-term concepts or ideas that reach beyond one's lifetime.[52] Even if violent action has or has not had certain consequences in the past, individual motivation and potential short-term gain may play a relatively stronger role in societies without the formalized central powers to override such concerns in favour of a course of action based on *long-term* memory and experience.

The bioarchaeological record

The questions of methodology and ethically sound terminology discussed so far are also at the core of human skeletal analysis. A number of caveats and limitations affecting the use of skeletal data have an immediate bearing on the validity and suitability of Pinker's collated data sets. Some of these aspects, including the lack of representativeness in the sample, have been touched upon in Ferguson's recent critiques of Pinker but deserve more detailed consideration.[53]

The missing Neolithic

Bioarchaeologists of prehistory have long known about the potential for violence in the period, long before Keeley's coverage of the subject, not least

---

[50]Martin Enserink, 'Searching for the Mark of Cain', *Science*, 289 (2000): 575–9; Knauft, 'Violence and Sociality in Human Evolution'.

[51]Gregor (ed.), *A Natural History of Peace*; Ingo W. Schröder and Bettine E. Schmidt, 'Introduction: Violent Imaginaries and Violent Practices', in Bettina E. Schmidt and Ingo W. Schröder (eds), *Anthropology of Violence and Conflict* (London: Routledge, 2001), 1–12.

[52]Steven A. LeBlanc and Katherine E. Register, *Constant Battles: Why We Fight* (New York: St. Martin's Griffin, 2003), 27.

[53]R. Brian Ferguson, 'Pinker's List', in Douglas Fry (ed.), *War, Peace, and Human Nature. The Convergence of Evolutionary and Cultural Views* (Oxford: Oxford University Press, 2013), 112–31; and R. Brian Ferguson, 'The Prehistory of War and Peace in Europe and the Near East', in Fry (ed.), *War, Peace, and Human Nature*, 191–240.

through Joachim Wahl and H. G. König's 1987 publication of the Neolithic
mass grave from Talheim, Germany (not mentioned by Pinker). The skeletal
remains from the site, dating to the later phase of the earliest Neolithic in the
region (c. 5000 BC), document the violent killing of thirty-four individuals,
including men, women and children who were consequently buried in a pit
without apparent care or consideration.[54] Overall, the current skeletal data
set for the Neolithic in Western and Northern Europe in particular, but also
for other regions in Europe, does in fact present a more comprehensive,
better understood and therefore more useful data set than the Mesolithic (c.
13,000–4,000 BC) assemblages Pinker has focused on.

   Chronologically, the Neolithic fills the period between Pinker's apparent
hunter-gatherer 'anarchy' (covered by the Palaeolithic and Mesolithic), and
what he terms the 'first agricultural civilizations with cities and governments'
(mostly emerging during the Bronze and Iron Ages). According to Pinker,
this earliest phase of permanently settled agriculturalists should mark the
beginnings of the decline of violent conflict. However, from bioarchaeological
studies we know that in the few regions where both good Mesolithic and
Neolithic skeletal remains are available, violence-related skeletal trauma
frequencies do not appear to vary much at all and do not represent the peak
Pinker is implying.[55] The omission of the Neolithic from Pinker's skeletal
data set, even though this period marks one of the most profound subsistence
and cultural changes in human history, is puzzling and unsettling, especially
in view of ready data availability. It may be explained through ignorance of
this data source, which seems unlikely. The omission may have more to do
with the problem of how to represent such a varied and extensive Neolithic
data set, which will be discussed in more detail in the following text, as well
as his reluctance to engage with primary data and a reliance on English-
language publications.

Differential diagnosis of violence-related
trauma and collated data sets

Bioarchaeologists diagnose pathologies, including skeletal evidence for
trauma, by looking at patterns of changes to the skeleton, discussing
potential causes for the changes observed and making a decision on the
most likely cause for the pattern observed with consideration of the wider
context of the remains (such as the chronological and biological age and

---

[54]Joachim Wahl und H. G. König, 'Anthropologisch-traumatologische Untersuchung der Menschlichen Skelettreste aus dem Bandkeramischen Massengrab bei Talheim, Kreis Heilbronn',
Fundberichte aus Baden-Württemberg, 12 (1987): 65–193.
[55]Fibiger et al., 'Patterns of Violence-Related Skull Trauma'; Pia Bennike, *Palaeopathology of
Danish Skeletons* (Copenhagen: Akademisk Forlag, 1985).

the archaeological context). In suspected cases where the implement of violence is still present, as in the case of embedded projectiles, this may be an obvious process. In all other cases, the likelihood of an observed injury to be diagnosed as intentional rather than accidental is related to observations on injury location (e.g. the head, while representing a small area of the whole body tends to be a prime target for violent assaults), as much as injury morphology (bone breaks a certain way depending on the type of impact, such as a blow with a blunt object). This analytical process takes into consideration clinical, forensic and experimental data as well as the skeleton's cultural context.[56] However, it may not always be possible to state with 100 per cent certainty that an injury was violence related; the more contextual and analytical detail is provided, the more secure the diagnosis is.

Collated skeletal trauma data needs to be treated as a constrained resource when representing vastly different publication dates that reflect different research methods and often a diversity of research questions. Evidence of violence trauma may have been an incidental finding rather than the primary focus and may have been identified and diagnosed according to disparate criteria. Bioarchaeological analytical methods are constantly changing, and violent trauma analysis in particular has undergone a rapid progression over the last couple of decades.[57] Much of this comes back to the question of the coherence of the data set and the criteria for its selection, which in Pinker's case reflects a clear focus on English-language publications and their preselected ready availability. A growing body of recent work on violence-related trauma in the Neolithic has involved, in addition to new data on recently discovered sites, the reanalysis of existing assemblages according to current analytical protocols.[58] This has resulted in a more robust and more readily useable and comparable data set, one that keeps growing, has revisited previously analysed collections and revised the diagnosis of cases of both evidence for *and* absence of violence-related injuries, largely ignored by Pinker.[59] Pinker's prehistoric archaeological site list could therefore easily be further supplemented with examples that do not show any sign of violent injury. Unequal geographical coverage and sample size impact on

---

[56]Fibiger et al., 'Patterns of Violence-Related Skull Trauma'; Meaghan Dyer and Linda Fibiger, 'Understanding Blunt Force Trauma and Violence in Neolithic Europe: The First Experiments Using a Skin-Skull-Brain Model and the Thames Beater', *Antiquity*, 91, no. 360 (2017): 1515–28.

[57]Vicki L. Wedel and Allison Galloway, *Broken Bones. Anthropological Analysis of Blunt Force Trauma*, 2nd edn (Springfield: Charles C. Thomas Publisher Ltd, 2014).

[58]Rick Schulting and Mike Wysocki, '"In this Chambered Tomb were Found Cleft Skulls . . .": An Assessment of the Evidence for Cranial Trauma in the British Neolithic', *Proceedings of the Prehistoric Society*, 71 (2005): 107–38; Martin Smith and Megan Brickley, *People of the Long Barrows. Life, Death and Burial in the Earlier Neolithic* (Stroud: The History Press, 2009), 102–12.

[59]Chris Knüsel and Martin Smith (eds), *The Routledge Handbook of the Bioarchaeology of Human Conflict* (Abingdon: Routledge, 2014).

bioarchaeological work as it does in Pinker's own account of the prevalence of violence. Unequal distribution of violence is a feature of the past and the present, with civil wars a particular confounding element for the assessment of violence in the latter, which is not sufficiently acknowledged by Pinker in his diachronic comparison. Often, large numbers of individuals are killed in a brutal and efficient manner and buried and reburied in multiple and poorly accessible locations. The trauma, fear and guilt of survivors as well as political agendas often make obtaining information about and locating the remains as well as assessing the total number of casualties problematic; political agendas may not even allow for crimes to become public knowledge and enter any statistics.[60]

Another important consideration is the mixing of data from event-related sites – such as those resulting from one-off violent conflict or massacres like Crow Creek, a pre-European contact Native American site dating to AD 1325 – which represents a large-scale violent event that may or may not be typical for the region and period – versus data from regular burial or cemetery sites, such as the earlier example of Mesolithic Vedbæk that may be more indicative of the day-to-day level of violence within a society.[61] These are discrete data sets on violent interaction that reflect rather different aspects of human behaviour and society, such as a large-scale massacre versus violent deaths within a community that may have resulted from a number of scenarios that could include, for example, one-to-one fighting, raiding and revenge killings. These different data may also produce quite different injury and fatality patterns that can be closely related to age or gender and include or exclude whole sections of society.[62] This brings the argument back to criticisms of Pinker's figures. The issue here is not just simply with numerical values but with the lack of information on what parts of society these figures actually represent.

Experiential qualities of violence and bioarchaeology

Despite affirmations to the contrary,[63] Pinker's account of prehistoric violence has neglected one of the most important aspects in this discussion, which is the significance of the experiential and contextual qualities of

---

[60]Roxana Ferllini, 'Recent Conflicts, Deaths and Simple Technologies: The Rwandan Case', in Knüsel and Smith (eds), *The Routledge Handbook of the Bioarchaeology*, 641–55; Christopher Knüsel and Martin J. Smith, 'The Osteology of Conflict – What Does It All Mean?', in Knüsel and Smith (eds), *The Routledge Handbook of the Bioarchaeology*, 657; My thanks to Alan Robinson for pointing this out.
[61]Knüsel and Smith, 'The Osteology of Conflict', 656–94.
[62]Linda Fibiger, 'Misplaced Childhood? Interpersonal Violence and Children in Neolithic Europe', in Knüsel and Smith (eds), *The Routledge Handbook of the Bioarchaeology*, 27–145.
[63]Pinker, *Better Angels*, 696.

any violent event. Throughout the book, Pinker refers to the impression of living in an age of violence versus the actual degree of violence present and experienced, but he fails to critically examine this question for his own work on prehistory. How did people experience life in the distant past that was their daily presence? We do not know whether the Mesolithic hunter-gatherer-fisher groups of Vedbæk viewed their lives as particularly violent, and with the still-limited Mesolithic skeletal data set available, we cannot say for certain how representative Vedbæk is of the wider European Mesolithic. Most importantly, though, it is more complex and challenging than Pinker suggests reconciling comparisons of diverse types and scale of violence occurring in chronologically and socioculturally diverse contexts. Is the immediacy of small group fighting, and its more immediate gains, more violent or cold-blooded than the mechanized wars of the twenty-first century? What are the important questions and by what standards do we judge a society more violent?

It is clear that fatality as the main measure of the extent of violence is a rather blunt and somewhat flawed tool to truly understand past violence, a reduction to something that can be measured universally through a simple number or percentage (though note the difficulties inherent in this approach as outlined in the introduction). Violent death certainly conveys an important aspect of conflict, but the true extent, cruelty and impact of violence cannot be understood without considering its aftermath, such as whether it occurred repeatedly. Injury recidivists, that is, those repeatedly sustaining injuries, may highlight sustained versus one-off exposure to violence and conflict, and reveal gender and age biases in recurring violent interactions.[64] Exploring aspects of care and treatment afforded to casualties may allow insights into societal support and social relations, and balance the picture to consider violence as process rather than event. Bioarchaeologists have most recently considered this issue through a more holistic approach that applies diagnostic criteria about the nature and impact of an injury resulting from clinical data while also considering the potential requirements of care resulting during the healing process or as a result of longer-lasting impairment.[65] A recent case study from Sweden considered cognitive and functional consequences of a traumatic head injury that would potentially have required short-term physical as well as longer-term social care. The authors conclude that 'the individual was part of a socially sustainable society where caring for the individual is a necessity for the society not to degrade'.[66]

---

[64]Redfern, *Injury and Trauma in Bioarchaeology*, 164–7.
[65]Lorna Tilley, *Theory and Practice in the Bioarchaeology of Care* (Cham: Springer, 2015).
[66]Anna Tornberg and Lars Jacobsson, 'Care and Consequences of Traumatic Brain Injury in Neolithic Sweden: A Case Study of Ante Mortem Skull Trauma and Brain Injury Addressed through the Bioarchaeology of Care', *International Journal of Osteoarchaeology*, 28 no. 2 (2018): 196.

Studies like these also help us to get away from the 'othering' we may unintentionally apply when considering the distant human past and make individual and collective experiences of violence more immediately relatable.[67] It also prevents us from falling into the trap of reducing violence to a single moment in time as manifested by a debilitating or fatal injury (Pinker's fatality count) and recognizes it as a process with significant consequences for the individual and his/her social network.

Conclusion

One could argue that many of the considerations and criticisms outlined earlier are addressing minor points of semantics that should not detract from Pinker's overarching thesis, but between the statistical and interdisciplinary shortcomings and his superficial cross-disciplinarity they do add up to a meaningful whole that should not be ignored. This has implications for Pinker's treatment not just of prehistory, but of the historic period as well. It is rather telling that Pinker's thesis, despite its prominence in both the popular and the academic sphere, does not feature prominently in archaeological or bioarchaeological/physical anthropological discourse on the nature of violence, but rather as a footnote about his misunderstanding of the complexity of the (bio)archaeological record and the identification of past lifeways.[68]

Archaeology's particularly close-up view of the past has always been inherently interdisciplinary, including the sciences and the humanities. For bioarchaeology, this can involve anatomy, palaeopathology, forensic anthropology, biomolecular chemistry, history of medicine and social anthropology, to name a few. Pinker's sweeping study, in contrast, provides a bird's-eye view that misses much of the detail. Anybody who is borrowing from, appropriating and ultimately 'colonizing' related disciplines, or indeed the distant past, should avoid postcolonial attitudes. Like the attempt to understand the meaning and motivations behind past human actions, true interdisciplinarity can indeed be a foreign country when navigated without the support and guidance of those firmly rooted in the subjects we are trying to navigate. Black and white narratives – in this case, the anarchic, prehistoric past steadily moving towards a more peaceful, civilized present – are a convenient approach to avoid outliers, variations and diversity, and offer the illusion of simplicity. Violence and conflict are anything but.

---

[67]Christoph Antweiler, 'Fremdheit, Identität und Ethnisierung: Instrumentalisierung des Anderen und ihre Relevanz für Archäologie und Ethnologie', in Tobias L. Kienlin (ed.), *Fremdheit – Perspectiven auf das Andere* (Boon: Verlag Rudolph Habelt, 2015), 25–40.

[68]Rebecca C. Redfern and Linda Fibiger, 'Bioarchaeological Evidence for Prehistoric Violence: Use and Misuse in the Popular Media', in Jane E. Buikstra (ed.), *Bioarchaeologists Speak Out: Deep Time Perspectives on Contemporary Issues* (Cham: Springer, 2018), 59–77; Knüsel and Smith, 'The Osteology of Conflict', 656–7.

8

Getting medieval on Steven Pinker

Violence and medieval England

Sara M. Butler

In *The Better Angels of Our Nature*, Steven Pinker puts forward a vision of the Middle Ages that is both grim and fearsome. He writes that '[m]edieval Christendom was a culture of cruelty' in which 'brutality' was 'woven into the fabric of daily existence'.[1] In a sketch from *Das Mittelalterliche Hausbuch* (The medieval housebook) depicting what Pinker describes as a scene from daily life, warlords terrorize the lower classes: 'a peasant is stabbed by a soldier; above him, another peasant is restrained by his shirttail while a woman, hands in the air, cries out. At the lower right, a peasant is being stabbed in a chapel while his possessions are plundered, and nearby another peasant in fetters is cudgeled by a knight.'[2] Violence pervaded every aspect of life: religion ('bloody crucifixes, threats of eternal damnation, and prurient depictions of mutilated saints'), travel ('[b]rigands made travel a threat to life and limb, and ransoming captives was big business'), domestic living ('even the little people, too – the hatters, the tailors, the shepherds – were all quick to draw their knives') and entertainment (throwing cats into bags, or beating pigs to death).[3] The government behaved no better

---

[1]Steven Pinker, *The Better Angels of Our Nature: Why Violence Has Declined* (New York: Penguin Books, 2011), 132, 1.
[2]Pinker, *Better Angels*, 65–6.
[3]Pinker, *Better Angels*, 67–8.

than its subjects. Medieval Europeans suffered 'centuries of institutionalized sadism', in which torture was practised as a cruel art and '[e]xecutions were orgies of sadism'.[4]

Admittedly, for Pinker, this hyperviolent portrayal of the Middle Ages is a usable past. He is eager to tell his audience a shocking story. Dusting off Norbert Elias' hoary thesis, Pinker sees history as a story of progress, with occasional fits and starts and some moments of distinct regression, in which humanity engages slowly but resolutely in a civilizing process. Not only have we refined our manners and hygiene (a subject upon which Pinker deliberates with glee and graphic detail) but we have learned the necessity of restraint when it comes to emotion and physical response. At the heart of this evolution is the discovery of empathy. Beginning in the Age of Reason, Pinker explains, '[p]eople began to *sympathize* with more of their fellow humans, and were no longer indifferent to their sufferings'.[5] In the twenty-first century, which Pinker describes as the Age of Empathy, our compassion extends even to the treatment of animals. As a result, according to Pinker, today we live in the most peaceful era in humanity's existence. For many, this story will seem implausible. After all, our capacity for destruction is unrivalled; in America, we hear about mass shootings on almost a daily basis; and political scientists regularly speak of the modern era as the Age of Genocide. How can it be possible that humans were ever more bloodthirsty than we are today?

To make this startling, seemingly counter-intuitive narrative a success, Pinker *needs* a barbaric Middle Ages. Indeed, without a violent point of departure, the book's central argument is untenable. Thus, it is not a surprise that Pinker discovers a barbaric Middle Ages when he goes looking. However, as I hope to demonstrate, this preposterous caricature of the medieval world depends entirely on Pinker's ignorance of the sources that inform his statistics, coupled with a meagre understanding of the medieval legal system.

The sources

Pinker's brazen confidence in his hypothesis is helped greatly by the fact that he knows nothing about the medieval era. Indeed, the very suggestion that our medieval ancestors were morally underdeveloped betrays his ignorance of the fundamentals of the Middle Ages. Medieval Christians prized charity (*caritas*), best understood as neighbourliness, as a key virtue. Men and women took seriously not only the church's Ten Commandments but also the Seven Corporal Works of Mercy, ubiquitous in the era's artwork and the basis for its acclaimed hospitality.[6] One quickly discovers that Pinker's tacit

---

[4]Pinker, *Better Angels*, 130, 132.
[5]Pinker, *Better Angels*, 133.
[6]Based on the teachings of Christ, the Seven Corporal Works enjoin good Christians to (1) feed

refusal to read the work of actual historians is a boon to his cause. Only five medieval historians have made their way into his bibliography (Geary, Groebner, Hanawalt, Kaeuper and Pérez), although their research plays a miniscule part in Pinker's historical analysis of the medieval era.[7]

To write a sensational history, you need sensational sources, and Pinker has had no difficulty finding sources about the Middle Ages that conform to his vision. His knowledge about violence in the medieval world is founded on four categories of source materials:

1. Grisly images of executions and torture devices, drawn from what Pinker refers to as 'coffee table books' about the Inquisition, as well as the website of an Italian torture 'museum' that purports to have a lofty but decidedly ahistorical goal. The museum's website declares with pride that '[t]he horror aroused in our visitors viewing the instruments allows us to make them our allies against torture'; in doing so, the exhibit 'lays bare the worst side of human nature: every man hides and holds back a potential butcher'.[8]

2. Arthurian romances, which Pinker treats as historical fact. Arthurian romances were intended to appeal to a knightly audience. A modern equivalent would be to regard the *Rambo* movies as an accurate depiction of the life of Vietnam veterans in America.

3. Bogus statistics. For the Middle Ages, Pinker draws on two highly unorthodox studies whose conspicuous titles publicize their spurious natures. In his *Great Big Book of Horrible Things*, and its accompanying website, 'Death by Mass Unpleasantness', self-proclaimed 'atrocitologist' Matthew White provides his reader with 'necrometrics' (death tolls from across history) that are at the same time improbably specific and unbelievably high.[9] Political

---

the hungry, (2) give water to the thirsty, (3) clothe the naked, (4) shelter the homeless, (5) visit the sick, (6) visit the imprisoned, or ransom the captive and (7) bury the dead.

[7]Patrick Geary, *The Myth of Nations: The Medieval Origins of Europe* (Princeton: Princeton University Press, 2002); Valentin Groebner, 'Losing Face, Saving Face: Noses and Honour in the Late Medieval Town', *History Workshop Journal*, 40 (1995): 1–15; Barbara A. Hanawalt, 'Violent Death in Fourteenth- and Early Fifteenth-Century England', *Contemporary Studies in Society & History*, 18, no. 3 (1976): 297–320; Richard W. Kaeuper, 'Chivalry and the "Civilizing Process"', in Richard W. Kaeuper (ed.), *Violence in Medieval Society* (Rochester: Boydell & Brewer, 2000), 21–35; and Joseph Pérez, *The Spanish Inquisition: A History* (New Haven: Yale University Press, 2006).

[8]For example, Robert Held, *Inquisition: A Selected Survey of the Collection of Torture Instruments from the Middle Ages to Our Times* (Aslockton: Avon & Arno, 1986), and Museo della Tortura e della Pena di Morte (San Gimignano, Italy), http://www.torturemuseum.it/en/, accessed 12 October 2017.

[9]Matthew White, *The Great Big Book of Horrible Things: The Definitive Chronicle of History's 100 Worst Atrocities* (New York: Norton, 2011). Since the writing of Pinker's book, White's website has migrated to: Matthew White, 'Necrometrics' (2010–2014), http://necrometrics.com/, accessed 7 January 2020.

scientist Rudolf J. Rummel's *Death by Government* coins the term 'democide' to describe the murderous activity of state systems. Each chapter heading takes its name from the death toll tied to a specific government (e.g. '61,911,000 Murdered: The Soviet Gulag State'; '10,214,000 Murdered: The Depraved Nationalist Regime').[10] His numbers are also inflated: Rummel claims that 350,000 Jews were killed in the Spanish Inquisition, which is 1.7 times higher than the actual Jewish population of Spain at that time.[11]

4. Flawed historical crime statistics, compiled and analysed by political scientist Ted R. Gurr and criminologist Manuel Eisner, both of whom rely on numbers furnished by medieval histories penned by James B. Given (thirteenth-century England) and Barbara A. Hanawalt (fourteenth-century England).[12] Both authors have made hyperbolic statements about the nature of violence in medieval England. Given claims that every person in thirteenth-century England, even 'if he did not personally witness a murder, knew or knew of someone who had been killed'.[13] Whereas Hanawalt argues that a person had a better chance of being murdered in medieval Oxford or London than of dying in an accident.[14] This is by far the most problematic of the four categories. While much of the other evidence, including White's and Rummel's statistics, can be easily dismissed as melodramatic nonsense, the same is not true of Gurr's and Eisner's works, which are academic in nature and which, on the surface, appear substantially more trustworthy. Nonetheless, the medieval data on which these studies are founded are inherently flawed: both Given and Hanawalt have been roundly criticized for their methodological approaches, and their statistics (although not their books) largely discredited.[15] I will elaborate on the disputes relating to their statistical usage in the following text. More important still: Gurr and Eisner have little understanding of the context from which these numbers have been plucked; Pinker has none.

[10]Rudolph J. Rummel, *Death by Government* (New Brunswick: Transaction Publishers, 1994).
[11]Pinker, *Better Angels*, 141; Helen Rawlings, *The Spanish Inquisition* (Malden: Blackwell, 2006), 48.
[12]James B. Given, *Society and Homicide in Thirteenth-Century England* (Stanford: Stanford University Press, 1977), and Barbara A. Hanawalt, *Crime and Conflict in English Communities, 1300-1348* (Cambridge, MA: Harvard University Press, 1979).
[13]Given, *Society and Homicide*, 40.
[14]Hanawalt, 'Violent Death', 302.
[15]In his review of Given's book, Hunnisett observed that his statistics 'are riddled with inaccuracies'. Roy F. Hunnisett, review of *Society and Homicide in Thirteenth-Century England*, *History*, 63, no. 209 (1978): 444–5, here 445.

The medieval numbers

Statistics are the linchpin in Pinker's analysis. They are also the bread and butter of a psychologist's research. Pinker rails against advocacy groups who use 'junk statistics' and make anecdote-driven claims; and yet, between his penchant for coffee table books and his failure to show any curiosity about the sources behind the statistics he employs, Pinker has fallen into the exact same trap.[16] Without question, Pinker's objective is praiseworthy. Tracking rates of violence over time and space holds much promise for a better understanding of the dynamics of humanity's relationship with violence, and especially discerning those social and cultural factors that drive the human species to commit violent acts. Thus, it should come as no surprise that Pinker is not the first scholar to attempt such a comparison. However, as criticisms levelled at Given and Hanawalt make clear, it is an unachievable goal. No matter how great our desire to construct practical data from medieval European sources, we cannot make them conform to our needs.

Criminologists measure violence by the number of homicides per 100,000 population per year. In an era with reliable census data, as well as solid record-keeping by the Bureau of Justice (or equivalent institutions in nations across the developed world), this approach produces reliable statistics that would seem to be an accurate reflection of modern rates of criminal violence. Yet, we need to acknowledge that the criminologist's tool was developed in response to modern data and a modern system of law. Medieval records present some insuperable obstacles, perhaps most significantly that we do not have accurate population figures for the period and estimates of population are problematic. Medieval England can serve as our example. The *Domesday Book* is as close as we can get to a medieval census, but its methodology is not conducive to population estimates. Its authors counted only heads of households, and thus dependents – women, children, singletons and the elderly, all of whom comprise a larger segment of the population than householders – are omitted. So, too, are members of religious orders and the personnel who served and lived in castles. Major cities, like London or Winchester, also do not appear in the survey. Poll tax data for three years in the fourteenth century likewise exist, but they suffer from many of the same complications.[17] Granted, none of this deterred Given from calculating estimates for his 1977 book, presumably the reason why both Gurr and

---

[16]Pinker, *Better Angels*, 401, 403.

[17]To offer some insight: in 1948, Josiah Cox Russell created population estimates for English cities using the 1,377 poll tax evidence. His estimates led many to believe that historians had exaggerated the impact of the Black Death. Russell's use of poll tax evidence supported a figure of 20 per cent population loss for the initial outbreak. See Josiah Cox Russell, *British Medieval Population* (Albuquerque: University of New Mexico Press, 1948), 198. No historian today would endorse such a low death rate.

Eisner have found his research so enthralling. Given's enterprise produces figures that are 'little more than guesswork', as mentioned by one critic.[18]

The deficit of population figures is just one impediment to producing crime rates for the medieval era. The corpus of medieval records is at best fragmentary, and it is not clear just what proportion of the records the extant rolls represent. For the county of Hampshire, for example, Carrie Smith explains that we have the reports of twelve coroners for the reigns of Edward III and Richard II, even though the Close Rolls (official collections of royal letters sent under seal) reveal that there were an additional forty-seven coroners elected during that seventy-two-year period.[19] Coroners' enrolments were created with a distinct purpose: they acted as a check on the work of the jurors of the so-called Hundreds Courts (an administrative unit of a county), who were fined if they failed to report any criminal activity. Thus, once the rolls fulfilled their purpose, they were cancelled and, one suspects, disposed of accordingly.[20] It is not clear why some records survive, nor is it possible to determine if the extant rolls are typical, or whether we should assume that they survived because there was something exceptional about them.[21]

To complicate matters further, the same case regularly appears multiple times in the surviving record, representing the defendant's progress through the various stages of the judicial process. In order to avoid inflating the numbers, it is necessary to identify and group all existing records relating to the same crime. However, even in an Excel spreadsheet sorted in manifold patterns, locating those cases can be a challenge largely because of medieval naming practices. For England, standardized names are a product of the post-medieval era. While some medieval men and women identified in the records do have established surnames, many others do not, such that a defendant in the common law records might be identified by his occupation ('John Smith'), by his village of origin ('John of Appletreewick'), by his current residence ('John Bythebrook'), in relation to his father ('John son of John Cook'), in relation to his mother ('John son of Maud widow of John the Cook') or by a defining characteristic ('Blind John'). Recognizing that all of these Johns are actually the same person entails a great deal of patient rereading of minute details, not aided in the least by the fact that standardized spelling was also an invention of the modern era. None of

---

[18]Edward Powell, 'Social Research and the Use of Medieval Criminal Records', *Michigan Law Review*, 79, no. 4 (1981): 967–78, here 975.

[19]Carrie Smith, 'Medieval Coroners' Rolls: Legal Fiction or Historical Fact?', in Diana E. S. Dunn (ed.), *Courts, Counties and the Capital in the Later Middle Ages* (New York: St. Martin's Press, 1996), 97–8.

[20]David Crook, *Records of the General Eyre*, Public Record Office Handbooks, no. 20 (London: Public Record Office, 1982), 36.

[21]For a more detailed discussion of medieval coroners' rolls, see Roy F. Hunnisett, *The Medieval Coroner* (Cambridge: Cambridge University Press, 1961), chap. 6.

this means that statistics drawn from medieval sources are unusable; rather, it means that they are always accompanied by a number of caveats which may (or may not) weaken the force of an argument. More important still, it makes comparisons with modern statistics untenable; medieval statistics simply lack the comprehensiveness and precision that defines modern record-keeping.

Even if we had accurate population totals, and all records had survived and were legible, we would still find ourselves in trouble. Given and Hanawalt based their data on indictments rather than verdicts. The reason why they chose this approach is understandable. Nearly 72 per cent of criminal perpetrators in medieval England fled, and because the English relied on communal policing – all males over the age of fourteen swore to police the community and each other – they were never tried.[22] Thus, trial verdicts represent an insignificant share of the crimes perpetrated. Calculating rates is further complicated by the fact that medieval juries were notoriously reluctant to convict. Conviction rates for homicide ranged between 12.5 per cent and 21 per cent (compared to a rate of 97.1 per cent for American criminal cases in 2015).[23] Leery of the death penalty, medieval juries typically saw indictment itself as a worthy punishment for most offenders because it meant time in prison awaiting trial, along with the discomfort and expense of a prison stay, as well as lost income and potentially irreparable damage to one's reputation within the community.[24] Knowing this, it makes sense that Given and Hanawalt preferred indictments rather than convictions for comparative analysis. Yet, this puts us in the difficult situation of comparing apples and oranges.

We have high standards today for indictment: even if the state's prosecutors have met the legal requirements for the evidentiary bar, they might still fail to convince a grand jury of the defendant's guilt, preventing the case from going forward to trial. At the level of the grand jury, medieval England's legal system had a substantially different process and standards. Foremost, medieval grand jurors were not impartial strangers summoned to court to assess evidence presented to them by a team of paid lawyers. Rather,

---

[22]Bernard William McLane, 'Juror Attitudes toward Local Disorder: The Evidence of the 1328 Trailbaston Proceedings', in James S. Cockburn and Thomas A. Green (eds), *Twelve Good Men and True* (Princeton: Princeton University Press, 1988), 36–64, here 56.

[23]John G. Bellamy, *The Criminal Trial in Later Medieval England* (Buffalo and Toronto: University of Toronto Press, 1998), 69; Patti B. Saris, et al., 'Overview of Federal Criminal Cases Fiscal Year 2015' (Washington, DC: United States Sentencing Commission, June 2016), 4, http://www.ussc.gov/sites/default/files/pdf/research-and-publications/research-publications/2016/FY15_Overview_Federal_Criminal_Cases.pdf, accessed 6 January 2017.

[24]Susanne Pohl-Zucker makes a similar statement for late medieval Württemberg and Zurich. Being indicted of a criminal offence brought one into contact with the executioner (whether the individual was executed or not), which 'shamed' the defendant and his family. See her *Making Manslaughter: Process, Punishment and Restitution in Württemberg and Zurich, 1376-1700* (Leiden: Brill, 2017), 93.

this group of twelve to twenty-four men of middling rank were the victims' neighbours and (most likely) social superiors, whose job it was to report crimes that had taken place in their community since the last judicial eyre. Their knowledge of local criminal activity derived predominantly from the complaints of private informants, rumours and local suspicions; moreover, unlike what we see in Roman-based law, there were no firm rules of evidence guiding either grand or petty jurors in their deliberations. All that was necessary was a unanimous verdict of the jury and how it got there remains a mystery for historians. Given the ease of accusation, it is no surprise that the English courts deemed malicious indictment a serious enough problem to necessitate the development of a specialized writ and accompanying juridical process.[25] Indeed, in the thirteenth century, false accusations of homicide were a popular tool employed by appellors (private prosecutors) to browbeat individuals into an out-of-court settlement in a death that may have been criminal; of course, it may also have been accidental, yet in a manner by which the family held the defendant accountable. Yearning for compensation rather than punishment, an astute accuser launched an appeal (private accusation) only after negotiations had stalled, as a means to draw the offender back into a productive conversation. Once the two reached an agreement, the accuser abandoned his appeal. The high numbers of appellors who failed to pursue their suits through to completion – according to Daniel Klerman, 57 per cent discontinued their appeals before the case even reached the eyre – attest to the efficacy of a false homicide charge to pushing through a successful out-of-court settlement.[26] False appeals became so common that the 1275 Statute of Westminster mandated a year's imprisonment for those who bring a false appeal of homicide or any other felony. This bold misuse of the accusation process, grossly inflating the numbers of accused criminals, contributes to the impracticality of a medieval/modern statistical comparison.

The loose requirements for formal accusations, when combined with a somewhat rudimentary investigative process founded on paltry resources, surely suggest that some of those acquitted were in fact innocent of the charges. Given the high rate of flight, those few who stuck around to stand trial likely chose to do so because (1) they were innocent or (2) they were guilty, but not enough so to be condemned by a jury of their peers to death. Either way, if we rely on indictments rather than convictions in our statistical analysis, we end up in the uncomfortable situation experienced by Given and Hanawalt of 'find[ing] the accused guilty *even if he has been acquitted*'.[27]

In addition, advances in modern medicine undoubtedly have had a weighty impact on rates of lethal violence. As Paul E. Hair remarked in his 1979 review of Given's book, in medieval England 'corpses were often produced by incidents which nowadays would simply lead to visits to a doctor or short spells in hospital'.[28] To name just a few wonders of the modern medical world that we take for granted: knowledge of germ theory and the value of surgical hygiene, blood transfusions, surgery with anaesthetics, X-ray and ultrasound technologies, antibiotics, and pain relief. Most people who are shot or stabbed today survive; the same was not true in the Middle Ages. Without anaesthetics, surgery intended to heal sent some patients into shock. Without antibiotics, festering wounds turned fatal. Even more problematic, medical theory of the time understood infection as a key stage in the healing process. If a wound did not infect naturally, English surgeons were advised to contaminate it in order to speed the process along.[29] And what about infanticide? The medieval world knew nothing about sudden infant death syndrome (SIDS), which today claims as many as 92.6 deaths per 100,000 live births per year.[30] Philip Gavitt contends that deaths by SIDS in the late medieval era were routinely mistaken for smothering deaths blamed on wet nurses.[31] The medieval church's repeated warnings about the dangers of 'overlaying' (accidentally smothering) one's child also need to be taken into consideration here. Where historians once saw overlaying as a 'polite fiction for deliberate infanticide', more recently those deaths have been reconsidered as unintentional, a by-product of the dangers of co-sleeping on uneven surfaces (straw beds), in buildings with poor ventilation systems.[32] Clearly, the differences in medical knowledge and technology alone make a statistical comparison between the two eras unworkable.

The greatest hurdle in assessing rates of crime (not just homicide) for medieval England is the simple fact that we cannot take medieval indictments

---

[27]Powell, 'Social Research', 969; emphasis in original.

[28]Paul E. Hair, review of *Society and Homicide in Thirteenth-Century England*, *Population Studies*, 33, no. 1 (1979): 196–7, here 196.

[29]R. Theodore Beck, *The Cutting Edge: Early History of the Surgeons of London* (London: Lund Humphries, 1974), 12. Whether to infect the wound was a subject of some controversy. See Carole Rawcliffe, *Medicine and Society in Later Medieval England* (London: Sandpiper Books, 1995), 74.

[30]Center for Disease Control and Prevention, 'Sudden Unexpected Infant Death and Sudden Infant Death Syndrome', US Department of Health and Human Services, https://www.cdc.gov/sids/data.htm, accessed 7 January 2020.

[31]Philip Gavitt, 'Infant Death in Late Medieval Florence: The Smothering Hypothesis Reconsidered', in Cathy Jorgensen Itnyre (ed.), *Medieval Family Roles: A Book of Essays* (New York: Garland, 1996), 137–57.

[32]Sara M. Butler, 'A Case of Indifference: Child Murder in Later Medieval England', *Journal of Women's History*, 19, no. 4 (2007): 59–82, here 67–8.

at face value. Private accusers frequently employed legal fiction as a strategy to work around the limitations of a rigid common law. To offer two typical examples:

(1) In general, litigants preferred the impartial justice and speedy resolution of the king's court to local judgement. Thus, they subtly enhanced the nature of their accusations in order to have their cases adjudicated by the king's justices. Asserting that it was a breach of the king's peace (*contra pacem*), that an assault transpired with force and arms (*vi et armis*) or that a theft exceeded 40 shillings in value were recognized legal fictions exercised to bring one's case into the king's jurisdiction.[33]

(2) Use of the 'bill of Middlesex' is perhaps the most widely acknowledged legal fiction. In order to have one's case of debt brought before the King's Bench (a substantially more efficient option than the Court of Common Pleas), the accused fabricated a suit for criminal trespass within Westminster, where the King's Bench had criminal jurisdiction as the local court. Once the defendant was in prison, the fictitious suit was dropped altogether, and the accuser moved forward with a suit of debt before the King's Bench.[34] In both of these situations, the criminal allegations were baseless.[35]

Private accusers were not alone in manipulating the law. When juries believed that the circumstances of a homicide did not warrant the death penalty, they were content to adapt the details of the record to secure a pardon. Thus, under the supportive guidance of the indicting jury, the man

---

[33]Stroud F. C. Milsom, 'Trespass from Henry III to Edward III', *Law Quarterly Review*, 74 (1958): 195–224, here 222–3; Michael Lobban, 'Legal Fictions before the Age of Reform', in Maksymilian Del Mar and William Twining (eds), *Legal Fictions in Theory and Practice* (Heidelberg: Springer, 2015), 199–223, here at 200.

[34]Stroud F. C. Milsom, *Historical Foundations of the Common Law* (London: Butterworths, 1969), 54–9.

[35]The medieval English were not the only Europeans at this time to fabricate crimes. In her analysis of late medieval French fear of crime, Claude Gauvard argues that 'litanies' of crimes were often inserted into political propaganda to make it more difficult for the king to pardon political felons. For example, in 1411, Armagnac mercenaries were said to have 'set fires, ransacked churches, kidnapped, killed, mutilated, raped married women and young girls and did all the evil anyone could do' (9). While these lists of crimes came to life in a political setting, they were typically incorporated into formal statements issued by the crown regarding a felon's death sentence. Moreover, when it comes to political crimes committed during the Hundred Years' War, these litanies were highly formulaic; the same lists appear over and over. How should a historian address these litanies when it comes to creating a statistical database? Which crimes did the convict actually commit? See Claude Gauvard, 'Fear of Crime in Late Medieval France', in Barbara A. Hanawalt and David Wallace (eds), *Medieval Crime and Social Control* (Minneapolis: University of Minnesota Press, 1999), 1–48.

who discovered his wife in flagrante with another man and then swiftly hacked the lover to death was transformed into a victim backed into a corner, lashing out only when he had no alternative because his life was in imminent danger.[36] Alteration of the facts of the case did not happen in all or even most indictments. Yet, without a side-by-side comparison of the case details across the legal record (from inquest to indictment to trial) – an accomplishment that is rarely possible because of the poor survival rate of records – there is no way to discern whether jurors tampered with the facts of the case. Legal fiction also pervades accusations of rape levelled against medieval England's clergy. Disgruntled with the inability of their parish clergy to live out their vows of celibacy, angry parishioners took the law into their own hands by accusing them of rape. In doing so, the accusers knew full well that their unruly priests would not be executed as criminals. A convicted cleric claimed 'benefit of clergy', an exemption from trial in the king's courts; instead, he had a right to be tried by his own peers, that is, fellow clergymen.[37] Thus, he was removed from the king's courts to the bishop's, where the list of punishments did not include execution because of the prohibition enjoined on the clergy not to shed blood. Rather, in the bishop's court, a randy clergyman would have to answer with penance for his (albeit consensual) sexual transgressions, which was in fact the purpose of indicting him in the first place.[38]

To make the situation even more complicated, crimes then did not necessarily mean the same thing as they do today. Take the crime of rape, for example. The Latin verb used to describe the crime of 'rape' is *rapio, rapere*, which means 'to seize'. Building on this broader sense of the term, the legal indictments employ it chiefly in two scenarios: (1) coitus without consent and (2) ravishment, that is, non-consensual abduction. In both cases, the consent at issue was not necessarily the victim's, but her husband's or her father's. The former category sometimes also included headstrong women who chose to marry against their fathers' will.[39] In the latter situation, most women had not only consented to their abductions but had their bags packed and were ready to go.[40] Indeed, all too often a woman's 'rapist' was a family

---

[36]Thomas A. Green, *Verdict According to Conscience: Perspectives on the English Criminal Trial Jury, 1200-1800* (Chicago: University of Chicago Press, 1985), 42–3.

[37]Only men could claim benefit of clergy. The right was not extended to women – not even nuns – until the seventeenth century.

[38]Robin L. Storey, 'Malicious Indictments of Clergy in the Fifteenth Century', in Michael J. Franklin and Christopher Harper-Bill (eds), *Medieval Ecclesiastical Studies: In Honour of Dorothy M. Owen* (Woodbridge: Boydell, 1995), 221–40.

[39]James A. Brundage, 'Rape and Marriage in the Medieval Canon Law', in James A. Brundage (ed.), *Sex, Law and Marriage in the Middle Ages* (Aldershot: Variorum, 1993), 62–75, here 74.

[40]Sue Sheridan Walker, 'Punishing Convicted Ravishers: Statutory Strictures and Actual Practice in Thirteenth- and Fourteenth-Century England', *Journal of Medieval History*, 13, no. 3 (1987): 237–49, here 238.

member helping her to leave an abusive marriage.[41] Close attention to the indictment's language can help us to discern which 'rapes' also comprised sexual assault. Presenting juries included 'lexical doublets', a phrase coined by Caroline Dunn, such as *rapuit et cognovit carnaliter* ('he raped her and carnally knew her') versus *rapuit et abduxit* ('he raped and abducted her') to clarify the nature of the offence.[42] However, all of the other aforementioned problems are still associated with the existing records.

Other offences that we today would categorize as criminal belonged in the medieval world to a more loosely defined civil jurisdiction and thus were not recorded among the crown pleas. Drawing blood, affray, assault, wounding, riot and mayhem[43] might be sued in a wide variety of courts, and thus appear scattered among the civil jurisdictions of local, royal and ecclesiastical courts. Criminal jurisdiction also failed to include those crimes perpetrated against or involving the clergy. Thus, any study concentrating exclusively on records of felony drawn from the king's courts cannot offer a complete picture of medieval violence.

Pinker has never seen a medieval court record, nor does he understand how the law worked in the Middle Ages. Therefore, it is no surprise that none of the aforementioned is factored into his discussion of the medieval numbers. When he measures medieval against modern statistics, he has no idea that they are measuring very different things; without valid statistics, Pinker's entire argument falls apart. He cannot maintain that violence has declined since the Middle Ages because we have no real evidence to prove that it has. Indeed, it is not at all clear just how violent the Middle Ages actually were.

The historiographic context

In Pinker's mind, convincing his audience of the brutality of the Middle Ages is somehow a herculean endeavour; yet, for medievalists, the more usual complaint is the seemingly natural conflation between 'medieval' and 'barbaric'. In large part, this is because Elias, while new to Pinker, is certainly not new to historians.[44] Elias' theory of the civilizing process is one of the foundational texts for studies of historical violence and has been re-energized through new conceptualizations multiple times since its publication

---

[41]Sara M. Butler, *Divorce in Medieval England: From One to Two Persons in Law* (New York: Routledge, 2013), 66–71.

[42]Caroline Dunn, *Stolen Women in Medieval England* (Cambridge: Cambridge University Press, 2013), 33.

[43]'Mayhem' was defined as the permanent maiming of an individual so that he was no longer able to defend himself.

[44]Pinker describes Norbert Elias as 'the most important thinker you have never heard of'. Pinker, *Better Angels*, 59.

in 1939 and translation into English in 1969. Without a doubt, the most thought provoking has been Michel Foucault's *Discipline and Punish: The Birth of the Prison* (1975). Foucault raised the stakes considerably, seeing medieval monarchies wielding terror as a tool of state building. In order to compel resistance to the ever-increasing reach of centralized government, the state sponsored public spectacles of violence, stamping punishment on the bodies of those who failed to show adequate respect when faced with authority.[45] Foucault's work does not appear in Pinker's bibliography; yet, with the book's focus on democide, his shadow hangs heavily over the study.

Grappling with Foucault's equally sensationalist and ahistorical views over the past forty-five years has prompted medievalists to question just how accurate his, and Elias', perception of the medieval era actually is. No one disagrees with the view that the medieval world was violent: it was. Medieval sermon stories regularly depict God taking out his vengeance upon man by spreading disease, brewing up storms, setting fires to homes and villages, and causing sudden death. Focus on the crucifixion and the suffering of Christ encouraged widespread self-violence among adherents, from starvation to flagellation and more, as the life of Henry Suso, a doctor of the church who slept on a bed of nails and wore a life-sized cross fastened to his back for a period of eight years, implies.[46] The church did not waver in assigning flogging or prison terms to a penitent when the nature of the sin required it. Secular law prescribed public hanging, burning, blinding and castration for felonies, and clergymen heartily recommended all devout Christians attend executions as a deterrent from choosing a criminal lifestyle. If violence is a learned trait, medieval men certainly learned it at home, as husbands were expected to govern their wives, children, and servants with a firm hand.[47] Yet, all of this is still a far cry from the budding panopticism outlined by Foucault.

The medieval historical community's response to Foucault's thesis might have warned Pinker off from writing his book, had he made the effort to read any of it.[48] Foucault's history is a paradigm of the danger inherent in arguing from theory rather than evidence, leaving his work open to scrutiny by archival scholars who have not hesitated to call attention to the yawning chasm between Foucauldian theory and actual historical experience. In reality, violence in the Middle Ages was hardly a 'spectacle'. The English sent only the most hardened criminals to their deaths. 'Hangman' was not

---

[45]Michel Foucault, *Discipline and Punish: The Birth of the Prison*, trans. Alan Sheridan (New York: Pantheon Books, 1977).

[46]For more on Henry Suso, see chapter 12 of Jerome Kroll and Bernard Bachrach, *The Mystic Mind: The Psychology of Medieval Mystics and Ascetics* (New York: Routledge, 2005).

[47]Sara M. Butler, *The Language of Abuse: Marital Violence in Later Medieval England* (Leiden: Brill, 2007).

[48]Trevor Dean provides an excellent step-by-step refutation of Foucault's *Discipline and Punish*. See chap. 6 of his *Crime in Medieval Europe* (Harlow: Longman, 2001).

even a profession in medieval England, as there was not enough work to keep a man employed.[49] Nor did the medieval English stand out from the rest of Europe in this respect. As Trevor Dean acknowledges, Europeans generally evinced a 'horror of spilling blood in punishment', such that 'when blood was spilt, it had be justified by the exceptional nature of the crime: especially inhuman acts, re-offending, a grave threat to public morality'.[50] Far from the 'orgies of sadism' that Pinker describes in such vivid detail, medieval executions were 'commonly hole-in-corner affairs, with few witnesses'; and because executions were typically staged at the gates to the city as a warning to visitors, any message regarding the power of the state bypassed the residents of the city altogether.[51] Perhaps most importantly, for those in attendance, rather than delighting in the pain of the executed, they participated in a heart-rending salvific drama intended to reconcile the penitent with the Christian community before death.[52] Treason trials were the one exception to the rule. They were intended to be gruesome in order to deter any future rebels from taking up the torch.[53] When Dafydd ap Gruffydd was executed, he was drawn to the site of execution, his entrails were burned while he was still alive, he was hanged, beheaded and then quartered, and his body parts were dispersed throughout England to be displayed as a warning.[54] However, only a handful of political traitors received this kind of treatment over the course of the Middle Ages, again, falling short of Pinker's imaginative bar.

Even the use of torture in the medieval period was tamer than either Foucault or Pinker present. It is important to note that the English did not employ torture, but during the thirteenth century, some Continental courts revived the Roman practice, exclusively for the purpose of extracting a confession, not as a punishment itself, as Pinker writes.[55] Torture was not part of the normal legal process; rather, it was a last resort, for those instances in which the defendant was presumed guilty, but the evidence did

---

[49]Henry Summerson, 'Attitudes to Capital Punishment in England, 1220-1350', in Michael Prestwich, Richard Britnell, and Robin Frame (eds), *Thirteenth Century England VIII: Proceedings of the Durham Conference 1999* (Woodbridge: Boydell, 2001), 123–33, here 128.

[50]Dean, *Crime in Medieval Europe*, 125.

[51]Summerson, 'Attitudes to Capital Punishment', 130. The statistics confirm that residents had few executions to attend. Between 1387 and 1400, Parisian Parlement heard more than 200 criminal cases, of which 4 ended in execution. See Patricia Turning, *Municipal Officials, Their Public, and the Negotiation of Justice in Medieval Languedoc: Fear not the Madness of the Raging Mob* (Leiden: Brill, 2013), 139.

[52]Trisha Olson, 'The Medieval Blood Sanction and the Divine Beneficence of Pain: 1100-1450', *Journal of Law and Religion*, 22, no. 1 (2006): 63–129.

[53]Katherine Royer, *The English Execution Narrative: 1200-1700* (London: Pickering and Chatto, 2014).

[54]Katherine Royer, 'The Body in Parts: Reading the Execution Ritual in Late Medieval England', *Historical Reflections*, 29, no. 2 (2003): 319–39, here 328–9.

[55]Pinker, *Better Angels*, 146.

not meet the *ius commune*'s high evidentiary standards of two eyewitnesses, or a confession. Furthermore, the law set restrictions on its implementation: torture was only to be used in capital crimes; the defendant was not to be maimed or killed; a physician had to be present at all times; torture might not be applied for longer than it takes to say a prayer; and so on.[56] When it came to the legal treatment of heretics or witches, crimes of a particularly worrying nature, a loosening of the rules inevitably transpired, but the inquisitor was not given carte blanche to do as he pleased.

Nor was violence directed chiefly at the body. Foucault rationalizes the use of corporal punishment by the medieval judicial system as a product of the feudal economy. With 'money and production . . . still at an early stage of development', in its search for meaningful punishment, the state settled on the body as 'the only property accessible'.[57] Pinker seems to be broadly in agreement with this thesis. Admittedly, the law codes of the era bolster this impression. As far back as the twelfth-century *Leis Willelme*, English law prescribed castration and blinding for rape, treason, poaching and a miscellany of other crimes. Yet, when put into context, a more lenient approach is discernible. Physical mutilation was devised as a merciful alternative to capital punishment, but finding instances outside of literature in which these penalties were actually carried out is not as easy as one might think.[58] More typically, the violence enacted by the state targeted one's purse, although even those sentences might be set aside when problematic, such as in instances of peace agreements, claims of poverty and confessions.[59] Even Robert Muchembled, whose own history of early modern violence mirrors much of what Pinker and Foucault have had to say, is compelled to recognize the non-violent punishments handed down by the medieval state, in which 'judicial fines were at the heart of the system'.[60] For readers of Elias, Foucault and Pinker, fines and compensation are a much less 'sexy' means of punishing offenders, but it was an effective means of law enforcement.

None of this historiography is meant to suggest that historians have unanimously rejected Elias, Foucault or Pinker. Among early modernists, in particular, there is a strong contingent of supporters for the view that society has become increasingly less violent over time, most recently: Robert

---

[56]Edward Peters, *Torture* (Philadelphia: University of Pennsylvania Press, 1985), chap. 2.

[57]Foucault, *Discipline and Punish*, 25.

[58]This is also true of the Continental sources. See Joanna Carraway Vitiello, *Public Justice and the Criminal Trial in Late Medieval Italy: Reggio Emilia in the Visconti Age* (Leiden: Brill, 2016), 164–5.

[59]Daniel Lord Smail, 'Violence and Predation in Late Medieval Mediterranean Europe', *Comparative Studies in Society and History*, 54, no. 1 (2012): 7–34; Vitiello, *Public Justice and the Criminal Trial*, 163.

[60]Robert Muchembled, *Le temps des supplices de l'obéisance sous les rois absolus, XVe-XVIIIe siècle* (Paris: Armand Colin, 1992), 28.

Muchembled (2011),[61] James Sharpe (2016)[62] and Matthew Lockwood (2017).[63] What do early modernists see in theories of decreasing violence that medievalists are missing? The explanation may well lie in the intensifying nature of violence in the sixteenth and seventeenth centuries. Much of the violence that has often been associated wrongly with the medieval world was in fact early modern. For example, flogging was not a penalty inflicted by the medieval state; rather, it was first introduced to common law courts under Henry VIII's 1530 Vagabonds Act (22 Hen. VIII, c. 12) as a deterrent for vagrancy. Parliament must have found the penalty effective because sixteenth- and seventeenth-century legislation expanded its application to include also bastard-bearing, begging, drunkenness, sex offences and even lunacy.[64] To be sure, the Tudor regime pioneered a wide variety of new forms of punishment bordering on the cruel and unusual. Under Henry VII, Parliament established human branding as a penal practice: a statute of 1487 required those who claimed benefit of clergy to be branded on the thumb with a T (thief) or an M (murderer) as a means of ensuring that the body of a convicted felon announced publicly his criminal past (in this respect, the convict effectively carries his 'paperwork' on his body). Sixteenth- and seventeenth-century officials enlarged the functionality of the practice, employing branding to signpost a broad diversity of criminal backgrounds: A (abjuror), V (vagabond), F (fraymaker) or B (blasphemer), with the brand itself appearing variously on the offender's thumb, cheek, forehead or chest. Nailing an offender's ear to the pillory was also a Tudor innovation. Convicted of seditious libel for spreading rumours about the death of the king, Thomas Barrie's infamous demise in 1538 from shock after standing on the pillory in the marketplace of Newbury for a day, both ears bored through with nails, would seem to be the first identifiable instance.[65] Removal of one's ears and hands materialized as a punishment for numerous crimes also during the reign of Henry VIII. Additionally, the notorious king was responsible for the introduction of indentured slavery and death by boiling. During his daughter Elizabeth's reign, Parliament passed a statute prescribing the cropping of ears and slitting of nostrils for those who engage in forgery.[66] English common law's increasingly violent

---

[61]Robert Muchembled, *A History of Violence: From the End of the Middle Ages to the Present* (London: Polity Press, 2011).
[62]James Sharpe, *A Fiery & Furious People: A History of Violence in England* (London: Arrow Books, 2016).
[63]Matthew Lockwood, *The Conquest of Death: Violence and the Birth of the Modern English State* (New Haven: Yale University Press, 2017).
[64]Guy Geltner, *Flogging Others: Corporal Punishment and Cultural Identity from Antiquity to the Present* (Amsterdam: Amsterdam University Press, 2014), 64–5.
[65]P. H. Ditchfield and William Page (eds), *A History of the County of Berkshire*, vol. II (London: Victoria County History, 1907), 93–4.
[66]Krista J. Kesselring, *Mercy and Authority in the Tudor State* (Cambridge: Cambridge University Press, 2003), 26–40.

punishments may have been patterned on a Continental trend. In the German world, the *Constitutio Criminalis Carolina* (c. 1532) 'paved the way for increased use of judicial torture and corporal punishment', an inclination that Guy Geltner observes also for the early modern French and Dutch.[67] Surely, judicial experimentation on such a grand scale reflects widespread tensions arising from the countless ills afflicting the early modern world: religious reformation, the witch craze, episodic outbreaks of plague and the sweating sickness, endemic war, and economic depression. Early modernists entrenched in this trying age presumably see everything that comes after it as a breath of fresh air. Of course, from the perspective of a medievalist, the mere existence of this period is enough to scotch Pinker's linear view of history.

Conclusion

What rankles medievalists most about Steven Pinker's book is that he is not particularly interested in the Middle Ages. Rather, the era is simply a starting point from which to apply a well-worn historical theory while adding his own psychological twist. However, in doing so, Steven Pinker dabbles in making history, without bothering to acknowledge that it is a discipline with its own rules and methods. One can imagine that Pinker might empathize with the historian's outrage if an amateur psychologist without even a rudimentary exposure to psychological theory tried to rebuild the pedestal from which Sigmund Freud had fallen years ago. Nevertheless, in this respect, historians need to acknowledge that Pinker is not the problem; he is merely a symptom. Among even educated people today, history is not often understood as a concrete discipline requiring training and experience, like physics or mathematics. Historians have not worked hard enough to convey to the world what we do: in particular, we do not just read the work of other historians and regurgitate it from a slightly different angle. In my case, being a historian means spending days and weeks in distant, sometimes inaccessible, archives, reading grimy, handwritten and abbreviated documents in Latin or Anglo-Norman Law French; reading reams upon reams of historians' work to make sure that I understand how my perspective fits in with theirs (or not); and being able to perform the historical analysis that makes sense of everything I read in the archives.

Despite the dubious nature of Pinker's history, the response to his book has an important lesson for historians: Pinker's message is reaching the masses, and ours is not. Why aren't academic histories read as voraciously as their popular counterparts in North America? Surely, *that* is the question we need to address next.

---

[67]Geltner, *Flogging Others*, 64–5.

9

History, violence and the Enlightenment

Philip Dwyer

In chapter four of *The Better Angels of Our Nature*, Steven Pinker explains one of the reasons why we live in the most peaceful era in human history. It all happened, not only in the West but in much of the rest of the world, during a 'narrow slice of history' from the late seventeenth century to the end of the eighteenth. He is referring to the period known as the Enlightenment, during which 'the first organized movements to abolish socially sanctioned forms of violence like despotism, slavery, duelling, judicial torture, superstitious killing, sadistic punishment, and cruelty to animals, together with the first stirrings of systematic pacifism', all came into being.[1] Institutionalized violence – by which Pinker means human sacrifice, torture and the persecution of heretics and witches – began to be questioned by Enlightenment thinkers, which led to the rapid abolition of those institutions.[2]

This change was not only inspired and driven by ideas – for Pinker, the Enlightenment was a 'coherent philosophy' – but also by a revolution in sensibilities, as people began to *sympathize* (Pinker's italics) and were no longer 'indifferent' to the suffering of others. These two forces – reason and sympathy – coalesced to form a 'new ideology' that placed 'life and happiness at the center of values', one that resulted ultimately in the triumph of 'reason' over superstition. The triumph of reason – which Pinker defines

---

[1]Steven Pinker, *The Better Angels of Our Nature: Why Violence has Declined* (New York: Allen Lane, 2011), xxiv, 133. My thanks to my colleague and co-editor Mark Micale for his incisive comments, and to Elizabeth Roberts-Pedersen for her helpful suggestions.
[2]Pinker, *Better Angels*, 180, 183.

as the 'application of knowledge and rationality to human affairs' – was ultimately responsible for the overall reduction in violence. Once reason triumphs, then its opposite, ignorance and superstition, will disappear. Ideas that 'gods demand sacrifices, witches cast spells, heretics go to hell, Jews poison wells, animals are insensate, children are possessed, Africans are brutish, and kings rule by divine right' are bound to be debunked as 'hogwash', thus undermining any rationale for violence.[3] This is what Pinker calls 'progress'. 'Reason' enables; indeed, it can *force* people to 'recognize the futility of cycles of violence' and to 'reframe violence as a problem to be solved'.[4]

This is the ur-statement, if you will, at the heart of *Better Angels*, the assertion that violence is a problem, that it is irrational and that it can be solved by applying rational thought. The mantra of 'reason' is not only used by Pinker as a historical explanation but carried over into his professional life. Pinker thus sets himself up, contra his critics, as the 'voice of reason', never more clearly expressed than in the book that appeared at the beginning of 2018, *Enlightenment Now: The Case for Reason, Science, Humanism, and Progress*. Written in part as a response to critics of *The Better Angels*, Pinker presents himself as the guardian of the values of the Enlightenment, because no one else was 'willing to defend them'.[5] Consider the hubris of that statement for a moment. Pinker has appointed himself the defender of the Enlightenment, seemingly discounting the many scholars who have dedicated years of their lives to researching, writing and explaining to broader audiences the meaning and significance of the Enlightenment.[6]

Like all polemicists bent on proving a point, there is just enough in these statements to lend them the air of credibility. Indeed, there are assertions that some not well versed in the historiography of the Enlightenment may agree with. But as I hope to demonstrate in what follows, Pinker mischaracterizes the history of the Enlightenment and what it actually represented. It was never a 'coherent philosophy' that remained unchallenged by thinkers in the eighteenth century, let alone in the twentieth. By presenting the Enlightenment as the era of 'reason' and humanism, he also mischaracterizes the Counter-Enlightenment by pitting ideologies like Jacobinism, Nazism and Bolshevism

---

[3]Pinker, *Better Angels*, 645.

[4]Pinker, *Better Angels*, xxvi.

[5]Andrew Anthony, 'Steven Pinker: "The way to deal with pollution is not to rail against consumption"', *The Guardian*, 11 February 2018, https://www.theguardian.com/science/2018/feb/11/steven-pinker-enlightenment-now-interview-inequality-consumption-environment.

[6]Apart from the oeuvre of Peter Gay, scholars who defend the Enlightenment, in a literature that consists of hundreds of books, include the following: Gertrude Himmelfarb, *The Roads to Modernity: The British, French, and American Enlightenments* (New York: Knopf, 2004); Tzvetan Todorov, *In Defense of the Enlightenment*, trans. Gila Walker (London: Atlantic Books, 2009); Anthony Pagden, *The Enlightenment: And Why It Still Matters* (Oxford: Oxford University Press, 2013), which admittedly appeared after Pinker's first book, and which is briefly mentioned in *Enlightenment Now*.

as the opposite of reason. This means that Pinker essentially argues that the Enlightenment = reason = a decline in violence, whereas the Counter-Enlightenment = a rejection of reason = an increase in violence. But as we shall see, those equations ignore a number of important historiographical questions, including debates about violence and modernity.

Finally, Pinker's ideas about reason and causation in history are naïve. The notion that ideas drive history is contentious, if not impossible, to prove, while the reasons some forms of violence diminished, like homicide and torture, are often tied to mundane practical reasons. Homicide and the use of judicial torture by European powers began to decline well before the second half of the eighteenth century, that is, well before Enlightenment thinking could have had any impact on the statistics. On the other hand, other forms of violence, like slavery, public executions and sexual assaults, persisted throughout the nineteenth and into the twentieth century. Although there has been a change in sensibilities towards some forms of violence over the course of the last 200 years, there is no demonstrable correlation between those sensibilities and actual rates of violence. Violence is a much more complex notion that is often driven not by superstition or unreason, but perfectly 'rational' motives, as the Nazis demonstrated to the world. In other words, one cannot clearly delineate between the rational and the irrational in human motivations.

Pinker's Enlightenment

Pinker's idea of the Enlightenment is a somewhat old-fashioned, if not simplistic, view of what was a vast and complex intellectual movement that persisted from the late seventeenth through to the early nineteenth century. In his understanding, the Enlightenment is a uniquely Western European development originating in the Renaissance and the Reformation. It was born of the experimental scientific culture that emerged out of Europe in the seventeenth and eighteenth centuries, and that was then exported to the rest of the world. One of Pinker's main arguments is that the Enlightenment embraced science, and in the process rejected religion or faith. It's an old chestnut, a simplified understanding of a complex process, that completely ignores the multifaceted role of religion and the Enlightenment, but I will come back to this point a little later in the chapter.[7] There is tacit acknowledgement of the diversity of Enlightenment thought, although in places Pinker contradicts himself about what exactly was the Enlightenment. At one point in *Enlightenment Now*, for example, Pinker calls it 'a

---

[7]See, Jonathan Sheehan, 'Enlightenment, Religion, and the Enigma of Secularization: A Review Essay', *American Historical Review*, 108 (2003): 1061–80, for an overview of the recent debates on the relationship between religion and the Enlightenment.

cornucopia of ideas, some of them contradictory', while at another he describes it as a coherent 'project'.[8] In an interview published in *Quillette*, an online magazine probably best described as right-wing 'contrarian', Pinker admitted that he used '"the Enlightenment" as a handy rubric for [a] set of ideals'.[9] Those *ideals* (Pinker's italics) are reason, science, and humanism. He then goes on to say, 'For all I know, if Voltaire or Leibniz or Kant stepped out of a time machine and commented on today's political controversies, we'd think they were out to lunch'. Which begs the question, what are those 'ideals' again?[10] If they are universal and timeless, then why would we think they were 'out to lunch'?

What is obvious in reading Pinker is that he seems utterly unaware of the massive historiography, spread across many disciplines – history, literature, politics, the history of science, sociology and economics – which have all adopted the Enlightenment as an object of study. In the last decade or two, the Enlightenment has been examined from all sorts of different perspectives – gender, the role of women, science, race, sexuality as well as geographical foci – leaving us with a far more complex view of it. The field is hugely contested and debated; it is not the fixed entity that Pinker seems to think it is. The works of Roger Chartier, Robert Darnton, Peter Gay, J. G. A. Pocock, Roy Porter, Daniel Roche and Franco Venturi, to mention some of the more mainstream intellectuals who write or have written about the Enlightenment, do not get a mention. Nor does Jonathan Israel's massive multi-volume treatment of the Enlightenment, which now spans seven volumes. Israel's views are contested but is difficult to avoid in any debates on the Enlightenment without mentioning him. This is, one might argue, par for the course; Pinker is not an historian, and like most people, the debates raging inside historical circles remain opaque, while the advances in the history of the Enlightenment over the last fifty years or so have seemingly failed to make a dent in mainstream understandings of the Enlightenment.

Much of what we once took for granted in the Enlightenment has been overturned. There is now a focus on the multiplicity of Enlightenments centred on national, confessional, regional and conceptual differences – the French, American, Austrian, English, Scottish, German, Islamic Enlightenment and so on. Nevertheless, the Eurocentric view of the Enlightenment has been widely questioned as the global turn has been applied to our understanding

---

[8]Steven Pinker, *Enlightenment Now: The Case for Reason, Science, Humanism, and Progress* (New York: Penguin Books, 2019), 8.

[9]"Steven Pinker: Counter-Enlightenment Convictions are "Surprisingly Resilient"', *Quillette Magazine*, 20 April 2018, https://quillette.com/2018/04/20/steven-pinker-counter-enlightenment-convictions-surprisingly-resilient/.

[10]A point also made by Aaron R. Hanlon, 'Steven Pinker's New Book on the Enlightenment Is a Huge Hit: Too Bad It Gets the Enlightenment Wrong', *Vox*, 17 May 2018, https://www.vox.com/the-big-idea/2018/5/17/17362548/pinker-enlightenment-now-two-cultures-rationality-war-debate.

of the eighteenth century so that we think of it today as also transnational, made up of different thinkers from different places around the world, all responding to global movements and trends.[11] Enlightenment scholarship has also produced a number of thematic books in recent years on the radical, religious, moderate, Catholic and secular Enlightenments.[12] There is also an acknowledgement that the significance of the Enlightenment changed over time so that what it meant in the eighteenth century was not the same as in the nineteenth or indeed in the twentieth century. Moreover, the views of eighteenth-century Enlightenment thinkers were necessarily very different to our own on a whole range of issue such as politics, free speech and tolerance.[13]

Nor does Pinker's understanding of the Enlightenment appear to be based upon an extensive reading of the primary sources. It's true that Pinker references some of the Enlightenment thinkers, such as Rousseau and Kant, as well as some conservative thinkers, such as Edmund Burke and Johann Gottfried Herder. Others like Locke, Spinoza, Newton, Voltaire, Montesquieu, Diderot and Beccaria are mentioned in places, but their work is often not specifically referred to. In other words, Enlightenment (and Counter-Enlightenment) thinkers are harnessed in the service of Pinker's own agenda. In the process, he passes over the nuances of the debates – and they are always complex – that took place during the Enlightenment, leading him to posit, as we shall see, a false dichotomy between science and religion, and reason and emotion.

The Enlightenment and violence

Pinker's ignorance of the scholarship might be forgiven if the Enlightenment was not *the* foundation stone around which he builds his case for declining rates of violence in the world in the modern era. It is also inexcusable in someone who sets himself up as the main defender of the Enlightenment.

---

[11]For an overview of recent scholarly trends, see Charles W. J. Withers, *Placing the Enlightenment: Thinking Geographically about the Age of Reason* (Chicago: University of Chicago Press, 2007), 1–6, 41; Sebastian Conrad, 'Enlightenment in Global History: A Historiographical Critique', *The American Historical Review*, 117, no. 4 (2012): 999–1027; and Annelien de Dijn, 'The Politics of Enlightenment: From Peter Gay to Jonathan Israel', *The Historical Journal*, 55, no. 3 (2012): 785–805.

[12]Margaret C. Jacob, *The Secular Enlightenment* (Princeton: Princeton University Press, 2019); Ulrich L. Lehner, *The Catholic Enlightenment: The Forgotten History of a Global Movement* (Oxford: Oxford University Press, 2016); David Sorkin, *The Religious Enlightenment: Protestants, Jews, and Catholics from London to Vienna* (Princeton: Princeton University Press, 2008); Jonathan Israel, *Radical Enlightenment: Philosophy and the Making of Modernity, 1650-1750* (Oxford: Oxford University Press, 2001).

[13]Dan Edelstein, *The Enlightenment: A Genealogy* (Chicago: University of Chicago Press, 2010), 52–60.

In *The Better Angels*, Pinker uses the Enlightenment to explain his putative decline in rates of violence. The question in fact, without Pinker ever really realizing it, revolves around causation in history: What drives history, and what drives changes in attitudes and practices? It is a question with which historians have grappled for generations. For Pinker, however, the answer is clear – ideas drive history and are responsible for the reduction in violence.[14]

There are two problems with this kind of thinking. The first is the difficulty, if not the impossibility, of demonstrating a causal link between reading, thinking and action. Pinker is assuming causality where arguably none exists, which in this instance is that Enlightenment thinking, based on reason, led to a reduction in violence, which to his mind is essentially irrational. To believe that one event or idea necessarily leads to another completely underestimates the complexity of history, and of reading and the internalization process.[15] Pinker is, admittedly, not entirely alone in this way of thinking, especially when it comes to the eighteenth century, and especially when it comes to the French Revolution. Scholars have fought over these points for decades.[16] Lynn Hunt, for example, has argued in a recent work that there is a correlation between empathy and our ability to imagine other cultural experiences, and that this would have contributed to a diminution in violence.[17] She goes so far as to argue that reading novels, and in particular epistolary novels, as well as 'reading accounts of torture', 'had physical effects that translated into brain changes'. These in turn 'came back out as new concepts about the organization of social and political life'.[18] Put another way, Hunt thinks that in order to account for historical change, historians have to account for changes to the individual mind, which could be put this way: reading (and listening) creates new understandings, which create new feelings, which engender change (an assertion she admits is difficult to prove or measure). Pinker largely adopts Hunt's arguments,

---

[14]Pinker, *Better Angels*, 477.
[15]Timothy Tackett, *The Coming of the Terror in the French Revolution* (Cambridge, MA: Belknap Press, 2015), 29–30, 33–8.
[16]Robert Darnton, 'An Enlightened Revolution?', *New York Review of Books* (24 October 1991), 33–6, put the question a little differently – 'how did the cultural system of the Old Regime contribute to the political explosion of 1789?' Roger Chartier, *Les Origines culturelles de la Révolution française* (Paris: Seuil, 1990), 86–115, posed the question differently again, 'Do books make revolutions?' Before Darnton, the same question was asked of the American Revolution by Bernard Bailyn, *The Ideological Origins of the American Revolution* (Cambridge, MA: Belknap Press, 1967). Decades before that, Daniel Mornet, *Les origines intellectuelles de la Révolution française, 1715-1787* (Paris: Armand Colin, 1933), argued that the intellectual origins of the Revolution could not simply be about books (*purement livresques*).
[17]Lynn Hunt, *Inventing Human Rights: A History* (New York: W. W. Norton and Co., 2006), 32.
[18]Hunt, *Inventing Human Rights*, 33.

reiterating that the increase in secular books and literacy rates helped set off the Humanitarian Revolution.[19]

Jonathan Israel is another scholar who believes that ideas drive history. He argues that what he calls the radical Enlightenment – democratic, republican and atheist thought – was 'incontrovertibly the one "big" cause of the French Revolution'.[20] Ideas alone according to Israel, were capable of inspiring the leaders of the Revolution on a political level. Both Hunt and Israel's views are highly contested. As a number of leading lights on the origins of the French Revolution have pointed out, discourses do not necessarily shape practices.[21] Some would argue that history changes thinking; thinking does not change history. Pinker presumes that ideas precede action – it serves his purpose – but it is impossible to prove that ideas impel change.

These debates typify the broader conundrum of determining causality in history. All sorts of other factors – social, political, economic – have to be taken into account when explaining why certain kinds of violence might have disappeared or declined, but others not. Along with thinking that the Enlightenment was responsible for a decline in violence is the assumption that humanist reformers were motivated by concern over the suffering of their fellow human beings, or indeed that the humanitarian movements of the eighteenth and nineteenth centuries should even be credited with the overthrow of things like public executions and slavery. But was that necessarily the case? The sources of change, according to some historians, have been entirely misidentified. It was not humanitarianism but other more pragmatic and far less idealistic reasons that came into play and that helped bring about changes in the practice of violence. Let me focus on three examples – torture, public executions and slavery – that demonstrate the impact of mundane practical factors, rather than lofty ideals, on some forms of violence and that also suggest alternative and more complex chronologies for its decline in the West.

The spectacle of the publicly tormented body was part and parcel of social life in Europe, at least before the French Revolution. European legal codes were inspired by ancient Roman traditions, which relied on torture for evidence. In France, there were two kinds of torture: 'preparatory torture', which took place in judicial chambers and which was designed to extract confessions; and 'preliminary torture', which took place in public on the body of the convicted criminal and which was designed to either extract

---

[19]Pinker, *Better Angels*, 172–7.
[20]Jonathan Israel, *Revolutionary Ideas: An Intellectual History of the French Revolution from the Rights of Man to Robespierre* (Princeton: Princeton University Press, 2014), 708.
[21]Roger Chartier, 'The Chimera of the Origin: Archaeology, Cultural History, and the French Revolution', in Jan Goldstein (ed.), *Foucault and the Writing of History* (Oxford: Blackwell, 1994), 175–7; Keith Michael Baker, *Inventing the French Revolution: Essays on French Political Culture in the Eighteenth Century* (Cambridge: Cambridge University Press, 1990), 5.

confessions or simply punish the convicted body.[22] Either way, there was a deep-seated belief in the interrelatedness of body, pain and truth in what Lisa Silverman has called the 'epistemology of pain'.[23]

This is meant to have shifted in the eighteenth century, when attitudes towards pain, death, violence and suffering supposedly changed. At least that was the commonly held view, largely influenced by Foucault's 1975, *Discipline and Punish*, which argued that sovereign power used the body as a stage on which to perform violence, such as spectacular public executions, in order to reinforce its legitimacy. This violence gave way to another kind of disciplinary power – prisons, barracks, schools and factories. I'm simplifying a complex argument that has inspired a generation of scholars, but we now think that Foucault didn't entirely get it right. It's true that between 1750 and 1850 imprisonment replaced most other punishments but there is a debate about whether this was due to the Enlightenment or whether it was due to earlier changes in the criminal justice system itself, brought about by legal reforms. Certainly, both torture and rates of execution were already declining in Europe during the seventeenth century, a period during which the utility of corporal punishment began to be called into question and states developed other more effective forms of social control. But to attribute that decline to the Enlightenment is, as John Langbein as pointed out, a 'fairy tale'.[24]

Langbein and others argue that European criminal procedure evolved much earlier, in the sixteenth and seventeenth centuries, and had to do with changing attitudes towards the law of proof, the legal history of infamy and the development of new criminal sanctions, including incarceration, which no longer required a confession be obtained by force. It's true that torture was officially abolished in most Western European countries between 1754 and 1788, but with a few exceptions this appears to have been largely symbolic.[25] In practise, torture had largely ceased to be used

---

[22]Lela Graybill, *The Visual Culture of Violence After the French Revolution* (London: Routledge, 2016), 11.

[23]Lisa Silverman, *Tortured Subjects: Pain, Truth, and the Body in Early Modern France* (Chicago: University of Chicago Press, 2001), 51–68.

[24]John H. Langbein, *Torture and the Law of Proof: Europe and England in the Ancien Régime* (Chicago: University of Chicago Press, 1977), 45–69; Bernard Schnapper, 'Les Peines arbitraires du XIIIe au XVIIIe siècle: Doctrines savantes et usages français', *Tijdschrift voor Rechtsgeschiedenis/Legal History Review*, 41, nos. 3–4 (1973): 237–77, and 42, nos. 1–2 (1974): 81–112; and John H. Langbein, 'The Legal History of Torture', in Sanford Levinson (ed.), *Torture: A Collection* (Oxford: Oxford University Press, 2006), 93–103. Response to Langbein in Edward Peters, *Torture*, expanded edn (Philadelphia: University of Pennsylvania Press, 1996). Lynn Hunt thinks that Langbein overstates his case (Lynn Hunt, 'The Paradoxical Origins of Human Rights', in Jeffrey N. Wasserstrom, Lynn Hunt and Marilyn B. Young (eds), *Human Rights and Revolutions* (Lanham: Rowman and Littlefield, 2007), 16–17, n. 25).

[25]Peters, *Torture*, 89–91; Langbein, 'The Legal History of Torture', 98–9. A few German states were slow on the uptake, with Baden abolishing torture in stages between 1767 and 1831. Hunt, *Inventing Human Rights*, 75–6; Langbein, *Torture*, 61–4, 177–9.

in many European countries by the seventeenth century. The last use of judicial torture in England, for example, occurred in 1640. France seems to have been an exception; although torture largely fell into disuse, it was still practised on occasion until it was officially abolished by the monarchy in 1788. The French revolutionaries felt the need to abolish it again in 1791, not because it was considered an atrocity but because it was inextricably linked with the 'social assumptions of absolutism'.[26]

Of course, it doesn't really make a difference whether torture is legal or not; if the state deems it necessary, it will use it. In Sweden, torture was never legal but was probably practised in the sixteenth and early seventeenth centuries.[27] It is naïve, therefore, to think, as Pinker seems to, that because torture has been abolished, it is no longer a problem. Despite a 1987 United Nations Convention Against Torture, which has been ratified by 130 countries, torture, or at least the 'cruel, inhuman or degrading treatment' covered by the Convention, is still practised in 141 countries around the world, including by the United States, Britain and Israel.[28] In other words, torture is almost universally condemned, and almost universally practised. Some have even attempted to justify its use with the theory of 'just torture'.[29]

As for public and sometimes spectacular capital punishments that historians often like to describe in great detail, the right of the state to use violence, and in some instances extreme forms of violence like breaking on the wheel and burning at the stake, was never really questioned by Enlightenment thinkers, let alone the public at large. Voltaire's famous *Treatise on Tolerance* – written after the death of Jean Calas, tortured and broken on the wheel – did not protest against the cruelty of the punishment, but rather against the religious bigotry that led to Calas' condemnation in the first place (Calas was a Protestant in as majority Catholic country). Certainly, the taste for viewing public executions and displayed bodies does not appear to have waned during the eighteenth and nineteenth centuries.[30] On the contrary, there is a good deal of evidence to suggest that executions were popular, or that at the very least they were capable of attracting large

[26]Graybill, *The Visual Culture of Violence*, 27.

[27]My thanks to Heikki Pihlajamäki for this.

[28]Amnesty International, 'Torture', https://www.amnesty.org/en/what-we-do/torture/; Oona Hathaway, 'The Promise and Limits of the International Law of Torture', in Levinson (ed.), *Torture*, 199–212, who finds that those who have ratified the treaty often behave worse than those who have not.

[29]Shunzo Majima, 'Just Torture?', *Journal of Military Ethics*, 11, no. 2 (2012): 136–48. See also, Michael Walzer, 'Political Action: The Problem of Dirty Hands', in Levinson (ed.), *Torture*, 61–76.

[30]See, Richard J. Evans, *Rituals of Retribution: Capital Punishment in Germany, 1600-1987* (London: Penguin, 1996), 135, 214, 193–6, 225–6; and Mark Hewitson, *Absolute War: Violence and Mass Warfare in the German Lands, 1792-1820* (Oxford: Oxford University Press, 2017), 128–31.

crowds, from across all social classes, well into the nineteenth century.[31] In Breslau in 1811, for example, thousands of locals flocked to see the publicly displayed corpses of recently executed victims.[32]

In France, executions were often carried out on the so-called 'justice days', which coincided with market days, in order to ensure a good turnout of people.[33] The guillotine, introduced in 1792 as a much more rational, efficient and humane form of killing, was meant to demonstrate just how enlightened were the French revolutionaries.[34] Executions attracted large crowds in France until it was largely hidden from public view from around 1870, and officially in 1939.[35] In the town of Béthune in northern France in 1909, for example, as many as 30,000 people gathered to watch the execution of the Pollet gang, who had terrorized the countryside for years. The crowds came from the surrounding region, including from Paris, as well as from Belgium and Germany. The French cinema company, Pathé Actualités, filmed and screened executions, including the Pollet gang, until 1909 when they were finally banned by the authorities.[36]

In London, right up to 1868 when public executions were finally banned (and not in 1783, as Pinker incorrectly writes), large crowds in the tens of thousands would also regularly turn out to watch hangings. And there were quite a few occasions in which to do so. At the same time that Enlightenment values were coming into their own, the English Parliament increased the number of crimes punishable by death fivefold, from about 50 in 1688 to about 240 in 1820.[37] Of course, many were able to avoid execution so that the number that occurred between 1770 and 1830 declined to a 'relatively modest' 7,000. In London, levels of execution appear to have been connected to moral panics about crime. In the first few decades of the nineteenth century, executions were taking place more frequently than any time since the Stuarts.[38] It is hardly something that can be reconciled with an

---

[31]Matthew White, '"Rogues of the Meaner Sort"? Old Bailey Executions and the Crowd in the Early Nineteenth Century', *The London Journal*, 33, no. 2 (2008): 135–53.

[32]Evans, *Rituals of Retribution*, 226.

[33]Graybill, *The Visual Culture of Violence*, 7.

[34]Daniel Arras, *La Guillotine* (Paris: Flammarion, 1987), 25–54.

[35]Emmanuel Taïeb, *La guillotine au secret. Les exécutions publiques en France, 1870-1939* (Paris: Belin, 2011).

[36]Albert Montagne, 'Crimes, faits divers, cinématographe et premiers interdits français en 1899 et 1909', *Criminocorpus*, http://journals.openedition.org/criminocorpus/207, accessed 18 August 2020.

[37]Simon Devereaux, 'The Promulgation of the Statutes in Late Hanoverian Britain', in David Lemmings (ed.), *The British and their Laws in the Eighteenth Century* (Woodbridge: Boydell Press, 2005), 85–6; Sharpe, *A Fiery & Furious People*, 393, 394, 396.

[38]Simon Devereaux, 'Execution and Pardon at the Old Bailey, 1730-1837', *American Journal of Legal History*, 57 (2017): 447–94; idem., 'The Bloodiest Code: Counting Executions and Pardons at the Old Bailey, 1730-1837', *Law, Crime and History*, 6 (1, 2016): 1–36; idem., 'Inexperienced Humanitarians? William Wilberforce, William Pitt, and the Executions Crisis of the 1780s', *Law and History Review*, 33 (2015): 839–85; idem., 'England's "Bloody Code"

'enlightened' attitude that was supposedly driving judicial and legal reform in the eighteenth and nineteenth centuries.

But here is the rub. By the 1830s, the system of capital punishment had more or less collapsed in England, and the number of executions and public hangings declined sharply. Why this was so remains one of the big questions in English penal history. Historians have suggested that this was largely due to a humanitarian reform movement, brought about in part by a change in sensibilities.[39] It is entirely possible that shifting attitudes had a role to play, but concern among the ruling elites about the behaviour and attitudes of the populace, as well as a belief that the condemned were no longer abiding by the preordained, Christian rituals, also had a role to play.[40] English observers considered the crowds who gathered to watch hangings to be far too turbulent and far too gay. It was the behaviour of the crowd along the processional route in London from Newgate prison to Tyburn, the traditional site of public executions, that was particularly concerning; the civil authorities feared that they had lost control of the process. It was one of the reasons why in 1783 public hangings were relocated from Tyburn to the front of Newgate prison. It was thus hoped that by containing the size of the crowd, public order would be restored. That was not to be; there were recurring incidents of crowd disorder. In 1849, Charles Dickens wrote to *The Times* after witnessing the hanging of Frederik and Maria Manning, railing not against the death penalty but rather against 'the wickedness and levity of the immense crowd'.[41]

The point is that changes were born of a complicated mixture of elements: changes in judicial processes, fear of the rabble at a time when the revolutionary potential of the mob was very much alive, as well as shifting cultural values – crowds had become indifferent to the spectacle of violence, or to put it another way, violence in 'progressive' societies no longer resulted in the required pedagogical outcome. This is not to say that crowds had lost

---

in Crisis and Transition: Executions at the Old Bailey, 1760-1837', *Journal of the Canadian Historical Association*, 24/2 (2013): 71–113; idem., 'Recasting the Theatre of Execution: The Abolition of the Tyburn Ritual', *Past & Present*, 202 (February 2009): 127–74.

[39]V. A. C. Gatrell, *The Hanging Tree: Execution and the English People, 1770-1868* (Oxford: Oxford University Press, 1994), 21, argues that the numbers of people being condemned to death and those being executed reached such alarming proportions that the system became 'unworkable and unbearable', but his explanation for the collapse of the system is wanting.

[40]The suffering victim was meant to imitate the suffering Christ, and thereby gain salvation through some sort of stoic acceptance of his fate. Punishment, then, was a ritual of. redemption. See, Paul Friedland, *Seeing Justice Done: The Age of Spectacular Capital Punishment in France* (Oxford: Oxford University Press, 2012), 91; Mitchel B. Merback, *The Thief, the Cross and the Wheel: Pain and the Spectacle of Punishment in Medieval and Renaissance Europe* (London: Reaktion Books, 1999), 19–20. This religious interpretation of executions has been contested by Pascal Bastien, *L'exécution publique a Paris au XVIIIe siècle: Une histoire des rituels judici-aires* (Seyssel: Champ Vallon, 2006).

[41]*The Times*, 13 November 1849. My thanks to Una McIlvenna for pointing this out.

interest in visible acts of brutality by the time the nineteenth century had come about. On the contrary, if the size of the crowds is anything to go by, it was evident that they were still very much fascinated by the spectacle of death.

Finally, let me briefly talk about slavery and the abolition movement. Slavery was built upon the omnipresence of violence. Indeed, it can only exist through the constant practice or fear of violence in order to maintain the slave population in servitude. We have no clear notion of whether levels of violence on the plantation increased in the course of the eighteenth century, but it was during this period, that is, in the decades after 1760, that the slave trade reached a peak. The French slave trade actually peaked in the years 1783–92/3, only to be interrupted by the outbreak of war between revolutionary France and the rest of Europe.[42] It's true that slavery was criticized by a number of French Enlightenment thinkers (Montesquieu, Raynal, Voltaire, Condorcet), but not usually for the ill-treatment meted out to the enslaved, or on moral grounds (as did Montesquieu). For some French Enlightenment thinkers, man was everywhere in chains; slavery was not qualitatively different to other forms of 'tyranny', the major preoccupation of thinkers at the beginning of the French Revolution.[43] This was different in England, where the Evangelical tradition, especially that of the Quakers, was at the forefront of the anti-slavery movement. Religion played an enormous role in England, and eventually in France, in the abolitionist movement, but the arguments against slavery were as much economic as moral. An effective argument had to be made that the abolition of slavery would not cost jobs and have an adverse impact on the economy.[44]

Even when it was abolished, illegal slavery continued to do a roaring trade, at least until around 1831, when France stepped up its measure against slavers. Illegal slavery was an open secret in many European ports, while slaving vessels continued to ply their trade between Africa and the Americas well into the 1880s.[45] A recent analysis of various cases of abolition around the world reveals the extent to which other motives, shrouded in the cloak of humanitarianism, played a role.[46] Ultimately, the abolition of slavery, as

---

[42]James A. Rawley, with Stephen D. Behrendt, *The Transatlantic Slave Trade: A History* (Lincoln: University of Nebraska Press, 2005), 15, 111, 113.

[43]Daniel P. Resnick, 'The Société des Amis des Noirs and the Abolition of Slavery', *French Historical Studies*, 7, no. 4 (1972): 558–69, here 561.

[44]Resnick, 'The Société des Amis des Noirs', 563–4; Alan Forrest, *The Death of the French Atlantic: Trade, War, and Slavery in the Age of Revolution* (Oxford: Oxford University Press), 109–11.

[45]Forrest, *The Death of the French Atlantic*, 248, 250–69; Marika Sherwood, 'The British Illegal Slave Trade, 1808-1830', *British Journal for Eighteenth-Century Studies*, 31, no. 2 (2008): 293–305, here 298–300.

[46]Hideaki Suzuki, 'Abolitions as a Global Experience: An Introduction'; and Benaz A. Mirzai, 'The Persian Gulf and Britain: The Suppression of the African Slave Trade', in Hideaki Suzuki (ed.), *Abolitions as a Global Experience* (Singapore: NUS Press, 2015), 7–9, and 113–29.

David Brion Davis wrote many years ago, has to do as much with political, economic and ideological motives as it does with humanitarian concerns.[47] There were certainly strong links between the abolition of slavery and the humanitarian movement, but other drivers also played a role and have to be taken into account. The British naval campaign against slavery from the mid-nineteenth century was motivated by a desire to enforce abolition, yes, but was also driven by the British desire to control the seas, as well as by a personal desire on the part of many navy captains for prize money. A 'bounty' was paid for every slave taken from a vessel. Between 1810 and 1828, the Royal Navy received over £570,000 in 'bounty' for captured slaves.[48] And we can always rely on the capitalist system to fill the void left by the abolition of the slave trade. When labour needs could no longer be met by slavery, other forms of bondage increased, targeting in particular workers in India and China in what became known as the 'coolie trade'. Within ninety years of the British abolishing slavery in 1807, more than 2 million people had become indentured labourers.[49] Even worse was the example of the Congo, where, between 1880 and 1920, around 10 million people were murdered, worked and starved to death. Pinker acknowledges this as a genocide, but not as a form of slave labour, which it patently was. Even the ending of slavery in the United States led to many being re-enslaved by another name right up to the 1940s.[50]

The rational and irrational in history

Just as Pinker mischaracterizes the Enlightenment, so too does he mischaracterize the Counter-Enlightenment, and he does so in much the same way, that is, by using outdated ideas and sources. In the case of the Counter-Enlightenment, Pinker relies on the Latvian-born British philosopher, Isaiah Berlin, who, writing in the late 1970s, was one of the first to popularize the term, 'Counter-Enlightenment', a twentieth-century invention.[51] Scholars have moved well beyond Isaiah Berlin's work to more

---

[47]David Brion Davis, *The Problem of Slavery in the Age of Revolution, 1770-1823* (Ithaca: Cornell University Press, 1975), 49.

[48]Sherwood, 'The British Illegal Slave Trade', 294.

[49]David Northrup, *Indentured Labor in the Age of Imperialism, 1834-1922* (Cambridge: Cambridge University Press, 1995), 156–61.

[50]Douglas A. Blackmon, *Slavery by Another Name: The Re-Enslavement of Black People in America from the Civil War to World War II* (New York: Doubleday, 2008).

[51]Isaiah Berlin, *Against the Current: Essays in the History of Ideas* (London: Hogarth Press, 1979), esp. 1–24. See, Eva Piirimäe, 'Berlin, Herder, and the Counter-Enlightenment', *Eighteenth-Century Studies*, 49, no. 1 (2015): 71–6. See also, Joseph Mali and Robert Wokler (eds), *Isaiah Berlin's Counter-Enlightenment* (Philadelphia: American Philosophical Society, 2003).

complex understandings of the 'Counter-Enlightenment',[52] but as is Pinker's wont, he doesn't take this into account, either because it doesn't suit him or because he simply hasn't read the literature. It's probably a bit of both, an example of the kind Daniel Smail talks about, of Pinker entering someone's house with muddy boots and acting in a bad manner by arrogantly sticking his feet on the table.

The Counter-Enlightenment is generally seen as either a movement among Christian writers who believed that the French *philosophes* were bent on the destruction of all religion or simply a movement that was in opposition to the Enlightenment. For Isaiah Berlin, as it is for Pinker, it was definitely the latter, a rejection of the principles of the Enlightenment, including objectivity and rationality.[53] The debate between enemies and advocates of the Enlightenment is hardly new. It dates back to at least the middle of the eighteenth century but was really sustained by two world shattering periods in time – the French Revolution and the Second World War (or more precisely, the violence of the two world wars, including the Bolshevik Revolution). As a result, thinkers essentially asked the same question of both events: Where did it all go wrong? For conservative thinkers in the first half of the nineteenth century reacting to the French Revolution, the answer was obvious, it was the fault of Rousseau. For radical thinkers in the second half of the twentieth century reacting to the Holocaust, the answer was just as obvious, it was the fault of Rousseau.[54]

I am simplifying things of course, but it exemplifies in some ways how people can arrive at the same conclusion from two diametrically opposed ideological positions. Early nineteenth-century conservative thinkers and radical twentieth-century thinkers, both grappling with extreme violence and what it meant to be 'modern', were wary of placing reason on a pedestal. In the decades after the Second World War, some argued that the Enlightenment had led to Nazism and Bolshevism. It is a criticism that first emerged out of Jacob Talman's 1952 book, *The Origins of Totalitarian Democracy*, which blamed the Enlightenment for the ideas that led to Hitler and Stalin. No one takes Talman's work very seriously today, in part because of the demolition job that Peter Gay carried out on it, but even Gay was unable to convince German intellectuals like Max Horkheimer and Theodor

---

[52]Darrin M. McMahon, *Enemies of the Enlightenment: The French Counter-Enlightenment and the Making of Modernity* (Oxford: Oxford University Press, 2001); Graeme Garrard, *Counter-Enlightenments: From the Eighteenth Century to the Present* (London: Routledge, 2005); Zeev Sternhell, *The Anti-Enlightenment Tradition*, trans. David Maisel (New Haven: Yale University Press, 2010).

[53]Pinker, *Better Angels*, 186; Isaiah Berlin, 'The Counter-Enlightenment', in Henry Hardy (ed.), *Against the Current: Essays in the History of Ideas* (New York: Penguin, 1982), 19–20. Berlin believes that he coined the term, but Sternhell, *The Anti-Enlightenment Tradition*, 3, shows that it was in existence at least fifteen years before.

[54]For a more detailed analysis of the debates, see Dijn, 'The Politics of Enlightenment', 787–8.

Adorno, who, writing in the 1960s, argued that totalitarianism was the result of rationalism taken to its extreme, so that the Enlightenment led to the Holocaust.[55] Zygmunt Baumann is probably the best-known proponent of the thesis that the Holocaust was deeply rooted in modern, Western civilization.[56]

This too is no longer taken very seriously by scholars, but at its heart, as already mentioned, people were questioning where 'progress', or to put it another way, where 'modernity' had gone wrong, that is, why a movement that was ostensibly based on reason could lead to the Terror, and to the horrors of the twentieth century. This goes to the heart of Pinker's own personal world view. He rejects the powerful illiberal current in Enlightenment thinking that includes, in the West at least, Jacobinism, Bolshevism and Nazism, all political ideologies that at their core believed humans and human society could be improved through violent means. They all not only advocated but practised violence in a methodical way to bring about revolutionary change in society. Pinker, on the other hand, cannot countenance the idea that there was a link between, ideology, the 'invention of reason', and 'reason' being used for violent ends, because for him violence is necessarily irrational.

That is, I would argue, to misunderstand the fundamental nature of violence. Violence serves a purpose and a function, no matter how 'irrational' or 'barbaric' or 'savage' an act might appear to the outside observer. This is as much the case today as it was in the past. Let me give you two (among countless) examples of how a seemingly irrational act of violence can be carried out in a cold, calculating way with rational objectives in mind.

During the 1947–8 war, which led to the creation of the state of Israel, a number of massacres were carried out by Jewish and Israeli forces, as well as a number of rapes and murders of Palestinian women. In addition, somewhere between 450 and 500 Palestinian villages were simply wiped off the face of the map. We know this because of the work of a group of what have been dubbed New Historians, Israelis who have challenged traditional views of history, the most prominent of whom is Benny Morris, whose study of the 1948 war is based on a massive archival study of largely Jewish sources.[57] As a result of those massacres and rapes, hundreds of thousands of Palestinians left their homes, often in fear of what might occur to them. It's an example of the use of massacre, seen throughout history, which might appear irrational from the outside, but which has a clearly defined purpose.

---

[55]A good summary of the anti-Enlightenment trend is in Hunt, 'The Paradoxical Origins of Human Rights', 4–5.

[56]Zygmunt Bauman, *Modernity and the Holocaust* (Cambridge: Polity Press, 1990). For a critique of this approach see, Marsha Healy, 'The Holocaust, Modernity and the Enlightenment', *Res Publica*, 3, no. 1 (1997): 35–59.

[57]Benny Morris, *1948: A History of the First Arab-Israeli War* (New Haven: Yale University Press, 2008).

Another example is the case of rape in warfare, which has, arguably, become much more systematic today than in previous centuries. In Mozambique, soldiers often forced local men to watch them raping women; the ritual mutilation of victims is carried out by cutting off noses, breasts, penises and so on; parents are constrained to maim or kill their children, to cook and eat them prior to their own execution.[58] They are all 'rational' and calculating techniques designed to instil terror into populations, and thereby prevent them from engaging in organized resistance. At the heart of attempts to understand human motivation behind violence is a question that can be asked of all political ideologies that descend into terror – what makes ordinary people choose violence?[59]

Of course, the process is complicated; it is not just about understanding rhetoric and ideas but also of placing them in their social and political context. A better line of questioning in my view is not to equate violence with the irrational but to posit whether reason can be 'irrational'? Can 'reason', however one defines it, lead to a reduction in violence, as Pinker maintains? Can 'reason' ever really be decoupled from irrational impulses? A number of scholars, using recent advances in the neurosciences, have sought to demonstrate that traditional divisions between 'reason' and 'emotion' are no longer tenable, and that emotions exert a significant impact on decision-making processes.[60]

Religion is an interesting example, something that Pinker rejects as a superstition. It's a common enough misconception, one that scholars held for many years, namely that the Enlightenment was by its very nature secularizing and therefore anti-religious. According to this view, thanks to the newly acquired capacity for science and critical thinking, people discarded religion in favour of rational thought. This we know was not the case; the Enlightenment never rejected sentiments and the passions, and was deeply imbricated in contemporary religious views, as well as, for some at least, delving into the occult through movements such as mesmerism and the *convulsionnaires*, people who congregated in cemeteries where they seemingly became possessed and went into ecstatic spasms.[61] By equating

---

[58]See, for example, K. B. Wilson, 'Cults of Violence and Counter-Violence in Mozambique', *Journal of Southern African Studies*, 18, no. 3 (September 1992): 527–82; and John Keane, *Violence and Democracy* (Cambridge: Cambridge University Press, 2004), 54–65.

[59]The question has motivated books as diverse as Marisa Linton, *Choosing Terror: Virtue, Friendship, and Authenticity in the French Revolution* (Oxford: Oxford University Press, 2013); and Christopher R. Browning, *Ordinary Men: Reserve Police Battalion 101 and the Final Solution in Poland* (New York: HarperCollins, 1992); and more recently Thomas Pegelow Kaplan, Jürgen Matthäus and Mark W. Hornburg (eds), *Beyond 'Ordinary Men': Christopher R. Browning and Holocaust Historiography* (Leiden: Ferdinand Schöningh, 2019).

[60]See, for example, Rose McDermott, 'The Feeling of Rationality: The Meaning of Neuroscientific Advances for Political Science', *Perspectives on Politics*, 2, no. 4 (2004): 691–706.

[61]Robert Darnton, *Mesmerism and the End of the Enlightenment in France* (Cambridge, MA: Harvard University Press, 1968); and B. Robert Kreiser, *Miracles, Convulsions, and Ecclesiastical Politics in Early Eighteenth-Century Paris* (Princeton: Princeton University Press, 1978).

religion with 'superstition', Pinker ignores the extent to which religion was hardwired into much of eighteenth-century Western culture, and the role that religion played in the Enlightenment.

The Enlightenment was not just a secularizing movement; many contemporaries were both religious *and* in favour of Enlightenment reform and Enlightenment thinking.[62] Since the 1930s, historians have been arguing that religion was not the opposite of reason and that it was not nearly as wide as some, like Peter Gay, imagined.[63] A number of prominent thinkers were themselves religious so that there was never a clear divide between religion and reason. In Scotland, the Enlightenment took place inside the churches where many clerics preached liberal ideas.[64] Some go so far as to argue that 'the Enlightenment was not only compatible with religious belief but conducive to it'.[65] In England, Enlightenment culture was not so much predominantly 'rationalist' as intensely Christian and Evangelical. Initial forms of Christian humanitarianism came into existence in the seventeenth century and were initially about helping the poor at home. Eventually, an amalgam of Christian morality and human rights inspired a broader notion of compassion and even pity for victims of oppression, such as slaves, and in the 1820s, towards Greeks under Ottoman rule.[66] Isaac Newton was profoundly religious.[67] David Hume, often cited by Pinker as an example of the kind of rational thinker typified by the Enlightenment, was not. He was an anti-rationalist. Similarly, John Locke believed that ideas were derived 'entirely from the senses' and that knowledge was only 'the Perception of the Agreement, or Dis-agreement, of any of our Ideas'.[68] In North America during the Revolution, the dictates of sentiment rather than reason were uppermost in many people's minds where emotional rhetoric was used to mobilize the people into action.[69] One could say the same of the French revolutionaries whose rhetoric was steeped in emotional appeals, and where sincerity and feeling were signs of virtue, and thus of political legitimacy.

---

[62]As was shown many years ago by Carl Lotus Becker, *The Heavenly City of the Eighteenth Century Philosophers* (New Haven: Yale University Press, 1932).

[63]See, Anton M. Matytsin and Dan Edelstein, 'Introduction', in Anton M. Matytsin and Dan Edelstein (eds), *Let There Be Enlightenment: The Religious and Mystical Sources of Rationality* (Baltimore: Johns Hopkins University Press, 2018), 1–6.

[64]Sorkin, *The Religious Enlightenment*.

[65]Sorkin, *The Religious Enlightenment*, 5, 3.

[66]See, for example, Howard G. Brown, *Mass Violence and the Self: From the French Wars of Religion to the Paris Commune* (Ithaca: Cornell University Press, 2018), who demonstrates how compassion and pity were born of reactions to mass violence.

[67]Jacob, *The Secular Enlightenment*, 32.

[68]Cited in Nicholas Hudson, 'Are We "Voltaire's Bastards?" John Ralston Saul and Post-Modern Representations of the Enlightenment', *Lumen*, 20 (2001): 111–21, here 115.

[69]Nicole Eustace, *Passion Is the Gale: Emotion, Power, and the Coming of the American Revolution* (Chapel Hill: University of North Carolina Press, 2008).

Conclusion

My focus here has not been to denounce 'reason' in history but rather to show that the Enlightenment was a good deal more complex than Pinker will allow for and that indeed it may not have been *the* turning point in the history of the decline of some forms of violence that Pinker, and other scholars, make it out to be. There is a good deal that indicates a turning point having more or less taken place by around 1650, much earlier than Pinker believes, and not as a result of Enlightenment thinkers, but rather as a result of other external factors that have to do with regional as well as global circumstances. This was the case for homicide, judicial torture, as well as duelling in the core European countries (but not on the periphery of Europe, it is worth underlining). On the other hand, other forms of violence, such as public executions, and slavery, which reached a peak by the end of the eighteenth century before being outlawed by Britain in 1807, continued well into the nineteenth century. Other forms of violence, such as torture and slavery, have never really gone away. In other words, there does not appear to be any clear correlation between reading, thinking and action, or between Enlightenment thinking and violence. Moreover, people, as I am sure Pinker would admit, can be both rational and irrational (or spiritual), practical and idealistic, concerned and indifferent to the fate of others. In short, people are motivated by somewhat contradictory impulses, but change can only come about by a combination of complex historical forces, most of which Pinker seems to ignore.

In some respects, Pinker falls into the category of the intellectual warrior, alongside – ironically since Pinker despises them – Marxists, postmodernists and those who advocate for a 'clash of civilizations', who have all appropriated, and in the process redefined, the Enlightenment for their own purposes.[70] Pinker's ideas around the Enlightenment recall the kind of naïve conception of progress, world peace and the belief that commerce and cosmopolitanism would act as a positive force for peace, which were common elements among eighteenth-century Enlightenment thinkers. Even the idea pursued by Pinker that the spread of democracy brings peace, since democracies do not fight each other, has its origins in the eighteenth century. Pinker's world view then seems to be a bit of a throwback to the eighteenth century, without really taking into account the barbarity of the twentieth century. The violence of the twentieth century really brings home the fact that people placed in extraordinary circumstances are more than capable of committing atrocities. This is as valid a statement of people's behaviour

---

[70]Conrad, 'Enlightenment in Global History', 1004, n. 19. See, Keith Michael Baker and Peter Hans Reill (eds), *What's Left of Enlightenment? A Postmodern Question* (Stanford: Stanford University Press, 2001).

today, as it is for past centuries. And this is where Pinker ultimately fails; he has little deep understanding of history and historical methodology. Without an intimate knowledge of the periods of history and the peoples he mentions, his work can never be more than a collection of generalizations based up on a misconception of history.

PART THREE

Places

10

The complexity of history

Russia and Steven Pinker's thesis

Nancy Shields Kollmann

It feels churlish to disagree with Steven Pinker's feel-good argument that face-to-face violence has declined in world history over the last six or so centuries. He does indeed show with statistical and anecdotal evidence that in many places the modern world is less hazardous to one's personal survival than life in premodern times, and that attitudes in many societies have changed. But historians can be a churlish bunch, and reading his book leaves me wanting more specificity and more difference, and leery of so long, broad and universalizing an argument. I find the most intriguing part of the book, in fact, to be the exceptions Pinker cites to his observed patterns. When I consider early modern Russia, what strikes me are the ways in which Russia took a very different approach to violence even though some of the same influences were at play.

Pinker writes on a vast scale – he argues that rates of face-to-face violence and organized warfare have fallen, and attitudes have turned against violence in 'civilized' societies, expanding from Europe into contemporary global society. As roots of these changes, he identifies phenomena familiar to historians thanks to burgeoning literature since the 1970s: early modern European state-building, 'the civilizing process' and the decline in homicide rates.[1]

---

[1]One of the earliest of Charles Tilly's many contributions to the study of state-building: Charles Tilly and Gabriel Ardant (eds), *The Formation of National States in Western Europe* (Princeton: Princeton University Press, 1975). On etiquette: Norbert Elias, *The Civilizing Process*, 2 vols. (New York: Urizen Books, 1978–82). On crime rates: Pieter Spierenburg, *The Spectacle of*

Central to Pinker's argument is the rise of a centralized state ('Leviathan') that claimed a monopoly of violence and enforced it through policing and judicial punishment. Important here is that the state was well-run, preferably in a way that moved towards democracy and pluralism over time; buy-in to the political system encouraged citizens to maintain peace. A second key element is the expansion of interregional commerce, which gave communities and individuals incentive to cooperate for individual and mutual benefit. 'Gentle commerce' also had the benefit of encouraging the growth of cities, which Pinker finds statistically less violent than rural communities. Third is the spread of civilized behaviour, initially inculcated through etiquette designed to corral violence among the king's men and create a 'courtly' culture of disciplined servants to the crown. Later, this trend was reinforced with Enlightenment claims for the universality of human rights, which in turn spawned a revulsion towards bodily harm to living creatures (animal and human) and eventually empathy for minority rights. As for the engines of these changes, Pinker relies on psychology, both group and individual, to argue that people, groups and states assess violence by cost-benefit analysis. They calculate the risks to their self-interest, honour and basic survival of engaging in, or deferring, violence. Thus, he also extols the rise of reason as a foundation on which individuals can make such calculations. From the sixteenth century, he argues, these forces joined together to launch a more 'civilized' world, where educated people living in urbanized democracies with healthy economies grew to avoid violence. Pinker marshalls ample statistical evidence of homicide rates, loss in war, frequency of armed combat, as well as anecdotal evidence of growing revulsion towards violence. In the very big picture, life in the stereotypical European civilized society has indeed improved.

Pinker also acknowledges exceptions. He notes that the dominant ideology of the nineteenth century – ethnic nationalism – undermines claims for universal rights, and he identifies geographical areas much less impacted by a decline of violence. In addition to isolated, often mountainous regions, he identifies a baleful arc of contemporary countries stretching from Central and East Africa through North India to Southeast Asia (p. 306) beset by a more violent status quo. Poverty, weak and corrupt states, and the absence of literacy and effective civic education deflect these areas from a more peaceable path. Most importantly, he argues that a decline in violence is 'not inevitable': these trends have always stemmed from rational choice and are not dependent on supposed inner demons of human nature. Societies

---

Suffering. Executions and the Evolution of Repression: From a Preindustrial Metropolis to the European Experience (Cambridge and London: Cambridge University Press, 1984); Richard van Dülmen, *Theatre of Horror: Crime and Punishment in Early Modern Germany*, trans. Elisabeth Neu (Cambridge: Polity Press, 1990); Peter Linebaugh, *The London Hanged: Crime and Civil Society In the Eighteenth Century* (Cambridge: Cambridge University Press, 1992).

and individuals could choose more war, more discrimination, more ethnic cleansing and more ambient violence if they find it in their self-interest. It is up to us.

In broad sweeps Pinker's argument does jibe with what many of us experience today. The historian in me, however, worries. His Euro-centrism raises a flag: he implies a single path into a peaceable modernity following the European model, leaving one to wonder about paths not taken, or the very concept of a determined path. And his focus on rational agency implies that other states or societies might have combined his cited factors and others to different ends. This seems to be the case for early modern Russia.

I have analysed the practice of the criminal law in early modern Russia from the sixteenth through the eighteenth centuries with the problem of violence as a main concern.[2] Violence was on my mind for two reasons: since the sixteenth century (and reiterated in Cold War rhetoric), Europeans have characterized Russians and their society as despotic, brutal and less civilized than the European 'West'.[3] Second, I had in mind the Foucauldian paradigm, supported by research by Spierenburg, Linebaugh, van Dülmen and others, that held that some European states well into the seventeenth century ruled through terror by staging 'spectacles of execution', compensating for the inability to rule through law, policing and civic cooperation with displays of official brutality. Eventually European states were able to abandon theatrical public executions, cruel and unusual punishments, judicial torture and other public displays of violence because of two interconnected trends: a growing state capacity to police deviant behaviour and to inculcate civic values in its citizens and a growing public acceptance of humanitarian ideals.[4]

Violence was not the only issue I was concerned with; I also analysed the degree to which the tsar's criminal courts ruled in accordance with law and legal procedure. I read the law and case law of homicide, recidivist theft and robbery, and major political and religious crime (in Muscovy's theocratic ideology, witchcraft, heresy, treason and rebellion all qualified as assaults on the state). Trial transcripts ranged from the early seventeenth century well into the eighteenth and covered the empire, involving not only the dominant East Slavic population but also subject peoples in Siberia, the Middle Volga (Tatar and Finno-Ugric peoples), Ukraine and even European foreigners in Russian service.

---

[2]Nancy Shields Kollmann, *Crime and Punishment in Early Modern Russia* (Cambridge: Cambridge University Press, 2012).

[3]Marshall Poe, '*A People Born to Slavery': Russia in Early Modern European Ethnography, 1476-1748* (Ithaca: Cornell University Press, 2000); Larry Wolff, *Inventing Eastern Europe: The Map of Civilization on the Mind of the Enlightenment* (Stanford: Stanford University Press, 1994).

[4]Michel Foucault, *Discipline and Punish: The Birth of the Prison*, trans. Alan Sheridan (New York: Vintage Books, 1979).

I found that the early modern Russian judicial system was in some ways less violent than its European counterparts. I cannot make this argument on the basis of statistics. Rates of crime are unavailable: no statistical data was kept (police forces were not functioning efficiently across the empire until late in the nineteenth century). Certain types of crime garnered especial attention over time, possibly suggesting new outbreaks. Predictably, Russia's earliest criminal law codes acknowledge prosecutions and punishment up to execution for murder, arson and other major crimes as well as for political and religious crimes. As the state began to amass bureaucratic control in the sixteenth century, recidivist burglary and theft, often identified with professional banditry in the countryside, rose to special concern. Legal procedure and criminal police institutions were created and endured through the seventeenth century. A massive legal compilation in 1649 for the first time gave detailed legal treatment to political and religious crime against the state, reflecting Muscovy's expanding control over peasant labour, taxation and daily life. In response, the seventeenth century saw a rising incidence of peasants fleeing landlords; when Peter I (ruled 1682–1725) instituted an onerous poll tax on peasants as well as new military recruitment for a massively increased standing army and new navy, runaway soldiers and sailors joined the ranks of runaway serfs as a focus of criminal prosecution. Persecutions of religious heterodoxy proliferated from the late seventeenth century after a theological schism in the Orthodox Church; for more than a century thereafter, official persecution of 'Old Believer' communities waxed and waned. The most recalcitrant of these schismatics were imprisoned and executed by burning as heretics. While we cannot attach rates of incidence to these crimes, it is clear that as the early modern Russian state expanded, it encountered violent challenges to its claims to control labour, collect taxes, maintain public order and enforce ideology.

Other early modern European states faced similar challenges, but Russia's modes of governance and criminal justice seem to have relied less on overt violence to meet them. We can see this in many spheres. One is the state's ability to monopolize the means of violence: in the fifteenth and sixteenth centuries, Moscow's rulers systematically integrated previously sovereign princes and local elites and their private retinues into the grand prince's army. Deprived of sovereign rights, such princes and elites in return received social status, land grants and other largesse. Well compensated in an environment with few other opportunities for gain, Russia's elite made its peace with service to the tsar and was remarkably stable well into the eighteenth century, with astoundingly few episodes of opposition to the dynasty.

In addition to monopolizing the means of violence in this way, Moscow's grand princes (self-titled tsars after 1547) assiduously condemned private violence among individuals, clans and other social groups; duelling and vendettas were forbidden and harshly punished. In their place, the state offered redress through litigation over insult to honour. All subjects of the tsar, from the highest church hierarchs and secular elites to serfs and even slaves, could litigate against people of all social ranks, and they did. Offences were usually verbal, occasionally including affronts such as knocking off a woman's hat or pulling a man's beard; such insults often occurred together with physical assault, but the crimes were tried separately. As a rule, winning litigants were compensated with a fine (its size rose according to the social rank of the insulted) and with the satisfaction of a restored reputation. When Europeans imported duelling in the late seventeenth century, the state immediately clamped down, punishing it as a capital crime. Peter I even ordered not only that a victorious dueller be executed by hanging but that the corpse of his rival also be strung up.[5]

In Russia, the reach of the criminal law was intentionally narrow: it involved murder and recidivist theft and robbery, arson and other heinous crimes, and high political and religious crime. Petty crimes that in some contemporary European countries were punished up to capital punishment were in Russia left to communities to deal with. Similarly, the reach of the central government was intentionally limited: it focused on monopolizing violence, collecting resources and dispensing the criminal law. Otherwise, as a multi-ethnic Eurasian 'empire of difference', the central government allowed subject peoples to retain language, religion, court systems, elites and public services as before. Similarly, the East Slavic peasant majority lived under the authority of landlords or village communes. All these communities were entitled to use corporal punishment for petty crime and disorder, according to local tradition. But none was allowed to impinge on the criminal process; if a murder, robbery, witchcraft accusation or other major crime occurred in a village, noble estate or native tribe, leaders were required to turn in suspects to the local governor for state justice. Those who tried to solve serious cases on their own, or administered torture, were punished harshly. Having defined the criminal law narrowly, the state worked assiduously to control that arena.[6]

The state also struggled, as all empires did, with policing officialdom to avoid corruption, violence and abuse. Truly egregious cases of corrupt governors, often in far-flung Siberia where the riches of the furs and the China trade tempted graft, were prosecuted harshly; as a preventive measure, the state rotated governors every two years, never sold venalities and never let local notables develop regional power. Since the state understood that

---

[5]On stability in the elite: Kollmann, *Crime and Punishment*, chaps. 14–15. On honour litigation: Nancy Shields Kollmann, *By Honor Bound: State and Society in Early Modern Russia* (Ithaca: Cornell University Press, 1999). On the petrine law on duelling: Kollmann, *Crime and Punishment*, 406.
[6]Nancy Shields Kollmann, *The Russian Empire, 1450-1801* (Oxford: Oxford University Press, 2017), Introduction.

in Siberia and steppe borderlands, subject peoples could disappear into the forest or prairie if the state demanded too much, governors were explicitly ordered not to abuse the locals. Such prescriptions hardly prevented violence against natives: initial stages of conquest were bloody and Russian garrisons ensured the constant threat of violence. But these approaches to local governance reflect the state's aversion to violence when it contradicted its goals.[7]

For similar reasons, the early modern Russian state sharply contrasts to many European counterparts in its approach to Christianization; the state refused to allow the Orthodox Church to forcibly convert non-Orthodox subjects, again for the pragmatic goal of not alienating the tax-paying populace. The Orthodox Church was not in any case a strongly missionary faith: it never developed a rhetoric of religiously sanctioned violence akin to crusades, and its moral philosophy advocated personal restraint, inner reformation and mercy. Exceptions were two periods of forcible conversion of Muslims in the Middle Volga and Bashkiria in the eighteenth century; these were fuelled to some extent by religious zeal connected to Catholic influence at court, but primarily by Russian migration into these valuable farming territories. Conversion served as a weapon with which to appropriate lands from uncooperative Muslims. But, as a rule, the state restrained forcible conversion precisely to maintain stable governance and taxation across the empire.[8]

Since Russia was an autocracy with no representative institutions or enfranchised social classes to provide leverage against the state, its legal system might be expected to have been arbitrary and despotic. Certainly, foreign visitors alleged as much. But my study shows that the criminal law was applied in a systematic manner according to the law. Law codes that included criminal punishments and procedure were issued in 1497, 1550 and 1649 and 1669, supplemented by myriad decrees from chanceries with judicial authority. These laws and decrees were laconic and practical, rarely theoretical or generalizable, but they provided judges with bases for trials and judgements. Judges themselves, however, were untrained in the law. Military officers were appointed to be Jacks-of-all-trades with adjudication a low priority among more pressing military, fiscal and administrative roles. Legal expertise, therefore, resided with the scribes assigned to their offices. Trained in the law according to uniform standards of procedure and paperwork emanating from Moscow, the local scribe kept judges on track with instructions on procedure and citations from the law

---

[7]Kollmann, *Crime and Punishment*, chap. 4.
[8]Forcible conversion: Kollmann, *Russian Empire*, 262–3, 397–402. Less violent religious rhetoric: Kollmann, *Crime and Punishment*, 424–5. Moral philosophy: Elise Kimerling Wirtschafter, *Religion and Enlightenment in Catherinian Russia: The Teachings of Metropolitan Platon* (DeKalb: Northern Illinois University Press, 2013).

regarding sentencing. Across the empire, transcripts of court cases follow the same model, use the same language, quote the same laws and reach the appropriate verdict – an amazing uniformity across a huge empire when compared to the legal multiplicity that many European countries faced at the time. The law distinguished levels of violence in punishment, reserving capital punishment for the highest crimes. To cite one example, a Tunguz tribe in eastern Siberia demanded that the judge turn over a Russian accused of killing one of their princes for execution by tribal justice. The governor insisted that the tsar's law prevailed; finding the man guilty of unintentional homicide, not murder, they sentenced him to a 'merciless' flogging, much to the dissatisfaction of the Tunguz.[9]

Other aspects of criminal practice also mitigated the use of violence. One was the provision of mercy: judges often reduced sentences in the tsar's name to respond to community appeals or otherwise maintain social stability.[10] In Russia, mercy reinforced the patrimonial tenet of Muscovite political ideology that the tsar was a just judge who protected his people from harm. Secondly, from the late seventeenth century, laws reduced the incidence of the death penalty, sending many capital criminals to exile to Siberia or other frontier towns. Exile was not an imprisonment system; the convict was kept in place by sheer distance and by branding for the most serious of them. While in exile, criminals worked: peasants farmed, artisans practised their crafts and many joined the local governor's militia. Reducing capital punishment in favour of exile addressed Russia's chronic shortage of labour.[11]

Even more unlike its European peers, Russia did not practise the elaborate, theatrical 'spectacles of suffering' for public executions that have garnered such attention in early modern European criminal law. In Russia, executions were simple affairs; the judge was expected to gather a crowd, often on a market day, as soon as possible after verdict. He was to have the verdict read aloud and then to execute promptly (generally by hanging or beheading). The 1649 law code prescribed that the condemned be given six weeks to repent, but case law shows that was rarely observed. Nor did courts take the time to assemble multiple condemned criminals for mass execution, or to build viewing bleachers and impressive scaffolds. They did not have formal rituals of last meals, forgiveness of the executioner, additional tortures on the stand and gruesome executions such as quartering. Rather, the terror of executions in Muscovy might have been in their speed; with Moscow so far away and cases dragging on for months and more with consultation between centre and local courts, communities needed to be reminded that the tsar's law really meant business. Judges were told 'not to delay the tsar's

---

[9]On judicial expertise, see Kollmann, *Crime and Punishment*, chap. 2. Tunguz case on 203.
[10]Kollmann, *Crime and Punishment*, chap. 7.
[11]Kollmann, *Crime and Punishment*, chap. 11.

work' (perhaps also a hedge against their being bribed), and they took pains to report back to Moscow how promptly they had indeed carried out an execution.

Russia's pragmatic approach to violence in the criminal process changed somewhat with exposure to European practice. Before the 1690s, a few incidences of the horrific punishment of quartering are cited, but they were exceptional.[12] Peter I came to power formally in 1682 as a ten-year-old and famously surrounded himself with European officers as he was growing up; not surprisingly, European-style tortures and executions begin to appear in his day. In 1696, a deserter was sentenced to breaking on the wheel, the first mention of such punishment in Russia; in 1697, Peter I staged a beheading in a theatrical manner, with the blood of the executed flowing over the exhumed body of a political accomplice of the convicted. But it was first-hand experience in Europe that brought the full 'spectacle of execution' model to Russia. Peter I witnessed a mass execution in Amsterdam during his embassy abroad (1697–8) and staged a similar spectacle in Moscow in 1698 when he dashed back to Russia to suppress a musketeer rebellion. Upwards to 1,000 people were tortured and over 700 were executed in mass groups in several 'days' of execution (others were flogged, exiled or otherwise punished). Breaking on the wheel, beheading with a sword (not the customary Russian axe) were European innovations here, as well as the vast scale of the spectacle itself. Hundreds were hanged from the Kremlin walls, their bodies left to sit all winter; hundreds more were beheaded; priests were broken on the wheel.[13]

During his reign, Peter I resorted to such spectacles in a few exceptional cases of high treason and official corruption, but in rural settings executions continued to be simple, speedy affairs. Conversely, however, Peter I further limited the use of the death penalty by requiring that each capital sentence be reviewed and by expanding the capital crimes to be punished with exile in Siberia or to forced labour on his many new construction projects (canals, harbours, St Petersburg). Going into the eighteenth century, Russia's use of the death penalty was declining.

Unlike any European counterpart, in the 1740s Russia abolished the death penalty entirely, replacing it with exile upon order of Peter I's daughter, Empress Elizabeth I (ruled 1741–61). There followed a great expansion of the exile and forced labour systems and a greater elaboration of brandings and bodily mutilation to mark capital criminals in exile. The motives of

---

[12]The horrific punishment of burning heretics inside wooded cages stuffed with incendiary material is recorded since the fifteenth century; the rebel Stepan Razin was quartered in 1671 and his body parts displayed on pikes for over a year.

[13]Kollmann, *Crime and Punishment*, chaps. 17–18 and 'Pictures at an Execution: Johann Georg Korb's "Execution of the Strel'tsy"', in Brian Boeck, Russell E. Martin and Daniel Rowland (eds), *Dubitando: Studies in History and Culture in Honor of Donald Ostrowski* (Bloomington: Slavica Publishers, 2012), 399–407.

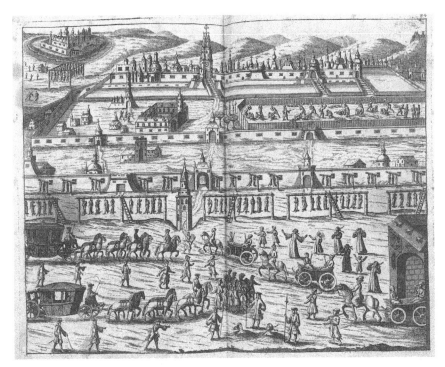

FIGURE 10.1 *Russia's first 'spectacle of execution': 'The execution of musketeers, Moscow 1698', published in Johann-Georg Korb,* Diarium itineris in Moscoviam *(Vienna, 1700). Library of the Hoover Institution, Stanford, CA.*

the abolition were never explained, nor was the abolition codified clearly; decrees made it appear that such exiled capital criminals were merely awaiting referral of their cases. But in fact, executions for common crime ended. Empress Elizabeth's motivation might have been religious, or she might have been reacting to the conditions of her coming to the throne. In the late 1730s, the ruling faction under Empress Anna Ioannovna (ruled 1730–40) had executed political rivals in a display of unprecedented violence that shocked the nobility, and another faction brought Elizabeth to power in a coup in rejection of that faction. Her abolition of the death penalty may have been intended to assuage noble fears. The nobility's continued Europeanization and the spread of Enlightenment humanitarian values under Catherine II (ruled 1762–96) ensured the continuation of the policy; Catherine, inspired by Beccaria, also lobbied for the abolition of torture (which occurred in 1801). Alexander I (ruled 1801–25) spoke proudly of imposing Russia's more benevolent law on newly acquired territories (such as Georgia) where capital punishment was still being practised. In the first half of the nineteenth century, brutality in the law was gradually lessened with privileged social ranks receiving immunity from corporal punishment, with the abolition of the branding of female exiles and eventually entirely, the ending of bodily mutilation and flogging, and other mitigations.[14]

This is not to say that executions disappeared entirely – although this was not stated explicitly in law until 1845, capital punishment was still allowed for treason, as seen in a few executions under Catherine II and famously in the execution of five Decembrist rebels in 1825. When capital punishment was finally presented systematically in the 1845 Criminal Code under the conservative Nicholas I (ruled 1825–55), it was limited only to attacks on the tsar himself, his family and the state; all other crimes, including heresy, parricide and murder, warranted exile or lesser punishments. Thus, the tsar epitomized the state and patrimonially protected his people from such a harsh punishment. Such an approach to the death penalty has a distinctly non-modern feel, combining religious fervour, Enlightenment humanitarianism and traditional Russian patriarchal ideology. The state continued with what one scholar calls a 'comparatively lenient' use of punishment. Jonathan Daly, in a comparative study of punishment regimes in late nineteenth-century United States, Russia and Europe, found that per capita Russia used execution, imprisonment and other forms of punishment notably less than its peers.[15]

Russia's judicial practice into the nineteenth century, therefore, would seem to reflect an aversion to violence. But few of Pinker's driving forces for such a case were at play here, and those that were – Western norms of etiquette and Enlightenment humanitarian ideals – emerged late and complemented what was already going on. The pacifying impulse of commerce hardly played a role: Russia was a resource-poor society with a serf-based autarkic economy where the state exerted as much control over productive resources and economic exchange as possible. Therein probably lies the greatest difference between Russia's relationship to judicial violence and that of contemporary Europe; Russia relied upon a more complicated relationship to violence than Pinker's smooth path of decline.

Human and material resources were always the key to state power in Russia, and the state wielded violence intentionally to mobilize them. Russia's early modern state consolidated in the fourteenth and fifteenth centuries by conquering and absorbing neighbours; by the end of the fifteenth century, it embarked on building a centralized state with a skeletal bureaucracy to govern new territories and to collect funds to support the growing cavalry army. Parallel to European states, Muscovy's claims on resources continuously expanded with military reform towards a gunpowder-armed

---

[14]Abby M. Schrader, *Languages of the Lash: Corporal Punishment and Identity in Imperial Russia* (De Kalb: Northern Illinois University Press, 2002).

[15]Jonathan Daly, 'Russian Punishments in the European Mirror', in Michael Melancon (ed.), *Russia in the European Context 1789-1914: A Member of the Family* (Gordonsville: Palgrave Macmillan, 2005), 161–88, here 176.

cavalry army and eventually a European-style standing army and with imperial expansion. Empire required greater resources, and also provided them. By the end of the seventeenth century, a skeletal network of fortresses stretching from European Russia to the Pacific solidified Russian tax-collecting authority over Siberia's fur-rich native tribes; conquests of Kazan (1552) and Astrakhan (1556) on the Volga expanded transit trade and opened the door to a slow but inexorable push across the steppe towards the Black and Caspian Seas and Caucasus. By the end of the eighteenth century, Russia was a major European geopolitical power, having captured the Black Sea littoral from the Ottoman Empire and dismembered Poland, bringing Ukrainian and Belorussian lands under Russian control. The only way all this success was possible was by a single-minded pursuit and control of resources, natural and human, to staff and equip the armies, support the elites and maintain the bureaucracy of empire.

Pursuing such a policy produced a multisided approach to violence. In contrast to the preceding discussion of seemingly less violence in the criminal law, one can cite many ways in which Russia was a violent state and society. Take torture, for example. Russia borrowed some aspects of the revived Roman law that spread across Europe in the sixteenth century, including judicial torture. European criminal codes such as the Habsburg 1532 *Carolina* surrounded the use of torture with limitations (witnesses, doctors, limitation on sessions, requirement that the tortured sign his confession the next day, etc.). But Russia lacked Europe's jurisprudential heritage; it had no guilds of lawyers or notaries, no law schools or seminaries, no legacy of Roman law or canon law, no university law faculties to turn to for expert advice (as the *Carolina* prescribed). Russia's criminal law mentioned torture only in passing, spelling out no limitations. Case law reveals that there was a de facto limit of three torture sessions in cases below highest crime, but with treason, heresy and witchcraft, torture was used without bound. Here, the Russian criminal court was a violent place indeed.[16]

It was not, however, a medieval torture chamber of the sort that Pinker so macabrely details. Russian courts did not use arcane instruments of torture, only flogging in strappado position. Pain could be increased with the placing of weights on the body; fire was used in the most serious cases. Muscovite torture was not elaborate and mechanical but suited for the task.

Over the sixteenth and seventeenth centuries, the state moved to control peasant mobility; about half of its peasants were landlords' serfs and the others were tied to their villages in areas too infertile to support gentry.

---

[16]On revival of Roman law: John H. Langbein, *Prosecuting Crime in the Renaissance: England, Germany, France* (Cambridge, MA: Harvard University Press, 1974). On judicial torture in Russia: Kollmann, *Crime and Punishment*, chap. 6; Valerie A. Kivelson, *Desperate Magic: The Moral Economy of Witchcraft in Seventeenth-Century Russia* (Ithaca: Cornell University Press, 2013).

Such forced immobility helped the state by providing a labour force for the cavalry army and military elite and by making taxation easier. Violence was endemic in serfdom and peasant justice. The exile system, also a state creation, was brutal and often deadly. And the state continued to wield violence after the 1740s prohibition on the death penalty when and where it needed to: it routinely declared martial law (replete with corporal and capital punishment) on the Caucasus, steppe and Central Asian borderlands to put down banditry, disorder and opposition.[17]

Society more broadly shows the same mixed picture. The Russian nobility and merchant class were absorbing European etiquette and Enlightenment values, and several imperial elites – Ukrainian noblemen and Cossacks, Polish noblemen, Baltic German Junkers – came into the empire already European in culture. But Russian nobles also fell for the fashion of duelling in the late eighteenth and early nineteenth century in defiance of repeated edicts. Furthermore, literacy and European values that might have encouraged a decline of violence according to Pinker were not disseminated to the mass of the population, who remained bound to peasant communes and customary law even after the emancipation of 1861 and a judicial reform that provided jury courts for the higher social ranks (1864). Furthermore, maintaining the imperial governing strategy of tolerating difference left many communities devoid of schools, public services, literacy, urbanization and a more differentiated economy. Only very late in the nineteenth century did the state attempt Russification to create some uniformity across the empire in language, education and culture; only a few decades after mid-nineteenth-century reforms did industrialization, urbanization, transportation networks and regional economic development expand, producing some of the softening effects (literacy, education, reason, commercial exchange) that Pinker cites. And these processes were abruptly ended by the 1917 revolution, with effects evident today. Pinker observes that Russia and Eastern Europe today constitute a more violent periphery outside the core European area (p. 89, 229), and in the twentieth century Russia suffered under a utopian ideology that wrecked unimaginable pain on the Soviet people.

The red thread uniting these disparate relationships to violence is the drive to mobilize resources. To ensure its survival, the Russian state single-mindedly controlled violence among individuals and groups, using the criminal law and litigations over honour. It garnered labour power by preferring exile over execution. It carried out executions swiftly to assert the tsar's power, but had neither time nor resources nor cultural inspiration to stage theatrical rituals. To keep up with European geopolitical rivals, it forcibly Europeanized the nobility and educated classes, but it maintained

---

[17]John LeDonne, 'Civilians under Military Justice during the Reign of Nicholas I', *Canadian-American Slavic Studies*, 7 (1973): 171–87.

serfdom for economic gain and political stability. Its 'politics of difference' imperial policy intervened little in daily life for its many and diverse colonial subjects, ensuring stability but leaving many to harsh customary discipline. The state rationally deployed or minimized violence to maximize its human resources as a strategic choice.

These reflections on the role of violence in Russia's early modern criminal law suggest that different states assess the utility of violence differently and use or limit it as it suits them. Just as Pinker himself notes that geographical isolation and poverty inhibit a decline in societal violence, a single-minded pursuit of limited resources pushed Russia to deploy violence in myriad ways, never approaching a steady march of decline. This messy, contingent outcome is the stuff of history.

11

A necrology of angels

Violence in Japanese history as a lens of critique

Michael Wert

As of 2019, it seems that enough time has elapsed since Pinker's *Better Angels* was published that we treat it properly, not as a work of scholarship, but of polemics and ideology, a primary source text revealing the context of its time.[1] At a time when capitalism's problems have become undeniable, along comes Pinker, who reassures capitalism's supporters that, despite all of capitalism's flaws, at least it does not cause violence. This is an old claim, going back to at least the nineteenth century. Thus, while *Better Angels* is a book of its time, it is also timeless. The excitement over the Pinker thesis, from the likes of Bill Gates, the Washington Post, et cetera, is akin to a séance; joining hands and calling upon the spirits of long-dead claims about the inherently peaceful nature of 'gentle commerce', the civilizing process, the Enlightenment and the West's progressive march towards greater wealth, non-violence and abandonment of ideology. Such assertions still have purchase among certain audiences, even as they are long proven wrong. Pinker is only the most recent in a scholarly tradition that includes Niall Ferguson's *Civilization* and David Landes' *The Wealth and Poverty of Nations: Why Some are So Rich and Some So Poor*, in which rational choice

---

[1]Analysis of his illogical arguments, misrepresentation of data and the like are legion. But this is a good summary: https://www.currentaffairs.org/2019/05/the-worlds-most-annoying-man.

by individuals and the greatness of Western technology play a defining role in determining wealth versus poverty or violence. In other words, the love that Bill Gates has for the Pinker thesis is easily explained – in Pinker's version of world history, Bill Gates is its prophet.

I propose using violence in Japanese history as a mirror, reflecting a parallel unfolding of history and historiography as it relates to violence. Along the way, my necrology of angels lists some dead claims about violence, the functions of history and ideology, and the putatively non-violent nature of capitalism, claims that have rung true since the nineteenth century for those unaware of their own ideological commitments. Violence throughout Japanese history is not unique; there are no Japanese characteristics to the violence that has occurred there. Violence in Japan does not offer us a case study of how Pinker's 'facts' are wrong; mine is not a positivistic critique.

My intellectual necrology follows three interconnected approaches that critique, by reflection of Pinker's thesis: historical metanarrative, structure and the individual agent. First, a similar argument about the 'civilizing process' has been made about early modern Japan that focuses on elite culture and privileged texts rather than popular culture or action. Second, I use late nineteenth- and early twentieth-century Japanese industrial capitalism to show how capitalism was symptomatically violent. In other words, violence is a symptom of the tensions inherent to capitalism. Despite genuine excitement for a constitutional government during the late nineteenth century, only by the 1920s did those dreams become realized for a small wealthy middle class, and, then, too little too late. Finally, since the Pinker thesis assigns responsibility to the free-floating individual, who has more or less 'self-control', we must consider at least one influence on an individual's action – ideological fantasy.

I do not mean ideology in the old-fashioned sense as something that is opposed to reality, a kind of false conscious that hides what is 'really going on', nor do I mean ideology in the political science usage as the political world view of a particular group or political party. In this older usage, 'ideology' has a negative connotation; for Pinker only the historical bad guys, fascism and communism, have ideology. Ideology, as he uses the concept, is visible – one can accept or reject it; thus, empathy, intelligence and self-control of the individual can trump ideology. Rather, ideology, as Zizek and others have defined it, is a framework that informs everyday life. The assertion that we are living in a time of great peace that was destined to come because of the Enlightenment, greater intelligence, increased prosperity and changing 'attitudes' that no longer glorify violence is, in fact, an ideological claim.

Scholars throughout the twentieth century have used philosophy, sociology and history to disprove many of the claims that inform Pinker's assumptions. For example, although Pinker claims that his approach is scientific, it is, in fact, scientistic; it apes the appearance of positivism to claim that reason and empirical facts 'are independent of the psychological make-up of the thinkers who attempt to grasp them'; this is largely a myth.

The sheer size of Pinker's book amounts to a scientistic version of 'if you say it enough, it becomes true' – a sentiment wonderfully captured by science journalist Tim Radford's theistic praise 'I don't know if he's right, but I do think this book is a winner'.[2] Reason never purged superstition, as Jason Josephson-Storm has shown, nor are we 'moving away from tribalism [and] authority'.[3]

The putative neutrality of 'facts' ignores how facts are deployed; they never represent themselves. Foucault put it best: 'once the historical sense is mastered by a suprahistorical perspective, metaphysics can bend it to its own purpose, and, by aligning it to the demands of objective science, it can impose its own "Egyptianism".'[4] Pinker reveals that even he is suspicious of his own teleological claims, 'this may seem Whiggish, presentist, and historically naïve . . . yet it is supported by facts'.[5]

The problem with teleology ('Whiggish') is not that it forecloses change from a putative root causation, but that by change over time, the current historical moment was ordained despite those changes. This 'moralizing of chronology', as Verlyn Klinkenborg eloquently stated it, is a problem not only for historians but even more so for scientists; 'nowadays science tries to keep watch for even the slightest trace of it, any suggestion that evolution has a direction tending to culminate in us . . . or in any other presumably desirable end point'.[6] The end point of teleology, quite literally the telos, ignores historical dead ends, and this is the primary complaint of historians about Pinker's thesis – that so much history is ignored. Worse, the optimism of telos casts things that go awry as mere tragic aberrations in an otherwise smooth progress towards peace. Slavoj Zizek stated the problem succinctly,

> The new breed of evolutionary optimists (Sam Harris, Steven Pinker) like to enumerate positive statistics . . . these are (mostly) true, but one can easily see problems that emerge with such a procedure. If one compares the status of Jews in Western Europe and in the Jews in the course of the last century, the progress is clear . . . but in between the holocaust happened.[7]

---

[2]Tim Radford, 'The Better Angels of Our Nature by Steven Pinker – Review', *The Guardian*, 19 November 2012.
[3]Jason Josephson-Storm, *The Myth of Disenchantment: Magic, Modernity, and the Birth of the Human Sciences* (Chicago: University of Chicago Press, 2017).
[4]Michel Foucault, 'Nietzsche, Genealogy, History', in *The Foucault Reader* (New York: Pantheon, 1984), 87. This is all the more applicable to Pinker for whom metaphysical language abounds, like 'psychological returnings'.
[5]Steven Pinker, *The Better Angels of Our Nature: The Decline of Violence in History and Its Causes* (London: Allen Lane, 2011), 938–40.
[6]Verlyn Klinkenborg, 'What Were Dinosaurs For?', *New York Review of Books*, 19 December 2019.
[7]Slavoj Zizek, *Sex and the Failed Absolute* (New York: Bloomsbury Academic, 2020), 7–8.

What accounts for bursts of violence in between chunks of seemingly peaceful time is that the potential for violence is part of the normal functions of society.

The form of the Pinker thesis is not new in historiography, and it has echoes in the Japanese history field. During the 1960s, it was known as 'modernization theory'. Many of the modernization theory supporters saw in Japanese history a similar progression towards capitalism and democracy as had been experienced in the West, different only in form and content, but with similar outcomes. Those modernization dreams were quickened by the Meiji Restoration (1868), the Meiji Constitution (1889), bureaucratization and the growth of party politics during the 1910s and 1920s, only to be dashed by the 'irrationality' and 'retrogression', an echo of Pinker's 'decivilization' claim, during wartime Japan of the 1930s and 1940s.[8] Led by Harvard historian Edwin Reischauer, who, not coincidentally, also served as John F. Kennedy's ambassador to Japan, these scholars transformed Japan from former enemy to geopolitical ally against the march of communism in Asia. A focus on the 'brighter side' of Japanese history, as one prominent Japanese historian advised, had informed modernization theory approach within the Japan field.[9]

The Pinker thesis is only slowly gaining attention in disciplines that focus on violence in East Asia. For example, like Pinker, Alex Bellamy studies trends in violence noting that at the height of the Cold War, East Asia accounted for 80 per cent of the globe's mass atrocities.[10] He agrees with Pinker regarding the ways in which premodern East Asia seems to reflect many of the trends Pinker identified as reasons for violence and its decline in premodern Europe.[11] Like Pinker, he sees the imposing of 'ideologies' as a major cause of macro violence during the modern period and economic development as a deciding factor in the decline of violence. Unlike Pinker, however, Bellamy clearly defines the focus of his study; mass atrocities that are incidents of intentional and direct violence against non-combatants that number at least 1,000. One of Pinker's biggest angelic natures, democracy, did not lead to a decrease in violence, argues Bellamy, but was a source of instability throughout Asia, in particular in East Timor and the Philippines; thus, the experience of modern Asia does not reflect all of the global trends outlined in

[8]See Sheldon Garon, 'Rethinking Modernization and Modernity in Japanese History: A Focus on State-Society Relations', *The Journal of Asian Studies*, 53, no. 2 (1994): 346–66.
[9]Marius Jansen, 'On Studying the Modernization of Japan', in Kokusai Kirisutokyo Daigaku and Ajia Bunka Kenkyu Iinkai (eds), *Studies on Modernization of Japan by Western Scholars* (Tokyo: International Christian University, 1962), 11.
[10]Alex Bellamy, *East Asia's Other Miracle: Explaining the Decline of Mass Atrocities* (Oxford: Oxford University Press, 2017), 1.
[11]Bellamy, *East Asia's Other Miracle*, 76.

Better Angels.[12] Moreover, the number of people killed in mass atrocities has gone down, despite population growth. This differs from statistics in the West, where the absolute numbers killed in mass atrocities rose throughout the first half of the twentieth century, even though the relative numbers have decreased, according to Pinker. In Asia, those declines have been more recent than Pinker observes for global trends.[13]

Macro violence in premodern Japan

Like other studies of the world before written history, general conclusions about violence are inconclusive. One talking head in NOVA's Pinker thesis documentary, *The Paradox of Violence*, asserted the following about skeletal finds around the world and the high rates of violence, 'the Paleolithic record is a horror show'. In a recent study of skeletal finds in ancient Japan, archaeologists discovered relatively low rates of violence. In fact, occurrences of violence decreased as more archaeological sites were found. The authors also noted that although there were several sites with high occurrences of violence, they might be uncommon instances of massacre, and should not be taken as representative, contradicting the suggestion made on *The Paradox of Violence.*[14]

The only type of violence that can be reasonably measured in early and medieval Japan to the sixteenth century is warfare and rebellion. As was the case throughout the medieval world, sparse data makes it difficult to determine warfare's demographic impact. Military campaigns from the tenth century until around the fourteenth century were mostly punitive in nature: quelling rebellions, pursuing enemies of the noble court in Kyoto, and policing land estates on behalf of the nobility. The first large-scale 'war', the so-called Gempei War (1180–5), pit the forces of two noble warrior families against each other in the name of imperial succession. Neither the Minamoto clan and its allies, who fought in the name of the retired emperor Go-Shirakawa, nor the Taira clan whose patriarch tried to usurp political power in Kyoto, fielded large armies. Skirmishes of several dozen socially elite warriors mounted on horses the size of modern ponies shot at each other as foot soldiers engaged each other and the riders. Outright death during combat was uncommon in many cases, and life-threatening

---

[12]Bellamy, *East Asia's Other Miracle*, 51.
[13]Bellamy, *East Asia's Other Miracle*, 76.
[14]Nakao Hisashi et al., 'Violence in the Prehistoric Period of Japan: The Spatio-Temporal Pattern of Skeletal Evidence for Violence in the Jomon Period', *Biology Letters*, 1 March 2016, https://doi.org/10.1098/rsbl.2016.0028.

casualties also appear to be low from extent war reports.[15] While political instability slightly affected the population, as warriors pillaged their way across the landscape to gather provisions, population growth between 700 and 1150 was static mostly due to famine and weak immunities against infections from the continent. In the early fourteenth century, the warrior regime issued an edict that banned warriors from stealing from local people, but even this was hardly a 'law' in the modern sense and was sometimes ignored if a warrior could prove that he was owed a debt from the victims.[16]

Political violence in and around Kyoto and central Japan during the political strife of the mid-fourteenth century resulted in more deaths, from collateral damage rather than combat, than previous eras in Japanese history. Armies grew to several hundred and even a thousand combatants. Famine spread during this same time, but with few reliable sources, as the most recent demographer of the medieval period argued, 'one can only infer a causal relationship between famine and war'.[17]

During the Warring States period (mid-fifteenth to late sixteenth centuries), which began with the Ōnin War (1467–77) that nearly destroyed Kyoto, death from warfare grew to its highest levels in premodern Japanese history. By the mid-sixteenth century, warlords across Japan fought to acquire and retain, territory, filling their armies with commoners and arming them with firearms and cannon. No longer small bands of elites on punitive missions, these armies could be as large as 50,000. Warfare included high collateral damage from burnt lands and burnt-down cities; nonetheless, the population continued to grow.[18]

Civil war ended under the conquerors Oda Nobunaga and Toyotomi Hideyoshi, but the largest international war in premodern world history was just beginning. After unifying Japan in the early 1590s, Hideyoshi invaded the Korean peninsula with the goal of conquering China. In 1592 and again in 1597, his armies clashed with Koreans, and, more significantly, the Ming Chinese army. The Japanese and Chinese militaries in Korea each outnumbered even the largest European armies at the time, around 100,000 and 120,000, respectively, not including Korean armies and guerilla units that may have numbered as high as 80,000. The Imjin War, as it was called in Korea, devastated the peninsula, and only ended when Hideyoshi died in Japan of natural causes. A third conqueror, Tokugawa Ieyasu, took over as hegemon in Japan, securing his rule by finally defeating Hideyoshi's son in 1615.

---

[15]William W. Farris, *Japan's Medieval Population: Famine, Fertility, and Warfare in a Transformative Age* (Honolulu: University of Hawai'i Press, 2009), 120.

[16]Farris, *Japan's Medieval Population*, 60.

[17]Farris, *Japan's Medieval Population*, 109.

[18]Farris, *Japan's Medieval Population*, 165.

Though not as demographically catastrophic as Japan's modern wars, the Warring States era and the invasion of Korea were marked by examples of brutality. Oda Nobunaga (1534–82) decimated Buddhist temples, killing nearly 10,000 clergy and lay followers. Buddhism continued to exist, but temples no longer held similar amounts of material wealth or military or political prowess as they did before Nobunaga's onslaught. During the Imjin War, Hideyoshi's armies cut off noses and ears in Korea to take back to Japan as evidence of their activities to receive rewards. The brutality of the Warring States period and the Imjin War might lead us to believe that medieval Japan was an extremely violent time, just as gory anecdotes led Pinker to assert the same about medieval Europe. But neither medieval Japan nor medieval Europe, as Sara Butler demonstrates in this volume, seem to have suffered catastrophic population loses from violence.[19]

What accounts for the relatively little violence in premodern Japan compared to modern Japan? Throughout premodern East Asian history, Buddhism influenced elite life. It had been integrated into how some states conceived of their ruling ideologies. Like many other religions, Buddhism places importance on the sanctity of life, making killing a sin. In Japan, compassion and mercy was paired with the concept of 'reason' (dōri). 'Compassion' was a term often used in premodern edicts and guides of how to address the handling of crimes on a warrior or noble person's land. Yet, as happened elsewhere throughout the Buddhist world, sovereigns used the protection of Buddhism and the state as an excuse to justify violence. Buddhist temple complexes also had access to violence specialists. It might appear, then, that ideology and group identity, to use Pinker's argument, were connected to violence.

But ideology as the horizon of symbols and values that inform daily life, in this case, what it meant to be an elite warrior man, the fantasy of combat, could rein in violent behaviour. Morten Oxenboell has suggested that warriors learned how to engage in violence by consuming famous war tales, fictionalized and performed stories about historical battles. In the past, historians used war tales as a source to understand actual combat. Recent scholarship, instead, uses war tales not as empirical sources, but to analyse noble elite culture, or, as Oxenboell does, to see what warrior men thought of their predecessors, and how to think of themselves as warrior men. Namely, war tales functioned as a means of enjoying violence as a mediated safe space, glorifying combat as a manly activity, while offering a model for how to properly conduct combat. Combat rituals described in war tales, such as calling out one's lineage, might have informed violent activity by warriors of a later era. For example, when the Mongols invaded Japan during the thirteenth century, mounted Japanese warriors confronted them

---

[19]Sara Butler, 'Getting Medieval on Steven Pinker', 125–41.

on the beaches by announcing their names and lineages, imitating scenes in war tales.[20] Thus, Oxenboell follows a wealth of broader scholarship on violence in history that shows how violence is not an inherent trait, but something affected by the unapparent influences that inform the 'common sense' of everyday life, in this case the values of warrior nobility.

The era of 'great peace'

The last warrior regime in Japanese history, referred to either as the Tokugawa or Edo Period (1603–1868), is best known in comparative history for two key features. The first feature is its supposed isolation from the rest of the world, voluntarily shutting off from Europe in order to curb the influence of Christianity and Europeans who might bring it. The second feature is its relative freedom from macro violence. Once the Tokugawa patriarch, Tokugawa Ieyasu, consolidated hegemony by winning the Battle of Sekigahara (1600), acquiring the title of shogun (1603), and defeated his last rival in a siege at Osaka Castle (1614–15), Japan experienced no warfare until the gradual collapse of the regime during the 1860s. A rebellion of nearly 10,000 in the southwest, the Shimabara Rebellion (1637–8), ended in about four months, after which no such rebellions posed any threat to the regime. Warlords and the Tokugawa clan, now ensconced in Edo (Tokyo) as the national hegemon, settled into a negotiated peace, free from the endemic warfare of the sixteenth century. The Tokugawa clan took much of the credit, deifying Ieyasu, and promoting their success in bringing 'great peace to the land'.

The phrase 'the great peace of the land' (*tenka taihei*) is doubly ideological. The Tokugawa regime used the concept to legitimize its rule, as a political ideology; the phrase 'great peace' appeared in the titles of atlases, in the language of edicts and in the contemporary histories of the period. But it continues to be ideological to this day, as the common knowledge, the 'academic consensus' about Japan, not only for the early modern period but in Japan in general. This second ideological deployment is the same one used by Pinker, namely as an unacknowledged assumption about history and the present, the 'unknown knowns', the things that we are not aware that we are aware of, as Zizek once said about how ideology operates, appropriating the language from Donald Rumsfeld's famous 'unknown's' quote.

On the surface, it seems like the title 'great peace' accurately describes the era. Nobody invaded Japan, warlords became 'lords' and while some commemorated their ancestor's loss to Tokugawa Ieyasu, a kind of early

---

[20]Morten Oxenboell, 'Epistemologies of Violence: Medieval Japanese War Tales', *History and Theory*, 56, no. 4 (2017): 44–59.

modern Japanese 'Lost Cause', no lord revolted against the Tokugawa regime. The Tokugawa shogunate acted as the centripetal force; lords lived every other year in Edo, while their wives and heirs lived there permanently as hostages meant to prevent rebellion. But the 270 or so domains located throughout Japan were relatively autonomous; some even drove diplomatic policy with close neighbours, especially the Korean kingdom. As long as lords played into the ceremony of deference to the shogunate, a government with sympathetic lords as advisers, then they were left to their own devices, thus 'performing the great peace', as one recent scholar described it.[21]

Warriors were to blame for much of the violence during the Warring States period, but during the first half of the seventeenth century, they flooded out of the countryside into their local castle town capitals, a trend no doubt welcomed by villagers. Nor could anyone act as both warrior and commoner, people had to choose a status, decisions largely unchangeable by their descendants. The famous 'sword hunts' of a previous hegemon, Toyotomi Hideyoshi, continued to be carried out by the Tokugawa regime, removing many weapons from the hands of non-warriors. With the means and carriers of violence largely monopolized by the regime, macro violence decreased in the countryside, while urbanization increased, especially in Edo, a city larger than any European capital. Travel became safer, commerce expanded and, as Suda Tsutomu has pointed out, the shogunate encouraged commoners to appeal grievances to local authorities rather than killing each other to solve problems – 'that was the wisdom of a society that avoided violence'.[22]

If the strong state is held up as one reason for declining violence, as suggested by historians of early modern Japan, so too has the 'civilizing process' been used to explain the pacification of samurai. The ideal government in premodern East Asian political philosophy required a balance between the 'civil' and the 'martial', with a slight preference for the former throughout Chinese and Korean history. Unlike China and Korea, Japan lacked a sizeable, purely civilian literati tradition. The civil nobility and clergy served as bureaucrats during much of premodern Japanese history, but, beginning in the seventeenth century, samurai served in such positions in the many domains and shogunate. Social historian Eiko Ikegami argued that warrior identity shifted from notions of honour and pride based on martial violence to one of self-control and education, from warrior to literate man. Ceremony had long been of interest to the most elite warriors; now even lowly warrior men were expected to know the basics. The state criminalized any form of personal fighting, including duelling, outlawed suicide upon the

[21]Luke Roberts, *Performing the Great Peace: Political Space and Open Secrets in Tokugawa Japan.* (Honolulu: University of Hawai'i Press, 2015).
[22]Suda Tsutomu, 'Advice from History', Meiji University online.

death of ones lord (*junshi*) and generally 'tamed' the samurai.[23] One samurai pundit of the early eighteenth century even complained of younger warriors, 'So many men now seem to have the pulse of a woman'.[24] Surely Pinker would approve of this feminization.

Complaints by older samurai, that the samurai of the ever-changing 'today' no longer knew what it meant to be a warrior, illustrate the main tension for samurai identity. They spoke to the need for violence to be maintained, even if in a restrained manner, as part of the warrior status group. Violence could not disappear entirely, but was, instead, proceduralized. Although fighting and duelling among samurai were punishable by death, regardless of the cause or who initiated the fight, a samurai had the right to cut down an offensive non-samurai, kill an adulterous wife and her lover, or avenge one's murdered father or uncle if one applied through local bureaucratic channels, gathered witnesses and received written permission to kill. The infamous 'ritual suicide' (*seppuku*) style of execution became institutionalized and was reserved for samurai alone. Even it became more civilized, shifting from actual disembowelment in the seventeenth century, to a simple gesture, reaching out for a short sword or a fan, that signalled an executor to cut off the head. By the end of the Tokugawa period, Ikegami asserts, 'the direct connection between samurai honor and the exercise of violence was gradually weakened, and a new ethic of the samurai as law-abiding "organizational men" had clearly emerged'.[25]

Growing disorder and violence occurred as the samurai became ever increasingly 'tamed', grotesque punishments receded from view and notions of benevolence prevailed. In other words, when thinking about 'taming' or 'civilizing' we would need to ask who is being tamed in the civilizing process; and, depending on how one defines 'violence', did Europe, or in this case, Japan, really experience less violence despite the surface appearance of more 'civilized' behaviour and the lack of 'war'? Moreover, were people in Europe so violent before the civilizing process? And, similarly, were samurai emotionally so aggressive, and informed by an honour that demanded violence, that they needed taming in the first place? The 'era of peace' argument might simply misrecognize the ideological claims of the Tokugawa regime that promoted itself as a bringer of peace, overemphasizing the barbaric nature of pre-Tokugawa warriors.[26] The Tokugawa samurai might have been more violent than their predecessors despite the lack of macro violence. Even Ikegami's example of a typical low-ranking warrior, a relatively poor samurai named

---

[23]Ikegami Eiko, *The Taming of the Samurai: Honorific Individualism and the Making of Modern Japan* (Cambridge, MA: Harvard University Press, 2003).
[24]Yamamoto Tsunetomo, *Hagakure*, trans. Alexander Bennett (Tokyo: Tuttle, 2014), 60.
[25]Ikegami, *The Taming of the Samurai*, 260.
[26]David Eason, 'The Culture of Disputes in Early Modern Japan, 1550-1700' (PhD diss, UCLA, 2009), 80.

Bunzaemon who led a tame life, 'never failed to write in his journal the talk of the town, all the local murders, love suicides, crimes of passion, and sexual scandals or acts of revenge. He also looked forward to testing his sword on corpses as part of his sword training'.[27]

Nor was it unusual, throughout the seventeenth century, that the educational 'scaffolding' for a teenage samurai included killing stray dogs, then practising sword skills on a criminal. Refusing to behead a criminal was seen as cowardice, and, in one chilling example, a samurai author 'vouched that beheading a fellow human being produced a pleasant feeling'.[28] Another writer, from the eighteenth century reflecting on the seventeenth century, noted that lowly aides or valets guilty of an offence presented samurai with opportunities to test their blades by conducting executions in the privacy of their own homes, but that such practices were either no longer maintained 'or else lords have become more benevolent and the old customs have died out'.[29]

The strong state might have led to decline in macro violence among the warriors, but even without a European Enlightenment the state also reduced both the intensity and the frequency of the most violent of punishments. As Daniel Botsman has shown, gory executions and grizzly torture gradually disappeared by the end of the seventeenth century, and those that remained were conducted out of sight. What is often forgotten in Norbert's Elias' account of the public disappearance of torture and punishment is not due to people no longer supporting violence, but simply not wanting to see it. As Barry Vaughn eloquently states it, Elias 'does not associate the onset of civilization with the extinction of violence, merely its occlusion'.[30]

If there was a decrease in certain forms of violence during early modern Japanese history, they occurred before interaction with the West. From the seventeenth century onwards, long before influence from Western penal reforms, evidence shows that the warrior regime taught officers and jailers to be compassionate rather than abuse, refrained from torturing pregnant women, and never executed children for murder.[31] Buddhist and Confucian notions of virtue, propriety, benevolence and mercy influenced the state's behaviour during the process of imprisonment and punishment, but those

---

[27]Ikegami, *The Taming of the Samurai*, 262–3.

[28]Beatrice Bodart-Bailey, *The Dog Shogun: The Personality and Policies of Tokugawa Tsunay-oshi* (Honolulu: University of Hawai'i Press, 2006), 130–1.

[29]From 'Tales from Long, Long ago', in Gerald Groemer, *Portraits of Edo and Early Modern Japan: The Shogun's Capital in Zuihitsu Writings 1657-1855* (Singapore: Palgrave Macmillan, 2019), 95.

[30]Barry Vaughan, 'The Civilizing Process and the Janus-Face of Modern Punishment'. *Theoretical Criminology*, 4, no. 1 (February 2000): 71–91. See also Philip Dwyer and Elizabeth Pederson in this volume.

[31]Daniel Botsman, *Punishment and Power in the Making of Modern Japan* (Princeton: Princeton University Press, 2013), 45.

same ideals led the regime to display beheaded heads, signalling to people that it was doing its duty to protect the people, in what Botsman calls 'bloody benevolence'. It was exactly in the name of humanity, benevolence and the concern for maintaining stability that, in the capital city Edo, the shogunate displayed heads as 'bodies as signs' for those passing in and out of the city. In other words, the regime's *political* ideology, as pacifiers of the realm, used violence to demonstrate the good that it was doing, just as modern states use violent incarceration practices to show citizens that the state is doing its job to project the people.

Early modern Japan seems to earn the epithet 'era of great peace'. But a pitfall of 'the era of peace' notion is that it usually referred to a peace among warriors through a lack of war; but what about everyone else? Urbanization led to economic dynamism, but in Edo, gangs of unemployed samurai attacked commoners for sport, and commoners formed gangs to retaliate; one scholar suggested that, until the eighteenth century, perhaps only the city of Osaka deserved the appellation 'pax Tokugawa'.[32] Another historian highlights the over 3,000 recorded peasants uprisings, two major insurrections and a couple of failed attempts to overthrow the shogunate, making this era seem 'anything but two and a half centuries of peace'.[33] Peasants who participated in uprisings typically did not target people and only sometimes destroyed property. They often amounted to little more than marches, nor were they 'revolutionary' in nature. But the frequency and degree of violence increased over time, from a low of 5.3 uprisings a year between 1590 and 1720, to nearly 24.4 a year from 1830 to 1871.[34] From the late eighteenth century onwards, those uprisings did not conform to the accepted norms, in which people were not harmed, but included personal assault, theft and arson. Instead of carrying farm tools as symbols of their status during uprisings, rather than as weapons, they now carried staves and swords. These new 'evil bands' (*akutō*), as they were called by rural folk, were comprised of young, disaffected men, who often organized themselves through semi-formal 'youth groups', originally meant to help rural society by planning and carrying out festivals, working on local public projects and acting as conflict mediators. They turned much of their ire against local authorities during times of economic hardship.[35] Both the degree and severity of these uprisings were caused by macro-structural changes in the economy; even as greater wealth was concentrated in the hands of

---

[32]Gary Leupp, 'Five Men of Naniwa: Gang Violence and Popular Culture in Genroku Osaka', in James L. McClain and Osamu A. Wakita (eds), *Osaka: The Merchant's Capital of Early Modern Japan* (Ithaca: Cornell University Press, 1999), 131.
[33]Peter Nosco, *Individuality in Early Modern Japan: Thinking for Oneself* (New York: Routledge, 2018), 43.
[34]Nosco, *Individuality in Early Modern Japan*, 43.
[35]Suda Tsutomu, *'Akutō' no Jūkyūseiki: Minshū Undō no Henshitsu to 'Kindai Ikōki'* (Tokyo: Aoki Shoten, 2002), 37–42.

merchants, greater insecurity led to violence among the poor. In other words, even if we accept that greater 'civilizing' occurred, and self-control pacified some people, structural 'gentle commerce' is always ungentle for someone else. Moreover, as Suda Tsutomu argues, it was not collective identity that contributed to this violence, contra-Pinker, who celebrates the individual over the group in the spread of non-violence, but the breakdown of the collective that characterized this phenomenon – individuals looked to help themselves ahead of the group.[36]

Indeed, youth violence persisted throughout the Tokugawa period. Contemporary observers noted that children engaged in large-scale mock wars, numbering several hundred at a time. They armed themselves with bamboo spears and challenged each other to fight. During the early nineteenth century, several such child 'wars' broke out in Edo. Similar to the uprisings, the increase in frequency and intensity of youth violence – 'an age of malevolent youth', as one scholar dubbed it – as best can be determined, coincided with disorder, natural disaster and economic woe that began during the 1890s.[37] We have no statistics about the population effects of such violence, whether or not these events led to a significant decrease in the population or inhibited population growth, but violence against infants – infanticide – was high enough in at least northeastern Japan to drastically affect population decline during the worst decades.[38] Nonetheless, what accounts for these seeming bursts of violence out of nowhere? Tokugawa Japan experienced increasing monetization and commercialization that benefitted the non-warrior wealthy elite. Yet economic gains for entrepreneurs did not translate into greater political participation. Moreover, every economic gain for one small group also included many economic losers: disaffected, underemployed youth with few opportunities. At the political top, a warrior hereditary caste, however tame they might have been, owed its existence to a violent past. That violence was celebrated in popular culture and could be appropriated by anyone to justify their resistance against the existing order.

The shift away from a bloodier seventeenth-century world began under the reign of the fifth shogun, Tokugawa Tsunayoshi (r. 1680–1709). Later, he was ridiculed for his 'laws of compassion', in which the harming of animals, especially stray dogs that had become a nuisance in Edo, was punishable by death. Kennels for the tens of thousands of dogs, paid for by Edo citizens, earned him the name 'dog shogun'. The laws also extended to compassionate treatment of humans. Ultimately, the laws were too strictly enforced, no

---

[36]Tsutomu, 'Akutō' no Jūkyūseiki, 71.
[37]W. Puck Brecher, 'Being a Brat: The Ethics of Child Disobedience in the Edo Period', in Peter Nosco (ed.), Values, Identity, and Equality in Eighteenth and Nineteenth Century Japan (Leiden: Brill, 2015), 94–6.
[38]See Fabian Drixler, Mabiki: Infanticide and Population Growth in Eastern Japan, 1660-1940 (Berkeley: University of California Press, 2013).

doubt expensive and unmanageable, and repealed immediately after his reign. In general, though, he tried to shift the martial–civil culture dyad more towards the side of culture. He cracked down on warrior behaviour, issuing new taxes, debasing coins and carrying out other reforms, ushering in a time of economic well-being and cultural flowering. At least one Confucian scholar lamented that during Tsunayoshi's time the killing of an offensive commoner on sight had become rare and that it had 'become fashionable to quibble that killing people is inhumane'.[39]

The accepted narrative about early modern Japan is that the era of peace ended during the nineteenth century. A series of interconnected events originated from inside and outside of Japan; Westerners, with the United States as the antagonist, forced unequal treaties upon the Japanese after several centuries of little contact with the West, subsequent anger towards the Tokugawa shogunate because of the treaties, newfound loyalist feelings towards the imperial institution, succession disputes within the Tokugawa clan, and natural disasters and economic woe, all culminated in an outbreak of domain civil wars, uprisings and assassinations. The Tokugawa shogunate collapsed in 1868, and resistance to the armies that fought in the name of the young Meiji emperor continued into 1869 (the Boshin War). The number of those killed in this Meiji Restoration era are unclear, but amount to around 30,000.

The Meiji Restoration

Slavoj Zizek, commenting upon the historiography of the French Revolution, wrote that no matter the political view, there is always a desire to explain away violence. On the conservative side, violence is seen as simply an anomaly on the march towards democracy, while liberals want to downplay violence altogether; 'everyone wants 1789 without 1793', just as people want coffee without the caffeine or chocolate without the sugar.[40] There is a similar attitude about the Meiji Restoration. A 2016 exhibition at the Edo-Tokyo museum that featured a famous samurai artist and swordsman, Yamaoka Tesshū, highlighted his role in the 'bloodless surrender of the Edo Castle', a slogan often used to characterize the Meiji Restoration as relatively non-violent or smooth. Historians typically characterize the Meiji Restoration as relatively bloodless compared to the French Revolution, a common description when comparing the Meiji Restoration to other foundational events in modern history. Not surprisingly, Japanese politicians often celebrate the Meiji Restoration in positive terms, such as during the 100th

---

[39]Bodart-Bailey, *The Dog Shogun*, 130, 145.
[40]Slavoj Zizek, *In Defense of Lost Causes* (London: Verso, 2017), 158.

anniversary in 1968, when, as Toyama Shigeki noted, politicians hoped that the centennial would reinvigorate patriotism among young people by showing them the Meiji energy that contributed to Japan's success.[41] In other words, a Japanese version of Zizek's observation might be that people want 1889, the promulgation of the Meiji Constitution, without 1869.

This second ideological deployment of 'great peace' began shortly after the Boshin War, in 1872, during the Iwakura Embassy to the West. Itō Hirobumi, one of the most powerful Meiji oligarchs, told an audience in San Francisco,

> Within a year a feudal system, firmly established centuries ago, has been completely abolished, without firing a gun or shedding a drop of blood. These wonderful results have been accomplished by the united action of a government and people, now pressing jointly forward in the peaceful paths of progress. What country in the middle ages broke down its feudal system without war?

Just like the Tokugawa 'era of peace', this new depiction of a uniquely peaceful Japan hides an undercurrent of ideological violence that shows up in unexpected bursts. Regardless how relatively peaceful the Boshin War might have been, what has been unresolved was the warrior fantasy that led to even more macro violence throughout the latter half of the nineteenth century.

An example of violence that seems to come from nowhere is best illustrated by an incident concerning the young and hopeful Mori Arinori, samurai member of the newly formed 'deliberative assembly', a group entirely comprised of samurai created to usher in a new modern government. In 1869, he proposed to the assembly that swords no longer be carried in public by anyone but police, military and government officials. The official who introduced the bill noted, with hesitation no doubt, that Mori simply wanted to point out that changes in government or law were not enough and that the very core of the people needed to be changed.

The reaction against Mori's proposal was swift and harsh. He was dismissed from the assembly, and had his rank demoted and his life threatened. Less well known is the assembly's debate about *seppuku*. More time was spent debating whether it should be abolished than on how to interact with Western countries (it was voted down 200 to 3). The elimination of the last vestiges of warrior identity, totems that anchored their internal sense of self for the samurai, fed into a series of violent conflicts that culminated in the Rebellion of the Southwest (1877). The Meiji Restoration hero and emperor-loyalist Saigō Takamori wanted the fledgling government to defend the country's

---

[41]For a full assessment of the 100th anniversary, see Toyama Shigeki, *Meiji Ishin to gendai* (Tokyo: Iwanami Shoten, 1968).

honour by forcing the Korean kingdom to recognize the new role of the Meiji emperor. The oligarchs rejected him. His followers, many samurai who wanted to preserve the right to wear two swords and maintain the distinctive samurai hairstyle, felt betrayed by the oligarchs, themselves now ex-samurai, who abolished these privileges. The government, recognizing the threat of warrior fantasies, even forbade the type of mass, hundred-child war games that pit a fictive Genji against the Heike, as all-too-violent re-enactments of the Gempei War, an overly 'boyish' activity that had caused problems during the Tokugawa period.[42]

The irony is that honour, which was meant to be interpreted as a pacifying, civilizing process, redefined during the Tokugawa period, according to Ikegami, as self-control and culture, informed mid-nineteenth civil conflicts among the warrior status group. Just as they felt the need to defend the honour of the emperor, on the one side, or the Tokugawa shogunate on the other, so too did influential leaders argue that Japan needed to defend its honour against Korea. These were not, to use Pinker's phrase, 'pockets of anarchy that lay beyond the reach of government [that] retained their violent cultures of honor'; it was, putatively, a 'tamed' culture of honour that had been part of the core of the warrior-dominated government that caused violence.

No doubt the end of the Meiji Restoration and the Boshin War was welcomed by those living in the areas affected by the violence. But as many philosophers throughout the twentieth century have argued, like Walter Benjamin, Michel Foucault or Frankfurt School thinkers, 'critical theorists', as Pinker hopes to scare quote them into oblivion, war does not bring an end to violence but merely changes it. 'Humanity does not gradually progress from combat to combat until it arrives at a universal reciprocity ... humanity installs each of its violences in a system of rules and thus proceeds from domination to domination ... and can be bent to any purpose', noted Foucault. Likewise, Walter Benjamin, who lived and died under fascism, reminds us, 'There is no document of civilization which is not at the same time a document of barbarism. And just as such a document is not free of barbarism, barbarism taints also the manner in which it was transmitted from one owner to another.'[43] Promises in the Charter Oath (1868) to rid Japan of the 'evil customs of the past', to 'seek knowledge ... to strengthen imperial rule', in addition to allowing people of all classes to pursue their own trade, and promises of a representative government, entered public discourse and found their way into the Imperial Rescript on Education (1890) and the constitution. Although good things certainly came from these documents, the emphasis on the emperor, the open question about who was

---

[42]Brecher, 'Being a Brat', 53.
[43]Foucault, 'Nietzsche, Genealogy, History', 85–6; Walter Benjamin, 'Thesis on History', in *Illuminations: Essays and Reflections* (New York: Harcourt, Brace & World, 1968), 256.

allowed to participate in government and in what capacities, and the issue of how a government eliminates 'evil customs', all speak to Benjamin's insight on the dark side of every progressive move forward.

The era of imperialism

The end of the warrior regime and the growth of an oligarchy, with pseudo representative government, incorporated new notions of hygiene, government reform, commercial development and international cooperation with the Western powers. Intellectuals tried to convince citizens to respect the emperor, cooperate with the government, reform their attitudes towards gender relations, control the self and replace premodern spirits with science, ideas encapsulated in the Meiji era (1868–1912) slogan 'Civilization and Enlightenment'. Public intellectuals like Fukuzawa Yukichi, who looked to the life and thought of Benjamin Franklin for inspiration, used the phrase to promote Western-style scientific inquiry and political liberalism. The concept was behind many Meiji period reforms, for example the impetus for penal reform stemmed from a desire to renegotiate unequal treaties that had been founded on Western views of Japan's uncivilized punishments. In civilizing Japan with more humane punishments, the Meiji oligarchs hoped to raise its status as a fellow civilized nation in the eyes of the Western powers.

The most significant change in what we might call 'modernity's violence' was its invisibility, masked by notions of scientific, bureaucratic and economic progress. Zizek described this dynamic as the interaction between 'subjective violence', which is visible and has an obvious agent (an army, a terrorist, a murder), and an 'objective', systemic and symbolic violence which is invisible yet is the root cause of subjective violence.[44] We can well imagine how this operates even now. A Western-based corporation needs raw materials from a non-Western country; it appropriates land directly, or benefits from land indirectly by purchasing materials from a company based in the target country. Land is taken from local people legally, bulldozed for use in providing raw materials in new (more efficient, profitable, etc.) supply chains, with any resistance from local people brutally oppressed. Subjective violence highlights either the violent, 'terroristic' resistance of locals or their violent repression by the non-Western government. What is ignored is the objective violence of the Western corporation on behalf of which all of the subjective violence occurs.

The systemic violence is always ideological and historical; it announces bad guys and good guys even if an ideologue is unaware of it. This is how Pinker operates: 'communism' is blamed for atrocities throughout the

---

[44]Slavoj Zizek, *Violence* (London: Profile, 2008), 1–2.

twentieth century, while capitalism ('gentle commerce') is celebrated as a counter to violence. The suffering of Indian textile workers or Chinese factory labour never enters Pinker's calculous of violence, nor are deaths from industrial pollution, such as the 1984 Bhopal gas accident caused by Union Carbide in India, which are as calculable as mortality from warfare, or the connection between imperialism and capitalism. Pinker is partly correct to point out that a leader's bellicose ambitions, and, by implication, macro violence, in a market economy, 'is constrained by stakeholders who control the means of production and who might oppose a disruption of international trade that's bad for business'. The stakeholders who control the means of production constrain the leader and his government, preventing violence to their disruptions of trade, but they support violence when seeking sources of raw materials and cheap labour.

Thus, the early Meiji oligarchs, looking to the West as a model, understood the connection between capitalism and violence – 'rich nation, strong military' became another popular slogan. The government removed legal and labour impediments to heavy industry, and, in return, heavy industry (mining, steel, ships) supplied the state with the means for building a military. Light industry spread throughout the countryside, in fine Ayn Randian fashion, unfettered by regulations. Predictably, salaries for silk mill workers, mostly girls and women, plummeted. Many labourers lived as indentured servants and received no pay at all. Unhealthy conditions during the daytime led to higher-than-normative rates of death from respiratory diseases like tuberculosis. They spent long nights locked in dormitories. On the military side, Otto von Bismarck warned the Japanese oligarchs about the empty meaning of law without the violence to support it: 'If the law of nations contained in it an advantage for them, the powerful would apply the law of nations to the letter, but when it lacked attraction, the law of nations was jettisoned, and military might employed, regardless of tactics.'[45]

The concepts behind these two slogans also informed Japan's imperial expansion. First, in the invasion of Taiwan (1874), Japan launched a punitive expedition against Taiwanese natives who attacked Ryukyuan fishermen. The government depicted this colonial moment as an act of 'civilizing' the Taiwanese aborigines.[46] Second, and more devastating, capitalism and its attending notions of scientific efficiency and profit killed millions of Chinese in addition to those killed in the subjective violence of warfare. It was not only ethnic pride, nationalism or racism that facilitated violence by Japan against the Chinese; it was also the logic of capitalism. Migrant workers

---

[45]See in Ando Nisuke, *Japan and International Law: Past, Present and Future: International Symposium to Mark the Centennial of the Japanese Association of International Law* (The Hague: Kluwer, 1999), 354–5.
[46]Robert Eskildsen, 'Of Civilization and Savages: The Mimetic Imperialism of Japan's 1874 Expedition to Taiwan', *The American Historical Review*, 107, no. 2 (April 2002): 388–418.

on transport ships in China were listed alongside 'soybeans and light machinery', rather than with passengers or crew.[47] At least 10,000 Chinese died in Japanese-run mines in China; conditions were only slightly better for miners in Japan. But the worst offenders might have been pharmaceutical companies. They profited from morphine sales to Europeans during the First World War, but had to legalize it in Korea after the war in order to keep profits high, creating 100,000 Korean addicts.[48] The situation was worse in Japan's puppet state, Manchukuo, where 5 million Chinese were addicted to drugs, and a little over half of all revenue came from drug sales.[49] Opium addicts were arrested, given amphetamines by the Manchukuo Welfare Ministry, and then sent to work to death in Japanese factories, all in the name of scientific development.[50] Lest we dismiss this as simply part of wartime violence, recent research points to the connection between the government, big business and opioid deaths even in the United States.[51]

Violence and deaths from more obvious sources, warfare, are slightly easier to calculate. First, warfare had been endemic to Japan's imperial legacy. Japan fought the Qing dynasty in the Sino-Japanese War (1894–5), taking control of Taiwan, and then engaged Russia in the Russo-Japanese War (1904–5) gaining control of Korea, first as a protectorate, and then as a colony (1910). The Sino-Japanese War only lasted six months before China capitulated, and the death toll was small compared to other events; approximately 15,000 died of fighting, wounds and disease. The Russo-Japanese War was much deadlier, with a total combatant mortality of 150,000 and nearly 20,000 civilians killed.

These first two modern international wars in East Asia established a foundation for Japan's growing empire and set the stage for the Asia-Pacific War. Japan's military, industrial and commercial interests grew throughout the Korean peninsula into northern China before the Great Depression. Railroads were key to this expansion, especially the South Manchurian Railroad Company, which, despite its name, operated a number of businesses including hotels, mills, warehouses and chemical research and development. The Japanese military had branches in both northern China and Korea to protect its businesses and civilians. Rampant warlordism in northern China contributed to the chaos, with some warlords aiding or fighting the Japanese in China, or both. The Japanese army in northern China, the Kwangtung army, assassinated one warlord and also faked an attack on Japan's railroad in order to pre-empt an invasion. Japan installed the last Qing emperor as

---

[47]Mark Driscoll, *Absolute Erotic, Absolute Grotesque: The Living, Dead, and Undead in Japan's Imperialism, 1895-1945* (Durham: Duke University Press, 2010), 55.
[48]Driscoll, *Absolute Erotic, Absolute Grotesque*, 117.
[49]Driscoll, *Absolute Erotic, Absolute Grotesque*, 237.
[50]See Driscoll, *Absolute Erotic, Absolute Grotesque*, 289–303.
[51]Michael Porter et al., 'A Recovery Squandered: US State of Competitiveness', Harvard Business School, December 2019, 28.

a leader of a puppet state called Manchukou. This set off the second Sino-Japanese War (1937–45).

The death tolls in the second Sino-Japanese War in Japan and China, including civilians, is difficult to measure. Numbers range from 20 million on the Chinese side, including those wounded but not killed, to as many as 35 million according to Chinese sources. Numbers were slightly more than 1.5 million on the Japan side. This does not include the over 90 million refugees, or those who died serving the Japanese empire in factories. Nor does it convey how Enlightenment values operating during this violence, namely social Darwinism, and efficient Fordist approaches to industries led to their death.

Article nine of the post-war constitution restrains any military ambitions that Japan might have, although that article was already being challenged by geopolitical interests shortly after it was written. The United States wanted Japan to rebuild its military to counter the rise of communism in East Asia. The self-defence forces were a legalistic compromise; it has the appearance of an army, navy and air force, but is technically not a 'military', nor does it engage in combat abroad.

But many conservatives in Japan want to change the constitution to free their self-defence force from any legal constraints and thus become what they call a 'normal country'. This might be a theme that ties together the threads of premodern, early modern and modern Japan, and perhaps, by extension, the world itself – a state's potential use of violence is the normal state of things. But states never use violence, whether through its penal system, police force or military, without some ideology, visible or otherwise, that justifies its use.

Conclusion

In this brief outline of violence throughout Japanese history, and, to a lesser extent, modern East Asian history, I hoped to point out several problems inherent with the Pinker thesis regarding two issues: first, the desire to show a linear trend from an extremely violent past to a less violent modern, present; second, the flaws in the assumptions about how history functions as a discipline of thought and argumentation.

Regarding the putatively violent past, there just is not enough reliable information to assert with authority precisely how violent the prehistorical, ancient and medieval periods were. What little information that exists suggests that the premodern period was not as violent as it might seem. Moreover, anecdotes are not a good substitute for statistical evidence. For example, as horrible as the attack on the Buddhist temples and monasteries might have been, we really can never be certain how many people were killed. The same can be said of Imjin War or, unexplored in this chapter, the

An Lushan rebellion (755–63) in China that supposedly resulted in up to an unlikely 36 million people killed.

In the case of Japan, the spikes in violence certainly seem non-linear. Before the seventeenth century, the waxing and waning of macro violence suggests that forces beyond notions of humanity, freedom and other such 'better angels' caused violent events. And when an 'era of peace' seemed to occur during the Tokugawa period, there was no Enlightenment streaming out of the European centre towards the non-European periphery. Marco violence in Japan declined compared to the Warring States period that preceded the 'era of peace', but a usefully ambiguous, negotiated peace existed between the warlords-turned-lords and the Tokugawa regime that led to stability, on the one hand, and the notions of benevolence and virtuous rule that led to creation of more peaceful bureaucracies on the other. Even so, if we include peasant uprisings and urban violence, in some way, the Tokugawa period might have been more violent than the centuries before it, including even the Warring States period. And like the Enlightenment values in Europe, notions of benevolence and virtue could, indeed, justify violence.

Like the Pinker thesis, notions of the always-already peaceful Tokugawa Japan, is clouded by ideology. It is probably no accident that Tokugawa Japan, often described as isolated in addition to being peaceful, is called 'early modern' Japan, in a state of bringing to the world a uniquely unique people and culture subjected to decidedly un-Enlightened militarists who brought Japan and East Asia into war. No, violence is part of modernity just as much as iPhone and freedom of speech. To claim that the Enlightenment, a time of 'almost modern', brings with it only good things cannot logically be true.

12

British imperial violence and the Middle East

Caroline Elkins

By the summer of 1938, the Arab Revolt in Mandatory Palestine had been raging for some two years and Britain had lost control of the situation. Both sides of the imperial divide terrorized Arab villagers, and the rebels dominated the countryside where they destroyed vast swaths of Palestine's infrastructure. As Britain scrambled to reassemble a new leadership cadre to take charge and crush the rebellion once and for all, a lone intelligence officer, Captain Orde Wingate, stepped forward with an idea to 'terrorize the terrorists . . . [to] catch them and just wipe them out'.[1] Officials at the highest level endorsed Wingate's brainchild – the Special Night Squads – and with it the plan '[t]o set up a system and undetected movement of troops and police by night, across country and into villages, surprising gangs, restoring confidence to peasants, and gaining government control of rural areas'.[2] For Wingate and his superior officers, translating Britain's superior 'national character' and prowess in training and natural aggression into a highly disciplined counterterror operation with the single goal of wiping out Arab rebels was the key to re-establishing British colonial control.

Wingate's Third Force took its brand of counterterrorism straight to the heart of the Arab villages. The Special Night Squads soon earned their

---

[1]Imperial War Museum (IWM), Sound Archive, Accession 4619, Fred Howbrook.
[2]IWM, Document Collection, 4623, Private Papers of Major General H. E. N. Bredin, 'Appreciation by Captain OC Wingate, of Force HQ Intelligence on 5.6.38 at NAZARETH of the possibilities of night movements by armed forces of the Crown with the object of putting an end to terrorism in Northern Palestine'.

legendary status when body counts and repression were the barometers for success. On their captain's orders, Wingate's men preferred inflicting bodily harm with blood-staining and dismembering bayonets and bombs rather than bullets; their leader's 'morality of punishment' also inspired them.[3] Reprisals became part of the Squads' repertoire, with oil-soaked sand stuffed into the mouths of uncooperative Arabs. Wingate boasted how 'anyone hanging about the line for an unlawful purpose was liable swiftly and silently to vanish away'.[4]

Britain's empire would become as renowned for creating civil wars as they would be for leaving them in its wake, and Palestine was no exception. The Special Night Squads would become a training ground for future Jewish insurgents, both against Britain and eventually the Arab population. So, too, did the Squads embrace a wide swath of British security forces, some of whom, like Corporal Fred Howbrook and Lieutenant Rex King-Clark, were professional soldiers trained to kill.[5] Others, when the Special Night Squads expanded, were like the inexperienced, job-seeking Sydney Burr, who, on a policing contract in Palestine, only knew Arabs as 'wogs' and casually recounted at the time how 'most of the information we get is extracted by third degree methods, it is the only way with these people'.[6] Many of these men were young, rough and ready recruits who were steeped in the Black and Tan traditions that suffused the Palestine Police Force after many within the Irish forces took up posts in the Mandate after 1922.

From the start, Arab politicians, including the president of the Palestine Arab Delegation to the League of Nations, Jamal al-Husayni, as well as European missionaries, local colonial officials, residents of Palestine, and military and police personnel documented Britain's repressive measures targeted primarily at the Palestinian Arab population – measures that were embraced not only by Special Night Squads but also at every level of British military, policing and colonial administrations.[7] Accounts of torture and humiliation, murder and systemized suffering were privately brought to Britain's successive high commissioners in Palestine, as well as to the Archbishop of the Anglican Church and Britain's War and Colonial

---

[3] John Bierman and Colin Smith, *Fire in the Night: Wingate of Burma, Ethiopia, and Zion* (New York: Random House, 1999), 115.

[4] Bierman and Smith, *Fire in the Night*, 115–16; and Liddell Hart Centre for Military Archives (LHCMA), King's College London, United Kingdom, Captain B.H. Liddell Hart Papers, GB0099, 11/1936-1938, Captain O.C. Wingate OCSNS, 'Report of Operations carried out by Special Night Squads on Night of 11/12 July 1938'.

[5] R. King-Clark, *Free for a Blast* (London: Grenville Publishing Company Limited, 1988), 157.

[6] IWM, Department of Documents, 88/8/1, Private Papers of S. Burr, Letter c. June 1937; for use of the term 'wogs' see multiple letters in the file, including 9 July 1937; 20 December 1937; c. March 1938, and c. April 1938.

[7] For example, see Middle East Centre Archive (MECA), St. Antony's College, Oxford, United Kingdom, GB165-0161, Jerusalem and East Mission, Boxes 61 and 66.

Offices.[8] A common refrain emerged as official responses rebounded in liberalism's echo chamber of denials – denials well-rehearsed in previous imperial dramas. In this instance, such lies and exaggerations, according to myriad British officials, were the handiwork of Arab propagandists, fuelled in no small way by the opportunistic inveigling of Europe's rising fascist tide that sought to discredit the good name of Britain and its empire.[9] Prime Minister Neville Chamberlain's Cabinet went so far as to dismiss the flow of allegations from Palestine as 'absolutely baseless', and declared that 'the character of the British soldier is too well known to require vindication'.[10]

Still, al-Husayni persisted and appealed to the League of Nations. Gesturing to the situation's gravity through historical analogy, he wrote:

Such atrocities of the dark ages, to which the human race, nowadays, look back with disgust and horror, of torturing men during criminal investigation and assaulting peaceful people and destroying their properties wholesale when peacefully lying within their homes are actions that have daily been perpetrated in the Holy Land during the greater part of the last three years.[11]

The letter's analogous flair then gave way to specificity. Among other excesses, al-Husayni described the 'scorching' of body parts with 'hot iron rods', 'severe beating with lashes', the 'pulling out [of] nails and scorching the skin under them by special appliances' and the 'pulling of the sexual organs'. He detailed the British forces' widespread ransacking and looting of homes, summary executions, disappearances, the denial of food and water to innocent civilians, the rape of women and girls, and the destruction of livestock. The diplomat then closed his appeal, reminding the League that, 'if the Mandatory [power of Britain] is innocent of these excesses then our demand for a neutral enquiry should be welcomed by all concerned'.[12]

While the outcome of al-Husayni's appeal hung in an international balance weighted by the *realpolitik* of fascism's advances, so too was it calibrated within liberalism's framework of permissible norms. These norms did not spring from Europe's pressing exigencies of the late 1930s, but rather were deeply rooted in the long durée of liberal imperialism's spread, particularly in Britain and its empire. There, stretching back before the

---

[8]Middle East Centre Archive (MECA), St. Antony's College, Oxford, United Kingdom, GB165-0161, Jerusalem and East Mission, Boxes 61 and 66.
[9]For example, Hansard, *House of Commons Debate* (*HCD*), vol. 341, cc 1988, 24 November 1938.
[10]TNA, WO 32/4562, Memorandum from G.D. Roseway to C.G.L. Syers, 12 January 1939.
[11] TNA, WO 32/4562, Letter from Jamaal Husseini, president, Palestine Arab Delegation, to His Excellency, the president of the Permanent Mandates Commission, 12 June 1939.
[12]TNA, WO/32/4562, Letter from Jamaal Husseini, president, Palestine Arab Delegation, to His Excellency, the president of the Permanent Mandates Commission, 12 June 1939.

Victorian era, conceptions of brown and Black subjects, the justifications for – if not the necessity of – violence and moral claims to a superior civilization created a tapestry of ideas that found expression in colonial administrations, imperial security forces, enabling legal scaffoldings, policies of divide and rule, and nationalist conceptions of Britain and the benevolent myths that belied them. So, too, did they find expression in the League's Permanent Mandate's Commission, which was as much a reflection of liberal imperialism's agenda as it was an oversight agent for its alleged transgressions.

The degree to which al-Husayni was aware of the mutually informing ideological, political and structural forces working against him is uncertain. Even so, this skilled and measured diplomat surely had some inclination of the ways in which interwar Palestine was a cauldron of ideas, institutions and personalities that had been incubated elsewhere in the imperial world. This world was one in which violence, even in its most severe forms, had evolved into a framework that was not simply justificatory but was also internalized by many of those wielding power, from the highest reaches of decision-making to the lowest levels of execution, as de rigueur.

By the eve of the Second World War, it was in Mandatory Palestine where decades of liberal imperialist ideas and practices that had matured across vast swaths of the British Empire would descend and consolidate in the most dramatic and consequential of ways. The reach and impact of these ideas and practices, as well as the individuals executing them, would extend well beyond al-Husayni's Palestine and the League's pending response to the repressive watermarks staining the Mandate's files to a post–Second World War future where Britain would systematically deploy violence – normalized over decades, if not centuries – in its last-gasp effort to hang onto empire and secure a place in the New World Order.

In the case of Palestine, and indeed much of the twentieth-century Anglo-colonial world, British liberalism gave rise to a framework of permissible norms and logics of violence in empire that myriad scholars often misunderstand, if they examine it at all. When Steven Pinker suggests that violence was on the decline and humanitarianism on the rise in the twentieth century, he offers the myth of British imperial benevolence, an academic fillip that can scarcely withstand empirical scrutiny. Pinker ignores copious amounts of historical evidence, including countless files documenting Britain's creation and deployment of violent repression in 1930s Palestine and elsewhere in the empire, not to mention the lived experiences of hundreds of millions of Black and brown people, some of whom offer detailed accounts of systematic violence throughout the twentieth-century British imperial world through memoirs, appeals to British and international commissions, letters to Colonial Office and newspaper articles, among other sources.

Had Pinker interrogated fully violence in the British Empire, and with it my 2005 publication, *Imperial Reckoning: The Untold Story of*

Britain's Gulag in Kenya, he would have been aware of the systemized violence that Britain deployed during the Mau Mau Emergency in colonial Kenya.[13] He might also, at a minimum, have gestured to the connections between 1950s Kenya and other theatres of British imperial violence such as those in Palestine, both before and after the Second World War. Had he widened his aperture, he might have located the genesis of twentieth-century British colonial violence in two processes – the birth of liberal imperialism and the evolution of legalized lawlessness in the empire. Together, they provided the ideological and legal apparatuses necessary for Britain's repeated deployment of systematized violence in far-flung corners of the globe.

Put another way, liberal imperialism, or the twinned birthing of liberalism and imperialism in the nineteenth century gave rise to liberal authoritarianism. In turn, this ideology, which underpinned Britain's civilizing mission, took form in various enabling legal scaffoldings, which included the evolution of martial law into emergency regulations, or statutory martial law, as well as the parallel consolidation of military doctrine and law around the issues of force. These reinforcing processes unfolded from the turn of the nineteenth century and continued through the interwar period into the era of decolonization after the Second World War. On the ground, various forms of systemized violence evolved in Sudan and the South African War, then the Easter Rising in Ireland, Amritsar, the evolution of air control in Iraq, the Egyptian uprising, the Irish War of Independence, the ongoing acts of revolutionary violence in Bengal, Western Wall violence and the Arab Revolt, where their coalesce and maturity created particular, British imperial-inspired forms of legalized lawlessness. Once crystalized, it's hardly surprising that these same policies and practices – often transferred from one hot spot to the next by shared cadres of colonial and military officers and footmen – unfolded in the late 1940s and 1950s on massive scales in colonies like Malaya, Kenya and Cyprus. There, detention without trial, torture, forced labour and starvation became routine tactics in suppressing the so-called terrorists demanding their independence from British colonial rule.

Locating the ideological framework for systematized violence in the British Empire takes us back to the nineteenth century. The extension of Britain's global power and domination brought with it history-defining debates about universal principles, free markets, the protection of property and rule of law, and, importantly, who was and was not entitled to the rights and responsibilities of citizenship. As liberal thought evolved in Europe, it intersected with the rise of empires. There was a mutually constitutive relationship between liberalism and imperialism that would have profound

---

[13]Caroline Elkins, *Imperial Reckoning: The Untold Story of Britain's Gulag in Kenya* (New York: Henry Holt, 2005).

consequences on British conceptions of liberty, progress and governance both at home and abroad.[14]

Defining much of British thought was the categorical assumption that a parochial Western liberalism, intrinsically universal, belonged to all people worldwide. Yet, there were deep contradictions in the liberal imperial project – contradictions that were increasingly understood through a racial lens. John Stuart Mill juxtaposed civilization and barbarism to create new ideological idioms. He advocated for a progressive notion of citizenship and a narrative of human development that was intimately bound with Britain's civilizing mission.[15] Good government in empire had to be adjusted to local 'stages of civilization', with Mill advocating for a paternalistic form of despotism to tutor empire's children. According to Mill, 'a civilized government, to be really advantageous to [subject populations], will require to be in a considerable degree despotic: one over which they do not themselves exercise control, and which imposes a great amount of forcible restraint upon their actions.'[16] In effect, England had a right, if not responsibility, to rule despotically to reform the barbarous populations of the world.

Universalist ideas gave way to culture and history conditioning human character. In an emerging global citizenry, inclusivity would come in stages, if ever. With Britain's political ascendancy over subject populations, Mill declared 'the same rules of international morality do not apply between civilized nations and between civilized nations and barbarians'.[17] While written in the mid-Victorian era, echoes of Mill's exclusion of 'barbarians' from the 'international morality' of the 'civilized nations' would resonate in twentieth-century justifications and denials of repression, as well as the denial of human rights laws to imperial subjects.[18] As empire expanded, and subject populations refused to conform to British conceptions of progress and civilizing largesse, Mill's liberal imperialism – which denied individual sovereignty to brown and Black peoples around the world, while holding

---

[14]The subsequent analysis draws upon a range of works, including Thomas R. Metcalf, *Ideologies of the Raj* (Cambridge: Cambridge University Press, 1994); Uday Singh Mehta, *Liberalism and Empire: A Study in Nineteenth-Century British Liberal Thought* (Chicago: Chicago University Press, 1999); Karuna Mantena, *Alibis of Empire: Henry Maine and the Ends of Liberal Imperialism* (Princeton: Princeton University Press, 2010); and Jennifer Pitts, *A Turn to Empire: The Rise of Imperial Liberalism in Britain and France* (Princeton: Princeton University Press, 2005).

[15]See, for example, Eileen P. Sullivan, 'Liberalism and Imperialism: J.S. Mill's Defense of the British Empire', *Journal of the History of Ideas*, 44 (1983): 599–617.

[16]John Stuart Mill, *Considerations on Representative Government* (New York: CreateSpace, 2014 (first published, 1861)), 4.

[17]As quoted in Sullivan, 'Liberalism and Imperialism', 610.

[18]Mantena makes a similar point in *Alibis of Empire*, 33.

out the promise of reform – opened the justificatory door to coercion as an instrument of colonial rule.[19]

A series of violent events in empire would harden notions of imperial subjects and their rights. The heroic civilizing mission, despite a rhetorical staying power that Pinker's work so ably embraces, would in practice be greatly eviscerated and replaced with a moral disillusionment and disavowal of liberalism's capacity to transform the backward peoples of empire, at least in part. In its place would enter a British imperial rule that, while still projecting its moral claims of the civilizing mission, accentuated and codified difference, and countenanced the threat and deployment of various forms of violence. The Indian Rebellion of 1857, followed by the Morant Bay Rebellion in Jamaica and with it the Governor Eyre crisis, would precipitate this volte-face. The Anglo-imperial pendulum swung in the conservative direction, with the likes of Thomas Carlyle and James Fitzjames Stephen leveraging the moment to further authoritarian views on imperial rule. They castigated Mill's 'sentimental liberalism', which reputedly undermined political stability in the empire and at home. For his part, Stephen was relentless, asserting an unapologetic racial superiority and advocating for absolute rule in the colonies and, with it the necessity of coercion. As far as Mill's beloved rule of law was concerned – a rule of law important to Pinker's thesis – James Fitzjames Stephen did not hedge, writing, 'Force is an absolutely essential element of all law whatever. Indeed, law is nothing but regulated force subjected to particular conditions and directed toward particular objects'.[20]

In retrospect, the liberal in Britain's liberal authoritarianism is often difficult to discern in empire. Initial acts of conquest would give way in the twentieth century to elaborate legal codes, the proliferation of police and security forces, circumscriptions on free-market economies for the colonized, and administrative apparatuses that marginalized and oppressed entire populations while fuelling racial and ethnic divisions within and between them. The lived realities of Britain's burden in the empire would be vastly different from the nation's self-representations, grounded as they were in a historical consciousness that was equally as deft at collective erasure and creating approbatory versions of the nation's past as it was in disseminating these ideas through liberalism's official and unofficial channels.

Had Pinker acknowledged liberalism's obfuscating abilities, he would have discovered the paradox between lived, imperial experiences of the colonized and the laudatory claims of Britain's civilizing mission. Indeed,

---

[19]See, for example, Nadia Urbinati, 'The Many Heads of the Hydra: J. S. Mill on Despotism', in Nadia Urbinati and Alex Zakaras (eds), *J. S. Mill's Political Thought: A Bicentennial Reassessment* (Cambridge: Cambridge University Press, 2007), 74–5.

[20]James Fitzjames Stephen, *Liberty, Equality, Fraternity*, ed. Stuart D. Warner (Indianapolis: Liberty Fund, 1993), 111.

the power of liberalism's obfuscations can be traced not only in the persistence of British imperial myths in today's Anglo-popular culture but also in scholarly works such as Pinker's that fail to interrogate the erasures and denials – like those put forth during the Arab Revolt – that litter Britain's colonial past. Nor do these works unpack the mutual constitution of liberalism and imperialism, and with it a dominant narrative of universal human emancipation, equality, rights and the civilizing mission that materialized simultaneously with an underbelly of repression as expressed in evolutionary thought, racism, class and sexism, among other things. The privileged media through which liberalism would do its work – including bureaucracy, mass media, law, literacy and the scholarly academy – became means of emancipation and inclusion, as well as tools of repression and obfuscation.

The evolution of legalized lawlessness, and its co-existence with an evolving military doctrine was, in many ways, an epiphenomenon of liberal authoritarianism. Racial and cultural difference become institutionalized at every level of executive, legislative and judicial rule in the British Empire. That military doctrine also reflected the 'rule of colonial difference' pervading British discourse, practices and institutions at home and in the empire should scarcely be surprising.[21] As Britain kept ticking off imperial, small wars and other eruptions of violence, its military increasingly considered best practices for dealing with the so-called recalcitrant natives, or terrorists, as was often the term. In turn, these practices would become part and parcel of the broader institutionalization of violence and were best captured in the work of Colonel Charles Callwell, who is a major figure in the study of counter-insurgency practices throughout the twentieth century. His *Small Wars: Their Principles and Practices* – originally written in 1896, and updated after he served as a staff officer and commander in the South African War – would become the starting point for nearly all counter-insurgency theorists and practitioners, even down to the present day.[22] Callwell's expansive work not only synthesized Britain's military engagements throughout the empire but also drew lessons from French, Spanish, American and Russian campaigns, among others. Together, these reference points would provide him with a range of historical examples that supported not only the perceived short-term effectiveness of unbridled force but also an ideological framework that understood such repressive measures to be a reflection of liberalism's underbelly.

For Callwell, when European troops were engaged in wars against the 'uncivilised' and 'savage' populations of the world, as opposed to civilized

---

[21]Partha Chatterjee, *The Nation and Its Fragments* (Princeton: Princeton University Press, 1993), 10.

[22]Colonel C. E. Callwell, *Small Wars: Their Principles and Practices* (Lincoln: University of Nebraska Press, 1996).

armies, a different set of rules were needed.[23] Callwell pointed to the 'moral force of civilisation' underwriting European superiority, and the need to teach 'savage' peoples 'a lesson which they will not forget'.[24] It was not only the strategic advantage of such measures that Callwell endorsed in waging total destruction against the enemy. Rather, he emphasized in his treatise the 'moral effect' that brutality wrought upon 'uncivilised' populations, writing:

> [The] object is not only to prove to the opposing force unmistakably which is the stronger, but also to inflict punishment on those who have taken up arms. . . . [The] enemy must be made to feel a moral inferiority throughout. . . . [Fanatics and savages] must be thoroughly brought to book and cowed or they will rise again.[25]

Callwell's 'moral effect' reflected the military's ease with fusing the White Man's Burden with battlefield strategies to produce a morality of violence that belied imperial confrontations around the globe. At once racist and perversely paternalistic, Callwell's moralistic terms, nonetheless, suggest the ways in which British military doctrine reproduced the Victorian-era norms of liberal imperialism, norms that understood the uses of violent measures to be a necessary part of ensuring order and civilizing the backward races of the world.[26] With its binaries of good versus evil framing justifications of violence in the empire, liberal imperialism was not simply an exculpatory ideology. It both shaped and reflected self and national understandings in parliamentary debates, media outlets, popular culture and commemorative acts, among other things. It also shaped military thinking and practices for Callwell and many of his successors – from the highest-ranking officials to the ordinary soldier – in future colonial conflicts.[27] In the years ahead, the main issue would be the legal and political frameworks necessary to accommodate Callwell's punitive violence. Once conventional warfare methods were jettisoned, 'It is then that the regular troops', according to Callwell, 'are forced to resort to cattle lifting and village burning and that the war assumes an aspect which may shock the humanitarian'.[28]

Turning historically to empire, there was a parallel evolution of legal and political norms that reflected the Britain's on-the-ground deployment of violence, as articulated in Callwell's treatise. Whereas government by

---

[23]The terms 'uncivilised' and 'savage' are deployed throughout Callwell's writings.

[24]Callwell, *Small Wars*, 102.

[25]Callwell, *Small Wars*, 41, 72, 148.

[26]Ian F. W. Becket suggests a similar point in *Modern Insurgencies and Counter-Insurgencies: Guerrillas and their Opponents since 1750* (London: Routledge, 2001), 25, 183.

[27]Daniel Whittingham, '"Savage Warfare": C. E. Callwell, the Roots of Counterinsurgency, and the Nineteenth-Century Context', in Matthew Hughes (ed.), *British Ways of Counterinsurgency: A Historical Perspective* (London: Routledge, 2013), 13–29, here 14.

[28]Callwell, *Small Wars*, 40.

consent increasingly defined England, Scotland and Wales in the nineteenth
century, order was imposed upon Ireland, for example, through a series of
Insurrection Acts, Habeas Corpus Suspension Acts, and deployments of
martial law. When these were not sufficient, Coercion Acts were introduced,
with measures to control arms, provide for special systems of trial, and
criminalize oath taking, among other things. At the time, the jurist and
constitutionalist theorist, Albert Dicey, made clear that the Coercion Acts
were fully incompatible with the rule of law and the ideals of civil liberties,
stating:

> in principle . . . thoroughly vicious . . . [it] in effect gave the Irish
> executive an unlimited power of arrest; it established in them a despotic
> government. . . . [It] could not be made permanent, and applied to the
> whole United Kingdom without depriving every citizen of security for his
> person freedom.[29]

Ultimately, the acts became the precursors for modern states of emergency
whose legal codes transferred repressive powers to civilian authorities
who, in turn, could declare a state of emergency, or the English equivalent
of a state of siege. This was distinct from the declaration of martial law,
and significantly for Ireland and other parts of the empire, little under the
Coercion Acts conferring emergency-like powers could be questioned in a
court of law.[30]

Looking elsewhere in the empire, the Defence of India Act was passed
in 1915, and was sweeping in its repressive scope. The act enabled India's
executive to pass any regulation to secure the public safety and defence
of the British Raj. In Bengal alone, some 800 orders were put into force,
eviscerating civil and political liberties, such as they existed.[31] When
Britain turned to arming the civilian state in Ireland with the Easter Rising
in 1916, and later what became the Irish War of Independence, they did
so through a host of highly authoritarian acts. Wielding a legally enabled
strategy of coercion, Whitehall and its Dublin Castle counterpart fuelled
a war that quickly descended into an intensified bloodbath of killings,
reprisals and counter-reprisals. It was also one that witnessed a deployment
of both military and police forces – including the notorious Black and
Tans and Auxiliaries – who helped carry out legalized reprisals in the
final months of the Irish War of Independence, along with a host of other

---

[29]A. V. Dicey, *The Case against Home Rule* (London: John Murray, 1886), 117.
[30]A. W. Brian Simpson, *Human Rights and the End of Empire: Britain and the Genesis of the European Convention* (Oxford: Oxford University Press, 2011), 78–80; and Gerard Hogan and Clive Walker, *Political Violence and the Law in Ireland* (Manchester: Manchester University Press, 1989), 12–14.
[31]Simpson, *Human Rights and the End of Empire*, 82.

repressive measures, before many of their members moved onto Palestine at the war's end.

Indeed, returning to the Mandate in the 1930s, the British government undertook a series of steps that consolidated decades of legalized lawlessness into a set of emergency powers that would become *the* model for future counter-insurgency campaigns. In 1931, the Palestine (Defence) Order in Council was passed and conferred upon the high commissioner a set of powers that exceeded any similar legislation to date. Based upon earlier codes in Ireland and India, and stretching back to the Irish Act of 1833, the Order in Council empowered the high commissioner to declare a state of emergency, and with it issue and amend regulations for arrest, detention without trial, censorship, deportation and trial by military courts, among other things. With the 1936 Arab general strike, the high commissioner declared a state of emergency in Palestine and issued the first of a series of emergency regulations and amending orders that included the power to demolish buildings, including villages and homes, and the imposition of the death penalty for discharging firearms and sabotaging phone and rail lines.[32]

Still, the military wanted more legal coverage to unleash an all-out assault on the Arab population. The top brass believed that the emergency regulations were inadequate, particularly in relationship to the punitive destruction of property and the unleashing of reprisals, which had been permissible in Ireland. After the Colonial Office's legal minds in London fretted, it was determined that martial law as it currently stood would, in fact, be too restrictive on the military and the punitive actions of its soldiers as the civil courts were still sitting in Palestine, and they could well challenge repressive military actions. In its place came the Palestine Martial Law (Defence) Order in Council of 26 September 1936, and subsequently a new Palestine (Defence) Order in Council on 18 March 1937. With it, Section 6 (1) stated the high commissioner:

[M]ay make such Regulations . . . as appear to him in his unfettered discretion to be necessary or expedient for securing the public safety, the defence of Palestine, the maintenance of public order and the suppression of mutiny, rebellion and riot, and for maintaining supplies and services essential to the life of the community.[33]

Shades of empire's Victorian-era past were cast into the Mandate's present when Stephen's nineteenth-century avowal that 'law is nothing but regulated force' was taken to its logical, liberal authoritarian conclusion in Palestine. There, the high commissioner, and with him, all security forces – including

---

[32]Simpson, *Human Rights and the End of Empire*, 84–5.
[33]Simpson, *Human Rights and the End of Empire*, 86.

the police and military – could do whatever they liked, which included all measures already on the books, as well as the punitive destruction of property, trial by military courts without right to appeal, and the sweeping away of any form of judicial review. Statutory martial law was now in effect, and when put into practice, army command – under the auspices of the high commissioner – would have the upper hand.[34] The legalization of lawlessness – ideologically rooted in the birthing of liberal imperialism, and having evolved over decades in various theatres of empire – was now fully matured.[35]

Operating in parallel with Britain's Colonial Office, the War Office ensured its field officers and soldiers a wide berth in defining and implementing the use of force. In 1929, the military manual was revised to take the events in Amritsar into account, though in practice little changed. The manual made clear that '[t]he existence of an armed insurrection would justify the use of any degree of force necessary effectually to meet and cope with the insurrection', and loosely defined 'collective punishments', 'reprisals' and 'retributions' – all of which, could well 'inflict suffering upon innocent individuals . . . [and were] indispensable as a last resort'.[36] Between the military's own code of conduct, and the civil emergency measures that offered legal coverage, Britain's troops, along with the local police force, operated virtually without restraint or fear of prosecution. When the steady stream of complaints and accounts of atrocities in late 1930s Palestine piled up on the desks of Palestine's chief secretary and officials back in London's Colonial and War Offices – where they would similarly amass during the multiple end-of-empire wars that shaped and defined the British Empire in the 1950s – almost nothing, legally, had to be done. In the time ahead, the few cases where prosecutions took place, acquittals were more the norm than the exception.

That aftermath of the Second World War is often viewed as the harbinger for human rights regimes; a recasting of humanitarian law in the wake of fascist atrocities perhaps led Pinker astray. Certain moments are seared into the historical consciousness of those seeking, ultimately, to put forward a facile understanding of the post–Second World War era and its relation to violence. One of the most iconic moments unfolded on the 10 December 1948 in the grandeur of Paris' Palais du Trocadero. There, forty-eight out of the United Nations' fifty-eight members, Britain among them, voted in favour of Resolution 217. Newspapers around the world heralded the

---

[34]Matthew Hughes, 'The Banality of Brutality: British Armed Forces and the Repression of the Arab Revolt in Palestine, 1936-39', *The English Historical Review*, CXXIV, 507 (April 2009): 318.
[35]Simpson, *Human Rights and the End of Empire*, 85–6.
[36]*Manual of Military Law* (London: HMSO, 1929), 103, 255; and Hughes, 'The Banality of Brutality', 316–17.

adopted Universal Declaration of Human Rights (UDHR) as a turning point
in history. For its protagonists like the UDHR's Drafting Committee Chair,
Eleanor Roosevelt, the Declaration's thirty articles were the culmination of
her husband's Four Freedoms, enshrining as they did universal beliefs in
the basic rights of individuals that he had championed in Congress before
America's entry into the Second World War. In addressing the General
Assembly on the eve of the Declaration's adoption, the former first lady
spoke to the promises of universal rights, suggesting, '[the Declaration] may
well become the international Magna Carta of all men everywhere. We hope
its proclamation by the General Assembly will be an event comparable to
the proclamation of the Declaration of Rights of Man . . . [and] the Bill of
Rights by the people of the United States'.[37] While she carried the human
rights torch for her late husband, Roosevelt was far more than a purveyor
of presidential legacy. There were few at the time who underestimated the
committee chair's role in navigating post-war high politics, while also being
attuned to the meaning of universal rights to the world's population. 'Where,
after all, do universal human rights begin?', Roosevelt would later ask. To
wit she replied:

> In small places, close to home – so close and so small that they cannot be
> seen on any maps of the world. . . . Such are the places where every man,
> woman, and child seeks equal justice, equal opportunity, equal dignity
> without discrimination. Unless these rights have meaning there, they have
> little meaning anywhere.[38]

To this day, 10 December is celebrated as Human Rights Day, ushering
in as it did a new article of faith in basic humanity and the need, above
all else, to protect inalienable rights which are intrinsically possessed, not
conferred.

At the time, the mood in Whitehall was sombre, though scarcely defeatist.
While for many in its halls individual rights and the civilizing mission's role
in bestowing them incrementally to empire's subjects had changed little, the
global esprit de corps was still shifting as a result of war and its devastations.
In the months leading up to the 10 December vote, British mandarins
manoeuvred between the Declaration – which like the Charter's preamble
had no legal enforcement – and its incipient Covenants which would be to
some degree legally enforceable. Fortunately for Britain, the Covenants were
taking significant negotiation time, and were ultimately decoupled from the
Declaration leaving one Labour MP, Eric Fletcher, incredulous:

---

[37]Eleanor Roosevelt, Adoption of the Declaration of Human Rights, Speech to the United Nations General Assembly, 9 December 1948, https://awpc.cattcenter.iastate.edu/2017/03/21/ado
ption-of-the-declaration-of-human-rights-dec-9-1948/.
[38]A. Reis Monteiro, *Ethics and Human Rights* (New York: Springer, 2014), 434.

> The [UN] charter contemplated that following the last war, some international machinery would be set up to define and protect human rights – the four freedoms, in the classic phrase of President Roosevelt. . . . It was felt, in the light of the experience of Fascism and Nazism, that there was an intimate link between the recognition of human rights and the preservation of the peace of the world.

Fletcher punctuated his concerns with an abiding point: 'I should regard it as a mere mockery and a sham to proceed with a pious declaration which would not be binding and enforceable.'[39] In the end, that's precisely what happened, at least in the near term. The Colonial Office was characteristically sanguine with the turn of events, with the colonial secretary, Arthur Creech Jones, writing, 'the conclusion of a Covenant and proposals for [its] implementation . . . may drag on for some time. From the colonial point of view this possibility would not appear to be particularly disadvantageous'.[40]

It would take another three decades for the Covenants to be hammered out and come into force, and even then, they would prove nearly as aspirational as the Declaration itself. Still, Articles 13, 21 and 25 of the Declaration – freedom of movement, participation in democratic government and social security – 'may be extremely difficult to reconcile' in the empire, in the words of the Colonial Office.[41] On this point, Creech Jones was blunt: the UDHR was potentially 'a source of embarrassment' as far as the empire was concerned.[42] Regardless, the fact that there were no legally binding mechanisms for the Declaration gutted it of much moral purpose for those who questioned the very premise of universal rights and rendered it at best an article of faith among the faithful. A year after the UDHR's celebrations had receded, Hersch Lauterpacht, Whewell Professor of International Law at Cambridge, and the first to write an English-language book advocating international protection of human rights, said as much when he lamented:

> At the time of the adopting of the Declaration there was no feeling of embarrassment at the incongruity between the enthusiastic acknowledgment of the fundamental character of the human rights proclaimed in the Declaration and the refusal to recognize them as a source of legal obligation binding in the sphere of conduct – a fact which in itself raises a cardinal issue of international morality.[43]

---

[39]*HCD*, Volume 447, columns 2263–5, 26 February 1948.
[40]Simpson, *Human Rights and the End of Empire*, 456.
[41]Simpson, *Human Rights and the End of Empire*, 458.
[42]Fabian Klose, '"Source of Embarrassment": Human Rights, State of Emergency, and the Wars of Decolonization', in Stefan-Ludwig Hoffman (ed.), *Human Rights in the Twentieth Century* (Cambridge: Cambridge University Press, 2011), 242.
[43]Simpson, *Human Rights and the End of Empire*, 460.

If Lauterpacht was disillusioned with the Declaration's non-binding nature, the protections afforded under the 1949 Geneva Conventions were more heartening to him and other UDHR sceptics, at least to those in the Western world. Running in parallel to the Declaration's negotiations, the Geneva Conventions' impetus and drafting were undertaken to strengthen the principles of humanity in war. The human rights moment that took form in the UDHR initially intersected with humanitarian law to create a 'legal-moral alteration' that moved from protecting soldiers' rights to those of civilians during wartime. This 'alteration', according to Boyd van Dijk, 'was partly a result of Allied wartime declarations condemning colonial-style counterinsurgency for 'civilized' Europeans, which would later boomerang back at them'.[44] The earlier Hague Conventions of 1899 and 1907, which did not strictly outlaw the use of reprisals, hostage taking and collective punishments and did not renounce the use of concentration camps, largely protected soldiers from civilians rather than the other way around. Moreover, colonial populations, according to international jurists and European politicians, were deemed uncivilized and therefore not party to international laws and protections during wartime.[45] In the interwar years, the International Committee for the Red Cross met in Monaco and Tokyo where its delegates crafted a far more capacious set of principles – including restrictions on aerial bombardments – to humanize war, though European powers rendered both drafts dead on arrival.

That the Tokyo Draft was resuscitated in the aftermath of the Second World War reflected changing, global sentiments towards the rules of war and civilians, civilians like those who had been subject to Nazi Germany's policies that had previously been reserved for colonized populations. It was a unique moment in time and Rooseveltian ideas of freedom gained traction in spheres beyond the UDHR negotiations. This spilling-over effect was apparent in the earliest drafts of the revised and expanded Geneva Conventions where the Norwegian jurist, Frede Castberg, among others, looked to apply wartime humanitarian law not just to interstate conflicts but also to civil and colonial wars. Such a move was a major departure, recognizing as it did universal claims to rights – claims couched in contemporary human rights discourse – and placing limitations on European colonizers' sovereignty in their empires.[46]

---

[44]Boyd van Dijk, 'Human Rights in War: On the Entangled Foundations of the 1949 Geneva Conventions', *The American Society of International Law*, 112, no. 4 (2018): 556.

[45]Frederic Megret, 'From "Savages" to "Unlawful Combatants": A Postcolonial Look at International Humanitarian Law's "Other"', in Ann Orford (ed.), *International Law and Its Others* (Cambridge: Cambridge University Press, 2006), 265–317; and Marco Sassoli, *International Humanitarian Law: Rules, Controversies, and Solutions to Problems Arising in Warfare* (Cheltenham: Edward Elgar Publishing, 2019), 1–14.

[46]van Dijk, 'Human Rights in War', 567–8.

In the end, however, inveigling by Britain, France and the United States – the former two countries bent on protecting their colonial privilege and strict rules of sovereignty, while the latter consumed with Cold War concerns – put a permanent redline to any significant human rights language or colonial protections in the Geneva Conventions' final documents. Those like Lauterpacht could laud the binding Conventions' 'instrument[s] laying down legal rights obligations as distinguished from a mere pronouncement of moral principles and ideal standards of conduct'.[47] Yet, whether these obligations and principles would change in any material way counter-insurgency efforts in the colonized world remained an open question. Eliminating all reference to universal human rights and replacing earlier draft language referring to 'colonial wars' with 'non-international armed conflicts', the Conventions' signatories also adopted Common Article 3, which, among other things, defined non-combatants and those who surrendered. The article also put forth their protections which included the prohibition, 'at any time and in any place whatsoever' of 'violence to life and person, in particular murder of all kinds, mutilation, cruel treatment and torture' as well as 'outrages upon dignity, in particular humiliating and degrading treatment'.[48]

With Common Article 3, contracting parties were only bound to the Conventions' terms in empire, and domestically for that matter, when 'non-international armed conflicts' arose. In practice, this meant that colonizers like Britain had discretion in determining the applicability of Common Article 3 to states of emergency or any other civil disturbance. Whitehall had great latitude in determining whether or not any of its end-of-empire wars met an undefined 'non-international armed conflict' standard that hinged on arbitrary measures of 'intensity'. There was no international supervisory board that determined whether or not an 'armed conflict' existed. It was the ambiguity of defining 'intensity' where violence existed in an 'armed conflict' that allowed Britain and other nations to sidestep Common Article 3 in their empires, and elsewhere, should they choose to do so.[49]

While the 1949 Geneva Conventions were a considerable departure from the Hague Conventions by providing numerous safeguards for both prisoners of war and civilians, the sensibility behind their final execution differed little from the racialized hierarchies and protection of sovereignty framing interpretations of earlier humanitarian laws. That there was a difference in historical context between the turn of the century and

---

[47]van Dijk, 'Human Rights in War', 555.
[48]'Geneva Convention Relative to the Treatment of Prisoners of War 12 August 1949', Article III, 91–2, https://www.un.org/en/genocideprevention/documents/atrocity-crimes/Doc.32_GC-III-EN.pdf, accessed 3 January 2020.
[49]M. Gandhi, 'Notes and Comments: Common Article 3 of Geneva Conventions, 1949 in the Era of International Criminal Tribunals', ISIL Year Book of International Humanitarian and Refugee Law, 2001, http://www.worldlii.org/int/journals/ISILYBIHRL/2001/11.html.

1949 was apparent, however, not only in the avoidance of explicit language referencing the 'civilized' and 'uncivilized' populations but also in the mere existence of Article 3, which gestured to one of the first infringements on colonial sovereignty, no matter how anaemic. At the same time, the jettisoning of any universal claims to rights, even for civilians at times of conflict, was yet another indication of the enduring, combined weight of colonial self-interest and the hierarchical conceptions of civilization and citizenship that underwrote it, as well as the legalized lawlessness upon which its perpetuation depended. Liberal imperialism, while tested in the brief efflorescence of human rights norms, emerged alive and well in the post-war era of international humanitarian law and its exclusions.

Insofar as Europe did produce one of the post-war period's most progressive and legally binding human rights documents with the European Convention on Human Rights (ECHR) so, too, did colonizing powers like Britain maintain their historic ability to dominate, coerce and exclude under the Convention's very rubric. Much like international humanitarian law, Europe's post-war human rights conventions emerged from the Second World War's totalitarian crises. Britain played a leading role in the Council of Europe and its Convention negotiations partly to counter charges against its isolationism from the continent which had increased in the wake of the country's imperial-oriented, economic policies and disinterest in integration. It would be an easy win for Ernest Bevin's beleaguered Foreign Office as the British government concentrated its efforts in ensuring European liberties and banned together with its continental counterparts to stave off communist subversion whose potential seemed limitless. Or, as Britain's representative to the Council of Europe's negotiations, Lord Layton, stressed:

> [The Convention is] a means of strengthening resistance in all our countries against insidious attempts to undermine our democratic way of life from within or without, and thus to give to Western Europe as a whole greater political stability.[50]

Britain was the first to sign the ECHR in March 1951, and while it did not come into force until September 1953 when Luxembourg offered the tenth ratification, the celebrations in Strasbourg were palpable, and its historic significance captured in the speech 'From the Europe of Dachau to the Europe of Strasbourg', which Paul Henri-Spaak, one of the continent's most ardent champions of integration, offered as a symbolic coda to the Council's efforts.[51]

---

[50]John Reynolds, *Empire, Emergency, and International Law* (Cambridge: Cambridge University Press, 2017), 118.
[51]Simpson, *Human Rights and the End of Empire*, 808–9.

Above all else, the ECHR was intended to be a set of European human rights laws, and Britain made every effort to ensure this was the case.[52] At the same time, there were deep concerns that the Convention, so necessary for the preservation of Western liberties, particularly as the Cold War advanced, could easily undermine the repressive measures necessary to snuff out rebellion or subversion elsewhere. The day after the Convention's signing, Labour's media-savvy Herbert Morrison replaced the ailing Bevin as foreign secretary, and he was determined to shore up Britain's obligations insofar as the ECHR and empire were concerned. His office would give away just enough to placate the human rights faithful while, at the same time, ensuring an international legal structure that not only facilitated but also legitimated the legalized lawlessness upon which many parts of Britain's empire depended.

At the time of ECHR negotiations, Britain was mired in multiple states of emergency, including that on the Malayan peninsula. When the Convention was signed, Article 63, or the 'colonial clause', waived the *a priori* application of its force in European empires. Yet, as far as the British government was concerned, the ECHR was the lesser of the two human rights' evils when it came to its colonial subjects as its allies in Europe were far more predictable than the wretched UN that was negotiating its own Covenants. Morrison could not have been clearer in his position: 'the sooner we disengage from an exercise [with the UN] which can only be embarrassing from the Colonial point of view the better'.[53] It's not surprising, therefore, that the Foreign Office took the decision to extend the ECHR to forty-five of its colonies and territories not because it was looking 'to improve the lot of colonial subjects', as one historian has observed, but rather 'to present British colonial policy and practice in a favourable light, by publicly committing colonial governments to respect for human rights and to furnish an argument for not accepting a UN Covenant if one was ever adopted'.[54]

Moreover, Britain gave up very little in extending the ECHR to its empire. First, there was no right of individual petition to the European Commission of Human Rights, the body that received complaints and, if there was merit, submitted them to the European Court of Human Rights after its establishment in April 1959. Up until 1966 when Britain accepted individual petition, government officials rationalized this logic claiming that

---

[52]There was significant negotiation and discussion occurring within the British government's ranks insofar as the ECHR effected its domestic jurisdiction. In particular, Britain wanted to retain the right to enforce future laws that could be brought into effect under DORAs, including detention without trial. By eliminating individual petition, British officials believed they had solved this issue, according to Andrew Moravcsik, 'The Origins of Human Rights Regimes: Democratic Delegation in Postwar Europe', *International Organization*, 54, no. 2 (Spring 2000): 238–43.

[53]Simpson, *Human Rights and End of Empire*, 813.

[54]Simpson, *Human Rights and End of Empire*, 825.

international law only applied to states. However, as A. W. Simpson points out, 'the United Kingdom's real reason was fear of repercussions in colonies and protectorates'.[55] Second, in the early drafting of the ECHR the British government introduced, and insisted upon, a derogation article that allowed a contracting party relief from the Convention in 'time of war or other public emergency threatening the interests of the people'.[56] Eventually enshrined as Article 15, states were permitted to derogate much of the Convention, with the exception of a handful of articles, the most notable of which was Article 3, or the 'Prohibition of torture', which stated: 'No one shall be subjected to torture or to inhuman or degrading treatment or punishment.'[57] In a stroke of a pen, derogation rendered most universal rights into contingent ones, even if these rights were already circumscribed through the nature of the ECHR's petition process. In the years ahead, similar derogations and contingent rights would be inscribed in the two United Nations' Covenants, much to Britain's approval.

Britain had been the first to ink the European Convention on Human Rights with its Article 15 poised to become one gigantic loophole for liberal imperialism's unrestrained use of force, whether against the so-called terrorists or their civilian supporters. The Colonial Office was well aware that the ECHR's extension to its overseas possessions was a public relations coup, though was also patently disingenuous as it was opting 'to send in a list of derogations which virtually nullify the whole thing', according to an internal memo.[58] Over time, the exceptional and temporary became the rule as colonies like Malaya and Kenya were beset with legally enabled emergency conditions where statutory martial law created police states aimed at quashing dissent while seeking to install politically acceptable regimes that would facilitate Britain's interests at the end of empire and beyond. Moreover, there were no limits on how many derogations a country could file using the minimal of evidence to support its invoking of Article 15. Within six weeks of the ECHR coming into force in much of its empire, Britain would derogate for Malaya and Singapore, with Kenya, British Guiana and Uganda's Bugandan Province soon to follow. In fact, the

---

[55]A. W. B. Simpson, 'Round Up the Usual Suspects: The Legacy of British Colonialism and the European Convention on Human Rights', *Loyola Law Review*, 41, no. 4 (Winter 1996): 685. Simpson also details the exact specifications in the ECHR whereby, 'Until 1966, only interstate application to the Commission were possible. Under article 25(1) of the Convention, the Commission was empowered to receive individual petitions from persons claiming to be the victims of violations, but only if the relevant state agreed. The acceptance of the jurisdiction of the European Court, established on 20 April 1959, was also optional. By 31 December 1959, nine contracting parties, including the Republic of Ireland, had accepted a right of individual petition, but not the United Kingdom'.
[56]Reynolds, *Empire*, 119.
[57] *European Convention on Human Rights*, Article 3, 'Prohibition on Torture', 7, https://www .echr.coe.int/Documents/Convention_ENG.pdf, accessed 3 January 2020.
[58]Reynolds, *Empire*, 131.

number of British derogations in the ECHR's first decade – nearly thirty in all – surpassed the combined total of all the other forty-five members of the Council of Europe for the first sixty years of the Convention's application. In effect, as legal scholar John Reynolds has pointed out, Britain ushered in a 'derogation regime' that would not only shape and define the lived experiences of millions of colonial subjects around the world but also normalize the exception in international law and practice.[59]

Long before derogations offered a fig leaf for regimes professing compliance with universal notions of human rights, Walter Benjamin observed in the aftermath of Palestine's Arab Revolt how '[t]he tradition of the oppressed teaches us that the "state of emergency" in which we live is not the exception but the rule'. He then went on to intone, 'We must attain a conception of history that accords with this insight.'[60] Indeed, there were important differences between the pre–Second World War era and its aftermath as the permissibility of detention without trial, collective punishments and the starvation of civilians, among other tactics, would be encoded in the derogation articles of post-war international human rights law, further excluded from humanitarian laws, and rendered part and parcel of a liberal imperialism that had ostensibly reformed with its claims to wartime 'partnership' with colonial subjects and rights rhetoric which, ultimately, bound nations like Britain to virtually nothing. Insofar as there were continuities between the pre- and post-war era, the ever-fetishized 'rule of law', as one historian points out, continued to be a 'potent fiction' and one that legitimated a range of repressive actions across Britain's empire.[61] In the war's aftermath, and as far as Morrison and Prime Minister Attlee's cabinet were concerned, the ECHR's derogation provisions together with the sidelining of individual petition rendered the Convention about as airtight as possible when it came to interference in their empire where the deployment of state-directed violence was exponentially expanding, and evolving, with each declaration of emergency.

In the end, the Permanent Mandates Commission never investigated British actions in Palestine. Jamal al-Husanyi's letter remained in the League's inbox, unanswered. The Second World War intervened before the Commission could respond, though chances are, as it had with multiple other previous complaints detailing British colonial violence in Palestine, the Commission would have dismissed al-Husanyi's as well. In fact, in an era of imperial internationalism, some might conclude that the Permanent

---

[59]Reynolds, *Empire*, passim.

[60]Walter Benjamin, *Selected Writings, Volume 4, 1938-1940*, trans. Edmund Jephcott, ed. Howard Eiland and Michael W. Jennings (Cambridge, MA: Belknap Press, 2003), 392.

[61]Edmund S. Morgan's 'that potent fiction' when referring to 'rule of law' as quoted in Nasser Hussain, *The Jurisprudence of Emergency: Colonialism and the Rule of Law* (Ann Arbor: The University of Michigan Press, 2003), 8.

Mandate's Commission was part of the problem, at least in Palestine, where it had chastised the British for having not been coercive enough in crushing the rebellion from the get-go.[62] In effect, the presumed oversight committee endorsed, with a similar moralizing refrain that echoed the likes of Wingate, Callwell and others, the use of violence against colonial subjects.

Still, al-Husanyi's letter was scarcely written in vain. It offers one footprint, along with thousands of others that litter the archives, of Britain's deployment of systematic violence in its twentieth-century empire. And, while al-Husanyi and Arab Palestinians never received a proper hearing of their complaints, other imperial subjects eventually would. In 2009, the British Empire was put on trial for the first time when, in London's High Court of Justice, five elderly Kikuyu claimants charged the British government with overseeing a system of torture and violence in the detention camps of late colonial Kenya. *Imperial Reckoning* was the historical basis for the case, and I was expert witness for the claimants. At the time of the filing, the Foreign and Commonwealth Office (FCO) – the named defendant in the case – vehemently denied any misdeeds in its former empire, much like the Chamberlain government in Palestine's yesteryear, and vowed to fight the case to the bitter end. This said, it also argued with equal vehemence that the international humanitarian law and the ECHR were not relevant in London's High Court – an argument that would have traction with presiding judge, Justice McCombe.

Pinker was surely aware of the historic Mau Mau case, as it was splashed across major newspapers in Britain. Yet, much like Foreign Secretary William Hague, he chose to dismiss the piles of evidence that tell a damning story of systematic violence in colonial Kenya – violence that was scarcely an anomaly to Britain's East African colony. Ultimately, however, after a four-year legal battle, the British government changed course. It became clear that after Justice McCombe ruled against the FCO's two strike-out motions, he was strongly inclined to believe that Britain had failed in its 'duty of care'. Put another way, according to McCombe's rulings, the colonial government in Kenya had failed in upholding Britain's civilizing mission, however idealized it was, or continued to be, in the justice's mind.

In June 2013, Foreign Secretary Hague rose in the House of Commons and offered Britain's first-ever acknowledgement, and apology, for its use of systematic violence in empire and with it a £20 million payout to over 5,000 Kikuyu victims of British torture in the detention camps of Kenya. In effect, the British government could no longer hide behind liberalism's obfuscations and moral claims that denied the imbrication of violence in its civilizing mission. The evidence – much of which was available to Pinker during his

---

[62]For a discussion of the League as 'an eminently Victorian institution', see Mark Mazower, *No Enchanted Palace: The End of Empire and the Ideological Origins of the United Nations* (Princeton: Princeton University Press, 2009), 21.

research – was simply too overwhelming. So, too, was the evidence from myriad other former British colonies – colonies like al-Husanyi's Palestine – available to Pinker, yet he chose to ignore it, or perhaps deny its validity. Yet, it's this very denial of evidence – particularly from hundreds of millions of former brown and Black colonial subjects – that renders works like Pinker's so damaging in the postcolonial present. Denied their lived experiences, these men and women are nonetheless etched in memories throughout the world, and it's these collective memories that scarcely need historians armed with archival data to jettison Pinker's Western-centric claims that violence declined in colonial landscapes during twentieth-century British rule.

PART FOUR

Themes

13

A history of violence and indigeneity

Pinker and the Native Americas

Matthew Restall

In March 2019, at the onset of the quincentennial of the Spanish-Aztec encounter, the president of Mexico, Andrés Manuel López Obrador, sent an open letter to the King of Spain and to the Pope, demanding an 'apology to the original peoples for violating their human rights, as they are known today, for committing massacres and enforcing the so-called Conquest with the sword and the cross'.[1]

Such an incident might appear to be reflective of the brave new world in which Steven Pinker argues we live, one where wars of conquest have been abolished and world leaders can insist on public acknowledgements of past atrocities. As Pinker points out, public apologies by religious and political leaders for acts of violence committed decades, even centuries, ago has been a steadily growing feature of international political culture since the 1980s.[2] In demanding or offering apologies for the invasions and atrocities

---

[1]'Envié ya una carta al rey de España y otra carta al Papa para que se haga un relato de agravios y se pida perdón a los pueblos originarios por las violaciones a lo que ahora se conoce como derechos humanos, hubieron matanzas, imposiciones, la llamada Conquista se hizo con la espada y con la cruz' (statement made on 25 March 2019, by Mexican president Andrés Manuel López Obrador, accessed at www.milenio.com/politica/amlo-pide-rey-espana-disculparse-co nquista-mexico-video).

[2]Steven Pinker, *The Better Angels of Our Nature: A History of Violence and Humanity* (New York: Viking, 2011), 654–60 (my page references are to the 2012 Penguin paperback edition).

of history, leaders are effectively commemorating the fact that such crimes existed in the violent past, but are not part of the peaceful present.

Although Spanish officials objected to López Obrador's remarks, their reaction nonetheless echoed that same assumption regarding violence in the past and the present. The Mexican president's letter hit the press just as Spaniards were weeks from voting in a general election, and so campaigning politicians from left and right denounced the demand as 'an affront to Spain' (as conservative leader Pablo Casado put it).[3] But defensive nationalism aside, remarks by Spanish politicians implied that present-day finger pointing over historical acts of violence was absurdly anachronistic – because the world *used to be* a violent place. According to this Pinkerish perspective, it makes no sense to target one nation for past crimes against others, because in past centuries *all* nations committed crimes of invasion and other outrages, whereas, today, all (or almost all) nations are committed to common non-violent goals.

When, later in 2019, López Obrador made remarks critical of the conquistador Hernando Cortés, the official historian of the conquistador's Spanish hometown protested that the president was indulging in 'presentism', in 'judging the events of five centuries ago by the standards of the 21st century'.[4] In other words, the Spanish historian made the Pinkerish assumption that the line between good and evil is not spatial but temporal or chronological. The triumph of 'the forces of civilization and enlightenment' (to quote the final line of Pinker's book) divides us from the brutish and nasty past, creating two worlds with completely different moral standards.[5]

The trans-Atlantic war of words between López Obrador and his Spanish detractors also evokes a more specific aspect of Pinker's argument, one that is the subject of this chapter. The Mexican president's letter can be seen as an act of deflection, similar to those employed by Pinker, particularly in his treatment in *The Better Angels of Our Nature* of the indigenous peoples of the Americas. By shifting to Spain and the Catholic Church all responsibility for depriving Native Americans of their human rights, López Obrador evaded the issue of anti-indigenous violence – broadly defined – during the last five centuries. Instead, the focus is kept, by López Obrador's supporters and critics both, on a past that is grossly misrepresented and misinterpreted.

That fact is neatly illustrated by the very Pinkerish reasons given by Madrid-based British journalist Michael Reid for why López Obrador's demand for

---

[3]Quoted in Bello (a column written by Michael Reid), 'Blaming the Conquistadors: Mexico's President Is Wrong to Seek an Apology for the Distant Past', *The Economist*, 4 April 2019, accessed at www.economist.com/the-americas/2019/04/04/blaming-the-conquistadors.
[4]Quote by Tomás García, municipal historian of Medellín, in Sam Jones and David Agren, 'Cortés: Still Divisive 500 years after Start of Conquest', *The Guardian*, 31 December 2019, longer version accessible at www.theguardian.com/world/2019/dec/31/hernan-cortes-mexico-s-pain-atlantic.
[5]Pinker, *Better Angels*, 841.

an apology was wrong – Pinkerish, that is, in using the same broad, common misconceptions about the history of the Americas that Pinker's book deploys and perpetuates. Indeed, Reid's two reasons correspond closely to the two aspects of Pinker's depiction of the Native American past. Reid's first reason is that the 'peoples in Mexico in 1519 were not the "original" ones but later arrivals. They, too, committed what nowadays would be called crimes against humanity – systematic human sacrifice in the case of the Mexica (Aztecs)'.[6] Similarly, Pinker characterizes all pre-Columbian indigenous societies, most particularly the Aztecs, as excessively violent – an outdated, colonialist (and neo-colonialist) stereotype.

Reid's second reason is that Spain's empire may not have been a 'spotless creation, but nor was it uniquely bad. Most of the Amerindians who died did so from diseases to which they had no immunity'.[7] That is not Pinker's position, but he does give European colonization in the Americas short shrift, giving the impression that it was less violent than were Native societies, with its most extreme manifestations restricted to genocidal moments in the history of the United States. The assignment of more space to the United States than the rest of the Americas is problematic in an obvious, general sense (suggesting an Anglocentrism and West-centrism), but also, more specifically, because the American past is effectively redeemed in the book by its role in the recent triumph of Enlightenment and civilization.

The effect is to deposit Native America in the dustbin of history, as if indigenous peoples were part of that brutish past, regrettably violent and regrettably annihilated by past Europeans, but not party to the triumph of our better angels.

'Undoubtedly a dangerous place': Pinker's Native America

How exactly, then, are Native Americans depicted in *The Better Angels of Our Nature*?[8] Native societies receive relatively little attention in the book; references, including indirect and passing ones, appear on roughly 4 per cent of the book's pages. But my concern is not with the quantity of such

---

[6]Reid/Bello, 'Blaming the Conquistadors'.
[7]Reid/Bello, 'Blaming the Conquistadors'. Such an argument, based on an oversimplified reading of Alfred Crosby's 'Columbian Exchange' thesis, was popular in the last half-century among apologists for European colonization in the Americas. Scholars understand the violence, slavery and dislocation of conquest and colonization to have exacerbated and often exceeded epidemic disease as population-decimating factors; see, for example, Catherine M. Cameron, Paul Kelton and Alan C. Swedlund (eds), *Beyond Germs: Native Depopulation in North America* (Tucson: University of Arizona Press, 2015).
[8]In this chapter, I use 'Native Americans' to refer to indigenous peoples of all the Americas, not just the region that is now the United States.

mentions – Pinker's purview, after all, is the whole of human history, and to criticize such a book for the space it devotes to this or that culture or region would be facile. My concern is rather with their type and tone, with the impression they give of indigenous American civilizations.

That impression is formed by the two aforementioned aspects – treatment of violence in Native America before contact with Europeans and violence in the Americas stemming from contact and colonization. First, most of the discussion of Native Americans in the book relates to the pre-Columbian period – the thousands of years prior to the initial arrival of European colonists in the Americas in the 1490s. The tone is set by the very first mention of a specific Native American, who is also the earliest indigenous human of any kind mentioned in the book. The crucial fact about this early American is presented thus: 'Kennewick Man was shot.'[9] Thus is the first seed planted of a link between violence and indigeneity that will take root and grow throughout the book.

The next reference to Native Americans begins by quoting the Declaration of Independence's complaint that the English king gave support to 'the merciless Indian Savages whose known rule of warfare, is an undistinguished destruction of all ages, sexes and conditions'. Noting that nowadays such a characterization seems 'archaic, indeed offensive', Pinker then goes on to argue that 'men in nonstate societies' did in fact routinely engage in precisely that kind of unrestrained violence, most notably committing massacres of whole villages, as well as acts of torture, rape, mutilation and cannibalism. Over a five-page passage, references are made to indigenous peoples in New Guinea and Australia, but also to those of New England, and to the Yanomamö and Inuit, with the overwhelming impression being threefold: that Native Americans and nonstate peoples are essentially the same category; that their societies were fundamentally and relentlessly violent; and that they existed overwhelmingly in the violent past, not the peaceful present.[10] All three impressions are patently false.

Across the 500 pages to follow, there are roughly a dozen further such references (coverage of Native Americans falls mostly in the book's first half), reinforcing that specious threefold impression. Cherry-picked cases of apparent acts of violence committed by nonstate Native peoples are equated with evidence of an age of violence or intrinsically violent cultures – a distinction Pinker makes for the West and for recent history, but neither for prehistory nor for Native America.[11] A graph quantifying 'percentage of deaths in warfare' divides societies into three nonstate categories and one

---

[9]Pinker, *Better Angels*, 3.

[10]Pinker, *Better Angels*, 51–6.

[11]As pointed out by Linda Fibiger, 'The Past as a Foreign Country: Bioarchaeological Perspectives on Pinker's "Prehistoric Anarchy"', *Historical Reflections/ Réflexions Historiques*, 44, no. 1 (Spring 2018): 13; see also her chapter in this volume.

state category. Native American groups top all three nonstate categories, seeming to give solid data support to the impression that they were humanity's most violent nonstate societies.[12]

When Pinker does briefly recognize the past existence of states in Native America, he turns not only to the Aztec Empire but to the most old-fashioned and stereotypically prejudicial notion of Aztec society – as one that made 'pre-Columbian Mexico . . . undoubtedly a dangerous place'. In that graph quantifying and ranking 'deaths in warfare', at the very top of the state category, is 'Ancient Mexico, before 1500 CE', comfortably beating out such contenders as 'World, 20th C (wars & genocides)' and 'Europe 1900-1960'. If you thought that the First and the Second World War, as well as the holocausts, purges and pogroms of the era, showed humanity at our most violent, you were wrong; the Aztecs have the twentieth-century beat. That apparent fact is presented again, as data, in another 'war deaths' graph, with 'Central Mexico, 1419-1519' handily surpassing 'Germany, 20th C'.[13]

Every time that the Aztecs appear in the book, they are depicted as among history's most extreme devotees of torture and sadistic violence, often with reference to alleged data that are wrong to absurd degrees – that are (to borrow Sara Butler's phrase in discussing a similar misrepresentation of Europe's Middle Ages) 'improbably specific and unbelievably high'.[14] We are told, for example, that 'the Aztecs sacrificed about forty people a day, 1.2 million people in all'. The impression given is that the Aztecs lowered all 'their victims into a fire, lifted them out before they died, and cut the beating hearts out of their chests'. The final appearance in the book of the Aztecs is as torturers of their own children.[15]

A reader whose grasp of Aztec (or Maya or Mesoamerican) culture is derived from video games and Mel Gibson's *Apocalypto* might accept that for a century the Aztecs cut out the beating hearts of forty people a day.[16] But no scholar of the Aztecs believes such patent nonsense nowadays, and very few ever have. So how does Pinker come to such a conclusion? Anyone well-read in Aztec history will quickly guess the answer, but the vast majority of readers cannot possibly be expected to do so. Pinker uses estimates of war

---

[12]Pinker, *Better Angels*, 59.

[13]Pinker, *Better Angels*, 59, 60, 64.

[14]Sara M. Butler, 'Getting Medieval on Steven Pinker: Violence and Medieval England', *Historical Reflexions/Réflexions Historiques*, 44, no. 1 (Spring 2018): 31.

[15]Pinker, *Better Angels*, 159, 162 (quote), 518. Note that the population of the Aztec capital of Tenochtitlan has also been exaggerated as being in the hundreds of thousands; it was more likely 50,000 to 60,000 (Matthew Restall, *When Montezuma Met Cortés: The True Story of the Meeting That Changed History* [New York: Ecco, 2018], 85, 376; Camilla Townsend, *Fifth Sun: A New History of the Aztecs* [New York: Oxford, 2019], 65), meaning that Pinker's numbers have the Aztecs 'sacrificing' the equivalent of 25–30 per cent of the city's population annually (for even more absurd numbers, see the following text).

[16]Mesoamerica is the well-studied civilizational area that includes Aztec, Maya and scores of other indigenous societies.

deaths and executions – the ritual execution of war captives traditionally called 'human sacrifice' in the West – compiled by Matthew White, a historian-librarian who is not a specialist in Aztec or Native American history, who himself used estimates compiled in the late-nineteenth to mid-twentieth centuries (increasingly seen by scholars as outdated).[17]

Those estimates were themselves extrapolations of claims made by Franciscan friars and other commentators in the Catholic Church decades after the fall of the Aztec Empire, claims designed to denigrate – literally, demonize – Aztec civilization and thus justify all and any methods used in the service of Spanish conquest and colonization. The earliest Europeans in the Americas arrived expecting to find monstrous humans and diabolistic cultures, and they were quick to imagine, invent and condemn indigenous peoples and societies as such.[18]

The extreme distortion of Native American civilizations was both quantitative and qualitative. That is, violence-related numbers were hugely exaggerated or simply made up. For example, Mexico's first bishop, the Franciscan Juan de Zumárraga, claimed that in one year he destroyed 20,000 Aztec 'idols', just as Aztec priests had 'sacrificed' that many annually – an invented number that soon turned into 20,000 *children*, and then an imagined 'offering up in tribute, in horrific inferno, more than one hundred thousand souls'.[19] Centuries of repetition and prejudice have drawn a direct line from Zumárraga to Pinker (which would have delighted the bishop). At the same time, the quality or type of violence that was supposedly found among the Aztecs (and other indigenous societies) was rendered as grotesque as possible from the Western perspective: it was heavily imbued with cannibalism (for which there is almost no evidence, all of it indirect and tainted by European filters); methods of torture or execution not used by Europeans were highlighted (heart-removal, for example); and all executions were styled 'human sacrifice' – an ethnocentric, judgement-laden term still overused in the West to describe killings in other cultures, regardless of whether they were intended as religious offerings or were executions of criminals or prisoners of war.

---

[17]Pinker relies entirely on Matthew White, a self-described 'popular history writer and atroci-tologist', in particular an 'in press' work missing from the bibliography, but presumably a reference to the White items that *are* listed, such as pages from his website and his *The Great Big Book of Horrible Things* (New York: Norton, 2011).

[18]The scholarship on this topic is vast, but the following passages should be accessible to any reader, and hopefully sufficient to pull the rug out from under Pinker's cursory but very nega-tive portrait of the Aztecs (none, it should be noted, available to Pinker when he was writing his book): David Carrasco, *The Aztecs: A Very Short Introduction* (Oxford: Oxford University Press, 2012), 61–9, and Restall, *When Montezuma Met Cortés*, 78–95; Townsend, *Fifth Sun*, is the most balanced history of Aztec civilization to date.

[19]Restall, *When Montezuma Met Cortés*, 82; 'horrific inferno' quote is my translation from Gaspar de Villagrá, *Historia de la Nueva Mexico* (Alcala: Luys Martínez Grande, 1610), folio 30r (an epic poem that captures well the viewpoint of the era).

In fact, the vast majority of religious offerings made in all indigenous societies (the Aztecs included) were flora and fauna. Neither the Nahuas (the larger ethnic group of which the Aztecs were a part) nor the Maya used a term that meant 'human sacrifice'; the term, like much of its meaning, was introduced by Europeans. Executions in the Aztec and Maya worlds were overwhelmingly war related, and war mixed political ambition and the 'goals of economic gain with cosmic justification' (just as it did – and arguably still does – in the West) (to quote archaeologist Elizabeth Graham). Thus, while the West has ranked the Aztecs as 'the biggest sacrificers in the world', in the words of historian of religion (and Harvard colleague of Pinker's) David Carrasco, 'there is no substantial archaeological or documentary proof that they ritually killed more people than any other civilization'.[20]

Public executions were no more a daily affair in Aztec cities than they were in European ones; quotidian life for Aztecs, as for other Mesoamericans, was marked by agricultural labour and the social rituals of community and family. As leading Aztec scholar Camilla Townsend recently noted, 'The Aztecs would never recognize themselves in the picture of their world that exists in the books and movies we have made.' That picture is a colonialist caricature, stripping the Aztecs of their humanity. We are so 'accustomed to being afraid of the Aztecs, even to being repulsed by them', that it has never occurred to us that we might simply identify with them, see them as fully human, flaws and all – as people capable of brutal violence but also of deep love, as people who invented ways to kill each other but also created spectacular cities and stunning works of art, as people who fought and wrote, who were cruel to each other and played music together, who savoured 'a good laugh, just as we do'.[21]

The numbers of war deaths in Aztec Mexico used by Pinker are therefore wildly exaggerated. But, more troublesome than that, the invention of those numbers and the deployment of them to tarnish the Aztecs as excessively violent barbarians is an old, pernicious colonialist tradition. I do not believe for a second that Pinker intended to perpetuate that tradition, nor do I blame him for swallowing a derogatory depiction that is widely reproduced. (Likewise, I see no reason not to give White the same benefit of the doubt.). Nonetheless, the origins and endpoint of the information–literature pathway taken by Pinker is clear, and highly misleading.

Certainly, there was violence in the Aztec world, as there was in the pre-Columbian Maya world and in all Native American societies; nobody denies that obvious fact. There is also evidence – most notably archaeological

---

[20]Elizabeth Graham, *Maya Christians and Their Churches in Sixteenth-Century Belize* (Gainesville: University Press of Florida, 2011), 40–3; Carrasco, *Aztecs*, 61; Restall, *When Montezuma Met Cortés*, 92.
[21]Townsend, *Fifth Sun*, quotes on 3, 212; also see 47–50; Matthew Restall, 'The Humans Behind the Sacrifice', *History Today*, April 2020, 96–7.

and art historical; from burials, murals and stone-carved monuments and glyphs – that there were periods of increased violence, usually war related, throughout the Mesoamerican past. But there is not a shred of solid, sustainable evidence that such periods made any Mesoamerican society more intrinsically violent than, say, medieval or early modern Europe. There is nothing to suggest either that daily life was especially violent or that political violence or warfare produced the massive fatalities claimed by Spanish ecclesiastics – who were purposefully biased and committed to a campaign of religious conversion that was ironically and hypocritically infused with methods of ritual violence.

On the contrary, warfare was controlled, restricted by season, and ritualized; for example, Aztecs and Mayas prioritized the capture of enemies over their slaughter in battle. Such captives were sometimes tortured, as depicted in the eighth-century murals in the Maya city of Bonampak, today in Southern Mexico. Or they were executed in public ceremonies that had political and religious significance, as evidenced by the skull racks found in some Mesoamerican sites, most notably in Tenochtitlan – today's Mexico City – where both stone-carved skulls and human crania have been excavated.[22]

But to take such evidence, exaggerate and highlight it, and make it the symbolic centrepiece of the depiction of an entire civilization (more accurately, a network of civilizations that developed over thousands of years), is blatant bigotry, colonialist prejudice and race-based propaganda. It is to follow – even unintentionally – in the footsteps of those Spanish ecclesiastics. It is to perpetuate the West's tradition of masking the violence of imperialism by classifying it as a pacification of inherently violent others, as bearing the burden of taming barbarians (think Thomas Macaulay trumpeting the British as 'the greatest and most highly civilized people that ever the world saw', in contrast to other nations, where 'the gutters foamed with blood').[23] It is the equivalent to summarizing Western civilization as stretching from the torture-execution (human sacrifice) of Christ across blood-soaked millennia into the age of the Holocaust, with little in between but thousands upon thousands being burned alive at the stake, guillotined, racked by the Inquisition, or hung, drawn and quartered in front of rapturous crowds.

---

[22]Mary Miller and Claudia Brittenham, *The Spectacle of the Late Maya Court: Reflections on the Murals of Bonampak* (Austin: University of Texas Press, 2013); Restall, *When Montezuma Met Cortés*, 93–4; Elizabeth Hill Boone (ed.), *The Aztec Templo Mayor* (Washington, DC: Dumbarton Oaks, 1987).
[23]Felipe Fernández-Armesto, *Out of Our Minds: What We Think and How We Came to Think It* (Oakland: University of California Press, 2019), 308 (quoting Macaulay's *History of England* [1849] and *Critical and Historical Essays* [1886]).

'Numerous expulsions and massacres':
Settler colonialism as solution

Consequently, this neo-colonialist perspective on Native Americans, unintentional as it may be, also correlates with how colonialism in the Americas is presented in *The Better Angels of Our Nature*. That topic – the broad history of European and Euro-American imperialism, and of the treatment and experience of Native Americans – receives less attention in the book than that of pre-Columbian Native America. There are early, passing references to the presence of Europeans in the hemisphere, but the impact of colonialism on subject populations is first raised in the form of entries in a table: 'Annihilation of the American Indians' is listed as one of the twenty-one greatest causes of violent death in human history.[24] These references would be easy to miss, as would subsequent, similar inclusions in lists of massacres and genocides (summarized as, for example, 'the numerous expulsions and massacres of Native Americans by settlers or governments in the Americas', or simply 'Genocide in the United States'). Of the dozen mentions of the topic, half take the form of inclusion in lists in text, table or graph.[25]

The other half of those dozen mentions take the form of a sentence or two (nothing as long as a paragraph), and almost all refer to the United States. In most cases, Pinker does not hold back from revealing the unflinching racism that underpinned the slaughter and abuse of Native Americans in the United States – from that 'merciless Indian savages' reference in the Declaration of Independence, to justifications of nineteenth-century massacres of Native families as exterminating 'nits' before they can make 'lice', to Theodore Roosevelt's infamous assertion that 'the only good Indians are the dead Indians'.[26]

The impression thus given of a deep and disturbing history of settler mistreatment of indigenous Americans serves Pinker's larger argument and, like much of his use of data and anecdotal discussion in the book, correlates solidly with historical evidence. One might have preferred to see even passing references to such topics as the decimation of the indigenous Caribbean and Mesoamerican populations in the sixteenth century, the enslavement of Native peoples across four centuries starting in the 1490s, and the genocide in California. But, again, carping on what is missing from a book of this scope is facile criticism.[27]

---

[24]Pinker, *Better Angels*, 235–6 (and also in the source notes to a follow-up graph on 238).
[25]Pinker, *Better Angels*, quotes from 390, 401; for all mentions, see 51–2, 113–14, 171, 197, 235, 238, 390, 393, 401–2, 463, 795.
[26]Pinker, *Better Angels*, 51, 393, 795.
[27]Furthermore, some of the important works that most readily come to mind on these topics have been published since Pinker finished his book; for example, Benjamin Madley, *An American Genocide: The United States and the California Indian Catastrophe, 1846-1873*

My objection, rather, is with the impression that is given by the sum of what Pinker *does* include and how he does it. First of all, the cursory coverage of settler violence and the violent impact of colonization throughout the Americas does not come close to balancing the more detailed and vividly anecdotal depiction of Native American societies, both 'nonstate' and 'state', as extremely violent. Second, consider the effect of that impression when combined with an example such as a graph showing homicide rates in New England declining dramatically from 1637 through the eighteenth century (because 'parts of the country became civilized as the anarchy of the frontier gave way – in part – to state control')[28]: the takeaway seems to be that while European settlement was a violent process, it was less violent than Native America before Europeans arrived, and that violence soon dissipated once the European 'Civilizing Process' took hold in the hemisphere.[29]

My third objection is that Native Americans only appear in the passages of the book that cover the modern era (by which I mean post-1900) as leftover hunter and gatherer groups on the margins of the civilized world – specifically Arctic Canada and the Amazon in the early-to-mid-twentieth century – and then only as examples of the intrinsic violence of nonstate and indigenous societies.[30] Otherwise, after encountering the Civilizing Process, Native Americans disappear. In effect, they cease to exist. A reader who did not know otherwise would conclude that Native Americans contributed to humanity's violent past, but that they are entirely absent from the civilized and peaceful present.

But, of course, Native Americans are not absent from the present. Their numbers in the United States – roughly 7 million – are comparable to the population of the same area before Europeans arrived there. The same is very broadly true of Maya speakers, of whom there are some 8 million today. Almost 2 million people speak Nahuatl, the language of the Aztecs, and four times that many people living in Andean nations speak Quechua, the language of the Inkas.

Not that the issue can be resolved by playing the numbers game, which too easily gives the impression of accurate and solid data where no such certainty lies – a game or methodology that underpins much of Pinker's

---

(New Haven: Yale University Press, 2016), and Andrés Reséndez, *The Other Slavery: The Uncovered Story of Indian Enslavement in America* (Boston: Houghton Mifflin Harcourt, 2016). Likewise, Roxanne Dunbar-Ortiz, *An Indigenous Peoples' History of the United States* (Boston: Beacon Press, 2014), would have served Pinker well had it been available as he wrote. Note that he does refer in passing to 'the appalling treatment of Native Americans by the Spanish in the Caribbean' (*Better Angels*, 402), as mentioned in the following text.
[28]Pinker, *Better Angels*, 113–14.
[29]Pinker borrows the phrase 'Civilizing Process' from Norbert Elias and a 1939 book with that title, using it with capital C and P as a core concept in his book – as discussed by other chapters in this volume. See the chapter by Philip Dwyer and Elizabeth Roberts-Pedersen, 'Steven Pinker, Norbert Elias and *The Civilizing Process*', 87–104.
[30]Pinker, *Better Angels*, 54–5, 64, 392.

argument.[31] Rather, beyond the glaring fact of the survival, growth and dynamism of indigenous peoples in the Americas today, and the implied denial of their very existence in Pinker's book, are this pair of crucial points: the persistence of Native populations and their cultures has been achieved in the face of massive, multifaceted violence against them by the very same civilization whose enlightened ideas and global triumph is the supposed reason for our peaceful twenty-first-century world; and yet, ironically, the West has much to learn – about things it claims to have invented, such as democracy, peaceful conflict resolution and environmental sustainability – from the indigenous cultures it (and Pinker) denigrates or denies. 'Indigenous peoples offer possibilities for life after empire', as Roxanne Dunbar-Ortiz has argued, 'possibilities that neither erase the crimes of colonialism nor require the disappearance of the original peoples colonized'.[32]

Pinker certainly recognizes that the global decline of violence, as he sees it, was not a toboggan run (his metaphor), but was marked by ups and downs (jagged lines, roller coasters, countercurrents etc.). But, by and large, examples that might complicate or problematize or even undermine the larger teleological thrust of his argument are absent or de-emphasized or deployed as exceptions that prove his rule. An example of that technique is his mention of Antonio de Montesinos, whose protests against 'the appalling treatment of Native Americans by the Spanish in the Caribbean' were the lone exception showing how 'until recently most people didn't think there was anything particularly wrong with genocide, as long as it didn't happen to them'.[33]

Although Pinker's larger point may be well taken, his decision to ignore the sixteenth-century debate in the Spanish Atlantic world over indigenous rights (its towering figure, Bartolomé de Las Casas, is not mentioned) has the effect of artificially flattening the ups and downs in the history of race-based and colonialist violence in the Americas. While a strong case can be made for the seventeenth and eighteenth centuries being less violent than the sixteenth in the main population centres of the Americas (such as central Mexico and central Peru), that is not true for the whole hemisphere.

Furthermore, there were larger trends in the late eighteenth and nineteenth centuries that surely went beyond the blip or bump of a temporary counter current. Old imperial and new national regimes generated systems of violence against subordinate populations that were underpinned by new ideologies of race- and class-based supremacy: sub-Saharan Africans were enslaved in the Americas in unprecedented numbers; independent Native American

---

[31]For the dangers and dark poignancy of such numbers in Native American history (specifically the Maya of modern Guatemala), see Diane M. Nelson, *Who Counts? The Mathematics of Death and Life after Genocide* (Durham: Duke University Press, 2015).

[32]Dunbar-Ortiz, *Indigenous Peoples' History*, 235.

[33]Pinker, *Better Angels*, 402.

polities were destroyed; new technologies of violence and surveillance were deployed to eliminate or control Native and mixed-race populations. For most people, especially those of Native and/or African descent, life got worse, not better.[34]

In fact, it got worse in precisely the era that followed that of the 'Enlightenment humanism' that Pinker argues was the turning point in human history, when the West began to lead the world out of the dark past and into a bright future. His recognition that 'Enlightenment humanism did not, at first, carry the day' serves only to trivialize the systematic violence and exploitation wrought by empires and nation states in the Americas and worldwide for two centuries following the American Declaration of Independence, whose 'philosophy' of 'humanism' is given foundational status by Pinker – ignoring, tellingly, that Declaration's exclusion from rights-bearing humanity of enslaved Africans and those 'Indian savages'.[35]

'Believe it or not': The implications of indigenous invisibility

Arguably, Pinker cannot be blamed for following so many others down the path of a prejudicial, colonialist view of Native Americans. His unrelenting focus is on violence in human history, and thus he inevitably and understandably presents indigenous societies as violent – along with all other past societies. Furthermore, the enormity of his world historical scope means he must rely on select sources that summarize fields, and some of those summaries are bound to mislead. That does not mean, however, that we can dismiss the gross misrepresentation of Native American history and culture in *The Better Angels of Our Nature*. That distorted portrait matters, for three reasons.

First, indigenous peoples in the Americas have faced and survived violence of all kinds – colonialist, genocidal, national-political and cultural – and continue to do so to this day. I alluded to this earlier, but it is worth stressing that race-based and often state-sponsored violence against Native

---

[34]There are entire fields of scholarship that could be cited here, but highly relevant is the scathing characterization of the Civilizing Process (as Pinker would call it) in nineteenth-century Latin America by E. Bradford Burns in his seminal *The Poverty of Progress: Latin America in the Nineteenth Century* (Berkeley: University of California Press, 1983); an accessible updated presentation of Burns' argument, placed in a larger historical context, is Julie A. Charlip and E. Bradford Burns, *Latin America: An Interpretive History* (London and New York: Pearson, 2016). Also see the various chapters on Latin America in Vols. III and IV of *The Cambridge World History of Violence* (Cambridge: Cambridge University Press, 2020).

[35]Pinker, *Better Angels*, 221. On Pinker's thesis and 'the paradox of the Enlightenment', see Philip Dwyer, 'Whitewashing History: Pinker's (Mis)Representation of the Enlightenment and Violence', *Historical Reflections/Réflexions historiques*, 44, no. 1 (Spring 2018): 54–65.

peoples has frequently been genocidal – not simply in a rhetorical sense but in line with the United Nations definition[36] – and that such violence *increased* in the centuries after Europe's Enlightenment ideas developed and spread, persisting through the late twentieth century as the world became – for some people – less violent. A vivid example, completely ignored in *The Better Angels*, is the staggering violence suffered by Maya families in Guatemala for most of the second half of the twentieth century. Pinker's book is full of the statistics of violent death, but he missed these: 200,000 people died in a thirty-six-year civil war in which every Maya family 'lost as least one person – so everyone is minus one'.[37]

By misrepresenting pre-Columbian and early modern (colonial-era) Native American societies, and ignoring modern Native Americans completely, Pinker (unwittingly) perpetuates the neo-colonialist perceptions of the indigenous past that underpin ongoing prejudice and mistreatment. If, as Butler notes, 'Pinker's message is reaching the masses, and ours is not', then any prejudicial notions that 'the masses' have regarding Native Americans past and present are being reinforced, not undone through pedagogy and enlightenment.[38]

Second, the Americas were an important centuries-long setting for the violent exercise and development of the imperialist capitalism of the West. Pinker views that history through the lens of his 'gentle commerce' and the 'civilizing' impact of 'Enlightenment humanism'. But if we view it from the Native American perspective, Western-led globalization looks a lot less gentle, and its 'Civilizing Process' a lot less civil. The effect is – ironically, in view of the focus of Pinker's book – to downplay the persistent violence of exploration, conquest and colonization, and the ways in which that violence echoes in the inequities of present-day political regimes and socio-economic structures – both within and between nations in the hemisphere.

Finally, the book's distorted portrait of Native Americans has implications for its core argument. A more accurate and sophisticated understanding of violence in Native America would show more variance across time and region, with variables such as climate change and outside invasion determining levels of violence – not inherent impulses or cultural imperatives. Region by region, there have been alternating periods of time that were marked by warfare or peace, deprivation or plenty, persecution or tolerance, going back not only through the five centuries since Europeans colonization began but through the millennia before that.

The relatively low levels of violence in the Americas today do not include and benefit all regions, and in the multi-century scale of things are

---

[36]Restall, *When Montezuma Met Cortés*, 328–30, 347–8; Dunbar-Ortiz, *Indigenous Peoples' History*, 9–10.
[37]Nelson, *Who Counts?*, 2.
[38]Butler, 'Getting Medieval', 38.

insufficient to show a permanent change. Thus, the larger pattern would be more cyclical than teleological. As a scholar of the recent genocidal war against the Guatemalan Maya observed, 'such violences tend to loop through time, less overcome than going latent for a spell.'[39] And even if anti-indigenous violence is cyclical on a statewide level, at the local level it can be omnipresent and unrelenting – for indigenous environmental activists in Brazil, Bolivia and Peru, for example; for villagers facing drugs cartels; for families in regions of the Americas where Native women are targeted and disappear decade after decade. If the story turns out to be less positive and inspiring for Native American societies, might that not be the case for all human societies? If so, the triumph of our nature's better angels, in Pinker's telling just a few generations old, would – terrifyingly – be temporary.

Pinker sets up his thesis from the opening paragraph of his books' preface as a happy surprise: 'Believe it or not – and I know that most people do not – violence has declined over long stretches of time, and today we may be living in the most peaceable era of our species' existence.'[40] It is bumper sticker brilliance, tailor-made for Twitter, and indeed was echoed in 2017 in an oft-quoted comment by Bill Gates ('Sounds crazy but it's true'; Pinker 'shows how the world is getting better' and 'this is the most peaceful time in human history').[41] But behind that you-won't-believe-it-but set-up is a less benign one, more of a you-already-know-this foundation stone: the West is better than the non-West. Thus, it is the West's triumph over other cultures that has made the world a better place. The persistence of that attitude was apparent in the discussions surrounding the quincentennial of Columbus' 1492 voyage, and it emerged similarly in the discussions – at the levels of national and international politics and media – of the quincentennial of the Spanish invasion of Aztec Mexico (as shown at the start of this chapter).

The slippage in Pinker's book between West/Other and present/past judgements is nowhere made starker than in his treatment of the Native Americas. Arguably, the Native American counternarrative is sufficient to pull the rug out from under Pinker's larger narrative, not least because of its connection to colonialism and neo-colonialism by the West, and the centrality of the West's triumph to Pinker's world view. But even if the Native American counternarrative cannot undo Pinker's larger narrative – especially such cornerstones as increased awareness of human rights, declines in homicide rates and the avoidance (thus far) of a Third World War – it

---

[39]Nelson, *Who Counts?*, 263.
[40]Pinker, *Better Angels*, xix.
[41]As of January 2020, Gates's fervent 2012 review of *Angels* was still accessible on www.gatesnotes.com/Books/The-Better-Angels-of-Our-Nature; his 20176 tweet is quoted in Mark S. Micale and Philip Dwyer, 'History, Violence, and Stephen [*sic*] Pinker', in *Historical Reflections/ Réflexions Historiques*, 44, no. 1 (Spring 2018): 3.

surely undermines the monolithic impression given by that narrative, calling for a closer consideration of counternarratives and their implications for the future.

Acknowledgements

I am grateful to Scott Doebler, Philip Dwyer, Kris Lane, Mark Micale and Robin Restall for contributing thoughts and comments made on earlier drafts.

14

The rise and rise of sexual violence

Joanna Bourke

Violent practices, technologies and symbols increasingly permeate our everyday lives. This is the fact that Pinker seeks to debunk. He attempts to do so in five ways: by selectively choosing his data; minimizing certain harms, adopting an evolutionary psychology approach, ignoring new forms of aggression and failing to acknowledge the political underpinnings of his own research. In this chapter, I will explore these shortcomings in relation to sexual violence.

The study of sexual violence is inherently difficult. We neither know how many people are victims nor how many are perpetrators. Every statistical database has flaws. Pinker had chosen to rely on the United States Bureau of Justice Statistics' National Crime Victimization Survey (NCVS). This is highly problematic since the sample used by the NCVS excludes some groups of people who are most at risk of sexual assault, including 'persons living on military bases and in institutional settings (such as correctional or hospital facilities) and persons who are homeless'.[1] The exclusion of prisoners is particularly telling since Pinker reports positively on increased incarceration rates in the United States, stating that one of the reasons for the decline of rape is that more 'first-time rapists' have been put 'behind bars'.[2] Indeed,

[1] Bureau of Justice Statistics, 'Data Collection: National Crime Victimization Study (NCVS)', 2015, at https://www.bjs.gov/index.cfm?ty=dcdetail&iid=245#Methodology, viewed 12 November 2019. Joanna Bourke is grateful for the generous support of the Wellcome Trust, Grant 205378/Z/16/Z.
[2] Steven Pinker, *The Better Angels of Our Nature: A History of Violence and Humanity* (London: Penguin Books, 2011), 486.

the level of incarceration in the United States is exceptional, with one in every thirty-seven adults under some form of 'correctional supervision'.[3] Incarceration is not 'race-blind': African Americans are imprisoned more than five times the rate of whites.[4] Given that sexually violent men are unlikely to give up their practices, as levels of incarceration have increased dramatically, so too have levels of sexual assault in prisons. The NCVS does not record such increases in prison-based sexual violence: some violated bodies are not valued as highly as others.

Pinker could have supplemented his use of NCVS data with other sources, which present a very different picture. Even if we ignore the fact that Pinker's statistics for sexual violence are drawn from British and American sources (while the World Health Organization finds that 35 per cent of women worldwide have experienced either physical or sexual violence)[5]; nevertheless, *reported* rapes are increasing dramatically. Between 1985 and 2007, rapes reported to the British police increased from 1,842 to 13,133. According to data released by HM Inspectorate of Constabulary on behalf of its rape-monitoring group, in 2015–16, police recorded 23,851 reports of adults being raped.[6] In France, there was a fourfold increase in the same period (from 2,823 to 10,128).[7]

Pinker's response to the increase in reported rape might very well be that the statistics actually prove his point: people are becoming more disapproving of sexual violence and less fearful of reporting assault. There is little evidence for this. Barriers to reporting sexual violence are still formidable. The Crime Survey for England and Wales in 2019 reported that 'sexual offences recorded by the police are not a reliable measure of trends in this type of crime',[8] because 'the majority of victims do not report the offence to the police'.[9] The Office for National Statistics estimated that

[3]NAACP, 'Criminal Justice Fact Sheet', at http://www.naacp.org/criminal-justice-fact-sheet/, seen 12 November 2019.

[4]NAACP, 'Criminal Justice Fact Sheet', at http://www.naacp.org/criminal-justice-fact-sheet/, seen 12 November 2019.

[5]World Health Organization, *Global and Regional Estimates of Violence against Women: Prevalence and Health Effects of and Non-Partner Sexual Violence* (Geneva: WHO, 2013), 2.

[6]Vikram Dodd and Helena Bengtsson, 'Reported Rapes Double in England and Wales in Four Years', *The Guardian*, 13 October 2016, at https://www.theguardian.com/society/2016/oct/13/reported-rapes-in-england-and-wales-double-in-five-years, viewed on 1 December 2017.

[7]Nicole Fayard and Yvette Rocheron, '"Moi quand on dit qu'une femme ment, eh bien, elle ment": The Administration of Rape in Twenty-First Century France and England and Wales', *French Politics, Culture and Society*, 29, no. 1 (Spring 2011): 74.

[8]Office for National Statistics, *Sexual Offences in England and Wales: Year Ending March 2019*, 51, at https://www.ons.gov.uk/peoplepopulationandcommunity/crimeandjustice/bulletins/crimeinenglandandwales/yearendingmarch2019, viewed 12 November 2019.

[9]Office for National Statistics, *Sexual Offending: Victimisation and the Path Through the Criminal Justice System*, 13 December 2018, at https://www.ons.gov.uk/peoplepopulationandcommunity/crimeandjustice/articles/sexualoffendingvictimisationandthepaththroughthecriminaljusticesystem/2018-12-13, viewed 12 November 2019.

fewer than one in five victims report the offence to the police,[10] while the Rape Crisis Federation of England and Wales found that only 12 per cent of the 50,000 women who contacted their services reported the crime of rape to the police.[11] Even the NCVS found that, between 1992 and 2000, 63 per cent of completed rapes, 65 per cent of attempted rapes and 74 per cent of completed and attempted sexual assaults against females were not reported to the police.[12] The British Crime Survey found even lower levels of reportage: less than 20 per cent of rape victims told the police.[13] Non-reportage is particularly high among minority women, the poor and disenfranchised, and prostitutes. It is also a problem for married women who have been victimized by their partners: lack of money and access to alternative housing, in addition to emotional dependency and concerns over retaining access to children, meant that victims often feel unable to pursue prosecution.

Statistical limitations are exacerbated by Pinker's narrow definition of 'violence'. This is the second problem with his argument. Pinker's definition of violence is largely drawn from legal precepts: there is a perpetrator, a cruel act, a harmful effect. Most violence today does not conform to this model. It is structural and institutional. It is about pervasive insecurity, poverty, disease and inequality. This kind of violence is powerful precisely because it has become naturalized: it is a 'fact of life' that seems impossible to challenge.[14] This partly explains why, as Pinker rightly emphasizes, modern lives are characterized by a free-floating anxiety about violence. These pervasive forms of sexual violence are not politically neutral: they are maintained by economic and social policies and sustained by legal and political processes. It is also something that has been challenged by activists such as Tamara Burke, who started the 'MeToo' movement precisely with the systemic sexual exploitation of African American and other minority women in mind. The sexualization of gender, racial and economic domination are a form of violence.

---

[10]Office for National Statistics, *Sexual Offending*.

[11]H. M. Crown Prosecution Service Inspectorate, *A Report on the Joint Inspection into the Investigation and Prosecution of Cases Involving Allegations of Rape* (London: H. M. Crown Prosecution Service Inspectorate, April 2002), 1.

[12]Callie Marie Rennison, *Rape and Sexual Assault: Reporting to Police and Medical Attention, 1992-2000* (Washington, DC: Bureau of Justice Statistics, 2002), 2.

[13]Andy Myhill and Jonathan Allen, *Rape and Sexual Assault of Women: The Extent and Nature of the Problem. Findings from the British Crime Survey* (London: Home Office Research, Development, and Statistics Directorate, March 2002), vii. Also see MOPAC, *Sexual Violence: The London Sexual Violence Needs Assessment 2016 for MOPAC and NHS England (London)* (London: MBARC, November 2016), 26, at www.london.gov.uk/sites/default/files/sexual_viole nce_needs_assessment_report_2016.pdf.

[14]I made this argument in my review of Pinker's book: Joanna Bourke, 'We Are Nicer Than We Think', *The Guardian*, 10 October 2011, at http://www.thetimes.co.uk/tto/news/article318 8732.ece, viewed 12 November 2019.

Furthermore, these are forms of violence that Pinker seems to think can be eradicated without the 'decivilizing' effects of protest such as occurred in the 1960s. For Pinker, violent protest is wrong, yet emancipatory politics for groups experiencing systemic violence may be the only way to effect change. Rights didn't simply emerge as part of a peaceful, civilizing process. In *Inventing Human Rights. A History* (2006), literary scholar Lynn Hunt would have us believe that the burgeoning expression of sympathy towards strangers was the outcome of the dramatic explosion in the publication and reading of novels. The epistolary novel taught readers to imagine that other people are similar to themselves. We all possess an inner space of feelings. The shared mystery of pain and pleasure promoted empathetic responses. In other words, she argues that fiction was the prime tool of an *education sentimentale*, changing human sensibilities.[15] But this does not fit the historical record: rights were more usually attained through protest, which was often violent. Rights do not arise out of universal, timeless moral truths, but are won in social struggles in the real world. For Pinker, violent protest is wrong; for peoples experiencing systemic sexual violence, it might be their only lifeline.

The third trap that Pinker falls into is the minimization of certain harms. He does this, in part, by failing to understand history. He states that 'one has to look long and hard through history and across cultures to find an acknowledgement of the harm of rape *from the viewpoint of the victim*'.[16] This is not the case. Rape was a heinous act precisely because it was known to inflict serious harm to victims. Medical jurisprudence textbooks were full of descriptions of the harm caused by rape, claiming (in the words of Alfred Swaine Taylor in his influential *Medical Jurisprudence* of 1861) that victims could 'sustain all the injury, morally and physically, which the perpetration of the crime can possibly bring down upon her'.[17]

The language used to articulate that harm was different in earlier periods, however. Prior to the 1860s, victims of *any* form of violence would not have used the word 'trauma' to refer to their emotional or psychological responses. That concept was invented by John Eric Erichsen, professor of surgery at University College Hospital in London, in 1866.[18] However, victims had other languages to communicate their pain. When the after-effects of rape were discussed, attention was paid to physical and moral realms. Women would 'mysteriously waste away, sicken, grow pale, thin, waxen, and finally quit the earth, and send their forms to early graves, – like blasted fruit falling

---

[15]Lynn Hunt, *Inventing Human Rights: A History* (New York: W. W. Norton and Co., 2006).
[16]Pinker, *Better Angels*, 476. Emphasis in the original.
[17]Alfred Swaine Taylor, *Medical Jurisprudence*, 12th edn (London: np, 1861), 687–98.
[18]John Eric Erichsen, *On Railway and Other Injuries of the Nervous System* (London: Walton and Maberly, 1866), 9. Also see John Eric Erichsen, *On Concussion of the Spine, Nervous Shock, and Other Obscure Injuries of the Nervous System in Their Clinical and Medico-Legal Aspects* (London: Longman, Green and Co., 1875), 195.

before half ripened' (as one author explained the aftermath of 'forced love' or marital rape in 1869).[19] Victims regularly referred to 'insensibility' to convey their distress. Rape victims were described as 'in a state of fever' (1822)[20], 'very ill, after lying in a fainting state some time' (1866)[21] and in a 'state of prostration' (1877).[22] These are very different ways to acknowledge the 'harm of rape from the point of view of the victim', but powerful ones indeed for their times.

There is another way Pinker minimizes harms. He contributes to rape myths by recycling long-standing prejudices about the prevalence of false accusations. The belief that 'women lie' about sexual assault is deeply embedded in our society, particularly within police forces and criminal justice systems. For example, one 2008 survey of 891 police officers in the south-eastern United States found that more than 50 per cent believed that half of women who complained of rape were liars and 10 per cent believed that the majority of complainants were lying.[23] Police 'unfound' (USA) or 'no-crime' (UK) large numbers of rape complaints, without investigation.[24] According to a recent study by legal expert Corey Rayburn Yung, American police departments 'substantially undercounted reported rapes'.[25] Police departments generated 'paper reductions in crime' in three ways: they designated an incident as 'unfounded' without carrying out any (or any thorough) investigation, classified a reported incident as a lesser offence and omitted to 'to create a written report that a victim made a rape complaint'.[26] Yung concluded that the number of police jurisdictions where undercounting took place had *increased* by over 61 per cent between 1995 and 2012.[27]

Pinker seems to share police scepticism about the veracity of rape complainants, and the weight that should be given to women's accounts of assault. He informs readers that rape is 'notoriously underreported, and at the same time often overreported (as in the highly publicized but ultimately

---

[19]Count de St. Leon, *Love and Its Hidden History*, 4th edn (Boston: William White and Co., 1869), 102.

[20]'Scotland: Perth Circuit Court', *The Times*, 21 September 1822, 3.

[21]'Crown Court', *The Times*, 8 March 1866, 11.

[22]'Outrage', *The Times*, 7 September 1877, 8. For a broader discussion, see my *Rape: A History from the 1860s to the Present* (London: Virago, 2007).

[23]Amy Dellinger Page, 'Gateway to Reform? Policy Implications of Police Officers' Attitudes Towards Rape', *American Journal of Criminal Justice*, 33, no. 1 (May 2008): 44–58. Also see Martin D. Schwartz, 'National Institute of Justice Visiting Fellowship: Police Investigation of Rape – Roadblocks and Solutions', *U.S. Department of Justice*, December 2012, at http://www.ncjrs.gov/pdffiles1/nij/grants/232667.pdf.

[24]Lisa R. Avalos, 'Policing Rape Complaints: When Reporting Rape Becomes a Crime', *Journal of Gender, Race, and Justice*, 20 (2017): 466–7.

[25]Corey Rayburn Yung, 'How to Lie with Rape Statistics: America's Hidden Rape Crisis', *Iowa Law Review*, 99 (2014): 1197.

[26]Yung, 'How to Lie with Rape Statistics', 1197.

[27]Yung, 'How to Lie with Rape Statistics', 1197.

disproven 2006 accusation against three Duke University lacrosse players)'.[28]
Such moral equivalence is not only dangerous: it is wrong. The extent of false
accusations has generated a vast amount of academic research. In 2000–3, for
example, the British Home Office commissioned a comprehensive research
project into the problem. Initially, the researchers concluded that 9 per cent
of reported rape accusations were false. However, on closer analysis, this
percentage dropped dramatically. They found that many of the cases listed
as 'no evidence of assault' were the result of someone other than the victim
making the accusation. In other words, a policeman or passer-by might see
a woman distressed or drunk, with her clothes ripped, and report it as a
suspected rape. However, when the woman was able to provide an account
for what happened, she stated that no assault had taken place. In other
instances, a woman regained consciousness in a public place or at home and,
unable to recall what happened, worried about whether she might have been
assaulted. The woman might approach the police not in order to claim rape,
but to check whether any crime had been committed. Once such cases had
been eliminated from the study, only 3 per cent of allegations should have
been categorized as false.[29] These statistics are in line with other studies.[30]
Contrary to the notion that men are at risk of being falsely accused, it is
significantly more common for actual rapists to get away with their actions.

Pinker's claim, therefore, that rape is 'over-reported' not only misstates
the known facts but also has real-life consequences: it bolsters the view
that women are prone to lie about being raped, influences the way the legal
system processes rape cases and prejudices perceptions of victims from the
moment they report being raped to the time they give evidence in court.

One of the reasons Pinker may underestimate the effect of repeating rape
myths is because he believes that women who report being sexual abused
are now treated with care and respect. 'Today', he writes, 'every level of the
criminal justice system has been mandated to take sexual assault seriously'.[31]

---

[28]Pinker, *Better Angels*, 484.
[29]Liz Kelly, Jo Lovett, and Linda Regan, *A Gap or a Chasm? Attrition in Reported Rape Cases*,
Home Office Research Study 293 (London: Home Office Research, Development and Statistics
Directorate, February 2005), xi and 46–7.
[30]Clare Gunby, Anna Carline and Caryl Beynon, 'Regretting It After: Focus Group Perspec-
tives on Alcohol Consumption, Nonconsensual Sex and False Allegations of Rape', *Social and
Legal Studies*, 22 (2013): 87 and 106; Kimberley A. Lonsway, Joanne Archambault and David
Lisak, 'False Reports: Moving beyond the Issue to Successfully Investigate and Prosecute Non-
Stranger Sexual Assaults', *The Voice*, 3, no. 1 (2009): 1–11, at http://www.ndaa.org/pdf/the_vo
ice_vol_3_no_1_2009.pdf; Philip N. S. Rumney, 'False Allegations of Rape', *Cambridge Law
Journal*, 65, no. 1 (2006): 128–58; Liz Kelly, 'The (In)credible Words of Women: False Allega-
tions in European Rape Research', *Violence Against Women*, 16, no. 12 (2010): 1345–55;
Kelly, Lovett, and Regan, *A Gap or a Chasm?*; David Lisak, Lori Gardiner, Sarah C. Nicksa
and Ashley M. Cote, 'False Allegations of Sexual Assault: An Analysis of Ten Years of Reported
Cases', *Violence Against Women*, 16, no. 12 (2010): 1318–34.
[31]Pinker, *Better Angels*, 482.

This is a classic case of conflating regulation with implementation. The law enforcement and justice systems may have been 'mandated' to take rape seriously, but that does not mean much in actual practice. A study by Kimberly A. Lonsway, Susan Welch and Louise F. Fitzgerald found that sensitivity training and education about rape improved the superficial behaviour of police officers, but not their attitudes towards rape victims.[32] Indeed, argues James F. Hodgskin, changes in police procedures are often simply a form of 'impression management', while 'internal operations, for the most part, go unchanged and unchallenged'.[33] Complaints about treatment by the police and in the courts are routine.[34] As noted earlier, even today substantial proportions of policemen and women do not take complainants' reports seriously. Rape complainants in some US jurisdictions are routinely given polygraph tests – a procedure that would be unimaginable for any other victim of crime.[35] In recent years, women who report being sexually assaulted or raped to the police risk finding themselves charged with 'perverting the course of justice'.[36] In 2017, there was evidence that the forensic samples taken from tens of thousands of rape victims were never even sent for testing.[37] Conviction rates are low and declining. In the United Kingdom in 1977, one in three of reported rapes resulted in a conviction. By 1985, this was 24 per cent or one in five and it was only one in ten by 1996.[38] Today, it is one in twenty. If people today abhor sexual violence more intensely than in the past, why is there a rapidly decline prosecution rates?

Pinker also claims that no one now 'argues that women *ought* to be humiliated at police stations and courtrooms, that husbands have a right to rape their wives, or that rapists should prey on women in apartment

---

[32]Kimberly A. Lonsway, Susan Welch and Louise F. Fitzgerald, 'Police Training in Sexual Assault Response: Process, Outcomes, and Elements of Change', *Criminal Justice and Behavior*, 28, no. 6 (2001): 695–730.

[33]James F. Hodgson, 'Policing Sexual Violence: A Case Study of *Jane Doe v. the Metropolitan Toronto Police*', in James F. Hodgson and Debra S. Kelley (eds), *Sexual Violence: Policies, Practices, and Challenges in the United States and Canada* (Westport: Praeger, 2002), 173.

[34]For example, see MOPAC, *Sexual Violence*, 29.

[35]Vivian B. Lord and Gary Rassel, 'Law Enforcement's Response to Sexual Assault: A Comparative Study of Nine Counties in North Carolina', in Hodgson and Kelley (eds), *Sexual Violence*, 166; T. W. Marsh, A. Geist and N. Caplan, *Rape and the Limits of Law Reform* (Boston: Auburn House, 1982).

[36]Avalos, 'Policing Rape Complaints', 460–71.

[37]Jill E. Daly, 'Gathering Dust on the Evidence Shelves of the US', *Women's Rights Law Reporter*, 25, no. 1 (Fall/Winter 2003): 17–36; Milli Kanani, 'Testing Justice', *Columbia Human Rights Law Review*, 42, no. 3 (Spring 2011): 943–92; Cassia Spohn, 'Untested Sexual Assault Kits: A National Dilemma', *Criminality and Public Policy*, 15, no. 2 (May 2016): 551–4; Tara Kalar, Elizabeth Meske, Alison Schimdt and Shirin Johnson, 'A Crisis of Complacency: Minnesota's Untested Rape Kit Backlog', *Bench and Bar of Minnesota*, 74 (2017): 22–8.

[38]Jessica Harris and Sharon Grace, *A Question of Evidence? Investigating and Prosecuting Rape in the 1990s* (London: Home Office Research Study 196, 1999), iii.

stairwells and parking garages'. Putting these three scenarios in the same sentence creates a misleading impression. After all, no one has ever argued that 'rapists should prey on women in apartment stairwells and parking garages': to include that phrase in the same sentence as husbands having a right to rape their wives makes that scenario seem equally ridiculous. However, until a few decades ago, many people *did* publicly argue that wives did not have the right to refuse to consent to sexual intercourse with their husbands. As late as 1991, a robust justification of the marital rape exemption was published in the *New Law Journal* by the distinguished legal academic Glanville Williams. In Williams' words:

> We are speaking of a biological activity, strongly baited by nature, which is regularly and pleasurably performed on a consensual basis by mankind. . . . Occasionally some husband continues to exercise what he regards as his right when his wife refuses him, the refusal most probably resulting from the fact that the pair have had a tiff. What is wrong with his demand is not so much the act requested, but its timing, or the manner of the demand.[39]

It wasn't until 1992 that the marital rape exemption was abolished in England; in Greece, it was in 2006; and it is still not a crime in more than forty countries. There continue to be formidable difficulties for wives who report being sexually abused by their husbands.

There are many other forms of sexual violence that many people *do* support. The military argues that hazing is necessary for the 'hardening' of soldiers and Marines. Hazing practices include sexual practices, such as forced public masturbation, imitating or performing fellatio, and 'greasings' (a naked man is smeared in machinery grease and buggered with a plastic tube). People don't necessarily feel distressed when the rights to sexual integrity are violated. The sexual abuses in Abu Ghraib were openly supported by many; there is a widespread support for torture, including sexualized forms of torture.

The Tailhook scandal is one example of many in which sexual abuse is minimized or accepted. At the Thirty-Fifth Annual Tailhook Association Symposium in Las Vegas in September 1991, a two-day debriefing of US Navy and Marine Corps aviation in Operation Desert Story, eighty-three women and seven men alleged sexual assault and harassment. Among other humiliations, they had been forced to walk down a corridor lined with men who groped them, a form of hazing that is common during 'crossing-the-line' ceremonies. In the subsequent public furore, the distinction between

---

[39]Glanville Williams, 'The Problem of Domestic Rape', *New Law Journal*, 141 (15 February 1991): 205; and 'The Problem of Domestic Rape', *New Law Journal*, 141 (22 February 1991): 246.

hazing and sexual abuse was blurred. For instance, writing in the *Marine Corps Gazette* in November 1992, leading American cultural conservative William S. Lind confessed to being puzzled by the public reaction to the abuse. 'After all', he wrote,

> no one was raped at Tailhook. From what was in the newspapers, it didn't sound much different from a Dartmouth fraternity on a Friday or Saturday night. Unless the women officers who are protesting their treatment so loudly went directly to flight school from a convent, they surely had some idea what to expect.[40]

Lind claimed that the public condemnation of the abuses at Tailhook were a classic example of 'fourth generation warfare' conducted by feminists against the American officer corps. Feminists 'are well on their way to their operational goal: the femininization of the Armed Forces'. If women in the military wanted to be treated as equals, Lind argued, then they had to accept the 'back-slapping, practical-joking, locker room atmosphere that usually prevails where men do dangerous jobs like flying combat aircraft'.[41]

Pinker is complacent about the violence that was part and parcel of imperialism. Of course, he details some of the major forms of suffering that resulted from imperial ventures, but these 'costs' are kept separate from his analysis of commerce as a civilizing force. According to Pinker, the trade of goods and services encourages people to treat others as beneficial to their own interests, and thus deserving of more consideration. Critic Randal R. Hendrickson summarizes the problem with this argument. He observes that Pinker is 'all but silent' on the forms of commerce that 'play to our demons'. Hendrickson notes:

> The colonialism of the newly civilized Europeans – surely a commercial activity, and often justified in enlightened terms of bringing civilization to untamed locals – is hardly mentioned.[42]

It is not necessary to look into the distant past to make this argument. After all, according to the International Labour Organization, at any given time in 2016, *40.3 million* people are living *in modern slavery*, including 24.9 million in forced labour and *15.4 million in forced marriages*. That means that there are 5.4 victims for every 1,000 people in the world. Of those in forced labour, 4.8 million are women engaged in forced sexual exploitation,

---

[40]W. S. Lind, 'Tailhook: The Larger Issue', *Marine Corps Gazette* (November 1992), 38.
[41]Lind, 'Tailhook: The Larger Issue', 38.
[42]Randal R. Hendrickson, 'Swords into Syllogisms', *The New Atlantis*, 38 (Winter/Spring 2013), 119.

or the commercial sex industry.[43] The millions of women who are trafficked in the sex trade are wiped from history: economic activities such as the sex trade 'call the gentleness of gentle commerce into question'.[44]

Pinker is equally complacent about forms of sexual violence that have only arisen in late twentieth and early twenty-first centuries: the invention and proliferation of technology-enhanced violence. He claims that the 'treatment of rape in popular culture' has 'changed beyond recognition' in positive ways. 'Today', he writes, 'when the film and television industries depict a rape, it is to generate sympathy for the victim and revulsion for her attacker'.[45] This is a surprising claim, given the amount of scholarship arguing that rape scenes in film and television are often included gratuitously or for titillation.

The sexualization of violence is especially prominent in video gaming, which Pinker correctly observes is 'the medium of the next generation, rivalling cinema and recorded music in revenue'.[46] Pinker believes that computer games 'overflow with violence and gender stereotypes' but that rape is 'conspicuously absent'.[47] This myth has been exploded in Anastasia Powell and Nicola Henry's book *Sexual Violence in a Digital Age*, which analyses structural inequalities as well as the gendered harms caused by technology-facilitated sexual violence, including virtual rape, image-based sexual abuse (such as 'revenge pornography') and online sexual harassment.[48] Other commentators have argued that threats of rape and other attacks are routine in the genre, as is the spread of violent sexual images.[49]

Video gaming and virtual spaces are prominent examples where sexual violence is rife. In 2013, a survey of male college students found that 22 per cent had engaged in technology-based sexually coercive behaviours.[50] In the

---

[43]See International Labour Organization, 'Global Estimates of Modern Slavery: Forced Labour and Forced Marriage', at https://www.ilo.org/global/topics/forced-labour/lang--en/index.htm, viewed 12 November 2019.

[44]Hendrickson, 'Swords into Syllogisms', 119.

[45]Pinker, *Better Angels*, 483.

[46]Pinker, *Better Angels*, 483.

[47]Pinker, *Better Angels*, 484.

[48]Anastasia Powell and Nicola Henry, *Sexual Violence in a Digital Age* (London: Palgrave, 2016). Also see Nicola Henry and Anastasia Powell, 'Technology-Facilitated Sexual Violence: A Literature Review of Empirical Research', *Trauma, Violence, & Abuse*, 19, no. 2 (June 2016): 195–208; and Nicola Henry and Anastasia Powell, 'Sexual Violence in the Digital Age: The Scope and Limits of Criminal Law', *Social and Legal Studies*, 25, no. 4 (2016): 397–418.

[49]This is a huge literature, but see Jessica Valenti, 'How the Web Became a Sexists' Paradise', *The Guardian*, 6 April 2007, 16, at https://www.theguardian.com/world/2007/apr/06/gender .blogging and Cheryl Lindsey Seelhoff, 'A Chilling Effect: The Oppression and Silencing of Women Journalists and Bloggers Worldwide', *Off Our Backs*, 37, no. 1 (2007): 18–21; Catherine Holahan, 'The Dark Side of Web Anonymity', *Bloomberg Businessweek*, 1 May 2008, at https://www.bloomberg.com/news/articles/2008-04-30/the-dark-side-of-web-anonymity.

[50]Martie P. Thompson and Deidra J. Morrison, 'Prospective Predictors of Technology-Based Sexual Coercion by College Males', *Psychology of Violence*, 3, no. 3 (2013): 233–46.

virtual environment *Second Life*, users can pay to sexually assault ('grief') other characters.[51] Some popular computer games (such as *Grand Theft Auto*) include rape scenarios. In his book *Second Lives: A Journey through Virtual Worlds*, Tim Guest estimated that around 6.5 per cent of logged-in residents have filed one or more abuse reports in *Second Life*. By the end of 2006, Linden Lab (creator of *Second Life*) was receiving 'close to 2,000 abuse reports a day'.[52] This is not a new phenomenon: the first recorded case of virtual rape occurred in 1993 among a cyberspace community called LambdaMOO, a multi-user, real-time, virtual world. In it, a user called Mr Bungle used his 'voodoo power' to sadistically attack and rape several female characters, who were made to look as though they were enjoying it.[53] Since that time, online sexual violence has proliferated. Feminists report systemic threats of death and sexual violence. 'Revenge porn' (when partners post to the internet sexually explicit photographs without consent) is popular. Cyber harassment is common.

Why should cybercrimes be regarded as violent? Because they have real-life effects on non-avatar people, inducing psychological disturbance (anxiety, depression, PTSD) and affecting life outcomes (sexual and social dysfunction, drug and alcohol abuse, self-harm, suicide). These forms of violence also generate major negative health outcomes for the victims' families, friends and communities. They cause women to police their own behaviour. Not only have women moved home, changed their jobs, and gone into hiding, they also 'shut down their blogs, avoid websites they formerly frequented, take down social networking profiles, refrain from engaging in online political commentary, and choose not to maintain potentially lucrative or personally rewarding online presences'.[54] These are 'real' harms, not virtual ones.

---

[51]Michael Bugeja, 'Avatar Rape', *Inside Higher Ed*, 25 February 2010, at http://www.insidehighered.com/views/2010/02/25/bugeja, viewed 12 November 2017.

[52]Tim Guest, *Second Lives: A Journey through Virtual Worlds* (London: Hutchinson, 2007), 227. Also see Melissa Mary Fenech Sander, 'Questions of Accountability and Illegality of Virtual Rape' (MSc thesis, Iowa State University, 2009).

[53]Julian Dibbell, 'A Rape in Cyberspace', *Village Voice*, xxxviii, 38, no. 51 (21 December 1993), at http://www. villagevoice.com/2005-10-18/special/a-rape-in-cyberspace/ and Julian Dibbell, 'A Rape in Cyberspace or How an Evil Clown, A Haitian Trickster Spirit, Two Wizards, and a Cast of Dozens Turned a Database into a Society', *Annual Survey of American Law* (1994): 471–89. Also see K. De Vries, 'Avatars Out of Control', in Serge Gutwirth (ed.), *Computers, Privacy, and Data Protection* (New York: Springer, 2011), 233–50; G. Young and M. T. Whitty, 'Games without Frontiers', *Computers in Human Behavior*, 26, no. 6 (2010): 1228; Michael Kasumovic and Rob Brooks, 'Virtual Rape in Grand Theft Auto 5: Learning the Limits of the Game', *The Conversation*, at https://theconversation.com/virtual-rape-in-grand-theft-auto-5-learning-the-limits-of-the-game-30520, viewed 1 December 2017; Mary Anne Franks, 'Unwilling Avatars: Idealism and Discrimination in Cyberspace', *Columbia Journal of Gender and Law*, 20, no. 1 (2011): 224–61; Jessica Wolfendale, 'My Avatar, My Self: Virtual Harm and Attachment', *Ethics and Information Technology*, 9, no. 2 (2007): 111–19.

[54]For a small sample of the evidence, see D. K. Citron, *Hate Crimes in Cyberspace* (Cambridge,

Finally, Pinker's employment of an evolutionary psychology model of sexual violence is problematic. His view of sexual violence is framed in terms of self-interested competitors, a 'genetic calculus' and a 'reproductive spreadsheet'.[55] He believes that the 'prevalence of rape in human history' and the 'invisibility of the victim in the legal treatment of rape' are

> all too comprehensible from the vantage point of the genetic interests that shaped human desires and sentiments over the course of evolution before our sensibilities were shaped by Enlightenment humanism.[56]

He notes that 'harassment, intimidation, and forced copulation are found in many species, including gorillas, orangutans, and chimpanzees'.[57] Rape, he contends, 'is not exactly a normal part of male sexuality [note that equivocal 'not *exactly*'], but it is made possible by the fact that male desire can be indiscriminate in its choice of a sexual partner and indifferent to the partner's inner life'.[58] There is also a slippage from the notion that 'Around 5 percent of rapes result in pregnancies, which suggests that rape can be an evolutionary advantage to the rapist'[59], to the view that this behaviour was the best strategy for men in evolutionary time.

Theorists hostile to the application of evolutionary insights to modern societies will remain sceptical. It is important to note, however, that feminist evolutionary scientists have challenged the *particular form* of evolutionary psychology that Pinker espouses. They point out the Western, male bias of its model of reproductive strategies.[60] As Pinker is aware, 'fitness' in the context of survival and reproduction is a much more complex phenomenon than his account allows for, most notably because it is affected not only

---

MA: Harvard University Press, 2014); Franks, 'Unwilling Avatars', 229; Danielle Keats Citron, 'Addressing Cyber Harassment: An Overview of Hate Crimes in Cyberspace', *Journal of Law, Technology, and the Internet*, 6 (2015): 1; Danielle Keats Citron, 'Cyber Civil Rights', *Boston University Law Review*, 89 (2009): 64–9; Danielle Keats Citron, 'Law's Expressive Value in Combating Cyber Gender Harassment', *Michigan Law Review*, 108 (2009): 373–5; Nicola Henry and Anastasia Powell, 'Embodied Harms: Gender, Shame, and Technology-Facilitated Sexual Violence', *Violence Against Women*, 21, no. 6 (March 2015): 758–79; Sander, 'Questions of Accountability and Illegality of Virtual Rape'.
[55]Pinker, *Better Angels*, 480.
[56]Pinker, *Better Angels*, 477.
[57]Pinker, *Better Angels*, 477.
[58]Pinker, *Better Angels*, 488.
[59]Pinker, *Better Angels*, 477.
[60]Patricia Adair Gowaty, 'Power Asymmetries between the Sexes, Mate Preferences, and Components of Fitness', in Cheryl Brown Travis (ed.), *Evolution, Gender, and Rape* (Cambridge, MA: MIT Press, 2003); Sarah Blaffer Hrdy, '"Raising Darwin's Consciousness": Female Sexuality and the Prehominid Origins of Patriarchy', *Human Nature*, 8, no. 1 (1997): 1–49; Sarah Blaffer Hrdy, *The Woman that Never Evolved: With a New Preface* (Cambridge, MA: Harvard University Press, 1999); Marlene Zuk, *Sexual Selection: What We Can and Can't Learn about Sex from Animals* (Berkeley: University of California Press, 2002).

by individual reproductive success in competitive environments (which may include forced sex or exploitative accumulation of material resources) but also by sexual selection (including taking into account the preferences of the opposite sex) and group selection (such as adhering to reproductive norms or restraining sexual impulses). Individual, group and sexual selection can, and often do, work against each other. For example, a trait or behaviour that can enhance sexual selection can also be non-adaptive in terms of individual fitness (e.g. certain sexual display behaviours increase the risk of being preyed upon). Equally, species often behave in ways that promote the survival and reproduction of the group, at the risk of individual survival and reproduction. Evolutionary psychologists of Pinker's variety tend to focus on individual environmental and genetic interactions, while downplaying sexual selection and group selection, because the latter are significantly more difficult to infer from evolutionary environments. But this does not mean that individual selection is actually dominant in terms of evolutionary mechanisms. Indeed, given the logic of the evolutionary account, the scarcity of the 'commodity' women possess – that is, child-bearing and raising – gives particularly strong preference to female tastes in sexual selection.[61] By focusing on only one of the mechanisms of selection, Pinker's paradigm privileges a male-biased, individualistic, neoliberal account of the evolution of the brain that is primarily about self-interest rather than the group.

Furthermore, Pinker's model of reproduction fails to acknowledge the evolutionary benefits of flexible responses, which may cut across gender lines.[62] For example, primatologists have observed that primate females are often aggressive in sex and promiscuous in soliciting it.[63] Evolutionary biologist Patricia Adair Gowaty and ecologist Stephen Hubbell developed a model that emphasizes flexibility of reproductive behaviour once factors such as environments, probabilities of encounters and survival, receptivity and life history are factored in. Rather than assuming that females will be 'coy' in their sexual encounters while males are promiscuous, they find that it depends on other contexts: if an individual's survival probability declines, so too will their 'choosiness', whether male or female.[64] As Gowaty and

---

[61]For further discussion, see Amy L. Wax, 'Evolution and the Bounds of Human', *Law and Philosophy*, 23, no. 6 (November 2004): 540.

[62]See Laurette T. Liesen, 'Women, Behavior, and Evolution: Understanding the Debate between Feminist Evolutionists and Evolutionary Psychologists', *Politics and the Life Sciences*, 26, no. 1 (March 2007): 51–70.

[63]Sarah Blaffer Hrdy, 'Empathy, Polyandry, and the Myth of the Coy Female', in Elliott Sober (ed.), *Conceptual Issues in Evolutionary Biology* (Cambridge, MA: MIT Press, 1994), 123–9; Hrdy, 'Raising Darwin's Consciousness', 8–22; Barbara Smuts, 'Male Aggression against Women: An Evolutionary Perspective', *Human Nature*, 3 (1992): 123–9; Barbara Smuts, 'The Evolutionary Origins of Patriarchy', *Human Nature*, 6 (1995): 1–32; Zuk, *Sexual Selection*.

[64]Patricia Adair Gowaty and Stephen P. Hubbell, 'Chance, Time Allocation, and the Evolution of Adaptively Flexible Sex Role Behavior', *Integrative and Comparative Biology*, 4 (2005): 931–44.

Hubbell conclude, 'Males, not just females, flexibly adjust choosy and indiscriminate behavior' and selection will 'sometimes select against choosy females and indiscriminate males'.[65]

Pinker's evolutionary approach also leads him to ignore the effect of sexual violence on certain women. He observes that rape 'entangles with three parties', which he claims are 'the rapist, the men who take a proprietary interest in the woman, and the woman herself'.[66] He reiterates this later, when noting that the 'second party to a rape is the woman's family, *particularly her father, brothers, and husband*'.[67] In these ways, Pinker omits the effects of rape (whether actual or threatened) on the lives of all women and other vulnerable people. Mothers, sisters, and daughters (to name just three) are harmed by this form of violence.

Many of these criticisms arise from Pinker's selective use of evidence from the psychological literature. To take one example: Pinker's particular evolutionary psychological approach would predict that women would be more harmed by sexual violence than would men. He cites the work of evolutionary psychologist David Buss, claiming that Buss 'shows that men underestimate how upsetting sexual aggression is to a female victim, while women overestimate how upsetting sexual aggression is to a male victim'.[68] In fact, Buss' research was done in the 1980s, and rather than showing a universal pattern differentiating male versus female responses, it is based on a sample of male and female undergraduates enrolled in a psychology course at a large Midwestern university. Participation in the survey earned the participants credits for their course.[69] These respondents are psychology's WEIRDs (i.e. Western, educated, undergraduate students from industrialized, rich and democratic countries). Furthermore, the questions that these students were asked to respond to carried within them a strong presumption for an evolutionary account of emotional responses to abuse – an account these students would have recognized given its prominence in psychology curricula of the time. The students were directed from the start that the project was investigating 'Conflict between Men and Women', as the sheet of paper they were given was entitled. All these factors strongly bias the survey.

Furthermore, Pinker does not report that Buss' study did *not* support the hypothesis that 'women would be upset and angered by the hypothesized

---

[65]Gowaty and Hubbell, 'Chance, Time Allocation, 940. Also see Steven Gangestad and Jeffrey Simpson, 'The Evolution of Human Mating: Trade-offs and Strategic Pluralism', *Behavioral and Brain Sciences*, 23 (2000): 575–6.

[66]Pinker, *Better Angels*, 477.

[67]Pinker, *Better Angels*, 478. My emphasis.

[68]Pinker, *Better Angels*, 488–9, referring to David M. Buss, 'Conflict between the Sexes: Strategic Interference and the Evocation of Anger and Upset', *Journal of Personality and Social Psychology*, 56, no. 5 (1989): 735–47.

[69]Buss, 'Conflict between the Sexes', 737.

feature of male reproductive strategy involving sexual aggressiveness'.[70] Indeed, Buss concluded that 'Overall, these results provide only partial support for the theory of conflict between the sexes on the basis of conflicting reproductive strategies'.[71] The evolutionary theory was only convincing in the experiment where the students were asked to speculate on how 'irritating, annoying, and upsetting' sexual aggressiveness would be to a person the man/woman was 'involved with'. As David Buller argues in *Adapting Minds: Evolutionary Psychology and the Persistent Quest for Human Nature* (2005), both Pinker's and Buss' methodologies are flawed and the evidence do not support their conclusions. 'Our minds', Buller concludes, 'are not adapted to the Pleistocene, but, like the immune system, are continually adapting, over both evolutionary time and individual lifetimes'.[72]

In conclusion, as I have tried to point out throughout this chapter, Pinker fails to recognize the ideological underpinnings of his research. The most common response of evolutionary psychologists is to accuse critics of committing a 'naturalistic fallacy', that is, deriving normative conclusions from scientific 'facts'. Even those of us who are careful not to assume that 'just because something *is*, does not mean that it *should be*', argue that it is important not to ignore the normative consequences of the so-called impartial knowledge. In the words of philosopher John Dupré:

> If evolution has in fact shaped our behavior it can only have done so by selecting physical structures, presumably in the brain, that cause the production of such behaviours. To say that a certain behavior, which some find morally objectionable, is caused by a physical structure in my brain, is in effect to remove at least part of my responsibility for it.[73]

Pinker's research has political consequences. If we accept his view that sexual violence has a biological basis, then this has normative consequences in terms of our responses to sexual violence. Of course, all research dealing with complex social and cultural phenomenon are, to some degree, ideological projects. But his neoliberal, evolutionary psychology defence of Western civilization needs more acknowledgement.

Pinker is keen to accuse his critics of ideological biases, while failing to acknowledge or even notice his own neoliberal defence of Western civilization. Feminist scientists are frequently forced to defend themselves against the accusation that they allow their politics to interfere with scientific objectivity. Gowaty explained to her critics that

---

[70]Buss, 'Conflict between the Sexes', 741.

[71]Buss, 'Conflict between the Sexes', 741.

[72]For example, see David Buller, *Adapting Minds: Evolutionary Psychology and the Persistent Quest for Human Nature* (Cambridge, MA: The MIT Press, 2005).

[73]John Dupré, *Human and Other Animals* (Oxford: Clarendon Press, 2002), 201.

Science is the practice of systematic observation and experiment as a means to test predictions from hypotheses while reducing or eliminating (i.e. controlling) the effects of perceived and possible biases on results and conclusions. So what it means to be self-consciously political is that one is thereby in a scientifically better position relative to those who are unaware of the political and social forces potentially affecting their science. . . . Buttressed with better controls, controls against potential biases we are able to perceive, makes our conclusions more reliable.[74]

Like Gowaty, Pinker's project is informed by his politics. Unlike Gowaty, by failing to acknowledge and then control for his own ideological bias, Pinker has missed an opportunity to convincingly explain the changing nature of violence in our societies.

---

[74]Patricia Adair Gowaty, 'Introduction: Darwinian Feminists and Feminist Evolutionists', in Gowaty (ed.), *Feminism and Evolutionary Biology: Boundaries, Intersections, and Frontiers* (New York: Chapman and Hall, 1997), 14.

15

Where angels fear to tread

Racialized policing, mass incarceration and executions as state violence in the post–civil rights era

Robert T. Chase

On 25 May 2020, George Floyd's murder was captured on video as Minneapolis police officer Derek Chauvin ground his knee against Floyd's neck for over eight minutes, despite Floyd calling out, 'Please, I can't breathe.' Arrested for allegedly passing off a $20 counterfeit bill at a convenience store, three police officers roughly handcuffed Floyd and pressed his face down against hard street pavement as Chauvin knelt with all his weight on Floyd's exposed neck. Meanwhile, a fourth officer prevented horrified onlookers from intervening even as they shouted that Floyd's nose had started to bleed profusely and as another pleaded, 'Bro, you've got him down, let him breathe at least, man.' Revealing the ubiquity of such state violence against Black communities, one of the onlookers exclaimed, 'One of my homies died the same way!' As the minutes ticked down with Officer Chauvin's knee still grinding on his exposed neck, Floyd breathlessly exclaimed, 'my stomach hurts, my neck hurts, everything hurts. . . . they're gonna kill me, man.' As Floyd slipped into unconsciousness and his body went limp, police officer Chauvin continued to press his knee against Floyd's neck for another two minutes, even after the medics that had finally arrived discovered that Floyd had no pulse.[1]

This moment of state violence repeats the traumatized refrain of 'I can't breathe' that Eric Garner pleaded over eleven times while New York police officer Daniel Pantaleo put him in a deadly chokehold simply for selling untaxed cigarettes during a July 2014 arrest. One month later, St Louis police officer Darren Wilson gunned down Michael Brown, an eighteen-year-old African American, and left his body in the street on a hot summer day on 9 August 2014 to demonstrate that state violence against Black bodies remains public spectacle in America. The political pundit, Charles Pierce, offered the pointed observation that leaving Brown's body was akin to what totalitarians regimes do when they want to demonstrate the exercise of state power through public execution:

> Dictators leave bodies in the street. Petty local satraps leave bodies in the street. Warlords leave bodies in the street. Those are the places where they leave bodies in the street, as object lessons, or to make a point, or because there isn't the money to take bodies away and burn them, or because nobody give a damn whether they are there or not.[2]

Just three months later, on 22 November 2014, twelve-year-old Tamir Rice was playing with a toy gun at the Cudell Recreation Center, a park in the City of Cleveland's Public Works Department, when Timothy Loehmann, a twenty-six-year-old white police officer, responded to a 911 call of a man brandishing a gun at the park by shooting and killing Rice almost immediately upon entering the park. In her masterly dissection of such police brutality, the scholar Keeanga-Yamahtta Taylor depicted the ever-growing list of deadly state violence against Black bodies as ubiquitous and nearly routine:

> Mike Brown was walking down the street. Eric Garner was standing on the corner. Rekia Boid was in a park with friends. Trayvon Martin was walking with a bag of Skittles and a can of iced tea. Sean Ball was leaving a bachelor party, anticipating his marriage the following day. Amadou Diallo was getting home from work. Their deaths, and the killings of so many others like them, prove that sometimes simply being Black can make you a suspect – or get you killed.[3]

---

[1]Christine Hauser, Derrick Bryson Taylor and Neil Vigdor, '"I Can't Breathe": Four Minneapolis Officers Fired after Black Man Dies in Custody', *New York Times*, 26 May 2020; Libor Jany, 'Minneapolis Police, Protesters Clash almost 24 Hours after George Floyd's Death in Custody', *Minneapolis Star Tribune*, 27 May 2020.

[2]Charles P. Pierce, 'The Body in the Street', *Esquire*, 22 August 2014.

[3]Keeanga-Yamahtta Taylor, *From #BlackLivesMatter to Black Liberation* (Chicago: Haymarket Books, 2015), 13.

Although African American make up only 12 per cent of the population, Black victims account for 23 per cent of the 1,003 people shot and killed by law enforcement in 2019.[4]

After the murder of Trayvon Martin in 2012, Black Lives Matter organized national protests in response to state and anti-Black violence. As a summer of national protest erupted over George Floyd's murder, so did the state violence against both journalists and Black Lives Matter protestors. Between 26 May and 2 June 2020 alone, there were 148 incidents of state police violence and arrests against both domestic and international journalists while they were covering the protest for George Floyd. In one particularly bad incident causing lasting damage, police shot Linda Tirado, a photojournalist covering the protests in Minneapolis, with a 'less-lethal' round resulting in the permanent loss of her left eye. Other cases of police brutality against journalists with visible press badges involved rubber bullets, tear gas, pepper spray at close distance directly into the face, claims of physical brutality with shields and batons, pushing, punching and throwing journalists to the concrete, and one disquieting incident of police shooting a journalist full of pepper bullets while still being live on TV as she gave the on-air live exclamation, 'I'm getting shot!'

While violence against journalists has increased globally since 2010, such state-sanctioned domestic violence by police against free speech and journalism in the United States earned much scrutiny, causing the countries of Germany, Australia and Turkey to offer official public calls that America respect press freedom. 'It's been shocking to all of us because of the scale of the violence', admitted Robert Mahoney, the deputy executive director of the Committee to Protect Journalists.

> We've now recorded more than 300 press-freedom violations in the past week of which the majority are attacks, physical assaults . . . and I hate to use the word unprecedented, but it is certainly something no one has seen probably since the 1960s when you had the civil rights movement, and violent repression of protests in which journalists were also caught up.[5]

More egregious still was the state violence against antiracist protestors, as one database documented at least 950 instances of police brutality against

---

[4]'Police Shootings Database', *Washington Post*, https://www.washingtonpost.com/graphics/investigations/police-shootings-database/, accessed 25 October 2020.
[5]Michael Safi, Caelainn Barr, Niamh McIntyre, Pamela Duncan and Sam Cutler, 'Analysis by Guardian and Bellingcat Finds 148 Arrests or Attacks on Media Covering George Floyd Protests in the US', *The Guardian*, 5 June 2020; Elahe Izadi and Paul Farhi, '"The Norms Have Broken Down": Shock as Journalists Are Arrested, Injured by Police while Trying to Cover the Story', *Washington Post*, 31 May 2020; Benjamin Mullin, 'Reports of Violence Against Journalists Mount as U.S. Protests Intensify', *Wall Street Journal*, 1 June 2020; Marc Tracy and Rachel Abrams, 'Police Target Journalists as Trump Blames "Lamestream Media" for Protests', *New York Times*, 1 June 2020.

civilians and journalists across the country during the five months of summer 2020 protests. In Portland alone, police spent more than $117,500 on teargas and 'less-lethal' munitions during just a six-week period. In one of the lasting cases of state violence, police shot the protestor Donavan La Bella with a 'less-lethal' munition that fractured his skull and left him with a severe injury requiring him to make ongoing and urgent hospital visits. 'It's like nonstop brutality. . . . the trauma is massive for a lot of people', said Tai Carpenter, board president of Don't Shoot Portland. 'Not only that when you're protesting violence to be met with violence . . . but also the fact that during COVID we're all isolated, a lot of people have to adjust to a new way of living, their livelihoods are affected and now they're realizing that their civil liberties do not matter at all.'[6] It is critical to note that none of these acts of state violence are random, rare or committed in isolation by solitary 'bad apple' cops, but rather they are part of a sustained and systematic system of anti-Black and anti-Brown violence that has been historically consistent as a violent expression of carceral state power.

Of course, this history of anti-Blackness and state violence does not exist in Steven Pinker's *The Better Angels of Our Nature* nor does any mention of state violence directed at Black Americans.[7] Instead, Pinker takes a 'colour-blind' narrative as critically integral to his claim of a post–civil rights era that represents a 'New Peace' symbolic of a less-violent post-1965 Western civilization. To begin this traditionally Whiggish reflection on what he terms the 'rights revolution' from the 1950s to the 1980s, Steven Pinker opens with an apocryphal narrative that the banning of grade-school playground dodgeball is a vital symbol of a new nonviolent age stemming from the rights revolution. For Pinker, this firvolous opening analogy about grade-school games definitively signals that 'yes, the fate of dodgeball is yet another sign of the historical decline of violence.' By drawing on Federal Bureau of Investigation reports of lynching and hate crime statistics, as well as polls showing a wider acceptance of school integration and interracial marriage, Pinker offers a few cherry-picked statistics that ignore the well-known and much publicized history of persistent state violence since 1965. Instead, Pinker cavalierly concludes that the demise of dodgeball 'is part of a

---

[6]Tobi Thomas, Adam Gabatt and Caelainn Barr, 'Nearly 1,000 Instances of Police Brutality Recorded in U.S. in Anti-Racism Protests', *The Guardian*, 29 October 2020.
[7]This chapter takes up anti-Blackness through the lens of what Ibram X. Kendi names as 'racist policy' and 'an anti-racist policy'. Kendi, who directs the Center for Antiracist Research at Boston University, writes, '[a] racist policy is any measure that produces or sustains racial inequity between racial groups. An antiracist policy is any measure that produces or sustains racial equity between racial groups. By policy, I mean written and unwritten laws, rules, procedures, processes, regulations, and guidelines that govern people. There is no such thing as a nonracist or race-neutral policy. Every policy in every institution in every community in every nation is producing or sustaining either racial inequity or equity between racial groups.' Ibram X. Kendi, *How to be An Antiracist* (New York: One World, 2019), 39–40.

current in which Western culture has been extending its distaste for violence farther and farther down the magnitude scale' from global war and genocide to 'rioting, lynching and hate crimes' so that the universal expansion of peaceful existence 'has spread to vulnerable classes of victims that in earlier era fell outside the circle of protection, such as racial minorities, women, children, homosexuals, and animals. The ban on dodgeball is weathervane for these winds of change'.[8]

Pinker's narrative on the decline of violence relies upon an intellectual leap that scholars have identified as a post–civil rights 'race neutral' framing that situates the victories of the Civil Rights Act of 1964 and the Voting Rights of 1965 as the inauguration of a less-violent and colour-blind era. Adherents to this colour-blind and a-world-less-violent narrative, such as Pinker, argue that racism and the racial violence that upholds it are no longer systemic, but rather narrowed to isolated incidents, individual 'bad apples' and increasingly rare. 'After 1965', Pinker happily declares, 'opposition to civil rights was moribund, anti-black riots were a distant memory and terrorism against blacks no longer received support from any significant community . . . . they have become a blessedly rare phenomenon in modern America'.[9]

When addressing matters of criminal justice at all, Pinker advances one of the most dismissed tropes of racialized criminalization by citing the rising incarceration rate after 1965 as one of his positive factors to make his argument that rape has declined – because 'first-time rapists' have been put 'behind bars'.[10] When he does take up race and policing, Pinker does not see such encounters as violent, but rather he dismisses racial profiling as a trivial matter. Pinker compares the 'lynching, night raids, anti-Black pogroms, and physical intimidation at the ballot box' of the Jim Crow South to 'a typical battle of today', which 'may consist of African American drivers pulled over more often on the highways', which he sees as more a nuisance than a threat of violence. Apparently unable to help himself, Pinker then blithely adds in parenthesis that 'when Clarence Thomas described his successful but contentious 1991 Supreme Court confirmation hearing as a "high-tech lynching," it was the epitome of tastelessness but also a sign of how far we have come'.[11] Such a framing of events obfuscates the persistent and growing power of state violence as a function of racial elimination.[12]

---

[8]Steven Pinker, *The Better Angels of Our Nature: Why Violence Has Declined* (New York: Viking, 2011), 380.

[9]Pinker, *Better Angels*, 388.

[10]Pinker, *Better Angels*, 403.

[11]Pinker, *Better Angels*, 381–2.

[12]Robin D. G. Kelley, 'Thug Nation: On State Violence and Disposability', in Jordan T. Camp and Christina Heatherton (eds), *Policing the Planet: Why the Policing Crisis Led to Black Lives Matter* (New York: Verso, 2016), 43–81, 57.

Writing in 2016, UCLA historian Robin D. G. Kelley revealed how language has been used to obfuscate state sanctioned violence. For example, the media frequently used the term 'thug' to criminalize Michael Brown, rather than see Brown's death at the hands of police as an act of state violence. 'What this sanitized national narrative occludes, are the chief issues that gave rise to the Civil Rights Movement in the first place: the violent subjugation of Black people by the state and its vigilante allies; taxation without representation and the denial of the franchise through terror and administrative means; and a government-dominated racial economy that suppressed Black wages, dispossessed Black people of land and property, excluded them from equal public accommodations, and subsidized white privilege by way of taxation. Violence held this precarious system together.'[12] And, as this chapter will demonstrate, violence continues to uphold post-1965 systematic racism through the state instruments of mass incarceration and racialized policing that amount to a persistent and ongoing pattern of carceral violence. This chapter takes up race and persistent and virulent patterns of state violence through the lens of carceral state scholar Ruth Wilson Gilmore's apt definition of systematic racism: 'Racism, specifically, is the state-sanctioned or extralegal production and exploitation of group-differentiated vulnerability to premature death.'[13] In contrast to Pinker's brand of dismissiveness, Keeanga-Yamahtta Taylor's analysis of Black Lives Matter makes a more astute argument that the modern-day criminal justice system enacts state violence to achieve post-1965 anti-Blackness. This chapter analyses police brutality and mass incarceration by taking up Taylor's argument that 'the focus on "state violence" strategically pivots away from a conventional analysis that would reduce racism to the intentions and actions of the individuals involved. The declaration of "state violence" legitimizes the corollary demand for state action.'[14] To counter Pinker's overly buoyant declaration that ending playground games of dodgeball is testament to a new era of universal non-violence, this chapter contends that post-1965 anti-Black and anti-Brown violence is continued through the full power of America's carceral states.

In *Caging Borders and Carceral States: Incarcerations, Immigration Detentions, and Resistance*, I define carceral states as follows: 'we, use the term "carceral states" to explore how geographical differences, regional histories, individual prison practices, state laws, and local responses to immigration and incarceration constructed a complicated carceral network that fused together a variety of actors at the state, local, regional, national, and even transnational levels.'[15] Put more directly, carceral

---

[13]Ruth Wilson Gilmore, *Golden Gulag: Prisons, Surplus, Crisis, and Opposition in Globalizing California* (Berkeley: University of California Press, 2007), 28.
[14]Taylor, *From #BlackLivesMatter to Black Liberation*, 167.
[15]Robert T. Chase (ed.), *Caging Borders and Carceral States: Incarcerations, Immigration Detentions, and Resistance* (Chapel Hill: University of North Carolina Press, 2019), 4.

networks are the interconnected and interlocking array of punitive tools of the state. These tools include policing, courts and sentencing guidelines, the prison, the parole and probation system, and immigration enforcement, detention and deportation. In the US context, these interlocking state powers are known as the 'policing powers' of the states, as enumerated as 'residual powers' in the Tenth Amendment to the Constitution, which granted exclusive control over prisons and policing to the individual states.[16] Through the powers of US federalism, the carceral states of mass incarceration and racialized policing make America's city streets a less safe and more violent place where many an angel would fear to tread.

Racialized policing and urban uprisings

Police violence, especially police brutality against Black and brown people, represents a silence, if not outright dismissal, in *The Better Angels of Our Nature*. In his assessment of 'race riots' of the mid-1960s in Los Angeles, Newark, Detroit and other cities, Pinker ignores that all of these urban uprisings were due to incidents of police brutality, which reflected what the historian Simon Balto characterizes as a long-standing historical practice where 'the local-level policing apparatus became thoroughly racialized, profoundly discriminatory, and deeply punitive'.[17] The history of policing in Chicago reveals how liberal reforms resulted in an accelerated policing capacity aimed against Black communities with the full force of state violence.

As Balto demonstrates in his study of policing in Chicago from Red Summer (1919) to Black Power (1969), state violence against Black neighbourhoods was a consistent mark of urban policing across the twentieth century. Beginning with the 1919 race riots of urban whites terrorizing Black communities, the Chicago Police Department (CPD) stood idly by as the violence ensued as 'members of the CPD repeatedly proved themselves to be defenders of whiteness and the color line, rather than protectors of all life and livelihood.'[18] Following Red Summer, the CPD operated in concert

---

[16]On the 'residual powers' of the Tenth Amendment in the framing of the US Constitution, see Jack N. Rakove, *Original Meanings: Politics and Ideas in the Making of the American Constitution* (New York: Alfred A. Knopf, 1996), 192. On policing powers, see Gary Gerstle, *Liberty and Coercion: The Paradox of American Government-From the Founding to the Present* (Princeton: Princeton University Press, 2015), 55–88.
[17]Simon Balto, *Occupied Territory: Policing Black Chicago from Red Summer to Black Power* (Chapel Hill: The University of North Carolina Press, 2019), 5.
[18]Balto, *Occupied Territory*, 29.

with Chicago's organized crime during the 1920s and 1930s to centre crime and vice in Black neighbourhoods, which demonstrated that the CPD's purpose was not to protect Black life, but to aggressively police it. When police turned to the crime that was concentrated in Black neighbourhoods, they increased their political power within Chicago's democratic machine politics. Out of that political arrangement, policing in Black neighbourhoods was predictably violent. Typical of such pre-1965 state violence included an incident where a police interrogation involved 'police officers strapping a prisoner to a chair, pulling his head back by the hair, and striking his Adam's apple with a blackjack (three times) with such force that "blood spurted half way across the room"'. In another police interrogation, several officers drove a Black suspect to a local dentist who 'selected an old dull drilling burr and began slowly drilling into the pump chamber of a lower rear molar in the region of a nerve' until the suspect 'confessed'.[19]

Horrified by such routine, everyday acts of state violence, the Civil Rights Congress delivered a petition to the United Nations Genocide Convention in 1951 with the blaring title 'We Charge Genocide: The Historic Petition to the United Nations for Relief from a Crime of the United States Government Against the Negro people'. Delivered by Paul Robeson and William Patterson, 'We Charge Genocide' was a book-length treatise documenting and decrying racial violence in the United States. Nearly 100 civil rights organizers and well-known intellectuals signed the petition, which cited segregation, lynching and police brutality as evidence of systematic racism against Black people in America. Framing police brutality as genocidal violence, civil rights organizations of the early 1950s held that state violence had just as much power to inculcate racial inequality as did Jim Crow-era lynching.

> Once the classic method of lynching was the rope. Now it is the policeman's bullet. To many an American the police are the government, certainly its most visible representative. We submit that the evidence suggests that the killing of Negroes has become police policy in the United States and that police policy is the most practical expression of government policy.[20]

In response to such strong criticism, the Chicago Police Department hired the reformer Orlando W. Wilson in 1960 'to help stabilize a reeling police department'.[21] Initially, Wilson attempted to bridge the widening gap between policing and Black communities through the implementation of such reforms as the 'Officer Friendly' programme, which put police

---

[19]Balto, *Occupied Territory*, 46.
[20]Balto, *Occupied Territory*, 105.
[21]Balto, *Occupied Territory*, 154.

officers into direct contact with schoolchildren, and community relations workshops where police and the community could dialogue. But as 'a stern law-and-order proponent', Wilson launched 'aggressive preventive patrol' and an attendant stop-and-seize programme, later becoming stop-and-frisk, after the 1961 Supreme Court decision in *Mapp v. Ohio* bared evidence obtained via unreasonable search and seizure. Wilson then turned to crime rates to construct a statistical rationale for the expansion of his department when he 'revolutionized the collecting and reporting of crime statistics-most importantly, by reporting *attempted* crimes rather than simply *executed crimes*'. This statistical 'feedback loop', as Balto names it, purposefully engineered an increase in the city's crime rate, which then substantiated the need to fund, and thereby grow, more urban policing. From 1965 to 1970, the number of CPD's patrolling officers grew by 25 per cent, and their funding doubled from $90 million in 1965 to $190 million in 1970.[22] 'It's a misconception that police simply enforce laws as they are', Balto concludes, 'rather, they routinely define the very nature and word of those laws'.[23] As the metric for successful police reform was arrests, the 'aggressive preventive patrol' made arrests 'the strategy's entire point'.

As a spate of new historical studies of urban policing in New York, San Francisco and Los Angeles makes abundantly clear, police reform and the targeting of Black communities occurred in tandem in cities everywhere.[24] Not only was police violence in urban centres rampant, but it was also consistently violent across the twentieth century. Everyday police brutality eventually stewed over, leading to urban rebellion during a wave of political violence during the late 1960s. The period that Pinker associates with 'a New Peace' of non-violence is, in fact, bookended by two of the nation's most well-known urban uprisings – notably, Los Angeles's Watts rebellion of 1965 and the LA uprising of 1992. As with most of the urban uprisings in America during the twentieth century, these street rebellions were precipitated by years of unaccountable state violence through police brutality and street execution. As Max Felker-Kantor demonstrates in his study of policing in Los Angeles, police shootings of Black people have historically received neither justice nor accountability. In the year leading up to the 1965 Watts rebellion, the Los Angeles Police Department (LAPD) 'committed sixty-four homicides of which sixty-two were ruled justifiable. In twenty-seven of the cases, the

---

[22]Balto, *Occupied Territory*, 164.
[23]Balto, *Occupied Territory*, 160.
[24]Christopher Lowen Agee, *The Streets of San Francisco: Policing and the Creation of a Cosmopolitan Liberal Politics, 1950-1972* (Chicago: University of Chicago Press, 2014); Max Felker-Kantor, *Policing Los Angeles: Race, Resistance, and the Rise of LAPD* (Chapel Hill: University of North Carolina Press, 2018); Clarence Taylor, *Fight the Power: African American and the Long History of Police Brutality in New York City* (New York: New York University Press, 2019); Carl Suddler, *Presumed Criminal: Black Youth and the Justice System in Postwar New York* (New York: New York University Press, 2019).

victim was shot in the back; twenty-five of the suspects were unarmed; and four had committed no crime when shot'.[25] Unmasking 'justifiable homicide' as racist state violence and outright murder becomes starkly frightening when we consider the LAPD's 77th Street Station's commonly used the acronym LSMFT, standing for 'Let's shoot a motherfucker tonight. Got your nigger knocker all shined up?'[26] Such sentiments weren't isolated to a few 'bad apples' but were widely shared by the LAPD as a whole and at the very top of the department. Indeed, no less than the infamous LAPD Chief (1950–65), William Parker, considered urban policing as a 'domestic war' where police represent 'a thin blue line of defense . . . upon which we must depend to defend the invasion from within'.[27]

The open disdain for Black life through the abuse of urban policing is not solely attributable to 'get tough' and 'law and order' conservatives. As *Policing Los Angeles* demonstrates, the mayoralty of liberal African American Mayor Tom Bradley (1973–93) ended with the Rodney King beating by four police officers, which was the spark that lit fire to Los Angeles's 1992 urban rebellion. Despite liberal attempts at such reforms as 'procedural fairness, better police-community relations, and more training, that sought to soften the power of the police', police brutality persisted because not even the Black liberal long-time Mayor Bradley attempted to 'fundamentally alter the basic power relations between the police and the city government on the on the one hand and black and brown communities on the other'.[28] This failure of political will ultimately resulted in Rodney King's beating at the hands of several police officers with batons as one of the officers instructed his fellow officers to 'hit his joints, hit the wrists, hit his elbows, hit his knees, hit his ankles'. That the city exploded in unrest on the news of the acquittal of the police officers in the summer of 1992 should come as no surprise – as scholars of carceral states have shown that what happened in Los Angeles in 1992 should be understood not as a lawless 'riot', but rather as a street rebellion against a criminal justice system that allowed anti-Black violence to continue unabated as justified lawfulness. Considering policing power's ability to make Black life disposable without legal consequence, Felker-Kantor concludes that historically the police retain what he named as 'the monopoly on legitimate violence'. 'Because the monopoly over the means of violence was core element of the police power', Felker-Kantor concluded, 'it enabled the LAPD to aggressively discipline perceived threats to social order, and, in the process, produce and enforce a hierarchical racial order'.[29]

---

[25] Felker-Kantor, *Policing Los Angeles*, 21.
[26] Felker-Kantor, *Policing Los Angeles*, 23.
[27] Parker quoted in Felker-Kantor, *Policing Los Angeles*, 5.
[28] Felker-Kantor, *Policing Los Angeles*, 3.
[29] Felker-Kantor, *Policing Los Angeles*, 5.

Pinker, however, dismisses urban uprisings as evidence of Black criminality and not as a function of state violence. 'African Americans were the rioters', Pinker reminds his readers, 'rather than the targets, death tolls were low (most rioters themselves killed by the police) and virtually all the targets were property rather than people. After 1950 the United States had no riots that singled out a race or ethnic group'.[30] First of all, such a dismissal ignores white rioting during the 1950s and again in the 1970s, when urban northern whites responded to racial integration of their schools and neighbourhoods with widespread violence, including a slew of virulent 'neighbourhood' incidents of urban white riots during 1950s–1960s Chicago and when 'anti-bussers' in 1970s Boston threw rocks at school buses filled with Black children.[31] Second, it dismisses Black urban unrest as rootless criminality, rather than understand 'riots' as what Martin Luther King called 'the voice of the unheard' where frustrated responses to ongoing police brutality can be better understood through the lens of pitched battles over political violence.

Following King's assassination in Memphis, Tennessee, on 4 April 1968, there were more than 125 Black urban uprisings that ended with over 15,000 police arrests and 50 deaths. As the Yale historian Elizabeth Hinton points out, the violence did not end there, but crested over four years in a wave of unrest. 'In the years that followed (1968-72)', Hinton reminds us, 'at least 960 segregated black communities witnessed 2,310 separate incidents of what journalists and state security officials described as "disturbances", "uprisings", "rebellions", "melees", "eruptions", or "riots". As in Minneapolis today, this type of collective violence almost always started with contact between residents and the frontline representatives of the state—the police—and then quickly moved on to other institutions'.[32] In light of ongoing struggles over policing, Hinton argued that historians should interpret post-1965 street violence in relationship to sustained and ubiquitous police brutality and 'not as a wave of criminality, but as a period of sustained political violence'.[33]

While the policing apparatus was already a time-tested machine for racial oppression before 1965, the federal government responded to urban unrest by declaring a new War on Crime that provided federal money to militarize police departments. The LAPD, for instance, saw its police budget double

---

[30]Pinker, *Better Angels*, 386.

[31]For white riots in 1950s Chicago, see Balto, *Occupied Territory*, 91–122; Arnold Hirsch, *Making the Second Ghetto: Race and Housing in Chicago, 1940-1960* (Chicago: University of Chicago Press, 1983); Arnold R. Hirsch, 'Massive Resistance in the Urban North: Trumbull Park, Chicago, 1953-1966', *Journal of American History*, 82, no. 2 (September 1995): 522–50. For the violence of white anti-bussers, see Ronald P. Formisano, *Boston Against Busing: Race, Class, and Ethnicity in the 1960s and 1970s* (Chapel Hill: University of North Carolina Press, 1991), 138–71.

[32]Elizabeth Hinton, 'The Minneapolis Uprising in Context', *Boston Review*, http://bostonreview.net/race/elizabeth-hinton-minneapolis-uprising-context.

[33]Hinton, 'The Minnesota Uprising in Context'.

from $88.7 million in 1966–7 to $198.5 million by 1972, which 'helped facilitate the LAPD's adoption of riot control plans, military hardware, and computerized systems.'[34] As part of a post-Vietnam embrace of domestic urban warfare, Chief Daryle Gates initiated the Special Weapons and Tactics (SWAT) unit, which drew on Los Angeles' proximity to California's defence industries. Gates' initiative led to the incorporation of military-style hardware, including tear gas and grenades, semi-automatic rifles, armoured vehicles and surveillance helicopters into the armamentarium of the LAPD, and to train the new SWAT units with tactical riot gear that turned beat police officers into deadly snipers. Meanwhile, from the air, the LAPD initiated a sky surveillance programme called Air Support to Regular Operations (ASTRO) where police helicopters roared over the city to claim a domestic policing victory that the US military could not earn in Vietnam.[35]

While Pinker points to the decline of warfare in a post-1945 'New Peace', urban policing after 1965 saw themselves in a pitched campaign of 'urban guerrilla warfare'. As a SWAT leader succinctly put it, 'Those people out there – the radicals, the revolutionaries, and the cop haters – are damned good at using shotguns and bombs, and setting up ambushes. We've got to be better.'[36] By 1982, at the height of the 'War on Drugs', 59 per cent of cities with a population above 50,000 had a SWAT unit, but by 1995, 89 per cent of such cities boasted a SWAT unit to wage domestic campaigns of wars on crime and drugs and, ultimately, wars on Black and brown people.[37] As an outgrowth of this militarized mentality to turn domestic policing into urban guerrilla warfare, Felkor-Kantor's study of the LAPD concludes that 'Anti-riot legislation, elite paramilitary units, and riot control plans enabled the LAPD to expand its capacity to operate as a military-style counterinsurgency force'.[38]

The post-1965 'new wars' on crime, drugs and terrorism, as opposed to the supposed 'New Peace' that Pinker asserts, didn't stop at the US border. During the height of the Cold War in the 1950s and 1960s, the American government exported policing as global counterinsurgent campaigns and constructed a transnational calculation where Cold War military tactics and strategies returned home to make a 'War on Crime' against people perceived

---

[34]Felker-Kantor, *Policing Los Angeles*, 50.

[35]Preceding ASTRO was the Office of Law Enforcement Assistance's (OLEA) second most expensive programme known as Project Sky Knight, which provided police surveillance and interdiction helicopters to the LA sheriff's office, which then contracted with eight cities within Los Angeles Country to also receive these police helicopters. Elizabeth Hinton, *From the War on Poverty to the War on Crime: The Making of Mass Incarceration in America* (Cambridge, MA: Harvard University Press, 2016), 90–1. On ASTRO, see Felker-Kantor, *Policing Los Angeles*, 54.

[36]SWAT leader quote from Felker-Kantor, *Policing Los Angeles*, 53.

[37]Radley Balko, *Rise of the Warrior Cop: The Militarization of America's Police Forces* (New York: PublicAffairs, 2014), 175.

[38]Felker-Kantor, *Policing Los Angeles*, 54.

as domestic insurgents in urban guerrilla warfare. In his study of this transnational connection, the Johns Hopkins sociologist Stuart Schrader puts it aptly: 'Across the globe, counterinsurgency was policing. At home, policing was counterinsurgency.'[39] Out of this arrangement of aggressive policing against Black and Brown communities arose mass incarceration and the carceral violence that comes with caging people.

The violence of mass incarceration

Mass incarceration is the post-1965 increase of the US prison population from 200,000 people to the modern-day prison population of 2.3 million and over 6.1 million under auspices of the carceral state through prisons, jails, probation and parole. To control that immense population, the carceral state in America now comprises 1,719 state prisons, 102 federal prisons, 2,259 juvenile correctional facilities, 3,283 local jails, 79 Indian Country jails and over 200 immigration detention facilities.[40] While Pinker posits that the post-1965 world represents a less-violent 'New Peace', the flip side of civil rights revolutions has been state violence through mass incarceration and policing. Mass incarceration is a coercive state response to the civil rights revolution that reached an unprecedented and dramatic zenith in 2016 with 2.3 million incarcerated citizens.[41]

Historians Naomi Murakawa and Elizabeth Hinton offer histories of 1960s-era liberalism that collectively advanced an earlier periodization for mass incarceration than Nixonian America where the Great Society's anti-poverty programmes contributed as much to the War on Crime as the

---

[39]Stuart Schrader, *Badges Without Borders: How Global Counterinsurgency Transformed American Policing* (Oakland: University of California Press, 2019), 25.

[40]Walter A. Ewing, Daniel E. Martinez and Ruben G. Rumbaut, 'The Criminalization of Immigration in the United States', American Immigration Council, July 2015, https://www.america nimmigrationcouncil.org/research/criminalization-immigration-united-states, accessed 12 December 2017; Jeremy Travis, Bruce Western and Steve Redburn (eds), *The Growth of Incarceration in the United States: Exploring Causes and Consequences* (Washington, DC: The National Academies Press, 2014); James J. Stephan, 'Census of State and Federal Correction Facilities, 2005', U.S. Department of Justice, Office of Justice Programs, NCJ222182, October 2008, NCJ 222182; Todd D. Minton, Scott Ginder, Susan M. Brumbaugh, Hope Smiley-McDonald and Harley Rohloff, Census of Jails: Population Changes, 1999–2013, U.S. Department of Justice, Office of Justice Programs, December 2015, NCJ 248627; Todd D. Minton, Jails in Indian Country, 2015, U.S. Department of Justice, Office of Justice Programs, November 2016, NCJ 250117.

[41]Following the economic recession of 2007–8, some states actively reduced the burdensome cost of their prison systems. Ten states reduced their incarcerated population by 10 per cent or more during the years 2006 to 2011. Peter Wagner and Bernadette Rabuy, Mass Incarceration: The Whole Pie, 2017, Prison Policy Initiative (PPI), 14 March 2017, https://www.prisonpolicy .org/reports/pie2017.html, accessed 12 December 2017.

concurrent War on Poverty.[42] In her evaluation of the Law Enforcement Administration Agency and its programmes, Hinton demonstrates that liberals pursued 'get tough' on crime measures even as the Johnson Administration built crime surveillance programmes into its anti-poverty measures. Both the Kennedy and Johnson Administrations (1961–9), according to Hinton, associated poverty with civil unrest and urban riots with crime. What made the subsequent mass incarceration so inevitable, however, was not simply that Johnson signed the 1968 Safe Street and Crime Act, but that Johnson's anti-poverty programmes established federal power in local urban spaces that stripped Black communities of decision-making and any significant role they might play in how their communities could address poverty and reduce crime.

Strikingly, the US incarceration rate remained stable from the 1920s to 1970s. Following the civil rights movement of the 1960s, however, the US incarceration rate more than quadrupled over the past four decades. This historically unprecedented incarceration rate draws disproportionately from minority and poor communities. When the Supreme Court handed down the 1954 *Brown v. Board of Education* decision, African American men went to prison at four times the rate of white men. Today that number has nearly doubled to seven times the rate of white men. By 2010, the incarceration rate was 2,207 for African Americans, 966 for Latinx and 380 for whites. Nearly sixty 60 per cent of the 2.3 million people in prison are African American or Latinx (858,000 Blacks and 464,000 Hispanics). The incarceration rates for African Americans are seven times the rate of whites, while Hispanics are incarcerated at three times the rate for non-Hispanic whites.[43] The historical context, as Heather Thompson makes clear in her seminal article 'Why Mass Incarceration Matters', is that from the Great Depression to the Great Society the number of people in federal and state prisons increased by 52,249 (1935–70), while in the post–civil rights era (1970–2005) the number of incarcerated people in US prisons and jails increased by 1.2 million.[44] Despite the civil rights revolution that eradicated Jim Crow segregation legislatively, the subsequent era of mass incarceration has turned the gains of the civil rights era into another age of severe racial disparity.[45]

---

[42]Naomi Murakawa, *The First Civil Right: How Liberals Built Prison America* (Oxford: Oxford University Press, 2014); Vesla Weaver, 'Frontlash: Race and the Development of Punitive Crime Policy', *Studies in American Political Development*, 21, Issue 2 (Fall 2007): 230–65; Hinton, *From the War on Poverty to the War on Crime*.

[43]National Research Council of the National Humanities, *The Growth of Incarceration in the United States Exploring Causes and Consequences* (Washington, DC: National Academies Press, 2014), 1–2.

[44]Heather Ann Thompson, 'Why Mass Incarceration Matters', *Journal of American History*, 97, no. 3 (December 2010): 704, 703–34.

[45]On the deep racial disparities of mass incarceration, see Michael Tonry, *Malign Neglect: Race, Crime, and Punishment in America* (New York: Oxford University Press, 1995); Jerome

With mass incarceration comes an increased capacity for state violence, as the prison has historically been a space where corporal punishment against prisoner bodies remained the primary disciplinary tool. Unlike Pinker's colour-blind narrative that ends civil rights activism against white supremacy and inequality with the passage of the Voting Rights Act in 1965, the development of Black Power expanded critiques of racial inequality to include Black poverty, northern urban segregation and police brutality. As Black Power activism of the late 1960s and early 1970s critiqued policing as systematic racism, prisoners looked to groups like the Black Panther Party to make the collective argument that prisons and policing were indeed violent instruments of white supremacy. During the 1960s and 1970s, prisoners made concrete demands to improve their immediate living and working conditions, which were generally deplorable, even as they simultaneously made claims that, as people under the full auspices of state control, they were entitled to both constitutional protections as citizens and basic human rights. Nationally, prison uprisings mirrored the urban unrest during the late 1960s as there were five prison uprisings in 1967, fifteen in 1968, twenty-seven in 1970, thirty-seven in 1971 and forty-eight in 1972 – the most prison uprisings in any year in US history.

The prison uprising that earned the most media attention during this period was the Attica uprising from 9 to 11 September 1971. On 9 September 1971, 1,281 prisoners at Attica Correctional Facility in Attica, New York, took control of the prison's D-yard, where they held thirty-nine prison guards and employees hostage during a tense stand-off with authorities that lasted nearly a week. While the immediate cause of the takeover was a struggle between a guard and a prisoner, politicized prisoners quickly organized into a collective democratic expression that organized fellow prisoners, protected the hostages, issued a list of grievances and called for thirty-three external observers to visit the prison. Many of the Attica prisoners' demands were practical ones: an end to unpaid or underpaid forced labour and respect for prisoners' basic legal and human rights. After four days of negotiations, Governor Nelson Rockefeller, who had risen to fame with tough-on-crime policies, ordered state police and national guardsmen to retake the prison.

In her gripping narrative, Heather Ann Thompson's *Blood in the Water: The Attica Prison Uprising of 1971 and Its Legacy* demonstrates that the state's retaking of the prison cemented state violence as the response to prisoners' demands for more humane treatment. Helicopters above

G. Miller, *Search and Destroy: African-American Males in the Criminal Justice System* (New York: Oxford University Press, 1996); Marc Mauer, *Race to Incarcerate* (New York: New Press, 1999); Bruce Western, *Punishment and Inequality in America* (New York: Russell Sage Foundation, 2006); Michelle Alexander, *The New Jim Crow: Mass Incarceration in the Age of Colorblindness* (New York: New Press, 2012); and Lawrence D. Bobo and Victor Thompson, 'Racialized Mass Incarceration: Poverty, Prejudice, and Punishment', in Hazel R. Markus and Paula Moya (eds), *Doing Race: 21 Essays for the 21st Century* (New York: W.W. Norton, 2010), 322–55.

the prison unleashed a thick fog of gas that caused 'tearing, nausea, and retching' and rendered the rebelling prisoners easy captives. But instead of rounding up the retching inmates, police and guardsmen – who after days of anxious waiting were now 'buzzing from a toxic cocktail of hatred, fear, and aggression' – unleashed a barrage of fire from hundreds of guns. 'The bullets were coming like rain', one prisoner said. Neither rebelling prisoners nor hostages were spared. In one chilling example, Thompson describes how four bullets ripped through guard and hostage Mike Smith's 'stomach, dead center right between his navel and genitals, exploded upon impact, which sent shrapnel downward to his spine'.[46] Joined by state police, correctional officers, local sheriffs and park police, the assembled siege 'removed their identification badges' and forcibly stormed the prison with batons swinging. Once the prison was retaken, prisoners were stripped naked, made to crawl through the mud and then proceeded through a police line where they were beaten with clubs. Perceived leaders of the uprising fared far worse, however. Thompson recounts how some of them were tortured for hours, sodomized with foreign objects and forced to play shotgun roulette. Sam Melville, whom witnesses claim survived the initial assault, was then executed point-blank. Much of this torture was racially motivated. One state trooper, for example, bragged of shooting a Black prisoner and then giving a White Power salute. The bloody assault ended with forty-three people dead – thirty-three prisoners and ten correctional employees who had been held as hostages – and eighty-nine wounded.

Despite this appalling demonstration of state violence, Rockefeller's government succeeded in preventing the public from learning that nearly all casualties were caused by state forces storming the prison, not by the prisoners. Indeed, the state would undertake a conspiracy to blame the deaths on the prisoners to paint them as butchers and discredit their political demands. At every turn of the investigation, the state – from the prison administrators to the state police to Governor Nelson Rockefeller – denies the surviving prisoners and the public the dignity of truth and full accountability. None of the men had died from knife wounds, for instance, even though state officials initially convinced the press, even the venerable *New York Times*, to publish that the throats of hostages had been slashed by inmates. Worse was the official claim and falsely reported story that prison guard Mike Smith had been castrated by Frank 'Big Black' Smith and had his testicles stuffed in his mouth, when, instead, Smith had been shot four times by troopers, and 'Big Black', who survived the assault, had subsequently been brutally tortured as state troopers and Corrections Officers placed a football under his chin and threatened him under pain of death not to let the ball drop as his naked body was beaten and sodomized with a screwdriver.

---

[46]Heather Ann Thompson, *Blood in the Water: The Attica Prison Uprising of 1971 and Its Legacy* (New York: Pantheon Books, 2016), 181.

When describing such state torture, Frank Smith tearfully told a courtroom during the Attica Brothers Legal Defense civil suit trial that, years later, he still felt 'just pain, unbearable pain. . . . I'm just, I'm full of pain'.[47] Heather Thompson concludes that such violence served as notice to American politicians that the project of mass incarceration was both deeply anti-Black and inherently violent.

'To countless white Americans in particular', Thompson concludes, 'Attica suggested that it was now time to rein in "those" black and brown people who had been so vocally challenging authority and pushing the civil rights envelope'.[48] The aftermath of the state's violence at Attica had created 'an anti-civil-rights and anti-rehabilitative ethos' such that 'any politician who wanted money for his or her district had learned that the way to get it was by expanding the local criminal just apparatus and by making it far more punitive'.[49] Today the prison massacre at Attica in the late summer of 1971, and the subsequent governmental cover-up, is a well-known moment in the history of violence in modern America. Nowhere in his over 800-page book, however, does Pinker even acknowledge, much less ponder, this painful event.

Moreover, state violence can be found not only in sensational and well-covered incidents such as Attica, but through the prison's power to exact everyday violence as a tool of punitive racial discipline. In my own work, *We Are Not Slaves: State Violence, Coerced Labor, and Prisoners' Rights in Postwar America* I offer a historical narrative of state violence in southern prisons from 1945 to 1990, particularly in Texas, where the prison system itself is an inherently violent space that consciously changes the shape, form and modalities of its punishment regime as a way to perpetually reproduce new arrangements of carceral violence and power. *We Are Not Slaves* draws upon court documents, affidavits, depositions, prisoner letters and over sixty oral histories to excavate how prison violence was state-orchestrated. I argue that the social structure of prison violence in the American South, particularly Texas, rendered prisoners to a state-orchestrated system of 'double enslavement – a slave for the state in prison fields and an enslaved body and servant within prison cells'.[50]

In Texas, the subject of my book, prisoner field drivers drew on the slave heritage of East Texas cotton plantations to drive the work of fellow prisoners. But within the prison, the prison administration deputized prisoners to act as guards, employing coercive and violent means to maintain control over the prisoner population. While prisoners worked

---

[47]Frank Smith quoted in Thompson, *Blood in the Water*, 488.
[48]Thompson, *Blood in the Water*, 561.
[49]Thompson, *Blood in the Water*, 561-2.
[50]Robert T. Chase, *We Are Not Slaves: State Violence, Coerced Labor, and Prisoners' Rights in Postwar America* (Chapel Hill: University of North Carolina Press, 2020), 105.

the fields as coerced slave labour, privileged prisoners known as 'building tenders' constructed an internal slave trade economy where they bought and sold the bodies of other prisoners as sexual slaves, subjects of coerced and often violent rape, and as domestic cell servants. During most of the twentieth century, the Texas prison administration allowed these selected prisoners to openly carry hand-made weapons so that they could insure prisoner discipline and administrative control. In return for their service, the prison administration provided these prisoners with certain privileges that allowed them control over the prison's system *sub rosa* internal economy. The prisoners whom the prison system placed in charge also ran an internal prison economy in which money, food, human beings, reputations, favours and sex all became commodities to be bought and sold. The building tender system was a hierarchical labour regime that constituted a vicious sex trade in which building tenders were given the tacit approval from the prison administration to use their power to rape other prisoners and engage in the buying and selling of prisoner bodies as a sexual commodity that signified cultural standing and societal power. In courtroom testimony to expose how the building tender system operated, one prisoner offered his astute estimation that connected such prison economies to state-orchestrated violence:

> See the whole thing [the building tender system] is a pretty physically-based thing. It's a very predatory system and this, I think, is a very important thing to note, that predatory is the common denominator for all of it. The strong prey upon the weak, and the weak are in a terrible position. . . . If they succumb to the predation, it only gets worse, and predation is social, it's sexual; it's economic.[51]

Despite the fact that Pinker published *The Better Angels of Our Nature* during the very height of mass incarceration, his account offers no reflection at all on the ways in which America's prisons were spaces suffused with rapacious sexual and everyday violence as a critical function of state power and racial degradation.

The death penalty as state violence

Finally, Steven Pinker is also blind to state executions as a source of deadly violence in the past and the present. In Pinker's world view, the decline of the lynching of Black American men as common public spectacle has rendered racially motivated hate crimes as having 'fallen into the statistical

---

[51]Chase, *We Are Not Slaves*, 102.

noise', yet his work remains conspicuously silent on the death penalty and state executions.[52] Before 1945, state executions in the United States arose in tandem with lynching as a violent tool to achieve Jim Crow and white supremacy. Between 1608 and 1945, states executed African Americans at the rate of half of all executions, although Southern states executed African American men at the rate of nearly 75 per cent. From the American Revolution to the Civil War, 'more than 66% of all executions occurred in the South and almost 80% in the South and Border states in combination'.[53] Study after study on the death penalty in the United States before 1945 characterizes state execution as one of 'the worst legacies of a criminal justice system that came to maturity as an instrument of Jim Crow racial subjugation'.[54] Lynching and state executions therefore worked in tandem together over time to produce the public association that linked Blackness to violent criminality, racial inferiority and inhuman immorality that made Black life itself something that white society refused to respect.[55] As Seth Kotch puts it in his study of state executions in North Carolina, 'lynching functioned like law' but 'the law also functioned like lynching: subjugating, constraining, and disrupting Black communities'.[56]

When, on 30 June 1972, the US Supreme Court rendered its 5-4 ruling on the case of *Furman v. Georgia*, it simultaneously created a national moratorium on the death penalty while opening the door for individual states to widen their use of capital punishment. On the one hand, Justice Potter Stewart's often-quoted concurring opinion that state executions were 'cruel and unusual in the same way being struck by lightning was cruel and unusual' cited race in these cases as that which 'can be discerned for the selection of these few to be sentenced to die', while simultaneously concluding that 'racial discrimination has not been proved'.[57] On the other hand, the Furman decision allowed individual states to craft new laws that

---

[52]Pinker, *Better Angels*, 385.

[53]Howard W. Allen and Jerome M. Clubb, *Race, Class, and the Death Penalty: Capital Punishment in American History* (Albany: State University of New York Press, 2008), 52.

[54]Stuart Banner, *The Death Penalty: An American History* (Cambridge, MA: Harvard University Press, 2002); Steven E. Barkan and Steven F. Cohn, 'Racial Prejudice and Support for the Death Penalty among Whites', *Journal of Research in Crime and Delinquency*, 31, no. 2 (May 1994): 202–9; Frank Baumgartner, Marty Davidson, Kaneesha R. Johnson et al., *Deadly Justice: A Statistical Portrait of the Death Penalty* (New York: Oxford University Press, 2017); William J. Bowers, Glenn L. Pierce and John F. McDevitt, *Legal Homicide: Death as Punishment in America, 1864-1982* (Boston: Northeastern University Press, 1984); David Garland, Randall McGowan and Michael Meranze, *America's Death Penalty: Between Past and Present* (New York: New York University Press, 2011). Seth Kotch, *Lethal State: A History of the Death Penalty in North Carolina* (Chapel Hill: University of North Carolina Press, 2020), 21.

[55]On the association of Blackness and criminality, see Khalil Gibran Muhammad, *The Condemnation of Blackness: Race, Crime and the Making of Modern Urban America* (Cambridge, MA: Harvard University Press, 2010). Kotch, *Lethal State*.

[56]Kotch, *Lethal State*, 25.

[57]*Furman v. Georgia*, 408 U.S. 238 (1972).

would retain capital punishment if they could satisfy the Eighth Amendment to the Constitution through the removal of arbitrary and discriminatory sentencing. Rather than initiate a new wave of human empathy, Furman instead initiated a renewed political furore for capital punishment. To cite but one example, a Harris Poll showed that more people (59 per cent in 1972 vs 48 per cent in 1969), not less, supported the death penalty immediately following the Furman decision.[58] It only took six months for Florida to restore the death penalty, and within three years, by 1975, thirty-one states once again instituted capital punishment by creating separate processes for conviction and sentencing, which was upheld by the Supreme Court in 1976 in *Gregg v. Georgia*.

Since 1975, states with the death penalty have put to death 1,526 people. About one-third of those put to death have been African American people. Southern states remain most likely to put people to death, accounting for 1,245 of state executions, and Texas alone has put to death 569 people. More than 8,500 people have been sentenced to death since the 1970s.[59] Although rates of execution have declined since 1965, it remains a symbolic and violent expression of the carceral state's power to eliminate people of colour. A recent study offers some telling statistics: 'Between 1976 and 2013, only seventeen white people were executed for killing a Black person while 230 black people were executed for killing a white person; black people were put to death more than twice as often for killing a white person (230 executions) than for killing a black person (108 executions).'[60] The political fervour for the death penalty since the 1970s continues to link Blackness with criminality and Black life as disposable. Rather than initiate a 'New Peace' of human empathy, the reimposition of the death penalty after 1975 reminds us of historian Seth Kotch's conclusion that 'any history of the death penalty is a history of failure'.[61]

Since 2010, nearly two dozen meticulously researched historical studies have clearly demonstrated beyond a doubt that racism and violence are endemic in the American criminal justice system. From urban policing, to border patrols, to mass incarceration, systematized violence has not only persisted but has intensified since 1965. To draw again on Ruth Wilson Gilmore, this history of persistent violence stemming from mid-to-late twentieth-century carceral states in America is indeed 'state-sanctioned or extralegal production and exploitation of group-differentiated vulnerability

---

[58]Kotch, *Lethal State*, 163.

[59]'Number of Execution by state and region since 1976', Death Penalty Information Center, https://deathpenaltyinfo.org/executions/executions-overview/number-of-executions-by-state-and-region-since-1976, accessed 20 December 2020.

[60]Frank R. Baumgartner et al., '#BlackLivesDon'tMatter: Race-of-Victim Effects in US Executions, 1976-2013', *Politics, Groups, and Identities*, 3, no. 2 (2015): 209–21.

[61]Kotch, *Lethal State*, 186.

to premature death'.[62] Yet Steven Pinker never acknowledges policing and prisons as sites of well-documented racial violence. He maintains instead that racial barbarities began to decline after 1965 and have since largely ceased in the United States, and blithely cites as a parallel to this happier age of race relations the banning of dodge ball, a game played by elementary school children in physical education classes. If the events of 2020 have taught us anything, it is that to ignore racialized policing, mass incarceration and capital punishment as sites of violence in America today is to deny that Black and Brown lives matter.

---

[62]Gilmore, *Golden Gulag*, 28.

16

The better angels of which nature?

Violence and environmental history in the modern world

Corey Ross

The Better Angels of Our Nature is an exceptional book: wide-ranging, erudite and enviably eloquent. Writing such grand syntheses is a daunting challenge at the best of times, and the challenges multiply quickly when transgressing disciplinary boundaries. The need to distil complexity and to write about things beyond one's own expertise makes such books far easier to criticize than to write. As the other chapters in this volume show, its core thesis about a long-term decline in violence offers plenty of scope for criticism, both conceptually and methodologically.

It might therefore seem churlish to focus on issues that Pinker's voluminous tome leaves out. But as Mark Micale has recently suggested, what the book omits is just as notable as what it includes.[1] Some of the silences reflect its decidedly Western-centric perspective, such as the inattention to imperial conquests and wars throughout Asia and Africa. Others stem from its narrow conception of violence itself. The focus on physical aggression between people offers little scope for considering the ways in which even the most 'civilized' (Elias) and cooperative societies have continued to engage in –

---

[1] Mark S. Micale, 'What Pinker Leaves Out', *Historical Reflections*, 44, no. 1 (September 2018): 128–39.

and indeed increased their reliance on – other forms of destructive and lethal behaviour that we might equally categorize under the heading of 'violence'.

How does the recent history of violence look if we include humankind's treatment of the biophysical environment? Despite its 800+ pages, Pinker's book has little to say about this question. It briefly hovers into view when he rejects the idea that climate change poses a major threat to international security, and it is touched upon again when citing research which suggests that ecological degradation has rarely been a significant factor in recent instances of armed conflict.[2] One simple explanation for why these matters get such short shrift is that they would make a long book even longer. A less generous interpretation might be that they cast an unwanted shadow on the rosy picture that Pinker wanted to paint. Either way, from the perspective of environmental history it is difficult to reconcile the optimistic tone of Pinker's thesis with what we know about recent relations between human societies and the rest of the material world. Indeed, an entire generation of research has highlighted how processes of industrialization, imperialism, population growth and mass consumption wrought unprecedented havoc on the global environment, living and inanimate alike.

This chapter suggests some of the ways in which we can enrich our understanding of the history of violence when we extend our attention to the non-human world. The benefits are about more than just covering additional ground, for this expanded focus also provides insights into how the treatment of people, environments and resources were interlinked. Social and ecological systems are always entangled. All human societies harness energy, take in resources and emit wastes, and one of the perennial questions is where the burdens fall and how they relate to existing customs, social hierarchies and structures of power. To what extent have various forms of exploitation been displaced from people on to other things? How do the different temporalities of biophysical and social processes shape patterns of violence? What were the cultural, technological and organizational linkages that tied the mass killing of people to large-scale environmental intervention? As the following sections will show, thinking about such questions not only affords new perspectives on the history of violence but also casts doubt on its alleged decline.

Violence slow and subtle

Over the past century, people have acquired a degree of control over nature that their ancestors could scarcely have imagined. Whether we look at

---

[2]Steven Pinker, *Better Angels of Our Nature: Why Violence Has Declined* (New York: Viking, 2011), 453–4.

the land, oceans, atmosphere or biosphere, the imprint of human activity is ubiquitous. So profound and comprehensive are the effects of human intervention as to qualify the recent past as a new era of natural history: the so-called Anthropocene.[3] Most of the processes that have driven this transformation are not new; humans have been farming, clearing, mining, hunting and polluting for a long time. The novelty lies in the scope and intensity of environmental change, which has amplified previously local problems into global ones. Humans have of course benefitted considerably from these changes in the form of higher living standards and longer lives (at least for many of us). But they also entailed considerable costs, which people have grown increasingly adept at shifting on to other things – whether to those less wealthy or powerful than themselves, or to the physical environment (or both). Insofar as humans have become masters of nature, they have done so by also becoming masters in the art of displacement.

One of the reasons why environmental interventions are rarely considered to be a form of 'violence' is because the damage they cause is often gradual rather than sudden, unnoticed rather than immediately evident. This does not make the effects any less harmful than if they happened all at once; if anything, it simply makes them harder to prevent and trickier to mitigate once they have started. The creeping, insidious consequences of biodiversity loss, soil deterioration, global warming and toxic pollution are far more serious – to humans and to other organisms – than the level of attention they attract. Unlike wars or immediate humanitarian crises, they do not make for spectacular images in a world of sensation-driven twenty-four-hour news cycles. Their comparative neglect in public discourse is not helped by the fact that the worst consequences tend to be borne by poor people, poor countries or future generations that lack the political or economic clout to change things. The burdens of mass environmental disruption are displaced across space and time, which blunts people's sensitivity to the harm being caused.

The literary scholar Rob Nixon has given a name to this phenomenon: 'slow violence'.[4] It is a fitting label that captures what he calls the 'attritional lethality' of the multiple environmental emergencies that humanity faces, while also highlighting the extent to which they are ignored because of

---

[3]Will Steffen, Jacques Grinevald, Paul Crutzen and John McNeill, 'The Anthropocene: Conceptual and Historical Perspectives', *Philosophical Transactions of the Royal Society*, 369, no. 1938 (March 2011): 842–67; John R. McNeill and Peter Engelke, *The Great Acceleration: An Environmental History of the Anthropocene since 1945* (Cambridge: Belknap, 2014); Gareth Austin (ed.), *Economic Development and Environmental History in the Anthropocene: Perspectives on Asia and Africa* (London: Bloomsbury, 2017); Christophe Bonneuil and Jean-Baptiste Fressoz, *The Shock of the Anthropocene: The Earth, History, and US* (London: Verso, 2016).
[4]Rob Nixon, *Slow Violence and the Environmentalism of the Poor* (Cambridge, MA: Harvard University Press, 2011).

the geographically and temporally dispersed nature of the consequences.[5] As Nixon shows, the gradual deterioration of environmental conditions and the declining access of local communities to resources have prompted environmental activists to give dramatic expression to the otherwise hidden ecological and social crises that such groups face. In recent years, scholars have repeatedly highlighted how state or private 'development' initiatives have driven environmental degradation and social inequality by sacrificing the health, land or water of local communities to the broader interests of global capital or centralized political control. Whenever such initiatives proceed without the knowledge or consent of those affected, it has become increasingly common to regard them as a form of environmental violence (whether 'slow' or otherwise).[6]

'Slow violence' has manifested itself in a multitude of forms. The history of mineral and oil extraction provides more than its share of examples. Over the past century, thousands of rural communities around the world have had to live with the harmful by-products of mining operations, and many have also had to cope with their toxic legacies long after they shut down. In the United States, abandoned mines still discharge around 50 million gallons of polluted water per day, which taints nearby ground and surface water supplies with elevated levels of heavy metals.[7] In China, the boom in rare-earth mining has left behind a denuded landscape pocked with toxic tailings pools across much of the south-eastern Jiangxi Province, while in inner Mongolia the wastes from the even bigger pits in Bayan Obo leach into surrounding watercourses, poisoning local people and animals.[8] Pollution levels are often even higher in many developing countries, where regulation has often been ineffective or unenforced. In Gabon, radioactive waste poisoned soil, water and human bodies for miles around the Franceville uranium mine, which dumped around 2 million tons of it directly into local rivers by 1975.[9] Contamination from the lead and zinc mine at Kabwe in Zambia, which operated almost entirely without regulation from 1902 to

[5]Nixon, *Slow Violence*, 8.

[6]The relevant literature is voluminous. For an overview of issues, see Stefania Barca, 'Telling the Right Story: Environmental Violence and Liberation Narratives', *Environment and History*, 20 (2014): 535–46.

[7]On mining and its legacies in the United States, see for example Timothy J. LeCain, *Mass Destruction: The Men and Giant Mines that Wired America and Scarred the Planet* (New Brunswick: Rutgers University Press, 2009); Chad Montrie, *To Save the Land and People: A History of Opposition to Surface Coal Mining in Appalachia* (Chapel Hill: University of North Carolina Press, 2003).

[8]Jason C. K. Lee and Zongguo Wen, 'Rare Earths from Mines to Metals: Comparing Environmental Impacts from China's Main Production Pathways', *Journal of Industrial Ecology*, 21, no. 5 (2016): 1277–90.

[9]Gabrielle Hecht, *Being Nuclear: Africans and the Global Uranium Trade* (Cambridge, MA: MIT Press, 2012), 239–48.

1994, resulted in lead levels in local children's blood up to ten times the recommended maximum.[10] The list of examples is long.

For many of the people living in such places, the discovery of oil or minerals beneath their feet has been more a blight than a blessing. Instead of deriving benefits from the riches pulled out of the earth, they find themselves victims of a 'resource curse'. The basic gist of this theory, which became widely influential in the 1990s, is that the more a state relies on a single abundant mineral resource, the more likely it is to be corrupt, undemocratic and militaristic.[11] Like all social theories, it is a generalization that does not apply equally everywhere; after all, some resource-rich countries have exemplary developmental and democratic credentials (Norway, Canada). But throughout much of the world, the pattern is striking. The problems are epitomized by the oil industry in Angola, where corruption and opaque payments brought huge profits for multinational oil firms while allowing political elites to pocket many of the proceeds for themselves. Most of Angola's production comes from the vast oilfields off the coast of Cabinda, a small exclave separated from the rest of the country by a narrow sliver of the Democratic Republic of the Congo. Despite its prodigious oil wealth, Cabinda has remained one of Angola's poorest provinces, and its inhabitants have received little from oil production apart from plummeting local fish stocks and drilling pollution. Indeed, the tensions surrounding oil revenues have only fuelled the secessionist struggle that has smouldered in Cabinda ever since the 1960s.[12] For resource-cursed societies like Cabinda, 'a mineral strike, though less immediately spectacular than a missile strike, is often more devastating in the long term, bringing in its wake environmental wreckage, territorial dispossession, political repression, and massacres by state forces doing double duty as security forces for unanswerable petroleum transnationals or mineral cartels'.[13]

The history of agricultural modernization has been another major source of slow-motion damage to land and people. Although the spread of industrial farming practices to the developing world since the 1950s and 1960s is generally credited with averting a world food crisis, the long-term problems associated with such practices are legion (soil degradation, fossil fuel dependence, unsustainable water use, loss of biodiversity and destruction of wildlife populations). Most pertinent to the theme of human violence is the use of chemical fertilizers and especially pesticides, which according to the World Health Organization caused around 1 million cases of poisoning and

---

[10]http://www.blacksmithinstitute.org/projects/display/3.
[11]Richard M. Auty, *Sustaining Development in Mineral Economies: The Resource Curse Thesis* (London: Routledge, 1993); Michael L. Ross, *The Oil Curse: How Petroleum Wealth Shapes the Development of Nations* (Princeton: Princeton University Press, 2012).
[12]Alban Monday Kouango, *Cabinda: un Koweit africain* (Paris: L'Harmattan, 2002); Kristin Reed, *Crude Existence: Environment and the Politics of Oil in Northern Angola* (Berkeley: University of California Press, 2009).
[13]Nixon, *Slow Violence*, 70.

around 20,000 deaths per year by the late 1980s, mostly due to long periods of exposure to harmful substances. While wealthy industrial countries used about 80 per cent of the world's pesticides, most of the poisonings and deaths occurred in developing countries where safety standards were poor and where manufacturers' guidelines for usage were frequently ignored (partly because users could not read them).[14] As Angus Wright highlighted in his searing indictment of the Green Revolution in Mexico, many such deaths were linked to corporate farms growing crops for Northern markets, where poor farm labourers were given little or no protective gear to shield them from the chemicals being sprayed around them.[15] Farm managers were more eager to keep down costs than to ensure the well-being of their employees, while manufacturers continued to market their products aggressively with little regard to how they were used after sale. Over the long term, poor labourers were essentially treated as little more than disposable bodies. The death of farm workers like Ramón Gonzalez, the eponymous victim of Wright's account, illustrates how the routine careless neglect of underprivileged groups constitutes a form of physical violence, one that is deeply embedded in structures of social inequality and environmental injustice.

Occasionally such creeping environmental and health crises have made a deep impression on public consciousness, especially when they posed a threat in wealthier and/or more democratically accountable countries. When Rachel Carson published *Silent Spring* in 1962, it shocked readers by demonstrating the extent of environmental contamination through the widespread use of modern pesticides, agro-chemicals and other industrial compounds. As the titled implied, birds were the proverbial canaries in the coalmine; populations of some species were plummeting due to the effects of DDT on the composition of eggshells, and the fact that this included the United States' national symbol (the bald eagle) greatly enhanced the book's popular impact. Yet what made the book so compelling at the time, and so foundational to the emergence of the modern environmental movement, was the way in which it broke down the barriers between humans and the rest of nature by showing how these toxins flowed throughout the entire web of the biophysical world, including human bodies. The message, in short, was that what is bad for nature is ultimately bad for humans. Annihilating pests, doubling crop yields or easing the burden of housework with space-age chemicals not only was the ticket to health and prosperity promised by states and corporations but also carried huge costs for ecosystems and for human well-being. Despite a well-funded campaign by the petrochemical industry to discredit Carson and her book, the message stuck, and the use

---

[14]David Pimentel, 'Green Revolution Agriculture and Chemical Hazards', *The Science of the Total Environment*, 188, Suppl. 1 (1996): S86–S98.
[15]Angus Wright, *The Death of Ramón Gonzalez: The Modern Agricultural Dilemma*, 2nd edn (Austin: University of Texas Press, 2005).

of many persistent organic pollutants (DDT, BHC) was banned or strictly limited.[16]

More often than not, these gradual assaults on the biophysical world were (and still are) under-recognized. This is especially true of the world's many 'sacrifice zones', ignored or forgotten corners whose degradation was considered acceptable for economic or political reasons, and which tended overwhelmingly to be inhabited by poor and underprivileged people (often ethnic minorities). Wealthy countries have their own version of such places: poor towns or neighbourhoods that breathe in the fumes of nearby refineries, drink the water into which upstream factories dispose of their effluents, or live with the toxic residues of industries long since disappeared.[17] At a global level they are correspondingly clustered in the developing world, from the ship-breaking yards of coastal Bangladesh to the e-waste recycling dumps of India to the oil-slathered marshes of the Niger Delta. 'Emerging' economies have perhaps the biggest problems of all. China's breakneck economic growth since the 1980s has been notorious for its environmental impact and for the manner in which it has been offloaded on to poor people near extraction or processing sites, not to mention the lungs of everyone who lives in its smog-mantled industrial cities. In all of these places, the poor are left to live with or clean up the noxious leftovers of economic activities that primarily benefit others.

Of all the slow-moving crises currently underway, climate change poses perhaps the greatest threat to health and well-being over the long term. The World Health Organization estimates that a changing climate will be responsible for 250,000 excess deaths annually over the coming decades, mostly as a result of malnutrition, malaria, diarrhoea and heat stress. Unsurprisingly, nearly all of these excess deaths will be in poor developing countries that have done the least to create the problem in the first place.[18] According to a recent United Nations report, such findings reflect the increasing risk of a kind of 'climate apartheid', where the rich pay to avoid the food and water shortages caused by climate crisis, while the poor face its full consequences.[19] In the meantime, failing rains, intensifying storms, melting ice and rising sea levels threaten to overwhelm entire regions and displace huge numbers of people. Most at risk are the coastal megacities of southern and eastern Asia, home to the world's largest concentration of humanity. Unlike Miami, New York or London, which may be able to spend their way out of the worst effects through massive infrastructural

---

[16]Linda Lear, *Rachel Carson: Witness for Nature* (London: Allen Lane, 1998); Lisa S. Sideries and Kathleen Dean Moore (eds), *Rachel Carson: Legacy and Challenge* (Albany: SUNY Press, 2008).
[17]Steve Lerner, *Sacrifice Zones: The Front Lines of Toxic Chemical Exposure in the United States* (Cambridge, MA: MIT Press, 2010).
[18]https://www.who.int/news-room/fact-sheets/detail/climate-change-and-health.
[19]https://news.un.org/en/story/2019/06/1041261.

investment, many of these cities are too poor to make this a realistic option. And some (notably Jakarta, Bangkok and Manila) face the added challenge of subsidence due to excessive groundwater extraction and urban sprawl, which means they are sinking as ocean levels rise.[20]

For at least one country the threat of global warming is downright existential. The Maldives, the world's lowest-lying state (with an average altitude of just over 1 metre and a peak altitude of under 2.5 metres), faces the threat of near-total inundation by the end of the current century. In October 2009, on the eve of the Copenhagen climate summit, its president held an underwater cabinet meeting with scuba-clad ministers in an effort to highlight the country's predicament.[21] Since then, the Maldives has served as a symbol of the inherent violence of fossil-fuel-driven climate change. It is among the most visible victims of the ongoing attack on the well-being and even survival of millions of people, present and future. As a micro-nation with zero clout on the world stage, it encapsulates how global power inequalities continue to determine the main winners and losers of the last two centuries of hydrocarbon-fuelled economic growth. The fact that there is little or nothing that the Maldives government can do by itself to avert its watery fate underlines the global nature of the problem and the need for international cooperation to address it. The current inevitability of a significant sea-level rise despite decades of warnings from scientists about greenhouse gas emissions also highlights the tendency of our political systems to postpone hard choices for as long as possible, especially if the drawbacks can be deferred to one's successors. What we are left with is the prospect that much (perhaps all) of a state's territory will be destroyed and many (perhaps all) of its inhabitants displaced as refugees due to the determination of more powerful states to pursue what they have perceived as their own economic and political interests even in the face of vociferous warnings about the damage that would be caused by this course of (in)action. This unintentional, unplanned and almost imperceptible process could hardly be more different from the spectacle of a violent military strike, but the end outcome is eerily similar.

Routine slaughter

One of the most fundamental aspects of the human remaking of nature has been the deliberate interference with the nature and distribution of plant and

---

[20]Henrike Brecht et al., 'Sea-Level Rise and Storm Surges: High Stakes for a Small Number of Developing Countries'; https://documents.worldbank.org/en/publication/documents-reports/documentdetail/156401468136816684/the-impact-of-sea-level-rise-on-developing-countries-a-comparative-analysis.

[21]See, for example, https://www.reuters.com/article/us-maldives-environment/maldives-sends-climate-sos-with-undersea-cabinet-idUSTRE59G0P120091017; Nixon, *Slow Violence*, 263–8.

animal species. The selection of cultivars and creatures according to their usefulness has been going on for millennia, and like most other processes of human-induced environmental change, the trend has accelerated over the past couple of centuries. In essence, it amounts to choosing winners and losers in the evolutionary struggle for survival. Some species have not fared well. Organisms perceived to have a negative use value – whatever we call a pest – have been deliberately targeted for elimination. Others have benefitted enormously: maize, wheat, swine, chickens and cattle are incomparably more prevalent thanks to human interference than they would otherwise be. Still others have undergone a form of unintentional selection, for example through overhunting or habitat destruction that happened for other reasons. Apart from house pets and a few categories of livestock (mainly animals kept for milking or traction), the common denominator for most of these organisms is that they are killed in fairly short order, usually for people to eat them or in order to keep them from eating or damaging the production of other things that people want to eat.[22]

In this sense, humans have been and continue to be an exceptionally violent species within the broader context of the biosphere. Is it fair to criticize Pinker's book for failing to recognize the vast scale of animal slaughter that humans inflict on a daily basis? The subject certainly lies beyond the book's core concerns, which remain resolutely, if understandably, anthropocentric in focus. The only exception is a subchapter in which Pinker discusses the rise of animal rights and the decline of cruelty to animals. These changes, he argues, formed part of the broader set of twentieth-century 'rights revolutions' in that the advocates of human and animal rights long regarded the two as closely linked. Insofar as we are all sentient creatures, the infliction of suffering on people or animals is a powerful analogy. Pinker even suggests that the rise of animal rights was a 'uniquely emblematic instance of the decline of violence', considering that its advocates (humans) were not affected by the changes themselves and therefore acted solely on the basis of ethical principles.[23] The transformation in animal rights over recent decades has undoubtedly been profound. From controls on the use of laboratory animals to the criminalization of blood sports to the adoption of more stringent standards of livestock husbandry, many societies have indeed come a long way from Descartes' notion of animals as clockwork mechanisms without souls or feelings.

Pinker is, then, undoubtedly correct to highlight the growing concern for animal welfare as a major cultural shift. In the early twenty-first century,

---

[22]Susan R. Schrepfer and Philip Scranton (eds), *Industrializing Organisms: Introducing Evolutionary History* (London: Routledge, 2004); Edmund Russell, *Evolutionary History: Uniting History and Biology to Understand Life on Earth* (Cambridge: Cambridge University Press, 2011).
[23]Pinker, *Better Angels*, 550.

it has even found expression within the discipline of history, furnishing at least part of the motivation behind the so-called 'animal turn' in research over the past ten to fifteen years.[24] Unfortunately, however, this welcome change of sensibility is not very characteristic of human–animal relations at a general level. The more we look beyond the favoured categories of companion creatures and charismatic species, and the farther we move from a Western-centric to a broader global perspective, the more violent these relations look. In short, the fate of most animals is not easily reconcilable with Pinker's thesis.[25]

The vast majority of animals in the world are either wild or domesticated for food purposes, and both categories have been killed on an unprecedented scale in recent times. While it is true that agricultural beasts are treated more humanely in many countries than they were just a few decades ago, we nonetheless confine and slaughter a huge number of them, and by no means are animal welfare standards a top priority for rural folk everywhere. It is difficult to determine the number of farm animals worldwide. Statistical returns to the United Nations Food and Agriculture Organization are notoriously unreliable; some countries scarcely have the means to do much more than guess, while others may over- or under-report for any number of political reasons. For what it is worth, the organization World Animal Protection currently estimates that over 70 billion animals are farmed and killed for food each year. That amounts to nearly ten animals for each human on the planet, and around two-thirds of them live in conditions that are deemed to cause 'suffering and distress' (generally by not allowing them to move freely).[26] When we realize that the combined biomass of humans and their domesticated animals is now greater than that of all wild terrestrial vertebrates,[27] and that the bulk of these domesticates are killed as soon as their feed-to-meat ratio has reached an optimum level, we get a rather different impression of human–animal relations than the story of animal rights suggests.

Chickens are subject to especially instrumental treatment, partly because of how the industry developed after the Second World War, and partly because they are widely deemed less intelligent or sentient than domesticated mammals. Most are raised in cramped battery houses and are killed when they are around forty days old. Despite their tender age at death, many

---

[24]See Dan Vandersommers, 'The "Animal Turn" in History', *Perspectives on History* (3 November 2016): https://www.historians.org/publications-and-directories/perspectives-on-history/november-2016/the-animal-turn-in-history; Benjamin Breen, 'Animal History: An Emerging Scholarly Trend', *JStor Daily* (29 October 2014), https://daily.jstor.org/animals-in-the-archive/.
[25]See also Micale, 'What Pinker Leaves Out', 131–3.
[26]https://www.worldanimalprotection.org/our-work/animals-farming-supporting-70-billion-animals.
[27]Vaclav Smil, 'Harvesting the Biosphere: The Human Impact', *Population and Development Review*, 37 (2011): 613–36.

already suffer from lesions, fractures, 'ammonia burn' (from the emissions of large amounts of accumulated faeces) and breathing difficulties due to the phenomenal growth rates they attain as a result of decades of careful genetic tuning and the development of supercharged feeds.[28] Over the past sixty to seventy years, the constant engineering of the modern broiler chicken has created animals so over-endowed with certain characteristics (in this case huge body mass, in particular the breast) and so unnaturally fast-growing (around sixty-five times their normal rate) that even their short lives are filled with chronic pain. Indeed, the current morphology, genetics and pathology of these creatures are so different from those of their ancestors that they are now completely unable to survive without human intervention.[29] Unfortunately for them, public concern about the inherent cruelty of the extreme breeding of pedigree dogs has not yet extended to the decidedly less adorable broiler chicken, by most estimates the most genetically manipulated creature on the planet.[30]

The number of livestock raised and killed each year varies greatly according to species and region. Statistical studies based on United Nations data estimate the following totals for animals slaughtered in 2016: 300 million cows, 450 million goats, 550 million sheep, 1.5 billion pigs and a staggering 66 billion chickens.[31] As one would expect, the highest numbers tend to be killed in the most populous countries such as China and the United States (with the notable exception of India). Per capita figures reveal a number of small and mid-sized countries that surpass even the historically high North American levels of slaughter (Uruguay, Australia and Ireland for cows; Germany, Denmark and Spain for pigs). Across much of sub-Saharan Africa and southern Asia, the number of farm animals killed per capita is still relatively low, and of course regional tastes and customs powerfully mould patterns of consumption. The near-absence of pigs across much of the Middle East, for instance, is mirrored in a corresponding predilection for chicken.

Despite recent efforts to improve slaughter practices, which have increasingly expanded into developing countries where meat consumption is rising, most of the killing still takes place in factory-style processing centres that often cause unnecessary stress before or during the actual act

---

[28]William Boyd, 'Science, Technology, and American Poultry Production', *Technology and Culture*, 42 (2001): 631–64.

[29]Carys E. Bennett et al., 'The Broiler Chicken as a Signal of a Human Reconfigured Biosphere', *Royal Society Open Science* (12 December 2018), https://royalsocietypublishing.org/doi/full/10.1098/rsos.180325.

[30]Roger Horowitz, 'Making the Chicken of Tomorrow: Reworking Poultry as Commodities and as Creatures, 1945-1990', in Schrepfer and Scranton (eds), *Industrializing Organisms*, 215–35; on pedigree dogs: https://www.independent.co.uk/voices/crufts-pedigree-dogs-animal-cruelty-lives-full-of-pain-why-glorify-them-a8248276.html.

[31]https://faunalytics.org/global-animal-slaughter-statistics-and-charts/.

of dispatch.[32] Within the confines of these industrial slaughterhouses, more animals are now killed for human consumption than ever before, and global totals continue to rise. Little of the carnage is ever seen by meat-eaters (especially, as it happens, in the same parts of the world in which modern animal rights have come furthest, namely North America and Europe), and those who see it tend to find it unappetizing. In a sense, this can be regarded as evidence that people have become more sensitive towards violence and killing in the recent past, as Pinker suggests. But as far as the overall treatment of animals is concerned, whatever sensitivities people have developed have not made most of them averse to eating creatures that have been killed out of their sight.

If the prospects for domesticated creatures are grim, wild animals have fared little better. It is now widely recognized that we are in the midst of the sixth great extinction event in Earth's history, the first being the End Ordovician some 444 million years ago, and the last one the End Cretaceous, which killed off the great dinosaurs (along with about three-quarters of all species at the time) and thereby opened up a world of new opportunities for mammals. What makes the current sixth extinction unique is that it is being driven mainly by the activities of one particular species, namely us humans.[33] When, precisely, this latest spasm of extinction began is a matter for debate, but it is clear that the rate of extinctions over the past century or so has climbed far higher than what scientists consider to be the longer-term 'background' rate. According to a recent study of 27,600 terrestrial vertebrate species (nearly half of known vertebrates), around 200 have gone extinct over the last century, disappearing at an average rate of about two species per year. This may not seem like much from the perspective of a human lifetime, but if these 200 species would have disappeared at the normal 'background' rate of the last 2 million years, the process would have taken 10,000 years rather than merely 100 (i.e. 100th the current rate).[34]

Some plant and animal species have of course been far more affected than others. Most extinctions and endangerments have taken place in isolated habitats such as islands (New Zealand has the world's highest rate of endangered species) or freshwater lakes (such as Lake Victoria in central Africa, which has witnessed a huge decline in endemic cichlid populations). Whereas mammals disappeared around 40 times faster than the background rate in the twentieth century, birds did so at 1,000 times the normal rate.[35] Most of the damage has been due to habitat loss resulting

---

[32]https://www.worldanimalprotection.org/our-work/previous-campaigns/humane-slaughter.
[33]See Elizabeth Kolbert, *The Sixth Extinction: An Unnatural History* (London: Bloomsbury, 2014); Edward O. Wilson, *Half-Earth: Our Planet's Fight for Life* (New York: Liveright, 2016).
[34]Gerardo Ceballos, Paul R. Ehrlich and Rodolfo Dirzo, 'Biological Annihilation via the Ongoing Sixth Mass Extinction Signaled by Vertebrate Population Losses and Declines', *PNAS*, 114, no. 30 (25 July 2017): E6089–96.
[35]John R. McNeill, *Something New under the Sun* (London: Penguin, 2000), 263.

from land clearance, pollution, the effects of invasive species and climate change, all of which have ultimately been driven by the rising pressures of human population and consumption. Particularly detrimental has been the 'great onslaught' on the world's tropical forests (especially in Amazonia and Southeast Asia), which are home to around half of all terrestrial species and which were reduced by a staggering 5.5 million square kilometres over the second half of the twentieth century.[36] One of the great worries of scientists and conservationists is that many of the biodiversity effects resulting from the past fragmentation of forests are yet to come; animal populations that can no longer establish contact with others for reproductive purposes will die out sooner or later.[37] In this context, one of the more alarming findings of recent research is that nearly half of all land mammals have lost over 80 per cent of their range between 1900 and 2015.

Over the past few generations, humans have been unwittingly setting the switches for a slow-motion biological train crash that could run long into the future. Although these processes may seem to have little to do with the subject of human violence per se, it is worth bearing in mind that they are causing an unprecedented loss of life (*and* its multitude of different forms) and that the pace at which this is happening, though gradual to human eyes, is downright traumatic on an evolutionary timescale. Again, to give a sense of the pace and scope of the changes, the World Wildlife Fund's 'Living Planet Index' calculates that global populations of wild animals fell by more than half from 1970 to 2014 – an astounding loss of life in what, for natural historians, amounts to no more than the blink of an eye.[38]

Indirect forms of killing through land clearance, pollution and habitat loss have done the most to threaten plant and animal life in the recent past. But hunting has also played a role, and indeed was a key factor for certain species. Although it may well be in decline in many countries (as Pinker notes[39]), hunting – and especially commercial hunting – has taken a gigantic toll over the past two centuries. Hunting-induced extinctions or near-extinctions go back millennia, but the pace has significantly quickened. The near disappearance of the American bison in the late nineteenth century is a legendary example. From a population of 30–50 million at the middle of the century, commercial hunting for hides had reduced them to fewer than 100 in the wild by 1902.[40] Charismatic trophy species such as African elephants have tended to avoid such perilous outcomes in part because of

---

[36]Michael Williams, *Deforesting the Earth: From Prehistory to Global Crisis* (Chicago: University of Chicago Press, 2003), 420–93.
[37]Ceballos, Ehrlich and Dirzo, 'Biological Annihilation'.
[38]See: https://s3.amazonaws.com/wwfassets/downloads/lpr2018_summary_report_spreads.pdf.
[39]Pinker, *Better Angels*, 562–3.
[40]Andrew C. Isenberg, *The Destruction of the Bison: An Environmental History, 1750-1920* (Cambridge: Cambridge University Press, 2000).

long-lasting conservation efforts, though the figures are nonetheless stark: estimates suggest that only around 350,000 remain from a population of as many as 10 million in 1930. Less famous, but scarcely less destructive, were campaigns to exterminate predators, which devastated populations of tigers, wolves, coyotes and other 'varmints'.[41] Complete extinctions are rarer but by no means unfamiliar. The passenger pigeon, the most populous bird in North America (and possibly the world) in the mid-nineteenth century, was extinct in the wild by 1900; Martha, the last of her kind, died in a Cincinnati zoo in 1914.[42] The list of recent entries could continue, including the South African quagga, the Tasmanian tiger, the Caribbean monk seal and the Carolina parakeet.

But extinctions and near-extinctions tell only part of the story of human predation, since most hunted species are not in immediate danger despite the fact that large numbers are killed. Moreover, the hunting of terrestrial vertebrates like those listed earlier also furnishes only part of the picture, since most hunting activity over the past century has in fact taken place at sea. The fishing industry is – despite all its technological paraphernalia – still a matter of hunting and capturing creatures in the wild. Even the growing aquaculture sector relies to a large extent on the capture of wild fish to feed to farmed ones. Since the initial industrialization of fishing in the late nineteenth century, the effects of this aquatic hunt have been profound. Life underwater is perhaps in even greater trouble than life on land, partly as a result of pollution and ocean acidification (driven by greenhouse gas emissions), but mostly due to the aggressive depletion of fish and whale populations.[43]

The best estimates of the global fish catch show a rise from 28 million tons in 1950 to a peak of 126 million tons in 1996, after which production tailed off and is unlikely ever to recover.[44] Global historical data on fish populations is fairly speculative, but the overall trend, and the huge impact of industrial fishing methods, can be glimpsed from studies carried out on well-documented waters like those around the United Kingdom, where the transition to steam power and heavier fishing gear was pioneered in the 1880–1890s. The results of a recent historical survey of trawler catches in

---

[41]Peter Boomgaard, *Frontiers of Fear: Tigers and People in the Malay World, 1600-1950* (New Haven: Yale University Press, 2001); Peter Coates, '"Unusually Cunning, Vicious, and Treacherous": The Extermination of the Wolf in United States History', in Mark Levene and Penny Roberts (eds), *The Massacre in History* (New York: Berghahn, 1999), 163–83; Jon Coleman, *Vicious: Wolves and Men in America* (New Haven: Yale University Press, 2004).

[42]Mark V. Barrow Jr, *Nature's Ghosts: Confronting Extinction from the Age of Jefferson to the Age of Ecology* (Chicago: University of Chicago Press, 2009), 96–100, 124–6.

[43]Callum M. Roberts, *The Unnatural History of the Sea* (Washington, DC: Island Press, 2007); Carmel Finley, *All the Boats on the Ocean: How Government Subsidies Led to Global Overfishing* (Chicago: University of Chicago Press, 2017).

[44]The best estimates, based on Food and Agriculture Organization data and other sources, are by the Sea Around Us project: http://www.seaaroundus.org/.

England and Wales implies an astounding historic decline in populations of demersal (bottom-dwelling) fish. Although overall annual production rose to a peak of slightly over 800,000 tons in the late 1930s, and although large catches were still common from the end of the Second World War until the early 1970s, these figures masked the enormous upsurge in effort (bigger and faster boats, better gear) required to achieve them. From 1889 to 2007, the catch per unit of fishing power (a better measure of the actual productivity of commercial fisheries, rather than just the overall catch) fell by 94 per cent (seventeen-fold), with an initial sharp drop marking the introduction of steam trawlers in the 1890s, followed by a gradual recovery from the 1920s to 1960s as fleets modernized, before ending with a near-complete collapse between the early 1960s and late 1980s.[45] Moreover, the stunning decline of demersal fish populations constitutes only a portion of the loss of sea life caused by industrial fishing. The use of heavy trawls – sometimes likened to underwater bulldozers – has completely transformed the seabed across vast swathes of the continental shelves, wrecking reef structures and converting once thriving and diverse marine ecosystems into endless mud flats. It is the aquatic equivalent of forest clear-cutting, and although it has been a boon to a few species that favour such conditions, it has ruined crucial shelter and spawning habitat for countless others, including some that are commercially valuable.[46]

Whale populations felt the lethal hand of human predation even more acutely than fish. The whaling industry had nearly died out in the late nineteenth century after most of the easily caught species (those not too large, not too fast and sufficiently buoyant to stay afloat once killed) had been all but wiped out. It was revived after the turn of the century by a series of technological innovations (the exploding harpoon cannon, followed by the stern-slipway factory ship) which together allowed whalers to target even the largest species of whales and to process them into valuable oil without even putting in to port. Altogether, it is estimated that some 1.5 million whales were killed in the Southern Ocean from 1904 to 1985, reducing their overall biomass from 43 million tons to around 6 million tons.[47] The outcome would have been even worse if conservationists had not stepped in to try to slow the killing. As early as the 1920s, steeply declining whale populations gave rise to coordinated attempts to set the industry on a more sustainable course, though to little overall effect. Quotas introduced by the International Whaling Commission (est. 1946) were largely ineffective, and

---

[45]Ruth H. Thurstan, Simon Brockington and Callum M. Roberts, 'The Effects of 118 Years of Industrial Fishing on UK Bottom Trawl Fisheries', *Nature Communications* (4 May 2010), 15. DOI:10.1038/ncomms1013.

[46]Roberts, *Unnatural History*, 145–60, 184–98.

[47]McNeill, *Something New*, 243; more generally J. N. Tønnessen and A. O. Johnsen, *The History of Modern Whaling* (London: Hurst, 1982).

even after the Commission shifted its focus towards conservation in 1964, its inability to enforce limits on recalcitrant nations critically undermined protective measures. Although matters had improved by around 1990, the result already amounted to a tragic failure of international conservation.[48] One can, of course, regard the gradual shift from exploitation towards conservation – which formed part of the wider movement to protect threatened species on land as well as sea – as evidence of a growing cultural aversion towards killing wild creatures. But most animals do not elicit the same level of sympathy as large, charismatic mammals. And even efforts to protect beloved species such as the blue or humpback whales illustrate a depressingly familiar pattern whereby attempts to preserve wildlife populations have tended to materialize long after serious damage has already been done.[49]

War, nature and violence

Before concluding, let us consider the environmental dimensions of a more conventional theme in the history of violence. It is often said that what characterized the era of 'total war' was the breakdown of boundaries between the military and civilian spheres, between the battlefront and the home front. Unlike previous wars, the world-spanning conflicts of the early twentieth century were won and lost not only on the battlefield but also in the factories and villages of belligerent countries. As societies sought to mobilize all of their resources for the production of violence, the deliberate targeting of enemy cities and civilians became an integral part of modern warfare. What is less commonly appreciated is how the boundaries between modern warfare and efforts to control nature also became increasingly blurred. As a number of studies have shown, these two endeavours evolved in a mutual relationship: while the growing capacity to manipulate the biophysical world expanded the scale of warfare, the pressures of 'total war' also led to more ambitious attempts to control the environment.[50]

Recent years have witnessed a surge of historical research on the connections between modern warfare and environmental change, from the extraction of strategic resources to problems of disease to the toxic

---

[48]Kurkpatrick Dorsey, *Whales and Nations: Environmental Diplomacy on the High Seas* (Seattle: University of Washington Press, 2013).

[49]Barrow, *Nature's Ghosts*; William M. Adams, *Against Extinction: The Story of Conservation* (London: Earthscan, 2004).

[50]See esp. Edmund Russell, *War and Nature: Fighting Humans and Insects with Chemicals from World War I to Silent Spring* (Cambridge: Cambridge University Press, 2001); Jacob Darwin Hamblin, *Arming Mother Nature: The Birth of Catastrophic Environmentalism* (Oxford: Oxford University Press, 2013).

legacies of industrialized conflict.[51] Some of the most intriguing insights have focused on the links between science and military power. The wars of the twentieth century encompassed more of the biophysical world than any previous conflicts in history. They rose thousands of feet into the sky, they plumbed the depths of the oceans and they stretched from the ice of the sub-Arctic to the tropical jungles of Asia. Achieving a greater knowledge of these environments was critical for mastering the many theatres of modern warfare. A better understanding of nature was also, of course, crucial for devising more effective means of killing. We are familiar with the story of the Manhattan Project, the race for nuclear weapons and even the long-term radioactive poisoning of nuclear test sites in the South Pacific (such as the American-controlled Marshall Islands, the French Polynesian atolls of Moruroa and Fangataufa). But the connections between science and military might have gone far beyond that. On a more general level, the development of weapons of mass destruction was tightly bound, both practically and ideologically, with large-scale interventions in the biophysical environment.

There was, for instance, an intimate link between the development of chemical weapons and the rise of modern pest control. Although nuclear arms serve as the very icon of a weapon of mass destruction, chemical weapons have actually killed far more people: 90,000 in the First World War and 350,000 in the Second (mostly resulting from the use of incendiary bombs, and not counting those who were murdered in Nazi gas chambers), compared to 100,000 victims of the two nuclear bombs.[52] Neither chemical weapons nor chemical pest control were new in the twentieth century. What was new was the scale on which people sought to destroy both human and natural foes.[53] As Edmund Russell argued in his innovative book on *War and Nature*, the two technologies co-evolved on numerous levels. Scientifically, they created overlapping fields of knowledge that drove each other forward and that expanded their operational scope. Institutionally, they were rooted in a nexus of interweaving civilian and military agencies in which breakthroughs in one area were rapidly transferred to the other.

---

[51]Richard P. Tucker et al. (eds), *Environmental Histories of the First World War* (Cambridge: Cambridge University Press, 2018); Simo Laakkonen et al. (eds), *The Long Shadows: A Global Environmental History of the Second World War* (Corvallis: Oregon State University Press, 2017); John R. McNeill and Corinna R. Unger (eds), *Environmental Histories of the Cold War* (Cambridge: Cambridge University Press, 2010); Richard P. Tucker and Edmund Russell (eds), *Natural Enemy, Natural Ally: Toward an Environmental History of Warfare* (Corvallis: Oregon State University Press, 2004); earlier insights into these connections were made by Michael Adas, *Machines as the Measure of Men: Science, Technology, and Ideologies of Western Dominance* (Ithaca: Cornell University Press, 1989).

[52]Russell, *War and Nature*, 3, 139–42. Most of the victims of incendiary bombs were in Japanese cities; in the Second World War, the only belligerents to use poison gas were Germany (in its extermination camps) and Japan (which reportedly deployed it in China).

[53]Russell, *War and Nature*, 7.

Ideologically, they generated a set of values that could be used to rationalize the large-scale annihilation of human and natural enemies alike.

These elemental connections between pesticides and chemical weapons span a large chunk of the twentieth century. The chemical arms race triggered by Germany's first deployment of chlorine gas in 1915 stimulated research into the use of lethal compounds not only as weapons but also as insecticides for agricultural or public health use. Between the wars, Germany's fearsome nerve gases were first stumbled upon by scientists searching for a more effective insect spray. During the Second World War, DDT was used as a chemical weapon of sorts by US forces desperate to reduce the number of military deaths caused by insect-borne diseases (at the time, malaria was claiming the lives of ten times more soldiers than combat in the Pacific theatre). After the war, DDT was used indiscriminately as a kind of miracle weapon against 'man's insect enemies', at least before Carson's intervention highlighted the enormous problems it caused. During the Cold War, as the two superpowers developed more potent chemical weapons for their respective arsenals, the US army spearheaded efforts to counter the problem of rising insect resistance to pesticides, which severely hampered the global campaign against malaria and was causing widespread difficulties on industrialized mono-cultural farms, whose vast fields planted in a single crop presented a veritable feast for certain pests.[54] In effect, the US army was engaged in an evolutionary arms race between bugs and scientists. The exigencies of large-scale technological warfare furnished a powerful motive for intervening more forcefully in nature, which itself provided potent new means for waging war.

Over the years, this alliance of environmental scientists and military planners devised ever-more ambitious means of enlisting nature in the waging of war. As the destructive potential of nuclear weapons increased, and as their actual deployment became correspondingly inconceivable, military leaders in the United States and Soviet Union sought other means to weaken and annihilate their enemies. Jacob Darwin Hamblin has shown in fascinating detail how American military agencies sought to devise an entirely new class of weapons for waging what NATO called 'environmental warfare': that is, the harnessing of geo-tectonic, climatic and biological processes for the goal of incapacitating enemy forces and killing as many people as possible.[55] Some of the ideas represented a variation on chemical or nuclear weapons, such as incendiary devices to set off enormous forest fires, or contaminating food crops and water supplies with the growing stockpile of radioactive waste. Others fell more under the category of biological weapons: spreading human and animal diseases or targeting specific links in enemy ecosystems to maximize economic or military disruption (such as through the introduction

---

[54]This paragraph is based on Russell, *War and Nature*, 87, 114–17, 155, passim.
[55]Hamblin, *Arming Mother Nature*.

of pests and bio-invaders that could devastate enemy crops or livestock herds). Still others were straight out of *Dr. Strangelove*: altering weather patterns to create floods or droughts, triggering artificial earthquakes and tsunamis with nuclear explosions and even using nuclear weapons to melt the polar icecaps and inundate low-lying cities. All of these initiatives extended the logic of 'total war' to the biophysical world as a whole.

Fortunately, the superpowers never used such nightmarish weapons against each other, but these projects nonetheless had important consequences, most of them unintended. For one thing, they raised suspicions that American and Soviet scientists were already more than capable of carrying out massive environmental interference, which encouraged rumours and accusations that they were doing so even when they were not. Not that they refrained entirely: the United States deliberately destroyed forests and enemy crops with chemicals during the Vietnam War, and indeed tried to meddle with the weather there as well.[56] The massive and sustained spraying of Agent Orange as a 'strategic defoliant' has had devastating long-term health and environmental effects in Vietnam. But the secrecy surrounding environmental warfare programmes also spawned all kinds of errant rumours about the United States spreading crop pests in the Eastern Bloc, the Soviets inadvertently unleashing epidemics on its own territory, or even the idea that the AIDS epidemic of the 1980s was the result of a US biological weapons experiment gone awry.

A second and perhaps more important consequence was the stimulation of a new awareness of the potential for worldwide human-induced environmental disaster. It is ironic that many of the scientists who sought to weaponize pests and diseases against enemy agricultural production were also some of the most vociferous proponents of biodiversity as a means of spreading risks and defending oneself against such threats. No less ironic is the way in which the global data and modelling systems that underpinned programmes to alter weather patterns and ocean currents were also what gave scientists a clearer line of sight on the global environmental changes (including greenhouse gas emissions) that were accelerating at the time. Years of research into environmental interactions and human vulnerabilities eventually fed into what Hamblin calls 'catastrophic environmentalism', or the idea that humans were unintentionally rushing headlong into a global environmental calamity. This mode of thinking is nowadays a hallmark of public discourse, one whose genealogy is usually traced back to the rise of environmental consciousness in reaction to the breakneck economic development and runaway population growth of the post-war era, and one whose history is conventionally signposted by events like the publication of

---

[56]Hamblin, *Arming Mother Nature*, 180–5, 202–6; see also Rebecca Pincus, '"To Prostitute the Elements": Weather Control and Weaponisation by US Department of Defense', *War & Society*, 36 (2017): 64–80.

Silent Spring, the fallout from Paul Ehrlich's best-selling *Population Bomb* or the Club of Rome's 1972 report on *The Limits to Growth*.[57] Far less widely recognized is the extent to which this modern environmental consciousness was rooted in Cold War attempts to wreak unprecedented levels of violence on enemy humans *and* nature.[58]

Conclusion

Among the various dimensions of violence that Pinker's account leaves out, the fate of the entire biophysical world beyond the flesh and blood of human bodies is a large omission. When we view the recent past through the lens of environmental history, the idea that violence has continually declined and that we are now living in the most peaceful time in human history seems at best an expression of tenacious optimism and at worst a case of wilful disregard. The history of the last two centuries – and in particular the decades since the middle of the twentieth century – has been characterized not so much by a greater sense of care for other living things as by an unprecedented assault on the global environment: its forests, soils, seas, animals and atmosphere. Despite the rise of environmental consciousness and rights-based animal protections, the recent past is marked by an increasingly determined effort by the world's most powerful human societies not just to alter nature to suit their needs but to subjugate it entirely, to place it at their disposal. At the same time, the quest to dominate nature has also given people an extraordinary capacity to wreak violence on each other, both of the 'slow' and of the more immediate variety. Worst of all, the damage is set to backfire. Human societies are, after all, an integral part of the biophysical environment. Despite our technological prowess, we still depend on an intricate web of natural processes to survive. When we meddle with these processes too persistently, when we exploit them too carelessly, we inevitably impair them. Environmental violence is ultimately violence towards humans as well.

---

[57]Paul R. Ehrlich, *The Population Bomb* (New York: Ballantine, 1968); Donna H. Meadows et al., *The Limits to Growth* (New York: Universe, 1972).
[58]This paragraph is drawn from Hamblin, *Arming Mother Nature*.

17

On cool reason and hot-blooded impulses

Violence and the history of emotion

Susan K. Morrissey

Emotion is not an explicit category of analysis in Steven Pinker's *The Better Angels of Our Nature: A History of Violence and Humanity*, but it is essential to his broader arguments. In positing the faculty of reason as the single most important driver of the alleged decline of violence in the West since the Enlightenment, he also attributes much of the underlying source of violence to untamed emotions, which he locates within the structures, systems and circuits of the brain and describes in terms of instincts, drives, urges and impulses. Though he does recognize the potentially positive, if more limited, roles of certain emotions, such as empathy, he consistently foregrounds the significance of the 'harder-boiled faculties' – reason, control, fairness – over the 'soft-hearted' empathy in overcoming what he calls the 'inner demons' of our nature. A binary opposition between reason and emotion thus shadows his historical narrative, in which reasoned self-control progressively displaces emotional anarchy, first among Western elites and then 'trickling down' unevenly to plebeians and the non-Western world. Pinker takes inspiration from Norbert Elias' *The Civilizing Process*, which was heavily influenced by Freud, an intellectual debt made explicit in the epigraph to chapter 3: 'It is impossible to overlook the extent to which civilization is built upon a renunciation of instinct.'[1] Drawing on Elias, Pinker also emphasizes the role of the state (the 'Leviathan') as integral to the array of forces he contends have combined to pacify our evolutionary heritage: a civilizing process, 'gentle commerce' (capitalism) and liberal-democratic norms, a humanitarian revolution, literacy and urbanization, and modern science and rationality.

In making a historical argument about the decline of violence, Pinker relies upon an ahistorical conceptualization of a universal human nature, including human emotions, accessed via the disciplines of evolutionary psychology, cognitive science and neuroscience. The book summarizes numerous psychological studies and experiments, with some relying on laboratory animals and many others, as he notes in passing, using readily available college students for their subjects.[2] For Pinker, universalism poses no contradiction: 'Among the beliefs about the world of which we can be highly confident', he writes, 'is that other people are conscious in the same way that we are. Other people are made of the same stuff, seek the same kinds of goals, and react with external signs of pleasure and pain to the kinds of events that cause pain and pleasure in each of us'.[3] For most historians, such beliefs seem patently naïve: our discipline is interested not only in temporality and change but also in cultural and historical contingency. One of the first lessons we often try to teach our students is *not* to presume that historical subjects are just like them: their motives and goals, their experiences of pain and pleasure, their consciousness of self, may in fact be radically different.[4]

In this volume and elsewhere, scholars have offered wide-ranging critiques of Pinker's thesis by presenting historical evidence to refute specific claims and by challenging his statistics, methods, definitions and so forth. This chapter instead draws on research in the history of emotion to interrogate some of his foundational categories and to suggest some alternative perspectives. I will begin with a brief overview of this burgeoning field, showing its relevance to an assessment of Pinker's claims, before turning to two case studies. The first probes Pinker's conceptualization of reason

---

[1]Steven Pinker, *The Better Angels of our Nature: A History of Violence and Humanity* (London: Allen Lane, 2011), 71; on 'harder-boiled faculties', 691; on 'hard-headed' reason versus 'soft-hearted' empathy, 784; on 'trickling down', 87.

[2]Pinker, *Better Angels*, 771.

[3]See also: 'Throughout this book I have assumed that human nature, in the sense of the cognitive and emotional inventory of our species, has been constant over the ten-thousand-year window in which declines of violence are visible, and that all differences in behavior among societies have strictly environmental causes.' Pinker, *Better Angels*, 218, 739.

[4]Even physical pain is highly variable in its experience, understanding and valuation across time and space. For recent discussions, see Rob Boddice, *Pain: A Very Short Introduction* (Oxford: Oxford University Press, 2017); Robert Boddice (ed.), *Pain and Emotion in Modern History* (Basingstoke: Palgrave Macmillan, 2014); and Joanna Bourke, *The Story of Pain: From Prayer to Painkillers* (Oxford: Oxford University Press, 2014).

as a critical force in countering the 'brawn' of human emotion, a binary opposition that not only underpins his thesis on the decline of violence but also reinforces his own authorial position as the voice of scientific reason. The second turns to the phenomenon of revenge, one of Pinker's five 'inner demons' that he likens to an evolutionary 'button'. His approach not only flattens and decontextualizes the history of revenge but also raises historical objections and ethical concerns.

The history of emotion

For Pinker, emotions are a biological universal, produced by the evolutionary processes of natural selection and designed to promote the survival and propagation of the genome. The emotion of disgust, for example, is not learned but innate, an adaptation that evolved as an avoidance response to dangerous animal products. Likewise innate are the fear of snakes (which is not learned, he asserts, but imperfectly unlearned in childhood), and a preference for the landscape of the savannah, humans' original habitat. In sum, emotions are 'adaptive, well-engineered software modules that work in harmony with the intellect and are indispensable to the functioning of the whole mind'.[5] While Pinker claims to reject a 'romantic' opposition between intellect and emotion, pointing out the lack of sharp lines separating thinking from feeling and the way emotion has its own 'cold logic', he nonetheless perpetuates a hierarchy in which emotion is, in his words, 'quintessentially irrational'. Agency effectively lies in biology with emotions 'triggered' by a 'propitious moment', and, in turn, triggering a 'cascade' of sub-goals (i.e. thinking and acting). As he summarizes: 'each human emotion mobilizes the mind and body to meet one of the challenges of living and reproducing in the cognitive niche.'[6] Two interconnected points are essential for our purposes. First, citing the influential but disputed findings of psychologist Paul Ekman, Pinker claims that 'the emotions of all normal members of our species are played on the same keyboard'; the so-called 'basic' emotions – the number is contested among those who accept the premise, but the original six were fear, anger, disgust, surprise, happiness and sadness – are accessible through universal patterns of facial expression. Second, cultural differences in emotional expression or behaviour are superficial, having no significant relation to how people actually feel. It simply does not matter whether a given language does or does not have a word for a specific emotion because emotions themselves are a biological substrate.[7] This framework provides

---

[5] Steven Pinker, How the Mind Works (New York: Norton, 1997), 370, 375–90.
[6] Pinker, How the Mind Works, 364, 373–4.
[7] Pinker, How the Mind Works, 365–9. While Pinker depicts Ekman's claims as widely accepted, other scholars describe widespread criticism and rejection, including among psychologists. For

the scaffolding of Pinker's argument, allowing him to impose the categories of modern psychology onto historical subjects, societies and processes.

The history of emotion, a distinctive subfield that emerged in the 1980s and expanded rapidly over the next decades, shares little common ground with Pinker's universalist approach.[8] This was not always the case. Historians had long referred in passing to emotions in their work, whether as a contributing factor in a historical subject's motivation or even as an ascribed quality of a group or society, but there had been little attempt – with a handful of major exceptions – to grapple explicitly with emotion as a conceptual category or historical force.[9] In some respects, this is not surprising: until the 1960s, professional historians had tended to privilege the operations of reason, focusing on high politics, war and diplomacy, and great men. The shift to social and then cultural history, the rise of women's and gender history, and conversations between historians and anthropologists helped to spark interest in emotion itself, which was conceived not as timeless, innate or irrational, but as culturally and historically constructed.

Central to the emergent field was the sphere of language, precisely what Pinker discounts as irrelevant, with scholars theorizing emotion as a complex, multifaceted process involving such factors as cognition and understanding, communication, social status and relations, power and (social) action in the world. A growing body of anthropological, historical and other humanistic research soon revealed major variations in emotional life and expression across time and space, with many languages possessing distinctive emotion concepts that do not translate easily and change over time. Even the English word 'emotion' only dates to the seventeenth century, when it was introduced from the French and began to displace an earlier language of passions and affections, before being appropriated as an overarching category by the new science of psychology in the nineteenth century.[10] This research further

---

the most fundamental assessment, see Ruth Leys, *The Ascent of Affect: Genealogy and Critique* (Chicago: University of Chicago Press, 2017), 76–128. For critical overviews, see Jan Plamper, *The History of Emotions: An Introduction* (Oxford: Oxford University Press, 2015), 147–63; and Rob Boddice, *The History of Emotions* (Manchester: Manchester University Press, 2018), 106–20.

[8]In addition to Plamper, *History of Emotions*, and Boddice, *History of Emotions*, see Barbara H. Rosenwein and Riccardo Cristiani, *What Is the History of Emotions?* (London: Polity, 2018); and Ute Frevert, *Emotions in History: Lost and Found* (Budapest: Central European University Press, 2011).

[9]The most important progenitors were the founders of the Annales School, Marc Bloch and Lucien Febvre, writing amid the rise of fascism. See especially Lucien Febvre, 'Sensibility and History: How to Reconstitute the Emotional Life of the Past', in Peter Burke (ed.), *A New Kind of History: From the Writings of Febvre*, trans. K. Folca (New York: Harper & Row, 1973), 12–26. It was originally published as 'La sensibilité et l'histoire: Comment reconstituer la vie affective d'autrefois', *Annales d'histoire sociale*, 3 (1941): 5–20. For further discussion of these figures and the prehistory of the field, see Plamper, *History of Emotion*, 40–60.

[10]The definition of emotion remains contested and fuzzy, even within psychology itself. Thomas Dixon, 'Emotion: The History of a Keyword in Crisis', *Emotion Review* (October 2012): 338–44.

highlights how emotion has functioned as a discursive category, one that modern Western culture has persistently relegated to the lower element in a series of interconnected binary oppositions: reason/emotion, rational/ irrational, mind/body, masculine/feminine, culture/nature, civilized/savage. It is worth stressing that these binaries are neither innate nor unchanging, but they are important here precisely because of their centrality to Pinker's thesis.

Historians of emotion take the relationship between the life sciences and the humanities very seriously. In his pathbreaking introduction to the field, Jan Plamper dissects the polarity between universalism and social constructivism with two long chapters dedicated to the life sciences and anthropology, respectively. The apogee of social constructivism occurred during the cultural turn of the 1990s, and Plamper depicts the dyad as more of a spectrum, a metaphor that holds open the possibility of productive compromise. After years of immersing himself in the science, however, he is pessimistic about the potential for substantive interdisciplinarity between historians and life scientists, citing less the divergence between universalism and constructivism than more fundamental differences in methods and research questions.[11] Other historians of emotion, like Rob Boddice, have pointed with more optimism to recent trends in neuroscience that emphasize the plasticity of the brain, a development with parallels in the fields of epigenetics and microevolution: scientific attention has been focusing increasingly on the complex entanglement of human biology with environment and experience, which has created an opening for a 'biocultural' view of the human being, in which the body itself is not a biological constant but 'worlded' and historical. As Boddice stresses, these approaches broadly mesh with historians' interest in the nexus of experience with historical change.[12] At the moment, then, a new dialogue between neuroscience and history has the potential to unfold amid a broader subversion of the polarity between nature and culture. Emotions are at the forefront of these considerations precisely because they intersect the material-neurological-bodily and the cultural-historical-experiential dimensions, thus holding the

---

See also Thomas Dixon, *From Passions to Emotion: The Creation of a Secular Psychological Category* (Cambridge: Cambridge University Press, 2003).

[11]Plamper emphasizes significant practical challenges: true interdisciplinarity would require the historian to cultivate a depth of knowledge in other fields that is difficult to achieve and maintain, all the more that the sciences tend to advance and discard hypotheses with some frequency as knowledge advances. See Plamper, *History of Emotion*, 163, 240–50.

[12]Boddice, *History of Emotion*, 142–67, 212–14; and Rob Boddice, *A History of Feelings* (London: Reaktion Books, 2019). See also the discussion in a roundtable of leading historians of emotion (Nicole Eustace, Eugenia Lean, Julie Livingston, Jan Plamper, William Reddy, and Barbara Rosenwein) in 'AHR Conversation: The Historical Study of Emotion', *The American Historical Review* (December 2012): 1487–531, esp. 1504–14.

potential to bridge the binary opposition itself.[13] Pinker – a universalist – is not engaged in this project.

The history of emotion is too large a field to summarize here, so I will briefly sketch some of its essential contours and leading figures in order to establish a framework through which we can critically assess Pinker's thesis. The first modern scholars to call explicitly for the history of emotions as a self-described field were Peter Stearns and Carol Stearns in the 1980s. Their major innovation was to distinguish emotion, which they defined as 'a complex set of interactions' involving both physiological and cognitive processes that give rise to feelings, from 'emotionology', a new term which encompassed 'the attitudes or standards that a society, or a definable group within a society, maintains toward basic emotions and their appropriate expression'. Whereas 'emotion' was not accessible to historical research, they argued, 'emotionology' certainly was. While this approach did occasionally veer towards a notion of emotion (and even 'basic emotions') as an implicitly innate and universal sphere, a kind of material substructure to emotional norms (emotionology) as cultural superstructure, it nonetheless opened a path for the historical study of emotional expression, attitudes and standards within a given society, insisting both on the historicity of these styles and on their active significance to all facets of experience, social life and historical change.[14] The term 'emotionology' never stuck, but the programmatic call encouraged new ways of approaching the social history of particular emotions, such as anger, fear or love, and opened up broader questions around emotional norms, including patterns of emotional restraint (control) or effusion, and the dynamics of change over time.

A decade later, the historian and anthropologist William Reddy made some of the most important and lasting interventions in the field, theorizing the character of emotion as simultaneously individual and social and effectively collapsing the nature/culture dyad. Rejecting the extremes of cultural relativism and seeking to develop a theory of emotional change, he argued against the effective partition of emotion as bodily affect from emotional expression as discursive construct. In its place, he advanced

---

[13]A prominent figure in neurohistory is Daniel Lord Smail, *On Deep History and the Brain* (Berkeley: University of California Press, 2008). See also his chapter in this volume, 'The Inner Demons of *The Better Angels of Our Nature*'. Peter N. Stearns has recently expressed concern that historians are failing to reach out sufficiently to their colleagues in the sciences. See his 'Shame, and a Challenge for Emotions History', *Emotion Review*, 8, no. 3 (July 2016): 197–206.

[14]See Peter N. Stearns and Carol Z. Stearns, 'Clarifying the History of Emotions and Emotional Standards', *The American Historical Review*, 90, no. 4 (October 1985): 813–36, here 813. See also Peter N. Stearns and Carol Z. Stearns, *Anger: The Struggle for Emotional Control in America's History* (Chicago: University of Chicago Press, 1989); Peter N. Stearns and Jan Lewis (eds), *An Emotional History of the United States* (New York: New York University Press, 1998); and Peter N. Stearns, *Shame: A Brief History* (Urbana, Chicago, and Springfield: University of Illinois Press, 2017).

the concept of 'emotives', arguing that emotion statements (such as 'I am angry'), are not merely descriptive or constative, but 'do things to the world. Emotives are themselves instruments for directly changing, building, hiding, intensifying emotions'.[15] As Boddice succinctly summarizes, an emotive 'represents an individual's attempt to translate inward feelings through cultural conventions in order to try to match the two. It is a process of navigation, finding a way to bring forth what one feels in accord with the expectations one is obliged to meet'.[16] Reddy emphasizes how emotives are generative, a mode of 'emotional self-shaping' and 'self-exploration', but also a source of suffering, in that they inevitably fail, to greater or lesser degrees, to encompass the feelings fully. Of similar importance was his concept of the 'emotional regime', defined as 'the set of normative emotions and the official rituals, practices, and emotives that express and inculcate them; a necessary underpinning of any stable political regime'.[17] Although some scholars have criticized how Reddy links emotional to political regimes, especially the modern nation-state, his conceptual apparatus remains foundational to the field.

Finally, the historian Barbara Rosenwein has elaborated another influential concept, 'emotional communities', which she defines as 'groups – usually but not always social groups – that have their own particular values, modes of feeling, and ways to express those feelings'. These groups are historically specific and highly variable in form and size; some may overlap, with individuals typically able to move among different ones. A crucial point, she stresses, is that 'emotional communities need not be "emotional". They simply share important norms concerning the emotions that they value and deplore and the modes of expressing them'.[18] In contrast to the implicitly top-down connotations of 'regimes', the concept of 'community' privileges a bottom-up model, one in which power is still at stake but also more dispersed within a given society. Though Rosenwein recognizes the various ways emotions are expressed, through language but also voice, gesture and bodily signs, she has developed methodologies around the identification and analysis of emotional vocabularies, including the complex ways multiple emotion words (broadly in the sense of emotives) can work together within

---

[15]William M. Reddy, 'Against Constructivism: The Historical Ethnography of Emotions', *Current Anthropology*, 38, no. 3 (June 1997): 327–51, here 331. He further developed these ideas in his monograph, *The Navigation of Feeling: A Framework for the History of Emotions* (New York: Cambridge University Press, 2001). See also his *The Invisible Code: Honor and Sentiment in Postrevolutionary France, 1815-1848* (Berkeley: University of California Press, 1997); and *The Making of Romantic Love: Longing and Sexuality in Europe, South Asia, and Japan, 900-1200 CE* (Chicago: University of Chicago Press, 2012).

[16]Boddice, *History of Emotion*, 63.

[17]Reddy, *Navigation of Feeling*, 129; Boddice, *History of Emotion*, 70; and 'AHR Conversation: The Historical Study of Emotion', 1497.

[18]Barbara H. Rosenwein, *Generations of Feeling: A History of Emotions, 600-1700* (Cambridge: Cambridge University Press, 2016), 3–4.

narratives.[19] In a recent monograph, she has analysed diverse emotional communities from the post-classical era into the early-modern period in Europe, exploring shifting understandings of particular emotions as well as varied valuations of expressivity and restraint. One explicit goal is to refute the notion of a linear historical progression towards increased emotional control.[20]

This last point is of particular relevance to a consideration of Pinker's thesis, especially his uncritical appropriation of Elias' civilizing process, which is a teleological account of a shift in emotional norms that depends upon a caricatured view of the medieval world as emotionally uncontrolled and childish, hence violent.[21] In a landmark article from 2002, 'Worrying about Emotions in History', Rosenwein, who is a medievalist, attacked this account, calling for modernists to rethink their views of both modernity and emotion. Though directed at Elias, her critique can be applied almost literally to Pinker's thesis:

> In brief, the narrative is this: the history of the West is the history of increasing emotional restraint. Greece and Rome may be quickly dismissed: did not Homer sing of the sweet delights of anger? The Middle Ages had the emotional life of a child: unadulterated, violent, public, unashamed. The modern period (variously defined) brought with it self-discipline, control, and suppression.[22]

Ironically, Pinker even quotes this very passage from Homer,[23] engaging here and elsewhere in precisely the kind of basic error that Rosenwein has identified in Elias' work: 'I came to the topic of the history of emotions because when I read Norbert Elias, rather late in my career, I knew that he

---

[19]As she notes, historians mainly work with the words left in the written record. Barbara H. Rosenwein, 'Problems and Methods in the History of Emotions', *Passions in Context: International Journal for the History and Theory of Emotion* (January 2010): 1–32. Other leading scholars in the field have pursued a related approach. See Ute Frevert et al., *Emotional Lexicons: Continuity and Change in the Vocabulary of Feeling* (Oxford: Oxford University Press, 2014).

[20]Rosenwein, *Generations of Feeling*.

[21]For further discussion, see also the chapter in this volume by Philip Dwyer and Elizabeth Roberts-Pedersen, 'Norbert Elias, Steven Pinker and the "Civilising Process"'. Pinker acknowledges in passing that 'the childishness of the medievals was surely exaggerated', but nonetheless relies on this metaphor, later applying it as well to the 'developing world'. Pinker, *Better Angels*, 82.

[22]Barbara H. Rosenwein, 'Worrying about Emotions in History', *The American Historical Review*, 107, no. 3 (June 2002): 821–45, esp. 827. Rosenwein also critiques the modernist lens of Peter Stearns and Carol Stearns (823–6). For a reply, see Peter N. Stearns, 'Modern Patterns in Emotion History', in Peter N. Stearns and Susan Matt (eds), *Doing Emotions History* (Urbana: University of Illinois Press, 2014), 17–40, esp. 22–4.

[23]Pinker, *Better Angels*, 56, 638. For a rereading of Homer's *Iliad* with an eye to revising our modern understanding of the text and its key emotions, including anger, see Boddice, *A History of Feelings*, 21–33.

was wrong. He was wrong for the most elementary of reasons: he didn't know how to read his sources. Rather than contextualize his texts, he culled phrases that conformed to his theory.'[24]

Rosenwein's insights help to illuminate a fundamental problem in Pinker's historical project that has implications for scientific research. Even as he denies a significant role for language in shaping human emotion, reading his sources without concern for the most basic historical methodology of source criticism, he fully assumes the transparency and universality of words – culling passages on violence, often dependent upon English translations, to match his desired historical narrative. The historian of early America, Nicole Eustace, has further argued that the insights gained from the historical study of emotion have real relevance for the practices of experimental psychology, which has wrongly presumed the universal and transparent meanings of the contemporary emotion words used in their research. 'Scientists need to understand', she writes, 'that the reason they can't locate "anger" in any one neural location is that the word (and the concept it encodes) is infinitely culturally malleable'. Far from being a radical social constructivist, Eustace accepts that there are 'loci for the processing of stimuli and that there are biological commonalities that underlie affect. Without that crucial caveat, the historical variability of emotion becomes meaningless, the simple result of random electrical activity in the brain'.[25]

While Rosenwein's main purpose was to reclaim the medieval world from its inaccurate representation as childlike, violent and uncontrolled, the (emotional) 'grand narrative' she critiques is not limited to the history of Europe but has multiple incarnations, most perniciously in the history of colonialism. In her work on revolutionary America, for example, Eustace was likewise

> struck by the traditional opposition between emotion and reason and by the oft-advanced proposition that civilized people were better at controlling their emotions than savage ones. For eighteenth-century British imperialists, this meant that Europeans were superior to Africans and Native Americans. . . . From the eighteenth century to the twentieth, to be civilized and modern was to be farther removed from unbridled emotion and untrammelled nature.[26]

Attentive to this binary, Eustace does not simply expose the discursive linkage of emotional restraint to narratives of progress and civilization but also demonstrates their active role in the exercise of social and political power, including the legitimation of mass violence against ('savage') Native

---

[24]'AHR Conversation: The Historical Study of Emotion', 1493.
[25]'AHR Conversation: The Historical Study of Emotion', 1507.
[26]'AHR Conversation: The Historical Study of Emotion', 1490.

Americans, in colonial and revolutionary America.[27] As a historian of Russia, these categories are deeply familiar to me as well: Russia has often been seen – and has seen itself – as 'backwards' in relation to a projected (mythic) 'Europe', a binary that has shaped stereotypes of excessive violence, savagery and cruelty (and helped to mask Western Europe's own violence, especially in the colony[28]). At the same time, Russia was also a colonial power that claimed the mantle of civilization in justifying its rule over Central Asia and the Caucasus.[29] The mapping of civilization, with its normative connotations around emotional control, has had a tremendous impact in the modern era. Operating through gendered, racialized, social, ethnic, national and other mechanisms, it articulates relations of power and has routinely served to legitimize – and veil – the violence of the 'civilized' against the 'savage', 'primitive' and/or 'immature'.

In his account of the making of modernity, Pinker relies uncritically on these same binaries, applies them across temporal, social and geographical contexts, and draws 'scientific' conclusions on their basis. Describing the people of medieval Europe as 'gross' with the habits of a three-year-old, he asserts that Western European elites progressively learned the habits of self-control and consideration, toning up this underused but innate human faculty. This civilizing process failed to take place, however, in 'the lower strata of the socioeconomic scale, and the inaccessible or inhospitable territories of the globe'.[30] His mapping of world civilization begins in Europe, where, along with the unruly lower classes, particular regions – Ireland and Finland followed by the south and the east – are progressively more 'stroppy' and violent, with 'rugged hills and valleys' producing 'blood-soaked' histories. Asserting that peaceable restraint has ostensibly spread outwards from Europe's northern industrial countries, Pinker observes that 'a gradient of lawlessness extending to eastern Europe and the mountainous Balkans is still visible'.[31] This mapping, which has a history, is neither objective nor value neutral.[32] The last reference, for example, plays on a pernicious stereotype of the Balkans as the home to

---

[27]Nicole Eustace, *Passion Is the Gale: Emotion, Power, and the Coming of the American Revolution* (Chapel Hill: University of North Carolina Press, 2008); and her *1812: War and the Passions of Patriotism* (Philadelphia: University of Pennsylvania Press, 2012).

[28]See Choi Chatterjee, 'Imperial Incarcerations: Ekaterina Breshko-Breshkovskaia, Vinayak Damodar Savarkar, and the Original Sins of Modernity', *Slavic Review*, 74, no. 4 (Winter 2015): 850–72.

[29]I refer to Europe here as an abstract projection associated with progress and modernity rather than as a literal geographical or historical entity. An influential text that shaped the image of Russia as Europe's 'other' was Marquis de Custine, *La Russie en 1839* (1843).

[30]Pinker, *Better Angels*, 82–7, 97.

[31]Pinker, *Better Angels*, 102, 104, 109.

[32]See Larry Wolff, *Inventing Eastern Europe: The Map of Civilization on the Mind of the Enlightenment* (Stanford: Stanford University Press, 1994). For some lasting implications, see Mark Steinberg, 'Emotions History in Eastern Europe', in Stearns and Matt (eds), *Doing Emotions History*, 74–99.

supposedly primitive peoples naturally prone to violence, a stereotype that has actively hindered historical understanding of the wars of the 1990s and the Bosnian genocide.[33]

Pinker then projects a similar absence of civilized self-control onto other regions of the world, including Africa and Asia, betraying abject ignorance about non-Western histories and cultures. In Pinker's narrative, colonialism becomes a mostly positive, civilizing force – bringing government and legality, however imperfect – with decolonization producing a 'decivilizing anarchy'.[34] Put simply, his account reproduces the self-justifying rhetoric of colonialism as a 'civilizing project' and whitewashes the myriad violences of colonialist regimes and their long-term impact on postcolonial societies, subjects that have been amply documented by historians such as Caroline Elkins.[35] His paternalistic voice comes through especially well in one passing comment, in which he blames violence and failures of political reform on a lack of the requisite (adult) norms of self-control. His word choice (here italicized) is revealing: 'They [unspoken norms of civilized behaviour] may explain why today it is so hard to *impose* liberal democracy on countries in the developing world that have not *outgrown* their superstitions, warlords, and feudal tribes.'[36] With violence given age-old, local, naturalized and biological roots in particular populations (thus projected onto 'them' and away from 'us'), there is little acknowledgement of other causal dynamics that might challenge this benign account of a pacific, peace-loving and rational West: racism, systemic economic exploitation, resource extraction, the international military industrial complex, active support for repressive governments and extensive military intervention and war-making. The history of emotions can help to expose the inner workings of Pinker's text, especially its iteration of a long-established and highly ideological conceptual framework built on the binary of reason/emotion, along with

---

[33]Ascribing the violence to 'ancient' hatreds, for example, obstructs recognition of the modern mechanisms of nationalist mobilization. The stereotype also informed the Western 'humanitarian' intervention. On the discursive construction of the Balkans as Europe's primitive other, see Maria Todorova, *Imagining the Balkans*, updated edn (New York: Oxford University Press, 2009); and Malica Bakić-Hayden, 'Nesting Orientalisms: The Case of Former Yugoslavia', *Slavic Review*, 54, no. 4 (Winter 1995): 917–31.

[34]Describing 'degenerations' in former colonies, he identifies two 'zones' in which, he claims, 'the Civilizing Process went into reverse: the developing world, and the 1960s'. Pinker, *Better Angels*, 97, 108, 376.

[35]For further discussion of colonial violence, see the chapter in this volume by Caroline Elkins, 'The "Moral Effect" of Legalized Lawlessness: British Imperial Violence and the Middle East'. See also her *Imperial Reckoning: The Untold Story of Britain's Gulag in Kenya* (New York: Owl Books, 2005). Much of this violence occurred far from the metropolitan centres, which allowed many people there to choose not to see it in the first place. Among the most brutal sites of mass European violence in a colonial setting was the Belgian Congo, which did briefly break through into the (Western) public eye. See Adam Hochschild, *King Leopold's Ghost: A Story of Greed, Terror and Heroism in Colonial Africa* (Boston: Houghton Mifflin, 1998).

[36]My emphases: note the coercive implications of 'impose' and the infantilization of 'outgrow'. Pinker, *Better Angels*, 223.

its myriad variations – self-control/instinctual effusion, civilization/savagery, progress/backwardness.

Cool reason

At the core of Pinker's analysis of violence is a notion of an innate human nature that is neither inherently evil nor inherently good, possessing both 'inner demons' – predation, dominance, revenge, sadism and ideology[37] – and 'better angels' – empathy, self-control, a moral sense and reason. It is the last factor that he sees as the primary driver of the supposed decline in violence. Because 'the other angels have been with us for as long as we have been human', he suggests, their role in countering our 'demons' is inevitably secondary. While empathy is 'a circle that may be stretched', and self-control 'a muscle that may be exercised', both are ultimately finite, constrained by (evolutionary) limits and neurophysiology. Reason, in contrast, is 'an open-ended combinatorial system, an engine for generating an unlimited number of new ideas. Once it is programmed with a basic self-interest and an ability to communicate with others, its own logic will impel it, in the fullness of time, to respect the interests of ever-increasing numbers of others. It is reason too that can always take note of the shortcomings of previous exercises of reasoning, and update and improve itself in response'.[38] In Pinker's narrative, therefore, the civilizing process 'toned up' the faculty of self-control he claims was so lacking in the violent medieval world; the Scientific Revolution and the Enlightenment then enabled a kind of re/programming generated by reason that – accelerated by factors such as literacy, urbanization and advances in intelligence (he emphasizes IQ) – promoted the forward march of progress, including the decline of violence. Note the governing metaphor he chooses – reason as (emotionless) computer.

This concept of reason underpins his linear, often triumphalist account of historical progress. Quoting in an epigraph the eponymous line from Martin Luther King's oft-cited 'I have a dream' speech, Pinker celebrates the grand 'logic' of reason unfolding over 'the fullness of time' achieving an ever-widening circle of inclusion.[39] However, he ignores King's own emphasis on the 'fierce urgency of now', which was articulated in the same

---

[37]'Ideology' differs qualitatively from these other categories, which are closer to what Pinker depicts as instincts or urges, and his logic seems to be that ideology (by which he means Marxism, socialism, nationalism, fascism) is simply irrational and bad. By defining ideology in this way, rather than as a coherent world view, he erases ideology from his own political stance. Pinker, *Better Angels*, 671–87.

[38]Pinker, *Better Angels*, 808–9.

[39]The full epigraph: 'I have a dream that one day this nation will rise up and live out the true meaning of its creed: "We hold these truths to be self-evident: that all men are created equal"'. Pinker, *Better Angels*, 456.

speech at the March on Washington in August 1963 and again four years later in his Sermon on Vietnam. Rejecting gradualism, King refused to wait patiently, insisted on the imperative to act and challenged systemic forms of oppression.[40] Taking King's quotation out of context, Pinker distorts its vision of historical change achieved through subaltern demand, a vision with a history and historiography,[41] and instead describes the 1960s as a time of 'decivilization'.[42] This vision was perhaps most forcefully articulated by Frederick Douglass in a 1857 speech:

> The whole history of the progress of human liberty shows that all concessions yet made to her august claims have been born of earnest struggle. . . . Those who profess to favor freedom and yet deprecate agitation are men who want crops without plowing up the ground; they want rain without thunder and lightning. . . . Power concedes nothing without a demand. It never did and it never will.[43]

For Pinker, in contrast, there is neither urgency nor demand but rather the benevolence of the gift: 'the Age of Reason and the Enlightenment brought many violent institutions to a sudden end', he thus writes, referring to slavery, torture and the death penalty.[44] Citing Thomas Jefferson's moral vision (without reference to his well-documented practices as a slave owner), he privileges the reasoned, humanitarian concerns of elites as the main motive force for progress.[45] Irrespective of the accuracy of such

---

[40]The Martin Luther King Jr. Research and Education Institute at Stanford University has reproduced the texts and audio of the two speeches. See https://kinginstitute.stanford.edu/king-papers/documents/i-have-dream-address-delivered-march-washington-jobs-and-freedom; and https://kinginstitute.stanford.edu/king-papers/documents/beyond-vietnam.

[41]For a recent intervention that centres Black agency through US history, see 'The 1619 Project', *The New York Times Magazine*, 18 August 2019, https://pulitzercenter.org/sites/default/files/ful l_issue_of_the_1619_project.pdf. See also Priyamvada Gopal's counter-history of the British empire, in which she documents the active political agency of colonial subjects and the enslaved in claiming emancipation and their critical roles in shaping the purportedly Western principles of freedom, equality and tolerance. Priyamvada Gopal, *Insurgent Empire: Anticolonial Resistance and British Dissent* (London: Verso, 2019).

[42]This section is followed by one on the 1990s – a pivotal period in the rise of mass incarceration in the United States – as a time of 'recivilization', driven in part by 'broken-windows' policing. See Pinker, *Better Angels*, 127–38, 138–54.

[43]Frederick Douglass, 'If There Is No Struggle, There Is No Progress', (1857), https://www.bla ckpast.org/african-american-history/1857-frederick-douglass-if-there-no-struggle-there-no-progress/.

[44]It is worth pointing out that these institutions continue to thrive across the world, including in the United States, but Pinker's mode of argumentation allows him to depict such facts as outliers, noise in the data or products of some form of 'backwardness'. Pinker, *Better Angels*, 190. For further discussion, see Philip Dwyer, 'Pinker's (Mis)Representation of the Enlightenment, History, and Violence', in this volume.

[45]Pinker, *Better Angels*, 186. On Jefferson and slavery, see Annette Gordon-Reed, *Thomas Jefferson and Sally Hemings: An American Controversy* (Charlottesville: University Press of Virginia, 1997); and her *The Hemingses of Monticello: An American Family* (New York: W.W. Norton,

claims, which innumerable historians have disputed, his description of the time frame as 'sudden' deserves particular scrutiny because it exposes his authorial position. To take just one obvious example, the 'sudden' abolition of slavery in the Americas took many decades after the Enlightenment (and a devastating civil war in the United States); that is, it took the entire lifetimes of countless enslaved human beings.[46] Of course, this objection may be dismissed as unscientific (and emotional): What are a few decades to the scientist scrutinizing human history over the millennia? Yet Pinker's birds-eye perspective reveals the essential quietism at the heart of his narrative, a quietism that forms part of an emotional economy: a *trust* in the self-correcting 'logic' of reason, a *confidence* in the benign effects of the state (the 'Leviathan') and an intense *satisfaction* at what 'we' have achieved. Pinker frequently uses the first-person plural pronoun, sometimes referring to humanity but often to a particular subset to which he numbers himself, an apparent descendant of the other great men he celebrates:

> When a large enough community of free, rational agents confers on how a society should run its affairs, steered by logical consistency and feedback from the world, their consensus will veer in certain directions. Just as we don't have to explain why molecular biologists discovered that DNA has four bases – given that they were doing their biology properly, and given that DNA really does have four bases, in the long run they could hardly have discovered anything else – we may not have to explain why enlightened thinkers would eventually argue against African slavery, cruel punishments, despotic monarchs, and the execution of witches and heretics. With enough scrutiny by disinterested, rational, and informed thinkers, these practices cannot be justified indefinitely.[47]

This perspective has contributed to the feelings of disquiet and outright indignation that his books have provoked among some readers (including among historians) and the feelings of adulation among others.[48] My language here is deliberate: feelings are central to the book – its arguments, its authorial tone, its claim to authoritative (scientific) status and its

---

2008). Pinker also neglects a large critical scholarship on humanitarianism, including as an affective position, that rejects the narrative of the gift. See, for example, Talal Asad, 'Reflections on Violence, Law, and Humanitarianism', *Critical Inquiry*, 41 (Winter 2015): 390–427.
[46]My point does not even address additional questions about the nature of the 'abolition' of slavery: its partial preservation in the Thirteenth Amendment of the US Constitution; Jim Crow and mass incarceration; and the systemic use of forced labour in colonial settings and many countries today, including the United States. See, for example, Michelle Alexander, *The New Jim Crow: Mass Incarceration in the Age of Colorblindness* (New York: New Press, 2010).
[47]Pinker, *Better Angels*, 217.
[48]Note the language of uplift and cheer in the blurbs of praise for Pinker's latest work, *Enlightenment Now: The Case for Reason, Science, Humanism, and Progress* (New York: Penguin Books, 2019).

reception. One critical reviewer even placed Pinker into a broad genre he called 'comfort history', designed to make readers feel better about the state of the world.[49] It is hardly coincidental that Pinker's final conclusion endorses our contemporary political and economic system by depicting capitalism ('gentle commerce') and liberal democracy as antidotes to violence (in contrast to the 'de-civilizing' protest movements of the 1960s and decolonization): 'the decline of violence is an accomplishment we can savor, and an impetus to cherish the forces of civilization and enlightenment that made it possible.'[50] A key mechanism at work here is an invitation to readers to identify themselves with Pinker's 'we' – the free, rational, enlightened and informed thinkers, who just happen to be, in his schema, the motive force of progress.[51]

Pinker positions himself as the cool and disinterested voice of scientific reason heroically combatting the forces of unreason, especially from humanists. This is made even more explicit in his latest volume, *Enlightenment Now*, which extends his arguments about the vast accomplishments of reason and the threats of 'counter-enlightenment' embodied in the irrational ideologies ('secular religions') of the far-right and, above all, the left, citing as an example a 'romantic Green movement' that 'subordinates human interests to a transcendent entity, the ecosystem'. In a chapter entitled 'progressophobia', he heatedly lashes out at his critics, not just by discounting them as motivated by irrationality and emotion (a 'phobia') but by caricaturing rather than addressing their concerns.[52] There is a long history of scientists claiming dispassionate objectivity, including in the modern discipline of history which formed in the nineteenth century with the development of new 'scientific' methods along with an ideal of the trained, professional historian as impartial arbiter, standing above the

---

[49]Stuart Carroll, 'Thinking with Violence', *History and Theory*, 55 (December 2017): 23–43. Similarly, Jennifer Mitzen argues that 'Pinker gradually feeds us a glossy modernity and clever statistics that steadily lead us away from political engagement by helping us feel good about ourselves and distant from the causes and victims of violence'. See her 'The Irony of Pinkerism', *Perspectives on Politics*, 11, no. 2 (June 2013): 525–8, here 528.

[50]Pinker, *Better Angels*, 841.

[51]In a blurb for *Enlightenment Now*, the billionaire businessman and philanthropist Bill Gates extols both books: 'The world *is* getting better, even if it doesn't always feel that way. I'm glad we have brilliant thinkers like Steven Pinker to help us see the big picture. *Enlightenment Now* . . . is my new favorite book of all time'. For a recent critique of elite philanthropy that also discusses 'Pinkering', a verb coined by TED Talk curator Bruno Giussani to denote the use of 'the long-run direction of human history to minimize, to delegitimize the concerns of those without power', see Anand Giridharadas, *Winners Take All: The Elite Charade of Changing the World* (New York: Alfred A. Knopf, 2018), 125–7.

[52]Rather than answering the substantive challenges raised in scholarly or other forums, he presents what he calls 'stylized versions of dialogues I have often had with questioners'. Pinker, *Enlightenment Now*, chaps. 3–4, esp. 32, 44–7.

fray, even as he – and it was most definitely a white man – was driven by passions.[53]

As Joanna Bourke, a fellow contributor to this volume, has recently emphasized, 'the scientific self is also a feeling self. The most heralded trait of scientists – "objectivity" – is itself an emotion involving a feeling of restraint and a striving for repetition.' She goes on to describe the 'emotional economy of science', including a 'disdain of "hot" language and a cultivation of composure'. In an article about the field of ballistics research during and after the Second World War, Bourke shows how scientists distanced themselves from the real subject of their work – the precise and devastating effect of weapons such as dumdum bullets and napalm upon the human body. In the process, 'violent agency' was attributed to the technologies or the military, but not to the people who actually developed, refined and 'improved' the weapons.

> Although the central job of ballistics scientists is the 'effective production of wounds', this is not regarded as violent, except to their victims, of course. In part, this lacuna is due to an ideological relationship forged between 'violence' and particular emotional states: anger, for instance. Indeed, one of the main criticisms ballistics scientists expressed about their paymasters (that is, the armed forces) is that the latter were swayed by emotion. In contrast, these scientists orchestrated cool, instrumental violence. Education, gender, class, status and whiteness were crucial in exempting them from any accusations of being violent men.[54]

Bourke's article is an excellent example of how the history of emotions has contributed to our understanding of both science and violence, and these scientists can perhaps be understood as forming an emotional community. She concludes with a call to expand our definitions of violence by being attentive to the ways some practices and people – in this case, ballistics scientists – are effectively excluded from the entire category.[55]

Her findings allow us to reflect back upon Pinker's celebration of cool reason – the 'we' of rational, disinterested thinkers – and his frequent attribution of violence to emotional heat, a binary that permits him to divorce the operations of reason from the production of violence.

---

[53]Bonnie G. Smith, 'Gender and the Practices of Scientific History', *The American Historical Review*, 100, no. 4 (October 1995): 1150–76; See also Bonnie G. Smith, *The Gender of History: Men, Women, and Historical Practice* (Cambridge, MA: Harvard University Press, 1998). On the cultivation of scientific insensibility in the nineteenth century using the example of medicine, see also Boddice, *History of Feelings*, chap. 5. See also Lorraine Daston and Peter Galison, *Objectivity* (New York: Zone Books, 2010).

[54]Joanna Bourke, 'Theorizing Ballistics: Ethics, Emotions, and Weapons Science', *History and Theory*, 55 (December 2017): 135–51, esp. here 138, 145, 148, 151.

[55]For some of her key works in the history of emotion, see Joanna Bourke, *Fear: A Cultural History* (London: Virago, 2005); and her *Wounding the World: How Military Violence and War Games Invade Our Lives* (London: Virago, 2014). See also her contribution to this volume, 'The Rise and Rise of Sexual Violence'.

'One would expect', he thus writes, 'that as collective rationality is honed over the ages, it will progressively whittle away at the shortsighted and hot-blooded impulses toward violence, and force us to treat a greater number of rational agents as we would have them treat us', a pacifying effect he believes has accelerated since 1945.[56] Ironically enough, he attributes the technologies of death – the very subject of Bourke's article – to hot emotions rather than the cool pleasures of scientific research (or the political economy of the military industrial complex): 'When people are rapacious or terrified', he remarks in passing, 'they develop the weapons they need; when cooler heads prevail, the weapons rust in peace'. Indeed, in his view, it is precisely the 'ability to set aside immediate experience, detach oneself from a parochial vantage point, and frame one's ideas in abstract, universal terms' that has led to 'better moral commitments, including an avoidance of violence'.[57] As Bourke demonstrates, however, such an ability to detach ourselves need not lead to such laudable ends but can instead serve to enable violence and render even its extreme forms invisible – the role of scientists in facilitating the mass use of napalm in Vietnam (by the United States) and Algeria (by France), the supposedly 'surgical strikes' of the Iraq War and modern drones, the US torture programme politely termed 'enhanced interrogation techniques'. Indeed, this very violence has been embedded in and explicitly justified by the same rhetoric of civilization (and savagery) reproduced by Pinker throughout his book.

Such arguments are anathema to Pinker, for whom reason and science (which he defines as 'the refining of reason to understand the world'[58]) are indelibly tied to progress and good. In responding to his critics, Pinker bemoans 'a demonization campaign' by humanities scholars that 'impugns' science, reason and Enlightenment values. Dismissing out of hand the very idea of any substantive connection between these fields and violence, he cites a 'twisted narrative' (with regard to scholarship on the Holocaust that identifies a lineage to Enlightenment rationality), 'pseudoscience' (with reference to scientific racism and eugenics), a 'universally deplored breach' in scientific practice and 'one-time failure to prevent harm' that yet 'may even have been defensible by the standards of the day' and is 'often misreported to pile up the indictment' (the Tuskegee syphilis study), and scattered bad apples more generally.[59] My point here is not to demonize rationality, science or modernity, blaming them for all social ills. Rather, it is to highlight the historical stakes of identifying violence and to suggest more nuanced understandings of its dynamics, both today and in the past: that

---

[56]His purpose in specifying 'rational agents' is unclear, as it contains the spectre of 'irrational' (savage?) agents. Pinker, *Better Angels*, 783.

[57]Pinker, *Better Angels*, 814, 793.

[58]Pinker, *Enlightenment Now*, 9.

[59]Pinker, *Enlightenment Now*, 396–405. See also Pinker, *Better Angels*, 777–8.

these dynamics include its imbrication with 'cool' reason does not invalidate the entire faculty of reason as such.

Reading Pinker through Bourke thus allows several observations. Excluding from the category of violence that which he does not wish to see and that which undermines his thesis, Pinker especially minimizes contemporary structural forms associated with capitalism, racism, the state, and science, whether in the expanding circle of environmental devastation or the system of mass incarceration, including the mass torture of solitary confinement.[60] His claim to cool, scientific objectivity – itself predicated on particular emotional norms – facilitates both the erasure of ideology from his own highly ideological position and its projection onto others.[61] To be sure, his impassioned attacks on his perceived foes – led by those he dismisses as eco- and social-justice warriors as well as the academic left – reveal an underswell of rather strong emotions.

Scripting revenge

Pinker opens his discussion of revenge, which is one of his five 'inner demons', with several paragraphs intended to display its universality: he quotes the Hebrew Bible, Homer (the same famous line on sweetness), Shakespeare's Shylock, the Yugoslav revolutionary Milovan Djilas, a nameless man from New Guinea and the Apache chief Geronimo. In his view, the 'urge for vengeance' forms a major cause of violence in everything from tribal warfare, homicide and school shootings to urban riots, terrorism and modern war, citing Pearl Harbor and 9/11. 'Revenge is not confined to political and tribal hotheads', he explains, 'but is an easily pushed button in everyone's brain'. The urge thus 'begins with the Rage circuit in the mid-brain-hypothalamus-amygdala pathway' and then, in humans, 'activates the insular cortex, which gives rise to feelings of pain, disgust, and anger'. Citing proverbs ('revenge is a dish best served cold'), apparently as conjoined illustration and evidence, Pinker describes how the reaction can then shift 'from an aversive anger to a cool and pleasurable seeking', noting in addition how 'revenge requires the disabling of empathy'.[62] Although the neurobiological understanding of the amygdala – raisin-sized masses of nerve cells in both halves of the brain – is in fact very much a work in progress, linked not just to threat responses

---

[60]For further discussion, see the contribution to this volume: Corey Ross, 'The better angels of which nature?: Violence and environmental history in the modern world,' 273–92.

[61]For an analysis of how his ideological position shapes his narrative, see Jeff Noonan, 'Liberalism, Capitalism, and the Conditions of Social Peace: A Critique of Steven Pinker's One-Sided Humanism', *International Critical Thought*, 9, no. 3 (2019): 394–410.

[62]He also posits the existence of a 'dimmer switch', that helps to reduce the urge, as well as the somewhat limited benefits of reconciliation and apology. See Pinker, *Better Angels*, 638–60, esp. 638–40.

but also to aspects of smell, vision and even musical perception, it has been the central spot on which universalist, essentialized and unchanging views of emotion have been pegged since the nineteenth century.[63] For Pinker, the urge for revenge is the product of evolutionary forces that have enduringly moulded our brains, and he locates its origins in the value of deterrence to survival – the threat to answer violence with violence. Along the best antidotes, in his view, are a strong state, civic norms and the self-control inculcated by the civilizing process.

Pinker's view of revenge is flat, inadequate to understanding its historical forms, cultural meanings and social operations. Half of his examples are literary – the *storytelling* of Homer, the Old Testament and Shakespeare – and the other half are configured as primitive, with Djilas described as 'born into a feuding clan of Montenegrins' (in homage to Balkan stereotypes). Pinker is right in one respect: forms of revenge do recur across many cultures, but they are better understood as meaningful narratives, scripts or strategies, which are shaped by specific emotional and cultural resources (sometimes including the Old Testament) and technologies (the media), and in which various emotives as well as logic and reason may play a role. In other words, the desire for, articulations of and practices of revenge emerge within the context of what we might call emotional communities. More broadly, historians integrate contextual (social, political, economic, cultural) dynamics and factors, agency and contingency, and relations of power and subordination. They thus address a major lacuna of Pinker's overall approach: his failure to theorize the social, that is, the ways supposedly individual psychological urges and drives are also somehow 'shared' by collectives and change over time.[64] To make this jump (and elide the problem), he relies on metaphors of epidemiology (contagion and infection), refers broadly to 'pathologies of thought' and 'groupthink' as especially characteristic of 'ideology', and routinely ascribes psychological deficiencies to people 'infected' with ideology, which effectively functions as his 'inner demon' for social processes. He summarizes thusly: 'An ideology cannot be identified with a part of the brain or even with a whole brain, because it is distributed across the brains of many people.'[65]

---

[63]One study even demonstrated the involvement of the amygdala in how jazz musicians can distinguish between improvization and music played from a score. See Plamper, *History of Emotion*, 1–4.

[64]One of the most thoughtful and influential explorations of how emotion works in a social context is Sara Ahmed, *The Cultural Politics of Emotion*, 2nd edn (New York: Routledge, 2015).

[65]'Ideology' (Nazism, Communism, etc.) is his go-to explanation for modern mass violence, though he also characterizes certain events (the burning of witches, the Holocaust) as madness or insanity. This approach obstructs historically nuanced explanations. Pinker, *Better Angels*, 194, 196, 672, 686, 613.

Let me give a brief historical example. In the late nineteenth and early twentieth centuries, small groups of activists espousing various political ideologies were developing the tactics of what is now often called terrorism, including targeted political assassinations, which they theorized as a method of political struggle (a 'weapon of the weak' against a powerful state) and as 'just vengeance' against state violence, colonial domination and/or systemic economic exploitation. It is worth stating (without endorsing their methods) that these were powerful and violent forces in people's lives, and that the tactic was grounded in a rational assessment of the balance of power. In an era marked by new technologies of media, transportation and communications, these groups also learned from one another, as did governments and police forces. Still, the character of these movements varied widely, with some becoming more brutal and others repudiating violence. In explaining their motivations, individuals often described political goals and ideals – freedom, suffrage, equality, human dignity – as well as personal experiences (including state violence), citing feelings not just of anger, pain or hatred but also love, sympathy and self-sacrifice. In sum, their political violence embodied both reason and emotion, self-control and spontaneity, in complex narratives that individuals and groups could tap and adapt, with these narratives (and emotional scripts) changing over time.[66] Pinker, in contrast, advances a different notion of universalized 'scripts for violence'. For him, such scripts are part of the 'human behavioral repertoire' that lie 'quiescent' until 'cued by propitious circumstances'.[67] By grounding the mechanisms of revenge within an ahistorical body, his model enables his birds-eye perspective on (supposed) meta-trends, but it cannot account for the complexities and nuances of micro-level histories, that is, for example, what might make some circumstances 'propitious' in the first place.

Significant ethical issues also result from universalist approaches: not even all political revenge is the same. A very different form of terrorism took form in this same period in the United States, especially, but not only, in the Jim Crow south: it involved systemic, state-sanctioned violence against African Americans, including lynching, which was likewise justified with reference to revenge (and the racialized binary of civilization/savagery). In this case, the 'grievances' were imaginary and constructed, propagating a politics (and emotional economy) of white victimization that served to legitimize, enact and uphold the institutions and manifold violences of white supremacy. To describe this expression of revenge as a 'button' like any other, just 'cued by propitious circumstances', obstructs a full telling of this history – its

---

[66]For an analysis of vengeance in Russian revolutionary terrorism with citation of the broader literature, see Susan K. Morrissey, 'Terrorism and *Ressentiment* in Revolutionary Russia', *Past & Present*, 264, no. 1 (February 2020): 191–226.
[67]Pinker, *Better Angels*, 587.

distinctive circumstances, racialized dynamics of power and subordination, historical subjectivities, emotional communities and sociopolitical legacies. In other words, the subject position is important: in order to understand a phenomenon such as revenge, including its emotional valence and relation to violence, it matters who is speaking or acting and why.[68] There are historical and ethical differences in the experiences, narratives and emotives of victims and perpetrators, bystanders and witnesses.[69]

This point brings me back to the examples originally cited by Pinker, especially his air of careless disregard. He describes the Hebrew Bible as obsessed with revenge but neglects to mention the distinctions it draws between sacred and personal vengeance – and the proscription of the latter. Shylock's words are quoted without thought for Shakespeare's literary and dramatic purpose, a topic with a lively scholarship on the complex significance of antisemitism. Lastly, Pinker quotes Geronimo at length – the blood, his joy in victory, his order to 'scalp the slain' – using his remark about rejoicing in revenge to comment blithely on its futility: after all, he had been defeated. Geronimo's words come from his autobiography, which is a complex, hybrid text based on carefully crafted oral testimony that he gave after some two decades as a prisoner of war, fully aware of his own personal defeat and a shared historical experience of forced displacement, mass murder and genocide; the text was also shaped by his interlocutors, the author and editor of the book, S. M. Barrett, an Oklahoma school superintendent, and an Apache translator, Asa Daklugie.[70] The narrative strategies of the source and the layers of historical context are equally immaterial to Pinker, who culls Geronimo's words from a secondary study in evolutionary psychology to evoke the savagery of (his) revenge as irrational urge. The violence of the 'civilizing' state hovers in the background, indistinct and tangential.

---

[68]For Pinker, these are incidental, a product of what he calls the moralization gap – the self-serving biases that are the 'evolutionary price' of being 'social animals'. Pinker, *Better Angels*, 587–99, esp. 590.

[69]For additional analysis, see Didier Fassin, 'On Resentment and *Ressentiment*: The Politics and Ethics of Moral Emotions', *Current Anthropology*, 54 (2013): 249–67. A similar point has also been made about evaluating trauma, which can be experienced by victims and perpetrators alike but is not necessarily the same thing: see Ruth Leys, *Trauma: A Genealogy* (Chicago: University of Chicago Press, 2000); Dominick LaCapra, *Writing History, Writing Trauma* (Baltimore: Johns Hopkins University Press, 2000); and Jeffrey C. Alexander, *Trauma: A Social Theory* (Cambridge: Cambridge University Press, 2012).

[70]*Geronimo's Story of His Life*, Taken down and edited by S. M. Barrett (New York, 1906). The passage Pinker quotes is on 53–4. Pinker's source is M. Daly and M. Wilson, *Homicide* (New York: A. de Gruyter, 1988). For further analysis, see Anita Huizar-Hernández, '"The Real Geronimo Got Away": Eluding Expectations in Geronimo: His Own Story; The Autobiography of a Great Patriot Warrior', *Studies in American Indian Literatures*, 29, no. 2 (Summer 2017): 49–70.

Conclusion

In applying the universalist categories of evolutionary psychology to historical subjects and processes, Pinker shapes a narrative of historical change around a reductive, ahistorical definition of violence – one with major, built-in blind spots, especially with regard to forms of systemic and state violence as well as the chequered historical relationship between science, reason, and violence. This narrative further depicts historical progress as emanating from the benevolent rationality of disinterested elites, such as himself; subaltern demand and resistance, in this telling, are sources of anarchy and violence. Finally, Pinker consistently represents himself as the voice of cool (scientific) reason, a discursive strategy that allows him to deny his own ideological position and political agenda and to accuse his critics of ideological bias and emotionality. The exposure of these mechanisms can help to explain the powerful attraction of his books for some readers and to facilitate different accounts of and responses to the history of violence.

Acknowledgements

I would like to thank Jan Plamper, Alexandra Oberländer and Mark Micale for their helpful feedback on this chapter.

PART FIVE

Coda

18

Pinker and contemporary historical consciousness

Mark S. Micale

Taken together, the preceding seventeen chapters constitute a definitive critique of *Better Angels of Our Nature* and *Enlightenment Now* – a critique whose overall verdict is resoundingly negative. Such cogent and learned evaluations speak for themselves. What I want to do here is articulate how historians – both inside and outside the academy – go about their work and contrast that against the modus operandi of Steven Pinker.

How historians work

Every branch of knowledge has certain methods and standards its practitioners generally agree upon. We historians see our role as interpreting recorded past events from the perspective of the present. We put much thought into choosing the subjects we study, making sure to describe and delimit them carefully. We define, as well as we can, the most important terms we employ. To understand a past event or person, practice or process, we believe that it's essential to learn as much as possible about the time and place in which the event occurred. Contextual knowledge is vital for genuine understanding. The bigger or more complicated a topic, the more challenging it becomes to generalize about it. Historians revel in the fine-grained particularities and peculiarities of the past; we enjoy colourful anecdotes about the past, yet we know that they are not primary evidence that can sustain an entire argument or interpretation. We base our understanding of a historical period on an examination of its physical remains; most often these are written documents, but they may also be photographs, films, artworks and other kinds of objects and artefacts. The skill that we probably value the most is the ability to critically evaluate what sorts of knowledge a scholar can and cannot obtain from a given source.

We believe passionately in intellectual expertise and deeply respect knowledge that has been obtained through close, systematic, and sometimes career-long, study. We hold that it is important to read and master what other scholars have said and published about our chosen subject (i.e. the historiography of a given topic or field). On both the college and graduate school levels, we teach our students that the past was as complicated as the present and that it therefore requires complex and nuanced judgements.

Truth about the past, and therefore our knowledge of it, can never be more than an approximation. The fragmentary nature of extant sources, the subjectivity of the individual doing the interpreting and the inescapable pastness of the past limit full comprehension. As in the sciences, the pursuit of this elusive truth is very much a collective enterprise, which is why we regularly organize all sorts of group undertakings and continually seek the input of our peers. We don't think that any one practitioner has all the answers. The notion of a single, totalized interpretation beyond critique or contestation, in any realm of intellectual endeavour, is foolhardy in our view. Years of study have instilled in us a sense of historical causation – a kind of intuitive awareness of how things do and do not happen.[1]

Within the past generation or two, academically trained historians have also become cognizant of the ways in which current conditions shape our views of the past. We try to guard against imposing twenty-first-century convictions and preferences on the often very different assumptions and conditions of the past.[2] Analogously, we recognize that the historian's own life experiences and ideological perspectives can influence our ideas and interpretations. We therefore think it is important to acknowledge, as much as possible, the beliefs that inform our work.

To further illuminate a project, historians sometimes decide that we need to draw on the methods, findings and insights of a collateral field of knowledge, such as anthropology, archaeology, linguistics or the law. It's not uncommon for us to spend years mastering a second discipline. And while we are proud to be professionals in our field, we admire and welcome the work of 'amateur' scholars from outside the academy. As an undergraduate, in the late 1970s I majored in history because I was inspired by the books of Barbara Tuchman about fourteenth-century Europe, the run-up to the

---

[1]L. B. Namier, 'History', in *Avenues of History* [1952], reproduced in Fritz Stern (ed.), *The Varieties of History: From Voltaire to the Present* (New York: Meridian Books, 1956), 375.
[2]Bernard Bailyn, *Illuminating History: A Retrospective of Seven Decades* (New York: W. W. Norton, 2020), 'Epilogue: The Elusive Past'.

First World War, and the career of Joseph Stilwell in China.[3] Tuchman was a gifted non-academic historian. Today, some of my favourite histories are books by non-academics like Russell Shorto and Adam Hochschild. One thing we insist upon is that writings such as these, spanning the divide between popular and scholarly audiences, abide by the basic intellectual standards outlined above.

Since approximately the end of the Second World War, the historical profession has been retreating from what is sometimes called philosophical historicism – the idea that history as a whole has a direction and is headed towards some ascertainable end point. Such linear and teleological schemes were once very common; indeed, they animated some of the major works of historiography and were central to thinkers such as Plato, Hegel and Marx. By contrast, most trained historians now would argue that the course actually taken by history has disproven such grand designs. We have become sceptical of the notion that events are destined to unfold inexorably in a single trajectory towards a universal goal. In fact, such meta-historical theories sometimes played out in ways that proved dangerous and destructive. In place of philosophical historicism, today we tend to emphasize contingency and discontinuity in history. We've become comfortable with the idea that multiple trends can operate at the same time – that, for instance, progress, regress and stasis can co-exist. We prefer to write history in the plural rather than the singular. That said, we still understand the basic need to generalize; we value big-picture accounts; and we are excited by ideas that are bold and innovative. When a historian does formulate such a new, compelling interpretation, we excitedly engage his or her work.[4]

A tally and a verdict

If the cognitive psychologist Steven Pinker had made an effort to learn about how professional students of history actually work, he would have known the things I just laid out. On the campus of Harvard University in Cambridge, Massachusetts, where Pinker teaches, the Department of Psychology is within easy walking distance of the Department of History. A short stroll from William James Hall on Kirkland Street to the university's main Widener

---

[3]Barbara W. Tuchman, *The Proud Tower: A Portrait of the World before the War, 1890-1914* (New York: Macmillan, 1966); Tuchman, *Stilwell and the American Experience in China, 1911-45* (New York: Macmillan, 1971); Tuchman, *A Distant Mirror: The Calamitous 14th Century* (New York: Knopf, 1976).

[4]Two examples of such works in my field of study are C. A. Bayly, *The Birth of the Modern World, 1780-1914* (Oxford: Blackwell, 2004) and Jürgen Osterhammel, *The Transformation of the World: A Global History of the Nineteenth Century*, trans. from the German by Patrick Camiller (Princeton: Princeton University Press, 2014).

Library passes directly by Robinson Hall, which houses Harvard's eminent history faculty, including two contributors to this volume. It seems not to have occurred to Pinker to stop in and consult his institutional colleagues about an entire field of knowledge in which he'd had no training, even as he was engaged in writing two large-scale books that claimed to identify and analyse important historical developments.

Consequently, Pinker's central argument about the progressive pacification of our species, and its related contention that the present is the most peaceful time in human history, are beset with a host of problems. Here is a brief summary of the deficiencies that the contributors to this volume have pinpointed in his work:

1. An overly narrow definition of violence as recorded statistical deaths from civilian and military causes.

2. Exaggeration of violence in certain past eras, to contrast it with the supposed peacefulness of the modern age.

3. A radical disregard for geo-chronological context.

4. The citation of raw quantitative data to impart a spurious pseudo-scientific quality to his presentation.

5. A tendency, in one topic after another, to ignore or dismiss copious quantities of counterevidence.

6. Failure to engage with the most important and respected scholarship on many subjects.

7. Exclusion of entire categories of violence that would complicate, if not contradict, his thesis, such as violence against indigenous people, colonial violence, prison violence, environmental violence and violence against animals.

8. Privileging of Western Europe and North America over the histories of Latin America, Africa, Asia and elsewhere in a work that aspires to explain behaviour worldwide.

9. Minimalization of the horrors of the twentieth century, including the First and the Second World War, the Holocaust, Stalin's Soviet Union, Mao's China and Pol Pot's Cambodia.

10. Failure to recognize the legacies of mass violence that endure long after the traumatic events have run their course.

11. Dismissal of newer forms of violence, and newly uncovered forms of past violence, such as the sexual abuse of children, wartime sexual violence, international human trafficking and cyber-violence.

12. Systematic unwillingness to acknowledge and examine the ideological orientations underlying his thinking and writing.

To this catalogue must be added Pinker's disturbing response to the reception his books have received. His reflexive, resentful dismissal of any critical comments seems to be combined with a complete incapacity for self-correction.

When evaluated by experts in field after field, *Better Angels of Our Nature* and *Enlightenment Now* have been found untrustworthy. Empirical, methodological, interpretative and argumentative problems confound Pinker's two forays into history. As Linda Fibiger above is the first to point out, Pinker's claims are not taken seriously by historians in any specialized field of study.[5] His work does violence to history.

Histories old and new

If *Better Angels of Our Nature* and *Enlightenment Now* fail as historical scholarship, and even as scientific hypothesis, Pinker's books may possess a certain power as ideological statements. But what ideology would that be? The contributors to this volume have distilled from his nearly 1,400 pages of text an underlying value system. In Pinker's world view, human progress is palpable, its signs all around us, in longer life spans, in increasing prosperity and in a worldwide rise in literacy. The protean engine of this progress is a combination of political freedom and market capitalism leavened by modern science, industry and technology. Since he is a psychologist by training, Pinker posits a psychological dimension to the process of human advancement: the ever-greater exercise of reason, intelligence and ingenuity combined with a growing capacity for altruism and empathy.

Against a prehistorical background of nature red tooth and claw, Pinker sees human violence waxing and waning through the centuries, but he believes that from the right vantage point, an overall trend towards pacification is discernible and undeniable. In the longue-durée ascent of our species, the eighteenth-century Enlightenment in Britain, Western and Central Europe, and the early United States played a pivotal role, he maintains; this was the breakaway moment when a constellation of ideas about nature, truth, reason, science, liberty, education, government, peace and happiness were for the first time widely and programmatically expressed. Enlightenment ideals, in his view, are still being worked out today; they are essentially responsible for what is best about our own time, and, if properly appreciated and cultivated, they bode well for the future of humanity. Pinker admits that cruel and violent acts continue to occur, but he thinks such tragedies take place less often, are less severe and are abhorred by more people than ever before. To him, outbreaks of brutality in our time represent reversions, or evolutionary throwbacks, to the bellicose tribal mentality of our prehistoric past.

---

[5]Fibiger, 'Steven Pinker's "prehistoric anarchy": A bioarcheological critique', chap. 7, 124.

In one version or another, the cluster of beliefs that Pinker subscribes to is common in the West – and elsewhere as well. It's a defensible philosophy. Had Pinker presented his vision as an autobiographical testament or as contemporary cultural criticism, rather than as history, he might have entitled his books *My Faith in Science and Reason* or perhaps *Three Cheers for Western Modernity!* or *Positivism and Progress*. These titles would have been more credible and less objectionable than the ones he chose.

If Pinker's work is essentially ideological-cum-historical, what, then, do genuine historians have to say in response? On first thought, it may seem that the most pertinent riposte to his progressivist world view is simply a recitation of recent events.[6] A worldwide disease pandemic, global market recessions, ceaseless gun violence, resurgent racism and nationalism, spiralling unemployment and homelessness, massive health inequalities, climate change–related natural disasters, egregious government corruption, deadly urban pollution and accelerated deforestation of the Amazon are just some of the day's headlines. To reconcile Pinker's theory with the current tumult in the world is difficult.

If we take a somewhat longer view, we see that democracy has not been faring very well lately: the end of the Cold War in 1989–91 was an unprecedented opportunity for bringing free representative government to the many former Soviet Bloc nations. But thirty years later, several of these Eastern European nations have fallen back into authoritarian politics, and post–Communist Russia itself is evermore repressive and autocratic. In China, Xi Jinping has been consolidating his dictatorship and cracking down on democracy's defenders in Hong Kong. Turkey, Brazil and the United States have suffered dangerous, demagogic leaders. Just as troubling to me, as a lifelong educator, is the poisoning of political news cultures in Western countries. In her incisive analysis *Democracy and Truth*, the intellectual historian Sophia Rosenfeld diagnoses 'the crisis of objective truth' unleashed in America by partisan television and social media sites that peddle bogus information and conspiracy theories around the clock.[7] Enlightenment's mantra – learning the truth so it can set us free – has never been more difficult to achieve; the current era of 'fake news' is enabled by the very technological modernity that Pinker seeks to lionize.[8]

On current events, of course, everyone has his or her own opinions. For this book, a more appropriate question might be: 'How do historians, as a community of professionals, respond to Pinker's philosophy of human

---

[6]Email message from David A. Bell to Philip Dwyer and Mark Micale, 25 May 2020.

[7]Sophia Rosenfeld, *Democracy and Truth: A Short History* (Philadelphia: University of Pennsylvania Press, 2018).

[8]Samuel Moyn, 'Hype for the Best: Why Does Steven Pinker Insist that Human Life Is on the Up?' *The New Republic*, 19 March 2018, review of Steven Pinker, *Enlightenment Now: The Case for Reason, Science, Humanism, and Progress* (New York: Penguin Books, 2019).

betterment?' To explore that issue, we need to pose a different question: not 'How best to research and write good history?' but 'Why study history at all?'

Through the centuries, that basic question has been asked frequently but has generated a variety of answers. Beginning in ancient Greece and continuing right up to the early twentieth century, one prominent, appealing genre of history chronicled the lives and dramatic actions of famous individuals, especially in politics, diplomacy and warfare. These accounts typically took the form of epic narratives and carried the implication that these legendary men – whether heroes or villains – exerted a determining influence on the course of history.

A second strand of history writing emerged from the world's great religions, including the hybrid Judeo-Christian tradition. The so-called providential histories perceive everything that happens in the past, present and future as the working out of the Creator's cosmological will or purpose. Although that plan might be inscrutable to humans, a guide to the divine master plan exists in major texts of that religion such as the Bible.

A third answer to the question 'Why study history?' was provided by the enlighteners of the eighteenth century. For Voltaire in France, Edward Gibbon in Britain and the Founding Fathers in early America, the past was pre-eminently populated by a voluminous cast of characters who exhibited a range of character traits worth studying. History in this view is the spectacle of these figures' virtuous (and in some cases, invidious) actions played out against the backdrop of events. One studied history, therefore, to learn 'the lessons of the past', especially regarding how to govern a nation, conduct a war, achieve prosperity and the like.

The nineteenth century, particularly in the British Isles during the long Victorian/Edwardian period (1837–1914), produced a fourth paradigm of historical meaning. This model has, since the 1930s, been labelled Whig history writing.[9] In the Whig outlook, history represents first and foremost a steady advance towards a future quasi-utopia in which the principal traits being chronicled will reach their fullest possible realization. In the nineteenth and early twentieth century, sweeping moral narratives of this sort focused on a variety of themes: freedom, happiness, enlightenment, constitutional monarchy, parliamentary democracy, science and technology, and civilization itself. These stories tended to divide people and events into good and bad. There might be challenges and setbacks along the way, but eventual triumph was a matter of historical destiny. Among the books and essays that fell into the Whig canon were William Whewell's *History of the Inductive Sciences from the Earliest to the Present Times* (1837), Henry Thomas Buckle's *History of Civilization in England* (1857), W. E. H. Lecky's

---

[9]Herbert Butterfield, *The Whig Interpretation of History* (London: G. Bell and Sons, 1931).

History of the Rise and Influence of the Spirit of Rationalism in Europe (1865), Lord Acton's *History of Freedom* (1907) and Benedetto Croce's *History as the Story of Liberty* (1938). In the Anglo-Whig view, the present was always the apex of a progressive movement.[10]

These paradigms shared a number of features: they all produced ambitious longitudinal narratives. They spanned centuries, if not millennia. The great change agents were invariably men. Furthermore, a single country or region – be it the classical Mediterranean, the ancient Middle East, the Christian West, Anglo-Saxon Northern Europe, Germany, Britain, France or the United States – was projected to be the hub of history from which civilization spread to the rest of the known human-inhabited world. Usually the epicentre was the historian-author's own country or continent. The things that were admirable in the tales these historians told typically served as a metaphor for what was seen as noble about the human species as a whole. For generations, countless textbooks of 'Western civilization' and histories of individual Western countries derived from the Whig historiographical tradition, albeit with various nationalistic twists.

Few professional practitioners today approach their work in any of these four ways. Although contemporary historians share with these earlier approaches a deep fascination with the past and a belief that we must assiduously study and learn from it, the content and practice of history writing have been fundamentally transformed in the past fifty years. This sea change was prompted by a simple realization: that all the earlier paradigms had excluded the experiences of the vast majority of human beings who lived in the past. Among those omitted were such numerically massive segments of people as women, peasants, workers and the poor. The earlier modes of history writing also excluded whole categories of people who – by dint of their national, ethnic or racial identity – constituted minority populations in the societies under study. Geographically speaking, those past accounts left out much, if not all, of the world outside the author's own civilizational orbit.

In dramatic contrast, thousands of scholars working over the past three generations have been researching, recovering and reconstructing the histories of the previously ignored and excluded. Women, peasants, industrial workers, the poor, immigrants, indigenous people, colonial subjects, Blacks, Hispanics, Asians, Jews, gay people and disabled people are just some of the ever-expanding number of historical subjects. Vast fields of empirical research have been opened up. The stories of these newly enfranchised groups are not secondary or supplementary; they have been granted equal space and equivalent integrity to the elite groups that formerly dominated historical accounts. Especially in English-speaking colleges and

---

[10]For a later and more sophisticated defence within English historiography, see 'History as Progress', in Edward Hallett Carr, *What Is History?* (New York: Knopf, 1961), chap. 5.

universities around the world, whole new curricula of history have been formulated. This enlargement of the discipline's content has been reinforced, particularly since the late twentieth century, by globalization; history has simultaneously been invigorated by the possibility of crafting truly global – rather than nation-based or continent-based – narratives. The avalanche of new scholarship has magisterially enlarged our understanding of the past, what it consists of and how it bears on contemporary public culture.

This new history does not entail just a broadened subject matter. It also raises lines of inquiry that are overtly political: Who was responsible for the omissions from the historical record? How did those individuals or institutions make their decisions? And to what ends?

For the aggregate of past human experiences to become written history in the present, selection, organization, analysis and interpretation are required. Those tasks, including the preliminary selection of subject matter, involve acts of inclusion and exclusion. Whose life experiences gain attention and whose are sidelined are not happenstance; the decisions are made by individual authors or a community of authors that formulate judgements on who is important enough to be recalled, studied and memorialized – that is, whose lives matter – and who should be forgotten or 'dis-remembered'.

These decisions are unavoidably ideological: in 1995, Michel-Rolph Trouillot provided a now classic discussion of this point in *Silencing the Past: Power and the Production of History*.[11] History, Trouillot saw, is not a neutral, non-ideological narrative that writes itself. Taking Christopher Columbus, the Haitian Revolution and the Mexican-American War's Battle of the Alamo as examples, he showed how histories have been written by the winners of conflicts who seek to centre and celebrate themselves while presenting the vanquished in ways that are distorted and deleterious or writing the defeated out of collective memory altogether.

It is no coincidence that Trouillot, who for many years directed the Institute for Global Studies at Johns Hopkins University, is Haitian by birth. The Haitian Revolution of 1791–1804 was the first successful slave revolt in world history and also the first time that a non-European people overthrew a European colonial regime in order to establish a new and independent nation. News of the uprising's success reverberated throughout North and South America, Britain and Western Europe, terrifying slave owners and inspiring emancipationist movements for much of the nineteenth century. Yet as late as the 1980s, when I undertook graduate studies at Yale in modern European history, there was no coverage of this momentous event. Was this a 200-year oversight or was it an archetypal example of 'ideological erasure'? Today, because of the remarkable reconceptualization of historical

---

[11]Michel-Rolph Trouillot, *Silencing the Past: Power and the Production of History* [1995], twentieth anniversary edition, second revised edition (Boston: Beacon Press, 2015).

scholarship, when historians teach 'the Age of the Atlantic Revolutions', the American, French and Haitian Revolutions receive equal time.

Pinker and contemporary historical consciousness

More and more historians realize that violence – and, in particular, the desire to conceal past violence – has been subjected to selective historical amnesia. In one instance after another, the human groups excluded from past histories were those who held subordinate status. It is not just that 'history is written by the victors', as the maxim (attributed to Winston Churchill) goes; the victories, we discover, were often secured with tremendous bloodshed. The violence often took place far from the centre of the dominant power (e.g. in the Zulu nation, the Tasmanian countryside, the Congo jungle, the Dakota hinterland) where it remained out of sight. Some of the violence occurred in closed institutional settings, such as prisons, camps, hospitals and asylums. Perpetrators of crimes often do everything they can to ensure that the event is forgotten. If compelled to acknowledge ignominious acts, they tend to explain and excuse it as a necessary step towards some greater goal, such religious conversion or a civilizing mission, or as a response to resistance and rebellion. Recovery of the hidden violence – which in some cases entailed entire systems of oppression in operation over centuries – is for the first time being constituted as a subject of independent historical study.

One of the most bracing changes this transvaluation has brought is the idea of imagining and investigating history from the perspective of the victim. With this reorientation, a new history is emerging, one that is fuller and more interesting and that delivers a truer sense of the past, including the good, the bad and the ugly. Great empire builders, from Alexander the Great to Napoleon Bonaparte, have been the stuff of ancient and modern legend; their heroic adventures look far different when viewed by the societies they conquered.[12] Military historians are now likely to spend as much time discussing the experience of civilians, including women, children, prisoners and refugees, as presenting the achievements of male combatants and their leaders. They may also attempt to reconstruct the enemy's point of view.[13] A book like Marcus Rediker's *The Slave Ship: A Human Story* (2007) enriched our understanding of the transatlantic slave trade by examining side by

---

[12]See, for example, David A. Bell's *The First Total War: Napoleon's Europe and the Birth of Modern Warfare as We Know It* (New York: Houghton Mifflin Company, 2007).
[13]For popular English-language war films that reflect this change of perspective, see *Heaven & Earth*, directed by Oliver Stone (1993); *Letters from Iwo Jima*, directed by Clint Eastwood (2006); and *Midway*, directed by Roland Emmerich (2019).

side the experiences of officers, sailors, slaves and former slaves.[14] A more topical example is the construction of America's transcontinental railroad in the 1860s. In generations of textbooks, this project was presented as a benchmark in American expansionism, a feat of private–public financing, and a miracle of engineering; today it is also examined for its impact on Chinese immigrant labour, Indian tribes living along its path and the buffalo that once dominated much of the terrain. Events of mass mortality, which previously received little or no attention outside of local or regional accounts, are now for the first time being integrated into global history. The Taiping Rebellion in southern China (1850–64), which resulted in 20 to 30 million deaths; the Paraguayan war of the 1860s, which did away with nearly 70 per cent of Paraguay's adult males; the so-called Holodomor of the early 1930s, which starved to death millions of ethnic Ukrainians; and the Hindu–Muslim massacres following the partitioning of India and Pakistan in 1947 are examples of this phenomenon.

Two fields that have been reshaped by this new approach are indigenous history and colonial/postcolonial studies. People in Europe and the Americas are familiar with the recent controversy over Christopher Columbus. The late fifteenth-century Italian explorer and navigator, the first European to voyage by sea to the Caribbean, was indubitably brave and intrepid. Change the viewing lens, however, and Columbus' 'discovery of America' is the start of a series of events, many of them carried out by Spanish 'conquistadors', that within fifty years decimated the indigenous Caribbean and Mesoamerican populations, some of which possessed rich cultures, including languages, books, and thousand-year histories.[15] In terms of biology and ecology, too, first contact with 'the New World' makes for a less-than-glorious story.[16]

Lest we think that genocides of native peoples were inadvertent and limited to the pre-eighteenth-century period (impressions left by Pinker), consider another example, this one less well known but recently highlighted in painful detail. It concerns the Mendocino Indian Wars along the coast of northern California during the third quarter of the nineteenth century. *American Genocide: The United States and the California Indian Catastrophe, 1846–73* was published in 2017 by the young UCLA historian Benjamin Madley. It is a work of profound research. It is also one of the

---

[14]Marcus Rediker, *The Slave Ship: A Human History* (New York: Penguin Books, 2007).

[15]Charles C. Mann, *1491: New Revelations of the Americas before Columbus* (New York: Vintage Books, 2006); Mann, *1493: Uncovering the New World Columbus Created* (New York: Knopf, 2011).

[16]Alfred W. Crosby, Jr, The *Columbian Exchange: Biological and Cultural Consequences of 1492* (Westport: Greenwood Publishing, 1973); Crosby, *Ecological Imperialism: The Biological Expansion of Europe, 900-1900* [1986], second edition (Cambridge: Cambridge University Press, 2004).

most depressing books that, as a resident of the state of California, I have read in years.[17]

Won from Mexico by way of conquest, the territory of California was formally annexed by the American government in 1848. That same year, gold was unexpectedly discovered in the hills northeast of Sacramento. In 1850, California entered the Union as 'a free non-slavery state'. As a result of this confluence of events, hundreds of thousands of white people, mostly young men in search of quick fortune, flooded into the northern half of the state during the 1850s. The newcomers sought land and water, which quickly brought them into conflict with the native inhabitants of the area who had lived there peacefully and productively for thousands of years. In 1769, before Spanish colonizers introduced new diseases into their environment, an estimated 310,000 Indians lived in California. When the Stars and Stripes were hoisted over the first state capitol building in 1850, the number had dropped to 150,000. By 1873, when the last of the 'Indian Wars' in the area came to an ignoble end, the Native American population had plummeted to 30,000, and the US Census of 1880 recorded just 16,277 Indians living in the entire state.

The violent history of settler–Indian relations across the North American continent is common knowledge. Madley's accomplishment is to provide the first comprehensive, incident-by-incident inventory of each shooting, hanging, kidnapping, ambush, massacre and battle as it unfolded during the years between 1846 and 1873.[18] Reconstructing this record of killings required a remarkable array of primary sources.[19]

Using as a pretence the occasional theft of ranchers' cattle and resistance to having their ancestral lands appropriated, recently arrived whites, Madley shows, embarked on an overtly exterminatory policy towards the indigenous inhabitants of northern California. The state militia, local volunteer militia groups, irregular bands of vigilante Indian fighters and, increasingly, the US army all undertook large-scale indiscriminate killings of the unarmed Indians. Not only land-hungry homesteaders but state legislators, local judges, state governors, the California Supreme Court and the US Senate, as well as the press and the burgeoning Euro-American public, supported Indian suppression and removal. Unrestrained violence that transgressed federal policy went unnoticed and unprosecuted by faraway Washington DC.

---

[17]Benjamin Madley, *American Genocide: The United States and the California Indian Catastrophe, 1846-1873* (New York and London: Oxford University Press, 2017).

[18]See his quantitative data at yalebooks.com/american-genocide-appendix.

[19]Madley's sources include newspapers, magazines, journals, letters, diaries, memoirs, biographies, autobiographies, scrapbooks, censuses, drawings, photographs, family histories, court documents, ethnographic reports, legislative texts and proceedings, local and regional histories, and correspondence between local, state and federal government officials. He found very few written Indian voices describing what took place during the 1850s and 1860s.

The most lethal of the raids occurred in the Mendocino Expedition of 1859–60 when roaming bands of settlers destroyed stores of food, torched villages in nighttime attacks and slew any members of the local Yuki tribes they could locate, regardless of gender or age. Indians who somehow survived the regional slaughter were shunted onto small agriculturally undesirable reservations. Some surviving women and children were seized for sale.[20]

Until the appearance of Madley's unflinching and full-scale account, this region of California figured in US textbooks only in connection with the Gold Rush, the early growth of San Francisco and the swashbuckling career of the explorer John C. Frémont. In stark contrast, Madley and others are excavating the truth about how the American West was really won. In one instance after another, a wave of massacres of a region's indigenous inhabitants was followed by generations of broken treatises, forced resettlement, deculturation and the placement of minors in non-Indian homes and boarding schools. The destructive trans-generational consequences of these traumas continue right up to the present when Native Americas are the US minority most disproportionately killed by the Covid-19 pandemic.

A second site of widespread government-sanctioned violence that long went under-recorded and unrecognized is colonial. The thirty-year period running from the late 1940s to the late 1970s was the age of decolonization on the African Continent. Undoing the late nineteenth-century 'Scramble for Africa', over fifty countries across Africa secured independence during these decades. Belgium, France, Italy, Portugal, Spain and the United Kingdom were the European powers involved.

Among the bloody 'end of empire' struggles was that of Kenya in the 1950s. In 1895, for commercial profit, the British laid claim to 'the East African Protectorate', renaming the territory 'British Kenya' in 1920 as they consolidated their control. Many people of the Kikuyu, Kenya's largest ethnic group, had lost arable land in the occupation; the British hold began to weaken in the early 1950s when about 20,000 Kikuyu men organized a violent insurrection that came to be called 'the Mau Mau Rebellion'. As in Star Wars, the empire struck back and crushed the rebellion, just as it did when confronted with restive local populations across its now-rapidly contracting world empire. Accounts of late colonial hostilities were written by (white male British) historians in London or Oxbridge, who relied uncritically on the Colonial Office's official reports. They acknowledged that rogue soldiers had gone too far in some acts of suppression of the Kikuyu but, they claimed, the regrettable incidents were limited and unavoidable.

---

[20]See also Jack Norton, *Genocide in Northwestern California: When Our Worlds Cried* (San Francisco: Indian Historian Press, 1979); Brendan C. Lindsay, *Murder State: California's Native American Genocide, 1846-1873* (Lincoln and London: University of Nebraska Press, 2012); and William B. Secrest, *When the Great Spirit Died: The Destruction of the California Indians, 1850-1860*, second edition (Sanger: Quill Driver Books, 2003).

Allegations of more serious and widespread human rights abuses, from first-hand witnesses, were dismissed. And, at any rate, Kenya obtained its independence on 12 December 1963.

Decades went by before the true story of British-Kenyan affairs came to the world's attention. The American historian Caroline Elkins' book *Imperial Reckoning: The Untold Story of Britain's Gulag in Kenya* tells a profoundly disturbing story – one that bears out in detail Trouillot's analysis of state power and the construction of history.[21] Elkins, a contributor to this volume, spent the better part of ten years researching the last decade of British colonial rule in Kenya. As they exited Kenya, the British destroyed thousands of files about the insurrection. Elkins, however, scoured libraries and archives to locate extant documents in Nairobi and London. She interviewed former colonial personnel. Most importantly, she learned to speak Swahili, which allowed her to interview over 300 survivors and their families who had lived in rural Kenya during the 1950s. By dint of her extraordinary perseverance, Elkins, now a professor at Harvard, pieced together a revealing chapter in African decolonialization from the perspective of the victimized population. Her book, published in 2005, won the Pulitzer Prize for General Non-Fiction.

Elkins found that British colonial authorities repressed the Mau Mau fighters through 'regularized and systematized violence'. They imprisoned without trials around 17,000 Kenyan fighters for two to six years. As a matter of policy, 'recalcitrant' prisoners were subjected to beatings, torture, castration, solitary isolation and hard labour intended to break their rebellious spirit; some were outright executed. The scale and scope of the repression vastly exceeded what had previously been known. Adapting tactics honed in earlier anti-colonial fights in Egypt, India and elsewhere, the authorities constructed dozens of makeshift detention centres and imprisoned between 160,000 and 320,000 Kikuyu in them. Several facilities were set up to incarcerate women. Dire conditions ensued with thousands of deaths from disease, malnutrition, exposure and forced labour. In addition, Elkins discovered, occupying colonial forces corralled as many as 1.5 million people – women and children included – into villages that for years stood barricaded with barbed wire and were heavily patrolled. Elkins' book – its British version is titled *Britain's Gulag* – likens the Kenyan penal network to Soviet repression in Siberia. The first popularly elected Black-majority government of Kenya closed the detention camps across the country and freed all political prisoners upon achieving independence.

Elkins' exposé reverberated through Britain, inspiring a trial in London that played out between 2009 and 2013. Spurred on by *Imperial Reckoning* and represented by international human rights lawyers, several elderly

---

[21]Caroline Elkins, *Imperial Reckoning: The Untold Story of Britain's Gulag in Kenya* (New York: Henry Holt and Company, 2005).

Kenyans sued the British government for past damages in London's High Court of Justice. Elkins, along with another historian, David M. Anderson from the University of Warwick, was an expert witness at the trial.[22] For years the Foreign and Commonwealth Office responded with indignant denials of any wrongdoing in its former empire. Then, following the discovery of a trove of incriminating colonial documents that had been concealed and classified for decades in British intelligence archives, on 6 June 2013 the government announced a settlement with the Mau Mau claimants. It issued an official apology to the people of Kenya, agreed to compensate 5,228 Kenyan survivors who were imprisoned and abused during the insurrection, and subsidized a monument to the victims of torture under British rule. The monument was unveiled in Nairobi's Uhuru Park in 2015.[23]

Benjamin Madley and Caroline Elkins are part of a new generation of researchers who, through intrepid historical research and a passionate commitment to finding out what really happened, are overturning old narratives and rewriting their subjects' histories.[24] It is important to emphasize that the atrocities being discovered and documented were in some cases perpetrated not by dictatorial totalitarian regimes but by Western liberal democracies. There is no mention of either set of events – the Mendocino wars or British brutality in Kenya – in Pinker's story of the world becoming less and less violent.

For a sobering account of our species' long history of genocidal violence, continuing to almost the present day, a thorough survey is Ben Kiernan's *Blood and Soil: A World History of Genocide and Extermination from Sparta to Darfur*.[25] Kiernan, a history professor at Yale and a specialist on the Cambodian genocide of 1975–9, concludes that race hatred, ideological warfare and religious sectarianism, combined with territorial expansionism, are the common motivations of past mass killings. Since the year 1400, genocides have occurred in every century and across the globe. Published in 2007, *Blood and Soil* includes full chapters on the English conquest of Ireland in the sixteenth century, the extermination of Indians by colonists and settlers of British North America in the seventeenth and eighteenth

---

[22]David Anderson, *Histories of the Hanged: Britain's Dirty War in Kenya and the End of Empire* (New York: W. W. Norton, 2005).

[23]For the story of the trial, see Marc Parry, 'Discovering the Brutal Truth about the British Empire', *The Guardian*, 18 August 2016.

[24]For another locus of colonial violence, this one involving a Continental European power in an earlier period, see Adam Hochschild's *King Leopold's Ghost: A Story of Greed, Terror, and Heroism in Colonial Africa* (Boston: Houghton Mifflin Co., 1998). One of the most sordid episodes in European colonialism, the story of the Belgian Congo was unfamiliar to many people until Hochschild's bestselling account.

[25]Ben Kiernan, *Blood and Soil: A World History of Genocide and Extermination from Sparta to Darfur* (New Haven: Yale University Press, 2007).

centuries, and massacres of Aborigines on the Australian frontier throughout the nineteenth century.

Systematic killings reached their deadliest concentration in the twentieth century – in Turkish-controlled Armenia, Nazi-occupied Central and Eastern Europe, Stalin's Soviet Union, Mao's China and Khmer Rouge's Cambodia. Modern technology, Kiernan observes time and again, gave these murderous campaigns a new scale and intensity. The years from the mid-1970s to the mid-1990s brought a succession of 'ethnic cleansings' – in Bosnia, Guatemala, Iraq, East Timor, Indonesia, Congo and Rwanda, not to mention the slaughter in Cambodia. Although Kiernan salutes the recent trend towards human rights accountability, including United Nations commissions of inquiry and International Criminal Court indictments, he devotes his closing ten pages to genocidal violence since 2000 and labels the killing of 300,000 African tribal farmers in Sudan's western Darfur region 'the opening genocide of the twenty-first century'.[26] He detects no diminution of genocidal movements and identifies a number of hotspots where worsening circumstances could fuel future conflicts. And the European Enlightenment? That eighteenth-century harbinger of hope plays no part whatsoever in Kiernan's 700-plus pages.[27]

The transformation of historical sensibility that has come about in the last half century is continuing. It is not just post-1960s radical activist-historians who are thinking anew about violence and our relation to it. While the editors and contributors were preparing this volume, one public statue after another, around the world, was being removed, defaced or destroyed. Why? Because these images in bronze memorialized figures such as the British arch-imperialist Cecil Rhodes, Belgium's brutal King Leopold II, an anti-Maori naval officer in New Zealand and leaders of the Confederate army who fought to maintain slavery in America. The roles those once-honoured men played in past violent actions have come under scrutiny and been found unacceptable. At stake, in the words of historians Jo Guldi and David Armitage, is 'the public future of the past'.[28]

While old statues have been toppled in a rejection of violence and injustice, new structures expressing a popular awakening have been rising. Among them are the following:

- A Memorial to the Murdered Jews of Europe in Berlin, Germany (2004)

---

[26]Kiernan, *Blood and Soil*, 595–6.
[27]See also Robert Gellately and Ben Kiernan (eds), *The Specter of Genocide: Mass Murder in Historical Perspective* (Cambridge and New York: Cambridge University Press, 2003); and Benjamin A. Valentino, *Final Solutions: Mass Killing and Genocide in the 20th Century* (Ithaca: Cornell University Press, 2004).
[28]Jo Guldi and David Armitage, *The History Manifesto* (New York and Cambridge: Cambridge University Press, 2014), 117.

- The Tuol Sleng Genocide Museum in Phnom Penh, Cambodia (2015)
- The War and Women's Rights Museum in Seoul, South Korea (2012)
- The 'Lynching Museum' in Montgomery, Alabama (2018)
- A monument to commemorate fallen Zulu warriors of the Anglo-Zulu Wars in Isandlwana, South Africa (1999)
- A memorial to Aboriginal and Torres Strait Islander men and women at the Australian War Memorial in Canberra (2019)
- The Mother and Child sculpture in honour of victims of sexual violence in conflicts around the world, in central London (2019)
- The National Museum of the American Indian (2004) and the National Museum of African-American History and Culture (2016), both on the Mall in Washington DC
- The Rwanda Genocide Center with museum and burial rounds in Kigali, Rwanda (1999)
- International slave trade museums on the Gaudeloupe Islands (2015) and in Liverpool, England (2007)
- The Parque de la Memoria, for victims of state-sponsored terrorism, in Buenos Aires, Argentina (2007)
- The Memorial to the Victims of Torture and Ill-Treatment in the Colonial Era in Nairobi, Kenya (2015)
- The Tacoma Chinese Reconciliation Park in Washington state recognizing the persecution of immigrants (2010)

There is even an Animals in War Memorial in Hyde Park, London, built in 2004. Memorials and mausoleums dedicated to national-political leaders and cemeteries and monuments remembering the war dead remain some of the most moving and widely visited sites throughout the world. These traditional memorializations, however, are now being joined by sculptures, statues, museums, commemorative sites and heritage parks devoted to civilian victims of mass violence who previously were rarely, if ever, commemorated. Many of these recently created sites have been established by government's that are trying for the first time to engage and grapple with their involvement in past tragedies or atrocities.[29]

---

[29]Not surprisingly, such initiatives have been resisted and resented by groups that would rather not educate people about these historical episodes, including revelations that might tarnish their public reputation and call into question their positive self-image. Some of the most vociferous opponents have been state governments that sponsor official patriotic histories and censor the study of past events that could compromise their authority. Investigations of historical violence can also risk revealing that the power, prosperity and peacefulness presently enjoyed by many democratic societies may have been achieved through decidedly uncivilized means.

An intellectual necrology[30]

By all indications, Steven Pinker remains oblivious to the growing shift in historical consciousness. Of the various competing paradigms of history writing, his *Better Angels of Our Nature* and *Enlightenment Now* are most rooted in nineteenth-century Whig literature. Pinker's neo-Whig frame of mind is manifested in elements such as these: a linear storytelling structure; an overarching progressivist interpretation; a willingness to subsume the great complexities of the past into a single moral trajectory; an evangelical belief that society today is freer, fairer, safer and richer than ever before; and an unbending faith that what is good and constructive in our species – that is, our 'angelic' side – will prevail over our darker, destructive capacities.

Whig scholars in the Victorian era envisioned the Anglo-Saxon races of Britain and Northern, Western and Central Europe as superior to the rest of humanity: progress, to them, depended on spreading European-cultivated values, institutions and behaviours to less fortunate and ostensibly inferior parts of humanity. One of Pinker's key contentions is that the evolution of societies towards an ever-kinder and gentler disposition is the single most important development in the history of our species. In his view, the Anglo-French Enlightenment of the eighteenth century was the brilliant before-and-after moment in this world historical process. Most of the change agents have been white male Westerners. The rest of the world follows, either receptive or resistant to Euro-American ideas; global history is Western history writ large. The index to *Better Angels of Our Nature* contains entries on certain aspects of violence with subheadings for individual European countries and then for 'the rest of the world', an indication of where the author's attention is focused and where it is not. Less economically and industrially developed regions, the so-called Global South, and societies with red-, yellow-, brown- and Black-skinned populations figure only tangentially in his calculations. Pinker's books, although hefty, are noteworthy for what they leave out.[31] The peoples denied voice and agency in his accounts are the same ones who often suffered great violence directed by the very Western governments he portrays as carriers of peace and progress. Pinker, unfortunately, is profoundly out of sync with contemporary historical thought.

Better Angels of Our Nature made its debut just over a decade ago. With a fluent writing style, a celebrity endorsement (by Bill Gates) and a provocatively counter-intuitive thesis, the book made a splash. For a few years, it seemed that Pinker might become a major voice in the public political and cultural discourse of our time. The early reception of his work,

---

[30]I thank Michael Wert for donating this term.
[31]Mark S. Micale, 'What Pinker Leaves Out', in Philip Dwyer and Mark S. Micale (eds), *Historical Reflections/Refléxions historiques*, 4, issue 1 (Spring, 2018): 128–39, reproduced in Dwyer and Micale (eds), *On Violence in History* (New York and Oxford: Berghahn, 2020), chap. 11.

however, came mainly in short journalistic reviews written in turnaround time by commentators with varying backgrounds. A second wave of readers with a deeper understanding of history has now given the book and its successor volume a closer appraisal. Ten years on, it has become apparent that Pinker's thesis about the decline of human violence and the growing peacefulness of our own time is built on a house of cards. After a closer look, and in light of an altered set of world circumstances, it's clear that his thesis does not withstand rigorous inspection. It is time to move on.

BIBLIOGRAPHY

Abbink, Jon. 'Preface: Violation and Violence as Cultural Phenomena', in Jon Abbink and Göran Aijmer (eds), *Meanings of Violence: A Cross Cultural Perspective*, xi–xvii. Oxford: Berg, 2000.

Adams, David (ed.). *The Seville Statement on Violence: Preparing the Ground for the Construction of Peace*. UNESCO, 1991.

Adams, William M. *Against Extinction: The Story of Conservation*. London: Earthscan, 2004.

Adas, Michael. *Machines as the Measure of Men: Science, Technology, and Ideologies of Western Dominance*. Ithaca: Cornell University Press, 1989.

Adler, Jeffrey S. '"Halting the Slaughter of the Innocents": The Civilizing Process and the Surge in Violence in Turn-of-the-Century Chicago', *Social Science History*, 25:1 (Spring 2001): 29–52.

Adler, Jeffrey S. *First in Violence, Deepest in Dirt: Homicide in Chicago, 1875–1920*. Cambridge, MA: Harvard University Press, 2006.

Agee, Christopher Lowen. *The Streets of San Francisco: Policing and the Creation of a Cosmopolitan Liberal Politics, 1950–1972*. Chicago: University of Chicago Press, 2014.

Ahmed, Sara. *The Cultural Politics of Emotion*. 2nd edn. New York: Routledge, 2015.

Aijmer, Göran. 'Introduction: The Idiom of Violence in Imagery and Discourse', in Göran Aijmer and Jon Abbink (eds), *Meanings of Violence: A Cross Cultural Perspective*, 1–21. Oxford: Berg, 2000.

Alexander, Jeffrey C. *Trauma: A Social Theory*. Cambridge: Cambridge University Press, 2012.

Alexander, Michelle. *The New Jim Crow: Mass Incarceration in the Age of Colorblindness*. New York: New Press, 2010.

Allen, Howard W. and Clubb, Jerome M. *Race, Class, and the Death Penalty: Capital Punishment in American History*. Albany: State University of New York Press, 2008.

Anderson, David. *Histories of the Hanged: Britain's Dirty War in Kenya and the End of Empire*. New York: W. W. Norton, 2005.

Anthony, Andrew. 'Steven Pinker: "The way to deal with pollution is not to rail against consumption"', *The Guardian*, 11 February 2018, https://www.theguard ian.com/science/2018/feb/11/steven-pinker-enlightenment-now-interview-inequ ality-consumption-environment

Angell, Norman. *The Great Illusion: A Study of the Relation of Military Power to National Advantage*. New York: G. Putnam's Sons, 1913.

Antweiler, Christoph. 'Fremdheit, Identität und Ethnisierung: Instrumentalisierung des Anderen und ihre Relevanz für Archäologie und Ethnologie', in Tobias L.

Kienlin (ed.), *Fremdheit – Perspectiven auf das Andere*, 25–40. Boon: Verlag Rudolph Habelt, 2015.

Archer, John. 'Introduction: Male Violence in Perspective', in John Archer (ed.), *Male Violence*, 1–20. London: Routledge, 1994.

Ardrey, Robert. *African Genesis: A Personal Investigation into the Animal Origins and Nature of Man*. London: Collins, 1961.

Arendt, Hannah. *The Origins of Totalitarianism*. Cleveland: Meridian, 1958.

Armit, Ian. 'Violence and Society in Deep Human Past', *The British Journal of Criminology*, 51:3 (2011): 499–517.

Arras, Daniel. *La Guillotine*. Paris: Flammarion, 1987.

Asad, Talal. 'Reflections on Violence, Law, and Humanitarianism', *Critical Inquiry*, 41 (Winter 2015): 390–427.

Austin, Gareth (ed.). *Economic Development and Environmental History in the Anthropocene: Perspectives on Asia and Africa*. London: Bloomsbury, 2017.

Auty, Richard M. *Sustaining Development in Mineral Economies: The Resource Curse Thesis*. London: Routledge, 1993.

Avalos, Lisa R. 'Policing Rape Complaints: When Reporting Rape Becomes a Crime', *Journal of Gender, Race, and Justice*, 20 (2017): 466–7.

Bailyn, Bernard. *The Ideological Origins of the American Revolution*. Cambridge, MA: Belknap Press, 1967.

Bailyn, Bernard. *Illuminating History: A Retrospective of Seven Decades*. New York: W. W. Norton, 2020.

Baker, Keith Michael. *Inventing the French Revolution: Essays on French Political Culture in the Eighteenth Century*. Cambridge: Cambridge University Press, 1990.

Baker, Keith Michael and Reill, Peter Hans (eds), *What's Left of Enlightenment? A Postmodern Question*. Stanford: Stanford University Press, 2001.

Bakić-Hayden, Malica. 'Nesting Orientalisms: The Case of Former Yugoslavia', *Slavic Review*, 54:4 (Winter 1995): 917–31.

Bales, Kevin. *Disposable People: New Slavery in the Global Economy*. Berkeley: University of California Press, 1999.

Balko, Radley. *Rise of the Warrior Cop: The Militarization of America's Police Forces*. New York: PublicAffairs, 2013.

Balto, Simon. *Occupied Territory: Policing Black Chicago from Red Summer to Black Power*. Chapel Hill: University of North Carolina Press, 2019.

Banner, Stuart. *The Death Penalty: An American History*. Cambridge, MA: Harvard University Press, 2002.

Barca, Stefania. 'Telling the Right Story: Environmental Violence and Liberation Narratives', *Environment and History*, 20 (2014): 535–46.

Barkan, Steven E. and Cohn, Steven F. 'Racial Prejudice and Support for the Death Penalty among Whites', *Journal of Research in Crime and Delinquency*, 31:2 (May 1994): 202–9.

Barrow Jr., Mark V. *Nature's Ghosts: Confronting Extinction from the Age of Jefferson to the Age of Ecology*. Chicago: University of Chicago Press, 2009.

Bastien, Pascal. *L'exécution publique a Paris au XVIIIe siècle: Une histoire des rituels judiciaires*. Seyssel: Champ Vallon, 2006.

Bauman, Zygmunt. *Modernity and the Holocaust*. Cambridge: Polity Press, 1990.

Baumgartner, Frank R., Davison, Marty, Johnson, Kaneesha R., Krishnamurthy, Arvind and Wilson, Colin P. '#BlackLivesDon'tMatter: Race-of-Victim Effects in US Executions, 1976-2013', *Politics, Groups, and Identities*, 3:2 (2015): 209–21.

Baumgartner, Frank R., Davison, Marty, Johnson, Kaneesha R., Krishnamurthy, Arvind and Wilson, Colin P. *Deadly Justice: A Statistical Portrait of the Death Penalty*. New York: Oxford University Press, 2018.

Bayly, C. A. *The Birth of the Modern World, 1780–1914: Global Connections and Comparisons*. Malden: Blackwell, 2004.

Beck, R. Theodore. *The Cutting Edge: Early History of the Surgeons of London*. London: Lund Humphries, 1974.

Becker, Carl Lotus. *The Heavenly City of the Eighteenth-Century Philosophers*. New Haven: Yale University Press, 1932.

Becket, Ian F. W. *Modern Insurgencies and Counter-Insurgencies: Guerrillas and their Opponents since 1750*. London: Routledge, 2001.

Bell, Daniel. *The Coming of Post-Industrial Society: A Venture in Social Forecasting*. New York: Basic Books, 1973.

Bell, David A. *The First Total War: Napoleon's Europe and the Birth of Modern Warfare as We Know It*. New York: Houghton Mifflin Company, 2007.

Bell, David A. 'The Power Point Philosophe: Waiting for Steven Pinker's Enlightenment', *The Nation*, 7 March 2018.

Bellamy, Alex. *East Asia's Other Miracle: Explaining the Decline of Mass Atrocities*. Oxford: Oxford University Press, 2017.

Bellamy, John G. *The Criminal Trial in Later Medieval England*. Buffalo and Toronto: University of Toronto Press, 1998.

Benjamin, Walter. 'Thesis on History', in Hannah Arendt (ed.), *Illuminations: Essays and Reflections*, 196–209. New York: Harcourt, Brace & World, 1968.

Benjamin, Walter. *Selected Writings*, trans. Edmund Jephcott, ed. Howard Eiland and Michael W. Jennings. Cambridge: Belknap Press, 2003.

Bennett, Carys E., Thomas, Richard, Williams, Mark, Zalasiewicz, Jan, Edgeworth, Matt, Miller, Holly, Coles, Ben, Foster, Alison, Burton, Emily J. and Marume, Upenyu. 'The Broiler Chicken as a Signal of a Human Reconfigured Biosphere', *Royal Society Open Science*, 12 December 2018, https://royalsocietypublishing.org/doi/full/10.1098/rsos.180325

Bennike, Pia. *Palaeopathology of Danish Skeletons*. Copenhagen: Akademisk Forlag, 1985.

Berlin, Isaiah. *Against the Current: Essays in the History of Ideas*. London: Hogarth Press, 1979.

Berlin, Isaiah. 'The Counter-Enlightenment', in Henry Hardy (ed.), *Against the Current: Essays in the History of Ideas*, 1–33. New York: Penguin, 1982.

Alexander Bevilacqua, *The Republic of Arab Letters: Islam and the European Enlightenment*. Cambridge, MA: Belknap Press, 2018.

Bierman, John and Smith, Colin. *Fire in the Night: Wingate of Burma, Ethiopia, and Zion*. New York: Random House, 1999.

Bishop, Chris. '"The 'Pear of Anguish'": Truth, Torture and Dark Medievalism', *International Journal of Cultural Studies*, 17:6 (2014): 591–602.

Blumstein, Alfred. 'Violence: A New Frontier for Scientific Research', *Science*, 289 (2000): 545.

Bobo, Lawrence D. and Thompson, Victor. 'Racialized Mass Incarceration: Poverty, Prejudice, and Punishment', in Hazel R. Markus and Paula Moya (eds), *Doing Race: 21 Essays for the 21st Century*, 322–55. New York: W.W. Norton, 2010.

Bocquet-Appel, Jean Pierre. 'Paleoanthropological Traces of a Neolithic Demographic Transition', *Current Anthropology*, 43 (2002): 637–50.

Bodart-Bailey, Beatrice. *The Dog Shogun: The Personality and Policies of Tokugawa Tsunayoshi*. Honolulu: University of Hawai'i Press, 2006.

Boddice, Robert (ed.). *Pain and Emotion in Modern History*. London: Palgrave Macmillan, 2014.

Boddice, Robert. *Pain: A Very Short Introduction*. Oxford: Oxford University Press, 2017.

Boddice, Robert. *The History of Emotions*. Manchester: Manchester University Press, 2018.

Boddice, Robert. *A History of Feelings*. London: Reaktion Books, 2019.

Bonneuil, Christophe and Fressoz, Jean-Baptiste. *The Shock of the Anthropocene: The Earth, History, and US*. London: Verso, 2016.

Bonta, Bruce. *Peaceful Peoples: An Annotated Bibliography*. Metuchen: Scarecrow, 1993.

Boomgaard, Peter. *Frontiers of Fear: Tigers and People in the Malay World, 1600–1950*. New Haven: Yale University Press, 2001.

Boone, Elizabeth Hill (ed.). *The Aztec Templo Mayor*. Washington, DC: Dumbarton Oaks, 1987.

Bossen, Claus. 'War as Practice, Power, and Processor: A Framework for the Analysis of War and Social Structural Change', in Ton Otto, Henrik Thrane and Helle Vandkilde (eds), *Warfare and Society: Archaeological and Social Anthropological Perspectives*, 89–102. Aarhus: Aarhus University Press, 2006.

Botsman, Daniel. *Punishment and Power in the Making of Modern Japan*. Princeton: Princeton University Press, 2013.

Bourke, Joanna. *Fear: A Cultural History*. Emeryville: Shoemaker Hoard, 2005.

Bourke, Joanna. *Rape: A History from the 1860s to the Present*. London: Virago, 2007.

Bourke, Joanna. *The Story of Pain: From Prayer to Painkillers*. Oxford: Oxford University Press, 2014.

Bourke, Joanna. *Wounding the World: How Military Violence and War Games Invade Our Lives*. London: Virago, 2014.

Bourke, Joanna. 'Theorizing Ballistics: Ethics, Emotions, and Weapons Science', *History and Theory*, 55 (December 2017): 135–51.

Bowers, William J., Pierce, Glenn L. and McDevitt, John F. *Legal Homicide: Death as Punishment in America, 1864–1982*. Boston: Northeastern University Press, 1984.

Boyd, William. 'Science, Technology, and American Poultry Production', *Technology and Culture*, 42 (2001): 631–64.

Brecher, W. Puck. 'Being a Brat: The Ethics of Child Disobedience in the Edo Period', in Peter Nosco (ed.), *Values, Identity, and Equality in Eighteenth and Nineteenth Century Japan*, 80–111. Leiden: Brill, 2015.

Breen, Benjamin. 'Animal History: An Emerging Scholarly Trend', *JStor Daily*, 29 October 2014, https://daily.jstor.org/animals-in-the-archive/

Brickman, Philip, Coates, Dan and Janoff-Bulman, Ronnie. 'Lottery Winners and Accident Victims: Is Happiness Relative?', *Journal of Personality and Social Psychology*, 36:8 (1978): 917–27.

Broadhurst, Roderic, Bouhours, Thierry and Bouhours, Brigitte. *Violence and the Civilising Process in Cambodia*. Cambridge: Cambridge University Press, 2015.

Brown, Howard G. *Mass Violence and the Self: From the French Wars of Religion to the Paris Commune*. Ithaca: Cornell University Press, 2018.

Brown, Warren. *Violence in Medieval Europe*. Harlow: Longman Pearson, 2011.

Browning, Christopher R. *Ordinary Men: Reserve Police Battalion 101 and the Final Solution in Poland*. New York: HarperCollins, 1992.

Brundage, James A. 'Rape and Marriage in the Medieval Canon Law', in James A. Brundage (ed.), *Sex, Law and Marriage in the Middle Ages*, 62–75. Aldershot: Variorum, 1993.

Buller, David J. *Adapting Minds: Evolutionary Psychology and the Persistent Quest for Human Nature*. Cambridge, MA: MIT Press, 2005.

Burgin, Angus. *The Great Persuasion: Reinventing Free Markets Since the Depression*. Cambridge, MA: Harvard University Press, 2012.

Burkitt, Ian. 'Civilization and Ambivalence', *British Journal of Sociology*, 47:1 (1996): 135–50.

Burns, E. Bradford. *Poverty of Progress: Latin America in the Nineteenth Century*. Berkeley: University of California Press, 1983.

Buss, David M. 'Conflict between the Sexes: Strategic Interference and the Evocation of Anger and Upset', *Journal of Personality and Social Psychology*, 56:5 (1989): 735–47.

Butler, Sara M. 'A Case of Indifference: Child Murder in Later Medieval England', *Journal of Women's History*, 19:4 (2007): 59–82.

Butler, Sara M. *The Language of Abuse: Marital Violence in Later Medieval England*. Leiden: Brill, 2007.

Butler, Sara M. *Divorce in Medieval England: From One to Two Persons in Law*. New York: Routledge, 2013.

Butler, Sara M. 'Getting Medieval on Steven Pinker: Violence and Medieval England', *Historical Reflections/Réflexions Historiques*, 44:1 (Spring 2018): 29–40.

Butterfield, Herbert. *The Whig Interpretation of History*. London: G. Bell and Sons, 1931.

Callwell, Colonel C. E. *Small Wars: Their Principles and Practices*. Lincoln: University of Nebraska Press, 1996.

Cameron, Catherine M., Kelton, Paul and Swedlund Alan C. (eds). *Beyond Germs: Native Depopulation in North America*. Tucson: University of Arizona Press, 2015.

Camp, Jordan T. and Heatherton, Christina (eds). *Policing the Planet: Why the Policing Crisis Led to Black Lives Matter*. New York: Verso, 2016.

Carr, E. H. *What Is History?* ed. R. W. Daves. 1961; Houndsmills: Macmillan, 1986.

Carrasco, David. *The Aztecs: A Very Short Introduction*. Oxford: Oxford University Press, 2012.

Carroll, Stuart. *Blood and Violence in Early Modern France*. Oxford: Oxford University Press, 2006.

Carroll, Stuart. 'Thinking with Violence', *History and Theory*, 55 (December 2017): 23–43.

Ceballos, Gerardo, Ehrlich, Paul R., and Dirzo, Rodolfo. 'Biological Annihilation via the Ongoing Sixth Mass Extinction Signaled by Vertebrate Population Losses and Declines', *PNAS*, 114:30 (25 July 2017): E6089–96.

Chalhoub, Sidney. 'The Politics of Ambiguity: Conditional Manumission, Labor Contracts, and Slave Emancipation in Brazil (1850s-1888)', *International Review of Social History*, 60:1 (2015): 161–91.

Charlip Julie A. and Burns, E. Bradford. *Latin America: An Interpretive History*. London and New York: Pearson, 2016.

Chartier, Roger. *Les Origines culturelles de la Révolution française*. Paris: Seuil, 1990.

Chartier, Roger. 'The Chimera of the Origin: Archaeology, Cultural History, and the French Revolution', in Jan Goldstein (ed.), *Foucault and the Writing of History*, 175–7. Oxford: Blackwell, 1994.

Chase, Robert T. (ed.). *Caging Borders and Carceral States: Incarcerations, Immigration Detentions, and Resistance*. Chapel Hill: University of North Carolina Press, 2019.

Chatterjee, Choi. 'Imperial Incarcerations: Ekaterina Breshko-Breshkovskaia, Vinayak Damodar Savarkar, and the Original Sins of Modernity', *Slavic Review*, 74:4 (Winter 2015): 850–72.

Chatterjee, Partha. *The Nation and Its Fragments*. Princeton: Princeton University Press, 1993.

Christensen, Jonas. 'Warfare in the European Neolithic', *Acta Archaeologica*, 75 (2004): 129–56.

Christian, David. *Maps of Time: An Introduction to Big History*. Berkeley: University of California Press, 2004.

Cirillo, Pasquale and Taleb, Nassim Nicholas. 'The Decline of Violent Conflicts: What Do The Data Really Say?' *Nobel Foundation Symposium 161: The Causes of Peace*, https://www.fooledbyrandomness.com/pinker.pdf

Cirillo, Pasquale and Taleb, Nassim Nicholas. 'On the Statistical Properties and Tail Risk of Violent Conflicts', *Physica A: Statistical Mechanics and Its Applications*, 452 (2016): 29–45.

Citron, Danielle Keats. 'Cyber Civil Rights', *Boston University Law Review*, 89 (2009): 64–9.

Citron, Danielle Keats. 'Law's Expressive Value in Combating Cyber Gender Harassment', *Michigan Law Review*, 108 (2009): 373–415.

Citron, Danielle Keats. *Hate Crimes in Cyberspace*. Cambridge, MA: Harvard University Press, 2014.

Citron, Danielle Keats. 'Addressing Cyber Harassment: An Overview of Hate Crimes in Cyberspace', *Journal of Law, Technology, and the Internet*, 6 (2015): 1–12.

Clare, Lee and Gebel, Hans Georg K. 'Introduction: Conflict and Warfare in the Near Eastern Neolithic', *Noe-Lithics*, 10:1 (2010): 3–5.

Coates, Peter. '"Unusually Cunning, Vicious, and Treacherous": The Extermination of the Wolf in United States History', in Mark Levene and Penny Roberts (eds), *The Massacre in History*, 163–83. New York: Berghahn, 1999.

Cockburn, J. S. 'Patterns of Violence in English Society: Homicide in Kent, 1560–1985', *Past and Present*, 130 (1991): 70–106.

Coleman, Jon. *Vicious: Wolves and Men in America*. New Haven: Yale University Press, 2004.

Conrad, Robert Edgar (ed.). *Children of God's Fire: A Documentary History of Black Slavery in Brazil*. Princeton: Princeton University Press, 1983.

Conrad, Robert Edgar. *The Destruction of Brazilian Slavery, 1850–1888*. 2nd edn. Malabar: Krieger, 1993.

Conrad, Sebastian. 'Enlightenment in Global History: A Historiographical Critique', *American Historical Review*, 117:4 (2012): 999–1027.

Cooney, Mark. 'From Warre to Tyranny: Lethal Conflict and the State', *American Sociological Review*, 62 (1997): 316–38.

Cooney, Mark. 'The Privatization of Violence', *Criminology*, 41:4 (2003): 1377–406.

Costa, Emilia Viotti da. *The Brazilian Empire: Myths and Histories*. Chapel Hill: University of North Carolina Press, 2000.

Crook, David. *Records of the General Eyre*, Public Record Office Handbooks, no. 20. London: Public Record Office, 1982.

Crosby, Alfred W. *The Columbian Exchange: Biological and Cultural Consequences of 1492*. Westport: Greenwood Publishing, 1973.

Crosby, Alfred W. *Ecological Imperialism: The Biological Expansion of Europe, 900-1900* [1986], second edition. Cambridge: Cambridge University Press, 2004.

Cummins, Robert A. 'Can Happiness Change? Theories and Evidence', in Kennon M. Sheldon and Richard E. Lucas (eds), *Stability of Happiness: Theories and Evidence on Whether Happiness Can Change*, 75–97. London: Academic Press, 2014.

Dakin, Douglas. *Turgot and the Ancien Régime in France*. London: Methuen, 1939.

Daly, Jill E. 'Gathering Dust on the Evidence Shelves of the US', *Women's Rights Law Reporter*, 25:1 (Fall/Winter 2003): 17–36.

Daly, Jonathan. 'Russian Punishments in the European Mirror', in Michael Melancon (ed.), *Russia in the European Context 1789-1914: A Member of the Family*, 161–88. Gordonsville: Palgrave Macmillan, 2005.

Daly, M. and Wilson, M. *Homicide*. New York: A. de Gruyter, 1988.

Darnton, Robert. *Mesmerism and the End of the Enlightenment in France*. Cambridge, MA: Harvard University Press, 1968.

Daston, Lorraine and Gallison, Peter. *Objectivity*. New York: Zone Books, 2010.

Davies, Jonathan. 'Introduction', in Jonathan Davies (ed.), *Aspects of Violence in Renaissance Europe*, 1–16. London and New York: Routledge, 2013.

Davis, David Brion. *The Problem of Slavery in Western Culture*. Ithaca: Cornell University Press, 1966.

Davis, David Brion. *The Problem of Slavery in the Age of Revolution*. Ithaca: Cornell University Press, 1975.

Davis, David Brion. *Inhuman Bondage: The Rise and Fall of Slavery in the New World*. New York: Oxford University Press, 2006.

Davis, David Brion. *Problem of Slavery in the Age of Emancipation*. New York: Knopf, 2014.

Dawson, Doyne. 'The Origins of War: Biological and Anthropological Theories', *History and Theory*, 35:1 (1996): 1–28.

de Dijn, Annelien. 'The Politics of Enlightenment: From Peter Gay to Jonathan Israel', *The Historical Journal*, 55:3 (2012): 785–805.

de Vries, Katja. 'Avatars Out of Control: Gazira Babeli, Pose Balls and "Rape" in Second Life', in Serge Gutwirth (ed.), *Computers, Privacy, and Data Protection*, 233–50. New York: Springer, 2011.

de Waal, Frans B. M. 'Primates – A Natural Heritage of Conflict Resolution', *Science*, 289 (2000): 586–90.

Dean, Trevor. *Crime in Medieval Europe*. Harlow: Longman, 2001.

Dentan, Robert K. 'Recent Studies on Violence: What's in and What's Out', *Reviews in Anthropology*, 37 (2008): 41–67.

Devereaux, Simon. 'The Promulgation of the Statutes in Late Hanoverian Britain', in David Lemmings (ed.), *The British and their Laws in the Eighteenth Century*, 85–6. Woodbridge: Boydell Press, 2005.

Devereaux, Simon. 'Recasting the Theatre of Execution: The Abolition of the Tyburn Ritual', *Past & Present*, 202 (February 2009): 127–74.

Devereaux, Simon. 'England's "Bloody Code" in Crisis and Transition: Executions at the Old Bailey, 1760–1837', *Journal of the Canadian Historical Association*, 24:2 (2013): 71–113.

Devereaux, Simon. 'Inexperienced Humanitarians? William Wilberforce, William Pitt, and the Executions Crisis of the 1780s', *Law and History Review*, 33 (2015): 839–85.

Devereaux, Simon. 'The Bloodiest Code: Counting Executions and Pardons at the Old Bailey, 1730–1837', *Law, Crime and History*, 6:1 (2016): 1–36.

Devereaux, Simon. 'Execution and Pardon at the Old Bailey, 1730–1837', *American Journal of Legal History*, 57 (2017): 447–94.

Dibbell, Julian. 'A Rape in Cyberspace Or How an Evil Clown, A Haitian Trickster Spirit, Two Wizards, and a Cast of Dozens Turned a Database into a Society', *Annual Survey of American Law*, 471 (1994): 471–89.

Dicey, A. V. *The Case against Home Rule*. London: John Murray, 1886.

Dijk, Boyd van. 'Human Rights in War: On the Entangled Foundations of the 1949 Geneva Conventions', *The American Society of International Law*, 112:4 (2018): 556.

Dinges, Martin. 'Gewalt und Zivilisationsprozess', *Traverse*, 2:1 (1995): 70–81.

Dinges, Martin. 'Formenwandel der Gewalt in der Neuzeit. Zur Kritik der Zivilisationstheorie von Norbert Elias', in Rolf Peter Sieferle and Helga Breuninger (eds), *Kulturen der Gewalt. Ritualisierung und Symbolisierung von Gewalt in der Geschichte*, 171–94. Frankfurt am Main: Campus, 1998.

Ditchfield, P. H. and Page, William (eds). *A History of the County of Berkshire*, 2 vols. London: Victoria County History, 1907.

Dixon, Thomas. *From Passions to Emotion: The Creation of a Secular Psychological Category*. Cambridge: Cambridge University Press, 2003.

Dixon, Thomas. 'Emotion: The History of a Keyword in Crisis', *Emotion Review* (October 2012): 338–44.

Djilas, Milovan. *The New Class: An Analysis of the Communist System*. New York: Praeger, 1957.

Dorsey, Kurkpatrick. *Whales and Nations: Environmental Diplomacy on the High Seas*. Seattle: University of Washington Press, 2013.

Drescher, Seymour. *Abolition: A History of Slavery and Antislavery*. Cambridge: Cambridge University Press, 2009.

Driscoll, Mark. *Absolute Erotic, Absolute Grotesque: The Living, Dead, and Undead in Japan's Imperialism, 1895–1945*. Durham: Duke University Press, 2010.

Drixler, Fabian. *Mabiki: Infanticide and Population Growth in Eastern Japan, 1660–1940*. Berkeley: University of California Press, 2013.

Duerr, Hans Peter. *Nacktheit und Scham*. Frankfurt am Main: Suhrkamp Verlag, 1988.

Duerr, Hans Peter. *Obszönität und Gewalt. Band 3: Der Mythos vom Zivilisationsprozeß*. Frankfurt am Main: Suhkampf, 1993.

Dülmen, Richard van. *Theatre of Horror: Crime and Punishment in Early Modern Germany*, trans. Elisabeth Neu. Cambridge: Polity Press, 1990.

Dunbar-Ortiz, Roxanne. *An Indigenous Peoples' History of the United States*. Boston: Beacon Press, 2014.

Dunn, Caroline. *Stolen Women in Medieval England*. Cambridge: Cambridge University Press, 2013.

Dunn, Diana E. S. (ed.). *Courts, Counties and the Capital in the Later Middle Ages*. New York: St. Martin's Press, 1996.

Dunning, Eric, Murphy, Patrick and Waddington, Ivan. 'Violence in the British Civilizing Process', in Eric Dunning and Stephen Mennell (eds), *Norbert Elias*, 4 vols, ii. 5–34. Sage: London, 2003.

Dunning, Eric and Hughes, Jason. *Norbert Elias and Modern Sociology: Knowledge, Interdependence, Power, Process*. London: Bloomsbury, 2013

Dupré, John. *Human and Other Animals*. Oxford: Clarendon Press, 2002.

Dwyer, Philip. 'Whitewashing History: Pinker's (Mis)Representation of the Enlightenment and Violence', *Historical Reflections/Réflexions historiques*, 44:1 (Spring 2018): 54–65.

Dwyer, Philip and Micale, Mark S. (eds), *On Violence in History*. New York: Berghahn, 2019.

Dwyer, Philip and Damousi, Joy (eds), *The Cambridge World History of Violence*. Cambridge: Cambridge University Press, 2020.

Dyer, Meaghan and Fibiger, Linda. 'Understanding Blunt Force Trauma and Violence in Neolithic Europe: The First Experiments using a Skin-Skull-Brain Model and the Thames Beater', *Antiquity*, 91:360 (2017): 1515–28.

Eason, David. 'The Culture of Disputes in Early Modern Japan, 1550–1700'. PhD diss, UCLA, 2009.

Edelstein, Dan. *The Enlightenment: A Genealogy*. Chicago: University of Chicago Press, 2010.

Ehrlich, Paul R. *The Population Bomb*. New York: Ballantine, 1968.

Eiko, Ikegami. *The Taming of the Samurai: Honorific Individualism and the Making of Modern Japan*. Cambridge, MA: Harvard University Press, 2003.

Eisner, Manuel. 'Modernization, Self-control and Lethal Violence: The Long-Term Dynamics of European Homicide Rates in Theoretical Perspective', *The British Journal of Criminology*, 41:4 (2001): 618–38.

Eisner, Manuel. 'Long-Term Historical Trends in Violent Crime', *Crime and Justice*, 30 (2003): 83–142.

Eisner, Manuel. 'From Swords to Words: Does Macro-Level Change in Self-Control Predict Long-Term Variations in Levels of Homicide?', *Crime and Justice*, 43:1 (2014): 65–134.

Eisner, Manuel. 'Interactive London Medieval Murder Map', Institute of Criminology, University of Cambridge, https://www.vrc.crim.cam.ac.uk/vrcr esearch/london-medieval-murder-map

Elias, Norbert. *The Civilizing Process: Sociogenetic and Psychogenetic Investigations*, trans. Edmund Jephcott. Oxford: Blackwell, 1994.

Elias, Norbert. *Reflections on a Life*, trans. Edmund Jephcott. Cambridge: Polity Press, 1994.

Elias, Norbert. *The Germans: Power Struggles and the Development of Habitus in the Nineteenth and Twentieth Centuries*, trans. Eric Dunning and Stephen Mennell. Oxford: Polity Press, 1996.

Elkins, Caroline. *Imperial Reckoning: The Untold Story of Britain's Gulag in Kenya*. New York: Henry Holt, 2005.

Eltis, David and Richardson, David. *Atlas of the Transatlantic Slave Trade*. New Haven: Yale University Press, 2010.

Ember, Carol R. and Ember, Melvin. 'War, Socialization, and Interpersonal Violence – A Cross-Cultural Study', *Journal of Conflict Resolution*, 38 (1994): 620–46.

Enserink, Martin. 'Searching for the Mark of Cain', *Science*, 289 (2000): 575–9.

Erichsen, John Eric. *On Railway and Other Injuries of the Nervous System*. London: Walton and Maberly, 1866.

Erichsen, John Eric. *On Concussion of the Spine, Nervous Shock, and Other Obscure Injuries of the Nervous System in Their Clinical and Medico-Legal Aspects*. London: Longman, Green and Co., 1875.

Eskildsen, Robert. 'Of Civilization and Savages: The Mimetic Imperialism of Japan's 1874 Expedition to Taiwan', *The American Historical Review*, 107:2 (April 2002): 388–418.

Eustace, Nicole. *Passion Is the Gale: Emotion, Power, and the Coming of the American Revolution*. Chapel Hill: University of North Carolina Press, 2008.

Eustace, Nicole. *1812: War and the Passions of Patriotism*. Philadelphia: University of Pennsylvania Press, 2012.

Eustace, Nicole, Lean, Eugenia, Livingston, Julie, Plamper, Jan, Reddy, William and Rosenwein, Barbara. 'AHR Conversation: The Historical Study of Emotion', *The American Historical Review*, 177:5 (December 2012): 1487–531.

Evans, Richard J. *Rituals of Retribution: Capital Punishment in Germany, 1600–1987*. London: Penguin, 1996.

Eze, Emmanuel Chukwudi (ed.). *Race and the Enlightenment: A Reader*. Cambridge, MA: Blackwell, 1997.

Fagan, Garrett G., Fibiger, Linda, Hudson, Mark and Trundle, Matthew (eds). *The Cambridge World History of Violence, Vol. I: The Prehistoric and Ancient Worlds*. Cambridge: Cambridge University Press, 2020.

Falk, Dean and Hildebolt, Charles. 'Annual War Deaths in Small-Scale versus State Societies Scale with Population Size Rather than Violence', *Current Anthropology*, 58:6 (2017): 805–13.

Farmer, Paul. 'On Suffering and Structural Violence: A View from Below', *Race/Ethnicity: Multidisciplinary Global Contexts*, 3:1 (2009): 11–28.

Farris, William W. *Japan's Medieval Population: Famine, Fertility, and Warfare in a Transformative Age*. Honolulu: University of Hawai'i Press, 2009.

Fassin, Didier. 'On Resentment and *Ressentiment*: The Politics and Ethics of Moral Emotions', *Current Anthropology*, 54 (2013): 249–67.

Fayard, Nicole and Rocheron, Yvette. '"Moi quand on dit qu'une femme ment, eh bien, elle ment": The Administration of Rape in Twenty-First Century France and England and Wales', *French Politics, Culture and Society*, 29:1 (Spring 2011): 68–92.

Fazal, Tanisha M. 'Dead Wrong?: Battle Deaths, Military Medicine, and Exaggerated Reports of War's Demise', *International Security*, 39:1 (Summer 2014): 95–125.

Febvre, Lucien. 'Sensibility and History: How to Reconstitute the Emotional Life of the Past', in Peter Burke (ed.), *A New Kind of History: From the Writings of Febvre*, trans. K. Folca, 12–26. New York: Routledge & Kegan Paul, 1973.

Felker-Kantor, Max. *Policing Los Angeles: Race, Resistance, and the Rise of the LAPD*. Chapel Hill: University of North Carolina Press, 2020.

Ferguson, Christopher J. and Beaver, Kevin M. 'Natural Born Killers: The Genetic Origins of Extreme Violence', *Aggression and Violent Behaviour*, 14 (2009): 286–94.

Ferguson, R. Brian. 'Introduction: Studying War', in R. Brian Ferguson (ed.), *Warfare, Culture and Environment*, 1–18. Orlando: Academic Press, 1984.

Ferguson, R. Brian. 'Explaining War', in Jonathan Haas (ed.), *The Anthropology of War*, 26–55. Cambridge: Cambridge University Press, 1990.

Ferguson, R. Brian. 'Pinker's List: Exaggerating Prehistoric War Mortality', in Fry (ed.), *War, Peace, and Human Nature*, 112–31.

Ferguson, R. Brian. 'The Prehistory of War and Peace in Europe and the Near East', in Fry (ed.), *War, Peace, and Human Nature*, 191–240.

Ferllini, Roxana. 'Recent Conflicts, Deaths and Simple Technologies: The Rwandan Case', in Knüsel and Smith (eds), *The Routledge Handbook of the Bioarchaeology of Human Conflict*, 641–55. Abingdon: Routledge, 2014.

Fernández-Armesto, Felipe. *Humankind: A Brief History*. Oxford and New York: Oxford University Press, 2004.

Fernández-Armesto, Felipe. *Out of Our Minds: What We Think and How We Came to Think It*. Oakland: University of California Press, 2019.

Fibiger, Linda, Ahlström, Torbjörn, Bennike, Pia and Schulting, Rick J. 'Patterns of Violence-Related Skull Trauma in Neolithic Southern Scandinavia', *American Journal of Physical Anthropology*, 150 (2013): 190–202.

Fibiger, Linda. 'Misplaced Childhood? Interpersonal Violence and Children in Neolithic Europe', in Knüsel and Smith (eds), *The Routledge Handbook of the Bioarchaeology*, 27–145.

Fibiger, Linda. 'Conflict and violence in the Neolithic of North-Western Europe', in Manuel Fernández-Götz and Nico Roymans (eds), *Conflict Archaeology: Materialities of Collective Violence in Late Prehistoric and Early Historic Europe*, 13–22. New York: Taylor & Francis, 2018.

Fibiger, Linda. 'The Past as a Foreign Country: Bioarchaeological Perspectives on Pinker's "Prehistoric Anarchy"', *Historical Reflections/ Réflexions Historiques*, 44:1 (Spring 2018): 76–100.

Fichte, J. G. *Foundations of Natural Right, according to the Principles of the Wissenschaftslehre* (1796), ed. Frederick Neuhouser, trans. Michael Baur. Cambridge University Press, 2000.

Finley, Carmel. *All the Boats on the Ocean: How Government Subsidies Led to Global Overfishing*. Chicago: University of Chicago Press, 2017.

Fletcher, Jonathan. 'Towards a Theory of Decivilizing Processes', *Amsterdams sociologisch Tijdschrift*, 22:2 (October 1995): 283–97.

Fletcher, Jonathan. *Violence and Civilization: An Introduction to the Work of Norbert Elias*. Cambridge: Polity Press, 1997.

Formisano, Ronald P. *Boston Against Busing: Race, Class, and Ethnicity in the 1960s and 1970s*. Chapel Hill: University of North Carolina Press, 1991.

Forrest, Alan. *The Death of the French Atlantic: Trade, War, and Slavery in the Age of Revolution*. Oxford: Oxford University Press, 2020.

Foucault, Michel. *Discipline and Punish: The Birth of the Prison*, trans. Alan Sheridan. New York: Pantheon Books, 1977.

Foucault, Michel. 'Nietzsche, Genealogy, History', in Paul Rabinow (ed.), *The Foucault Reader*, 76–100. New York: Pantheon, 1984.

Franklin, Michael J. and Harper-Bill, Christopher (eds). *Medieval Ecclesiastical Studies: In Honour of Dorothy M. Owen*. Woodbridge: Boydell, 1995.

Franks, Mary Anne. 'Unwilling Avatars: Idealism and Discrimination in Cyberspace', *Columbia Journal of Gender and Law*, 20:1 (2011): 224–61.

Fredrickson, George M. *Racism: A Short History*. Princeton: Princeton University Press, 2003.

Freedman, Lawrence (ed.). *War*. Oxford: Oxford University Press, 1994.

Freud, Sigmund. *Civilization and Its Discontents*, trans. Joan Riviere. London: Hogarth Press, 1930.

Frevert, Ute. *Emotions in History: Lost and Found*. Budapest: Central European University Press, 2011.

Frevert, Ute, Bailey, Christian, Eitler, Pascal, Gammerl, Benno, Hitzer, Bettina, Pernau, Margrit, Scheer, Monique, Schmidt, Anne and Verheyen, Nina. *Emotional Lexicons: Continuity and Change in the Vocabulary of Feeling*. Oxford: Oxford University Press, 2014.

Friedland, Paul. *Seeing Justice Done: The Age of Spectacular Capital Punishment in France*. Oxford: Oxford University Press, 2012.

Fry, Douglas. 'Maintaining Social Tranquility: Internal and External Loci of Aggression Control', in Sponsel and Gregor (eds), *The Anthropology of Peace and Nonviolence*, 133–54.

Fry, Douglas (ed.). *War, Peace, and Human Nature: The Convergence of Evolutionary and Cultural Views*. Oxford: Oxford University Press, 2013.

Galtung, Johan. 'Violence, Peace, and Peace Research', *Journal of Peace Research*, 6:3 (1969): 167–91.

Gangestad, Steven and Simpson, Jeffrey. 'The Evolution of Human Mating: Trade-offs and Strategic Pluralism', *Behavioral and Brain Sciences*, 23 (2000): 575–6.

Garland, David, McGowan, Randall and Meranze, Michael. *America's Death Penalty: Between Past and Present*. New York: New York University Press, 2011.

Garon, Sheldon. 'Rethinking Modernization and Modernity in Japanese History: A Focus on State-Society Relations', *The Journal of Asian Studies*, 53:2 (1994): 346–66.

Garrard, Graeme. *Counter-Enlightenments: From the Eighteenth Century to the Present*. London: Routledge, 2005.

Gat, Azar. *War in Human Civilization*. Oxford: Oxford University Press, 2006.

Gatrell, V. A. C. *The Hanging Tree: Execution and the English People, 1770–1868*. Oxford: Oxford University Press, 1994.

Gauvard, Claude. 'Fear of Crime in Late Medieval France', in Barbara A. Hanawalt and David Wallace (eds), *Medieval Crime and Social Control*, 1–48. Minneapolis: University of Minnesota Press, 1999.

Gavitt, Philip. 'Infant Death in Late Medieval Florence: The Smothering Hypothesis Reconsidered', in Cathy Jorgensen Itnyre (ed.), *Medieval Family Roles: A Book of Essays*, 137–57. New York: Garland, 1996.

Gay, Peter. *The Cultivation of Hatred: The Bourgeois Experience Victoria to Freud*, vol. 3. New York: Norton, 1993.

Geary, Patrick. *The Myth of Nations: The Medieval Origins of Europe*. Princeton: Princeton University Press, 2002.

Gellately, Robert and Kiernan, Ben (eds). *The Specter of Genocide: Mass Murder in Historical Perspective*. Cambridge and New York: Cambridge University Press, 2003.

Geltner, Guy. *Flogging Others: Corporal Punishment and Cultural Identity from Antiquity to the Present*. Amsterdam: Amsterdam University Press, 2014.

Geronimo's Story of His Life, Taken Down and Edited by S. M. Barrett. New York, 1906.

Gerstle, Gary. *Liberty and Coercion: The Paradox of American Government-From the Founding to the Present*. Princeton: Princeton University Press, 2015.

Giddens, Anthony. '*The Society of Individuals*: Norbert Elias, Michael Schröter and Edmund Jephcott', *American Journal of Sociology*, 98:2 (1992): 133–4.

Gilmore, Ruth Wilson. *Golden Gulag: Prisons, Surplus, Crisis, and Opposition in Globalizing California*. Berkeley: University of California Press, 2007.

Ginsberg, Morris. *The Idea of Progress: A Reevaluation*. Westport: Greenwood Press, 1972.

Giridharadas, Anand. *Winners Take All: The Elite Charade of Changing the World*. New York: Alfred A. Knopf, 2018.

Given, James B. *Society and Homicide in Thirteenth-Century England*. Stanford: Stanford University Press, 1977.

Godfrey, Barry, Emsley, Clive and Dunstall, Graeme (eds). *Comparative Histories of Crime*. Cullompton: Willan Publishing, 2003.

Goldschmidt, Walter. 'Peacemaking and Institutions of Peace in Tribal Societies', in Leslie E. Sponsel and Thomas Gregor (eds), *The Anthropology of Peace and Nonviolence*, 109–31. Boulder: Lynner Rienner Publishers, 1994.

Goldstein, Joshua S. *War and Gender: How Gender Shapes the War System and Vice Versa*. Cambridge: Cambridge University Press, 2001.

Goldstein, Joshua S. *Winning the War on War: The Decline of Armed Conflict Worldwide*. London: Dutton, 2011.

Gómez, José María, Verdú, Miguel, González-Megías, Adela and Méndez, Marcos. 'The Phylogenetic Roots of Human Lethal Violence', *Nature*, S38 (2016): 233–7.

Goody, Jack. *The Theft of History*. Cambridge: Cambridge University Press, 2006.

Gopal, Priyamvada. *Insurgent Empire: Anticolonial Resistance and British Dissent*. London: Verso, 2019.

Gordon, Daniel. 'The Canonization of Norbert Elias in France: A Critical Perspective', *French Politics, Culture & Society*, 20:1 (2002): 68–94.

Gordon-Reed, Annette. *Thomas Jefferson and Sally Hemings: An American Controversy*. Charlottesville: University Press of Virginia, 1997.

Gordon-Reed, Annette. *The Hemingses of Monticello: An American Family*. New York: W.W. Norton, 2008.

Goudsblom, Johan, Jones, Eric and Mennell, Stephen. *The Course of Human History: Economic Growth, Social Process and Civilization*. London: Routledge, 1996.

Gould, Stephen Jay. 'Nonmoral Nature', *Natural History*, 91:2 (February 1982): 19–26.

Gould, Stephen Jay. *The Mismeasure of Man*, revised edn. New York: Norton, 1996.

Gouldner, Alvin W. 'Doubts About the Uselessness of Men and the Meaning of the Civilizing Process', *Theory and Society*, 10:3 (May 1981): 413–18.

Gowaty, Patricia Adair. 'Introduction: Darwinian Feminists and Feminist Evolutionists', in Patricia Adair Gowaty (ed.), *Feminism and Evolutionary Biology: Boundaries, Intersections, and Frontiers*, 1–17. New York: Chapman and Hall, 1997.

Gowaty, Patricia Adair. 'Power Asymmetries Between the Sexes, Mate Preferences, and Components of Fitness', in Cheryl Brown Travis (ed.), *Evolution, Gender, and Rape*, 61–86. Cambridge, MA: MIT Press, 2003.

Gowaty, Patricia Adair and Hubbell, Stephen P. 'Chance, Time Allocation, and the Evolution of Adaptively Flexible Sex Role Behavior', *Integrative and Comparative Biology*, 4 (2005): 931–44.

Graham, Elizabeth. *Maya Christians and Their Churches in Sixteenth-Century Belize*. Gainesville: University Press of Florida, 2011.

Graybill, Lela. *The Visual Culture of Violence After the French Revolution*. London: Routledge, 2016.

Green, Nile. *The Love of Strangers: What Six Muslim Students Learned in Jane Austen's London*. Princeton: Princeton University Press, 2016.

Green, Thomas A. *Verdict According to Conscience: Perspectives on the English Criminal Trial Jury, 1200–1800*. Chicago: University of Chicago Press, 1985.

Gregory, Brad S. *Salvation at Stake: Christian Martyrdom in Early Modern Europe*. Cambridge, MA: Harvard University Press, 1999.

Groebner, Valentin. 'Losing Face, Saving Face: Noses and Honour in the Late Medieval Town', *History Workshop Journal*, 40 (1995): 1–15.

Groemer, Gerald. *Portraits of Edo and Early Modern Japan: The Shogun's Capital in Zuihitsu Writings 1657–1855*. Singapore: Palgrave Macmillan, 2019.

Grossman, Dave. *On Combat: The Psychology and Physiology of Deadly Conflict in War and Peace*. Millstadt: Warrior Science Publications, 2004.

Guest, Tim. *Second Lives: A Journey Through Virtual Worlds*. London: Hutchinson, 2007.

Guldi, Jo and Armitage, David. *The History Manifesto*. New York and Cambridge: Cambridge University Press, 2014.

Gunby, Clare, Carline, Anna and Beynon, Caryl. 'Regretting It after: Focus Group Perspectives on Alcohol Consumption, Nonconsensual Sex and False Allegations of Rape', *Social and Legal Studies*, 22:1 (2012): 87–106.

Gurr, Robert Ted. 'Historical Trends in Violent Crimes: A Critical Review of the Evidence', *Crime and Justice: An Annual Review of Research*, 3 (1981): 295–353.

Haidt, Jonathan. *The Righteous Mind: Why Good People Are Divided by Politics and Religion*. New York: Pantheon Books, 2012.

Hamblin, Jacob Darwin. *Arming Mother Nature: The Birth of Catastrophic Environmentalism*. Oxford: Oxford University Press, 2013.

Hammer Jr., C. I. 'Patterns of Homicide in a Medieval University Town: Fourteenth-Century Oxford', *Past and Present*, 78 (1978): 3–23.

Hanawalt, Barbara A. *Crime and Conflict in English Communities, 1300–1348*. Cambridge, MA: Harvard University Press, 1979.

Hanawalt, Barbara A. 'Violent Death in Fourteenth- and early Fifteenth-Century England', *Contemporary Studies in Society & History*, 18:3 (1976): 297–320.

Hanawalt, Barbara A. 'Obverse of the Civilizing Process in Medieval England', *IAHCCJ Bulletin*, 20 (Spring 1995): 49–60.

Hannaford, Ivan. *Race: The History of an Idea in the West*. Washington, DC: Woodrow Wilson Center Press, 1996.

Harari, Yuval N. *Sapiens: A Brief History of Humankind*. London: Harvill Secker, 2014.

Harcourt, Bernard E. *Illusion of Order: The False Promise of Broken Windows Policing*. Cambridge, MA: Harvard University Press, 2001.

Harris, Jessica and Grace, Sharon. *A Question of Evidence? Investigating and Prosecuting Rape in the 1990s*. London: Home Office Research Study 196, 1999.

Harris, Marvin and Kotak, Conrad. 'The Structural Significance of Brazilian Categories', *Sociologica*, 25 (1963): 203–8.

Harrison, Simon. 'War', in Alan Barnard and Jonathan Spencer (eds), *Encyclopedia of Social and Cultural Anthropology*, 561–2. London: Routledge, 2002.

Harvey, David. 'Neoliberalism as Creative Destruction', *Annals of the American Academy of Political and Social Science*, DCX (March 2007): 22–44.

Hathaway, Oona. 'The Promise and Limits of the International Law of Torture', in Levinson (ed.), *Torture*, 199–212,

Headey, Bruce. 'The Set-Point Theory of Well-Being Needs Replacing: On the Brink of a Scientific Revolution?', *SSRN Electronic Journal* (2007), doi:10.2139/ssrn.1096451

Healy, Marsha. 'The Holocaust, Modernity and the Enlightenment', *Res Publica*, 3:1 (1997): 35–59.

Hecht, Gabrielle. *Being Nuclear: Africans and the Global Uranium Trade*. Cambridge, MA: MIT Press, 2012.

Helbling, Jürg. 'War and Peace in Societies Without Central Power', in Otto, Thrane and Vandkilde (eds), *Warfare and Society*, 113–39.

Held, Robert, Bertoni, Marcello and Gil, Amor. *Inquisition: A Bilingual Guide to the Exhibition of Torture Instruments from the Middle Ages to the Industrial Era, Presented in Various European Cities in 1983–87*. Florence: Qua d'Arno, 1985.

Henry, Nicola and Powell, Anastasia. 'Embodied Harms: Gender, Shame, and Technology-Facilitated Sexual Violence', *Violence Against Women*, 21:6 (March 2015): 758–79.

Henry, Nicola and Powell, Anastasia. 'Sexual Violence in the Digital Age: The Scope and Limits of Criminal Law', *Social and Legal Studies*, 25:4 (2016): 397–418.

Henry, Nicola and Powell, Anastasia. 'Technology-Facilitated Sexual Violence. A Literature Review of Empirical Research', *Trauma, Violence, & Abuse*, 19:2 (June 2016): 195–208.

Hewitson, Mark. *Absolute War: Violence and Mass Warfare in the German Lands, 1792–1820*. Oxford: Oxford University Press, 2017.

Himmelfarb, Gertrude. *The Roads to Modernity: The British, French, and American Enlightenments*. New York: Knopf, 2004.

Hinton, Elizabeth Kai. *From the War on Poverty to the War on Crime: The Making of Mass Incarceration in America*. Cambridge, MA: Harvard University Press, 2016.

Hirsch, Arnold, *Making the Second Ghetto: Race and Housing in Chicago, 1940–1960*. Chicago: University of Chicago Press, 1988.

Hirsch, Arnold R. 'Massive Resistance in the Urban North: Trumbull Park, Chicago, 1953–1966', *Journal of American History*, 82:2 (September 1955): 522–50.

Hochschild, Adam. *King Leopold's Ghost: A Story of Greed, Terror and Heroism in Colonial Africa*. Boston: Houghton Mifflin, 1998.

Hochschild, Adam. *Bury the Chains: Prophets and Rebels in the Fight to Free an Empire's Slaves*. Boston: Houghton Mifflin, 2005.

Hodgson, James F. 'Policing Sexual Violence: A Case Study of *Jane Doe v. the Metropolitan Toronto Police*', in Hodgson and Kelley (eds), *Sexual Violence*, 173–90.

Hodgson, James F. and Kelley, Debra S. (eds). *Sexual Violence: Policies, Practices, and Challenges in the United States and Canada*. Westport: Praeger, 2002.

Hogan, Gerard and Walker, Clive. *Political Violence and the Law in Ireland*. Manchester: Manchester University Press, 1989.

Holahan, Catherine. 'The Dark Side of Web Anonymity', *Bloomberg Businessweek*, 1 May 2008, https://www.bloomberg.com/news/articles/2008-04-30/the-dark-side-of-web-anonymity

Hopgood, Stephen. *The Endtimes of Human Rights*. Ithaca: Cornell University Press, 2013.

Horowitz, Roger. 'Making the Chicken of Tomorrow: Reworking Poultry as Commodities and as Creatures, 1945–1990', in Schrepfer and Scranton (eds), *Industrializing Organisms*, 215–35.

Hrdy, Sarah Blaffer. 'Empathy, Polyandry, and the Myth of the Coy Female', in Elliott Sober (ed.), *Conceptual Issues in Evolutionary Biology*, 123–9. Cambridge, MA: MIT Press, 1994.

Hrdy, Sarah Blaffer. '"Raising Darwin's Consciousness": Female Sexuality and the Prehominid Origins of Patriarchy', *Human Nature*, 8 (1997): 1–49.

Hrdy, Sarah Blaffer. *The Woman that Never Evolved: With a New Preface*. Cambridge, MA: Harvard University Press, 1999.

Hudson, Nicholas. 'Are We "Voltaire's Bastards?" John Ralston Saul and Post-Modern Representations of the Enlightenment', *Lumen*, 20 (2001): 111–21.

Hughes, Matthew. 'The Banality of Brutality: British Armed Forces and the Repression of the Arab Revolt in Palestine, 1936–39', *The English Historical Review*, CXXIV, 507 (April 2009): 313–54.

Hughes, Matthew (ed.). *British Ways of Counterinsurgency: A Historical Perspective*. London: Routledge, 2013.

Huizar-Hernández, Anita. '"The Real Geronimo Got Away": Eluding Expectations in Geronimo: His Own Story; The Autobiography of a Great Patriot Warrior', *Studies in American Indian Literatures*, 29:2 (Summer 2017): 49–70.

Hull, Isabel V. *Sexuality, State, and Civil Society in Germany, 1700-1815*. Ithaca: Cornell University Press, 1996.

Hunnisett, Roy F. *The Medieval Coroner*. Cambridge: Cambridge University Press, 1961.

Hunt, Lynn. *Inventing Human Rights. A History*. New York: W. W. Norton and Co., 2006.

Hunt, Lynn. 'The Paradoxical Origins of Human Rights', in Jeffrey N. Wasserstrom, Lynn Hunt, and Marilyn B. Young (eds), *Human Rights and Revolutions*. Lanham: Rowman and Littlefield, 2007.

Hussain, Nasser. *The Jurisprudence of Emergency: Colonialism and the Rule of Law*. Ann Arbor: The University of Michigan Press, 2003.

Huxley, Aldous. *Brave New World*. New York: Alfred Knopf, 2013.

Ikegami, Eiko. *The Taming of the Samurai: Honorific Individualism and the Making of Modern Japan*. Cambridge, MA: Harvard University Press, 1995.

Ingrao, Christian. *Believe and Destroy: Intellectuals in the SS War Machine*. Cambridge: Polity, 2013.

İşcan, Mehmet Yaşar and Kennedy Kenneth, A. R. (eds). *Reconstruction of Life from the Skeleton*. New York: Alan R. Liss, 1989.

Isenberg, Andrew C. *The Destruction of the Bison: An Environmental History, 1750–1920*. Cambridge: Cambridge University Press, 2000.

Israel, Jonathan. *Radical Enlightenment: Philosophy and the Making of Modernity, 1650–1750*. Oxford: Oxford University Press, 2001.

Israel, Jonathan. *Revolutionary Ideas: An Intellectual History of the French Revolution from the Rights of Man to Robespierre*. Princeton: Princeton University Press, 2014.

Jacob, Margaret C. *The Secular Enlightenment*. Princeton: Princeton University Press, 2019.

Jaeger, C. Stephen. *The Origins of Courtliness: Civilizing Trends and the Formation of Courtly Ideals, 939–1210*. Philadelphia: University of Pennsylvania Press, 1985.

Jansen, Marius. 'On Studying the Modernization of Japan', in Kokusai Kirisutokyo Daigaku and Ajia Bunka Kenkyu Iinkai (eds), *Studies on Modernization of Japan by Western Scholars*, 1–11. Tokyo: International Christian University, 1962.

Jenks, Susanne. 'The Writ and the Exception *de odio et atia*', *Journal of Legal History*, 23:1 (2002): 1–22.

Johnson, Eric A. and Monkkonen, Eric H. (eds). *The Civilization of Crime. Violence in Town and Country since the Middle Ages*. Urbana and Chicago: University of Illinois Press, 1996.

Johnson, Eric A. *Nazi Terror: The Gestapo, Jews and Ordinary Germans*. New York: Basic Books, 1999.

Jones, Daniel Stedman. *Masters of the Universe: Hayek, Friedman, and the Birth of Neoliberal Politics*. Princeton: Princeton University Press, 2012.

Josephson-Storm, Jason. *The Myth of Disenchantment: Magic, Modernity, and the Birth of the Human Sciences*. Chicago: University of Chicago Press, 2017.

Judt, Tony. *Postwar; A History of Europe Since 1945*. New York: Penguin, 2007.

Jurmain, Robert and Kilgore, Lyn. 'Sex-Related Patterns of Trauma in Humans and African Apes', in Anne L. Grauer and Patricia Stuart-Macadam (eds), *Sex and Gender in Paleopathological Perspective*, 11–26. Cambridge: Cambridge University Press, 1998.

Kaeuper, Richard W. 'Chivalry and the "Civilizing Process"', in Richard W. Kaeuper (ed.), *Violence in Medieval Society*, 22f–38. Rochester: Boydell & Brewer, 2000.

Kalar, Tara, Meske, Elizabeth, Schimdt, Alison and Johnson, Shirin. 'A Crisis of Complacency: Minnesota's Untested Rape Kit Backlog', *Bench and Bar of Minnesota*, 74 (2017): 22–8.

Kaldor, Mary. *New and Old Wars: Organized Violence in a Global* Era. Cambridge: Polity, 1999.

Kamen, Henry. *The Spanish Inquisition: An Historical Revision*. London: Phoenix Giant, 1998.

Kanani, Milli. 'Testing Justice', *Columbia Human Rights Law Review*, 42:3 (Spring 2011): 943–92.

Kaplan, Steven L. *Bread, Politics and Political Economy in the Reign of Louis XV*, 2 vols. The Hague: Martinus Nijhoff, 1976.

Kaplan, Thomas Pegelow, Matthäus, Jürgen and Hornburg, Mark W. (eds). *Beyond 'Ordinary Men': Christopher R. Browning and Holocaust Historiography*. Leiden: Ferdinand Schöningh, 2019.

Karonen, Petri. 'Trygg eller livsfarlig? Våldsbrottsligheten i Finlands städer 1540–1660', *Historisk Tidskrift för Finland*, 80:1 (1995): 1.11.

Karonen, Petri. 'A Life versus Christian Reconciliation: Violence and the Process of Civilization in the Kingdom of Sweden, 1540–1700', in Ylikangas, Karonen and Lehti (eds), *Five Centuries of Violence in Finland and the Baltic Area*, 85–132.

Kaspersson, Maria. '"The Great Murder Mystery" or Explaining Declining Homicide Rates', in Godfrey, Emsley and Dunstall (eds), *Comparative Histories of Crime*, 72–88.

Keane, John. *Violence and Democracy*. Cambridge: Cambridge University Press, 2004.

Keegan, John. *A History of Warfare*. New York: Knopf, 1993.

Keeley, Lawrence H. *War before Civilization: The Myth of the Peaceful Savage*. New York, Oxford: Oxford University Press, 1996.

Kelley, Robin D. G. 'Thug Nation: On State Violence and Disposability', in Jordan T. Camp and Christina Heatherton (eds), *Policing the Planet: Why the Policing Crisis Led to Black Lives Matter*, 15–33. New York: Verso, 2016.

Kelly, Liz, Lovett, Jo and Regan, Linda. *A Gap or a Chasm? Attrition in Reported Rape Cases*, Home Office Research Study 293. London: Home Office Research, Development and Statistics Directorate, February 2005.

Kelly, Liz. 'The (In)credible Words of Women: False Allegations in European Rape Research', *Violence Against Women*, 16:12 (2010): 1345–55.

Kendi, Ibram X. *How to be An Antiracist*. New York: One World, 2019.

Kerin, James R. 'Combat', in *Encyclopedia of Violence, Peace and Conflict*, 2nd edn, ed. Lester R. Kurtz, 349. San Diego: Academic Press, 1998.

Kesselring, Krista J. *Mercy and Authority in the Tudor State*. Cambridge: Cambridge University Press, 2003.

Kiernan, Ben. *Blood and Soil: A World History of Genocide and Extermination from Sparta to Darfur*. New Haven: Yale University Press, 2007.

Kim, Nam C. 'Angels, Illusions, Hydras, and Chimeras: Violence and Humanity', *Reviews in Anthropology*, 41:4 (2012): 239–72.

King-Clark, R. *Free for a Blast*. London: Grenville Publishing Company Limited, 1988.

Kissane, Bill. *Nations Torn Asunder: The Challenge of Civil War*. Oxford: Oxford University Press, 2016.

Kivelson, Valerie A. *Desperate Magic: The Moral Economy of Witchcraft in Seventeenth-Century Russia*. Ithaca: Cornell University Press, 2013.

Klein, Herbert S. and Luna, Francisco Vidal. *Slavery in Brazil*. Cambridge: Cambridge University Press, 2010.

Klerman, Daniel. 'Settlement and Decline of Private Prosecution in Thirteenth-Century England', *Law and History Review*, 19:1 (2001): 1–65.

Klose, Fabian. '"Source of Embarrassment": Human Rights, State of Emergency, and the Wars of Decolonization', in Stefan-Ludwig Hoffman (ed.), *Human Rights in the Twentieth Century*, 237–57. Cambridge: Cambridge University Press, 2011.

Knauft, Bruce. 'Violence and Sociality in Human Evolution', *Current Anthropology*, 32 (1991): 391–428.

Knüsel, Christopher and Smith, Martin J. (eds). 'Introduction: The Bioarcheology of Conflict', in Knüsel and Smith (eds), *The Routledge Handbook of the Bioarchaeology*, 3–24.

Knüsel, Christopher and Smith, Martin J. 'The Osteology of Conflict – What Does It All Mean?', in Knüsel and Smith (eds), *The Routledge Handbook of the Bioarchaeology*, 656–94.

Koerner, Lisbeth. *Linnaeus: Nature and Nation*. Cambridge, MA: Harvard University Press, 1999.

Koh, Harold Hongju. 'The New Global Slave Trade', in Kate E. Tunstall (ed.), *Displacement, Asylum, Migration*, 232–55. Oxford: Oxford University Press.

Kolbert, Elizabeth. *The Sixth Extinction: An Unnatural History*. London: Bloomsbury, 2014.

Kollmann, Nancy Shields. *By Honor Bound: State and Society in Early Modern Russia*. Ithaca: Cornell University Press, 1999.

Kollmann, Nancy Shields. *Crime and Punishment in Early Modern Russia*. Cambridge: Cambridge University Press, 2012.

Kollmann, Nancy Shields. 'Pictures at an Execution: Johann Georg Korb's "Execution of the Strel'tsy"', in Brian Boeck, Russell E. Martin and Daniel Rowland (eds), *Dubitando: Studies in History and Culture in Honor of Donald Ostrowski*, 399–407. Bloomington: Slavica Publishers, 2012.

Kollmann, Nancy Shields. *The Russian Empire, 1450–1801*. Oxford: Oxford University Press, 2017.

Kotch, Seth. *Lethal State: A History of the Death Penalty in North Carolina*. Chapel Hill: University of North Carolina Press, 2020.

Kouango, Alban Monday. *Cabinda: un Koweit africain*. Paris: L'Harmattan, 2002.

Kreiser, B. Robert. *Miracles, Convulsions, and Ecclesiastical Politics in Early Eighteenth-Century Paris*. Princeton: Princeton University Press, 1978.

Krieken, Robert van. 'Violence, Self-discipline and Modernity: Beyond the Civilizing Process', *Sociological Review*, 37 (1989): 193–218.

Krieken, Robert van. *Norbert Elias*. London: Routledge, 1998.

Krieken, Robert van. 'Norbert Elias and Emotions in History', in David Lemmings and Ann Brooks (eds), *Emotions and Social Change: Historical and Sociological Perspectives*, 19–42. London: Routledge, 2014.

Kristiansen, Kristian. 'Towards a New Paradigm? The Third Science Revolution and its Possible Consequences in Archaeology', *Current Swedish Archaeology*, 22 (2014): 11–34.

Krogh, Tyge. *A Lutheran Plague: Murdering to Die in the Eighteenth Century*, 1–5. Leiden: Brill, 2012.

Krohn-Hansen, Christian. 'The Anthropology of Violent Interaction', *Journal of Anthropological Research*, 50 (1994): 367–81.

Kroll, Jerome and Bachrach, Bernard. *The Mystic Mind: The Psychology of Medieval Mystics and Ascetics*. New York: Routledge, 2005.

Krüger, Gesine. *Kriegsbewältigung und Geschichtsbewußtsein: Realität, Deutung und Verarbeitung des deutschen Kolonialkriegs in Namibia 1904 bis 1907*. Göttingen: Vandenhoeck and Ruprecht, 1999.

Kühn, Manfed. *Johann Gottlieb Fichte: Ein deutscher Philisoph, 1762–1814*. Munich: Beck, 2012.

La Vopa, Anthony J. *Fichte: The Calling of the Self and Philosophy*. Cambridge: Cambridge University Press, 2001.

Laakkonen, Simo, Tucker, Richard P. and Vuorisalo, Timo (eds). *The Long Shadows: A Global Environmental History of the Second World War*. Corvallis: Oregon State University Press, 2017.

LaCapra, Dominick. *Writing History, Writing Trauma*. Baltimore: Johns Hopkins University Press, 2000.

Lacroix, Justine and Pranchère, Jean-Yves. *Le Procès des droits de l'homme: Généalogie du scepticisme démocratique*. Paris: Seuil, 2016.

Langbein, John H. *Prosecuting Crime in the Renaissance: England, Germany, France*. Cambridge, MA: Harvard University Press, 1974.

Langbein, John H. *Torture and the Law of Proof: Europe and England in the Ancien Régime*. Chicago: University of Chicago Press, 1977.

Langbein, John H. 'The Legal History of Torture', in Sanford Levinson (ed.), *Torture: A Collection*, 93–103. Oxford: Oxford University Press, 2006.

Lear, Linda. *Rachel Carson: Witness for Nature*. London: Allen Lane, 1998.

LeBlanc, Steven A. and Register, Katherine E. *Constant Battles: Why We Fight*. New York: St. Martin's Griffin, 2003.

LeCain, Timothy J. *Mass Destruction: The Men and Giant Mines that Wired America and Scarred the Planet*. New Brunswick: Rutgers University Press, 2009.

LeDonne, John. 'Civilians under Military Justice during the Reign of Nicholas I', *Canadian-American Slavic Studies*, 7 (1973): 171–87.

Lee, Jason C. K. and Wen, Zongguo. 'Rare Earths from Mines to Metals: Comparing Environmental Impacts from China's Main Production Pathways', *Journal of Industrial Ecology*, 21:5 (2016): 1277–90.

Lee, Wayne E. *Waging War: Conflict, Culture, and Innovation in World History*. Oxford and New York: Oxford University Press, 2016.

Lehner, Ulrich L. *The Catholic Enlightenment: The Forgotten History of a Global Movement*. Oxford: Oxford University Press, 2016.

Leibniz, Gottfried Wilhelm. *Theodicy: Essays on the Goodness of God, the Freedom of Man, and the Origin of Evil*, ed. Austin M. Farrer, trans. E. M. Huggard. New York: Cosmo Classics, 2009 [1710].

Lerner, Steve. *Sacrifice Zones: The Front Lines of Toxic Chemical Exposure in the United States*. Cambridge, MA: MIT Press, 2010.

Leupp, Gary. 'Five Men of Naniwa: Gang Violence and Popular Culture in Genroku Osaka', in James L. McClain and Osamu A. Wakita (eds), *Osaka: The Merchant's Capital of Early Modern Japan*. Ithaca: Cornell University Press, 1999.

Levine, Robert M. and Crocitti, John J. (eds). *The Brazil Reader: History, Culture, Politics*. Durham: Duke University Press, 1999.

Levinson, Sanford. 'Contemplating Torture: An Introduction', in Sanford Levinson (ed.), *Torture: A Collection*, 23–43. Oxford: Oxford University Press, 2004.

Leys, Ruth. *Trauma: A Genealogy*. Chicago: University of Chicago Press, 2000.

Leys, Ruth. *The Ascent of Affect: Genealogy and Critique*. Chicago: University of Chicago Press, 2017.

Liesen, Laurette T. 'Women, Behavior, and Evolution: Understanding the Debate Between Feminist Evolutionists and Evolutionary Psychologists', *Politics and the Life Sciences*, 26:1 (March 2007): 51–70.

Liliequist, Jonas. 'Violence, Honour and Manliness in Early Modern Northern Sweden', in Mirkka Lappalainen and Pekka Hirvonen (eds), *Crime and Control in Europe from the Past to the Present*, 174–207. Helsinki: Hakapaino, 1999.

Lindsay, Brendan C. *Murder State: California's Native American Genocide, 1846–1873*. Lincoln and London: University of Nebraska Press, 2012.

Lindström, Dag. 'Homicide in Scandinavia: Long-term Trends and Their Interpretations', in Sophie Body-Gendrot and Pieter Spierenburg (eds), *Violence in Europe: Historical and Contemporary Perspectives*, 41–64, here 48f. New York: Springer, 2008.

Linebaugh, Peter. *The London Hanged: Crime and Civil Society in the Eighteenth Century*. Cambridge: Cambridge University Press, 1992.

Linton, Marisa. *Choosing Terror: Virtue, Friendship, and Authenticity in the French Revolution*. Oxford: Oxford University Press, 2013.

Lisak, David, Lori, Gardiner, Nicksa, Sarah C. and Cote, Ashley M. 'False Allegations of Sexual Assault: An Analysis of Ten Years of Reported Cases', *Violence Against Women*, 16:12 (2010): 1318–34.

Lobban, Michael. 'Legal Fictions before the Age of Reform', in Maksymilian Del Mar and William Twining (eds), *Legal Fictions in Theory and Practice*, 199–223. Heidelberg: Springer, 2015.

Lockwood, Matthew. *The Conquest of Death. Violence and the Birth of the Modern English State*. New Haven and London: Yale University Press, 2017.

Lonsway, Kimberly A., Welch, Susan and Fitzgerald, Louise F. 'Police Training in Sexual Assault Response: Process, Outcomes, and Elements of Change', *Criminal Justice and Behavior*, 28:6 (2001): 695–730.

Lord, Vivian B. and Rassel, Gary. 'Law Enforcement's Response to Sexual Assault: A Comparative Study of Nine Counties in North Carolina', in Hodgson and Kelley (eds), *Sexual Violence*, 155–72.

Lucas, Richard E. 'Adaptation and the Set-Point Model of Subjective Well-Being', *Current Directions in Psychological Science*, 16:2 (2007): 75–9.

Lykken, David and Tellegen, Auke. 'Happiness Is a Stochastic Phenomenon', *Psychological Science*, 7:3 (1996): 186–9.

Madley, Benjamin. *An American Genocide: The United States and the California Indian Catastrophe, 1846–1873*. New Haven: Yale University Press, 2016.

Majima, Shunzo. 'Just Torture?', *Journal of Military Ethics*, 11:2 (2012): 136–48.

Malešević, Siniša. 'Forms of Brutality: Towards A Historical Sociology of Violence', *European Journal of Social Theory*, 16:3 (July 2013): 1–19.

Malešević, Siniša. *The Rise of Organised Brutality: A Historical Sociology of Violence*, 134. Cambridge: Cambridge University Press, 2017.

Mali, Joseph and Wokler, Robert (eds). *Isaiah Berlin's Counter-Enlightenment*. Philadelphia: American Philosophical Society, 2003.

Mann, Charles C. *1491: New Revelations of the Americas before Columbus*. New York: Vintage Books, 2006.

Mann, Charles C. *1493: Uncovering the New World Columbus Created*. New York: Knopf, 2011.

Mann, Michael. 'Have Wars and Violence Declined?', *Theory and Society*, 47:2 (January 2018): 37–60.

Mannix, Daniel. *The History of Torture*. Phoenix Mill, Stroud, Gloucestershire: Sutton, 2003.

Mantena, Karuna. *Alibis of Empire: Henry Maine and the Ends of Liberal Imperialism*. Princeton: Princeton University Press, 2010.

Markus, Hazel R. and Moya, Paula (eds). *Doing Race: 21 Essays for the 21st Century*. New York: W.W. Norton, 2010.

Marsh, T. W., Geist, A. and Caplan, N. *Rape and the Limits of Law Reform*. Boston: Auburn House, 1982.

Martin, Debra L. and Frayer, David W. 'Introduction', in Debra L. Martin and David W. Frayer (eds), *Troubled Times: Violence and Warfare in the Past*, xiii–xxi. Amsterdam: Gordon and Breach, 1997.

Marx, Anthony W. *Making Race and Nation: A Comparison of the United States, South Africa, and Brazil*. Cambridge: Cambridge University Press, 1998.

Maschner, Herbert D. G. and Reedy-Maschner, Katherine L. 'Raid, Retreat, Defend (repeat): The Archaeology and Ethnohistory of Warfare on the North Pacific Rim', *Journal of Anthropological Archaeology*, 17 (1998): 19–51.

Matytsin, Anton M. and Edelstein, Dan. 'Introduction', in Anton M. Matytsin and Dan Edelstein (eds), *Let There Be Enlightenment: The Religious and Mystical Sources of Rationality*, 1–6. Baltimore: Johns Hopkins University Press, 2018

Mauer, Marc. *Race to Incarcerate*. New York: New Press, 1999.

Mayer, Peter. 'Comparative Reflections on *The Civilizing Process*', in Lemmings and Brooks (eds.) *Emotions and Social Change*, 233–51.

Mazower, Mark. *No Enchanted Palace: The End of Empire and the Ideological Origins of the United Nations*. Princeton: Princeton University Press, 2009.

McDermott, Rose. 'The Feeling of Rationality: The Meaning of Neuroscientific Advances for Political Science', *Perspectives on Politics*, 2:4 (2004): 691–706.

McKinnon, Andrew M. 'The Sacramental Mechanism: Religion and the Civilizing Process in Christian Western Europe with Particular Reference to the Peace of God Movement and its Aftermath', in Andrew McKinnon and Marta Trzebiatowska (eds), *Sociological Theory and the Question of Religion*, 105–26. Farnham: Taylor & Francis, 2014.

McLane, Bernard William. 'Juror Attitudes toward Local Disorder: The Evidence of the 1328 Trailbaston Proceedings', in James S. Cockburn and Thomas A. Green (eds), *Twelve Good Men and True*, 36–64. Princeton: Princeton University Press, 1988.

McMahon, Darrin M. *Enemies of the Enlightenment: The French Counter-Enlightenment and the Making of Modernity*. New York: Oxford University Press, 2001.

McMahon, Darrin M. *Happiness: A History*, 466–80. New York: Atlantic Monthly Press, 2006.

McMahon, Richard, Eibach, Joachim and Roth, Randolph. 'Making Sense of Violence? Reflections on the History of Interpersonal Violence in Europe', *Crime, History and Societies*, 17:2 (2013): 5–26.

McNeill, John R. *Something New Under the Sun*. London: Penguin, 2000.

McNeill, John R. and Unger, Corinna R. (eds). *Environmental Histories of the Cold War*. Cambridge: Cambridge University Press, 2010.

McNeill, John R. and Engelke, Peter. *The Great Acceleration: An Environmental History of the Anthropocene since 1945*. Cambridge, MA: Belknap, 2014.

Meadows, Donella H., Meadows, Dennis L., Randers, Jorgen and Behrens III, William W. *The Limits to Growth*. New York: Universe, 1972.

Megret, Frederic. 'From "Savages" to "Unlawful Combatants": A postcolonial look at International Humanitarian Law's "Other"', in Orford (ed.), *International Law and Its Others*, 265–317.

Mehta, Uday Singh. *Liberalism and Empire: A Study in Nineteenth-Century British Liberal Thought*. Chicago: Chicago University Press, 1999.

Melzer, Arthur M., Weinberger, Jerry and Zinman, M. Richard (eds). *History and the Idea of Progress*. Ithaca: Cornell University Press, 1995.

Mennell, Stephen. 'Decivilizing Processes: Theoretical Significance and Some Lines for Research', *International Sociology*, 5:2 (1990): 205–23.

Mennell, Stephen and Goudsblom, Johan. 'Civilizing Processes—Myth or Reality? A Comment on Duerr's Critique of Elias', *Comparative Studies in Society and History*, 39:4 (1997): 729–33.

Mennell, Stephen. *The American Civilizing Process*. Cambridge: Polity, 2007.

Merback, Mitchel B. *The Thief, the Cross and the Wheel: Pain and the Spectacle of Punishment in Medieval and Renaissance Europe*. London: Reaktion Books, 1999.

Merbs, Charles F. 'Trauma', in İşcan and Kennedy (eds), *Reconstruction of Life from the Skeleton*, 161–89.

Mercier, Hugo and Sperber, Dan. *The Enigma of Reason*. Cambridge, MA: Harvard University Press, 2017.

Metcalf, Thomas R. *Ideologies of the Raj*. Cambridge: Cambridge University Press, 1994.

Micale, Mark S. 'What Pinker Leaves Out', *Historical Reflections*, 44:1 (September 2018): 128–39.

Micale, Mark S. and Dwyer, Philip. 'History, Violence, and Stephen Pinker', *Historical Reflections/Réflexions Historiques*, 44:1 (Spring 2018): 1–5.

Mill, John Stuart. *Considerations on Representative Government*. New York: CreateSpace, 2014, first published, 1861.

Miller, Jerome G. *Search and Destroy: African-American Male Sin the Criminal Justice System*. New York: Oxford University Press, 1996.

Miller, Mary and Brittenham, Claudia. *The Spectacle of the Late Maya Court: Reflections on the Murals of Bonampak*. Austin: University of Texas Press, 2013.

Milsom, Stroud F. C. 'Trespass from Henry III to Edward III', *Law Quarterly Review*, 74 (1958): 195–224.

Milsom, Stroud F. C. *Historical Foundations of the Common Law*, 54–9. London: Butterworths, 1969.

Mirzai, Benaz A. 'The Persian Gulf and Britain: The Suppression of the African Slave Trade', in Hideaki Suzuki (ed.), *Abolitions as a Global Experience*, 113–29. Singapore: NUS Press, 2015.

Mitzen, Jennifer. 'The Irony of Pinkerism', *Perspectives on Politics*, 11:2 (June 2013): 525–8.

Molloy, Barry (ed.). *The Cutting Edge: Archaeological Studies in Combat and Weaponry*. Cheltenham: History Press, 2007.

Molloy, Barry and Grossman, Dave. 'Why Can't Johnny Kill?: The Psychology and Physiology of Interpersonal Combat', in Molloy (ed.), *The Cutting Edge*, 188–202.

Monkkonen, Eric. 'New Standards for Historical Homicide Research', *Crime, History and Societies*, 5:2 (2001): 5–26.

Montagne, Albert. 'Crimes, faits divers, cinématographe et premiers interdits français en 1899 et 1909', *Criminocorpus*, http://journals.openedition.org/criminocorpus/207, accessed 18 August 2020.

Monteiro, A. Reis. *Ethics and Human Rights*. New York: Springer, 2014.

Montesquieu, Charles Louis de Secondat, baron de La Brède et de. *Lettres persanes*, 2 vols. Paris: Bureaux de la Publication, 1880.

Montrie, Chad. *To Save the Land and People: A History of Opposition to Surface Coal Mining in Appalachia*. Chapel Hill: University of North Carolina Press, 2003.

Moravcsik, Andrew. 'The Origins of Human Rights Regimes: Democratic Delegation in Postwar Europe', *International Organization*, 54:2 (Spring 2000): 238–43.

Mornet, Daniel. *Les origines intellectuelles de la Révolution française, 1715–1787*. Paris: Armand Colin, 1933.

Morris, Benny. *1948: A History of the First Arab-Israeli War*. New Haven: Yale University Press, 2008.

Morris, Ian. *War!: What Is It Good For?: Conflict and the Progress of Civilization from Primates to Robots*. New York: Farrar, Straus and Giroux, 2014.

Morrissey, Susan K. 'Terrorism and *Ressentiment* in Revolutionary Russia', *Past and Present*, 246:1 (2019): 191–226.

Moyn, Samuel. *Origins of the Other: Emmanuel Lévinas between Revelation and Ethics*. Ithaca: Cornell University Press, 2005.

Moyn, Samuel. *The Last Utopia: Human Rights in History*. Cambridge, MA: Belknap Press, 2010.

Moyn, Samuel. 'Hype for the Best: Why Does Steven Pinker Insist that Human Life Is On the Up and Up?' *The New Republic*, 19 March 2018.

Moyn, Samuel. *Not Enough: Human Rights in an Unequal World*. Cambridge, MA: Belknap Press, 2018.

Muchembled, Robert. *Le temps des supplices de l'obéisance sous les rois absolus, XVe-XVIIIe siècle*. Paris: Armand Colin, 1992.

Muchembled, Robert. *A History of Violence. From the End of the Middle Ages to the Present*. Cambridge: Polity Press, 2012.

Muhammad, Khalil Gibran. *The Condemnation of Blackness: Race, Crime and the Making of Modern Urban America*. Cambridge, MA: Harvard University Press, 2010.

Müller, Jan-Werner. *What Is Populism?*. Philadelphia: University of Pennsylvania Press, 2016.

Munkler, Herfried. *The New Wars*, trans. Patrick Camiller. Oxford: Polity, 2005.

Murakawa, Naomi. *The First Civil Right: How Liberals Built Prison America*. Oxford: Oxford University Press, 2014.

Murray, Kenneth R., Grossman, Dave and Kentridge, Robert W. 'Behavioral Psychology of Killing', in Kurtz (ed.), *Encyclopedia of Violence*, 166–73.

Myers, David G. and Diener, E. (eds). 'Who Is Happy?', *Psychological Science*, 6:1 (1995): 10–19.

Myhill, Andy and Allen, Jonathan. *Rape and Sexual Assault of Women: The Extent and Nature of the Problem. Findings from the British Crime Survey*. London: Home Office Research, Development, and Statistics Directorate, March 2002.

Nabuco, Joaquim. *Abolitionism: The Brazilian Antislavery Struggle* (1883), trans. and ed. Robert Conrad. Urbana: University of Illinois Press, 1977.

Nakao, Hisashi, Tamura, Kohei, Arimatsu, Yui, Nakagawa, Tomomi, Matsumoto, Naoko and Matsugi, Takehiko. 'Violence in the Prehistoric Period of Japan: The Spatio-Temporal Pattern of Skeletal Evidence for Violence in the Jomon Period', *Biology Letters*, 1 March 2016, https://doi.org/10.1098/rsbl.2016.0028

Nakhimovsky, Isaac. *The Closed Commercial State: Perpetual Peace and Commercial Society from Rousseau to Fichte*. Princeton: Princeton University Press, 2011.

Namier, L. B. 'History', in *Avenues of History* [1952], reproduced in Fritz Stern (ed.), *The Varieties of History: From Voltaire to the Present*. New York: Meridian Books, 1956.

Natarajan, Deepa, Vries, Han de, Saaltink, Dirk-Jan, de Boer, Sietse F. and Koolhass, Jaap M. 'Delineation of Violence from Functional Aggression in Mice: An Ethological Approach', *Behavior Genetics*, 39 (2009): 73–90.

Nelson, Diane M. *Who Counts? The Mathematics of Death and Life after Genocide*. Durham: Duke University Press, 2015.

Netterstrøm, Jeppe Büchert. 'Criminalization of Homicide in Early Modern Denmark (16th to 17th centuries)', *Scandinavian Journal of History*, 42:4 (2017): 459–75.

Niewöhner, Jörg. 'Epigenetics: Embedded Bodies and the Molecularisation of Biography and Milieu', *BioSocieties*, 6:3 (13 June 2011): 279–98.

Nilsson, Sven A. *De stora krigens tid. Om Sverige som militärstat och bondesamhälle*. Uppsala: Uppsala universitet, 1990.

Nisbet, Robert A. *History of the Idea of Progress*. New York: Basic Books, 1980.

Nisuke, Ando. *Japan and International Law: Past, Present and Future: International Symposium to Mark the Centennial of the Japanese Association of International Law*. The Hague: Kluwer, 1999.

Nivette, Amy E. 'Violence in Non-state Societies: A Review', *The British Journal of Criminology*, 51:3 (2011): 578–98.

Nixon, Rob. *Slow Violence and the Environmentalism of the Poor*. Cambridge, MA: Harvard University Press, 2011.

Noonan, Jeff. 'Liberalism, Capitalism, and the Conditions of Social Peace: A Critique of Steven Pinker's One-Sided Humanism', *International Critical Thought* (2019), doi: 10.1080/21598282.2019.1649170

Northrup, David. *Indentured Labor in the Age of Imperialism, 1834–1922*. Cambridge: Cambridge University Press, 1995.

Norton, Jack. *Genocide in Northwestern California: When Our Worlds Cried*. San Francisco: Indian Historian Press, 1979.

Nosco, Peter. *Individuality in Early Modern Japan: Thinking for Oneself*. New York: Routledge, 2018.

Nussbaum, Martha C. *Creating Capabilities: The Human Development Approach*. Cambridge: Belknap Press of Harvard University Press, 2011.

Nystrom, Pia. 'Aggression and Nonhuman Primates', in Mike Parker Pearson and Nick J. N. Thorpe (eds), *Warfare, Violence and Slavery in Prehistory*, 35–40. Oxford: Archaeopress, 2005.

O'Connell, Robert. *Ride of the Second Horseman: The Birth and Death of War*. Oxford: Gordon & Breach, 1995.

Oka, Rahul C., Kissel, Marc, Golitko, Mark, Sheridan, Susan Guise, Kim, Nam C. and Fuentes, Agustín. 'Population is the Main Driver of War Group Size and

Conflict Casualties', *Proceedings of the National Academy of Sciences*, 114, no. 52 (2017): E11101–10.

Olson, Trisha. 'The Medieval Blood Sanction and the Divine Beneficence of Pain: 1100–1450', *Journal of Law and Religion*, 22:1 (2006): 63–129.

O'Mara, Margaret. *The Code: Silicon Valley and the Making of America*. New York: Penguin Press, 2019.

Orford, Ann (ed.). *International Law and Its Others*. Cambridge: Cambridge University Press, 2006.

Orwell, George. *1984*. New York: Signet Classic, 1977.

Österberg, Eva. 'Criminality, Social Control, and the Early Modern State: Evidence and Interpretations in Scandinavian Historiography', in Eric A. Johnsson and Eric H. Monkkonen (eds), *The Civilization of Crime: Violence in Town and Country since the Middle Ages*, 35–62. Urbana and Chicago: University of Illinois Press, 1996.

Österberg, Eva and Sogner, Sølvie (eds). *People Meet the Law. Control and Conflict-Handling in the Courts: The Nordic Countries in the Post-Reformation and Pre-Industrial Period*. Oslo: Universitetsforlaget, 2000.

Osterhammel, Jürgen. *The Transformation of the World: A Global History of the Nineteenth Century*, trans. Patrick Camiller. Princeton: Princeton University Press, 2014.

Osterhammel, Jürgen. *Unfabling the East: The Enlightenment's Encounter with Asia*, trans. Robert Savage. 1998; Princeton: Princeton University Press, 2018.

Otterbein, Keith F. 'The Origins of War', *Critical Review*, 2 (1997): 251–77.

Otterbein, Keith F. 'Killing of Captured Enemies: A Cross-Cultural Study', *Current Anthropology*, 41 (2000): 439–43.

Otterbein, Keith F. *How War Began*. College Station: Texas A&M University Press, 2004.

Otto, Ton. 'Conceptions of Warfare in Western Thought and Research: An Introduction', in Otto, Thrane and Vandkilde (eds), *Warfare and Society*, 23–8.

Oxenboell, Morten. 'Epistemologies of Violence: Medieval Japanese War Tales', *History and Theory*, 56:4 (2017): 44–59.

Pagden, Anthony. *The Enlightenment: And Why It Still Matters*. Oxford: Oxford University Press, 2013.

Page, Amy Dellinger. 'Gateway to Reform? Policy Implications of Police Officers' Attitudes Towards Rape', *American Journal of Criminal Justice*, 33:1 (May 2008): 44–58.

Painter, Nell Irvin. *The History of White People*. New York: Norton, 2010.

Pearson, Mike Parker and Thorpe, I. J. N. (eds). *Warfare, Violence and Slavery in Prehistory*. Oxford: Archaeopress, 2005.

Pepperell, Nicole. 'The Unease with Civilization: Norbert Elias and the Violence of the Civilizing Process', *Thesis Eleven: Critical Theory and Historical Sociology*, 137:1 (2016): 3–21.

Pérez, Joseph. *The Spanish Inquisition*. New Haven: Yale University Press, 2006.

Peters, Edward. *Torture*, expanded edn. Philadelphia: University of Pennsylvania Press, 1996.

Peterson, David. 'Reality Denial: Apologetics for Western-Imperial Violence', https://www.globalresearch.ca/reality-denial-apologetics-for-western-imperial-violence/32066

Piirimäe, Eva. 'Berlin, Herder, and the Counter-Enlightenment', *Eighteenth-Century Studies*, 49:1 (2015): 71–6.

Pimentel, David. 'Green Revolution Agriculture and Chemical Hazards', *The Science of the Total Environment*, 188:Suppl. 1 (1996): S86–S98.

Pincus, Rebecca. '"To Prostitute the Elements": Weather Control and Weaponisation by US Department of Defense', *War & Society*, 36 (2017): 64–80.

Pinker, Steven. *How the Mind Works*. New York: Norton, 1997.

Pinker, Steven. *The Blank Slate: The Modern Denial of Human Nature*. New York: Viking, 2002.

Pinker, Steven. *The Better Angels of Our Nature: The Decline of Violence in History and Its Causes*. London: Allen Lane, 2011.

Pinker, Steven. *Enlightenment Now: The Case for Reason, Science, Humanism, and Progress*. New York: Penguin Books, 2019.

Pitts, Jennifer. *A Turn to Empire: The Rise of Imperial Liberalism in Britain and France*. Princeton: Princeton University Press, 2005.

Plamper, Jan. *The History of Emotions: An Introduction*, trans. Keith Tribe. Oxford: Oxford University Press, 2015.

Poe, Marshall. *'A People Born to Slavery': Russia in Early Modern European Ethnography, 1476–1748*. Ithaca: Cornell University Press, 2000.

Pohl-Zucker, Susanne. *Making Manslaughter: Process, Punishment and Restitution in Württemberg and Zurich, 1376–1700*. Leiden: Brill, 2017.

Pollard, Sidney. *The Idea of Progress: History and Society*. New York: Basic Books, 1969.

Posner, Eric A. *The Twilight of Human Rights Law*. Oxford: Oxford University Press, 2014.

Powell, Anastasia and Henry, Nicola. *Sexual Violence in a Digital Age*. London: Palgrave, 2016.

Powell, Edward. 'Social Research and the Use of Medieval Criminal Records', *Michigan Law Review*, 79:4 (1981): 967–78.

Prestwich, Michael, Britnell, Richard and Frame, Robin (eds). *Thirteenth Century England VIII: Proceedings of the Durham Conference 1999*. Woodbridge: Boydell, 2001.

Rakove, Jack N. *Original Meanings: Politics and Ideas in the Making of the American Constitution*. New York: Alfred A. Knopf, 1996.

Ralph, Sarah (ed.). *The Archaeology of Violence: Interdisciplinary Approaches*. Albany: State University of New York Press, 2012.

Rawcliffe, Carole. *Medicine and Society in Later Medieval England*. London: Sandpiper Books, 1995.

Rawley, James A. with Behrendt, Stephen D. *The Transatlantic Slave Trade: A History*. Lincoln: University of Nebraska Press, 2005.

Rawlings, Helen. *The Spanish Inquisition*. Malden: Blackwell, 2006.

Reddy, William M. 'Against Constructivism: The Historical Ethnography of Emotions', *Current Anthropology*, 38:3 (June 1997): 327–51, here 331.

Reddy, William M. *The Invisible Code: Honor and Sentiment in Postrevolutionary France, 1815–1848*. Berkeley: University of California Press, 1997.

Reddy, William M. *The Navigation of Feeling: A Framework for the History of Emotions*. New York: Cambridge University Press, 2001.

Reddy, William M. *The Making of Romantic Love: Longing and Sexuality in Europe, South Asia, and Japan, 900–1200 CE*. Chicago: University of Chicago Press, 2012.

Redfern, Rebecca C. *Injury and Trauma in Bioarchaeology: Interpreting Violence in Past Lives*. Cambridge: Cambridge University Press, 2017.

Redfern, Rebecca C. and Fibiger, Linda. 'Bioarchaeological Evidence for Prehistoric Violence: Use and Misuse in the Popular Media', in Jane E. Buikstra (ed.), *Bioarchaeologists Speak Out: Deep Time Perspectives on Contemporary Issues*, 59–77. Cham: Springer, 2018.

Rediker, Marcus. *The Slave Ship: A Human History*. New York: Penguin Books, 2007.

Reed, Kristin. *Crude Existence: Environment and the Politics of Oil in Northern Angola*. Berkeley: University of California Press, 2009.

Reed, Paul F. and Geib, Phil R. 'Sedentism, Social Change, Warfare, and the Bow in the Ancient Pueblo Southwest', *Evolutionary Anthropology*, 22:3 (2013): 103–10.

Reis, João José. *Slave Rebellion in Brazil: The Muslim Uprising of 1835 in Bahia*, trans. Arthur Brakel. 1986; Baltmore: Johns Hopkins University Press, 1993.

Rennison, Callie Marie. *Rape and Sexual Assault: Reporting to Police and Medical Attention, 1992–2000*. Washington, DC: Bureau of Justice Statistics, 2002.

Reséndez, Andrés. *The Other Slavery: The Uncovered Story of Indian Enslavement in America*. Boston: Houghton Mifflin Harcourt, 2016.

Resnick, Daniel P. 'The Société des Amis des Noirs and the Abolition of Slavery', *French Historical Studies*, 7:4 (1972): 558–69.

Restall, Matthew. *When Montezuma Met Cortés: The True Story of the Meeting That Changed History*. New York: Ecco, 2018.

Restall, Matthew. 'The Humans Behind the Sacrifice', *History Today* (April 2020): 96–7.

Reynolds, John. *Empire, Emergency, and International Law*. Cambridge: Cambridge University Press, 2017.

Riches, David (ed.), *The Anthropology of Violence*. Oxford: Basil Blackwell, 1986.

Rifā'ah Rāfi' al-Ṭahṭāwī. *An Imam in Paris: Account of a Stay in France by an Egyptian Cleric (1826–1831)*, trans. Daniel L. Newman. London: Saqi, 2004.

Robb, John. 'Violence and Gender in Early Italy', in Martin and Frayer (eds), *Troubled Times*, 111–44.

Roberts, Callum M. *The Unnatural History of the Sea*. Washington, DC: Island Press, 2007.

Roberts, Luke. *Performing the Great Peace: Political Space and Open Secrets in Tokugawa Japan*. Honolulu: University of Hawai'i Press, 2015.

Robinson, R. J. '"The Civilizing Process": Some Remarks on Elias's Social History', *Sociology*, 21:1 (1987): 1–17.

Rosanvallon, Pierre. *The Demands of Liberty: Civil Society in France since the Revolution*, trans. Arthur Goldhammer. Cambridge, MA: Harvard University Press, 2007.

Rosenfeld, Sophia. *Democracy and Truth: A Short History*. Philadelphia: University of Pennsylvania Press, 2019.

Rosenwein, Barbara H. 'Worrying about Emotions in History', *The American Historical Review*, 107:3 (June 2002): 821–45.

Rosenwein, Barbara H. 'The Uses of Biology: A Response to J. Carter Wood's "the Limits of Culture?"', *Cultural and Social History*, 4:4 (2007): 553–8.

Rosenwein, Barbara H. 'Problems and Methods in the History of Emotions', *Passions in Context: International Journal for the History and Theory of Emotion*, 1:1 (January 2010): 1–32, published online at http://www.passionsincontext.de, accessed 16 March 2018.

Rosenwein, Barbara H. *Generations of Feeling: A History of Emotions, 600-1700*. Cambridge: Cambridge University Press, 2016.

Rosenwein, Barbara H. and Cristiani, Riccardo. *What Is the History of Emotions?* Cambridge: Polity, 2018.

Ross, Michael L. *The Oil Curse: How Petroleum Wealth Shapes the Development of Nations*. Princeton: Princeton University Press, 2012.

Roth, Randolph. 'Homicide in Early Modern England 1549–1800: The Need for Quantitative Synthesis', *Crime, History and Societies*, 5:2 (2001): 33–67.

Roth, Randoph. *American Homicide*. Cambridge, MA: Harvard University Press, 2009.

Roth, Randolph. 'Does Better Angels of Our Nature Hold Up as History?', *Historical Reflections/Réflexions Historiques*, 44:1 (2018): 94–5.

Royer, Katherine. 'The Body in Parts: Reading the Execution Ritual in Late Medieval England', *Historical Reflections*, 29:2 (2003): 319–39.

Royer, Katherine. *The English Execution Narrative: 1200–1700*. London: Pickering and Chatto, 2014.

Rummel, Rudolph J. *Death by Government*. New Brunswick: Transaction Publishers, 1994.

Rumney, Philip N. S. 'False Allegations of Rape', *Cambridge Law Journal*, 65:1 (2006): 128–58.

Russell, Edmund. *War and Nature: Fighting Humans and Insects with Chemicals from World War I to Silent Spring*. Cambridge: Cambridge University Press, 2001.

Russell, Edmund. *Evolutionary History: Uniting History and Biology to Understand Life on Earth*. Cambridge: Cambridge University Press, 2011.

Russell, Josiah Cox. *British Medieval Population*. Albuquerque: University of New Mexico Press, 1948.

Russell, Penny. *Savage or Civilised? Manners in Colonial Australia*. Sydney: NewSouth Books, 2010.

St. Leon, Count de. *Love and Its Hidden History*, 4th edn. Boston: William White and Co., 1869.

Sander, Melissa Mary Fenech. 'Questions of Accountability and Illegality of Virtual Rape'. MSc thesis, Iowa State University, 2009.

Sapolsky, Robert M. *Behave: The Biology of Humans at Our Best and Worst*. New York: Penguin, 2017.

Sassoli, Marco. *International Humanitarian Law: Rules, Controversies, and Solutions to Problems Arising in Warfare*, 1–14. Cheltenham: Edward Elgar Publishing, 2019.

Scarre, Chris (ed.). *The Human Past: World Prehistory & the Development of Human Societies*, 2nd edn. London and New York: Thames & Hudson, 2009.

Scheper-Hughes, Nancy and Wacquant, Loïc (eds). *Commodifying Bodies*. London: Sage, 2002.

Schmidt, Bettina E. and Schröder, Ingo W. (eds). *Anthropology of Violence and Conflict*. London: Routledge, 2001.

Schnapper, Bernard. 'Les Peines arbitraires du XIIIe au XVIIIe siècle: Doctrines savantes et usages français', *Tijdschrift voor Rechtsgeschiedenis/Legal History Review*, 41:3–4 (1973): 237–77, and 42:1–2 (1974): 81–112.

Schrader, Abby M. *Languages of the Lash: Corporal Punishment and Identity in Imperial Russia*. De Kalb: Northern Illinois University Press, 2002.

Schrader, Stuart, *Badges without Borders: How Global Counterinsurgency Transformed American Policing*. Los Angles: University of California Press, 2019.

Schrepfer, Susan R. and Scranton, Philip (eds). *Industrializing Organisms: Introducing Evolutionary History*. London: Routledge, 2004.

Schröder, Ingo W. and Schmidt, Bettine E. 'Introduction: Violent Imaginaries and Violent Practices', in Schmidt and Schröder (eds), *Anthropology of Violence and Conflict*, 1–12.

Schulting, Rick and Wysocki, Mike. '"In this Chambered Tomb were Found Cleft Skulls...": An Assessment of the Evidence for Cranial Trauma in the British Neolithic', *Proceedings of the Prehistoric Society*, 71 (2005): 107–38.

Schwartz, Stuart B. *Sugar Plantations in the Formation of Brazilian Society: Bahia, 1550–1835*. Cambridge: Cambridge University Press, 1985.

Schwartz, Stuart B. *Slaves, Peasants, and Rebels: Reconsidering Brazilian Historiography*. Urbana: University of Illinois Press, 1992.

Schwerhoff, Gerd. 'Zivilisationsprozess und Geschichtswissenschaft. Norbert Elias' Forschungsparadigma in historischer Perspektive', *Historische Zeitschrift*, 266 (1998): 561–605.

Schwerhoff, Gerd. 'Criminalised Violence and the Process of Civilization: A Reappraisal', *Crime, History and Societies*, 6:2 (2002): 103–26.

Schwerhoff, Gerd. 'Violence and the Honour Code: From Social Integration to Social Distinction?', *Crime, History and Societies*, 17:2 (2013): 27–46.

Scott, Rebecca. *Slave Emancipation in Cuba: The Transition to Free Labor, 1860–1899*. Pittsburgh: University of Pittsburgh Press, 2000.

Secrest, William B. *When the Great Spirit Died: The Destruction of the California Indians, 1850–1860*, second edn. Sanger: Quill Driver Books, 2003.

Seelhoff, Cheryl Lindsey. 'A Chilling Effect: The Oppression and Silencing of Women Journalists and Bloggers Worldwide', *Off Our Backs*, 37:1 (2007): 18–21.

Sen, Amartya. *Development as Freedom*. New York: Knopf, 1999.

Sharpe, James. 'Crime in England: Long-Term Trends and the Problem of Modernization', in Johnsson and Monkkonen (eds), *The Civilization of Crime*, 17–34.

Sharpe, James. *A Fiery & Furious People: A History of Violence in England*. London: Random House, 2016.

Sharpe, R. R. (ed.). *Calendar of Coroners Rolls of the City of London, AD 1300–1378*. London: R. Clay and sons, 1913.

Sheehan, Jonathan. 'Enlightenment, Religion, and the Enigma of Secularization: A Review Essay', *American Historical Review*, 108 (2003): 1061–80.

Sheehan, Jonathan and Wahrman, Dror. *Invisible Hands: Self-Organization and the Eighteenth Century*. Chicago: Chicago University Press, 2015.

Shelley, Louise. *Human Trafficking: A Global Perspective*. Cambridge: Cambridge University Press, 2010.

Shepherd, Jonathan. 'Violent Crime in Bristol: An Accident and Emergency Department Perspective', *The British Journal of Criminology*, 30:3 (1990): 289–305.

Sherwood, Marika. 'The British Illegal Slave Trade, 1808–1830', *British Journal for Eighteenth-Century Studies*, 31:2 (2008): 293–305.

Shryock, Andrew and Smail, Daniel Lord (eds). *Deep History: The Architecture of Past and Present*. Berkeley: University of California Press, 2011.

Sideries, Lisa S. and Moore, Kathleen Dean (eds). *Rachel Carson: Legacy and Challenge*. Albany: SUNY Press, 2008.

Sikkink, Kathryn. *Evidence for Hope: Making Human Rights Work in the 21st Century*. Princeton: Princeton University Press, 2017.

Silverman, Lisa. *Tortured Subjects: Pain, Truth, and the Body in Early Modern France*. Chicago: University of Chicago Press, 2001.

Simmons, Beth A. *Mobilizing for Human Rights: International Law in Domestic Politics*. Cambridge: Cambridge University Press, 2009.

Simpson, A. W. Brian. 'Round Up the Usual Suspects: The Legacy of British Colonialism and the European Convention on Human Rights', *Loyola Law Review*, 41:4 (Winter 1996): 629–711.

Simpson, A. W. Brian. *Human Rights and the End of Empire: Britain and the Genesis of the European Convention*. Oxford: Oxford University Press, 2011.

Singer, Peter. *Animal Liberation: A New Ethics for Our Treatment of Animals*. New York: HarperCollins, 1975.

Skidmore, Thomas E. *Brazil: Five Centuries of Change*, 2nd edn. New York: Oxford University Press, 2010.

Sklar, Kathryn Kish. 'Human Rights Discourse in Women's Rights Conventions in the United States, 1848–70', in Slotte and Halme-Tuomisaari (eds), *Revisiting the Origins of Human Rights*, 163–88.

Slaboch, Matthew W. *A Road to Nowhere: The Idea of Progress and Its Critics*. Philadelphia: University of Pennsylvania Press, 2018.

Slotte, Pamela and Halme-Tuomisaari, Miia (eds). *Revisiting the Origins of Human Rights*. Cambridge: Cambridge University Press, 2015.

Smail, Daniel Lord. *On Deep History and the Brain*. Berkeley: University of California Press, 2008.

Smail, Daniel Lord. 'Violence and Predation in Late Medieval Mediterranean Europe', *Comparative Studies in Society and History*, 54:1 (2012): 7–34.

Smil, Vaclav. 'Harvesting the Biosphere: The Human Impact', *Population and Development Review*, 37 (2011): 613–36.

Smith, Bonnie G. 'Gender and the Practices of Scientific History', *The American Historical Review*, 100:4 (October 1995): 1150–76.

Smith, Bonnie G. *The Gender of History: Men, Women, and Historical Practice*. Cambridge, MA: Harvard University Press, 1998.

Smith, Carrie. 'Medieval Coroners' Rolls: Legal Fiction or Historical Fact?', in Dunn (ed.), *Courts, Counties and the Capital in the Later Middle Ages*, 97–8.

Smith, Helmut Walser. *The Continuities of German History: Nation, Religion, and Race across the Long Nineteenth Century*. Cambridge: Cambridge University Press, 2008.

Smith, Martin and Brickley, Megan. *People of the Long Barrows: Life, Death and Burial in the Earlier Neolithic*. Stroud: The History Press, 2009.

Smith, Martin, Schulting, Rick and Fibiger, Linda. 'Settled Lives, Unsettled Times – Neolithic Violence', in Fagan, Fibiger, Hudson and Trundle (eds), *The Cambridge World History of Violence, Vol. I: The Prehistoric and Ancient Worlds*, 79–98.

Smuts, Barbara. 'Male Aggression Against Women: An Evolutionary Perspective', *Human Nature*, 3 (1992): 1–44.

Smuts, Barbara. 'The Evolutionary Origins of Patriarchy', *Human Nature*, 6 (1995): 1–32.

Sorkin, David. *The Religious Enlightenment: Protestants, Jews, and Catholics from London to Vienna*. Princeton: Princeton University Press, 2008.

Spierenburg, Pieter. *The Spectacle of Suffering. Executions and the Evolution of Repression: From a Preindustrial Metropolis to the European Experience*. Cambridge and London: Cambridge University Press, 1984.

Spierenburg, Pieter. 'Faces of Violence: Homicide Trends and Cultural Meanings, Amsterdam, 1431–1816', *Journal of Social History*, 27:4 (1994): 701–16.

Spierenburg, Pieter. 'Elias and the History of Crime and Criminal Justice: A Brief Evaluation', *IAHCCJ Bulletin*, 20 (Spring 1995): 17–30.

Spierenburg, Pieter. 'Long-Term Trends in Homicide: Theoretical Reflections and Dutch Evidence, Fifteenth to Twentieth Centuries', in Johnsson and Monkkonen (eds), *The Civilization of Crime*, 63–105.

Spierenburg, Pieter. 'Violence and the Civilizing Process: Does it Work', *Crime, History and Societies*, 5:2 (2001): 87–105.

Spierenburg, Pieter. *A History of Murder: Personal Violence in Europe from the Middle Ages to the Present*. Cambridge: Polity Press, 2008.

Spierenburg, Pieter. 'Toward a Global History of Homicide and Organized Murder', *Crime, Histoire & Sociétés / Crime, History & Societies*, 18:2 (2014): 99–106.

Spohn, Cassia. 'Untested Sexual Assault Kits: A National Dilemma', *Criminality and Public Policy*, 15:2 (May 2016): 551–4.

Stearns, Peter N. and Stearns, Carol Z. 'Clarifying the History of Emotions and Emotional Standards', *The American Historical Review*, 90:4 (October 1985): 813–36.

Stearns, Peter N. and Stearns, Carol Z. *Anger: The Struggle for Emotional Control in America's History*. Chicago: University of Chicago Press, 1989.

Stearns, Peter N. and Lewis, Jan (eds). *An Emotional History of the United States*. New York: New York University Press, 1998.

Stearns, Peter N. 'Modern Patterns in Emotion History', in Peter N. Stearns and Susan Matt (eds), *Doing Emotions History*, 17–40, esp. 22–4. Urbana: University of Illinois Press, 2014.

Stearns Peter N. 'Shame, and a Challenge for Emotions History', *Emotion Review*, 8:3 (July 2016): 197–206.

Stearns, Peter N. *Shame: A Brief History*. Urbana, Chicago, and Springfield: University of Illinois Press, 2017.

Steffen, Will, Grinevald, Jacques, Crutzen, Paul and McNeill, John. 'The Anthropocene: Conceptual and Historical Perspectives', *Philosophical Transactions of the Royal Society*, 369:1938 (March 2011): 842–67.

Steinberg, Mark. 'Emotions History in Eastern Europe', in Stearns and Matt (ed.), *Doing Emotions History*, 74–99.

Stephen, James Fitzjames. *Liberty, Equality, Fraternity*, ed. Stuart D. Warner. Indianapolis: Liberty Fund, 1993.

Sternhell, Zeev. *The Anti-Enlightenment Tradition*, trans. David Maisel. New Haven: Yale University Press, 2010.

'Steven Pinker: Counter-Enlightenment Convictions are "Surprisingly Resilient"', *Quillette Magazine*, 20 April 2018, https://quillette.com/2018/04/20/steven-p inker-counter-enlightenment-convictions-surprisingly-resilient/

Stevenson, Ana. 'The "Great Doctrine of Human Rights": Articulation and Authentication in the Nineteenth-Century U.S. Antislavery and Women's Rights Movements', *Humanity*, 8:3 (2017): 413–39.

Stocking, George. *Victorian Anthropology*. New York: Free Press, 1987.

Stone, Lawrence. 'Interpersonal Violence in English Society 1300–1980', *Past and Present*, 101 (1983): 22–33.

Storey, Robin L. 'Malicious Indictments of Clergy in the Fifteenth Century', in Franklin and Harper-Bill (eds), *Medieval Ecclesiastical Studies*, 221–40.

Strange, Carolyn and Cribb, Robert. 'Historical Perspectives on Honour, Violence and Emotion', in Strange, Cribb, and Forth (eds), *Honour, Violence and Emotions in History*, 1–22.

Strange, Carolyn, Cribb, Robert and Forth, Christopher E. (eds). *Honour, Violence and Emotions in History*. London: Bloomsbury, 2014.

Strathern, Andrew J. and Stewart, Pamela J. 'Anthropology of Violence and Conflict, Overview', in Lester Kurtz (ed.), *Encyclopedia of Violence, Peace and Conflict*, 2nd edn, 75–86. San Diego: Academic Press, 2008.

Stringer, Chris and Andrews, Peter. *The Complete World of Human Evolution*. London: Thames & Hudson, 2005.

Suddler, Carl. *Presumed Criminal: Black Youth and the Justice System in Postwar New York*. New York: New York University Press, 2019.

Sullivan, Eileen P. 'Liberalism and Imperialism: J.S. Mill's Defense of the British Empire', *Journal of the History of Ideas*, 44 (1983): 599–617.

Summerson, Henry. 'Attitudes to Capital Punishment in England, 1220–1350', in Prestwich, Britnell, and Frame (eds), *Thirteenth Century England VIII*, 123–33.

Suzuki, Hideaki. 'Abolitions as a Global Experience: An Introduction', in Suzuki (ed.), *Abolitions as a Global Experience*, 1–24.

Tackett, Timothy. *The Coming of the Terror in the French Revolution*. Cambridge, MA: Belknap Press, 2015.

Taïeb, Emmanuel. *La guillotine au secret. Les exécutions publiques en France, 1870–1939*. Paris: Belin, 2011.

Taylor, Clarence. *Fight the Power: African Americans and the Long History of Police Brutality in New York City*. New York: New York University Press, 2019.

Taylor, Keeanga-Yamahtta. *From #BlackLivesMatter to Black Liberation*. Chicago: Haymarket Books, 2016.

Thomas, Keith. *In Pursuit of Civility: Manners and Civilization in Early Modern Europe*. New Haven and London: Yale University Press, 2018.

Thome, Helmut. 'Modernization and Crime: What Is the Explanation?', *IAHCCJ Bulletin*, 20 (Spring 1995): 31–48.

Thome, Helmut. 'Explaining Long Term Trends in Violent Crime', *Crime, History and Societies*, 5:2 (2001): 69–86.

Thompson, Heather Ann. 'Why Mass Incarceration Matters', *Journal of American History*, 97:3 (December 2010): 703–34.

Thompson, Heather Ann. *Blood in the Water: The Attica Prison Uprising of 1971 and Its Legacy*. New York: Pantheon Books, 2016.

Thompson, Martie P. and Morrison, Deidra J. 'Prospective Predictors of Technology-Based Sexual Coercion by College Males', *Psychology of Violence*, 3:3 (2013): 233–46.

Thorpe, I. J. N. 'Anthropology, Archaeology, and the Origins of Warfare', *World Archaeology*, 35:1 (2003): 145–65.

Thurstan, Ruth H., Brockington, Simon and Roberts, Callum M. 'The Effects of 118 Years of Industrial Fishing on UK Bottom Trawl Fisheries', *Nature Communications* (4 May 2010): 15, doi:10.1038/ncomms1013

Tilley, Lorna. *Theory and Practice in the Bioarchaeology of Care*. Cham: Springer, 2015.

Tilly, Charles and Ardant, Gabriel (eds). *The Formation of National States in Western Europe*. Princeton: Princeton University Press, 1975.

Todorov, Tzvetan. *In Defense of the Enlightenment*, trans. Gila Walker. London: Atlantic Books, 2009.

Todorova, Maria. *Imagining the Balkans*, updated edn. New York: Oxford University Press, 2009.

Tønnessen, J. N. and Johnsen, A. O. *The History of Modern Whaling*. London: Hurst, 1982.

Tonry, Michael H. *Malign Neglect: Race, Crime, and Punishment in America*. New York: Oxford University Press, 1995.

Tornberg, Anna and Jacobsson, Lars. 'Care and Consequences of Traumatic Brain Injury in Neolithic Sweden: A Case Study of Ante Mortem Skull Trauma and Brain Injury Addressed through the Bioarchaeology of Care', *International Journal of Osteoarchaeology*, 28:2 (2018): 188–98.

Townsend, Camilla. *Fifth Sun: A New History of the Aztecs*. New York: Oxford, 2019.

Toyama, Shigeki. *Meiji Ishin to gendai*. Tokyo: Iwanami Shoten, 1968.

Travis, Jeremy, Western, Bruce and Redburn, Steve. *The Growth of Incarceration in the United States: Exploring Causes and Consequences*. Washington, DC: National Academies Press, 2014.

Trigger, Bruce. *A History of Archaeological Thought*. Cambridge: Cambridge University Press, 2006.

Trouillot, Michel-Rolph. 'Anthropology and the Savage Slot: The Poetics and Politics of Otherness', in Richard G. Fox (ed.), *Recapturing Anthropology: Working in the Present*, 17–44. Santa Fe: School of American Research Press, 1991.

Trouillot, Michel-Rolph. *Silencing the Past: Power and the Production of History* [1995], 20th anniversary edition, second revised edn. Boston: Beacon Press, 2015.

Tsunetomo, Yamamoto. *Hagakure*, trans. Alexander Bennett. Tokyo: Tuttle, 2014.

Tsutomu, Suda. *'Akutō' no Jūkyūseiki: Minshū Undō no Henshitsu to 'Kindai Ikōki'*. Tokyo: Aoki Shoten, 2002.

Tuchman, Barbara W. *The Proud Tower: A Portrait of the World before the War, 1890–1914*. New York: Macmillan, 1966.

Tuchman, Barbara W. *Stilwell and the American Experience in China, 1911–45*. New York: Macmillan, 1971.

Tuchman, Barbara W. *A Distant Mirror: The Calamitous 14th Century*. New York: Knopf, 1976.

Tucker, Richard P. and Russell, Edmund (eds). *Natural Enemy, Natural Ally: Toward an Environmental History of Warfare*. Corvallis: Oregon State University Press, 2004.

Tucker, Richard P., Keller, Tait, McNeill, J. R. and Schmid, Martin, (eds). *Environmental Histories of the First World War*. Cambridge: Cambridge University Press, 2018.

Turner, Fred. *From Counterculture to Cyberculture: Stewart Brand, the Whole Earth Network, and the Rise of Digital Utopianism*. Chicago: University of Chicago Press, 2006.

Turning, Patricia. *Municipal Officials, Their Public, and the Negotiation of Justice in Medieval Languedoc: Fear not the Madness of the Raging Mob*. Leiden: Brill, 2013.

Tuzin, Donald F. 'The Spectre of Peace in Unlikely Places: Concept and Paradox in the Anthropology of Peace', in Thomas Gregor (ed.), *A Natural History of Peace*, 3–33. Nashville: Vanderbilt University Press, 1996.

Urbinati, Nadia. 'The Many Heads of the Hydra: J. S. Mill on Despotism', in Nadia Urbinati and Alex Zakaras (eds), *J. S. Mill's Political Thought: A Bicentennial Reassessment*, 74–5. Cambridge: Cambridge University Press, 2007.

Valentino, Benjamin A. *Final Solutions: Mass Killing and Genocide in the 20th Century*. Ithaca: Cornell University Press, 2004.

Valéry, Paul. 'La crise de l'esprit', *Nouvelle Revue Française*, 13 (1919): 321–37.

Vandersommers, Dan. 'The "Animal Turn" in History', *Perspectives on History*, 3 November 2016, https://www.historians.org/publications-and-directories/pers pectives-on-history/november-2016/the-animal-turn-in-history

Vaughan, Barry. 'The Civilizing Process and the Janus-Face of Modern Punishment', *Theoretical Criminology*, 4:1 (February 2000): 71–91.

Villa, Monique. *Slaves Among Us: The Hidden World of Human Trafficking*. London: Rowman and Littlefield, 2019.

Vitiello, Joanna Carraway. *Public Justice and the Criminal Trial in Late Medieval Italy: Reggio Emilia in the Visconti Age*. Leiden: Brill, 2016.

Voltaire. *Candide, or Optimism*, trans. John Butt. London: Penguin, 1947 [1759].

Wahl, Joachim and König, H. G. 'Anthropologisch-traumatologische Untersuchung der Menschlichen Skelettreste aus dem Bandkeramischen Massengrab bei Talheim, Kreis Heilbronn', *Fundberichte aus Baden-Württemberg*, 12 (1987): 65–193.

Walker, Philip L. 'A Bioarchaeological Perspective on the History of Violence', *Annual Review of Anthropology*, 30 (2001): 573–96.

Walker, Sue Sheridan. 'Punishing Convicted Ravishers: Statutory Strictures and Actual Practice in Thirteenth- and Fourteenth-Century England', *Journal of Medieval History*, 13:3 (1987): 237–49.

Walzer, Michael. 'Political Action: The Problem of Dirty Hands', in Levinson (ed.), *Torture*, 61–76.

Warbourton, David. 'Aspects of War and Warfare in Western Philosophy and History', in Otto, Thrane and Vandkilde (eds), *Warfare and Society*, 37–55.

Wax, Amy L. 'Evolution and the Bounds of Human', *Law and Philosophy*, 23:6 (November 2004): 527–91.

Weaver, Vesla. 'Frontlash: Race and the Development of Punitive Crime Policy', *Studies in American Political Development*, 21 (Fall 2007): 230–65.

Wedel, Vicki L. and Galloway, Allison. *Broken Bones: Anthropological Analysis of Blunt Force Trauma*, 2nd edn. Springfield: Charles C. Thomas Publisher Ltd, 2014.

Weitz, Eric D. *A Century of Genocide: Utopias of Race and Nation*. 2003; Princeton: Princeton University Press, 2015.

Weitz, Eric D. 'Self-Determination: How a German Enlightenment Idea Became the Slogan of National Liberation and a Human Right', *American Historical Review*, 120:2 (2015): 462–96.

Weitz, Eric D. *A World Divided: The Global Struggle for Human Rights in the Age of Nation-States*. Princeton: Princeton University Press, 2019.

Western, Bruce. *Punishment and Inequality in America*. New York: Russell Sage Foundation, 2006.

White, Matthew. '"Rogues of the Meaner Sort"? Old Bailey Executions and the Crowd in the Early Nineteenth Century', *The London Journal*, 33:2 (2008): 135–53.

White, Matthew. *The Great Big Book of Horrible Things: The Definitive Chronicle of History's 100 Worst Atrocities*. New York: Norton, 2011.

Whitt, Hugh P. 'The Civilizing Process and Its Discontents: Suicide and Crimes against Persons in France, 1825–1830', *American Journal of Sociology*, 116 (2010): 130–86.

Whittingham, Daniel. '"Savage Warfare": C. E. Callwell, the Roots of Counterinsurgency, and the Nineteenth-Century Context', in Hughes (ed.), *British Ways of Counterinsurgency*, 13–29,

Willey, Patrick S. *Prehistoric Warfare on the Great Plains: Skeletal Analysis of the Crow Creek Massacre Victims*. New York: Garland, 1990.

Williams, Eric. *Capitalism and Slavery*. Chapel Hill: University of North Carolina Press, 1944.

Williams, Glanville. 'The Problem of Domestic Rape', *New Law Journal*, 141 (15 February 1991): 204–5.

Williams, Michael. *Deforesting the Earth: From Prehistory to Global Crisis*. Chicago: University of Chicago Press, 2003.

Wilson, Edward O. *Half-Earth: Our Planet's Fight for Life*. New York: Liveright, 2016.

Wilson, K. B. 'Cults of Violence and Counter-Violence in Mozambique', *Journal of Southern African Studies*, 18:3 (September 1992): 527–82.

Wirtschafter, Elise Kimerling. *Religion and Enlightenment in Catherinian Russia: The Teachings of Metropolitan Platon*. DeKalb: Northern Illinois University Press, 2013.

Withers, Charles W. J. *Placing the Enlightenment: Thinking Geographically about the Age of Reason*. Chicago: University of Chicago Press, 2007.

Wolfe, Patrick. *Traces of History: Elementary Structures of Race*. London: Verso, 2016.

Wolfendale, Jessica. 'My Avatar, My Self: Virtual Harm and Attachment', *Ethics and Information Technology*, 9:2 (2007): 111–19.

Wolff, Larry. *Inventing Eastern Europe: The Map of Civilization on the Mind of the Enlightenment*. Stanford: Stanford University Press, 1994.

Wood, J. Carter. *Violence and Crime in Nineteenth-Century England: The Shadow of Our Refinement*. London: Routledge, 2004.

World Health Organization, *Global and Regional Estimates of Violence Against Women: Prevalence and Health Effects of and Non-Partner Sexual Violence*. Geneva: WHO, 2013.

Wouters, Cas. *Informalization: Manners and Emotions Since 1890*. Los Angeles: SAGE Publications, 2007.

Wrangham, Richard W. 'The Evolution of Coalitionary Killing', *Yearbook of Physical Anthropology*, 42 (1999): 1–30.

Wright, Angus. *The Death of Ramón Gonzalez: The Modern Agricultural Dilemma*, 2nd edn. Austin: University of Texas Press, 2005.

Wright, Quincy. 'Definitions of War', in Freedman (ed.), *War*, 69–70.

Wulf, Andrea. *The Invention of Nature: Alexander von Humboldt's World*. New York: Knopf, 2016.

Ylikangas, Heikki. 'Major Fluctuations in Crimes of Violence in Finland: A Historical Analysis', *Scandinavian Journal of History*, 1:1 (1976): 81–103.

Ylikangas, Heikki. 'Reasons for the Reduction of Violence in Finland in the Seventeenth Century', in Lappalainen and Hirvonen (eds), *Crime and Control in Europe*, 165–73.

Ylikangas, Heikki, Johansen, Jens Christian V., Johansson, Kenneth and Næss, Hans Eyvind. 'Family, State, and Patterns of Criminality: Major Tendencies in the Work of the Courts, 1550–1850', in Eva Österberg and Sølvie Sogner (eds), *People Meet the Law: Control and Conflict-Handling in the Courts. The Nordic Countries in the Post-Reformation and Pre-Industrial Period*, 57–139. Oslo: Universitetsforlaget, 2000.

Ylikangas, Heikki, Karonen, Petri and Lehti, Martti (eds). *Five Centuries of Violence in Finland and the Baltic Area*. Columbus: Ohio State University Press, 2001.

Ylikangas, Heikki. 'What Happened to Violence? An Analysis of the Development of Violence from Medieval Times to the Early Modern Era Based on Finnish Source Material', in Ylikangas, Karonen and Lehti (eds), *Five Centuries of Violence in Finland and the Baltic*, 1–84.

Young, G. and Whitty, M. T. 'Games Without Frontiers', in *Computers in Human Behavior*, 26:6 (2010): 1228–36.

Yung, Corey Rayburn. 'How to Lie with Rape Statistics: America's Hidden Rape Crisis', *Iowa Law Review*, 99:3 (2014): 1197–256.

Zamiatin, Evgeniĭ Ivanovich. *We*. New York: Modern Library, 2006.

Zizek, Slavoj. *Violence*. London: Profile, 2008.

Zizek, Slavoj. *In Defense of Lost Causes*. London: Verso, 2017.

Zizek, Slavoj. *Sex and the Failed Absolute*. New York: Bloomsbury Academic, 2020.

Zollikofer, Christoph E., Ponce De Leon, Marcia S., Vandermeersch, Bernard and Lévêque, François. 'Evidence for Interpersonal Violence in the St. Cesaire Neanderthal', *Proceedings of the National Academy of Sciences of the United States of America*, 99 (2002): 6444–8.

Zuk, Marlene. *Sexual Selection: What We Can and Can't Learn About Sex from Animals*. Berkeley: University of California Press, 2002.

INDEX

www.ingramcontent.com/pod-product-compliance
Ingram Content Group UK Ltd.
Pitfield, Milton Keynes, MK11 3LW, UK
UKHW020652280225
455688UK00004B/99